Research Anthology on Advancements in Cybersecurity Education

Information Resources Management Association
USA

Published in the United States of America by
    IGI Global
    Information Science Reference (an imprint of IGI Global)
    701 E. Chocolate Avenue
    Hershey PA, USA 17033
    Tel: 717-533-8845
    Fax: 717-533-8661
    E-mail: cust@igi-global.com
    Web site: http://www.igi-global.com

Library of Congress Cataloging-in-Publication Data

Names: Information Resources Management Association, editor.
Title: Research anthology on advancements in cybersecurity education /
  Information Resources Management Association, editor.
Description: Hershey PA : Information Science Reference, [2022] | Includes
  bibliographical references and index. | Summary: "This research
  reference book of contributed chapters discusses innovative concepts,
  theories, and developments for not only teaching cybersecurity, but also
  for driving awareness of efforts that can be achieved to further secure
  sensitive data"-- Provided by publisher.
Identifiers: LCCN 2021038926 (print) | LCCN 2021038927 (ebook) | ISBN
  9781668435540 (hardcover) | ISBN 9781668435557 (ebook)
Subjects: LCSH: Computer security--Study and teaching. | Computer
  networks--Security measures--Study and teaching.
Classification: LCC QA76.9.A25 R4347 2022 (print) | LCC QA76.9.A25
  (ebook) | DDC 005.8--dc23/eng/20211007
LC record available at https://lccn.loc.gov/2021038926
LC ebook record available at https://lccn.loc.gov/2021038927

British Cataloguing in Publication Data
A Cataloguing in Publication record for this book is available from the British Library.

The views expressed in this book are those of the authors, but not necessarily of the publisher.

For electronic access to this publication, please contact: eresources@igi-global.com.

List of Contributors

Table of Contents

Section 3
Curriculum and Program Development

Section 4
Teaching Practices, Models, and Technologies

Preface

The efficiency of online activities has driven individuals to conduct such tasks as shopping, banking, utilizing medical records, and more online. While convenient, these services also pose significant risks to an individual's personal information, allowing criminals with expert hacking skills to infiltrate and steal valuable data. As such, the need for cybersecurity professionals has increased as businesses seek to implement safer systems and individuals work to better secure their personal data. In order to develop competent cybersecurity professionals, educational programs and curriculum strategies must be investigated and continuously updated to ensure they have the proper skills to combat modern criminal practices.

Thus, the *Research Anthology on Advancements in Cybersecurity Education* seeks to fill the void for an all-encompassing and comprehensive reference book covering the latest and emerging research, concepts, and theories for working professionals. This one-volume reference collection of reprinted IGI Global book chapters and journal articles that have been handpicked by the editor and editorial team of this research anthology on this topic will empower cybersecurity professionals, teachers, curriculum developers, instructional designers, administrators, security analysts, researchers, academicians, universities, and students with an advanced understanding of critical issues and advancements of cybersecurity education.

The *Research Anthology on Advancements in Cybersecurity Education* is organized into four sections that provide comprehensive coverage of important topics. The sections are:

1. Awareness and Understanding the Need for Cybersecurity Education;
2. Certifications, Competencies, and Skill Development;
3. Curriculum and Program Development; and
4. Teaching Practices, Models, and Technologies.

The following paragraphs provide a summary of what to expect from this invaluable reference tool.

Section 1, "Awareness and Understanding the Need for Cybersecurity Education," opens the book with a discussion on importance of security awareness and why it is crucial to build a cyber aware society. The opening chapter in this section, "Security Awareness in the Internet of Everything," by Prof. Viacheslav Izosimov of Semcon Sweden AB, Sweden and Prof. Martin Törngren from KTH Royal Institute of Technology, Sweden, advocates that security awareness of users and developers is the foundation to the deployment of an interconnected system of systems and provides recommendations for steps forward highlighting the roles of people, organizations, and authorities. Another chapter, "How to Educate to Build an Effective Cyber Resilient Society," by Prof. Jorge Barbosa of Coimbra Polytechnic - ISEC, Coimbra, Portugal, develops possible strategies that can contribute to the cyber resilience of society in the area of cyber education. The closing chapter in this section, "The Different Aspects of Information Security Education," by Prof. Suchinthi Fernando of Rutgers University, USA, discusses the importance of information security education for everyone and shows how instead of being intimidated by it, different categories of users can obtain varying depths of information security education based on their cyber-activities and need for knowledge.

Section 2, "Certifications, Competencies, and Skill Development," discusses strategies and practices for building professional cybersecurity skills and competencies as well as certification courses that aid in the professional development of security practitioners. The opening chapter in this section, "How Can a Cybersecurity Student Become a Cybersecurity Professional and Succeed in a Cybersecurity Career?" by Profs. Sandra Blanke, Paul Christian Nielsen, and Brian Wrozek of the University of Dallas, USA, provides aspiring cybersecurity students a clear understanding of the various educational pathways they can choose to achieve their goals and describes educational categories while including an assessment of each that students will want to consider based on their own situation. Another chapter in this section, "The Role of Cybersecurity Certifications," by Prof. Adrian Davis of ObjectTech Group, UK, looks at the burgeoning field of certification for individuals in the field of information security or cybersecurity and examines how these certifications are produced, the subjects they cover, and how they integrate and the various audiences to which the certifications are aimed. The next chapter, "The Role of Cybersecurity Certifications," by Prof. Adrian Davis of ObjectTech Group, UK, looks at the burgeoning field of certification for individuals in the field of information security or cybersecurity and examines how these certifications are produced, the subjects they cover, and how they integrate and the various audiences to which the certifications are aimed. The following chapter, "Certifications in Cybersecurity Workforce Development: A Case Study," by Prof. Ping Wang of Robert Morris University, USA and Prof. Hubert D'Cruze from the University of Maryland, USA, analyzes the CISSP certification requirements, domains, and objectives and attempts to map them to the cybersecurity industry competencies and the US national cybersecurity workforce framework (NCWF). Another chapter in this section, "Cyber Security Competency Model Based on Learning Theories and Learning Continuum Hierarchy," by Prof. Winfred Yaokumah of Pentecost University College, Ghana, proposes a cybersecurity competency model that integrates learning theories (cognitive, affective, and psychomotor), learning continuum hierarchy (awareness and training), and cybersecurity domain knowledge. An additional chapter in this section, "Online Calling Cards and Professional Profiles in Cybersecurity From Social Media," by Prof. Shalin Hai-Jew of Kansas State University, USA, explores some aspects of cybersecurity professional profiles ("calling cards") available on the open Social Web and what may be learned about respective skills and capabilities from these glimmers of the person(s) behind the profiles. The next chapter, "Opinions of the Software and Supply Chain Assurance Forum on Education, Training, and Certifications," by Beatrix Boyens of Adaptive Management Concepts, USA, provides an overview of discussions held at the Software and Supply Chain Assurance (SSCA) forum held May 1-2, 2018, in McLean, Virginia; the two-day event focused on education and training for software assurance (SwA) and Cyber-Supply Chain Risk Management (C-SCRM). A closing chapter in this section, "A Cybersecurity Skills Framework," by Prof. Peter James Fischer of the Institute of Information Security Professionals, UK, traces the evolution of cybersecurity skills requirements and development over the past 40 years, from the early days of computer security (Compusec) to the present day. Another chapter, "Why One Should Learn Ethical Hacking," by Prof. Sunita Vikrant Dhavale of the Defence Institute of Advanced Technology, India, presents the importance of learning hacking techniques by each and every person dealing with cyber operations and explains various basic terminologies used in the ethical hacking domain and also provides step-by-step instructions for setting up an ethical hacking lab in order to carry out the attacks mentioned in further chapters of this book. The final chapter in this section, "Teaching Offensive Lab Skills: How to Make It Worth the Risk?" by Prof. Zouheir Trabelsi of UAE University, UAE and Profs. Margaret McCoey and Yang Wang from La Salle University, USA, identifies and discusses the learning outcomes to be achieved because of hands-on lab exercises using ethical hacking and the ethical implications associated with including such labs in the information security curriculum.

Section 3, "Curriculum and Program Development," offers best practices for developing modern curricula that teaches cybersecurity professionals fundamental skills and the latest techniques needed to succeed in their field. The opening chapter in this section, "A Holistic View of Cybersecurity Education Requirements," by Prof. Steven M. Furnell of the University of Plymouth, UK & Edith Cowan University, Australia and Prof. Ismini Vasileiou from the University of Plymouth, UK, establishes the need for cybersecurity awareness, training, and education in order to enable us to understand and meet our security obligations. Another opening chapter in this section, "Developing the Social, Political, Economic, and Criminological Awareness of Cybersecurity Experts: A Proposal and Discussion of Non-Technical Topics for Inclusion in Cybersecurity Education," by Udo Richard Averweg of eThekwini Municipality, South Africa and Prof. Marcus Leaning from the University of Winchester, UK, considers a number of exemplary issues that are considered worthy of inclusion in the development of future cybersecurity workers and provides an overview of the issues of the "dark side of the net" that cause problems for global cybersecurity and international business risk. The next chapter, "Cybersecurity Curricular Guidelines," by Prof. Matt Bishop of the University of California – Davis, USA; Prof. Diana Burley from The George Washington University, USA; and Prof. Lynn A. Futcher of Nelson Mandela University, South Africa, discusses the Cybersecurity Curricular Guidelines, a joint effort of the ACM, IEEE Computer Society, AIS SIGSAC, and IFIP WG 11.8, which has eight knowledge areas broken down into knowledge units and topics. The following chapter, "Developing Cyber Security Competences Through Simulation-Based Learning," by Prof. Bistra Konstantinova Vassileva of the University of Economics, Bulgaria, provides a current overview of the existing body of the literature in the field of simulation-based learning and the key cybersecurity issues to develop a methodological business-oriented and evidence-based learning framework which will provide students or trainees with the opportunity to develop practical skills in the field of cybersecurity issues through a virtual business simulator. An additional chapter in this section, "Opportunities and Challenges of Cybersecurity for Undergraduate Information Systems Programs," by Prof. Shouhong Wang of the University of Massachusetts Dartmouth, USA and Prof. Hai Wang from Saint Mary's University, Canada, investigates the opportunities and challenges of cybersecurity for information systems (IS) programs and proposes a curriculum structure of cybersecurity track for IS programs. The next chapter, "Enhancing a SCRM Curriculum With Cybersecurity," by Profs. Art Conklin and Chris Bronk of the University of Houston, USA, provides additional skillsets for future supply chain professionals to assist firms in including software-related cybersecurity risk as a component in SCRM. An additional chapter, "All the World's a Stage: Achieving Deliberate Practice and Performance Improvement Through Story-Based Learning," by Dr. Brian S. Grant of Raytheon Technologies, USA, provides a case study where a systematic, organized method of storytelling, presented as the story-based learning model, is used to design a series of integrated and engaging activities for cybersecurity training (to protect computer systems and networks) that fosters deliberate practice and improves performance. A concluding chapter, "A Collaborative Cybersecurity Education Program," by Profs. Gerald Quirchmayr and Thomas Schaberreiter of the University of Vienna, Austria; Prof. Teemu J. Tokola from the University of Oulu, Finland; Profs. Ludwig Englbrecht and Günther Pernul from the University of Regensburg, Germany; Prof. Sokratis K. Katsikas of Norwegian University of Science and Technology, Norway & Open University of Cyprus, Cyprus; Prof. Bart Preneel from Katholieke Universiteit Leuven, Belgium & imec, Belgium; and Prof. Qiang Tang of Luxembourg Institute of Science and Technology, Luxembourg, presents an implementation of a cybersecurity education program that aims to address some issues identified in current cybersecurity teaching in higher education on a European level, like the fragmentation of cybersecurity expertise or resource shortage, resulting in few higher education institutions to offer full degree programs. The final chapter in this section, "Techniques and Tools for Trainers and Practitioners," by Drs. Melanie Oldham and Abigail McAlpine of Bob's Business, UK, considers how to adopt the right approach to cybersecurity training for organizations, with training modules that cater to end-users, and which are designed to ensure maximum retention of information by presenting short, humorous, animated scenarios that are relatable for the target audience.

Section 4, "Teaching Practices, Models, and Technologies," relates cybersecurity directly to education by examining various guidelines and practices while providing ideas for implementation to create a thorough cybersecurity education. The opening chapter in this section, "Delivering Cybersecurity Education Effectively," by Prof. Alastair Irons of the University of Sunderland, UK, draws on current research and best practice into teaching in cybersecurity in higher education and provides a theoretical and pedagogical foundation for helping tutors make decisions about what topics to include and approaches to teaching and assessing the cybersecurity curriculum. Another opening chapter in this section, "A Practical Exploration of Cybersecurity Faculty Development With Microteaching," by Prof. Darrell Norman Burrell of The Florida Institute of Technology, Melbourne, USA; Prof. Ashley Dattola from Capella University, Minneapolis, USA; Prof. Maurice E. Dawson of Illinois Institute of Technology, Chicago, USA; and Prof. Calvin Nobles from Temple University, Philadelphia, USA, discusses the implementation and use of microteaching and how it can provide a quality improvement approach to help cybersecurity instructors on all levels improve their ability to teach effectively. Another chapter, "Teaching Graduate Technology Management Students With Innovative Learning Approaches Around Cybersecurity," by Prof. Darrell Norman Burrell of The Florida Institute of Technology, USA, intends to influence the practice of cybersecurity education through the use of innovative applied and engaged learning approaches. The next chapter, "The Cybersecurity Awareness Training Model (CATRAM)," by Prof. Regner Sabillon from the Universitat Oberta de Catalunya, Spain, presents the outcome of one empirical research study that assesses the implementation and validation of the cybersecurity awareness training model (CATRAM), designed as a multiple-case study in a Canadian higher education institution. An additional chapter, "The Three-Dimensional Model for a Community," by Profs. Gregory B. White and Natalie Sjelin from CIAS, The University of Texas at San Antonio, USA, provides an overview of the development and importance of the 3-D model and will describe the scope areas that were included. A concluding chapter in this section, "Evolutionary and Ideation Concepts for Cybersecurity Education," by Prof. David A. Gould of City University of Seattle, USA; Prof. Gregory Block from Syracuse University, USA; and Prof. Simon Cleveland of Georgetown University, USA, presents the general evolutionary algorithm and pairs it with an ideation technique (SCAMPER) to illustrate how certain evolutionary processes can be applied to cybersecurity education and learning. The following chapter, "Effectiveness of Increasing Realism Into Cybersecurity Training," by Prof. Robert Beveridge of Robert Morris University, USA, describes how cybersecurity is a field that is growing at an exponential rate in light of many highly publicized incidences of cyber-attacks against organizations and the need to hire experienced cybersecurity professionals is increasing. The final chapter in this section, "Design of Cyberspace Security Talents Training System Based on Knowledge Graph," by Prof. Yang Zhao of

JiLin University, China; Profs. Xi Chen and Fangming Ruan from Guizhou Normal University, China; and Prof. Lvyang Zhang from Yiwu Industrial and Commercial College, China, puts forward the training scheme of network security talents, discusses the relationship between knowledge atlas and network space security, gives the construction and distribution of network space full knowledge atlas, and then constructs an education big data architecture for cyberspace security based on knowledge graph around the use of knowledge.

Although the primary organization of the contents in this work is based on its four sections offering a progression of coverage of the important concepts, methodologies, technologies, applications, social issues, and emerging trends, the reader can also identify specific contents by utilizing the extensive indexing system listed at the end. As a comprehensive collection of research on the latest findings related to cybersecurity education, the *Research Anthology on Advancements in Cybersecurity Education* provides teachers, cybersecurity professionals, security analysts, curriculum developers, instructional designers, administrators, researchers, academicians, universities, students, and all audiences with a complete understanding of the challenges that face those working with cybersecurity education. Given the need for a better understanding of cybersecurity in all areas professionally and academically, this extensive book presents the latest research and best practices to address the challenges and provide further opportunities for improvement.

Section 1
Awareness and Understanding the Need for Cybersecurity Education

Chapter 1
Security Awareness in the Internet of Everything

Viacheslav Izosimov
Semcon Sweden AB, Sweden

Martin Törngren
KTH Royal Institute of Technology, Sweden

ABSTRACT

Our societal infrastructure is transforming into a connected cyber-physical system of systems, providing numerous opportunities and new capabilities, yet also posing new and reinforced risks that require explicit consideration. This chapter addresses risks specifically related to cyber-security. One contributing factor, often neglected, is the level of security education of the users. Another factor, often overlooked, concerns security-awareness of the engineers developing cyber-physical systems. Authors present results of interviews with developers and surveys showing that increase in security-awareness and understanding of security risks, evaluated as low, are the first steps to mitigate the risks. Authors also conducted practical evaluation investigating system connectivity and vulnerabilities in complex multi-step attack scenarios. This chapter advocates that security awareness of users and developers is the foundation to deployment of interconnected system of systems, and provides recommendations for steps forward highlighting the roles of people, organizations and authorities.

INTRODUCTION

Joe[1] was driving a long-hauler on his way to Michigan. Suddenly, the truck electronics started acting crazy showing speeds above 90 mph, lots of failures on the display, beeping all over. He pulls off the truck onto the sideway. That day most of the trucks stopped all over the country, not possible to fix or repair on a short notice... This led to goods not being delivered, with empty supermarkets, empty gas stations, stopped production plants, and other economically negative consequences. What was the reason for these events? A good friend recommended installing a great app for fuel consumption monitoring.

DOI: 10.4018/978-1-6684-3554-0.ch001

Joe did and so did many drivers. The app was helpful until the very last update… Luckily, some trucks were still operational and the reserve vehicles were put to help.

The system will not be more secure than the knowledge in security of its creators. Security knowledge and awareness of engineers that implement or install a system can be as critical as the choice of a crypto algorithm and a proper key management infrastructure. Security-awareness of system users and operators are critical to ensure that the system is not compromised. Irrespective of the technical quality, any solution becomes effectively unsecure if the user leaks out passwords or blindly accepts installation of malicious software.

The focus of this chapter will be on smart cyber-physical systems (CPS) in Internet of Things (IoT) that provide services critical for society. Examples of these smart systems include connected passenger cars, intelligent transportation systems, smart household appliances and alike. This chapter considers them together with their drivers, operators, installation engineers and other persons directly and indirectly involved into their creation and during operation. These systems live in the Internet or exist as part of an era of connectivity and dependencies represented by infrastructures such as 3G/4G/5G, global navigation and positioning systems, providing and requesting services. The IoTs are nowadays part of infrastructures in healthcare, energy, transportation and many others. The level of interaction in these infrastructures has increased substantially with advances in development and enhancement of "clouding", connecting to and making use of cloud computing services. This type of connectivity nowadays raises concerns for robustness and trustworthiness. A fault or a malicious attack on one of system's components, even the least critical at first glance, may affect other, critical, ones. A trend is, thus, emerging towards "edge computing", as a way to decentralize the cloud and reduce some of the risks associated with the clouding. For example, Satyanarayanan et al. (2013) advocate for cloudlets as a viable connectivity alternative to clouds in hostile environment, ultimately considering the whole Internet or its parts as possibly hostile, e.g. in the event of a cyberwar, natural disaster or during military operations.

The chapter will also look into examples of "not yet smart" systems and will advocate that they must be designed with the same level of security requirements as those connected to the Internet. Otherwise, these "not yet smart" systems pose potential serious threats to society when they unintentionally find their ways to the connected world, in situations often unexpected. In a modern society, it is nearly impossible to avoid these connections, due to actions of users, due to system complexity and sometimes due to security negligence of system developers.

According to the Roundtable on Cyber-Physical Security, Peisert et al. (2014), developers and users are responsible for security of an embedded product. Tariq, Brynielsson & Artman (2014) studied the problem of users' security awareness in where they conducted a number of semi-structured interviews in a large telecommunication organization.

The authors of this chapter decided to use a similar approach to evaluate security-awareness of developers, engineers and academics, by conducting a number of interviews and surveys. The chapter will give some insight into the study of user awareness in a user-centric survey.

To evaluate state of practice in security of existing systems, authors conducted two practical attacks feasible, in particular, due to security-unawareness of system developers and users. The attacks involve a connected smart product, a modern commercial vehicle, e.g. Joe's truck, and an off-line critical facility.

The objectives of this chapter are to:

- Present background and relevant literature on cyber-physical security and security awareness;

- Present and discuss results of the authors' interview study with developers and security experts (with the short version published in Izosimov & Törngren (2016));
- Present and discuss results of the authors' survey study with developers and users (with the short version published in Izosimov & Törngren (2016));
- Present and evaluate two practical attack scenarios, for a smart connected car and for an offline facility (more detailed version is published in Izosimov et al. (2016));
- Discuss a possible course of action for organizations and authorities, with focus on development and usage of embedded smart products and connected services;
- In addition, tell stories to give some insights to educational effort towards developers and to the development environments in large- and medium-size companies;
- And, finally, list examples of the attacks matched against the security-awareness and roles of developers and users (operators).

BACKGROUND

Evolving of Internet of Things (IoTs) pose substantial security challenges both technically and with respect to the users and developers. For example, Elkhodr, Shahrestani & Cheung (2013) discussed several possible attacks in IoTs, considering such specific IoT aspects as object naming, interoperability and identity management. Roman, Najera & Lopez (2011) highlighted challenges for dealing with security in IoTs, in particular, those related to scalability of solutions and dramatically increased amount of interactions. In some special cases of IoTs, for example, in smart power grids, security was considered on a physical connectivity level, Lee, Gerla & Oh (2012), and at a system level, Mo et al. (2012) and Cui et al. (2012). Mo et al. (2012) presented an interesting attack model for smart power grid systems. In Cui et al. (2012), a particular case for coordinated data-injection attack on power grid was discussed. Authors suggested a detection mechanism for this attack and pointed out the fact that the attack detection can be computationally sophisticated for a large grid. This is, in fact, one of the greatest challenges in any IoT infrastructure. IoT complexity makes it hard to have full technical understanding of smart product and services. MSB (2014) presented guidelines on security processes in industrial automation, where people played a great role. This report is a good reference to practical implementation of IoTs for industrial automation domain.

In IoT systems, "software security" plays an important role. In particular, risks related to software, Peisert et al. (2014), Sobel & McGraw (2010), Li et al. (2014), are seen as one of the largest contributing factors to lack of security in the overall system. Complexity, heterogeneity and complex software frameworks make software essentially critical for system security. At the same time, software tools drastically reduce threshold and minimize time needed for an attacker to prepare an efficient attack on a software level. In recent past, however, hardware security started to gain a momentum, not least due to increased hardware complexity, largely distributed development and manufacturing chains. For example, a whole variety of hardware manipulation methods were established, from a simple hardware counterfeit, Leest & Tuyls (2013) to highly sophisticated Hardware Trojans, Mitra, Wong & Wong (2015), Tehranipoor & Koushanfar (2010), Tsoutsos & Maniatakos (2014). This triggered US Government to react and to establish new trade policies for hardware, Mitra, Wong & Wong (2015). The third one, communication security was always a great concern for research community. Researchers documented and studied attacks on various communication protocols, network infrastructures and interfaces, on military communications, Stillman & DeFiore (1980), mobile networks, Zhang & Fang (2005), wireless, Sakarindr & Ansari (2007), peer-to-peer interfaces such as Bluetooth, Carettoni, Merloni & Zanero (2007), Dunning (2010) and attacks on supporting functions such as GPS, Larcom & Liu (2013).

However, a majority of attacks in IoTs and cyber-physical systems (CPS) involve more than a single attack "type", are often very sophisticated and done in several steps. Complexity of attacks was outlined in, for example, Kwon, Liu & Hwang (2013), where a tight connection to physical environment in a stealthy deception attack on CPS systems was pointed out. In the cyber-world, a related example is a distributed denial-of-service (DDoS) attack or flooding attack, Eom et al. (2008), where attackers follow an "attack tree" structure, trying different attack paths until either an attack is successful or is detected. In cyber-physical and IoT worlds, attacks are not only complex but they are also very heterogeneous, often with high involvement of human actors in a number of different roles.

In this chapter, security evaluation is based on Anderson (2008) book, which provides insights into both cyber and embedded aspects of security. The book contains a number of inspiring examples interesting for both researchers and practitioners. Further, the security understanding is complemented with the latest publications on a number of hackers' forums, BlackHat conference outlines and the Escar conference recent publications on security in automobiles.

A governmental organization in the UK conducted a study similar to the study presented in this book chapter. The UK study covers the cyber-security domain (at a country level) targeting the security awareness of the organizations and their management, GOV.UK (2018). However, the UK study does not cover embedded and cyber-physical systems, nor IoT systems. This book chapter uses a similar approach from the research point of view but applies it to embedded systems domain, e.g. interviews and surveys, further extending the scope with the practical evaluation of attack scenarios. Note, however, that the statistical methods used in the UK cyber-security study are not applicable to the work presented in this book chapter due to small population sizes. Authors of this book chapter did not have comparable resources to the governmental organizations for covering all the organizations across the country. The study presented in this book chapter provides motivation why these studies are necessary and should be sponsored and initiated by the governmental authorities to evaluate security awareness of both users and developers of IoT systems. The present study advocates for the need of regular (on a yearly basis) representative public studies within the IoT embedded and cyber-physical system domain, similar in size to the UK cyber-security study, because the study information is critical for planning prioritized measures on a country level towards overall national cyber-security resilience. Political decisions and budget spending must be motivated by the objective facts and not by the subjective and often bias guesses.

Back to 2006, Manjak (2006) conducted a study on using social engineering to increase cyber-security awareness of users of personal computers and the university computer network. In this study, the University at Albany, the State University of New York (SUNY), put a lot of effort into reducing security incidents by informing and "engineering" students and employees to adapt proper computer usage, to learn computer ethics and to comply with basic principles of cyber-security hygiene. The first attempt failed, with barely no effect demonstrated. The users tend not to accept the guilt and blamed the IT department and computers' software for permitting infections. However, the first failed attempt played a critical role in enabling the second attempt, a lot more successful. In the second attempt to increase security-awareness, SUNY decided to use more interactive methods and even involved basketball players of the local team to propagate the important information to students. The effort also propagated to the employees of the campus. The measurement of the second attempt revealed drastically reduced number of cyber-security incidents, at students' personal computers, employees' computers and for the overall computer network. Further, users demonstrated a lot less risky network behavior that contributed to the overall positive outcome. Hence, the education of users played a significant role in the increase of their security-awareness. As human beings do not change whether they work with the personal computer or an IoT device, the findings should re-apply onto the domain of embedded and cyber-physical systems. The increase in security-awareness requires education and an overall information strategy, in the case of this book chapter, the education and the strategy at the national level.

While a (limited) number of security-awareness studies for IT cyber-security are available for general public and researchers, e.g. GOV.UK (2018), Manjak (2006), authors could not find studies on security-awareness of developers and users of embedded and cyber-physical systems in IoT. To the best of the authors' knowledge, the study in this book chapter appears to be one of the first of its kind targeting embedded and cyber-physical IoT systems.

The authors have, however, found evidences for the existence of similar studies. For example, the ENISA (2017) report provides evidences of a study on security-awareness in the IoT domain while omitting the study details directly summarizing the conclusions. The ENISA report conclusions confirm findings of the authors of this book chapter, and will be matched against authors' findings in Conclusions. Another example is the study from Japan, IPA (2010), proving recommendations for developers and users of IoT systems, where the awareness is in focus. Similar examples are the more recent recommendations such as ACEA (2017). ACEA (2017) guidelines dedicate the whole section to training of security-awareness. National Institute of Standards and Technology (NIST) at the US Department of Commerce has an extensive program for IoT security, NIST (2018). The Draft NISTIR 8228, for example, states, "Many organizations are not necessarily aware of the large number of IoT devices they are already using and how IoT devices may affect cybersecurity and privacy risks differently than conventional information technology (IT) devices do." The source of this statement is not provided. However, it may point to the publically-unavailable security-awareness studies within the NIST. In 2017, in Sweden, Swedish Civil Contingencies Agency (MSB) organized a seminar on security awareness, partly considering security awareness in the IoT systems (the material is available online in MSB (2017)). Thus, the importance of security-awareness of developers and users of IoT systems is clearly perceived as an issue, yet very little detailed information is available about the level of security awareness. Further, a number of organizations offer a great chunk of programs for security trainings to increase security-awareness as, for example, in the healthcare sector with many of these programs targeting IoT and embedded systems. Hence, the authors dedicate this book chapter to bridge this information gap on security awareness even if the study in this book chapter as such is limited to a small portion of population.

Examples of attacks against embedded and cyber-physical IoT systems are highlighted in Appendix 3, with awareness of developers and users helping to prevent these attacks.

INTERVIEWS

This section presents interview study on developers' understanding of embedded security, evaluating responses from security experts in the area since they are the ones who spread the security knowledge and setup directions of future development in the security domain. The interview study is limited to 15 individuals and serve as an introduction to the topic of security awareness. 15 respondents is a too small portion of the population to make statistically significant conclusions.

At first, the goal of the interview study was to see the present status of embedded security understanding in industry, by managers and developers responsible for development of products and services. Second, the interview study compared understanding of embedded security between respondents from industry and academia. In the interviews, the authors use two questionnaires for academic and non-academic (industry, service organizations, authorities, etc.) audience with 8 questions. In total, the authors interviewed 10 non-academic respondents (from transportation, telecom, healthcare and machine industry) and 5 academic (from universities and a research institute), sending out more than 50 questionnaires. In general, the questionnaire triggered a large interest in the organizations.

The interviews were conducted in the period from October to December 2014. The questions were sent out in advance and most of the respondents had time to prepare their answers (and even ask for permissions from managers). The interviews were performed anonymous with the direct textual transcription of the answers such that the answers could not be linked to a particular respondent or their organization, via the voice, pictures, or by any other means. Most of the interviews were performed face-to-face; authors had two respondents together in one of the interviews (counted as a single respondent in the study); and one interview was conducted over telephone. Each interview took about one hour, with some, however, lasting for as much as 3 hours and with some as short as 20 minutes.

Question 1: What Do You Consider as Main Security Threats for Your Products / Services? How Have You Identified These Threats?

The rationale behind this question was to trigger discussion with the respondent and to evaluate in an "open" fashion relation of the respondent to security in general and to embedded security in particular. The question was complemented during discussion with requests for confirmation on importance of system-level, software-level and hardware-level security. The relation to the actual product or services was important in case of a non-academic respondent. Many of the respondents took the question with a bit of uncertainty on what the actual answer can be, that is, what is "between the lines". However, after some clarification, the discussion could start and usually respondents felt more comfortable closer to the end of the interview.

Most of the respondents considered computer security important for products and services, except the only one who claimed that, because his/her products are not connected to the Internet, considering embedded or computer security is not necessary.

In total, 14 respondents out of 15 considered computer security important. Several of respondents pointed out advanced persistent threat (APT) as one of the main threats to their products and organizations. In particular, not because of the APT as such but because other attackers (for example, criminal organizations) can utilize holes and backdoors identified or created by APT. One respondent claimed that one large APT has a record of about 2000 unreported holes in common operating systems such as Windows or Linux. Another respondent claimed that another APT had installed a similar amount of backdoors into embedded systems as a measure to counterbalance the first APT in case of a potential cyber-war.

Respondents pointed out "usual criminals" and criminal organizations are one of the most common attackers even for embedded systems. According to respondents, the organizations themselves and employees can also act intentionally or unintentionally as attackers on products of their customers. One respondent pointed out that, in general, individuals with the ability to create dangerous software, both intentionally and unintentionally, can become part of an attack if they themselves use the software (or someone else uses their software to conduct an attack). These individuals that "play" can become a source of an attack, often unintentionally. The respondent provided curious scanning of ports on a PLC (Programmable Logic Controller) of a power station as an example. It can lead to overload of that PLC and cause a failure of that station with substantial economic consequences.

To the surprise, terrorists were not named as one of the major attack sources. Respondents claimed that the physical terrorist attack is still scarier to general public than an online attack from an unknown source. According to the respondents, the terrorists are the only ones who want to happily risk or even miss their lives during an attack. The online terrorist attack does not offer this possibility, or, at least, this is not possible directly.

With respect to attacks on individuals and their privacy, a variety of home services were named as one of the main attack sources expected to grow in future.

Some of the respondents claimed that basically everyone is a potential source of an attack, intentionally or unintentionally. The source of this attack will be exceptionally hard to trace and link to this particular teenager.

With respect to a technical "attack level", the majority of respondents see system-level, software-level or communications as the ones responsible for the most of security violations. Hardware related security problems, however, were claimed as "exotic" and "an academic exercise", not connected to real-life.

The following citation can summarize the discussion on Question 1:

"If we, Europeans, are afraid of external attacks, in North America, they are afraid of own employees and, in India, they are afraid of their suppliers."

Thus, the subjective factor of fear and social and national background play often an important role in naming a potential source of attack, which should be accounted for in constructing a globally balanced attack vector for embedded systems in IoTs.

With regard to the second part of the question "How have you identified these threats?" respondents had difficulty to point out direct sources. Among identifications of the threats, respondents used public sources, incident reporting within their organizations, conducted their own reasoning, information from red alert teams, information obtained from public incident databases. Some used "stomach feeling" and some did not provide information about sources of their conclusions at all.

Question 2: How Does Your Organization Handle Security Threats?

With respect to this question, 9 out of 15 respondents had a clear strategy on acting upon identified security threats. However, only 5 out of 15 suggested suitable efficient methods to react quickly upon the detected threat. In particular, respondents from telecom were the best, with clear examples on acting and defeating threats that could affect their products. Many organizations, however, had it difficult to imagine the necessary steps to prioritize critical threats and run escalation procedures.

One of the best answers included dedicated response teams and mechanisms for triggering alert sequences, clear routings for incident response and corporate policies. Some had even a dedicated security competence centrum, which permanently works with the security threats and ensures a proper education of organization personnel to be able to react quickly and efficiently. One of the answers also suggested securing intrusion information for tracing and identification of attackers.

Other answers included suggestions of stopping writing code in C and using Java instead. Some suggested that corporate management should take clear security responsibility and it is important to stop "placing data on people" who cannot be trusted. Some respondents suggested regular updates as a primary measure to deal with security issues, some wanted to build-in security from the beginning such that "things would run smoothly on their own" without any intervention.

This citation can summarize the results obtained on Question 2: "The worst that can happen. If nothing happens for a while and suddenly everything collapses and you don't know why." That recalls Joe's story with his truck.

Question 3: How Do You Identify and Follow Up on New Security Attacks? Perform Analysis of Their Criticality?

Question 3 is related to Question 2 and was supposed to support the discussion arisen from the previous question. According to authors' evaluation, 10 of 15 respondents work to classify and identify new threats, which is somewhat better than in the case of Question 2. Answers included dedicated response teams that work on scanning for identification of potentially related attacks and doing prioritization. Some have dedicated processes in the organization that are regularly executed to identify new relevant threats and propagate the information throughout the organization. Some do "hacking" of the own software. Some acquire (or even buy) attack software and develop it further to perform assessment of their own products. Many respondents participate in forums and conferences, dedicated security societies and communities, read research articles and online forum publications. Some have a number of research projects on security and supply M.Sc. thesis students with security evaluation assignments. Many (but not all) perform risk analysis and do cost estimations, that is, to react or not on the attack. However, 5 out of 15 respondents (including the one who does not consider security important) do not do much for following up on the new threats.

With respect to the second part of the question "Perform analysis of their criticality?" answers of the respondents were rather limited. In some more advanced cases, e.g. from telecom, the red alert team dictated the criticality and set deadlines to fix the breach identified. Several respondents answered "everything is critical". Other respondents pointed out incident databases for criticality levels. In general, the majority of the respondents had difficulty to answer on this part of the question.

Question 4: How Important Embedded Security for Your Organization Compared to IT Security / Cybersecurity?

With this question, the idea was to clarify relationship between embedded security and cyber-/IT-security. Discussion also included evaluation whether respondents differentiate between these two "securities". 3 out of 15 thought that IT security is the same as embedded security (including the one who did not consider security important). 5 out of 15 were sure that embedded security is different from IT security. 7 out of 15 were not sure about the relationship.

With respect to importance of embedded security versus cyber-security, 3 out of 15 considered that cyber-security is the most important and, the same, 3 out of 15, considered that embedded security is, instead, the most important. Other, 9 out of 15 considered that both "securities" are equally important (or unimportant according to that one respondent that did not consider security important for his/her product because of no connectivity).

To summarize the answer, "there is no border line" any longer as one of the respondents stated.

Question 5: Which Security Attributes Are the Most Important for Your Product / Service? How Do You Ensure "Traceability" of This Attribute in Development, Operation and Maintenance?

With this question authors wanted to identify which attributes are the most important to the respondents, in particular, according to CIA (Confidentiality, Integrity and Availability) classification. Most of the respondents had a clear idea about these attributes. 9 out of 15 stated that all three attributes are equally important. Other, remaining answers, included:

- Integrity alone was the most critical for one respondent and availability was the most critical for another one.
- Intellectual property was named once.
- Reliability was critical for the one that considered security as not important.
- One respondent pointed out "trademark" as the most critical.
- Importance of accountability was also emphasized.

One respondent had an interesting perspective with respect to customers' view on security attributes. According to him/her "customers do not have a foggiest idea what is important for security – it is important to them that things should run smoothly".

Majority of respondents were united on importance of classification of all the threat vectors according to CIA, performing CIA ranking. A few respondents also stated that for individual applications, CIA weights could be different.

With respect to the second part of the question "How do you ensure "traceability" of this attribute in development, operation and maintenance?" again respondents found it difficult to answer. Internal processes were pointed out as one possible answer and to integrate security from the beginning into the development process was another "good" answer. The majority of the respondent again could not provide a clear answer on the second part of the question.

Question 6: If Relevant, What Is the Relation Between Security and Safety for Your Products / Services?

Purpose of this question was to study interrelation between safety and security. Majority of respondents (9 out of 15) see a clear connection between security and safety, especially for embedded systems. 6 out of 15, however, either do not work with safety-critical products (for example, in case of telecom) or do not see a clear connection (including the one that does not consider security important). In particular, some of these answers included "all is safety – no security", "we have not seen safety issues due to security problems" and "for our system, the relation is not very clear". To summarize the majority of answers, an interesting statement was provided from a healthcare domain: "huge risk when you put this thing into a human body" when talking about embedded systems used in transplants and connected automated insulin injectors.

Question 7: Which Security Standards Exist in Your Application Domain? And Question 8: Which of These Standards Do You Use for Your Products / Services?

The purpose with these questions was to identify important security standards (including safety standards that contain security-related clauses). Originally, authors' separated these questions in the discussion, for the standards that exist in the domain and for the standards that are, actually, in use by the respondents. It turned out that these two questions could be merged into a single question. For those who did not use security standards, existence of them was not important. Those who knew about standards existence were, actually, using the standards that they knew about. The lists of existing standard and standards in use were almost identical. In addition, academic respondents were not interested in standards at all. On contrary, industry respondents were very much interested in standards. Even the one who did not consider security important for his/her product (see the discussion in Question 1) was clear that, if the security standard existed in his/her domain, then it would be used.

To summarize, 9 out of 15 use standards at least on a "business level". Of those 9, 7 use "technical" security standards. 5 out 15 do not use any security standard and do not consider them important (4 out of those 5 were, in fact, academics). The remaining 1 respondent was the one who considered security standards important but did not have them in his/her domain and that is why was not using them. The majority of respondents were using ISO 27000 family of standards (on a "business level"). From technical standards, respondents named encryption standards, NIST standards, common criteria, CWE (Common Weakness Enumeration), IEC 61508 (with a clause on security for safety), IEC 62443, ISO 17799, SS-3492, FDA "thresholds" (that include even security aspects), security protocols from the suppliers and few other alternatives.

INTERVIEW SUMMARY AND SURVEY STUDY

The overall summary of the interview study is presented in the "Interviews" column in Table 1. In particular, only 33% consider valid security methods and, respectively, follow up on new threats. Less than 50% use security standards during technical work (it can be attributed to lack of security standards in many areas). Respondents did not consider hardware-based attacks seriously despite evidences and US export regulations.

During the work in the interview study, it became clear that industry is attracted to questions of embedded security, while more work is necessary to distribute the security knowledge. Hence, it was proposed to organize a larger industrial event. Academic and industry speakers, knowledgeable in security, were invited. In particular, speakers were invited who could give introduction into hardware security topic. About 100 participants registered, with the majority coming from industry and some from academia and other organizations. Authors summarized talks of the event, discussed with the speakers, asked questions of interest and conducted the survey study presented in this section.

During introduction to the conference, main outcomes from the interview study were presented and conference participants were requested to complete survey to re-validate the findings. In columns "Survey" in Table 1, authors outline results obtained. The greatest differences are in questions (2), (9) and (10). The respondents of the survey were more uncertain about their security strategies and considered less security standards in business and technical levels. The reason for lower numbers of security standards can be that, during interviews, respondents could clarify what it was meant with the security standards and could elaborate more, which could have effect. The final survey result is, nevertheless, alarming, especially for use of the standards.

Table 1. Summary of interviews (15 respondents) and survey (55 respondents – all, academic and industry), % yes answers

Topic	Interviews	Survey (All)	Survey (Acad.)	Survey (Ind.)
1. Security is important	93	**95**	100	98
2. Use a valid and clear security strategy	60	**29**	13	27
3. Consider valid security methods	33	**44**	38	42
4. Classify and identify new threats	66	**45**	50	35
5. Follow up on new threats	33	**46**	63	35
6. Embedded and IT security are equally important	60	**96**	100	98
7. CIA attributes are all important	60	**63**	63	60
8. Safety can be affected by security threats	60	**98**	100	98
9. Use security standards: business level	60	**17**	25	13
10. Use security standards: technical level	47	**12**	13	13

Interestingly, 96% considered embedded and IT security equally important and 98% that safety can be affected by security threats. It was only 60% for both in the interview study. This case can be attributed to way the interviews were conducted, when, during discussion, respondents could bring up their multi-grained view of the problem. Usage of valid security methods was slightly increased to 44% (from 33% in the interview study). Still the number is rather low. With respect to threats, for threat classification and following new threats, 45 and 46% were obtained, respectively, which can be considered somewhat similar to the interview study with 66 and 33% (considering similarity of the questions, 66 and 33% would effectively produce average of 50%). Thus, about 50% do not work with the security threats, which is alarming, considering that this is an independent outcome from the interviews and the survey.

Authors were interested to compare relationship between academic and industrial respondents. The comparison is shown in Table 1, "Survey (Acad.)" against "Survey (Ind.)". The results match well except two questions related to classification and following on new threats. For academic respondents, 50 and 63% identify and follow new threats, while for industry, this is only 35%. This makes findings even more alarming, e.g. only 1/3 of industry respondents work with security threats. This means that, to transfer to Joe's example, his truck may well be one of the trucks without functionality to withstand new types of security attacks, and can easily fall a victim to an emerging attack category!

With respect to a technical "attack level", the majority of interview respondents see system-level, software-level or communications as the ones responsible for the most of security violations. Hardware related security problems, however, were claimed as "exotic" and "an academic exercise", not connected to real-life. This is not true since a number of issues were reported with respect to hardware counterfeits Leest & Tuyls (2013), hardware backdoors, Tsoutsos & Maniatakos (2014), and alike, and import regulations were even introduced by the United States against counterfeited hardware components Mitra, Wong & Wong (2015).

Authors also wanted to study views on the attackers. Initially, the categories of attackers were obtained from the interview study. Several of respondents pointed out advanced persistent threat (APT), e.g. attackers with large resources like countries, as one of the main threats to their products and organizations. In particular, not because of the APT as such but because other attackers (for example, criminal organizations) can utilize holes and backdoors identified or created by APT. APTs are not interested to close these holes since they use the holes for their own purposes. Criminals and criminal organizations were named as one of the most common attackers even for embedded systems according to the respondents. They have relatively large resources and courage to conduct variety of attacks with the purpose to make money out of it. The organizations themselves and employees can also act intentionally or unintentionally as attackers on products of their customers. An employee can attack his/her organization for one reason or another due to, for example, conflict at work or urgent need of money. Individuals with the ability to create dangerous software (e.g. hackers or crackers), both intentionally and unintentionally, can become part of an attack if they themselves use the software (or someone else uses their software to conduct an attack). For example, curious scanning of ports on a PLC (Programmable Logic Controller) of a power station can lead to overload of that PLC and cause a failure of that station with substantial economic consequences.

Similar to the interview study, terrorists were not named as one of the major attack sources. The general claim here was that the physical terrorist attack is still scarier to general public than an online attack from an unknown source. Another reason is also that terrorists are the only attackers who want to happily risk or even miss their lives during an attack, while the online terrorist attack does not offer this possibility, at least, not directly.

The list of attackers was extended with competitors and users, who might potentially either initiate the attacks or become a part of the attack scenario.

Table 2. Considered attackers by survey respondents (academic, industry and users), %

Attackers	Acad.	Ind.	Users
1. Advanced Persistent Threat (APT)	13	7	14
2. Terrorists	25	20	7
3. Hackers	88	63	68
4. Users	38	44	14 (21)
5. Employees (in case of users "Colleagues")	25	17	7
6. Competitors	50	46	-
7. Others	38	17	11
Criminals were pointed out as the most common type of attackers in the interview study (while were purposely omitted in the survey). They were, for example, more "popular" than the "Others" category in the survey. 57% of users also consider that criminals are a common type of attackers. Survey and interview studies are complementary.			

Authors systematized list of attackers and formed survey questions for evaluation. The results from the survey study are presented in Table 2, columns "Acad." and "Ind.". As can be seen, "hackers" are leading with 63% for industry and 88% academia. The second place is competitors, 46 and 50%, respectively. The third place is users, with 44 and 38%. This finding is rather controversial. Organizations consider their main users as a threat to their businesses and products! Academic respondents also consider more of other types of attacks (38%) than industry (17%). Advanced Persistent Threat (APT) is considered as rather lower priority attacker category for both academic and industry respondents, while is ranked high for other organizations (second highest after hackers). Note also that authors purposely omitted criminals, which were pointed out as the main category of attackers in the interview study, to study the level of influence on the audience in the survey. Interestingly, criminals were not pointed out by any of the respondents (there was a possibility to write additional information) and the "others" is still 22% (considering all 55 respondents). 22% is less than the level of "popularity" of criminals in the interview study. This shows that surveys should be used carefully and results from the survey are necessary to complement with the detailed interviews, highlighting fine-grained aspects in the answers.

Finally, authors were interested to know opinion about inclusion of security-related information into user manuals, since according to the opinion of the authors, users must be aware of security implications due to smart products that they use. 89% of respondents in the survey study considered that manuals must include security-related information. According to check on the present manuals, however, manufacturers and service providers, for some reason, do not provide sufficient security related information to the users. This is clearly an indication that possible security risks can arise due to users' unawareness of the fact that the products that they use can be maliciously manipulated or due to resulting lack of knowledge on possible countermeasures. To follow up this question, authors have conducted additional survey study targeting users of smart systems.

The user-related survey included 28 respondents from the younger generation that use smart products every day. The following results were obtained (in % Yes answers) as shown in Table 3.

Table 3. Users survey, %

Do you consider security important for your personal devices and all systems that you use at home and while in public?	96%
Are you aware of security recommendations for these devices?	32%
Do you consider these security recommendations sufficient?	29%
Do you follow these security recommendations?	14%
Do you agree that product user manuals (guides) should provide security information to you?	96%
In your devices, do you consider attacks against privacy more critical than against integrity? (**integrity:** absence of improper system alterations – potentially hazardous)	46%

Authors could conclude that users are aware about security. However, very small fraction of users is aware of security recommendations for their smart products (32%) and, as the result, only 29% consider these recommendations sufficient and only 14% follow the recommendations. 96% of respondents consider essential providing of security information into the user manuals. To transfer to Joe's example, only few of the truck drivers would follow security recommendations!

Finally, a common misconception is that users are the most concern about their privacy. As this survey illustrates, this is not true. Only 46% consider privacy attacks more critical than integrity attacks. A quested was also added about attackers into the survey. Part of the results is depicted in Table 2, column "Users". Hackers are on top of the list. Then, in fact, criminals have received 57% (criminals are omitted in Table 2). This matches well the interview study outcome. Users consider themselves as attacker as well but only 14% (compare to 44% as perceived by the industry). 21% of respondents consider also that other users are attackers. Advanced Persistent Threat (APT) has obtained 14%. Colleagues and terrorists obtained the same value of 7% each. Further, 11% of users consider relatives as potential attackers.

In the interviews and survey, due to very limited population base, authors could not find it possible to differentiate between different industries without disclosure of the anonymity of the respondents or without falling into a trap of making generalizations from too small samples. However, authors would like to point out telecommunication industry that clearly demonstrated superiority in the security-awareness; authors could trace this superiority in the survey exercise as well. Not only telecommunication industry, most industries will contribute to the IoT products and, consequently, to their security. Engineers with security background in telecommunication are presently hot on the job market and attractive due to their understanding of the cyber-security. New upcoming regulations, customer requests or attacks faced force IoT companies, both new start-ups and traditional, to obtain staff competences in the security for IoT systems.

Authors wrote two small stories on how security knowledge and awareness can propagate between industries in Appendix 1 and Appendix 2. The story in Appendix 1 tells about inter-industrial knowledge exchange and security awareness training activity organized by the governmental agency. In that story, governmental agency contributed to establishing the knowledge transfer and enabling the education effort for security-awareness. The story is Appendix 2 tells about security knowledge transfers between industries and successive increase of security-awareness within a given industry (with automotive as an example) once started. The story in Appendix 2 also outlines the environment that many developers face in their companies with lack of resources and support for security activities. Security awareness at all levels, starting from the top management, play an important role for making a reasonably secure product or providing a service with a good security level. In that story both media and research contributed to success and knowledge transfers from other industries and academia.

TWO EXAMPLES OF PRACTICAL ATTACKS

To evaluate practical aspects of attacking embedded systems, the authors studied an app attack on a modern smart car and an attack on an offline critical facility.

App Attack on a Modern Car

In this section, an app attack on a modern smart car will be presented (authors have studied this attack in collaboration with one large automotive manufacturer).[2] First, the attacker creates a malicious app that bypasses security mechanisms of Google App Store or Apple App Store. Second, through social engineering the attacker encourages users to download the app on their mobile phones, using ads, twits and similar. Third, mobile phone, when it is connected via a wireless interface to a car (via Bluetooth, for example), performs scanning of connection profiles, looking for possible backdoors. When one or more backdoors are identified, the app is updated with the new functionality (to explore that backdoor) across multiple mobile phones.

The next step now is to perform modifications of the infotainment cluster. Since a limited number of suppliers provide implementation of the cluster and standard solutions are often used (Linux, Android, iOS or QNX), the already known "attack portfolio" can be re-used. When the infotainment cluster is hijacked and software is updated, there will be a number of interesting options available by showing incorrect fuel level, incorrect speed, motor temperature, activating microphone to listen to communication inside the car, creating a number of sounds (for example, a crash sound, which will force the driver to act dangerously), etc. Indeed, the attacker can stop here. However, more options will be available if the attack continues. The attacker can exercise gateway functionality to a CAN bus. Once the gateway is bypassed, a full control of the car can be taken.

The app can then establish communication via a network of proxies, using mobile phones of users that no nothing about presence of malicious functionality on their phones. Thus, a fleet of cars can be compromised at once, at virtually no cost. The attackers themselves may not be interested to deal with the fleet of compromised vehicles, but they can sell it further on to interested groups and organizations.

A simplified version of a car attack can be also executed via workshops, thus, without the need to compromise drivers' mobile phones. In this case, a workshop network is compromised at first and then an attack is executed directly via workshop tools.

One interesting version of attack on a passenger car was reported in US, where one insurance company installed an Internet-connected monitoring tool on the internal OBDII contact to monitor drivers' behavior in exchange of the reduced insurance fee. (OBDII is a physical interface inside the car used for car diagnostics at the workshops and assessment of the vehicle by authorities.) Virtually no security was provided at this tool and it was easily compromised, Brewster (2015).

Attack on an Offline Facility

This section presents a second attack example, a facility that, due to security reasons, is not connected to the Internet.[3] Four ways to get in are possible.

- **The First Case:** Facilities are served with people. Their mobile phones, in particular, private phones, can be utilized in a similar fashion as above (e.g. by installing a malicious app). Mobile phones can use a variety of interfaces to explore the facility (maybe, someone will want to charge a mobile phone via a USB port, for example?). In this case, innocent users will become victims of an attacker and will act on attacker's behalf similar to the automotive case above.
- **The Second Case:** The attack is performed in a more technical fashion. Equipment used in these facilities needs to undergo updates, software fixes, upgrades, or new equipment should be installed. It is often taken away from the facilities and then it gets connected to the Internet, in one way or another, and can be, hence, compromised. In this case, the attacker will have to identify suppliers of equipment to facilities first. They will, then, compromise network of the supplier(s) and, introduce malicious functionality into supplier's development chain. This variant of attack scenario is more like a cyber-attack, even though the facility is not connected to the Internet. Embedded systems of this facility are an attack target, which makes it an embedded system attack at the end.

- **The Third Case:** The attacker will go further on into the "supply chain" and will install back-doors either in software that can be potentially used in these facilities or in hardware (also known as "Hardware Trojans"). This attack requires, however, substantial resources and direct access to development and manufacturing chain.

However, it will allow to compromise not one but many facilities at once. Alternatively, instead of creating backdoors themselves, the attacker will use already existing backdoors, purposely or not purposely created by others, for example, by an Advanced Persistent Threat (APT), which will save a lot of time and effort. This attack variant is more of an emerging trend than a current state of practice. However, such attacks were already reported where attackers were, for example, using existing hardware backdoors Mitra, Wong & Wong (2015).

- **The Last, Fourth Case:** the attacker will try to explore unknown and unintentional bridges from non-critical system elements to a critical one. It can happen that the air conditioning or ventilation system is connected to the Internet (since it was considered as non-critical, and excluded from the security work). The attacker will first compromise this system and then try to exploit potential bridges between the system and the critical off-line systems at the facility. If the ventilation system is not connected to the Internet, installation of a malicious component inside the system during, for example, routine maintenance is another possible option for an attacker.

Comparison

The traditional concept with drawing "borders" or "circles" does not work any longer in the IoT world due to enormous complexity, super-connectivity and unlimited computational capabilities to anyone. Thresholds to execute the above attacks are constantly reduced, both in terms of time and knowledge.

Table 4 illustrates the automotive app attack and the off-line critical facility attack (with the second variant of this attack focusing on the supplier's network). As it can be seen, the attack on a critical off-line facility takes 7 steps to perform compared to the automotive app attack that takes 10 steps. Moreover, off-line facility's assets can be more interesting for the attacker. The app attack on a modern car is complex and can be difficult to perform, which, however, according to the case study on this attack, is fully feasible. By far, not all the attackers will be interested to accomplish all 10 steps. Some attackers will stop at the info-cluster level (at 8 steps). For some attackers, installation of a malicious app on the driver's mobile phone can be already sufficient (with only 4 steps necessary). The hypothesis of the authors is that attacks with fewer steps are, in general, more common since they take less effort and less time.

Note that, in the automotive scenario, the attacker used users' unawareness of mobile phone security and smart car security. Insufficient security awareness of developers (both of the info-cluster and the internal CAN network) contributed to susceptibility to the attacks. In the off-line facility scenario, suppliers are unaware of connection between security of the facility and security of their network. Maintenance personnel of the facility are unaware of security implication of outsourcing of the maintenance work to the external suppliers. In turn, operators of the facility are not aware that the equipment of the facility has been compromised. They consider the facility as "fully secure" due to disconnection from the Internet and will not be ready, hence, to react in the event of unleashed attack.

Table 4. Attack steps

	Smart Car Attack	**Offline Facility Attack**
# Steps	1. Create app 2. Place app to an app store 3. Social engineering 4. App installation 5. Scanning Bluetooth 6. Update app 7. Enable "right" profile 8. Hijacking info-cluster 9. Scanning gateways 10. Opening CAN bus	1. Identify suppliers 2. Get into suppliers net 3. Development chain modification 4. Wait until update 5. Update equipment 6. Activate code inside 7. Unleash attack
Severity	Vehicles fleet in danger, society-critical	Critical facility in danger, society-critical

DISCUSSION

In Joe's example, some of the truck manufacturers obviously did not consider possible security threats, of those "less secure" trucks not all drivers followed security recommendations and the attack, if executed, is quite likely to be successful for those truck drivers and their trucks…

How can we stop attacks at people's homes and critical IoT (and offline) facilities? Indeed, proposing technically sound security solutions is one possible way forward. However, these security solutions should acknowledge responsibilities of developers and service provides as well as the level of security education of users and operators. Otherwise, even a super-smart security solution can fail due to that classical case of "a password exchanged to a muffin" or unsecure implementations. A number of steps are necessary. At first, a proper attack vector for a product should be determined within, for example, a manual exercise. Security risks and countermeasures should be suggested and integrated into development. It is beneficial if the independent reviews can be conducted on both the security evaluation and the level of implementation of countermeasures. Such approaches, as the recently suggested SAHARA approach for automotive systems, Macher et al. (2015), can be used to provide a systematic analysis and ranking of security risks, including their relation to safety properties of a system. Companies and organizations should strive for security culture with security education of personnel, security monitoring and alert response teams. Standards on both technical and business levels should be facilitated and demanded. Manuals and guides for customers should include sufficient information on the product security and actions that must be undertaken in case of security breaching. Products that are imported to the country should be subjected to security evaluation on compliance to basic security principles both technically and in form of proper manuals and installation guides. Users and operators should be regularly updated on the subject of embedded security, by facilitating reporting on embedded and IoT security "issues" and publishing information on security violations. In general, education on embedded security should be taken to each high school classroom, where pupils can learn about embedded security and their own responsibilities as members of the society. Emerging IoT society will not leave any member unattended and everyone can become a victim. The whole society must be prepared to act in the IoT world, with security thinking in mind.

Some of the interview respondents claimed that basically everyone is a potential source of an attack, intentionally or unintentionally. This brings us to the example of using victim's mobile phone to perform an attack, without victim being aware of that (as discussed in the attack scenarios presented in the previous section). Moreover, since, in IoT, unlimited connectivity and computational capacity will be available to everyone, it means that anyone can potentially become an attacker. For example, any unhappy teenager will be soon potentially able to run a DDoS on public services (similar to MSB2 (2014)) to ensure that the qualification exam after high school will be cancelled. The source of this attack will be exceptionally hard to trace and link to this particular teenager.

These changes will not happen by themselves and it is a responsibility of authorities to facilitate them. Authorities can impose rules and create facilitating regulations. However, they cannot make any single product secure and make each user or operator aware of security issues in that product. Therefore, acting on the educational level and launching security investigations to demonstrate susceptibility of infrastructural components and certain products can be a possible solution. Another possible solution is to establish a voluntary country-level embedded and IoT security standard and voluntary security marking for smart products and services that comply with this standard.

The majority of interview respondents (of those who use security standards) seems to be relying on their own adaptations of the standards, often derived from one or several "common" sources. As one respondent has stated "own requirements are best". The reflection to this is that "own requirements" can be a dangerous path because, in security, it is often good to use something that has been thoroughly validated by the experts on presence of security flaws. A good example here is the "open" encryption standards that can be scrutinized by the security community before deployment. Own "custom-made" solutions become often easily compromised due to lack of independent reviews.

Lack of proper security standards is clearly present, in particular, those standards that are domain-specific. Academia is not interested in helping in standardization work, while industry is very much interested in standardization. Academic respondents focus more on research and education aspects in security, studying new threats and security methods. This is, however, not a very healthy trend because standards are one of possible ways for researchers to influence development of embedded products and incorporate their knowledge into multiples of IoT products. A dialog here can benefit both researchers and industry, facilitating information exchange and development.

With issues happening in the security domain and constant reporting on security implications, users' security awareness should increase and, at some turning point, embedded security will become a competitive feature of a product or an infrastructure. In this case, manufacturers and operators will be interested themselves to ensure that they receive this voluntary "security marking" to increase sales, which, in turn, will initiate a positive feedback-loop leading to the overall security increase. However, it has been warned that security marking alone may not work, Peisert et al. (2014), and may create a "false sense of security".

With new threats constantly emerging, the evaluation must include a "dynamic" security aspect with organizations constantly reacting and taking actions to secure products and services against these new threats. This is what some of the interview respondents have proposed. In addition, voluntary security assessments on smart products and evaluations of manuals and guidelines can be effective. Penetration testing of critical infrastructures and evaluation of processes in development organization can be beneficial to ensure that defects are detected before they are utilized in malicious purposes or cause safety-critical faulty behavior.

When all around is smart and connected, it is ultimately users' or operators' responsibility to ensure own security, which demands a good level of understanding of embedded security by practically everyone. Each person will become responsible for his smart vacuum cleaner at home, for her smart car, smart watch and alike – but users must be informed about security (and related safety) risks and ways of reducing them. This is ultimately a duty of developers, which is, unfortunately, not the case today, at least with respect to consumer products as the study indicated.

Authors wrote two fictional stories, in Appendix 1 and Appendix 2, on how security-awareness and security knowledge can propagate between the developers, between industries and within the same industry domain. The role of governmental authorities and research are essential to make those stories a success story.

FUTURE RESEARCH DIRECTIONS

Similar to "classic" IT cyber-security, the authors consider apparent that the focus in embedded/cyber-physical security will eventually shift to security-awareness. The emphasis will shift from technical or algorithmic paradigms to socio-technical, giving people back their important role. Deployment of Internet of Things (IoT) applications has accelerated in past few years, with research boosting around Cloud Computing, Systems of Systems and Cyber-Physical Systems. Due to lack of security-awareness, security related aspects have not been addressed so far. But security-awareness is strongly emphasized now in many research agendas in related areas, for example, the ECSEL SRA, AENEAS, ARTEMIS & EPoSS (2018). Until the proposed research and industry agenda in IoT security is achieved, many of currently deployed solutions will lack systematic approaches to reliability and security. This makes current deployment of Internet-based solutions susceptible for massive attacks and makes them highly non-resilient. Despite the fact that many of critical entities, such as factories, aircraft, critical country infrastructures, commercial vehicles, etc. are nowadays connected, the approaches used so far cannot protect them. This results in an increased trend of failures in these infrastructural components, *seldom with consequences*, e.g. leading to "blackouts" discussed in newspapers, and *mostly without consequences*, e.g. leading to, at glance, non-critical service disruptions, with the latter ones, in fact, potentially more severe. The successful multi-step attacks may manifest themselves in those slight deviations from the normal, eventually resulting in accomplishment of the goals set by the attacker, without noticing.

Addressing security is also central for achieving safety of future connected systems such as automated transportation systems, where lacking availability, compromised integrity and unintended functions, can cause direct harm to human lives, AENEAS, ARTEMIS & EPoSS (2018).

This book chapter opens up a "door" towards possible solutions at the level of society as such, motivating for the need of security research towards human phycology and sociology as a corner-stone to the truly viable IoT security solutions. The present research in this direction of security awareness, for embedded and cyber-physical systems, is not extensive by any means, thus, opening up for great opportunities and discoveries. The book chapter can serve as a first aid in future steps to be taken.

The following can be examples of future research opportunities:

- Establish and conduct national-wise studies in the IoT domain, accounting for statistically significant portion of the population.
- Formalize and classify boundaries of systems of interests and systems of influence in the IoT domain, and define their dynamic behavior for both defenders and attackers as the roles, interfaces, windows and circles change.
- Establish game theories to enable behavioral studies of developers' and users' security-awareness vs. attackers' maturity and effort in the complex IoT environment.

- Create viable economic models of incentives on both "defense" and "attack" sides in IoT.
- Define the proper function of law in IoT and what acts can influence the "game" and support the model of incentives, what should be the legal sanctions, and what punishment to permit.

CONCLUSION

There is clearly a gap in security understanding of developers. Security standards are also lacking, and those that are available are not used. Nearly all respondents (including users), however, consider security important which can drive development of embedded security and help with introduction of appropriate methods and standards. However, there is presently a gap in security "education" of the users of smart products and services, with security information often lacking in the manuals, which are supposed to be the main source of users' product and service information. Security-aware developers and users can directly or indirectly prevent or reduce the risk of attacks on embedded and cyber-physical IoT systems. Appendix 3 lists examples of the attacks matched against the security-awareness and roles of developers and users (operators) in prevention of these attacks.

Note that the study presented in this book chapter is limited due to small population size. Authors did not have the possibility to perform a study similar to GOV.UK (2018). For that, a similar effort, supported and authorized on a ministry level, is required. Authors' ambition is that the study in its current form will motivate the effort of a large-scale investigation. The results are alarming and pose the risks to national security. Hence, authors would recommend statistically significant investigations on a yearly basis, similar to the GOV.UK (2018) study, to be able to measure and control security-awareness of both developers and users. When performing large scale statistical study, it is important to construct questions in different ways to address categories of respondents in the most appropriate manner. Recall also from Manjak (2006) that a decent information strategy is necessary to "outreach" both developers and users, with the "winning team" showing the lead.

ENISA (2017) report comes to a similar conclusion as in this book chapter, specifying Gap 2: "Lack of awareness and knowledge", stating namely "There is an overall lack of awareness regarding the need of security in IoT devices", which leads to measure 4.2.4: "Human Resources Security Training and Awareness" and recommendation 6.2: "Raise awareness for the need for IoT security". The recommendation is intended for IoT industry, providers, manufacturers, associations, academia, consumer groups and even regulators. ENISA (2017) states "Many security incidents could be avoided if developers and manufacturers were aware of the risks they face on a daily basis" and recommends 3 steps:

- "Security education and training needs to be established in industries"
- "End users and consumers have to be educated"
- "Among the developer community, awareness needs to be raised to adopt fundamental security principles"

In this book chapter, the recommendations, as derived from the discussion, are somewhat more extensive:

- Companies and organizations should strive for security culture with security education of personnel, security monitoring and alert response teams

- Standards on both technical and business levels should be facilitated and demanded
- Manuals and guides for customers should include sufficient information on the product security and actions that must be undertaken in case of security breaching
- Products that are imported to the country should be subjected to security evaluation on compliance
- Users and operators should be regularly updated on the subject of embedded security, e.g. facilitate mandatory publishing of information on security violations
- Education on embedded security should be taken to each high school classroom
- Authorities should impose rules of the "game" and create security facilitating regulations

DISCLAIMER

The opinion and views contained in this book chapter are those of the authors and do not represent the official opinion of Swedish Civil Contingencies Agency (MSB).

ACKNOWLEDGMENT

This research was supported by the Swedish Civil Contingencies Agency (MSB).

REFERENCES

ACEA. (2017). *ACEA principles of automobile cybersecurity.* Retrieved from https://www.acea.be/publications/article/acea-principles-of-automobile-cybersecurity

AENEAS, ARTEMIS, & EPoSS. (2018). *Strategic Research Agenda for Electronic Components and Systems.* Retrieved from https://efecs.eu/publication/download/ecs-sra-2018.pdf

Anderson, R. J. (2008). *Security engineering: A guide to building dependable distributed systems* (2nd ed.). Hoboken, NJ: John Wiley & Sons.

Brewster, T. (2015). *Security: Hacker says attacks on 'insecure' progressive insurance dongle in 2 million US cars could spawn road carnage.* Retrieved from https://www.forbes.com/sites/thomasbrewster/2015/01/15/researcher-says-progressive-insurance-dongle-totally-insecure

Carettoni, L., Merloni, C., & Zanero, S. (2007). Studying Bluetooth malware propagation: The BlueBag project. *IEEE Security and Privacy, 5*(2), 17–25. doi:10.1109/MSP.2007.43

Cui, S., Han, Z., Kar, S., Kim, T. T., Poor, H. V., & Tajer, A. (2012). Coordinated data-injection attack and detection in the smart grid: A detailed look at enriching detection solutions. *IEEE Signal Processing Magazine, 29*(5), 106–115. doi:10.1109/MSP.2012.2185911

Dunning, J. P. (2010). Taming the Blue Beast: A survey of Bluetooth based threats. *IEEE Security and Privacy, 8*(2), 20–27. doi:10.1109/MSP.2010.3

Elkhodr, M., Shahrestani, S., & Cheung, H. (2013). The Internet of Things: Vision & challenges. In *Proceedings of the IEEE TENCON Spring Conference* (pp. 218-222). Washington, DC: IEEE Computer Society.

ENISA. (2017). *Baseline security recommendations for IoT in the context of critical information infrastructures*. Heraklion, Greece: European Union Agency for Network and Information Security.

Eom, J.-H., Han, Y.-J., Park, S.-H., & Chung, T.-M. (2008). Active cyber attack model for network system's vulnerability assessment. In *Proceedings of International Conference on Information Science and Security* (pp. 153-158). Washington, DC: IEEE Computer Society. 10.1109/ICISS.2008.36

GOV.UK. (2018). *Cyber security breaches survey 2018*. Retrieved from https://www.gov.uk/government/statistics/cyber-security-breaches-survey-2018

IPA. (2010). *Approaches for embedded system information security (2010 revised edition): Know your organization's security level by checking 16 points*. Retrieved from https://www.ipa.go.jp/files/000014118.pdf

Izosimov, V., Asvestopoulos, A., Blomkvist, O., & Törngren, M. (2016). Security-aware development of cyber-physical systems illustrated with automotive case study. In *Proceedings of 2016 Design, Automation & Test in Europe Conference & Exhibition* (pp. 818–821). San Jose, CA: EDA Consortium. doi:10.3850/9783981537079_0756

Izosimov, V., & Törngren, M. (2016). Security Evaluation of Cyber-Physical Systems in Society Critical Internet of Things. In *Proceedings of the Final Conference on Trustworthy Manufacturing and Utilization of Secure Devices TRUDEVICE 2016*. Barcelona: UPCommons.

Kwon, C., Liu, W., & Hwang, I. (2013). Security analysis for cyber-physical systems against stealthy deception attacks. In *Proceedings of American Control Conference* (pp. 3344–3349). Washington, DC: IEEE Computer Society.

Larcom, J. A., & Liu, H. (2013). Modeling and characterization of GPS spoofing, In *Proceedings of IEEE International Conference on Technologies for Homeland Security* (pp. 729-734). Washington, DC: IEEE Computer Society.

Lee, E.-K., Gerla, M., & Oh, S. Y. (2012). Physical layer security in wireless smart grid. *IEEE Communications Magazine*, *50*(8), 46–52. doi:10.1109/MCOM.2012.6257526

Leest van der, V., & Tuyls, P. (2013). Anti-counterfeiting with hardware intrinsic security, In Proceedings of 2013 Design, Automation & Test in Europe Conference & Exhibition (pp. 1137-1142). San Jose, CA: EDA Consortium.

Li, Y., Hui, P., Jin, D., Su, L., & Zeng, L. (2014). Optimal distributed malware defense in mobile networks with heterogeneous devices. *IEEE Transactions on Mobile Computing*, *13*(2), 377–391. doi:10.1109/TMC.2012.255

Macher, G., Sporer, H., Berlach, R., Armengaud, E., & Kreiner, C. (2015). SAHARA: A security-aware hazard and risk analysis method. In *Proceedings of 2015 Design, Automation & Test in Europe Conference & Exhibition* (pp. 621–624). San Jose, CA: EDA Consortium. doi:10.7873/DATE.2015.0622

Manjak, M. (2006). Social engineering your employees to Information Security. In *Global Information Assurance Certification Gold Papers for Security Essentials*. Swansea, UK: SANS Institute.

Mitra, S., Wong, H.-S. P., & Wong, S. (2015). *Stopping hardware Trojans in their tracks*. Retrieved from https://spectrum.ieee.org/semiconductors/design/stopping-hardware-trojans-in-their-tracks

Mo, Y., Kim, T. H.-H., Brancik, K., Dickinson, D., Lee, H., Perrig, A., & Sinopoli, B. (2012). Cyber-physical security of a smart grid infrastructure. *Proceedings of the IEEE*, *100*(1), 195-209.

MSB2. (2014). *International case report on cyber security incidents: Reflections on three cyber incidents in the Netherlands, Germany and Sweden*. Retrieved from https://www.msb.se/RibData/Filer/pdf/27482.pdf

MSB. (2014). *Guide to increased security in industrial information and control systems*. Karlstad, Sweden: Swedish Civil Contingencies Agency.

MSB. (2017). *Informationssäkerhet och bedrägerier*. Retrieved from https://www.msb.se/sv/Forebyggande/Informationssakerhet/Stod-inom-informationssakerhet/Informationssakerhet-och-bedragerier/

NIST. (2018). *NIST Cybersecurity for IoT Program*. Retrieved from https://www.nist.gov/programs-projects/nist-cybersecurity-iot-program

Peisert, S., Margulies, J., Nicol, D. M., Khurana, H., & Sawall, C. (2014). Designed-in security for cyber-physical systems. *IEEE Security and Privacy*, *12*(5), 9–12. doi:10.1109/MSP.2014.90

Roman, R., Najera, P., & Lopez, J. (2011). Securing the Internet of Things. *Computer*, *44*(9), 51–58. doi:10.1109/MC.2011.291

Sakarindr, P., & Ansari, N. (2007). Security services in group communications over wireless infrastructure, mobile ad hoc, and wireless sensor networks. *IEEE Transactions on Wireless Communications*, *14*(5), 8–20. doi:10.1109/MWC.2007.4396938

Satyanarayanan, M., Lewis, G., Morris, E., Simanta, S., Boleng, J., & Ha, K. (2013). The role of cloudlets in hostile environments. *IEEE Pervasive Computing*, *12*(4), 40–49. doi:10.1109/MPRV.2013.77

Sobel, A. E. K., & McGraw, G. (2010). Interview: Software security in the real world. *Computer*, *43*(9), 47–53. doi:10.1109/MC.2010.256

Stillman, R., & DeFiore, C.R. (1980). Computer security and networking protocols: Technical issues in military data communications networks. *IEEE Transactions on Communications, 28*(9), 1472-1477.

Tariq, M. A., Brynielsson, J., & Artman, H. (2014). The security awareness paradox: A case study, In *Proceedings of the IEEE/ACM International Conference on Advances in Social Networks Analysis and Mining* (pp. 704-711). Piscataway, NJ: IEEE Press. 10.1109/ASONAM.2014.6921663

Tehranipoor, M., & Koushanfar, F. (2010). A Survey of Hardware Trojan Taxonomy and Detection. *IEEE Design & Test of Computers*, *27*(1), 10–25. doi:10.1109/MDT.2010.7

Tsoutsos, N. G., & Maniatakos, M. (2014). Fabrication attacks: Zero-overhead malicious modifications enabling modern microprocessor privilege escalation. *IEEE Transactions on Emerging Topics in Computing*, *2*(1), 81–93. doi:10.1109/TETC.2013.2287186

Zhang, M., & Fang, Y. (2005). Security analysis and enhancements of 3GPP authentication and key agreement protocol. *IEEE Transactions on Wireless Communications*, *4*(2), 734–742. doi:10.1109/TWC.2004.842941

KEY TERMS AND DEFINITIONS

Advanced Persistent Threat: A malicious threat by a well-organized group, often government, with virtually unlimited resources, to target persistently and effectively the assets of the selected attack target with highly sophisticated stealthy attacking measures over an unlimited period of time.

Asset: The artefact with a distinct value (monetary, information, service) in the system of interest.

Attack Scenario: A scenario that describes steps and ways the attacker may use vulnerability (deficiency in the system design or services).

Breach: A security-related incident, often caused by exploited vulnerability, potentially resulting in theft and damage to the system and its services.

Cyber-Physical Systems: The system controlled by computers (or so-called embedded computing systems), tightly integrated with the external surrounding environment, including their users, Internet, physical environment, where its physical components are deeply intertwined with hardware and software components, often acting in different temporal and spatial scales, interacting in multiple ways internally and with the external environment, exhibiting multiple modes and distinct behaviors.

Cybersecurity: The protection of computer systems from theft and damage to their assets and from manipulation and distraction of their services.

Red Alert Team: The team of people in an organization dedicated to identify vulnerabilities, follow-up on the security threats and issue security alerts across the organization, suggesting counter-measures to balance the security threats and enforcing procedures and methods to fix vulnerabilities.

Safety: The protection from harm to health of people (or, in some cases, also economic damage).

Security Awareness: Knowledge and attitude of an individual, a group of people, an organization to protection of assets (physical, information, economic) of the individual, the group of people, the organization.

Threat: An intent to cause harm to an individual, a group of people, to steal or to damage property, to manipulate the system, to disrupt or to halt services, motivated by a value of the assets in question.

ENDNOTES

[1]   Joe is a fictional character. Any resemblance to actual persons, living or dead, or actual events is purely coincidental.

[2]   Note that the detailed technical information on the attack is omitted in this chapter, and details can be found in Izosimov et al. (2016).

[3]   Note that authors have not executed this attack, only empirically studied possibilities of execution of the attack steps. The practical evaluation of this attack was left to the responsible organizations.

This research was previously published in Harnessing the Internet of Everything (IoE) for Accelerated Innovation Opportunities; pages 272-301, copyright year 2019 by Engineering Science Reference (an imprint of IGI Global).

APPENDIX 1: THE WORKSHOP STORY

This appendix gives insights to possible positive effect of the educational effort for developers. Simon is a developer who is invited to the educational effort, a workshop, together with other developers. Simon is a fictional character. Any resemblance to actual persons, living or dead, or actual events is purely coincidental.

Simon was invited to participate in a security workshop after he took part in the interview security study done at one university. The study was initiated by the governmental agency who was also hosting the workshop. Workshop was attended in part by interview respondents, in part by other security experts and in part by employees interested in embedded security questions, like Simon. In general, workshop participants took the outcome of the interview study positively. In particular, that one respondent who did not consider security important got a lot of attention from the audience, Simon was also surprised. Audience was united about difficulties in separation between embedded security and cyber security and acknowledged cyber-embedded interrelation within complex CPS systems. The need for standardization in security domain was also discussed. The workshop involved several other presentations, on security of industrial control systems (SCADA), security in telecommunications and a number of presentations on security research work on securing energy systems, IT security challenges, information security, cryptography and security in healthcare.

During the lunch break, Simon participated in an exercise on prioritization of attack vectors for society-critical IoT systems. As an attack target, his team chose a railroad and an air traffic control. Workshop participants received 4 attackers' portraits, "kidz" (somewhat lost teenagers who want to show off), "security researcher" (who want to show that his/her security principles works), "terrorists" (who want to force society to accept the "proper truth") and "advance persistent threat (APT)" (who want to cause substantial economic damage without being detected). Simon's team managed to create attack vectors within the lunch break with respect to these 4 attackers and constructed 4 multi-step attack scenarios with various numbers of steps. In one of them (the APT), the scenario would run over a longer period of time to "compromise" the entire railroad infrastructure with, for example, forcing train delays and causing a number of small but visible accidents. In case of terrorists, the attack target was changed to the emergency phone number system. Workshop participants from other team than Simon's considered this target more attractive for terrorists with a possibility of more direct personal involvement. A complex attack scenario composed of physical, cyber and embedded attack steps was suggested. It involved blocking ambulances and other emergency vehicles for a long period of time by remote braking in into the alarm system, smart sensors, cameras and alike combined with distributed physical attacks, using weapons and bombing, and massive DDoS on respective online emergency services and service phone numbers. In general, Simon and his team could quickly identify main attack components, estimate probability of attacks and construct attack scenarios, and all within less than an hour. Simon had always troubles in understanding of security and often felt hopeless to execute commands of the red alert team. This exercise helped him to gain self-confidence and demonstrated that people like him have the ability to construct, analyze and document complex attack scenarios in a tight time frame, at a good level of details, and suggest possible countermeasures to effectively stop the attacker. Jointly, during the follow-up 30-minute workshop slot, workshop organizers provided feedback (in audience discussion), prioritized attacks and selected countermeasures of those suggested by the workshop participants.

This type of exercise helped Simon and other developers to gain security understanding. Designers like Simon themselves should become a backbone of the society for prevention of attacks and their creativity can become a good support for creating proper mechanisms for securing complex IoT systems. People are naturally capable of dealing with complex and loosely defined problems and, if certain training is provided, are able to efficiently manage security threats, perform prioritization and selection of countermeasures. Attackers are themselves humans (or, at least, virtual human instantiations) and it is reasonable to quest them with human defenders. At the workshop, the term "apprenticeship" was also named with the suggestion that designers experienced in security should train "apprentices" to ensure development of security knowledge and methods within the respective organizations. Simon decided to talk to his manager and to request a mentor from the red alert team, who could meet him every second week and talk about embedded security.

On a technical side, tool support is, as well, necessary for defenders to act efficiently and resolve quickly computation-intensive and data search-intensive tasks, by using, for example, cloud computational capacity, as the attacker would do. However, absence of tools should not be used as a motivation of not doing exercises on constructing attack vectors for individual organizations, products and services. About 20 people, including Simon, could easily organize themselves and conduct exercise within less than an hour using only a pen and a paper.

After the workshop, Simon confronted his top management on the need of security training within his company. The management did not accept his proposition and declined to invest into security education of the employees. Simon decided to quit his work after confronting the management and went on to increase his knowledge in the area, which he apparently liked the most, embedded security for IoT systems. Simon is now a well-paid consultant delivering security advice and security training to a broad range of companies within his industry sector with his old company as one of the primary clients.

Thanks to the governmental agency that enabled this possibility for training and knowledge exchange and thanks to Simon who confronted his management and took that difficult decision. According to Simon, the interest for his training and consultancy is drastically increasing and he is again hiring more security consultants in his privately-owned company.

APPENDIX 2: THE TRAVELLING MAN STORY

This appendix gives insights to the development environment of large and medium-sized organizations. The story is created to provide support on the question of why security awareness can propagate between the developers and within and in-between development organizations. Mike, Ben, Laura, Alexander, Michael, Kim and Peter are fictional characters. Any resemblance to actual persons, living or dead, or actual events is purely coincidental. Choose of automotive industry is of pure coincidence and the story is imagination of the authors of this book chapter.

Mike worked at a large automotive manufacturer in a Board of Directors trying to figure out how to take the company out of the crises after the Lehman Brothers crash in 2008. Two years later still the order intake was low and the company was bleeding money, cache flow was never near to the pre-crisis level. One morning Mike found on his desk the so-called Oakland article about researchers hacking an unknown passenger car. Mike had no idea who put it on his desk.

Mike was not in mood going over the financial numbers again, that seemed to be hopeless, and he started reading the article. "Gosh! Do we do anything about security in our company except the IT security?" That seemed to be a problem different from that cash flow what he was trying to solve in the last two years, he really needed a break. He called in Ben, a research director, asking whether anyone is doing research on the vehicle security.

Apparently of more than 100 research projects, there was only one targeting automotive security and that one was about to be closed as most of other research projects, to save the precious cash flow, according to directive. Ben was rather eager to close the security project quicker than planned as a research overspending and that project seemed to be not bringing any value to the customers, comparted to, for example, HMI projects or the diesel engine software optimization projects. Research projects were rather difficult to close as there are always more than one party involved and some obligations and promises were made to the funding agencies. Still Ben was doing his best to prevent starting new research projects and closing down existing or simply reducing the company's participation to nearly 0 man-hours; the diesel project he would, of course, keep.

Cash flow was not at all good, Ben as many other didn't get any extra bonus that year. The security project had already no company's engineers involved, only a part-time project manager, Laura, who was about to go on maternity leave and that was a perfect time to finally close the project. Still the project was for some reason backed by Aftersales, and they were the guys with a strong influence. "Mike, I promise I close this deem project tomorrow!" said Ben to Mike in a phone call, "Anyway, our customers don't care about security! This is not important for them! We all know!" "In fact, Ben, I've just read a research article this morning and I want to give you a different order." "What? Mike, do you read research articles?" "I did spend some time at university doing my PhD as you know." Mike proudly replied and smiled. That was clearly not Ben's case, who got to his Research position after many years working in a factory directly after College, slowly advancing in his career. In the job interview, Ben promised to do only "industrial" research that would help to sell more and cheaper cars, particularly focusing on diesel engines and cheaper production processes. That was a real selling point to the top management, as diesel engines were the most popular among the customers who also wanted to have vehicles at as low cost as possible, and Ben got the Research Director position a bit more than a year ago.

"Ben, yes, we have cash flow problems but I also see that in case we survive, security may become one of the priorities. Give the guys what they need. Put them also in contact with the IT department. Our vehicles are connected but we have done some savings on security as you know. Just connect and drive, that may be too risky. No security regulation whatsoever that demand any security but still… Better we change it." Ben replied "OK, as you like. Anyhow, Aftersales for some reason do not want to close the security project. I had like 10 meetings with them already trying to explain the situation. They are the only ones who put engineering resources." Mike got some rather awful stomach feeling "Add engineers from other projects, ensure that this security project has resources!" Ben replied "Sure, you are the boss!" Ben closed down some other projects this day, including his favorite diesel project, and moved engineers to the security project. Laura was choked about the news and so was Alexander who kept working on the project from a partner organization. Alexander was a research engineer from university's telecom department (or what was left from that department after the IT crash in early 2000s) and was adapting telecommunication knowledge in cyber-security to automotive domain. Laura kept good track of the backlog and all got to work directly, the company demo was just in a month ahead. She first thought to escape the shame when the baby is born…

Several years later, Alexander worked in a completely different project, in a completely different place. Yes, many years have passed, with some large-scale recalls due to security breaches as, for example, the Jeep re-call. The automotive manufacturer where he worked years ago did not face recalls due to security. Mike helped to establish a proper security policy based on Alexander's input, IT department took responsibility even for the vehicle security (Alexander could find a good connection there as many of the staff members worked previously in telecommunication), they made changes to the Telematics unit and Alexander's research ideas went straight into production. One idea that Alexander liked the most was to ensure that only the vehicle itself can establish external connections and to limit the connectivity window to the minimum. This approach was applied even to older vehicles, already in operation, thus, improving their security virtually at no cost.

Alexander was now at Tier-1, doing some system engineering. Security was not all a priority as the customers, large automotive manufacturers, did not previously require any work for security despite all the directives and regulations that were approved world-wide this summer, in Europe, in the US and in China. That was frustrating. Alexander knew that it would change one day. This morning his project received an updated compliance matrix to fill in. "Wow!" was Alexander's first impression when he looked at it. He could see all his 190 security policy points. "Hmm. Apparently, it becomes an industry-wide standard." To reply for the compliance was an easy task and no one had doubts since the management was aware of the new security regulations in place after the summer. Media run a large campaign to inform about oncoming changes and nearly everyone got affected at a personal level, even top management and their family members.

However, none really worked with security in the Tier-1 company, except one crypto-guy who was encrypting the software images. The customer wanted a quick delivery just in 3 weeks of initial security work products. Alexander run around to see whether anyone had competence at security, e.g. from a previous job or research at university. And he could find. Michael, Kim and Peter. Michael worked in a telecommunication company before and was equally puzzled as Alexander why security was not a priority in automotive industry; he also watched Jeep and other hacking films. Kim did research on security some years ago at university, published well-cited articles at highly renowned conferences and highly-ranked security journals. Kim thought that she would work with security after employment but quickly found herself doing some other "more important" work tasks. Kim wanted to come back to university, which turned out to be quite impossible, and she stayed. Peter worked in the aero-space domain with security aspects and was at some point head-hunted by the HR department as an expert. His security work was mostly on the shelves and he was unsure why the company wanted to keep him at all.

Michael took the cyber-security manager role. Kim was appointed to Security Expert. Peter assumed the role of Cyber-security Line Manager. The integration of security into the product started from an early concept phase for the first time ever… Thanks to both media with their public effort that helped to get easy acceptance from the top management and thanks to the automotive manufacturer customer who required the cyber-security in their products. And thanks to Mike who spent one morning off the cash flow problem. (We still don't know who put the Oakland research article on his desk that morning.) As Ben has retired, the research projects are again flourishing. Mike has taken the Research Director role after finally solving the cash flow problem, supported the company's transition to electrical vehicles and the autonomous driving is a next target. Mike already promoted several security research projects on AI within the organization and more to come, thanks to NHTSA and other organizations requiring security in automotive domain.

APPENDIX 3: SECURITY-AWARENESS AND ATTACK TYPES

This appendix lists possible examples of attack scenarios against IoT infrastructures in Table 5. For each example, the role of users and developers is considered, e.g. a security-aware developer and/or user (operator) can prevent or reduce the risk of the attack when considering design or operational measures. Note that the list of attack scenarios is not complete and is provided for illustrative purposes.

Table 5. Attack scenarios and security-awareness

Attack Scenario or Category	Human involvement (e.g. user)	Possibility for prevention via security-awareness
Attacks on object naming, interoperability and identity	Modification of the identity of the IoT components, performing "theft" of this identity and using of this identity for masquerading. The attack can as well target user (operator) identity.	Designers aware of this type of attack can consider measures to prevent the attack or make it impractical. Users (operators) if aware of this attack scenario can take actions to protect own identify and identity of the IoT elements.
Scalability attacks	Attacks that explore multiple interfaces and multiple components of the IoT infrastructure with overload measures using the internal properties (sources) of the IoT infrastructure.	Designers aware of this type attack can investigate scalability properties of the IoT infrastructure, thus, making this attack impossible. Users (operators) if aware may observe the attack and take specified preventive actions.
Coordinated data-injection attacks	Attack against measurement support (sensors) of the IoT infrastructure to provoke the desired state in the infrastructure and trigger the desired action from the operator (users).	Developers if aware can consider data-injection attacks within the analysis of the system. Users (operators) if aware of the attack can decide not trigger the "desired" operation and use reporting channel to get confirmation of the action before undertaking it.
Heterogeneous complex software frameworks attacks	The attack that targets deficiencies of software frameworks, platforms used in IoT infrastructures (for example, it can target operating system, communication stack software)	Developers if aware can take actions to "design away" deficiencies of framework and platforms or to enable dedicated mechanisms. Users if aware may decide not to expose their elements to risky conditions to avoid the "entry point"
Hardware-level attack on largely distributed development and manufacturing chains	The attack targets the supply chain of hardware components enabling the attacker to install desired functionality into the hardware (e.g. Hardware Trojans).	Developers may build it mechanisms in the design to indicate modifications and the organizations may introduce dedicated assessment and testing mechanisms to the supply chain. User (operator) if aware may examine the hardware component before using it whether the component may look suspicions, as well trace supply sources of that component.
Attacks on communication protocols, network infrastructures and interfaces	General attack type that attempts to explore weaknesses of communication protocols (at different levels), systematic deficiencies of network infrastructures or known issues with the interfaces used.	Developers if aware may decide not to use communication protocols or interfaces with known security risks, or may correct deficiencies or close the backdoors before deployment. Users (operators) may decide not to use IoT devices that deploy risky mechanisms or protocols, or ensure that the connectivity is limited to the minimum necessary level.
Mobile network attacks	The attack that takes over mobile communication parts of the IoT infrastructure, for example, with rogue base stations.	Developers can consider this possibility in their designs and "harden" the designs against the attack, e.g. using application measures. Users if aware can observe suspicious switching between the base stations in IoT components.

continues on following page

Attack Scenario or Category	Human involvement (e.g. user)	Possibility for prevention via security-awareness
Wireless network attacks	The attack that takes over wireless network (or networks) of the IoT infrastructure, with for example, faked or hijacked access points.	Developers can consider this possibility in their designs and "harden" the designs against the attack, e.g. using additional dedicated wireless security protocols. Users if aware can observe suspicious switching between the access points in IoT components, and regularly examine the connections.
Peer-to-peer interface attacks (incl. Bluetooth attack)	The attack that penetrates (and explores) peer-to-peer interface attempting to enable or introduce functionality desired by the attacker.	Developers can consider this possibility in their designs and restrict the designs against the attack, e.g. by disabling unnecessary access modes. Users if aware can observe on-going attack when the attacker explores the interface, and switch-off the connectivity, report the case.
Navigation attacks (incl. GPS attack)	The attack that takes over navigation capability of the system.	Designers can build in complementary redundancy measures for navigation (e.g. based on wireless connectivity). Users if informed may rely less on the navigation capability, double-checking the actual position.
Sophisticated multi-step attacks	Combined attack that involves multiple steps, many of the steps are often related to social engineering of users	Designers can build in resilience against this type of attack performing system analysis, conducting penetration testing and clearly defining the role of the users and operators in the system. Users can resist social engineering better if informed about possibility exposure to this kind of attack, thus, making virtually impossible for an attacker to advance the attack.
Stealthy deception attacks	The attack that establishes a coherent (but fake) system view to users of the system when overtaking the system	Designers can build in resilience against this type of attack performing system analysis, defining manual steps for operators and users. Users can look for suspicious patters and "freezing" of system information.
Distributed multi-choice denial-of-service (DDoS) attacks (incl. multi-choice flooding attack)	Attack type that systematically explores weak links throughout large infrastructure (several infrastructures), users that have access to the infrastructure are also systematically explored	Designers can build in mechanisms for identification, cut down and blocking sources of the attack in early attack phases. Users can take measures not to reduce the risk of exploitation of themselves and their devices as a "weak link" during advancement of the attack via the attack tree.
Heterogeneous multi-role social engineering attacks	Attack type that directly targets users or a whole organization (even several organizations e.g. over the supply chain), sometime involving identity thief of top management (even CEO).	Organizations can build in protection mechanisms into their organizations to prevent this type of attack. Employees can trigger an alarm in case the social engineering attack has taken place (e.g. if team members, their management, purchase department are affected).

Chapter 2
How to Educate to Build an Effective Cyber Resilient Society

Jorge Barbosa

Coimbra Polytechnic - ISEC, Coimbra, Portugal

ABSTRACT

The possibility that computers, in particular, personal computers, can be used for harmful actions affecting global computer systems as a whole, due to two main reasons: (1) hardware and / or software failures, which are caused by problems related to their manufacture which must be solved by their respective manufacturers and (2) failures due to actions or inactions of their users, in particular people with low computer skills, people of very low age groups, e.g. children, or very old age groups, e.g. ageing people, or others without a minimum of computer skills. This problem is aggravated by the continuous proliferation of equipment, namely mobile devices, IOT devices and others that have Internet connectivity, namely through a browser. There are the possible ways in the area of cyber education that can contribute to cyber resilience of society and these are developed in this work.

INTRODUCTION

Today's society, especially in the more developed countries, is almost entirely based on so-called information and knowledge technologies. Virtually all actions, both individual and collective, and both privately and institutionally, use in one way or another a computer in some of the processes they use in their daily lives and almost all of these computers are connected to the Internet.

Although these connection to the Internet has many advantages and it must be continued to use and develop its potential, like almost all human achievements, this use constitutes a double-edged sword. When used in its normal sense, it creates and brings enormous advantages to the daily lives of citizens and societies. The problem is when these potential and the objectives to be achieved are misused and used for actions contrary to the basic objective and that result in harmful actions for the whole society and its populations.

DOI: 10.4018/978-1-6684-3554-0.ch002

The possibility that computers, in particular personal computers, can be used for harmful actions has essentially been due to two main reasons: (1) hardware and / or software failures, which are caused by problems related to their manufacture and that must be solved by the respective manufacturers and (2) failures due to actions or inactions of their users, in particular people with low computer skills, people of very low age groups, e.g. children, or elderly-aged groups, e.g. ageing people, or others without a minimum knowledge of computer skills.

These people do not have a real and objective perception that computers can be used for harmful actions and the implications in the whole world information society.

This problem is aggravated by the continuous proliferation of equipment, namely mobile devices, IOT devices and others that have Internet connectivity through a browser.

As it is not very foreseeable that computers no longer have to give rise to computer failures that allow their use in these types of nefarious activities, the author is of the opinion that only a very profound change in the awareness of the population of these issues through massive cyber-education programs for safety applications to all age groups, professions and educational levels, that can be applied worldwide, can minimize this serious problem, thus creating, in the future, a more cyber-resilient society. The possible ways in the area of education that can contribute to this resilience are analyzed in this work.

CYBER ACTIONS AT PRESENT

Cyber actions of various types have increased annually in a dizzying way.

Many cybersecurity agencies and organizations, both governmental and private, that monitor this type of activity, have produced periodic reports all coinciding with the fact that the number of harmful cyber actions grow from year to year in a frightening way.

The actions reported refer to actions of common cyber-crime, more sophisticated actions targeting banking and financial institutions, actions to obtain personal data, namely personal banking and financial data, and even actions of cyber war or cyber espionage, such as military or industry, the latter seemingly unleashed by states or by organizations and individuals apparently connected to more obscure structures in some states.

One aspect that has also been emphasized in these reports is the sophistication of the attacks and the techniques used in them. This sophistication has been such that many of the software agents used are very hard to detect, and are often only detected when they are activated and trigger some of the actions for which they have been designed and "installed" in a sub-reciprocal way on the computers that make up the software network from which the computer attack will later be triggered. They are true stealth software agents that even technical computer users hardly ever detect, let alone most ordinary users who have only a minimum of computer knowledge and even so from the user's point of view.

The origin of these attacks has also diversified and the countries where they leave also have increased in number. However, this information may not be entirely correct given that one of the major problems is the identification and attribution of cyber-attacks. This results from the fact that most attacks come from botnet computers, which were in advance of actions for the software agents that will later be used in the attacks. As already mentioned, most of the time, its legitimate owners are totally unaware of the role that their equipment had or could have in these actions. It should be noted that most of the time users actively participate although unknowingly and innocently in the actions that allow them to install on their computers these agents of malicious software. Often these actions are motivated by the greed of many users. In return for a pseudo gain or any benefit, users install software that also installs pernicious software. Also, users are invited to click on addresses whose actual action is to install such malicious software with the opening of mails, most often with a bait that appeals to greed or that uses half-truths, imitation of mails from real institutions like banks, government institutions or service companies.

Furthermore, these computers are not normally, or at least many of them are not, located in the same country where the real authors of the cyber action are located, because the borders of the Internet are not the same geographical borders of the countries but, rather the cyberspace. In this way and to a certain extent the location and identification of the botnet's constituent computers is not very useful. The location and identification of the masters computers, that is, those that were used to constitute the botnet and later may be used to trigger the attacks through actions that "wake" the botnet's computers to attack according to the software planted on them and then activated, is very difficult. The location and identification of these master computers is one of the most big and difficult problem in cyber security.

The DDoS cyber-attacks are one of the simplest and most efficient ways to perform computer attacks in particular when you want to embarrass or even prevent access to servers connected to the internet, such as WEB servers. In these types of attacks hundreds or even thousands of computers, previously infected with a software agent that will be used in this attack, are deployed in an authentic computer attack network that is made up of the so-called botnet (Bantim, 2012). Basically, in this type of attack, Internet-connected services and websites are rendered unusable by channeling a large amount of Internet traffic to the attacked server at the same time, thus making normal server operation unviable and even causing it to be turned off (see Figure 1).

Figure 1. A botnet (Bantim, 2012)

The Last Biggest Attack

There are several preferred "targets" for these types of attacks which are round and half targeted. One of them, which has been attacked several times, is GitHub. This service provides hosting and code management and is also widely used to host service information.

One of the largest attacks on this service took place on February 28, 2018. This attack surpassed all previous attacks. Before long, this service was receiving 1.35 terabits / second of traffic from thousands of sites via 126.9 million packets per second (Kottler, 2018).

Figure 2. Scheme of the attack used against GitHub (Simões, 2018)

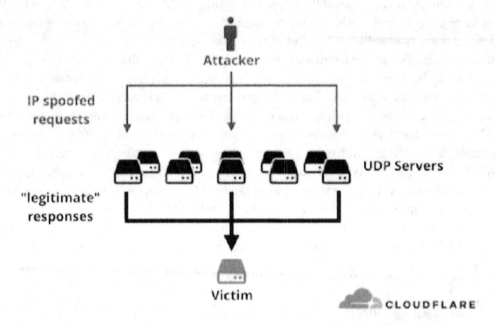

One of the peculiarities of this attack is that no botnet was used. Instead, hundreds of Memcached Servers that were available on the Internet were used. This is shown in Figure 2 (Sam Kottler, 2018). The tactic used in this attack was at an early stage and the attacking servers pretended to be GitHub's own servers, thus sending a simple command to the original servers (Simões, 2018).

They responded with an error and in these data exchanges the exchanged data volumes grew exponentially driving GitHub's own servers 50 times the initial data volume. Through this technique, where a botnet was not used, a huge amount of data was generated and greatly affected the servers by this amplification effect.

Using the services of Akamai Prolexic, which they resorted to after the first ten minutes of the attack, GitHub managed to counteract this attack after just five minutes. Akamai pulled all the traffic and separated what was identified as bad / malicious traffic, thus preventing that traffic from reaching GitHub's servers. The graph in Figure 3 (Sam Kottler, 2018) shows the traffic at the time of the attack, highlighting the peak reached at 1.35 Tbps / s.

The first part of the attack hit 1.35 Tbps and there was a second peak of 400Gbps shortly after 18:00 UTC. This graph provided by Akamai shows the incoming traffic in bits per second that has been peaked.

In the graph shown in Figure 4, the inbound versus outbound throughput over transit links are shown (Kottler, 2018).

Monitoring of transit bandwidth levels and load balancer response codes indicated a full recovery at 17:30 UTC. This data is shown in Figure 5 (Sam Kottler, 2018).

Figure 3. Traffic at the time of the attack (Kottler, 2018)

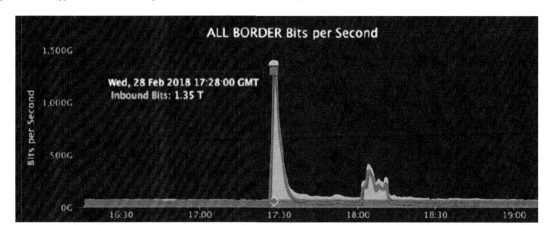

Figure 4. Inbound versus outbound throughput over transit links (Kottler, 2018)

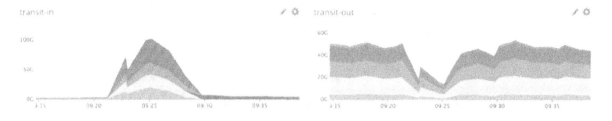

Figure 5. Monitoring of transit bandwidth levels and load balancer response codes (Kottler, 2018)

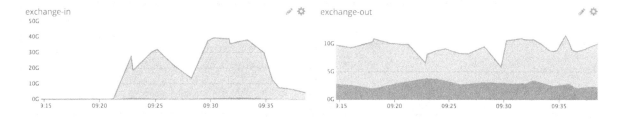

Monitoring the Internet Attacks

Companies in the cyber security area routinely disclose these reports in a public way on their websites. An example of this is Kaspersky which provides very detailed and real-time technical information on the activity it monitors. An example of this is the graphics shown in the following figures (Kupreev, 2019).

According to these reports on monitoring such attacks, such as reports by Kaspersky (Oleg Kupreev, 2019), the attacks on an annual basis increase in the number of attacks and their sophistication.

Taken from this report, Figure 6 shows data for these attacks in the last quarter of 2018 and in the first quarter of 2019. It should be noted that on March 16, 2019, there was a peak in the number of attacks, and 699 attacks were detected only on this day.

Figure 6. Attacks in the last quarter of 2018 and in the first quarter of 2019 (Kupreev, 2019)

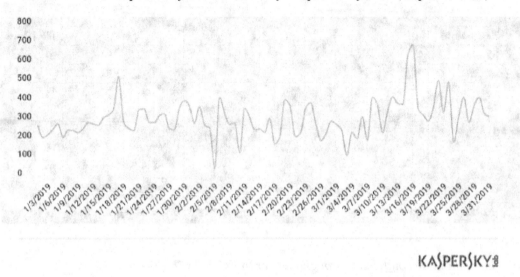

It is also observed in the Figure 7, that the geographical distribution of both bot computers and masters have diversified, making it very difficult to detect them in advance and consequently minimize effects.

Figure 7. Geographical distribution of both bot computers and masters (Kupreev, 2019)

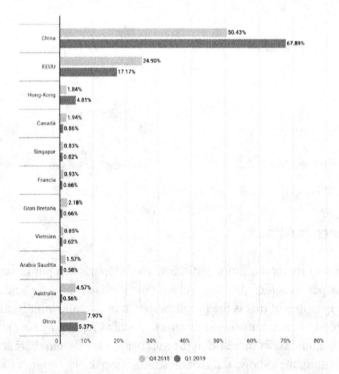

The daily intensity of the attacks is also growing strongly. Figure 8 shows a graph obtained in real time on the Kaspersky website about Cyberthreat Real-Time Map. In this graph, we observe the computer attacks and their main types for The United States at the date and time when this graph was obtained on that site (Cyberthreat Real-Time Map, 2019). At this day, The United States were the 6th most attacked country.

Figure 8. Geographical distribution of both bot computers and masters (Kupreev, 2019)

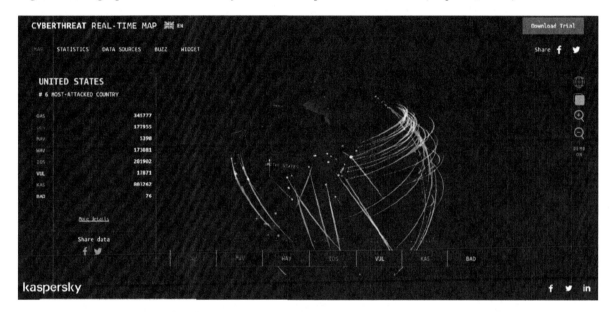

Another very interesting report is the FORTINET Landscape Report (FORTINET, 2019). This report is published quarterly and is known as the LTI, Threat Landscape Index. The latest report refers to the first quarter of 2019, Q1 2019 Quarterly (FORTINET, 2019). This report is not a survey about Internet Threats but analyzes the principal threads occurred in each quarter. According to the authors, "We developed the Fortinet Threat Landscape Index (TLI) in mid-2018 to answer the seemingly simple, yet deceptively difficult, question of "Is it getting better or worse out there?" Generally speaking, the TLI is based on the premise that things are getting worse if more of our sensors detect a wider variety of threats or a higher volume (doubly so if we see both). If the opposite is true, then the cyber landscape is less threatening. Perhaps most importantly, it shows the rate of those changes over time and helps draw attention to the forces driving them."

In Figure 9, we can see the Fortinet Threat Landscape Index and sub-indices of the main types of threads occurred during the first quarter of 2019.

This data and information absolutely confirm the perception what computer technicians and engineers linked to computer security commonly have about this problem. In the face of them, the author really considers that this is a big problem that we currently face.

Figure 9. Fortinet threat Landscape Index (top) and subindices for botnets, exploits, and malware (bottom) (Fortinet, 2019)

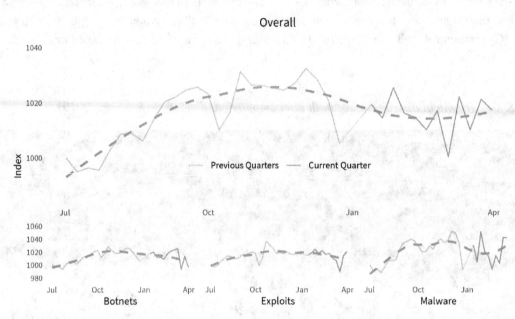

However, we also have the perception that the importance of the problem and the need for its resolution or at least its mitigation is only understood by these technicians. Almost all other actors in cyberspace will not give them the slightest importance, nor do they find it useful to waste a lot of time on such a subject. This is really very worrying, as it is these other actors who own and use a big number of different types of equipment: computers, smartphones, IOT devices, etc. These are the devices that can be and are usually used for attacks. The users not worrying about it, and the devices will be virtually all unprotected and at the mercy of being regimented to the botnet armies.

It is therefore very urgent to reverse this situation!

The Cyber War Scenario

With regards to cyber-attacks, the issue that currently make fear and concerns in many security and defense organizations, either related to security and defense structures or with the civil society organizations, is whether these "cyber-attacks" on systems do not come from individual actors alone. or small groups and targeting isolated systems only.

If such "attacks" come from strongly structured organizations with a large number of elements, constituting a cyber army that objectively and purposefully acts together to "destroy" the informatics system of any state through simultaneous and multiple attacks on its computer systems, this state can paralyze, become overwhelmed and even lose its sovereignty.

These actions organized and concerted, by some country, for the affectation and even destruction of the computer systems connected to the critical infrastructures of another country, using exclusively computer means, are referred to as Cyberwar. It can be considered its division into Cyber Attack and Cyber Defense (Barbosa, 2018).

As cyberwar actions consist of exploiting computer and software vulnerabilities, it is necessary that these computer failures are not known. That is, their knowledge is not yet in the public domain, so that manufacturers systems can correct them and as a result of this correction the computer systems are no longer susceptible to attacks from them. A previously unknown or presupposed unknown vulnerability is addressed as a Zero Day Vulnerability, ZDV. This designation means that it can be exploited as it is still in "Day Zero" of public knowledge, i.e. not yet known or at least this discovery has not yet been publicly announced, and as such systems may be permeable to error and failure arising therefrom.

For the flaws arising from these bugs to be usable and exploitable, it is necessary for a computer program that triggers some harmful action based on the exploitation of these vulnerabilities to be specifically developed and placed on the adversary computer to be affected, for example a computer in a banking system that you want to affect. This software is called Exploit and if it is developed for a ZDV, then it will be called Zero Day Exploit, ZDE. This software is secretly planted on the attacking computers of the attacking computer and generally takes no action at all. It lies dormant on the computer where it was planted as a zombie that will be activated later, usually remotely via the Internet, only when the attacker has planned it. These zombies can therefore remain long planted on a computer undetected and waiting for a possible need for use by the offending country (Clark, 2010).

One of the most famous cyber warfare actions thought to have been triggered using ZDE's, in particular three, was the action against Iranian nuclear centrifuges known as Stuxnet, the name given to the first discovered ZDE that was used in this action (Zetter, 2014).

Given that the targets are more specific and localized, these cyber warfare actions are more likely to be triggered using ZDE's than DDoS or similar attacks. However, these attacks can also be used in such actions, as for example thought to be the case of the so-called Estonian War in 2007 and other mostly cyber-war actions attributed to Russia (Friedman, 2014) and (Farmer, 2018).

Thus, the apprehensions described in this article will then also underlie these cyber warfare actions. What has then been said is also applicable in these cases.

Past and Current Actions and Studies Related to This Problem

The perception of this problem is no longer from now!

However, not all actors who have responsibilities such as government entities, universities, internet regulatory and monitoring entities and so on, deal with it in the same way and with the same importance.

This concern is not the same in all countries right away. There are some who are genuinely concerned with the problem and are trying to deal with it objectively, clearly and with assertiveness; other countries do not have this policy. However, this is serious and cannot be seen in this way as the Internet is not limited to geographical boundaries that delimit countries. Its action extends across the entire cyberspace, i.e. the entire network and computers worldwide. Thus, it is not because a country does not deal with the problem that it does not exist and does not affect it. Worse than that, it affects all other countries, including those who eventually try to deal with the problem.

There are several actions or initiatives that addressing this major problem promote actions in this area with a purpose of raising awareness and showing this problem.

Among these initiatives, we highlight the following:

- **National Initiative for Cybersecurity Education (NICE) CiberSecurity Workforce Framework** (NICE Framework) **(William Newhouse, August 2017)**: "A reference framework that describes the interdisciplinary nature of cyber security work. It serves as a fundamental reference resource for describing and sharing information about cybersecurity work and the knowledge, specific skills, and broad skills (KSAs) needed to complete tasks that can strengthen an organization's cyber security posture.

NICE fulfills this mission by coordinating with government, academic, and industry partners to build on existing successful programs, facilitate change and innovation, and bring leadership and vision to increase the number of skilled cybersecurity professionals helping to keep our nation secure."

- **Europeans' attitudes towards cyber security, Eurobarometer 464A (European Commission, 2017) and (Europeans' attitudes towards cyber security, 2017):** "The special Eurobarometer 464a on the attitudes of Europeans towards cyber security was published on 13 September. The survey reflects consistent rates of increase in online activity, with ever more respondents in the EU using the internet for their daily activities. At the same time, there are increasing concerns about security aspects and also higher incidents of cybercrimes compared to previous surveys.

The results of the survey show that a large majority (87%) of European Union citizens regard cybercrime as an important challenge to the internal security of the EU: 56% think that cybercrime is a very important challenge and 31% see it as fairly important (based on more than 28 000 face-to-face interviews). In 2015, 80% (42% and 38%, respectively) were of the same opinion.

Nearly half of respondents (49%) think enough is being done by law enforcement agencies (LEAs) in their respective countries to combat cybercrime, although only 13% agree completely and a significant proportion (14%) say they do not know. For comparison, the following percentages think that LEAs do enough to fight: terrorism 63%, drug trafficking 53%, and corruption 43%.

The two most common concerns when using the Internet for online banking or purchases are about the misuse of personal data (45%) and the security of online payments (42%). This is a steady increase from 2013 (37% and 35%) via 2015 (43% and 42%, respectively)."

- **European Cyber Security Month, ECSM (European Cyber Security Month, 2019):** An initiative supported by the European Commission and by the European Union Agency for Cybersecurity, ENISA. This year it will take place on 1st – 31st October 2019, on the theme *Cyber Security is a Shared Responsibility.*

According to the documentation of this initiative, "ECSM is the EU's annual awareness campaign that takes place each October across Europe. The aim is to raise awareness of cyber security threats, promote cyber security among citizens and organizations; and provide resources to protect themselves online, through education and sharing of good practices."

In this context, the Portuguese National Cybersecurity Center (CNCS) has organized debates with cyber education sessions on the main them Cyber Hygiene. Although this designation may be strange and uncommon, there is much doctrine about "hygienic" needs in the area of safety and there is no shortage of analogies about "hand washing" and "vaccination", all in favor of creating a culture of security, with rules that help prevent cyber-attacks and (computer) viruses and malware. From the CNCS perspective, these rules must be shared by all users and must be taught at an earlier age.

- **Digital Education Action Plan - Action 7 Cybersecurity in Education - Raising awareness of teachers and students (European Commission, n.d.):** This is another initiative of the European Union and the aim of this initiative is to promote the Cyber Education. The focus will be on three main axes What, Why and How, namely the following.

What

This action aims to increase awareness of the risks faced when being online and to support capacity building of educators in online safety. Two initiatives are foreseen:

- An EU-wide awareness-raising campaign on cyber culture, which will promote online safety, media literacy and 'cyber hygiene' for children, parents/carers and teachers;
- A blended course (online and face-to-face) for teachers on cybersecurity and pedagogical approaches to teaching cybersecurity in primary and secondary education.

Why

1 in 3 internet users is a child.

Around half of 11-16-year-olds in the EU have encountered one or more of the most frequent internet risks.

51% of European citizens do not feel informed about how to deal with cyber threats.

There is an urgent need to raise public awareness of the potential risks of being online and to develop skills to act in safe and responsible ways.

How

A range of activities and events will take place in Europe and beyond, including on Safer Internet Day, to help raise awareness of online safety issues at home, school, work and in the community.

6,000 teachers at primary and secondary level will be trained on cybersecurity and on pedagogical approaches to cybersecurity.

The European Strategy for a Better internet for children combines financial support, legislation and self-regulation and involves Member States, industry and civil society. Under this framework, the commission co-funds a pan-European network of Safer internet centers, coordinated at EU level by insafe and inHoPE. The betterinternetforkids.eu website serves as a single entry point for online tools and services for EU citizens and the Safer internet community."

- **NATO Cooperative Cyber Defense Center of Excellence, NATO CCD COE, Tallinn, Estonia (GEERS, 2011) and (Anon):** The issue of educating people is a major concern, and as such is one of the fundamental vectors of the NATO strategy as regards to cyber defense. In this respect, various actions related to this issue of cyber defense education and training of the military and civilian populations of the alliance countries have been carried out by this military alliance. It is the conviction of the alliance that the commitment of the civilian population to cyber defense is a vital issue for the establishment of an effective and real capacity for self-defense. Hence, there is a growing concern about cyber defense education for its civilian populations. These actions include training and performing exercises integrating not only their military, but also members of the civilian populations of NATO countries.

For this purpose, NATO therefore regularly conducts exercises such as the annual exercise known as the Cyber Coalition Exercise, which aims to promote the inclusion of cyber defense exercises in all Alliance exercises, such as Crisis Management Exercise, CMX. With the aim of promoting cyber education, and through the NATO CCD COE in Estonia, the NATO Cyber Range is promoted.

- **Portuguese Cybersecurity Awareness and Training Program (CNCS, 2019):** The Portuguese National Cybersecurity Center, with the mission of promoting the sharing of knowledge and a national cybersecurity culture, has developed the Cybersecurity Awareness and Training Program, through which it aims to increase the education and awareness of the citizens and employees of the organizations to address the dangers of uninformed use of cyberspace through awareness-raising and cybersecurity training in different parts of the country, from north to south, including the islands, with the support of partners;
- **MOOC – Cyber Security in Schools:** The Portuguese Directorate-General for Education, in collaboration with the University of Lisbon, the Cyber Attorney's Office of the Attorney General's Office, the Directorate-General for Education and Science Statistics (DGEEC) and the Portuguese Computer Science Teachers Association, promotes the online training course "Cybersecurity in Schools", in MOOC format (Massive Open Online Course), within the scope of SeguraNet Awareness Center. This course is intended for members of the Directorate of Public and Private Schools, ICT coordinators / administrators who are most directly involved in cybersecurity issues and the security forces in schools. However, it is open to all teachers of basic and secondary education, to senior technicians, psychologists, social workers, etc. and to anyone interested in this subject.

The main objective of this MOOC is to make schools and the wider educational community aware of cybersecurity issues and to promote critical, responsible and secure use of the Internet, mobile devices and virtual environments. Generally speaking, this training course will cover the following objectives:

- Encourage reflection on security opportunities and challenges in the digital world;
- Value the safe use of networks, information systems and digital devices;
- Empower for the safe use of the Internet, mobile devices and virtual environments;
- Promote good cybersecurity practices in educational communities.
- **We Need to Modernize Cybersecurity Education to Include Vital Skills (Morello, 2019):** In this post the author expresses several concerns related to a more modern approach and in keeping with the current dangers of unprepared internet use. In the approach clues and indications of what in the reader's opinion is necessary to do are given. Regarding the various types of target audiences, however, the author is very general about what to do.
- **Cybersecurity, a relevant issue in children's education (Vitor Manso, 2019):** The author focuses on the use of the internet by children. Key aspects such as password security, suitability of age-appropriate computer applications, the use of social networks, supervised use by adults and digital education are mentioned;

- **Kids need to learn about cybersecurity, but teachers only have so much time in the day (Joanne Orlando, 2019):** According to the author, "While we do need more education on cyber security, the school curriculum is already overflowing, and teachers are expected to take on this program voluntarily. It seems schools are routinely being expected to manage more societal issues - road safety, teeth brushing, and how to have sex safely. We need to carefully consider whether we can ask teachers to take this on too."

- **A Parents' Guide to Cybersecurity (Connectsafely, 2019):** In this guide, a Top 5 Questions Parents About Cybersecurity are placed and analyzed:
  - "**What are the biggest security threats to kids?** Children and teens can be caught by the same kinds of security problems that affect adults (drive-by downloads, links to malicious sites, viruses and malware, etc.). But there are some special ways criminals get to kids, such as links to "fan sites" that contain malicious links or "free stuff," messages that look like they're from friends, offers of free music or movies or ring tones or anything else that a child might be tempted to download;
  - **How do I talk with my child about security?** Actually, security is one of those topics that are pretty easy to talk with kids about, because, just like adults, they don't want to be exploited, tricked or ripped off either. Just talk with them about how there are some people who try to take advantage of others by stealing their money or their information. Explain that not everything is what it appears to be – why it's important to think before we connect. Don't make it a one-time conversation; revisit it from time to time. Ask them what they think and if they've gotten anything suspicious lately. Your kids might know more about cybersecurity than you think;
  - **How do we protect our family's computers?** It's important to use up-to-date security software and make sure that your operating system and the software you use are up to date. Software companies sometimes find and then fix security flaws via updates. Follow the rest of the advice in this guide – such as being careful about the websites you and your kids visit and links you and they click on – and always make sure you have strong passwords;
  - **How do we protect our mobile devices?** There are security apps for mobile devices, but the best way to protect mobile devices is to use a PIN (personal identification number or password), to be careful about what apps you use and to have a way of wiping your data if your phone is lost or stolen. Visit ConnectSafely's security center at connectsafely.org/security to find out about apps that will remotely wipe or lock your phone and help you find it if it's missing;
  - **Why do we always hear "Never share your passwords"?** Because it can be tempting to share passwords with friends, and it's not sound cybersecurity. The more widely passwords are shared, the more your data, identity and property are out of your control. Sometimes friends become ex friends or are just careless with all that's behind your password, so it's important that passwords are kept private, easy to remember and hard to guess. Talk with your kids about why it isn't a good idea to share their passwords – except possibly with you. But if you want to model not sharing passwords, you can check your kids' accounts with them rather than knowing and using their passwords when they're unaware you're in their accounts. For more on this, visit passwords.connectsafely.org." in (Connectsafely, 2019).

DEALING WITH THE BIG PROBLEM

Functional Cyber Violence

The malicious actions, which the author calls functional cyber violence owing to their harmful effects on the functioning of societies, may be due to different motivations. They may be due to simple acts of play, most often to show pseudo-computer proficiency attacks that we call cyber-attacks of vanity. They may also be due to actions of cybercrime, aiming to obtain economic returns, and here we highlight actions of capture of corporate server attacks of DDoS to incapacitate remote systems or at much higher-level attacks aimed at attacking the so-called national sovereignty of some state. This is called cyber warfare.

Whatever their type, these actions have in common some factors. They are usually hidden actions and they are usually executed remotely. That is to say, they are not actions triggered locally where one has and uses physical access to the computational systems, and they are executed exploiting faults in the computational systems. Another very important aspect is that, in general, the target to be achieved is not a specific target. Here some of the types mentioned are excepted. For example, it may be a deliberate intention to attack a particular institution or company, and then the targets will obviously be specific. Another situation of specific targets usually occurs in cyber warfare. In this case, the preferred targets are computer systems of the so-called critical infrastructures. That is, the computer systems that control and manage electricity, potable water, food logistics fuel systems and also banking and financial systems. These targets are chosen to provoke civil chaos and even paralyze societies by depriving them of the aforementioned means.

However, not all attacks are targeted at specific targets. Many are targeted indiscriminately, whether occasional attacks or not, especially those due to cyber-vanity or cyber-crime. In these cases, the attacks are massive and use massive and indiscriminate means of distribution such as e-mail systems.

The ordinary and not very informatically proficient user tends to face these attacks and this type of activity as something that only concerns computer science. Even at the level of higher sectors of society, such as police, legal and even governmental structures, they often have this same perception and their actions are negatively influenced by this as perhaps a wrong perception of the problem.

For example, in a large number of attacks, namely non-DDoS attacks, so systems can be attacked, they must be vulnerable to such attacks because they have some software or hardware failure that allows such attack by using the so-called exploits, i.e. software that exploits these same flaws. This is a matter for IT since the problem may not only come from there.

It also comes from another indirect and unconscious facilitator of computer attacks. This side is made up of dozens of computer users who have no idea that their means can be used in cyber-violence and, as such, act as simple unconscious and innocent pawns in this type of activity. This problem arises from the fact that the computer systems to attack must be vulnerable to attack but to be attacked you need two things: the means of attack itself and the weapon to use this means of attack. Compared to a classic firearm, we would say that you need two things: the ammunition itself and the weapon that fires this ammunition. The perspective here is the same: whether in attacks using exploits or DDoS, it takes the computer to target these attacks. These media are then the computers of ordinary users who unknowingly are empowering them.

Many of the computer media, from a personal or business computer, a smartphone or some similar device, have hardware or software failures not resolved by the respective manufacturers. These faults have possibly been resolved by them but not corrected by the owners of those systems personal. These owners may not have a policy of correct use of access passwords and so a very considerable number of "weapons" may be available for use in cyber-attacks.

We can consider that in general all attacks go through two temporally distinct phases, which are the preparation phase of the attack and the attack phase itself. The phase of preparation, and excluding occasional attacks, is usually a phase that requires a lot of time for its implementation and consists of the installation in computer software systems that will interact with the systems to attack.

The Framework for the Actions

Although attacks on critical infrastructures or command and control systems of military systems are, by their magnitude and the fact that they may call into question the sovereignty of countries, which are very worrying and serious and included in the so-called Cyber War, other types of attacks by their constancy and intensity are also very worrying and exhausting for civil societies.

There has also been a growing increase in the relevance of these attacks. Of concern is the possibility of a mixed attack, i.e. specific targets but using, for example, DDoS attacks, and targeting the banking and financial systems of some countries, similar to those that occurred in Estonia in 2007. On the other hand, they have had another framework of a cyber war against this country, which could paralyze the banking systems used every day causing chaos in the affected countries (Friedman, 2014).

The possibility of these attacks occurs not only due to the existence of security problems as a result of failures in personal computers that allow the installation of software that constitutes them as a bot of some botnet. This possibility stems mainly from the common users and their unconsciousness and unconcern, although not necessarily purposeful, to protect their systems. These common users are essentially concerned with the possible existence of viruses on their computers that in one way or another may affect their files, the operation of their computer and other aspects related to them. Even so, despite the personal affectation and damage they may have, only a small number of users take protection measures. And, normally, these actions are defensive, that is are taken when a problem appears, and are not preventive actions and as such taken by anticipation.

In addition to these aspects, it should be noted that the software to be used in a remote computer attack to some system, when this attack is well planned and the software well designed, does not affect the computer where it is housed as this is not its purpose. As such, it is not easily detected by computer owners because they do not notice any harmful action on their own computer. Even bot software detection by computer security software is difficult if there has not been any previous attack in which this bot software has already been used. Therefore, may remain incognito on the zombie computer.

In this way, it is verified that although the existence of computer crashes, both hardware and software, is serious, the problem is more centralized and as such its resolution will also be centralized and later made available.

If this aspect alone is already troubling, it is further aggravated by the diversity of equipment, Smartphones, IOT devices, etc. Most of these devices have an internal browser, often with username and standard access passwords and as such easily accessible. As an example of this, we have the computer attack that occurred in September 2016 in which the simple domestic surveillance camera browsers were used to trigger a mass attack of DDoS (Franceschi-Bicchierai, 2016).

That cyberattack was powered by something the internet had never seen before: an army made of more than one million hacked Internet of Things devices. The hackers, whose identity is still unknown, used not one, but two networks made of around 980,000 and 500,000 hacked devices, mostly internet-connected cameras. The attackers used all those cameras and other unsecured online devices to connect to the journalist Brian Krebs website KrebsOnSecurity.com, pummeling the site with requests in an attempt to make it collapse, in (Franceschi-Bicchierai, 2016).

The Importance of the Type of Users Profile

One face of this multifaceted problem is the users themselves. As we have already mentioned, the vast majority of these users are not very computer literate, usually have a minimum knowledge of how to operate and handle their equipment and even this knowledge is usually from the user perspective. They have a very wide age range and can range from children to older people. It is also not because they are too young or too old that their equipment cannot be penetrated and used to trigger cyber-attacks. The economic and social level is also not important for considering users as potential unconscious suppliers of equipment to be used for attacks.

Another worrying issue related to this diversity of users is the fact that many of them are children who use mobile devices such as smartphones, pads and other similar equipment. Because of their age and unconcern, they do not have any notion of the danger that their mobile equipment can cause in terms of cyber security. It is not because these devices are child-operated that do not become dangerous and cannot be used in cyber attacks.

Failures to facilitate computer attacks can also originate and cause problems with network equipment for residential Internet access. Let us cite the fact that there is a European manufacturer of a router for residential Internet access where the access password was created based on the public SSID. Then, the password is easily determinable by reversing the creation process. These kinds of equipment were massively installed by an internet access provider without changing the original password. This made these routers fully accessible to anyone. Clients always had the possibility of a posteriori changing these passwords but as most of them were not computer-literate people they did not have the notion of what they should and should do, much less how to do it. Subsequently these suppliers changed this procedure and the equipment became available with unique passwords. However, for a long time these devices have been exposed and permeable and perhaps many will still be, leading to their undue use.

That is to say, all computers of any kind are usable, and therefore any actions to be taken must take into account all such types of users and cannot exclude themselves a priori.

How can This Problem be Solved?

Therefore, problems that may arise due to actions and mainly non-actions of cyber protection by ordinary users are much more difficult to resolve than those due to hardware or software failures. This is due to the fact that personal computers or mobile devices are spread worldwide and are of several different types. That is to say, it is a decentralized problem and requires for its resolution that preventive actions be taken locally in these systems, which is not easy to do and may not be possible to be done by some entity.

It must be their owners to take such protective measures.

So, the question is how to do this or better how do the owners do this?

The author is of the opinion that only with massive actions of education in cyber security, can these problems be achieved, and if not eliminated, at least minimized.

The approach to be taken in these actions must be global, i.e. it cannot be considered that this is a problem to be solved only by computer scientists. No, it is not. The level of involvement of these technicians is very important and essential but given the universalist and already mentioned nature of the worldwide dissemination of devices with internet access, the actions have to be much more comprehensive, and involve all types of users whatever their level of education, economic level or age group.

Thus, ordinary users have to become the central target of these e-safety education campaigns.

We believe that in most countries, this position is not usually followed. When awareness-raising and e-safety education campaigns are in place, they are usually targeted at narrow population groups, such as university students and age groups in their twenties.

Now it is not only these users of the internet. Globally, and this trend is growing and even unstoppable, anyone on any side is already or will very soon come to be an internet user. If we add too little information and training in the area, we have a perfect storm with results that could include the existence of an increasing number of easily captured devices used for concerted actions of cyber-attacks.

It is common and also understandable that these users have only a posture and behavior solely to protect their devices, namely the protection of your files, i.e. their text documents and their photos files. That is, these people have only an understandable local and particular concern with the surrounding computing environment and not with the overall aspect as is the global computing infrastructure in its various components.

Education campaigns also must focus on this aspect. Any computer regardless of its characteristics, its computational power, location, etc., which is connected to the internet, becomes part of a whole and can be used to negatively affect this whole.

Raise awareness of Internet access providers and device manufacturers with browsers or built-in net access.

CONCLUSION

The problem of computer attacks and their effects on the daily life of civil society is one of the most worrying issues in today's societies, which are almost entirely dependent on the information society.

The role of the users of this information society, namely that of ordinary users, that is, those who are not very computer literate, is very significant. Although most of the time, and for most people, this is a problem that only computer engineers and technicians must deal with, and as such should only be solved, this is not the case. The role of these technicians is to find solutions to these problems, but the application of these solutions does not concern them directly, but to all users of computer equipment: computers, smartphones, pads, etc., by protecting their equipment and to operate them in a safe manner.

This apparently stress-free solution to the problem is not easy to achieve. The devices are used by any kind of people: are used by children, older people and others; by people with low, medium or high levels of knowledge and intellectual levels; by people with higher, middle or basic education; by academics or not; and by people from all social levels. This various factors / conditions, makes the problem universal.

However, belonging or not to one of these "groups" does not give these users a lower or greater digital proficiency, and everything is within that diversity of users.

The diversity of equipment also contributes to the problem. To be used in a computer attack, the equipment does not necessarily have to be top of the range. It does not have to have a great computational power or certain other special technical characteristics. Only being connected to the internet is enough. Thus, desktops, laptops, smartphones and even IOT devices can theoretically be used in these attacks.

The above example of using thousands of simple home surveillance cameras used to launch the largest known DDoS computer attack to date is one such example.

The solution, therefore, is to promote effective, proficient and effective cyber education that regardless of these group "classifications" can make it possible to form a resilient cyber society as much as possible.

The actions that have been taking place in the field of the promotion of computer security education are interesting and useful, but it seems to us that they are more topical actions, very localized actions, very focused on age groups, fringes of society or very narrow academic background, and as such they prove ineffective or at least inefficient in practice.

Some directions are pointed out that, through mass and universal cyber education, taking into account the diversity of the type of users and equipment, allow their cyber education or at least their awareness of such a need in order to promote the search for solutions for the protection of computer systems, in particular those which in this context turn out to be the most unprotected.

REFERENCES

Bantim, R. (2012). O que é botnet? Techtudo. Retrieved from https://www.techtudo.com.br/artigos/noticia/2012/03/o-que-e-botnet.html

Barbosa, J. (2018). *Pequenas potências militares convencionais, Grandes potências militares ciberné-llcus - Abordagem da utilização de meios informáticos na defesa/ataque militar moderno.* Coimbra, Portugal: IDN.

Clark, R. A. (2010). *Cyber War: the next threat to national security and what to do about.* NY: HarperCollins Publishers Inc.

CNCS. (2019). Programa de Sensibilização e Treino em Cibersegurança. Retrieved from https://www.cncs.gov.pt/atividades/programa-de-sensibilizacao-e-treino-em-ciberseguranca/

European Commission. (2017). Special Eurobarometer 464a - Europeans' attitudes towards cyber security. European Union, Directorate-General for Migration and Home Affairs. Brussels: EU. doi:10.2837/82418

European Commission. (n.d.). Digital Education Action Plan - Action 7 Cybersecurity in Education - Raising awareness of teachers and students. Retrieved from https://ec.europa.eu/education/education-in-the-eu/european-education-area/digital-education-action-plan-action-7-cybersecurity-in-education_en

Connectsafely. (2019). A Parents' Guide to Cybersecurity. Retrieved from https://www.connectsafely.org/wp-content/uploads/securityguide.pdf

Cyberthreat Real-Time Map. (2019). Retrieved from https://cybermap.kaspersky.com/pt

European Cyber Security Month. (2019). Retrieved from https://cybersecuritymonth.eu/

Europeans' attitudes towards cyber security. (2017). European Commission. Retrieved from https://ec.europa.eu/home-affairs/news/europeans'-attitudes-towards-cyber-security_en

Farmer, B. (2018). Russia was behind 'malicious' cyber attack on Ukraine, Foreign Office says. The Telegraph. Retrieved from https://www.telegraph.co.uk/news/2018/02/15/russia-behind-malicious-cyber-attack-ukraine-foreign-office/

Fortinet. (2019). *Q1 2019 Quarterly Threat Landscape Report*. Fortinet.

Franceschi-Bicchierai, L. (2016). How 1.5 Million Connected Cameras Were Hijacked to Make an Unprecedented Botnet. The Vice Site. Retrieved from https://www.vice.com/en_us/article/8q8dab/15-million-connected-cameras-ddos-botnet-brian-krebs

Friedman, P. S. (2014). *Cybersecurity and Cyberwar - What everyone needs to know*. N.Y: Oxford University Press.

Geers, K. (2011). Strategic cyber security NATO Cooperative Cyber Defence Centre of Excellence. Tallinn, Estonia: CCD COE Publication.

Kottler, S. (2018). February 28th DDoS Incident Report. The GitHub Blog. Retrieved from https://github.blog/2018-03-01-ddos-incident-report

Manso, V. (2019). Cibersegurança, uma questão relevante na educação das crianças. Associação Nacional para a Inovação e Desenvolvimento. Retrieved from https://www.m4p.pt/pt/destaques/artigos-de-opiniao/item/41-ciberseguranca-uma-questao-relevante-na-educacao-das-criancas

Morello, J. (2019). We Need To Modernize Cybersecurity Education To Include Vital Skills. *Forbes*.

NATO Cooperative Cyber Defence Centre of Excellence. (n.d.). Retrieved from https://ccdcoe.org/

Newhouse, W., Keith, S., Scribner, B., & Witte, G. (2017). *National initiative for cybersecurity education (NICE) cybersecurity workforce framework*. NIST; doi:10.6028/NIST.SP.800-181

Oleg Kupreev, E. B. (2019). Ataques DDoS en el primer trimestre de 2019. Kaspersky Lab. Retrieved from https://securelist.lat/ddos-report-q1-2019/88828/

Orlando, J. (2019). Kids need to learn about cybersecurity, but teachers only have so much time in the day. The Conversation AU. Retrieved from http://theconversation.com/kids-need-to-learn-about-cybersecurity-but-teachers-only-have-so-much-time in the day 112136

Simões, P. (2018). GitHub sobreviveu ao maior ataque DDoS alguma vez registado. PplWare. Retrieved from https://pplware.sapo.pt/internet/github-sobreviveu-maior-ataque-ddos/

Zetter, K. (2014). *Countdown to Zero Day: Stuxnet and the launch of the world's first digital weapon*. NY: Crown Publishers.

Chapter 3
The Different Aspects of Information Security Education

Suchinthi Fernando
Rutgers University, USA

ABSTRACT

This chapter discusses the importance of information security education for everyone, ranging from organizations to professionals and students, all the way through to individual users of information and communication systems. It discusses the different subject areas in information security and shows how instead of being intimidated by it, different categories of users can obtain varying depths of information security education based on their cyber-activities and need for knowledge. Information security professionals would require an in-depth knowledge in all aspects of information security, and information technology professionals and students would require an overall education in these areas, while most users of information and communication systems would only require a basic education to help protect their information assets in cyberspace.

INTRODUCTION

Information is power. All important decisions, whether personal or corporate decisions, short-term or strategic long-term decisions, are made based on information available at a given time. The importance of acquiring and managing up-to-the-minute and accurate information has become more and more important in this digital era leading up to the fourth industrial revolution, where information technology prevails over all other types of technology. Managing information entails not only maintaining the integrity of the information, but also preserving its confidentiality to gain that much required edge over competitors, or ensuring that the privacy of any groups or individuals is not violated. As important as it is to obtain the latest information in order to gain that competitive advantage, it is even more important to ensure that that information does not fall into the wrong hands, since the damage caused by an information security breach, both financially as well as to the reputation of an organisation or any individual, could be phenomenal. As the race for acquiring information gets heated leading to all out cyber warfare, the difficulty of managing information also increases exponentially.

DOI: 10.4018/978-1-6684-3554-0.ch003

Cyber-security has become a focal point of most organisations, where they strive to provide information security and assurance by creating more resilient structures and systems to keep the never-ending, ever-increasing threats and attacks at bay. Where they previously used to focus only on other aspects of information technology, such as faster networks with higher bandwidths, higher processing speed and power, timely and cost effective software delivery, etc., information technology now revolves around information security, where secure networks, stronger encryption protocols, stronger and more robust systems, secure software development, etc. have taken the centre stage. The software and information industry has finally come to the realization that information security is not something that can be plugged in at the end, but is, in fact, an integral component of information technology that needs to be considered and planned for from the start, incorporated into the design of systems and software, and where the implementation of software systems should be carried out around the established information security standards and procedures. Thus, information security is now finally acknowledged as a journey and not simply as an end destination. Almost all corporations now incorporate information security at all levels and in all branches of business by setting up the required perimeter, hardware and software security systems in place and laying out information security policies and procedures.

The weakest link in all these security measures, however, is the users of these information systems. No matter how strong the technological security measures are, or how well conceived the security policies, procedures and protocols are, if these policies, procedures and protocols are not properly administered or followed, therein lies the biggest vulnerability of any system. The human aspect of information security is the leading cause of information security breaches, and is the component that is most commonly and easily exploited, whether it is in the form of intrusions from the outside or insider threats. This stands true whether it is a corporation, a government, or an individual – the weakest component in an information system is its users. The only way to guard against this is to ensure that information users are properly educated and made aware in the ways of securing information, and thereby, securing their lives.

Living in this digitized age, using all kinds of communication devices which allow people to access and share information in a multitude of ways, without at least a basic awareness of information security is analogous to being in the driver's seat in a car on a busy highway without knowing how to drive. This does not mean that one must shy away from all technology and not be socially active in this digital world. As extensive as the subject of information security is, the fear of not being able to acquire all that knowledge should not deter people from using the technology available to them. Instead, they should gear themselves up by learning what they need to learn about information security, so they may be ready to function in this digital era without having to face major threats.

Information security covers a vast range of subject areas, but not each user needs to be thoroughly educated in each of these different areas. Based on what their job entails and the level of engagement they have with the information, and the criticality of the information they deal with, their information security education can be catered to suit each user role accordingly. Some users might require in-depth knowledge of certain areas, while needing only a basic understanding in others, whereas other users might need only basic awareness overall, and others need an all-round detailed understanding. Regardless of a user's job within a certain organisation, all individual users of information and communication systems should also be cognizant in information security so they may know how to protect their privacy and not put their lives at risk. The mission of this chapter is to discuss the importance of information security education, the different aspects of such an education, and the varying depths and levels of information security education and awareness required by different types of users based on their user roles within an information system. This chapter aims to provide information users with a basic education on information security, and list best practices to help them stay protected in cyberspace.

BACKGROUND

Information security is an essential and timely component in information technology (IT) education, especially in the present digital era of the fourth industrial revolution. Yet, even though the teaching of basic IT skills such as basic programming, database and web development, etc. has become an integral part of education regardless of whether or not the students major in computer or information sciences, information security is most often overlooked and left out (Senanayake & Fernando, 2017). This is quite an unfortunate situation as information security has much broader scope than IT, and is, in fact, an integral part of any information and communication system which stores information and allows its users to access and share that information. According to Harris and Maymi (2016), today's fast-paced growth of the IT industry, which does not allow sufficient time for educating people on how to properly maintain and safeguard their information, leaves less time for information security professionals to discover new security practices and procedures, while, unfortunately, giving more time for adversaries to learn how to circumvent the security mechanisms in place (Harris & Maymi, 2016). Information systems should enable proper and secure access to and communication of information to authorized users through authorized channels instead of simply allowing access to anyone. Thus, users of information systems should receive sufficient education in information security to enable them to properly utilize the system, while ensuring their privacy, as well as the confidentiality and integrity of the information. Education in information security, therefore, is required not only by students and professionals, but also by any and all users of information and communication systems.

When it comes to possible information security vulnerabilities and threats, ignorance is not bliss. Unfortunately, risk and uncertainty are difficult concepts for people to evaluate (West, 2008), as the human brain perceives security somewhat differently from its reality (Schneier, 2008). While the reality of security is mathematical, based on the probability of different risks and the effectiveness of different countermeasures, the feeling of security is based on the individual person's psychological reactions to these (Schneier, 2008). This divergence between the reality and the brain's perception of security leads to gaps between the required and implemented security countermeasures, where if the threat is perceived to be greater than what it actually is, one can feel paranoid even when they are secure, resulting in expensive, unnecessary security mechanisms, whereas when they fail to comprehend the real intensity of the risk they may become complacent and undermine it, thereby increasing their vulnerability to attacks. Gains in security involve trade-offs in terms of money, time, convenience, capabilities or liberties, and humans make these trade-offs intuitively, exaggerating some risks or costs, while downplaying others (Schneier, 2008). When aspects of trade-off such as the severity of risk, probability of risk, magnitude of the costs, effectiveness of countermeasures at mitigating the risk, and comparison of disparate risks and costs are evaluated incorrectly, perceived trade-offs also diverge from the actual trade-offs. Schneier (2008) categorizes behavioural heuristics as risk, probability, cost, and decision heuristics, where risk heuristics also include Prospect Theory by Kahneman and Tversky (1979), where people accept small sure gains rather than risking or chancing a larger gain, whereas they risk larger losses rather than accepting smaller sure losses (Kahneman & Tversky, 1979), among others. West (2008) further states that some of the predictable and exploitable characteristics in the human decision-making process are their belief of being less at risk, risk homeostasis or maintaining an acceptable degree of risk in their minds and thus increasing risky behaviour to suit increased security measures (for e.g.: driving faster to compensate for wearing a seatbelt, etc.), and cognitive miserliness (i.e.: having only a limited capacity for information processing and multitasking). These lead to feeling less motivated by abstract concepts such as security, and to making quick, uninformed decisions based on learned rules and heuristics instead. Hence, security only becomes a priority when people start to have problems with it (West, 2008). Therefore, an important part of information security education is teaching users that anyone could fall victim to an information security attack at any time. It is important to perceive risk accurately, in order to implement necessary countermeasures to avert that risk. As tighter security mechanisms help to keep vulnerabilities and attacks at bay, and thereby, keep risk below the 'accident zone', periodic risk perception renewals are also required in order to maintain risk perception in the human mind at an acceptable level, so that people will maintain security mechanisms above an acceptable threshold (Gonzalez & Sawicka, 2002).

When the concept of information security was first developed, it focused mainly around technological aspects such as network security and cryptography, etc. (Bishop, 2003), but as the realization that the users of the system were the weakest link and that human errors played the biggest role in information security breaches was dawned, so was the importance of the human aspect pertaining to security recognized (Fernando, 2014). As the focus of information security thus shifted from being technology-oriented to management-oriented (Lacey, 2009), international standards such as ISO/IEC 270001 (2005) etc. also emphasized the need to take human resource security into consideration when managing information security. As explained by Vroom and von Solms (2003), effective information security requires not only physical and technical controls, but also operational controls, which concern the behaviour and actions of users with regards to information security and are listed under security policies, procedures and guidelines. They further state that even though these policies, etc. are audited to ensure their effectiveness, instead of also auditing the performance of users, their adherence to these policies, procedures and guidelines are simply assumed (Vroom & von Solms, 2003). This is inadequate as people often find ways to work around such established policies, etc. instead of actually following them. In order to succeed in business in today's world, ensuring that access to information is strictly limited to the personnel who need to know it in order to perform their assigned tasks is mandatory (Schweitzer, 1996), leading to the implementation of the latest and strongest security mechanisms to limit unauthorized access to information by most organisations. In such cases, tricking people to reveal confidential information is much easier than penetrating the myriad of layers of technological security mechanisms that are put in place. In fact, most information security attacks such as social engineering, spear phishing, or willing or unwilling, knowing or unknowing collusion from an insider, etc. require a human element in order to succeed (Williams, 2011).

Another interesting observation is that 60%-70% of attacks originate, not from intrusions from the outside, but from 'trusted folk' already inside the system (Lynch, 2006). This number increases further when including users with non-malicious intent wittingly or unwittingly involved in attacks (Grimes, 2010). An intrusion is an activity violating system's security policy (Ning, Jajodia & Wang, 2003), while an insider threat is when trusted users with legitimate access abuse system privileges (Liu, Martin, Hetherington & Matzner, 2005), or when individuals possessing substantial internal access to system enact intentionally disruptive, unethical or illegal behaviour (Mills, Grimaila, Peterson & Butts, 2011), Thus, expensive and sophisticated intrusion detection systems are rendered worthless against these insider attacks, which are nearly to completely indistinguishable from normal actions as inside attackers already have authorization to use and access the system, and these actions are not too different from the normal operation of applications and processes (Liu, et al., 2005). Thus, malicious insider activities such as exploitation, extraction, manipulation, reconnaissance, entrenchment, etc. could easily pass off as normal activities such as database administration, word processing, web browsing, command-prompt interaction, etc. Therefore, it is advised to design security systems by accepting that the adversaries are already inside the system (Sabett, 2011). According to Foley (2011), the components required for a proactive and sustainable security program include preventive, detective, corrective and feedback mechanisms, from credentialing users and restricting their access through authorization of identity, time and place, to auditing, reviewing, monitoring, increasing security awareness and deterring inappropriate activity, to updating credentials, restricting or removing access based on the user's contribution to the compromise, severity of the compromise, and the risk of incident being repeated, to dynamic, reactive and planned feedback to create solutions (Foley, 2011).

In today's world where nearly everyone is digitally interconnected with each other, and where the Internet of Things (IoT) plays a very important role in the day to day life of people as they utilize the Internet for most of their activities including shopping, banking, managing their health, ordering their meals, etc. (Kim & Solomon, 2016), companies and organisation dealing with vast amounts of data and information are not the only subjects at risk of information security breaches, but any person connected to a network through a communication device of any sorts could be a victim of information security attacks (Senanayake & Fernando, 2017). Hence, it is of the utmost importance for any person using information systems for any purpose, whether professional or personal, to be cognizant in information security and be aware of threats and vulnerabilities they could be faced with, and thus, to acquire at least the basic knowledge on countermeasures against these threats and vulnerabilities. ISO/IEC 270001 (2005) emphasizes the importance of training, awareness and competence of users of an information security management system; while Peltier (2002) states that the user's level of awareness should be taken into consideration when developing security awareness programs (Peltier, 2002). This chapter intends to show that different users can obtain varying levels of education in different areas of information security education based on their job tasks and user roles and aims to bridge the gaps currently existing in most information systems and organisations by encouraging information system users to obtain the required education or awareness in order to minimize the risk of falling victim to cybercrimes.

DIFFERENT ASPECTS OF INFORMATION SECURITY

Information Security Subject Areas

The Certified Information Systems Security Professional (CISSP) certification defines eight CISSP domains as Security and Risk Management, Asset Security, Security Engineering, Communication and Network Security, Identity and Access Management, Security Assessment and Testing, Security Operations, and Software Development Security (Harris & Maymi, 2016).

The author identifies the basic subject areas of an overall information security education as listed below.

Subject Areas of an Information Security Education

- **Risk Assessment and Management:** Assessing potential risk factors to determine the appropriate level of security.

- ○ Proper identification of all assets (including facility, hardware, software, data, human assets, knowledge, etc.).
- ○ Valuation of assets (determine the value of assets based on the cost of acquiring new assets to replace assets if lost/damaged, cost of developing/getting the assets back to original state, cost of maintaining assets, cost of lost productivity when assets are unavailable, cost of replacing corrupt/lost data, value to owners and users, value to adversaries, value of intellectual property, price others are willing to pay for it, liability issues if assets are compromised, usefulness of assets, etc.).
- ○ Identify threats to assets, their exposure rates and probabilities of risk.
  - ▪ Major risk categories include physical damage (for e.g.: fire, water, vandalism, power loss, natural disasters, etc.), human errors (i.e.: accidental/intentional action or inaction that disrupts productivity), equipment malfunction (i.e.: failure of systems and peripheral devices), inside and outside attacks (i.e.: hacking, cracking, attacking), misuse of data (for e.g.: sharing trade secrets, fraud, espionage, theft, etc.), loss of data (intentional/unintentional through destructive means), and application errors (for e.g.: computation, input, buffer overflows, etc.) (Harris & Maymi, 2016).
- ○ Classify threats by category and calculate actual magnitude of potential loss in order to rank severity of identified vulnerabilities and prioritize potential risks.
- ○ Identify possible security countermeasures to reduce identified risks to an acceptable level.
- ○ Establish required level of security by implementing the suited security countermeasures selected through cost/benefit comparison (comparing security budget with the required protection; i.e.: the safeguard should only be implemented if the cost of loss of assets is greater than the cost of the safeguard).
- **Security Architecture and Models:** How the security model is determined based on security requirements and priorities of the organisation.
  - ○ Classify data/information based on their criticality (i.e.: level of secrecy, value to the organisation, value to outside sources, the loss/damage that would occur should the data/information be disclosed/compromised, etc.).
  - ○ Establish the role of trust, process activity, device maintenance, etc. within the organisation, and operating states, kernel functions, memory mapping, etc. of the systems used within the organisation.
  - ○ Establish different user roles within the organisation.
  - ○ Determine the security clearance levels of personnel based on their job descriptions (tasks needed to perform), need-to-know, department, occupation, level within the organisational hierarchy, and the least privileges required by them.
  - ○ Determine the Security Model to be adapted by the organisation based on which factors/objectives of information security (i.e.: main factors such as confidentiality, integrity, availability, and other factors such as accountability and non-repudiation) matter the most to the organisation (Harris & Maymi, 2016).
    - ▪ The most basic security model for when confidentiality is prioritized over other aspects is the Bell-laPadula model, which ensures no read-up and no write-down.
    - ▪ If integrity is the priority, the Biba model ensures no read-down and no write-up.

- Other security models include Clark-Wilson model, Information Flow model, Non-interference model, Brewer and Nash (Chinese Wall) model, Graham-Denning model, and Harrison-Ruzzo-Ullman model, etc.
  - ○ Implement the organisation's security model based on security clearance levels of users and classification levels of data/information objects.
- **Security Management Practices:** How the organisation's security system is established and managed.
  - ○ Evaluate business objectives, security risks, user productivity, functionality requirements and objectives of the organisation.
  - ○ Establish security policies, procedures, standards, baselines, and best practices stating what to do and how to do it in order to ensure organisation's security.
  - ○ Establish guidelines on how to act in unforeseen, unanticipated circumstances.
  - ○ Determine the security consciousness and awareness levels of users; categorize users based on their level of understanding and observance of security principles, policies, procedures, guidelines and best practices, and conduct personnel security training and awareness.
    - Conduct periodic risk perception renewals to ensure that risk perception and security consciousness of users remain within an acceptable level.
- **Access Control Systems and Methodology:** Controlling access to information based on privileges assigned to a specific user or user role.
  - ○ Authentication to verify user's identity/credentials to ensure they are who they claim to be.
    - Something the user knows (for e.g.: signature, password, personal identification number/PIN, passcode, key phrase, etc.).
    - Something the user has (for e.g.: key, swipe card, token, etc.).
    - Something the user is (biometrics, for e.g.: fingerprint, facial scan, voice print, iris scan, retina scan, palm scan, hand geometry, hand topology, signature dynamics, keyboard dynamics, etc.). Biometric authentication systems require proper calibration to reduce false negatives and false positives.
  - ○ Verifying user's authorization to access the requested information.
    - Verify if the user has the need-to-know and authorization to access that information/data object based on the organisation's security model, by comparing the user's security clearance level with the information/data object's classification level.
    - Verify the methods or modes through which the user is allowed to access that information (for e.g.: through a graphical user interface, command line interface, direct access to the back-end database, etc.).
    - Validate what actions the user is allowed to perform on the information (i.e.: enter/input/create new information, view/read, update, or delete existing information).
    - Best method is to default to 'no access' and to allow access only to those users that have been explicitly authorized access rather than to first allow access to anyone who meets the criteria and then deny access to blacklisted users.
  - ○ Proper identification and authentication of user and verification of authorization ensures accountability of users to their actions.
  - ○ Single Sign-On (SSO) systems such as Kerberos allow users to access many interconnected systems during the session by signing on once.

- ○ Access control models include Discretionary Access Control (DAC), Mandatory Access Control (MAC), and Role-Based Access Control (RBAC).
- ○ Access control should happen at different levels and layers of the security system through physical, technical and administrative controls, starting with access to the facility at the security perimeter, access to the building, access to the user's computer, access to the system and network limited by access control lists (ACLs) implemented on firewalls, constrained user interfaces which limit access only to data/information objects a user is authorized to access, etc.
- ○ Penetration testing should be conducted on the system periodically to ensure that access control mechanisms are solid and not easily penetrable.
- **Telecommunications and Network Security:** How network structures and communication systems are designed and implemented to ensure secure communication of information.
  - ○ Network structure includes the architecture and design of the network and the material used for constructing it (Kim & Solomon, 2016).
    - ▪ Type of network (i.e.: wide area network/WAN, local area network/LAN, metropolitan area network/MAN, etc.), topology of the network (for e.g.: ring, bus, mesh, star topology, etc.), access technologies (for e.g.: Ethernet, token ring, Carrier-sense multiple access/CSMA with collision detection or collision avoidance, etc.), and wireless technologies (for e.g.: frequency hopping or direct sequence spread spectrum, etc.).
    - ▪ Wireless medium or cabling (for e.g.: coaxial or twisted pair copper cables, fibre optics, etc.) optimized for different parts of the network to ensure the least noise, attenuation, crosstalk, etc., while staying within a reasonable budget based on distance/length of cabling needed, fire rating of cabling material, network structure, type of transmission (whether analog or digital, asynchronous or synchronous, broadband or baseband), etc.
    - ▪ Intranets, Extranets, Network Address Translation (NAT), Internet Protocol (IP) addressing formats (i.e.: version 4 – Ipv4 or version 6 – Ipv6), subnets and subnet masks.
    - ▪ Firewall types (i.e.: Packet Filtering, Stateful Inspection, Application Proxy, etc.).
    - ▪ Firewall architectures for segregation and isolation of different network domains based on who has access to information in each domain and criticality of information (for e.g.: Bastion host, Screened host, Screened subnet with a demilitarized zone/DMZ between the public and private network portions, etc.).
    - ▪ Type of encryption, i.e. Link encryption (encrypt all data including headers, routing data, addresses, etc., along a communication path, requiring decryption at each hop, but providing extra protection against packet sniffers) or End-to-End encryption (where headers, addresses, routing data, etc. are not encrypted, thus eliminating the need for decryption at each hop).
  - ○ Establish the devices (for e.g.: hubs, switches, routers, repeaters, bridges, gateways, etc.) to be used at different layers/levels of the network.
    - ▪ The International Standards Organisation's Open Systems Interconnected (ISO/OSI) 7-layered reference model consists of physical layer, data-link layer, network layer, transport layer, session layer, presentation layer, and application layer.
    - ▪ The Transmission Control Protocol / Internet Protocol (TCP/IP) 4-layered network model consists of network interface layer, internet layer, transport layer, and application layer.

- Implement networking protocols best suited for the level of security needed based on who accesses information through the system, ways in which information is accessed, and how critical the information is.
    - Networking protocols at transport layer include Transmission Control Protocol (TCP) and User Datagram Protocol (UDP), while protocols at the internet or network layer include Internet Protocol (IP), etc.
    - Other protocols include Dynamic Host Configuration Protocol (DHCP), Internet Control Message Protocol (ICMP), Internet Message Access Protocol (IMAP), Simple Mail Transfer Protocol (SMTP), Post Office Protocol (POP), Simple Network Management Protocol (SNMP), Point to Point Protocol (PPP), Layer 2 Tunnelling Protocol (L2TP), Internet Protocol Security (IPSec), Transport Layer Security (TLS), Secure Socket Layer (SSL), Wireless Access Protocol (WAP), File Transfer Protocol (FTP), FTP over TLS/SSL (FTPS), Secure FTP (SFTP), Hypertext Transfer Protocol (HTTP), HTTP over TLS/SSL (HTTPS), etc.
- Establish the ports for certain protocols and services as best suited for the organisation.
    - Common ports include ports 20 and 21 for FTP, 25 for SMTP, 80 for HTTP, 110 for POP, 143 for IMAP, etc.
    - Close all ports which are not being utilized, so as to not allow adversaries the chance to attack through those ports.
- Establish network connection methods.
    - Dedicated Links, Switching (i.e.: Packet Switching or Circuit Switching), Frame Relay, and Virtual Circuits.
    - Remote Access, Virtual Private Network (VPN) and Tunnelling.
- Establish policies on network usage.
    - Times at which network access is allowed to ensure that no untimely access is possible, and to identify attempts to access the network at unusual times.
    - Locations/terminals through which network access is allowed, remote access policies, etc. to limit access to the network from specified terminals/locations, and to identify attempts to access the network from unspecified remote locations, etc.
    - Amount of network access allowed in one session, and number of sessions allowed per day, etc., so that access can be limited as needed, and excessive access or changes in access patterns could be identified.
- **Cryptography:** The art and science of disguising data.
    - Being Greek for 'hidden secret', cryptography is the way of storing and transmitting data in a form that can only be read and processed by its intended users/recipients.
    - Information can be protected by encoding/encrypting/enciphering it into an unreadable format, so as to hide it from unauthorized users.
    - The authorized users or intended recipients of the transmitted coded message can decode/decrypt/decipher it with the proper key.
    - The roots of cryptography run as far back as Egyptian hieroglyphics. Cryptography later evolved into a mechanism to securely pass messages through hostile environments (Harris & Maymi, 2016).
        - Used during wars by Spartans (i.e.: Scytale cipher, a papyrus sheet which can be read only if wrapped around a staff of the proper diameter), Greeks (for e.g.: messages tat-

tooed on carrier's shaved head and covered by the growing hair, etc.), Mary, Queen of Scott's, and Benedict Arnold, all the way through to the Enigma machine used by the Germans during World War II (the cracking of which by the Turing machine is said to have shortened the war by two years).

- Early ciphers included 'Atbash Cipher' (a Hebrew cryptographic method which flips the alphabet over), and 'Caesar Cipher' (where Julius Caesar shifted the alphabet to the right by three positions).

○ Types of ciphers include substitution ciphers (where letters of the plaintext are substituted with different characters to create the cipher-text), transposition ciphers (where letters of the plaintext are scrambled to create the cipher-text), running key cipher (where the key may be hidden in the physical world and could for e.g. refer to a certain letter in a certain word in a certain line on a certain page of a certain book, etc.), and concealment cipher (where a certain agreed upon key, such as every third letter of the message, is used).

- Atbash Cipher, Caesar cipher, Vigenere Cipher, One Time Pad, etc. are examples of substitution ciphers.

○ Steganography is the method of hiding data in another media such as in an image, audio or video file.

○ Current encryption algorithms apply complex mathematical formulae in a specific sequence to plaintext in order to encrypt it.

○ The strength of the cryptosystem depends on the encryption algorithm (the more complex the algorithm, the more difficult it is to crack, and the higher the security), secrecy and length of the key (the longer it is, the more difficult it is for an adversary to guess it), and initializing vectors for key generation, etc.

- The stronger the cryptosystem, the more effort is needed to break it.
- A cryptosystem is considered strong if it is still secure when the encryption algorithm is made public and only the key is kept secret.

○ Stream ciphers perform mathematical functions on individual bits in a stream (where a key determines which functions are applied in what order), whereas block ciphers divide the plaintext message into blocks of bits and perform substitution, transposition, and other mathematical functions to it (where the algorithm dictates the functions to be used and the key dictates the order in which they should be used).

○ Cryptosystem can use symmetric keys (same key for decrypting as for encrypting) and asymmetric keys (different, but related key for decrypting than for encrypting).

- Symmetric keys are faster than asymmetric keys.
- By having a private key and public key combination (where the private key is secret and known only to its owner, and the public key is known by other users) asymmetric keys are much more secure, but carry significant overhead and are slower compared to symmetric keys.
- In addition to added security (by not sharing the private key), asymmetric keys also enable verification of sender's identity as the sender's private key acts as the sender's signature. In order to both ensure security and verify sender's identity, the message will have to be encrypted twice (once using the sender's private key, and once using the receiver's public key) and also decrypted twice (using the receiver's private key, and the sender's public key). Double encryption and double decryption adds further overhead

to the performance of asymmetric keys, but also verify the identities of both parties in secure communication.

- Symmetric cryptographic systems include Data Encryption Standard (DES), Triple-DES (3DES), etc., while asymmetric encryption algorithms include RSA (named after its inventors Rivest, Shamir, and Adleman), El Gamal, Elliptic Curve Cryptosystems (ECCs), etc.
- Hybrid methods utilize both symmetric and asymmetric keys to get the best of both worlds, by encrypting a symmetric session key using secure asymmetric keys, and then using the faster, symmetric session key for both encrypting and decrypting messages communicated within that session (thereby making the communication faster and more efficient due to lack of extra overhead), and then destroying that session key at the end of the communication session (to ensure further security).
  - Public Key Infrastructure (PKI) uses the services of a Certificate Authority (CA) to vouch for the trustworthiness of parties (especially servers) included in communication (especially in client-server communications), by issuing a certificate verifying their identity. The CA is a third party trusted by both communicating parties.
  - Hashing is a form of one-way encryption (where decryption is not possible, but message integrity can be verified by comparing against the original hash/message digest).
    - Password files should be stored in either encrypted or hashed form. It is best to hash the passwords and store the hash instead of the password itself. Then, each time the user enters their username and password combination, the entered password will be hashed and this hash will be compared against the stored hash corresponding to the entered username. If it is exactly the same, then the entered password is correct (as the smallest change to the plaintext will make a significant change in the hash) and the user is authenticated.
    - A hash value encrypted with the sender's private key creates their digital signature.
    - Hashing algorithms include MD5, Secure Hashing Algorithm (SHA) and HAVAL, etc.
  - Cryptanalysis is the science of studying and breaking the secrecy of encryption algorithms.
    - Frequency analysis is comparing the most frequently used letters and words in the cipher-text to those in the alphabet of the plaintext, to figure out patterns and thereby figure out the key and break the cipher.
  - Key management is important to ensure the trust on which cryptography is based.
    - Keys need to be securely distributed (protected during transmission, etc.) to the correct entities and continuously updated.
    - Key Escrows help by maintaining back-up keys in case they need to be recovered.
    - Multiparty control of emergency key reduces potential for abuse.
  - Message and e-mail encryption standards include Multipurpose Internet Mail Extension (MIME), Privacy-Enhanced Mail (PEM), Message Security Protocol (MSP), Pretty Good Privacy (PGP), etc.
- **Physical Security:** The physical elements contributing to information security.
  - Information security begins with securing the perimeter and restricting access to secure areas within the facility.
    - Closed Circuit Television (CCTV), motion detectors, sensors, alarms, security guards, fences, walls, etc. help enforce perimeter security and physical access control.

- Monitoring activities, examining devices taken inside and outside of the facility, signing out material, etc. help to reduce and deter theft of physical items.
- Intrusion detection systems (for e.g.: proximity detection, photoelectric/photometric detection, wave pattern detection, passive infrared/IR, acoustical-seismic detection, electromechanical detection, vibration detection, etc.) and intrusion prevention systems help to detect and deter intruders. Alarms should notify law enforcement officials of intrusions.

○ Authorization methods and controls such as biometrics, individual access badges, magnetic swipe cards, wireless proximity readers (recognizing presence of approaching object), and tokens, etc., locked cases on individual computers, placing the most sensitive assets in guarded controlled zones, etc. add extra layers of security, and thereby multiple barriers that need to be circumvented in order to access resources.

○ Proper facility construction, protection from fire and water damage, proper heating, ventilation and air-conditioning (HVAC) controls, antitheft mechanisms, etc. are required to protect all assets of the organisation including human assets.

○ Main threats to physical security include theft, interruption of services, physical damage, compromised system integrity, unauthorized information disclosure, etc. (Harris & Maymi, 2016).

- Location, visibility and accessibility of facility (i.e.: natural camouflage or attracting intruders), likelihood of natural disasters, construction material (fire protection/combustibility levels), load borne by walls, beams and columns, reinforcement for secured areas, implementation of physical controls such as fences, gates, locks, lighting, etc. should be considered before building the facility.
- Placement of doors, windows, secure hinges, fire rating, resistance to forcible entry, directional opening (opening out from the facility), electric locks reverting to disabled state for safe evacuation in power outages (if a 'safety first' approach is followed), bulletproof/shatterproof glass, etc.
- Load and weight bearing floors and ceilings, non-conducting surfaces and anti-static flooring, etc. Eliminate drop ceilings so intruders cannot lift ceiling panel and climb over partitioning walls.
- Back-up and alternate electrical power supplies, back-up procedures in cases of power loss (as disabled IDS makes intrusion easier), clean and steady power source (without interference/line noise, fluctuation, electromagnetic interference/EMI, radio frequency interference/RFI, or transient noise.), proper placement of distribution panels and circuit breakers to allow easy access.
- Surge protectors, orderly shutting down of devices, power line monitors, regulators, grounded connections, shielded lines (magnetic induction), three-prong connections and adapters. Avoid fluorescent lights (to eliminate RFI). Avoid plugging outlet strips and extension cords to each other.
- Proper placement of water and gas lines, shut-off valves, positive flow (where material flows out of and not into the building).
- Positive air pressure in HVAC systems, protected intake vents, dedicated power lines, emergency shut-off valves and switches, proper placement, etc.

- Fire detection and suppression through proper placement of the best suited type of sensors and detectors (i.e.: smoke activated, heat activated, or flame activated) and sprinklers (for e.g.: wet pipe, dry pipe, pre-action, deluge, etc.). Alternatives to sprinklers are to shut down air circulation, use carbon dioxide (CO_2), and alert fire station.
    - Illuminated and visible exit signs and unblocked fire exit doors to ensure safe evacuation in emergencies.
    - Regular monitoring of HVAC controls, climate controlled atmosphere, and reduced contaminants (corrosion, blockage, hazardous gases, etc.).
  - Location of facility components is important.
    - Data centres should not be located in top floors (in case of fire) or in basements (in case of floods), but at the core of the building (easy access to emergency crews).
    - Secure assets located in semi-secluded areas with limited accessibility.
    - Computer and equipment rooms located near wiring distribution centres, and having only a single access door (impossible to access through public areas).
  - Cipher (programmable) locks such as door delays (alarms triggered if held open too long), key-override (special key combination for emergencies overrides normal procedure), master-keying (supervisory personnel can change access codes), and hostage alarm (key combination alerting guards/police when under duress), etc., increase security.
  - Device locks for hardware include switch controls (covering on/off switches), slot locks (mounted bracket and steel cable securing system to stationary component), port controls (blocking access to drives/unused serial and parallel ports), peripheral switch controls (on/off switch between unit and slot), and cable traps (prevent removal of input and output devices by passing cables through lockable unit), etc.
  - Stationary, revolving doors and turnstiles for mantraps (small room with two doors, both needing authentication, but having entered through the first, the person is locked inside while guards verify their identity and unlock the second).
  - Weight detectors to prevent piggybacking (entering through a door that was opened for another person).
  - Physical access needs to be audited (date and time of access attempt, entry point, user identification, unsuccessful attempts, attempts at unauthorized times, etc.).
- **Applications and Systems Development Security:** Secure software development.
  - Integrate information security into the software development life cycle beginning with the requirements gathering phase (identify required level of security), moving on to the analysis and design phase (incorporate suitable security measures in the software design), through to the implementation phase (develop the designed security features), testing and debugging phases (also test security mechanisms for accuracy and correctness), deployment phase (configure security mechanisms properly), all the way through to the maintenance phase (constantly test, assess and update security mechanisms to suit current security needs).
  - Multiple layers of software security starting with the front-end user interface (validate user input to filter out invalid input or malicious code), through to the back-end database (screen and parse data before inserting it into the database).
  - Proper separation of user roles through the software system's user interface by only enabling and making visible the options for functionality that particular user/user role is authorized for.

- Not seeing other possible functionality available only to other users is an extra layer of security as not knowing about their existence helps limit users only to functionality that is allowed to them.
  ○ Options for users to select input from (i.e.: radio buttons, check boxes, drop-down menus, etc.) whenever applicable to reduce possible input errors.
  ○ Adopt best practices for programming/software development to ensure no room has been left for unforeseen security breaches.
    - Close back-doors/maintenance hooks (i.e.: alternate channels created by programmers to enable easy testing of the module instead of navigating through the proper access path each time) and other covert paths, which, if remained opened, would also allow unauthorized users access to the system.
    - Check for other programming loopholes which could lead to information security problems/breaches (for e.g.: buffer overflows, which can be exploited to enter lengthy inputs which overflow the buffer's boundaries and overwrite other memory locations adjacent to it, etc.).
- **Operations Security:** Ensure smooth operation of routine activities to allow the system to run in a secure manner.
  ○ Continually assess personnel and job functions, and provide training.
  ○ Monitor and audit activity, and ensure resource protection.
  ○ Security mechanisms can be categorized as preventive (to prevent an intrusion from happening), detective (to detect an intrusion once it has happened), deterrent (to deter or discourage intruders from attempting intrusion), corrective (to correct presently problematic mechanisms), and recovery (mechanisms such as data back-ups to help recover from attacks/intrusions).
  ○ Ensure standards compliance and due care.
  ○ Administrative management of personnel.
    - Enforce separation of duties (by breaking up high risk activities into multiple separate components to be carried out by different personnel) to ensure that a single user alone cannot compromise the organisation's security.
    - Job rotation to ensure that another person would be knowledgeable and experienced in handling the tasks of any person who is unavailable, and would thereby be able to step in.
    - Enforce 'least privilege' and 'need-to-know' principles to ensure users only have access to information and system resources they need to perform their tasks.
    - Mandatory vacations to allow the organisation time to find and correct any fraudulent activities should any have happened.
  ○ Change management to ensure smooth transition when required.
  ○ Back-up and recovery systems.
- **Business Continuity Planning and Disaster Recovery Planning:** How business impact analysis is performed to help recover from disasters and continue business.
  ○ Development, implementation and maintenance of a short term disaster recovery plan to deal with the disaster and its ramifications while still in emergency mode right after the disaster has struck.

- Minimize effects of a disaster by creating contingency plans to ensure that resources, personnel and processes can resume operation in a timely manner.
  - Longer term business continuity plan for continuing critical business operations in a different mode, through alternate channels, possibly at a different location, until regular conditions are available again.
  - Crisis management to deal with customers, suppliers, shareholders, and other stakeholders, in order to restore the organisation's reputation and regain the trust of these third parties.
  - Different back-up and recovery alternatives.
    - Concurrent/simultaneous soft back-ups such as to a Redundant Array of Inexpensive Disks (RAID), allow quick recovery to the latest data/information.
    - Frequent back-ups to storage media kept in a different location (within the facility) from the servers and other system resources allow somewhat fast recovery to recent data/information.
    - Less frequent, periodic hard back-ups where storage media is moved to a different location outside the facility, allow recovery (albeit not to the most recent data/information) from disasters which destroy the facility.
  - Proper, easy to reach, easily comprehensible documentation clearly detailing out the steps in recovery and restoration of assets.
  - Determine whether the organisation will adopt a 'safety first' approach (where human lives will be prioritized over the security of other assets) or a 'security first' approach (where the highly critical nature of data/information requires the prioritization of their security).
    - A safety first approach is preferable, allowing people to evacuate from the facility, even though the security of other assets could be compromised.
    - At high security organisations such as military organisations which deal with high risk data, unfortunately the facility would revert to complete lock-down to ensure that the security of its information assets cannot be compromised, even though that could also mean that personnel would also be trapped inside the facility during the disaster.
  - Periodic testing and drills to ensure people know how to respond in emergencies (based on emergency evacuation procedures, etc.) without panicking.
- **Security Laws, Investigations and Ethics:** The different components of Cyber-law.
  - Enforce software licensing and privacy to ensure that intellectual property rights are not violated.
  - Educate users on security laws, regulations and ethics which they should abide by, liability and ramifications of actions, etc.
  - Surveillance, search, seizure, and intrusion of privacy.
    - Constant surveillance or monitoring of user activity may intrude on user's privacy, but might be required at times though not very ethical.
  - Different types of digital evidence and their admissibility in court.
  - Incident handling practices to conduct forensic investigations with the least disruption to productivity and business operations (Volonino & Anzaldua, 2008).
  - Identification and prosecution of perpetrators, and protection of assets.
  - Software crimes and conducting digital forensic investigations without compromising the evidence, and while maintaining chain of custody, etc.

- **Information Security Attacks:** Methods and forms of attacks and possible countermeasures.
  - Eavesdropping, network sniffing, wiretapping, intercepting/capturing data passing over the network, etc., are passive attacks, where the attacker is not affecting protocol, algorithm, key, message, or encryption system.
    - Passive attacks are hard to detect, thus should be prevented rather than detected.
    - Passive attacks are usually for reconnaissance before an active attack
  - Altering messages, modifying system files, masquerading/spoofing, etc., are active attacks, where the attacker does something with the gathered data instead of simply reading it.
  - Tools such as protocol analysers, port scanners, operating system (OS) fingerprint scanners, vulnerability scanners, exploit software, war-diallers, password crackers, keystroke loggers, etc., and malicious software such as viruses, worms, Trojan horses, rootkits, spyware, etc. could be used in information security attacks.
  - Access control monitoring helps to keep track of attempts to log in (especially unsuccessful attempts), and thereby help identify any intrusion attempts.
  - Honey pots are open (not locked-down) computers with their services enabled, but with no real company information, used to entice would-be attackers.
    - Enticement does not induce an attacker to commit the crime and is thus, legal. Entrapment, however, is inducing to committing a crime, and is thereby unethical and illegal.

Table 1 describes some of the more complex information security attacks and the security components they compromise.

Varying Depths and Areas of Information Security Education for Different Users

The information security subject areas listed in the previous section may seem daunting and intimidating, but not all users need to acquire knowledge about all these areas. While information security professionals require an in-depth knowledge in these to enable them to perform risk analysis, identify countermeasures, and implement solid security practices to help protect the facility, network, system, and information, by efficiently and predictably balancing risk with service (Harris & Maymi, 2016), software engineers, other IT professionals and students of computer and information sciences, etc. would require an overall understanding in information security, along with further exploration of certain identified domains. Even though each user of an information and communication system needs to be educated in information security in today's digitally interconnected world, for most users, a basic education on how to protect oneself and one's information assets in cyberspace would suffice.

Figure 1 depicts the varying depths of information security education in different subject areas required for different user roles based on their tasks in cyberspace.

Table 1. Complex information security attacks

Name	Description	Security Aspects Compromised
Man-in-the-middle	• Attack on asynchronous keys. • Man-in-the-middle intercepts the 1st user's public key before it reaches the 2nd user, replaces it with their public key and sends to the 2nd user, and masquerades as the 1st user to the 2nd user. • He then does the same with the 2nd user's public key, and masquerades as the 2nd user to the 1st user. • The users believe they are communicating with each other, but they are both communicating with the man-in-the-middle instead. • Can be averted by using a certificate signed by a trusted third party such as a CA.	Compromises confidentiality, integrity, and availability of the system.
Dictionary attack	• Attack on user authentication. • Run commonly-used passwords (or known words existing in a dictionary) through the encryption system to compare with passwords in the password file to find passwords.	Compromises the password and the authentication mechanism.
Brute-force attack	• Attack on user authentication. • Continually try different combinations of input until the correct password is uncovered. • Once part of the password is revealed through dictionary attack, it is easier to figure out the rest of the password through brute-force as there are fewer combinations required.	Compromises the password and the authentication mechanism.
Birthday attack	• Attack on the cryptographic system. • Mathematically exploiting the probability of finding a collision in the hash function by repeatedly evaluating the function through brute-force to compromise the hashed password files.	Compromises the hash algorithm, the passwords and the authentication mechanism.
Denial of Service (DoS) and Distributed Denial of Service (DDoS)	• Attack on network resources. • Flooding the network with unnecessary requests and occupying system resources by unnecessary tasks so as to deny service to legitimate users. • If all or most attacks originate from the same IP address, the system can track down and block requests from that IP address. • DDoS attack is when the requests originate from multiple different distributed locations and spoofed IP addresses so as to avoid detection.	Compromises the availability of system resources such as network, etc.
Phishing and Spear Phishing	• Attack on private information. • Trick users into providing private information such as credit card information, passwords, etc. via e-mails or instant messages, where the message appears to come from a legitimate source. • The obtained information is then used for identity theft. • Can be avoided by validating credentials before communicating, and by refraining from clicking on unknown links, etc. • Spear Phishing targets a specific organisation to gain unauthorized access into the system.	Compromises confidentiality of data and the authentication mechanism.
Pharming	• Attack on private information and DNS. • Poison the DNS to spoof IP addresses and thereby redirect users to a fake/bogus website where they would unknowingly provide their private information to the fake server/attacker. • Targets large groups of users simultaneously.	Compromises integrity of the DNS, and confidentiality of personal data.
Session Hijacking	• Attack on communication session. • Monitor connection to determine sequence numbers used by the two users, and generate traffic as if coming from one party. • Overload a legitimate user with excess packets to make them drop out of the session and steal the session from that user, and thereby take control of an existing communication between two users.	Compromises network and system availability.
Replay attack	• Attack on data transmission. • Capture data in transit and replay it later. • Can be prevented by enforcing time stamps, provided that the clocks of both parties in communication are synchronized.	Compromises network availability and the authorization mechanism.

continues on following page

Table 1. Continued

Name	Description	Security Aspects Compromised
Social Engineering	• Attack on human sociability and trust. • Trick people into unintentionally and unknowingly revealing confidential information.	Compromises data confidentiality.
Phreaking	• Attack on the telephone system. • Exploit bugs and glitches existing in the telephone system to gain unauthorized access to the system.	Compromises the authorization mechanism.
War-dialling	• Attack on the telephone system. • Insert a long list of phone numbers into a war-dialling program to find a modem that can be exploited to gain unauthorized access to.	Compromises the authorization mechanism.
Emanations capturing	• Attack on physical security of the facility. • Capturing electrical waves emanated into the surrounding environment to intercept transmitted information.	Compromises data confidentiality.
Asynchronous attack	• Attack on system booting. • Replace the boot-up instruction file with a malicious file during the time difference between when the system checks for the file and when it executes those instructions.	Compromises system availability and integrity.
Keystroke monitoring	• Attack on user authentication. • Review and record keystrokes entered by the user during an active session to figure out the user's authentication credentials.	Compromises the password and the authentication mechanism.
Shoulder surfing	• Attack on user authentication. • Look over the user's shoulder while the user is keying in their password/PIN to figure out the user's authentication credentials.	Compromises the password and the authentication mechanism.

Source: Compiled by the author with data obtained from Harris and Maymi (2016) and Kim and Solomon (2016)

SOLUTIONS AND RECOMMENDATIONS

As a solution to the problem of being intimidated by the vast subject that entails information security, users can identify the aspects and depth of information security education they need based on their cyber-activities, as shown in Figure 1 in the previous section. Thus, information security professionals would need to study each of the subject areas shown in Figure 1 in-depth in order to understand the theoretical concepts behind information security, be able to identify information security risks, evaluate available information security tools, select the best tools and countermeasures for averting identified risks, gain experience and develop skills in using such tools in order to best configure and utilize them to suit the necessity and to constantly keep up with the information security of the organisation and information system. Information security policy makers should focus more on the areas of risk assessment and management, security architecture and models, security management practices, operations security, disaster recovery and business continuity planning, etc., while cryptologists and other such information security researchers will be focusing on new cryptographic methods, access control methodologies, and so on. Networking engineers and administrators will focus on the telecommunications and networking concepts, tools, architecture, models, etc., in order to figure out how best to design and implement the network of the system, whereas civil engineers, architects and builders will be focusing on how best to design and build the facility in the safest and most secure manner. Software engineers and software architects should study about secure software development and incorporate these practices in their work, while forensic experts and investigators, as well as law enforcement officials, should be knowledgeable about the security laws and other legal aspects of information security. While IT professionals and students of computer and information sciences require an overall understanding about each of these subject areas, all users of information systems should receive at least a basic awareness in information security in order to allow them to protect their information assets in cyberspace.

In addition, the information security best practices listed below would help users in further protecting their information assets.

Figure 1. Varying depths and areas of information security education for different users
Source: Compiled by the author

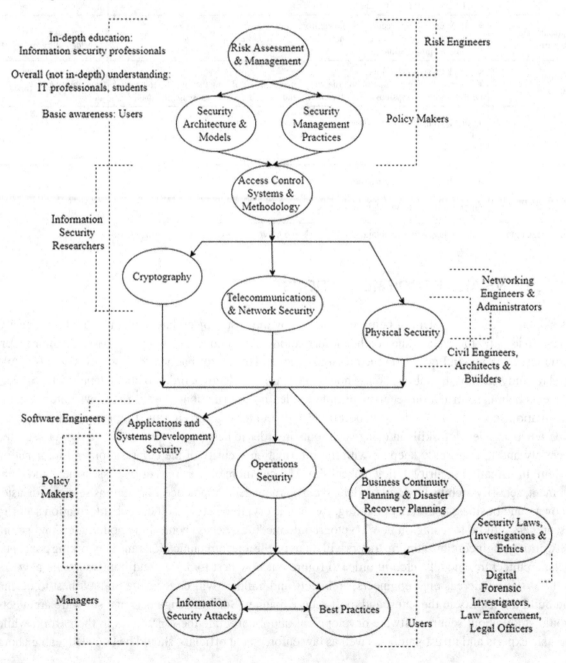

Information Security Best Practices

- **Separation of Tasks:** Separating work-related tasks from personal tasks to ensure that only work-related cyber behaviour will be monitored (Fernando, 2014).
  - Avoiding personal web browsing, personal e-mails or instant messaging while engaged in work-related activities would help preserve the user's privacy better as their personal information will not be travelling across public networks, etc.
- **Password Security Behaviour:** Best practices for managing password security.
  - Adopt strong passwords with special characters, numbers, and both uppercase and lowercase letters, which are not obvious, and are difficult to guess.
  - Change password frequently, as the chances of a password being intercepted grow higher the longer a password is in use.
    - Avoid reusing former passwords.
  - Avoid saving, writing down, or storing passwords in places easily accessible by others.
    - Use an algorithm that is meaningful in some sense to generate passwords that are not easily forgotten.
    - Avoid incorporating name, date of birth, address, etc. and other such personal information that can be easily found by others within one's password.
  - Avoid sharing the same password across different applications.
  - Avoid sharing passwords with others.
- **Data Back-Up Behaviour:** Frequently and periodically perform data back-ups (both work and personal data) in multiple forms and in multiple storage media to enable recovery of data should it be needed.
- **Data Sanitization Behaviour:** Ensure that unnecessary copies (both hard and soft copies) of data are destroyed (Bishop, Bhumiratana, Crawford, & Levitt, 2004).
  - Regularly sanitize external storage media.
  - Control access by others to personal storage media.
  - Minimize using storage media belonging to others, and when used ensure that they are scanned before use and sanitized after use before returning them.
  - Periodically delete temporary files, cookies, browsing history, saved passwords, etc.
- **Network Security Behaviour:** Best practices concerning network security.
  - Ensure that firewalls are enabled.
    - If firewalls were disabled or relaxed to allow different applications access to the system, and if privileges were escalated to allow installation of software, etc., reset escalated privileges and re-enable firewalls after installation of programs.
  - Periodically update antivirus software and scan computer disks and drives.
  - Check for authenticity of websites (requesting certificates by trusted CAs), e-mail attachments, etc. before clicking on links or opening attachments.
  - Validate credentials of the other party before correspondence.
- **Physical Security Behaviour:** Best practices concerning physical security (Fernando, 2014).
  - Be aware of the surrounding (whether other people are around, whether one's computer monitor is visible to others, etc.).
  - Lock computers when leaving the desk.
  - Lock cupboards, desks, office, home, vehicle, etc.

- ◦ Ensure that confidential or personal items (documents, computers, storage media, password hints, etc.) are not left unattended.
- ◦ Avoid sharing personal items with others whenever possible (for e.g.: lending or borrowing keys, etc.), and exercise caution should such a need arise.
- ◦ Avoid using unknown items without validation.

FUTURE RESEARCH DIRECTIONS

Information security has always been and will continue to be a game between the good and evil doers. As one strives to strengthen their security system by patching up holes, eliminating vulnerabilities, improving the strength and efficiency in encryption algorithms, networking protocols, etc., another would find a way to circumvent that new security mechanism. Unfortunately, in most cases, the tools used for ethical hacking and penetration testing by organisations to test the strength of their security systems are themselves used by adversaries to intrude into those systems. Yet, in order to ensure the protection of people and their information assets in cyberspace, new research concerning cryptography (such as lattice encryption, etc.), network security, data sanitization, digital forensics, access control, and other areas of information security should and will continue to emerge.

CONCLUSION

Even though there are many facets to information security, and acquiring an education in information security is not a simple task, it is mandatory to be cognizant in information security in order to protect oneself and one's information assets in cyberspace. Being intimidated by the vast subject range of information security is no reason to stay away from today's heavily interconnected cyber-world. Instead, one can obtain an awareness and basic education in information security that would suffice to help stay protected in cyberspace. As the depth and areas of information security education required by different users vary based on their user roles and cyber-activities, those users who require in-depth education in certain areas of information security can obtain such in-depth education, while other users can obtain only a basic awareness and understanding as deemed appropriate.

REFERENCES

Bishop, M. (2003). *Computer Security – Art and Science*. Boston, MA: Pearson Education.

Bishop, M., Bhumiratana, B., Crawford, R., & Levitt, K. (2004). How to sanitize data. *Proceedings of the 13th IEEE International Workshops on Enabling Technologies: Infrastructure for Collaborative Enterprises*.

Fernando, S. (2014). *Internal Control of Secure Information and Communication Practices through Detection of User Behavioural Patterns*. Niigata, Japan: Nagaoka University of Technology.

Foley, K. (2011). Maintaining a proactive and sustainable security program while hosting and processing personally identifiable information. *Information Systems Security Association Journal, 9*(5), 25–32.

Gonzalez, J. J., & Sawicka, A. (2002). A framework for human factors in information security. *Proceedings of 2002 World Scientific and Engineering Academic Society International Conference on Information Security.*

Grimes, R. A. (2010). How to thwart employee cybercrime. *Insider Threat Deep Drive – Combating the Enemy Within, InfoWorld – Special Report*, 2-7. Retrieved August 5, 2012, from http://resources.idgenterprise.com/original/AST-0001528_insiderthreat_2_v1.pdf

Harris, S., & Maymi, F. (2016). *CISSP All-in-One Exam Guide* (7th ed.). New York, NY: McGraw-Hill Education.

ISO/IEC 270001. (2005). *Information technology – Security techniques – Information security management systems – Requirements.* Geneva, Switzerland: ISO.

Kahneman, D., & Tversky, A. (1979). Prospect theory: An analysis of decision under risk. *Economoetrica, 47*(2), 263–291. doi:10.2307/1914185

Kim, D., & Solomon, M. G. (2016). *Fundamentals of Information Systems Security* (3rd ed.). Burlington, MA: Jones & Bartlett Learning.

Lacey, D. (2009). *Managing the Human Factor in Information Security: How to win over staff and influence business.* West Sussex, England: Wiley.

Liu, A., Martin, C., Hetherington, T., & Matzner, S. (2005). A comparison of system call feature representations for insider threat detection. In *Proceedings of the 2005 IEEE Workshop on Information Assurance.* West Point, NY: United States Military Academy. 10.1109/IAW.2005.1495972

Lynch, D. M. (2006). Securing against insider attacks. *Information Security and Risk Management*, 39-47. Retrieved August 5, 2012, from http://www.csb.uncw.edu/people/ivancevichd/classes/MSA%20516/Supplemental%20Readings/Supplemental%20Reading%20for%20Wed,%2011-5/Insider%20Attacks.pdf

Mills, R. F., Grimaila, M. R., Peterson, G. L., & Butts, J. W. (2011). A scenario-based approach to mitigating the insider threat. *Information Systems Security Association Journal, 9*(5), 12–19.

Ning, P., Jajodia, S., & Wang, X. S. (2003). *Intrusion Detection in Distributed Systems – An Abstraction-Based Approach.* Norwell, MA: Kluwer Academic Publishers.

Peltier, T. R. (2002). *Information Security Policies, Procedures and Standards: Guidelines for Effective Information Security Management.* Boca Raton, FL: Auerback Publications.

Sabett, R. V. (2011). Have you seen the latest and greatest "security game changer"? *Journal of Information Systems Security Association, 9*(5), 5.

Schneier, B. (2008). *The psychology of security.* Retrieved August 5, 2012, from http://www.schneier.com/essay-155.html

Schweitzer, J. A. (1996). *Protecting Business Information.* Newton, MA: Butterworth-Heinemann.

Senanayake, T., & Fernando, S. (2017). Information Security Education: Watching your steps in cyberspace. *Proceedings of the International Science and Technology Conference 2017.*

Volonino, L., & Anzaldua, R. (2008). *Computer Forensics for Dummies.* Indianapolis, IN: Wiley Publishing.

Vroom, C., & von Solms, R. (2003). Information security: Auditing the behaviour of the employee. *IFIP TC11 18th International Conference on Information Security (SEC2003).*

West, R. (2008). The psychology of security. *Communications of the ACM, 51*(4), 34–41. doi:10.1145/1330311.1330320

Williams, B. R. (2011). Do it differently. *Journal of Information Systems Security Association, 9*(5), 6.

KEY TERMS AND DEFINITIONS

Authentication: Validating the identity of a subject. Proving that a subject is actually who they claim to be.

Authorization: Granting privileges and allowing access to objects for specified subjects.

Availability: The ability to use services and resources when requested.

Cipher-Text: Data that is encoded into an unreadable format.

Confidentiality: The ability to ensure secrecy and prevent unauthorized disclosure of information.

Countermeasure: A safeguard to mitigate potential risk by eliminating the vulnerability.

Identity: The name by which a subject can be uniquely identified.

Integrity: The correctness and accuracy of data or information.

Plaintext: Un-coded data that is human- or machine-readable.

Section 2
Certifications, Competencies, and Skill Development

Chapter 4

How Can a Cybersecurity Student Become a Cybersecurity Professional and Succeed in a Cybersecurity Career?

Sandra Blanke
University of Dallas, USA

Paul Christian Nielsen
University of Dallas, USA

Brian Wrozek
University of Dallas, USA

ABSTRACT

The need for cybersecurity professionals extends across government and private industries. Estimates place the shortage of cybersecurity professionals at 1.8 million by 2022. This chapter provides aspiring cybersecurity students a clear understanding of the various educational pathways they can choose to achieve their goals. The authors describe educational categories and include an assessment of each that students will want to consider based on their own situation. The authors discuss how the study of cybersecurity can be accomplished from a computer science, engineering, and business perspective. Students with STEM skills can accomplish their goals in numerous cybersecurity roles including cyber engineer, architect, and other technical roles. Finally, students with cyber business interest can accomplish their goals with a focus on strategy, compliance, awareness, and others. Organizations need employees with all these skills. This chapter concludes with the recommendation for continual learning, the value of networking, and the encouragement for students to start creating a cyber career.

DOI: 10.4018/978-1-6684-3554-0.ch004

INTRODUCTION

As cybersecurity professionals and educators, the authors are often asked by students and other individuals currently in information technology and other career fields; "How Can I Become a Cybersecurity Professional"? This question is being asked because there are numerous publications reporting a very large gap in cybersecurity expertise and for those with cybersecurity skills there are six figure salary opportunities. Steve Morgan (2016) the Founder and CEO at Cybersecurity Ventures and Editor-In-Chief of the *Cybersecurity Market Report* and *Forbes* contributor reported "if you are thinking about a career change in 2016, then you might want to have a look at the burgeoning cybersecurity market which is expected to grow from US$75 billion in 2015 to US$170 billion by 2020 … a career can mean a six-figure salary, job security and the potential for upward mobility."

Jeff Kauflin (2017) an author for Forbes Staff focusing on leadership and careers reports "behind every new hack or data breach, there's a company scrambling to put out the fire. That's good news for job seekers with cybersecurity security skills. Employers can't hire them fast enough." ISACA (2016) estimates a global 2 million workforce gap by 2019 and Cisco Continuum (2017) reports cybersecurity will have a workforce gap of 1.8 million by 2022.

These statistics are prompting many individuals to consider moving into cybersecurity. Some have solid backgrounds in supportive fields such as information systems administration, networking, software development, and testing. Others seek to make major career changes from largely unrelated fields such as accounting, marketing, sales, and manufacturing. A successful transition to cybersecurity promises a strong demand for these needed skills, high pay, and job stability for the foreseeable future.

This chapter was written to provide the aspiring cybersecurity professional with an overview of the initial study of Information Assurance that was introduced in May, 1988 in Presidential Decision Directive 63 (PDD 63). Prospective cybersecurity students need to understand the purpose, the complexity, and the importance of reducing vulnerabilities in our national infrastructure, risk management strategies and other important areas of cybersecurity education. This objective can only be accomplished by developing the number of cybersecurity professionals.

Prospective students will learn of the many cybersecurity job titles, skills and resources that have been created and can be used to assist the student. Numerous cybersecurity education categories are discussed and a realistic review of each are provided including advantages and disadvantages of each. Students are provided recommendations on how to prepare for either a technical or non-technical position in cybersecurity as well as recommendations to begin their cybersecurity career.

BACKGROUND

Creation of the Study of Cybersecurity Education

In May 1988 the Presidential Decision Directive 63 (PDD 63), within the Clinton Administration, created the Policy on Critical Infrastructure Protection and the initial development of the Centers of Academic Excellence in Information Assurance (IA) Education (CAE-IAE) Program. The CAE program was initially developed by the National Security Agency (NSA) in 1998 and in 2004 the Department of Homeland security joined as a partner. "The goal of the program is to reduce vulnerability in our national information infrastructure by promoting higher education in cyber defense and producing professionals with cyber defense expertise for the nation" (National Centers of Academic Excellence in Cyber Defense, 2016).

In 2008, the CAE in IA research was added to encourage doctoral research in cybersecurity. In 2010, Two-year institutions, technical schools, and government training centers were added (National Centers of Academic Excellence in Cyber Defense, 2016). In 2016, the CAE-Cyber Operations designation was announced and in 2017 it restructured to have two designation programs. The CAE-Cyber Operations Fundamental and the CAE-Cyber Operations Advanced (CAE-Cyber Operations Announcements, 2017). To date, there are over 200 colleges and universities designated as CAEs that develop and train individuals with cybersecurity responsibilities within the government and private industries (National Centers of Academic Excellence in Cyber Defense, 2016).

Sizing the Cybersecurity Expertise Gaps

In an effort to accurately identify the cybersecurity expertise gaps, the U.S. Commerce Department's National Institute of Standards and Technology (NIST) funded CyberSeek™

(Cybersecurity Supply/Demand Heat Map, n.d.). Rodney Petersen (2016), director of the National Initiative for Cybersecurity Education (NICE) reported the development of CyberSeek™ and explained that it is an interactive online tool designed to assist cybersecurity job seekers find job openings and for employers to identify the type of skilled workers they need. CyberSeek™ was developed by CompTia, a nonprofit trade association for IT professionals and organizations.

By using the CyberSeek™ heat map, on January 20, 2018 the report indicates 285,681 cybersecurity job openings and a total of 746,858 total employed in the cybersecurity workforce. Focusing on Texas, there are 20,007 total cybersecurity job openings and 64,671 total employed in the cybersecurity work-force. Initiating the report for California shows there are 31,731 cybersecurity job openings and 83,413 total employed in the cybersecurity workforce. The top cybersecurity job titles reported by CyberSeek™ include Cybersecurity Engineer, Cybersecurity analyst, network engineer/architect, cybersecurity manager/ administrator, software developer/engineer, systems engineer, vulnerability analyst/penetration tester, IT auditor and cybersecurity architect.

As is evident from the job titles reported by CyberSeek,™ cybersecurity is a broad field. Many of the positions are technical while others are less technical and management focused. The cybersecurity field has its own language, tools, and a certain level of hands-on experience that has proven to take time, dedication, and focus to develop.

BREACHES, CONFUSION OF JOB TITLES, SKILLS GAP, AND OPPORTUNITIES

Too Many Cybersecurity Breach Incidents

Data breaches are occurring at an accelerated rate. Risk Based Security's annual Data Breach QuickView report 4,149 data breaches in 2016 setting an all-time high in number of records exposed at 4.2 billion (Reported data breaches expose over 4 billion records, 2017). The Identity Theft Resource Center (ITRC) is a non-profit organization that helps victims of identity theft. ITRC recorded a 40% increase in data breaches in 2016 despite the fact that these incidents are traditionally under-reported (Data breaches increase 40 percent, 2016).

The non-profit organization Online Trust Alliance (OTA) released their ninth annual study "2017 cybersecurity Incident and Breach Response Guide." OTA reported 82,000 cybersecurity incidents negatively impacted organizations in 2016. The OTA counts cybersecurity incidents that do not necessarily result in the loss of personal or financial information such as ransomware infections or denial of service (DOS) attacks. The OTA estimates that the number of incidents could approach 250,000 if all were publicly reported but many companies do not disclose incidents of cyber-attack for fear of reputation harm. (Consumer Data Breaches Level Off While Other Incidents Skyrocket, 2017).

Wide Range of Skills to Be Developed

The cybersecurity profession is still young and does not have the benefit of years of organizational alignment, reporting experience, or usage of standard job titles and job descriptions. In many organizations, cybersecurity has been added to the Information Technology (IT) department reporting directly to the Chief Information Officer (CIO). Cybersecurity issues and individuals hired may be viewed from a technology perspective based on the IT reporting structure. For a number of positions within cybersecurity having a technology background is important and is a requirement for employment.

For example, the Cybersecurity Network Engineer needs experience and knowledge in networking and protocols to fully understand the cybersecurity risks to design and secure the network. The systems auditor will need to understand the business processes, procedures and have a working knowledge of the technical environment. As an example, an auditor will need a strong working knowledge of a Linux or Windows operating system to properly assess the system security controls.

Confusion Regarding Job Roles, Titles, and Duties

There is tremendous confusion around job roles, titles and duties. The cybersecurity industry lacks the maturity and terminology discipline found in other professions and occupations. Terms like architect, engineer and analyst are used interchangeably for a variety of job responsibilities. The fact that cybersecurity reports to IT and other organizations with existing and more familiar job titles may be one of the reasons jobs titles are being used interchangeably and across departments. In an effort to reduce this confusion, the National Institute of Standards and Technology (NIST) in the U.S. Department of Commerce lead an effort and in 2012 published the National Initiative for Cybersecurity Education (NICE) Cybersecurity Workforce Framework.

The goal of the NICE Workforce framework (NIST SP 800-181) was to provide the early stages of a common language to discuss and understand work and skill requirements of cybersecurity professionals. The framework is organized into seven high-level functional categories (Table 1). Each functional category is then supplemented with specialty areas and job titles within each specialty area.

Over time the NICE Cybersecurity Workforce framework will most likely be helpful to all organizations, however from these authors perspective it has been slow to be accepted in the public sector. Additionally, there is still the issue of the shortage of qualified cybersecurity candidates. One of the main issues with staffing cybersecurity job positions is that the technical skills required for these jobs are the same skills required for many other science, technology, engineering and math (STEM) related jobs. The U.S. Department of Commerce Economics and Statistics Administration Office of the Chief Economist reports in the STEM Jobs: 2017 update while the "STEM occupations are projected to grow

Table 1. National Initiative for Cybersecurity Education (NICE) workforce framework

NIST: NICE Framework Workforce (7-Categories)
Securely Provision
Operate and Maintain
Protect and Defend
Investigate
Oversee and Govern
Analyze
Collect and Operate

by 8.9 percent from 2014 to 2024, compared to 6.4 percent growth for non-STEM occupations" today – there is still a shortage of STEM resources and, therefore, qualified cybersecurity candidates.

Since the world of identity fraud, ransomware, hackers, cybersecurity terrorist, insider and portable device abuse shows no signs of slowing down or going away, the field of cybersecurity is growing and is a wonderful opportunity for those with interest, aptitude and the willingness to work hard, study, and learn the appropriate software, tools or other resources in use for a particular area of cybersecurity interest. Individuals in cybersecurity will need a passion for continual learning and a realization that no one in this field knows everything.

Cybersecurity Education Categories

Cybersecurity capabilities are built on a solid understanding of the theory, practice and implementation of cybersecurity principles. Familiarity and proficiency with the technical tools of the trade separate the professional from the novice. So how does one obtain these skills if they are coming from a non-technical background? The most obvious and acceptable method sought by potential employers is on-the-job experience, but for the aspiring student of security that is usually the missing element. This is especially true for those who have no work experience or for those transitioning from unrelated careers into cybersecurity. A number of different methods have been used to fill these gaps including:

- Self-paced free online books and youtube videos;
- Off the shelf software and cybersecurity tools;
- Undergrad cybersecurity programs at Center of Academic Excellence Cyber Defense Education (CAE-CDE) accredited schools – and non-CAE schools;
- Graduate cybersecurity programs at Center of Academic Excellence Cyber Defense Education (CAE-CDE) accredited business, computer science and engineering schools;
- Vendor training from cybersecurity focused educators and cybersecurity vendors; and
- Others.

The chapter explores each of these different methods with a realistic examination of the probably of success defined by a successful interview and being selected for the cybersecurity position.

Self-Paced Free Online Books and YouTube Videos

The internet has provided a wide variety of free online resources in the form of e-books, blogs, and YouTube videos that provide training in the multiple disciplines of security. There are several advantages to this approach as well as some serious drawbacks.

Advantages include

- Low or no cost associated with this form of training; and
- Training is self-paced and available any time or place that has an internet connection.

Disadvantages include

- There is wide variance in accuracy, currency and quality of the training;
- Training material may disappear at any time;
- These is little or no guidance on what to study or in what order;
- Adopting this approach requires considerable self-discipline; and
- There is rarely any credible tangible proof of proficiency.

The effectiveness of self-paced online study of freely available material is mixed. On one hand, making the effort shows an employer the candidates' interest in the topics and determination to gain the needed exposure and training for at least an entry level position. However, it also raises the question of commitment – investing ones capital (money) as well as time tends to have more weight to a potential employer. Employers do not generally possess any independent validation or verification of the candidate's effort other than testing for knowledge.

Some employers do require proficiency validation before progressing through to a job offer; however, those that do not have a formal testing program in place are not likely to create testing for self-trained individuals. Instead, the potential employer may use interviewers or an interviewer panel with subject matter expertise from within the hiring company. Here again, there can be widely variable results depending on the motivation and skill levels of those performing the interviews. Without an insider (mentor) to move a resume through the hiring process and provide a vote of confidence to skeptical interviewers, job offers from this approach would be a rare occurrence.

Emerging Self-Study Programs

Recently, there have been a number of dedicated cybersecurity training sites appearing on the internet that offer the advantage of more structured curriculum with higher quality training resources. Some of these sites are following the open online university model with materials such as online video lectures produced by individuals that are from established and known educational institutions and are often well known in cybersecurity circles. Some programs are associated with accredited schools and some even offer certificates showing completion of courses within their programs. The cost of these programs varies depending on the number and type of classes taken and whether a certificate would be provided.

It is important to note that these programs are not the same as online degree programs offered by universities and do not result in an accredited degree. So far, the marketplace has not fully embraced this training model as meeting the requirements for employment however some of the programs are providing good supplemental training for those who already have a more traditional degree or who are already working in the cybersecurity field.

For those interested, one such site is Cybrary which has free membership and boasts about 1.4 million users. The site focuses on cybersecurity and IT training and has both free and paid training resources. Some of the offerings are directed toward obtaining certifications while others provide general training suitable for meeting the continuing education units (CEU) credits most certifications require ("Free and Open Source Learning for Cybersecurity, IT").

Advantages include

- Low or moderate cost associated with this form of training;
- There is better structure and some peer review of the presented materials;
- The training is usually self-paced and available any time or place where there is internet service;
- Some programs are associated with known educational entities;
- Some programs may offer certificates of completion; and
- More opportunity to become exposed to other security professionals.

Disadvantages include

- The marketplace has not fully embraced this form of training as a primary foundation;
- Accuracy, currency and quality of the training remains questionable;
- Adopting this approach also requires considerable self-discipline; and
- Students may be subject to additional marketing or cost requirements once enrolled.

The potential student must be very selective in the programs and material to which they commit. A potential employer will question the quality of this form of training and will likely test the candidate on their knowledge. Errors and mistakes at this stage will not lead to employment. Unless used as a supplement for existing cybersecurity employees, this approach would lead to entry-level jobs at best. The current list of available programs have not yet developed a positive enough reputation through placing successful students in meaningful positions to attract the attention of hiring managers. The list of available programs is growing which may indicate growing acceptance. During the research for this chapter, the authors reviewed a blog by Zaharia (2016) that appears to be valuable for those considering online cybersecurity courses.

Off the Shelf Software and Cybersecurity Tools: Self Training

Another approach is to obtain and learn off the shelf cybersecurity oriented tools and software. Most students of security will have limited resources when it comes to acquiring professional grade software and the infrastructure needed to support that software. Fortunately, there are many tools used by security practitioners that are available for free or are inexpensive. These tools can be used in many different environments including some home environments. Acquiring and learning these tools has some value in the marketplace, but also serves the purpose of improving the student's understanding of the security environment.

The key for the student is to use this as an opportunity for gaining depth of knowledge of not only the tool, but the environment in which the tool functions. An example of a widely used tool would be

Wireshark (www.wireshark.org). This free tool allows the capture and analysis of computer network traffic. It is a powerful tool which can be used to learn about the networks and the protocols that are widely used in today's Transmission Control Protocol/Internet Protocol (TCP/IP) networks.

Some caution should be used when adopting this approach of acquiring and learning security tools. Many security tools can be used for illicit and illegal purposes just as easily as for educational or legitimate business purposes. Most businesses expressly forbid the use of these types of tools on their networks without appropriate written permission. Without written permission, using these types of tools will normally lead to being disciplined up to and including termination. While this is not usually the case in home environments, it can become an issue if your home environment is connected to the internet through an internet service provider most of whom have service agreements prohibiting the use of such tools. It is always wise to ensure you do not begin entry into the security world with a lawsuit or other legal issues.

However, taking appropriate cautions provides a great deal of knowledge that can be gained by becoming proficient with several of the tools of the trade. Three good tools available for free are NMap, WireShark and NetWitness. These tools may require a free registration by the tool vendor. There are also a large number of other tools classed as 'security tools' which should be avoided by those new to the cybersecurity space. Many of these are open source, free and widely available. Some are collections of tools arranged in suites designed for use by professional penetration testers or other experienced security professionals. They are also widely used by hackers and others with illegal and illegitimate intentions. Just loading some of these on a work laptop for example could be cause for dismissal. When in doubt, leave it out. Get advice and written permission, especially if you are using networks and equipment owned by others.

Advantages include

- Free or inexpensive is very appealing;
- Many small and medium sized companies leverage free and low cost security related products as a cost savings strategy in their environments;
- The student can begin to develop the common vocabulary and experience shared by others in the security field; and
- The student can work at their own pace and at any time.

Disadvantages include

- No exposure to enterprise class products that would provide better opportunities in larger corporations;
- There is seldom a support network to answer questions or provide guidance;
- The student may not select the tools most likely to be found in the cybersecurity space and consequently invest time in the wrong areas of study;
- The student must have the self-discipline to commit the time and research necessary to learn the material;
- There is seldom any recognizable confirmation of competence that can lead to a job interview; and
- Stating that one has studied independently will not usually generate significant interest from hiring managers.

For the student with a passion for the subject of cybersecurity, limited financial resources and adequate time, a self-paced open source approach to learning may be the only option. In general this approach does not usually translate into a position in cybersecurity without a mentor on the inside to promote capabilities to a hiring manager. The investment in time to gain the proficiencies needed to talk through an interview is often more than a student can afford. Again, if this is the only option, then the recommendation is to start the learning process early and select tools that are approved prior to use on any network.

Center of Academic Excellence Cyber Defense: Undergrad

Center of Academic Excellence Cyber Defense Education (CAE-CDE) recognized schools offer a better option for those with the required time and financial resources. These programs are especially valuable for those individuals that perform better in a structured environment or those who are new to the field of cybersecurity. Recognized degrees have long been a standard for indicating at least a basic under-standing of a particular discipline. The same is true of a degree in cybersecurity. For many a degree is the minimum requirement into an entry level position where the employee can gain additional practical experience and begin the advancement process through the career opportunities offered in the field.

Advantages include

- Broad exposure to the many disciplines that encompass the field of security;
- Exposure to other security students and professionals;
- Exposure to multiple disciplines in the security space allowing a choice of focus;
- An opportunity to start building a reputation and professional network;
- A support structure for study and learning;
- Possible scholarship opportunities;
- An recognized degree; and
- Some programs offer assistance in finding employment opportunities.

Disadvantages include

- Time – most undergraduate degree programs take approximately four years to complete;
- Cost of education varies greatly, but inexpensive programs are rare;
- Students may incur considerable debt by the time they complete a degree;
- Undergraduate degree programs require study outside the primary area of interest to obtain the degree; and
- Many undergraduate programs are not designed for working adult schedules and provide the best opportunities for those not currently in the workforce.

Selecting a program that has obtained the CAE-CDE designation ensures the student will have exposure to the major areas identified by Department of Homeland Security, National Security Agency and private organizations as essential for performing activities in the security space. This designation is a differentiator for programs offering cybersecurity degrees. Students wanting to work in the cybersecurity profession should strongly consider schools with this designation over those that do not have the designation. This is not to say non-CAE schools do not have good programs, but rather their programs do not have the benefit of a standard framework vetted by the CAE-CDE structured program.

Center of Academic Excellence Cyber Defense: Graduate

Over the last decade the number and quality of graduate cybersecurity programs offered by universities with the CAE-CDE designation has grown, however they still remain a small percentage of schools offering cybersecurity degrees. Graduate business schools, engineering and computer science programs may carry the CAE-CDE designation.

There are several designations for graduate schools that participate in the Center of Academic Excellence Cyber programs. In addition to the CAE-CDE designation, there are CAE-Research (CAE-R) and CAE-Cyber Operations Advanced. The CAE-R schools will typically be a Department of Defense (DoD) school, a Ph.D producing military academy or another higher level designation. Research schools (designated as CAE-R) are designed to advance the science of security by applying academic rigor to problems allowing the creation or development of solutions.

The output of research institutions may be the basis of additional academic research or may lead to the development of products or the formation of companies that may implement the solutions developed. The students in these programs may have a unique research job title. Graduates from research oriented universities may remain in academia obtaining a terminal degree (Ph.D.), work in government or continue their research within commercial entities developing or enhancing products for the marketplace (CAE-CDE, 2018).

Schools with the CAE-Cyber Operations Advanced designations are based within a graduate computer science, electrical engineering or computer engineering department which is capable of promoting a technically deep and relevant program in cybersecurity. Graduates from these programs are expected to exhibit in-depth foundational knowledge that allows them to function within the specialized field of cyber operations (CAE-Cyber Operations Advanced, 2018). The educational requirements are broad as well as deep requiring exposure to the social, legal, policy and ethical aspects encountered in cyber operations.

These topics are often in addition to traditional disciplines like math, computer science, engineering, IT and others. "A curriculum suitable to satisfy the academic requirements for designation as a cyber operations program may include courses from multiple colleges within a university and from multiple programs and disciplines, or, in the case of a defined cyber operations degree program, it can be demonstrated that the relevant information from these disciplines has been integrated into the cyber operations program courses" (CAE-Cyber Operations Advanced).

CAE-Cyber Operations Advanced may be viewed as an applied cybersecurity education. Within the applied programs, there are two general approaches, although the distinction is not as clear. The first approach focuses on providing the basic and or advanced skills needed to advance a student's career in the cybersecurity space. CAE-Cyber Operations Advanced designated programs are designed to do this for more experienced cyber professionals with an interest in the STEM aspects of cybersecurity.

The second type of applied program seeks to provide the cybersecurity skills needed to advance into new cybersecurity practitioner positions. These are CAE-CDE designated business schools that provide the needed management, marketing, financial, communications, governance, and leadership tools to new or already experienced security professionals. These programs may assume that the student already has significant experience in cybersecurity and is seeking advancement into senior managerial roles. While some basic management related topics may be required, the focus remains on the development of applied cybersecurity skills.

Students are required to meet the acceptance criteria and may be required to take foundational level courses in related fields such as cybersecurity, software development, systems administration or computer networks.

Advantages include

- Broad exposure to the many disciplines that encompass the field of cybersecurity;
- Exposure to other cybersecurity students and professionals;
- An opportunity to start or continue building a cybersecurity related reputation and professional network;
- A support structure for study and learning;
- Possible scholarship opportunities
- Possible intern or government job opportunities
- Many graduate programs are designed for working adults and provide opportunities for afterhours and online courses so the student can continue working if needed; and
- An accredited degree, however some programs will allow completion of core security courses for a certificate rather than a full graduate degree.

Disadvantages include

- Time – most graduate degree programs take approximately two to three years to complete;
- A master of science (ms) in cybersecurity is generally two years while an masters of business administration in cybersecurity would be approximately three years to complete;
- Graduate degree programs may require study outside the primary area of interest to obtain the degree such as management, leadership, finance and or marketing;
- Cost of education varies greatly, but inexpensive programs are rare;
- Students may incur considerable debt by the time a graduate degree is completed; and
- Students need to understand completion of this degree is the next important step in preparing for a cybersecurity job and ongoing learning are required to stay current on cybersecurity trends and issues.

Cybersecurity Product Vendor Training

An often overlooked learning opportunity for new cybersecurity students is training offered by vendors and manufacturers of cybersecurity products. While much of this training is associated with the sales process, it can have multiple benefits for students. For those without a formal introduction to security terminology, vendor training can begin to familiarize students with the many specialized terms used in the security space. Although it is likely to be overwhelming at first, prolonged exposure provides context that would be difficult to acquire in self-directed study.

While most vendor presentations are focused on a product or series of products they are selling, an important component of the sales pitch is identifying the industry problem they are attempting to solve and how their product addresses that need. Often the presentation will include comparisons with competing products. These can become excellent talking points during an interview, especially when the interviewer is looking for specific product experience. Even without great depth of experience, being able to identify the problem being addressed and the other available solutions creates an opportunity for a conversation that is relevant to the interviewer.

Advantages include

- Usually free, sometimes sponsored by your current employer;
- Potentially broad exposure to the many disciplines that encompass the field of security;
- Exposure to other security professionals and security clients;
- An opportunity to learn about the problems that exist in the security space and the solutions that are being created and marketed to address the problems;
- Potential employment.

Disadvantages include

- It may not be possible to go directly into the preferred line of security practice;
- One may become stuck in a specific area of practice (if it's the job one desires - then it's a positive);
- Products change rapidly in order to stay relevant to solving a cybersecurity problem; and
- Some technical aspects are difficult to grasp for those outside the cybersecurity environment.

Vendors may provide an indirect avenue into cybersecurity employment. This may be a good opportunity for someone transitioning from another career into cybersecurity. As an example, someone with sales experience but limited direct security experience could seek to sell security products. Given the highly technical nature of most security product solutions, sales personnel are often accompanied by a technical sales engineer to answer the complex technical questions. Again, this is a learning opportunity. With time, enough knowledge could be gained to either move into a technical sales support position or another position that is more cybersecurity than sales. Gaining specific product experience is frequently a path to employment within a customers' organization that uses the product.

Cybersecurity Certifications

There is no shortage of cybersecurity certifications from which to select. A quick Google search indicates there are many cybersecurity certifications to choose from offered by non-profit or commercial organizations. The question is; what certifications will provide the most value to the student and help them be more qualified for a cybersecurity position? A number of certifications require on the job experience, background checks, references, and hands-on tools use. As an example, one of the most widely recognized and accepted cybersecurity certifications is the Certified Information Systems Security Professional (CISSP) managed by The International Information System Security Certification Consortium (ISC^2.)

This certification requires five years of cumulative, paid full-time work experience in at least two of the eight cybersecurity domains defined by ISC^2 and provided in Table 2. One year may be satisfied with a four-year college degree or an advanced degree from a U.S. National Center of Academic Excellence in Information Assurance Education (CAE/IAE). Candidates may also satisfy one year of full time work if they hold an approved credential. As an example, The Certified Cloud Security Professional (CCSP), Certified cybersecurity Forensic Professional (CCFP), Certified Ethical Hacker v8 or higher and other approved credentials.

Table 2. Information System Security Certification Consortium (ISC²)

ISC2 CISSP Domains
Security & Risk Management
Asset Security
Security Engineering
Communication and Network Security
Identify and Access Management
Security Assessment and Testing
Security Operations
Software Development Security

Source: ISC².org

There are many other certifications available. Some offer lower entry requirements and provide only general background information in security. Others offer very specialized certifications designed to show proficiency in a particular area of security, for example the Certified Ethical Hacker (CEH). For students that lack strong on the job experience, the combination of formal training and targeted certifications may be a successful ticket to interviews.

For students considering a certification it is recommended that students review the criteria for completion and determine the students' qualifications to meet the criteria. Additionally, the authors recommend students work on one certification at a time. If a student is completing an academic program in cybersecurity they should first complete their academic program and then pursue a certification offered by a non-profit or commercial organization. Working on too many educational or certification programs at once are overwhelming and not allow the student to fully engage and learn from either program.

International Student Challenges and Opportunities

International students face some additional challenges when approaching the cybersecurity job market. Bottom line with cybersecurity is that non-U.S. citizens will most likely not be hired by the U.S. government, defense contractors that work with and sell to the U.S. government or other industries that sell product or work with the U.S. government. While government and government contractors represent a significant portion of the cybersecurity job market, there are other industries will hire qualified international individuals.

As one vertical industry example, the authors have worked with healthcare organizations and know these organizations will hire individuals with H1B status in cybersecurity positions. Healthcare in the U.S. is guided by HIPAA and HITECH and therefore required to secure confidential patient information. Almost every device in a healthcare organization can access the internet and therefore is at risk of being breached. With the primary focus on patient care and patient lives traditional healthcare experts (doctors, nurses, lab technicians, insurance experts, others) expertise is focused on patient care and not cybersecurity technology. Healthcare, retail, finance, education and other industries are very good options for cybersecurity.

SOLUTIONS AND RECOMMENDATIONS TO PREPARING FOR A CYBERSECURITY CAREER

To obtain current hiring information from Chief Information Security Officers (CISO) these research authors completed a convenience survey of Texas CISO. Respondents were asked what experience level they were expecting to acquire; 20% indicated they are looking to hire interns and individuals with less than one year of experience in the coming months; 36% indicated they were expecting to acquire individuals with one to five years of experience. When asked; what type of skills the CISO expected to hire; 36% percent indicated non-technical job titles while the remainder is focused on technical jobs. When asked if the CISO would hire interns; 43% responded "yes" and 43% responded "maybe". Overall these survey results indicate a favorable position for students with little to no experience being considered in an entry level cybersecurity position.

Cybersecurity students should prepare for a cyber career by first critically reviewing their past experiences and determine if prior work experience or aptitude leads the student to either a technical or non-technical cybersecurity position. The listing below is a sample of job titles that are typically used for non-technical cybersecurity positions and do not generally require technical backgrounds. These positions should be considered for those in the work force with management experience, excellent written and oral communications, organizational skills, interpersonal skills, negotiation skills, leadership, strategic planning, public speaking, process design, project management or regulatory and compliance skills and interests:

- Governance / Compliance auditor
- Cybersecurity Policy developer
- Cybersecurity Program manager
- Cybersecurity Awareness / Education / Training facilitator
- Crisis or Risk management leader

The listing below is a sampling of job titles that are typically used for technical cybersecurity positions and will most likely require either a computer science degree, telecommunications, engineering, or prior work experience in one of these areas:

- Network security
- Computer security
- Software security
- Data analyst / scientist
- Security Operations Center analyst (this may be considered an entry position and employers will provide on the job training)

Students should also review the cybersecurity educational categories and determine which ones meet their needs and in what priority order best suit the students' needs. While starting to work on the educational categories students should review LinkedIn and job boards to stay current on cyber topics and skills required by the hiring companies. Students should learn the details of the NIST Cybersecurity framework, the NICE workforce framework and all details of technologies and tools.

From a social networking perspective students should join cyber associations (ISACA, ISSA, others), join MeetUps on specific technologies of interest and identify mentors from the universities, cyber associations and their current work environment. Students should work with a career counselor and the career development organizations at their work location or school to develop a professional resume, interview and communication skills.

Students should know that building a cybersecurity career does not happen overnight – it takes time and it is well worth the effort. Stay positive; accept positions along the career path way that will provide related skills; plan on building cybersecurity expertise for years to come. Working students should excel in their current work environment and look for ways to get involved in cybersecurity to build the case for rotating to the actual cybersecurity team when openings arise. CISOs like to rotate internally because they are getting someone who has a proven track record and already know the company culture. It is also a good way to leverage existing relationships with internal groups.

FUTURE RESEARCH DIRECTION

Authors of this chapter surveyed CISOs that responded they are hiring experienced cyber professionals and they are willing to hire and train interns and entry level cyber individuals. Future research will continue along these lines to CISOs to learn of their hiring needs, gaps and recommendations to support and train the student and employee who is passionate to learn and develop a professional career in cybersecurity. Current graduate students and graduate cybersecurity students will be surveyed to learn of their cyber career success and additional training needs as they continue developing their professional cybersecurity careers. Educational opportunities will be aligned to meet the needs of the cybersecurity student.

CONCLUSION

After reading this chapter, aspiring and current cybersecurity students should understand that the study of cybersecurity is growing and there are many opportunities for serious and passionate students to become a successful cybersecurity professional. There are many options for obtaining the requisite knowledge to enter the field; however, there are qualitative differences such as: from free self-paced internet information, off the shelf software, undergraduate programs, graduate programs, vendor training and other resources. Adopting a traditional approach of leveraging known accredited degree programs remains the most likely to produce the desired results. Self-paced, free and informal, non-accredited training is a very useful method of enhancing knowledge and staying current as the cyber professional progresses through their career.

Cybersecurity students and professionals alike will need to continually refine their cybersecurity knowledge and utilize the many educational tools to stay current. Cybersecurity is dynamic; threats constantly evolve and the cyber professional must continue to meet the challenges. The cybersecurity student will want to align their time, commitment, interest and goals to the educational categories that best satisfy their needs. Networking with professionals and educators in cybersecurity and joining professional cybersecurity associations' are excellent ways for cyber students to begin their career into the cyber security community. Getting started now on their chosen educational path is extremely valuable in providing the best opportunities for developing cyber expertise necessary to secure an interview and developing an exciting career in cybersecurity.

REFERENCES

CAE-CDE. (2018, February 1). Retrieved on March 23, 2018, from: https://www.caecommunity.org/about-us/what-cae

CAE-Cyber Operations Advanced. (2018, January 22). Retrieved on March 23, 2018, from: https://www.nsa.gov/resources/educators/centers-academic-excellence/cyber-operations/advanced/index.shtml

CAE-Cyber operations announcements. (2017, November 6). Retrieved on February 9, 2018, from: https://www.nsa.gov/resources/educators/centers-academic-excellence/cyber-operations/announcements.shtml

Certified information systems security professional (CISSP). (2018). Retrieved on January 4, 2018, from: https://www.isc2.org/Certifications/CISSP

Cisco. (2017). Retrieved on March 1, 2018, from: https://continuum.cisco.com/2017/06/09/cybersecurity-will-have-a-workforce-gap-of-1-8-million-by-2022/

Consumer data breaches level off while other incidents skyrocket. (2017, January 25). Retrieved on December 18, 2017, from: https://otalliance.org/news-events/press-releases/consumer-data-breaches-level-while-other-incidents-skyrocket

CyberSeek™ Heat Map. (2017). Retrieved on September 4, 2017, from: http://cyberseek.org/heatmap.html

Data breaches increase 40 percent in 2016, finds new report from identity theft resource center and Cyberscout. (2017, January 19). Retrieved on November 11, 2017, from: http://www.idtheftcenter.org/2016databreaches.html

Free and open source learning for cyber security, IT and more. (2017). Retrieved on December 23, 2017, from: from https://www.cybrary.it/

Kauflin, J. (2017, March 16). The Fast-Growing Job With a Huge Skills Gap: Cyber Security. *Forbes*. Retrieved on August 4, 2017, from: https://www.forbes.com/sites/jeffkauflin/2017/03/16/the-fast-growing-job-with-a-huge-skills-gap-cyber-security/#35c3769c5163

Morgan, S. (2016, January 2). One Million Cybersecurity Jobs Opening in 2016. *Forbes*. Retrieved on June 2, 2016, from: https://www.forbes.com/sites/stevemorgan/2016/01/02/one-million-cybersecurity-job-openings-in-2016/#532b27bc27ea

National centers of academic excellence in cybersecurity defense. (2017). *National Security Agency*. Retrieved on July 23, 2017, from: https://www.nsa.gov/resources/educators/centers-academic-excellence/cyber-defense/

National information assurance training and education center (n.d.). *National Information Assurance Training and Education Center*. Retrieved on July 23, 2017, from: http://niatec.info/ViewPage.aspx?id=104

NIST announces CyberSeek™ and interactive resource for cybersecurity. (2016). *Comptia*. Retrieved on March 23, 2017, from: https://www.comptia.org/about-us/newsroom/press-releases/2016/11/01/nist-announces-cyberseek-an-interactive-resource-for-cybersecurity-career-information

NIST framework for improving critical infrastructure cybersecurity. (2017, December 5). Retrieved on January 3, 2018, from: https://www.nist.gov/sites/default/files/documents/2017/12/05/draft-2_framework-v1-1_without-markup.pdf

NIST publishes NICE cybersecurity workforce framework. (2017, August 7). Retrieved on December 4, 2017, from: https://www.nist.gov/news-events/news/2017/08/nist-publishes-nice-cybersecurity-workforce-framework-categorizing-and

Ponemon Institute 2017 cost of data breach study. (2017, June). *IBM Corporation*. Retrieved on October 7, 2017, from: https://www-01.ibm.com/common/ssi/cgi-bin/ssialias?htmlfid=SEL03130WWEN&

Reported data breaches expose over 4 billion records. (2017, January 25). Retrieved on April 15, 2017, from: https://www.riskbasedsecurity.com/2017/01/2016-reported-data-breaches-expose-over-4-billion-records/

U.S. Department of Commerce Economics and Statistics Administration Office of the Chief Economist STEM Jobs. 2017 Update. (2017). Retrieved on October 10, 2017, from: http://www.esa.doc.gov/sites/default/files/stem-jobs-2017-update.pdf

Zaharia, A. (2016, May 17). 50+ useful cyber security online courses you should explore. *Heimdal Security*. Retrieved on June 22, 2017, from: https://heimdalsecurity.com/blog/50-cyber-security-online-courses-you-should-know-about/

ADDITIONAL READING

Forbes Tech / Security. (n.d.). Retrieved on June 2, 2017, from: https://www.forbes.com/security/#51f790164552

Harris, S., & Maymi, F. (2016). *CISSP Exam Guide* (7th ed.). New York: McGraw-Hill Education.

Information Systems Security Association International (ISSA). (2017). *The ISSA Journal*. Retrieved on June 22, 2017, from: http://www.issa.org/?page=ISSAJournal

InfoSecurity Magazine. (2017). Retrieved on September 30, 2017, from: https://www.infosecurity-magazine.com/

Journal, I. S. A. C. A. (2017). Retrieved on September 2017, from: https://www.isaca.org/About-ISACA/-ISACA-Newsletter/Pages/@-isaca-volume-1-10-january-2018.aspx

Kim, D., & Solomon, M. G. (2018). *Fundamentals of Information Systems Security*. Burlington, MA: Jones & Bartlett Learning.

National Initiative for Cybersecurity Careers and Studies (NICCS). (2017). Retrieved on August 4, 2017, from: https://niccs.us-cert.gov/training

OWASP – Top 10 Application Security Risks (2017). Retrieved on December 3, 2017, from: https://www.owasp.org/index.php/Top_10-2017_Top_10

SANS Newsletters and Newsbites (2017). Retrieved on December 3, 2017, from: https://www.sans.org/newsletters/newsbites/xix/90

KEY TERMS AND DEFINITIONS

Assessment: An assessment is a methodical evaluation of processes and/or controls to determine whether they are functioning as intended. Assessments may be driven by industry requirements such as the payment card data security standard (PCI-DSS) or may be performed as part of a well-managed security program.

Cybersecurity: Includes process, procedures, technologies, and controls designed to protect systems, networks, and data.

Cybersecurity Framework: Risk based approach to managing cybersecurity risk. This framework includes the framework core, implementation tiers, and profiles.

Governance (GRC): Governance is the process of managing through the use of controls which can include policies, procedures and other management tools. Governance is the "G" in GRC with "R" being risk and "C" being compliance. These three functions of management are designed to improve oversight and coordination in larger and diverse organizations. GRC requires significant involvement by many departments and is often facilitated by complex implementations of software tools.

H1B: H1B is a type of work visa defined under the Immigration and Nationality Act which allows foreign nationals with specialty skills to work in the U.S. There are many job categories that fall under this program including engineering, software development, and information technology.

Health Information Technology for Economic and Clinical Act (HITECH): Provides additional economic incentives to move the health care industry toward electronic records including enhanced requirements for privacy and data protection.

Health Insurance Portability and Accountability Act (HITECH): There are several security implications to this federal regulation most of which relate to the security rule provisions which require the protection of electronic health records.

Information Assurance: The process of protecting information assets and information. This term is still widely used in the public sector but has been replaced with cyber security in most of the private sector.

National Initiative for Cybersecurity Education (NICE): NICE promotes nationwide initiatives to increase the number of people with knowledge, skills, and abilities to perform the tasks required to perform cybersecurity responsibilities.

National Institute for Standards and Technology (NIST): Organization within the U.S. Department of Commerce. NIST promotes U.S. innovation, standards, and technology that enhances economic security.

Risk Management: Ongoing process of identifying, assessing, prioritizing, and reducing risk.

Science, Technology, Engineering, and Math (STEM): STEM is education based in the specific disciplines of science, technology, engineering, and math.

Vulnerability: A vulnerability is any weakness in a product, process or system which could potentially be exploited to reduce the security or function of that product, process, or system.

This research was previously published in Global Cyber Security Labor Shortage and International Business Risk; pages 111-128, copyright year 2019 by Business Science Reference (an imprint of IGI Global).

Chapter 5
The Role of Cybersecurity Certifications

Adrian Davis
ObjectTech Group, UK

ABSTRACT

The chapter looks at the burgeoning field of certification for individuals in the field of information security or cybersecurity. Individual information security certifications cover a wide range of topics from the deeply technical to the managerial. These certifications are used as a visible indication of an individual's status and knowledge, used to define experience and status, used in job descriptions and screening, and may define expectations placed on the individual. This chapter examines how these certifications are produced, the subjects they cover, and how they integrate and the various audiences to which the certifications are aimed. The role, the perceived and real value, and benefits of certification within the field of information security both from an individual and an organizational perspective are discussed. Finally, some conclusions on certification are presented.

INTRODUCTION

Information security[1] certifications now form a significant part of the wider information security industry, with a powerful influence on individuals and organizations within that industry. Certifications are often a prerequisite for senior jobs, working in government or for employment in specific roles; they are also widespread across the industry. The major certification bodies – (ISC)[2], ISACA, EC Council and SANS – claim to have trained or have as members well over 500,000 individuals in total. Certification is also a big business, with annual reports from two of the major players in the field ((ISC)[2], 2017 and ISACA, 2017a) both indicating revenue for each of over US$50 million from education, examinations, membership and publications.

DOI: 10.4018/978-1-6684-3554-0.ch005

Before embarking on a review of these certifications, the definition of certification as used in this chapter should be provided. This chapter uses the term certification with the following meaning: "the act of certifying or state of being certified" (Collins, 2018) here we use the last part of the definition to indicate that an individual is in the state of being certified, i.e. they hold a certificate, which is an official document received when a course of study or training is completed.

The chapter is structured as follows. A very brief background is given to explain the rise of information security certifications. This is followed by a review of certification bodies and their characteristics, then an in-depth review of information security certifications at the time of publication. The discussion continues by examining the role of certifications from a personal and organizational perspective, the perceived value and benefit and then the misuse and abuse to which certifications can be put. Finally, some future trends in the field of information security certification are highlighted.

A BRIEF HISTORY OF INFORMATION SECURITY CERTIFICATIONS

Information security – originally computer security – came from an IT background. It was considered to be an IT specialism for a number of years and so didn't really require much in the way of oversight, a single unified voice, certification or qualifications. Typically, certifications were created by one or more groups of willing, interested and altruistic individuals either responding to a perceived need or trying to set a standard that could be readily understood. By setting standards, these groups hoped to both define what made an individual competent and knowledgeable in the field of information security and provide a mechanism to identify those who were perhaps less than capable. There was not the need to submit to scrutiny or oversight as the numbers involved were small, the individuals knew each other and the roles many of the individuals worked in required some form of government vetting and clearance – and most, if not all of the groups were based in the United States. From these beginnings rose the information security certification industry we see today.

Today, there is no one "global body" that can truly claim to represent information security and the individuals in the field. Whilst there are a number of organizations who have global membership and reach, they do not capture everyone who works in the field, nor does everyone in the field want to hold the certifications they offer. Thanks to its multi-disciplinary nature, information/cyber security is a "big tent" and covers more than just technical roles. Thirty-five roles (CyberSN, 2018) related to security have been identified, ranging from the highly technical security analyst to CEO. These example roles – and all 35 – will have widely differing requirements for skills, knowledge and experience; yet all will require some knowledge of information/cyber security. However, for many non-technical roles, possession of certain certifications will not be possible, as they will not possess the relevant skills and experience – and they might never gain them. Examples of these individuals could include those people working in marketing, PR and finance for information security organizations.

From an academic perspective, information security is a new discipline that has been recognized as such for about thirty years or so. It is multi-disciplinary in nature, covering both technical and non-technical subjects, including programming, hardware design and function, networking, economics, law and business as well as security-related topics such as cryptography and risk management. As a result, it has been difficult to create educational pathways for students that meet both academic standards and industry needs.

Typically, universities have also found difficulties in establishing undergraduate degree courses in the subject, as it has been difficult to understand the needs of industry, establish demand for such degrees and create information security courses with enough differentiation from those degrees, such as computing, already offered. Additionally, many of the topics are covered in computer science or related degrees, with security has been offered as an optional module near the end of the course. However, the last few years, cybersecurity undergraduate degrees have started to be developed and offered to prospective students, some in response to the government cybersecurity guidelines and some in response to industry needs.

The first information security degrees were postgraduate, and this trend has continued, with a significant number of universities offering this option to students. One advantage of this approach is that the student will have experience and/or subject knowledge, meaning that the course can focus on the security aspects rather than the fundamentals of IT and networking.

So, the multi-disciplinary nature of information security has both created opportunity for multiple certifications and differing educational approaches. But information security defies easy categorization: is it a technical discipline, where knowledge of the inner workings of IT and cryptography are a must, or is it a hybrid discipline, where knowledge of people, process and technology are a must? Whilst this author is of the latter opinion, the sheer diversity of the field and the roles in it means that probably both are valid perspectives: and therein lies the problem. What are the fundamentals that matter? What are the fundamentals that everyone should know? How should individuals prove their knowledge and skill?

Contributing to this issue is that the certification bodies have been created from and possess different philosophies and perspectives. For example, ISACA, given its audit background, typically defines tasks that certification holders should be able to perform and then tests against those tasks; ISACA also has its own standard (COBIT, ISACA 2012) against which performance can be measured. These different starting points and perspectives mean that the certification bodies prioritize different domains of knowledge, different experience and different approaches (such as technically-oriented or management-oriented).

Additionally, although standards bodies such as BSI, NIST and ISO have published numerous information security standards, many of those focus on the technical and managerial, not the individual, perspective. It can be argued that ISO 27021:2017 Competence requirements for information security management systems professionals (ISO 2017) does state the competences (meaning the combination of knowledge and skills, CEN (2014)) required or expected of professionals managing an ISMS; however, it does not specify a personal certification or qualification scheme.

As information security has evolved, this lack of a unifying voice for the profession, coupled with dissatisfaction about certifications and low barriers of entry has meant that numerous bodies have stepped into the vacuum and created education, training, certifications and qualifications they believe will be of use. Each certification body has its own views on what is important, what is required and what individuals should know and be able to do to gain the certification and declare themselves to be capable of working in information security. Alongside this, professional and certification bodies in other industries are offering information security education, training and certifications to their membership.

The preceding paragraphs should not be taken as criticism of the institutions or individuals involved: rather, they indicate the evolving and changing natures of this topic, of information security careers and of the knowledge and skill requirements, characteristic of an emerging profession. With such uncertainty and fluidity, it can be very difficult for academic institutions and certification bodies to create pathways, qualifications, certifications and frameworks whilst having the confidence that these developments will have long-term viability and recognition. Allied to this is the rapid technological change and developments in technology which are challenging to keep abreast of, integrate into formal education and to estimate their impact and relevance.

Undoubtedly, the power of the market has also played a part in creating the range and number of information security certifications currently available. Creating a certification can result in significant revenue opportunities associated with the sale of associated education, training, memberships and publications. Additionally, at the time of writing, all things "cyber" are in vogue, so many organizations are seeking to capitalize on this trend by offering "cyber" courses and the like.

Having briefly discussed the history of information security certifications, we now turn our attention to the certification bodies that administer the certifications currently available and their core activities.

CERTIFICATION BODIES

Behind the certifications are organizations, termed certification bodies, that produce, administer, market and sell certifications. They may also offer and administer membership, membership benefits and continuing education opportunities. This section focuses upon three key activities the certification bodies deliver, namely certification; membership; and certification maintenance and update.

Certification

The major certification bodies all follow a similar process. An individual wanting to gain a certification must know, learn or refresh a body of knowledge. The bodies offer various pathways to learn the body of knowledge, ranging from self-study to online courses to face-to-face training. There is also typically a range of published (both physical and electronic) books, study guides, presentations and practice tests. Training is carried by authorized instructors or authorized training partners (collectively termed authorized providers), who are supplied with the most current education materials. The individual is then examined by a written examination and, in some cases, a practical hands-on examination as well. Once the individual passes the examination(s), a certificate detailing what the individual has obtained is produced.

Membership

Many certification bodies offer membership as a result of a successful examination result. Membership is usually conditional on meeting eligibility criteria and signing up to a code of ethics. However, unlike many professional bodies, the certification bodies typically only have two levels of membership: the first is full membership, where an individual has the requisite years of experience and holds a certification; the second where an individual holds the certification but hasn't obtained the experience required to be a full member (sometimes termed "Associate"). The certification bodies do not necessarily offer the path of progression offered by true professional bodies; once the certification is obtained, there is no further progression – once a member, always a member – although other certifications can be obtained.

These bodies typically require that an individual maintains their membership. This is usually achieved by paying an annual fee and, in many cases, obtaining a certain number of hours of continuing professional education (CPE) or similar. The guidelines for what actually qualifies as a CPE can be complex (see for example CompTIA no date, GIAC 2018 and ISACA 2018a) but the intention is to drive individuals to undertake education and activities outside the normal performance of their role, so that the individuals develop and grow throughout their membership.

Typically, an individual will either have an annual target of continuing professional education to attain or will have to reach a target over a three-year cycle, with yearly minima and maxima. The minima and maxima are set to stop individuals doing nothing for two years and then collecting all their CPE in one go. Individuals are responsible for maintaining their record of CPE obtained and many organizations randomly audit a percentage of their members annually to check if CPE are being recorded in accordance with published guidelines.

To aid members in obtaining CPE credits, all the bodies offer a range of webcasts, podcasts, events and quizzes, many of which are free to members; they also offer CPE credits for volunteering and mentoring. Other organizations can offer CPE opportunities, such as conference, training and education providers.

Codes of ethics are prevalent across the industry. Undoubtedly, due to the knowledge and access possessed by individuals working in information security, those individuals could cause significant harm to people, IT systems, organizations and even governments. Such codes of ethics are designed to set out and reinforce a set of behaviors an individual is expected to demonstrate and usually have sanctions (or disciplinary measures) for breaching the code. Usually the sanction is expulsion from the membership and loss of the certification. Disciplinary action is usually organized and overseen by the certification body acting on complaints or reports of violations of the code of ethics. Sample codes of ethics are shown in Table 1.

The table above highlights three interesting points. First, that the code of ethics may be publicly available, so that anyone can read it; second, there is an altruistic imperative to serve clients/stakeholders, protect the wider community and advance the profession as viewed by the certification body. Third, they are not focused solely on the protection or use of technology; the codes are focused on the human side of information security.

Efforts have been made to harmonize these codes of ethics (see Cybersecurity Credentials Collaborative, 2015a) but they have not yet reached fruition. The harmonized code binds the individual certification bodies' code of ethics together and provides a code of ethics which is applicable industry-wide. The harmonized code covers four main areas: integrity, objectivity, confidentiality and professional competence.

Certification Maintenance and Update

The certification bodies discussed in this chapter invest significant resources in updating and enhancing their certification and associated materials. Using (ISC)^2 as an example, all of their certifications are on a two or three-year update cycle. For an individual certification, there is a methodical process, which concentrates on the examination and ensures it tests the tasks that are performed by security professionals who are engaged in the profession. The tasks are defined by workshops comprised of members, non-members and experts which produce Job Task Analyses (JTA). The JTA are then used to develop the examination and its associated questions. Once the examination is updated, a separate team will be given the outputs of the JTA (the knowledge required) to produce educational material covering the knowledge required. Considerable effort is expended in the running the JTA, producing the examination and the educational material and in keeping the examination and education teams apart. Of interest is the fact that the examination is developed first – then the education.

Certification bodies administer certifications and we now turn our attention to reviewing those certifications.

Table 1. Codes of ethics published by selected certification bodies (note ISACA present their code as a numeric list)

(ISC)²	GIAC	ISACA
• Protect society, the common good, necessary public trust and confidence, and the infrastructure. • Act honorably, honestly, justly, responsibly, and legally. • Provide diligent and competent service to principles. • Advance and protect the profession.	Respect for the Public • I will accept responsibility in making decisions with consideration for the security and welfare of the community. • I will not engage in or be a party to unethical or unlawful acts that negatively affect the community, my professional reputation, or the information security discipline. Respect for the Certification • I will not share, disseminate, or otherwise distribute confidential or proprietary information pertaining to the GIAC certification process. • I will not use my certification, or objects or information associated with my certification (such as certificates or logos) to represent any individual or entity other than myself as being certified by GIAC. Respect for my Employer • I will deliver capable service that is consistent with the expectations of my certification and position. • I will protect confidential and proprietary information with which I come into contact. • I will minimize risks to the confidentiality, integrity, or availability of an information technology solution, consistent with risk management practice. Respect for Myself • I will avoid conflicts of interest. • I will not misuse any information or privileges I am afforded as part of my responsibilities. • I will not misrepresent my abilities or my work to the community, my employer, or my peers.	1. Support the implementation of, and encourage compliance with, appropriate standards and procedures for the effective governance and management of enterprise information systems and technology, including: audit, control, security and risk management. 2. Perform their duties with objectivity, due diligence and professional care, in accordance with professional standards. 3. Serve in the interest of stakeholders in a lawful manner, while maintaining high standards of conduct and character, and not discrediting their profession or the Association. 4. Maintain the privacy and confidentiality of information obtained in the course of their activities unless disclosure is required by legal authority. Such information shall not be used for personal benefit or released to inappropriate parties. 5. Maintain competency in their respective fields and agree to undertake only those activities they can reasonably expect to complete with the necessary skills, knowledge and competence. 6. Inform appropriate parties of the results of work performed including the disclosure of all significant facts known to them that, if not disclosed, may distort the reporting of the results. 7. Support the professional education of stakeholders in enhancing their understanding of the governance and management of enterprise information systems and technology, including: audit, control, security and risk management.

INFORMATION SECURITY CERTIFICATIONS

As of writing, one survey (Wikipedia 2018) has identified 102 recognized information security-related certifications; there are also other professional certifications, awarded by bodies such as the BCS, The Chartered Institute for IT, the Security Institute and the IEEE, which also award certifications and/or membership to individuals who work in this field.

Not all these recognized information security certifications are as well-known or recognized by the industry as others. Rather than survey the entire one hundred certifications, this section focuses on the better known and most popular (in terms of certification holders) information security certifications, which are shown in Table 2.

Table 2. Well known information security certifications (in alphabetical order of awarding body)

Certification	Certification Body	Experience Requirements	Exam	Code of Ethics	Maintenance Requirements
CISSP	(ISC)²	Five years or more	Yes	Yes	Yes
SSCP	(ISC)²	One year	Yes	Yes	Yes
CCSP	(ISC)²	Five years or more	Yes	Yes	Yes
CISMP	BCS	None	Yes		
Security+	CompTIA	None (but recommended)	Yes	Yes	Yes
CEH	EC Council	Two years or more	Yes	Yes	Yes
GIAC Certifications	GIAC	Varies	Yes	Yes	Yes
GSE	GIAC	Must hold GIAC certifications	Yes	Yes	Yes
CISM	ISACA	5 years or more	Yes	Yes	Yes
CISA	ISACA	5 years or more	Yes	Yes	Yes
CSXP	ISACA	Not stated	Yes	Yes	Yes

The rest of this chapter discusses these certifications, and highlight points of interest, similarity and divergence. To aid the reader, the following sections provide an overview of the certifications available, divided into three categories: technical, managerial and specialist. These categories are based on the predominant content of the certification, so the divisions are somewhat arbitrary in that many certifications contain elements of all three categories. However, this approach provides a useful framework to comprehend the scale and breadth of information security certifications and the related industry.

Alongside the certification bodies are a number of professional bodies that offer membership and certification in information security for individuals working in information security, along with professional bodies for IT and other professions; these are also covered to provide as full a picture as possible.

Note that the following paragraphs focus only on those certifications which are considered to be relevant to information security; thus many IT certifications, which may have some information security component, will be ignored. Vendor certifications will also not be covered.

TECHNICAL CERTIFICATIONS

Technical certifications are those which focus on particular technologies, hardware and software associated with information security. These certifications are typically very focused, covering a particular technology or software package; they may also require the student to display practical knowledge and skills by conducting tasks in a controlled environment (such as an online laboratory).

The SANS Institute probably offers the widest variety of information security courses, numbering over 55 (SANS 2018), covering everything from information security fundamentals to security awareness to securing code in Java/EE. SANS began by offering hands-on technical training and has expanded to cover the non-technical to meet demand and to reflect the changes in the information security industry. SANS major strength is in delivering very intensive five- or six-day face-to-face training courses, led by an instructor, although many of the courses are now available online. SANS uses a small group of rigorously selected instructors (about 100) to deliver their courses; the instructors perform their teaching in addition to their day jobs, meaning that the instructors are current and have deep experience in the topics they teach.

SANS courses are aligned to and can be used to obtain certifications from Global Information Assurance Certification (GIAC). GIAC offers 28 certifications (GIAC 2016), covering five domains: cyber defense, application security, penetration testing, digital forensics and management, legal and audit. For each certification gained, an individual can submit a research paper on the subject of the certification; if accepted, the individual gains a GIAC Gold certification. Additionally, once an individual has completed a set of prerequisites, including GIAC Gold, they may sit both an exam and a hands-on practical to become a GIAC Security Expert (GSE). GIAC certifications require either maintenance by CPE accumulation or by retaking the examination; the GSE can only be renewed by examination.

Whereas SANS has a deserved reputation for advanced technical training, CompTIA has aimed its cybersecurity certification at the entry-level and thus filled an important area. CompTIA offer a range of IT and information security certifications and their entry-level offering in information security is the Security+. This certification covers network security; compliance and operational security; threats and vulnerabilities; application, data and host security; access control and identity management; and cryptography (CompTIA 2016). Security+ has a set of maintenance requirements, including an annual maintenance fee and a three-year continuing education cycle; there is also an option to resit the examination. This certificate is also part of a certification pathway for an individual aspiring to have a career in IT or information security (CompTIA 2018).

ISACA offer their CSXP (CybersecurityNexus Practitioner, ISACA 2015), which is designed to evaluate an individual's ability to perform cybersecurity tasks, through hands-on testing. CSXP is unique in that no formal training is offered by ISACA; instead, individuals are told what they should be able to achieve and the tools and techniques they will need to apply. This approach is designed to overcome the limitations of written examinations and provide both individuals and organizations with a robust assessment of what an individual can achieve in a practical sense. CSXP uses a three-year cycle for certificate maintenance, with all holders required to resit the examination at the end of the cycle. ISACA do not state the experience required to sit the exam; however, the list of tasks and tools is extensive and indicates to your author that at least two years' experience is needed.

MANAGERIAL CERTIFICATIONS

Moving on from the technical certifications, the second category of certifications are the managerial. These typically take a broader view of information security, and are focused on processes, standards, business context and the management of information security in an organization. Technical knowledge is assumed or is provided at a higher level than provided for in the technical certifications.

There are two certifications that dominate this category: the Certified Information Systems Security Professional (CISSP) from (ISC)^2 and the Certified Information Security Manager (CISM) from ISACA. Both are aimed at individuals with five or more years' experience and both require an individual to know (and recall) a Common Body of Knowledge. Both are gained by examination, proof of experience, and for the CISSP, endorsement by an (ISC)^2 member. This last condition, which is unique to (ISC)^2 as far as the author knows, means the individual seeking a certification from (ISC)^2 must have their application countersigned by an existing (ISC)^2 member. This has three important implications: first, should an individual falsify the proof of experience, then the endorser may lose their certification, so the endorser should know the individual or check the veracity of the individual; second, it encourages individuals to build networks and engage with (ISC)[2] members before they gain their certification; and third, it creates a tight-knit community where groups of certificate holders know and trust each other.

There is much debate about which of these certifications is better, or what they cover. Table 3 highlights the knowledge domains for each certification.

Table 3. The CISSP and CISM knowledge domains

CISSP Domains ((ISC)[2] 2018)	CISM Domains (ISACA 2017b)
Security and Risk Management	Information Security Governance
Asset Security	Information Risk Management
Security Engineering	Information Security Program Development and Management
Communication and Network Security	Information Security Incident Management
Identity and Access Management	
Security Assessment and Testing	
Security Operations	
Software Development Security	

CISSP was launched in 1994 ((ISC)[2] 2018) and has a deserved reputation within the industry for setting the standard for individuals working at intermediate and senior roles in information security. The CISSP requires individuals to know both the technical aspects of information security, with detailed sections on networking protocols, cryptography and access control, and the non-technical aspects, such as risk management, auditing and legal aspects. These are all presented in the Common Body of Knowledge (CBK), which all individuals aspiring to the CISSP should know. The CISSP has been accused of being "a mile wide and an inch deep", but there is no doubt it attempts to be comprehensive and authoritative.

CISM on the other hand is built around tasks an individual is expected to be able to achieve and the associated knowledge an individual should possess to achieve the task. This, it can be argued, provides more structure to the learning and also reflects better the tasks and activities an information security manager may be asked to accomplish.

In addition to possessing the knowledge related to the topics covered by the domains listed above, individuals wishing to gain the certification must be able to show relevant experience in at least two of the domains. CISSP and CISM both require a minimum of five years' experience in the domains, although individuals can pass the examination and then gain the experience.

Both CISSP and CISM offer several study methods, including self-study, online learning and face-to-face teaching. The latter, with the use of intensive "boot camp" training has garnered some criticism in that an individual can spend four or five days cramming and then sit the exam – and emerge at the end of a (very) intensive week with the certification. The boot camp model is very popular with time-poor individuals working in information security, as it provides a quick method of gaining the desired certification. However, as in all training, the process can be gamed by an individual who intensively studies for the week, and then regurgitates the facts to pass the exam, yet may have little hands-on or real-world experience, or ability to apply the knowledge insightfully.

Alongside the CISSP and CISM, there are newer certifications aimed at individuals working at more senior levels of the industry, or those individuals aspiring to reach such levels. Typical of these is the EISM (Information Security Manager) and CCISO (Certified Chief Information Security Officer, offered by the EC-Council. The EISM uses the same courseware and training as the CCISO certification, but goes onto less depth, as does the corresponding exam. Both the EISM and CCISO are built around five domains (EC Council 2018a), as shown in Table 4.

Table 4. The CISSP, CISM and CCISO knowledge domains

CISSP Domains ((ISC)² 2018)	CISM Domains (ISACA 2017b)	EISM/CCISO Domains (EC Council 2018a)
Security and Risk Management	Information Security Governance	Governance (Policy, Legal, and Compliance)
Asset Security	Information Risk Management	IS Management Controls and Audit Management
Security Engineering	Information Security Program Development and Management	Management of Projects, Technology, and Operations
Communication and Network Security	Information Security Incident Management	Information Security Core Concepts
Identity and Access Management		Strategic Planning and Finance
Security Assessment and Testing		
Security Operations		
Software Development Security		

At this point, it is worth stating that all three certifications cover similar ground but are differently organized and take different perspectives. For example, all three certifications cover well-known standards such as ISO/IEC 27001, ISO/IEC 27005 and NIST; all three cover incident management; all three cover similar technologies such as access control; and all three require five years' experience.

SPECIALIST CERTIFICATIONS

The third category, specialist certifications, differs from the previous two in that they are not technology-focused, nor do they take a broad view of information security. These specialist certifications may cover particular activities, such as auditing or hacking, or cover particular technologies from technical, information security and business contexts.

There are number of specialist certifications of particular relevance to individuals working in information security, namely CISA, CCSK, CCSP, CEH (and related certifications) and OCSP.

The first and the longest serving is the CISA (Certified Information Systems Auditor) launched by ISACA in 1978 (ISACA 2018b). This certification is almost an industry prerequisite for individuals wanting to develop and further a career in IT and information security auditing. CISA, in a manner similar to CISM, has five knowledge domains:

- The Process of Auditing Information Systems

- Governance and Management of IT
- Information Systems Acquisition, Development and Implementation
- Information Systems Operations, Maintenance and Service Management
- Protection of Information Assets.

With the move to cloud computing and the introduction of the "as a Service" model, certifications covering cloud security were an obvious opportunity for the certification bodies. The first true cloud security certification was the CCSK, offered by the Cloud Security Alliance (Cloud Security Alliance 2011), and now updated to version 4. CCSK has a body of knowledge based on the CSA Cloud Security Guidance v4 (Cloud Security Alliance 2017a), the CSA Cloud Control Matrix (Cloud Security Alliance 2017b) and the ENISA Cloud Computing Risk Assessment report (ENISA 2009). The Cloud Security Guidance covers 14 domains, listed below:

1. Cloud Computing Concepts and Architectures
2. Governance and Enterprise Risk Management
3. Legal Issues, Contracts and Electronic Discovery
4. Compliance and Audit Management
5. Information Governance
6. Management Plane and Business Continuity
7. Infrastructure Security
8. Virtualization and Containers
9. Incident Response
10. Application Security
11. Data Security and Encryption
12. Identity, Entitlement and Access Management
13. Security as a Service
14. Related Technologies

Domain 14, Related technologies, covers topics such as Big Data, Internet of Things and serverless computing. The CCSK does not require any maintenance, but holders of the certification are encouraged to retake the latest version, to keep their knowledge up to date.

Following on from the CCSK, the Cloud Security Alliance collaborated with (ISC)² to create the Certified Cloud Security Professional (CCSP). The CCSP has much in common with the CSSK and the CISSP but takes a more strategic view than the CCSK and includes privacy and traditional security approaches. The CCSP (like the CISSP) has a CBK which covers six domains, namely Architectural Concepts & Design Requirements; Cloud Data Security; Cloud Platform and Infrastructure Security; Cloud Application Security; Operations; and Legal & Compliance ((ISC)² 2015). The certification is gained by examination and has maintenance requirements similar to the CISSP, with a three-year cycle requiring 90 CPE.

Next in this overview of technical certifications is the Certified Ethical Hacker (CEH), awarded by the EC Council. CEH was launched in 2002 (EC Council 2017) and the latest version, version 10, covers the following domains (EC Council 2018b):

1. Background

2. Analysis/Assessment
3. Security
4. Tools/Systems/Programs
5. Procedures/Methodology
6. Regulation/Policy
7. Ethics.

Gaining the CEH is through a written exam; certificate holders can also take the CEH (Practical), launched in 2018. The CEH (Practical) is a hands-on examination where the individual has to perform various hacking techniques such as packet sniffing, SQL Injection and cryptographic attacks. CEH and CEH (Practical) provide a route to move to the EC Security Analyst and EC Security Analyst (Practical) and then the expert-level Licensed Penetration Tester (Master). Of interest is the emphasis on hands-on practical examination as an adjunct to the written tests. EC Council also have a code of ethics and typically require a certificate holder has to maintain the credential over a two or three-year cycle, in which varying numbers of CPE must be earned.

The technical certification section is rounded off by OSCP (Offensive Security Certified Professional), offered by Offensive Security (Offensive Security, 2018a). OSCP requires an individual to conduct a full penetration test of an unknown system, using Kali Linux. The individual is given 24 hours to complete the test and create a penetration test report, with in-depth notes and screenshots detailing their findings. Points are awarded for each compromised host, based on their difficulty and level of access obtained. OSCP (and other certifications offered by Offensive Security) do not have a maintenance requirement; once passed they never expire.

The prerequisite course for OSCP, entitled Penetration Testing with Kali Linux, has the following syllabus: (Offensive Security 2018b):

1. Getting Comfortable with Kali Linux
2. The Essential Tools
3. Passive Information Gathering
4. Active Information Gathering
5. Vulnerability Scanning
6. Buffer Overflows
7. Win32 Buffer Overflow Exploitation
8. Linux Buffer Overflow Exploitation
9. Working with Exploits
10. File Transfers
11. Privilege Escalation
12. Client Side Attacks
13. Web Application Attacks
14. Password Attacks
15. Port Redirection and Tunnelling
16. The Metasploit Framework
17. Bypassing Antivirus Software
18. Assembling the Pieces: Penetration Test Breakdown.

The prerequisite syllabus is very detailed and focused on the technical aspects of conducting a penetration test.

PROFESSIONAL MEMBERSHIP

Professional bodies cover a significant number of human activities and typically follow a common path, in that an individual will progress from a junior to a senior level of membership. This progression may be marked by gaining experience, by the gaining of knowledge or skill and by the passing of exams. Using a UK body (BCS, The Chartered Institute for IT) as an example, membership of a professional body typically follows the route shown in Figure 1.

Figure 1. Typical professional pathway
(after BCS, 2014)

	Student	Associate	Member	Chartered Member	Fellow/ Chartered Fellow
Qualifications		Degree in unrelated subject OR Non-degree OR undergraduate degree	Undergraduate degree		
Experience/ years	0	0 – 10	3 – 5	5+	10+
Career level	Foundational	Operational	Operational	Tactical	Strategic
Typical titles			Team Leader Manager Lecturer	Team Leader Deputy Head of... Senior Manager Senior Lecturer Reader	Head of... Professor Director Partner

So, as Figure 1 illustrates for an individual, joining a professional body provides a clear path for progression, with way points and criteria for advancement clearly defined. In some professions, medicine and accountancy being two examples, professional qualifications and certifications are required to practice, so the professional body also provides the "licence to practice".

The key to moving upwards through the membership is experience and passing the requisite criteria. For some professions, that may mean passing exams to join and move upwards or passing interviews to gain the next level of membership. As a result, progression is often seen as a milestone for an individual.

Within information security, there are two well-known professional bodies. The first is CREST which provides technical certifications for individuals working in penetration testing, threat intelligence, incident response and security architecture. CREST (CREST 2016) offers individuals a pathway from Practitioner (entry-level) through Registered (competent to work independently without supervision) to Certified (technically competent to run major projects and teams). At each level, examinations have to be passed and each level requires documented evidence of experience – Practitioner requiring 2,500 hours, Registered requiring at least 6,000 hours and Certified requiring at least 10,000 hours of relevant experience (CREST 2017). CREST examinations can include both written and practical components. CREST also provides accreditation for organizations working in particular segments of the information security industry and standards for topics such as penetration testing.

The second professional body is the IISP, Institute of Information Security Professionals. Like CREST, the IISP was formed in the UK and offers individual and corporate membership. The individual membership pathway has four levels (IISP 2018a) from Student to Fellow. Supporting the membership pathway is the Skills Framework, which can be used to guide individuals as they develop. The Skills Framework can also indicate to individuals when they can progress through the membership; it is also used to assess individuals to ensure they hold the correct membership.

As discussed in the previous chapter, the IISP Skills Framework is composed of 10 skills areas and disciplines, as follows (IISP 2018b):

1.   Information security governance and management
2.   Threat assessment and information risk management
3.   Implementing secure systems
4.   Assurance, audit, compliance and testing
5.   Operational security management
6.   Incident management, investigation and digital forensics
7.   Security discipline (not used)
8.   Business resilience
9.   Information security research
10.   Management, leadership, business and communications
11.   Contributions to the information security profession and professional development.

Each of these skills areas and disciplines are broken down into skills groups. For each skill group, a descriptor indicates what an individual should know and be able to accomplish, using levels from 1 (basic knowledge) to 6 (expert/lead practitioner).

Within IT and engineering, professional bodies such as BCS, the Chartered Institute for IT (BCS), the Institution for Engineering Technology (IET) and the Institute of Electrical and Electronics Engineers (IEEE) count information security individuals within their membership and also provide information security education and training for their members. The BCS, The Chartered Institute for IT, also offers an entry-level information security certificate, the Certificate in Information Security Management Principles (CISMP). This certificate is aimed at IT professionals either wishing to expand their knowledge or individuals who wish to move into the information security field. The knowledge is divided into nine modules (BCS, 2017):

1.   Information Security Management Principles
2.   Information Risk
3.   Information Security Framework
4.   Procedural/People Security Controls
5.   Technical Security Controls

6. Software Development and Lifecycle
7. Physical and Environmental Security Controls
8. Disaster Recovery and Business Continuity Management
9. Other Technical Aspects.

The knowledge is tested by examination; once passed there are no further requirements on the individual. CISMP is a stepping stone into practitioner-level qualifications (which examine particular aspects of information security in more detail) and ultimately the UK Government Certified Professional scheme (originally CESG Certified Professional, now Certified Professional; NCSC 2016).

AN ALTERNATIVE VIEW OF CERTIFICATIONS

Besides grouping the certifications by their content, they can also be grouped by the level of experience and knowledge the individual is expected to possess. Certification bodies typically use three categories – entry-level, intermediate and senior – and Table 5 illustrates both typical definitions and where popular (and previously discussed certifications) are placed.

Table 5. Information security certifications grouped by level of experience required (in alphabetical order of certification body)

Entry-Level	Intermediate	Senior
No previous experience required	Typically require two or more years' experience	Typically require five or more years' experience
(ISC)² SSCP BCS CISMP CSA CCSK CompTIA Security+ ISACA CSX Cybersecurity Fundamentals certificate GIAC Information Security Fundamentals	CompTIA Cybersecurity Analyst+ EC Council Certified Ethical Hacker GIAC Security Essentials ISACA CXSP (assumed)	(ISC)² CISSP (and concentrations) (ISC)² CCSP ISACA CISM ISACA CISA EC Council CCISO EC Council LPT(M) GIAC Security Expert

The table serves an important purpose, in that it dispels a common myth that there are no entry-level certifications for information security. Thanks to their status, certifications such as CISSP and CISA dominate discussions and job descriptions (see the section entitled Misuse and Abuse), so new entrants and career changers believe that an individual must have a CISSP or similar to work in information security. This misconception does deter individuals from joining the information security workforce.

It also highlights that a pathway exists for individuals who wish to develop their skills and knowledge by taking and passing relevant certifications through their career. An individual can use certifications to define certain points in a career, because the stated experience requirements and successful completion of the examination(s) can be used to highlight increasing knowledge and skill.

The table provides an insight into how certifications can be combined to produce a roadmap for an individual. Many certifications are stand-alone, so it can be difficult for an individual to choose the certification that provides the greatest benefit and to create a pathway to move from entry-level to senior

Figure 2. Example certification pathways from entry to senior level

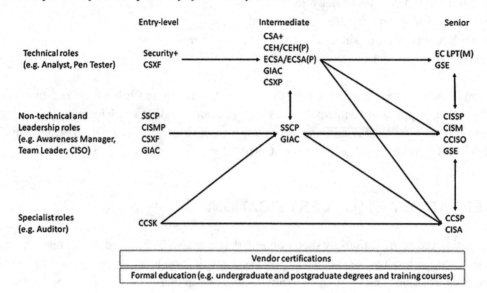

certifications. Figure 2 illustrates how the certifications discussed in this chapter can be combined to produce such a pathway.

Figure 2 above again confirms the complexity and multiplicity of certifications and highlights how an individual, who can meet the relevant criteria, can demonstrate their progress and development. It also indicates how an individual can plan their development; for example, if an individual comes from a technical role and aspires to a leadership role, then they examine the prerequisites for a management certification and plan to gain the relevant experience and knowledge, through education and practice.

Having examined certifications in detail, we now turn to the role of certification to an individual and their career and to an organization and its information security.

ROLE OF CERTIFICATION: INDIVIDUAL

For an individual, certification typically comes after university-level education, and may occur quite a few years after the conclusion of formal education, as Figure 3 shows.

The figure highlights that for many individuals, certification comes after formal education and occurs during their career. Note that certifications may be taken in addition to other education qualifications and that, multiple certifications may be taken by an individual during their career. Individuals typically view certifications as a mechanism to achieve one or more of the following:

1. Develop a career
2. Get a new job
3. Get my bosses' job
4. Get a pay rise
5. Get a promotion
6. Keep the individual's current job

7.   Prove professional knowledge and experience
8.   Keep up with peers
9.   Move into a new career
10. Earn CPE.

Note the list above is neither is in priority order nor will stay the same throughout an individual's career. However, the decision to obtain a certification will often be driven by one or more of the above; as will the reasoning behind the decision.

Figure 3. Relationship of education and certification
(after Davis, 2017)

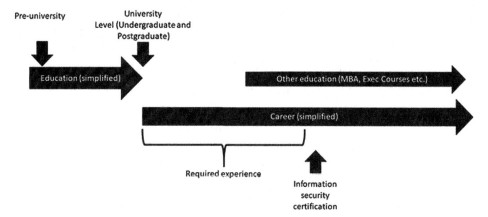

Certifications are often seen as a mechanism to advance an individual's career. The acquisition of a defined set of information security knowledge, coupled with an independent assessment of that knowledge is seen as a passport to success. In some cases, particular roles or jobs require the possession of a particular certification (for example Government roles), so gaining a certification allows the individual to enter that particular field. This places a heavy burden on the individual from two directions: concerns over actually obtaining the certification and concerns that failure may impair the individual's immediate and future prospects. It is worth noting that many individuals who decide to sit (or write) a certification examination may have not studied for a number of years, and so have to relearn the tools and techniques of effective studying and revision, as well as the actual education material related to the certification.

Certifications are also viewed as a mechanism to enter the information security industry. Due to the wide currency afforded certain certifications, many new entrants believe they must obtain the senior certification before they start in any information security role; they also do not realize that there are entry-level certifications, or courses of education that would be of more relevance.

ROLE OF CERTIFICATION: ORGANIZATIONAL

From an organizational perspective, a certification can indicate a number of things about an individual or an employee. First, possession indicates that an individual can pass an exam or a set of entry criteria, as discussed above. Second, it shows that an individual is prepared to spend time and effort, and in some cases, considerable sums of money, to gain knowledge and skills and develop themselves in their chosen field. Third, the possession of a certification may indicate a desire to either be seen as an expert in a field, or a desire to become such an expert; the certification is a spring-board to achieve that. Fourth, the individual possesses a set of knowledge as defined by the certification body and has ready access to that knowledge. Fifth, the certification possessed will indicate (to some extent) the level of knowledge and experience of the individual from entry-level to expert. Finally, the certification may also indicate the behavior the individual should demonstrate, and the organization can expect.

As well as these positive indicators, there are negative ones. Possession of a certification cannot tell an organization whether the individual is the right fit for the role, the organization and the team; the specific, detailed experience an individual has in the field; their delivery successes and failures; and whether the individual which actually listen to their new bosses and peers.

For organizations, certifications provide a useful standard or benchmark to evaluate candidates for roles, produce job descriptions and set levels of seniority. Thanks to the criteria for obtaining certifications, which are widely known and available, a certification can be used very quickly to determine both a candidate's experience and suitability for a post (but see "misuse and abuse below"); the possession (or not) can also be used as a sifting mechanism to select suitable candidates for interview and beyond.

Offering routes to certification can also be a powerful tool to retain and motivate staff. Many of the certifications require an investment in time and money to obtain and maintain, so having the financial and/or resource support of an employer is often welcomed. Tying promotion opportunities, pay rises and other recognition to gaining certifications or promoting individuals who gain a certification are typical approaches.

For an organization, employing certified individuals can be used to indicate that information security is a management concern and that the organization has committed to invest in expertise.

Professionalization and Certification

There is a debate within information security as to whether it is a profession and whether individuals who work in the field and who have gained certifications can call themselves "information security professionals". Certification bodies, with their entry requirements, membership obligations and codes of ethics believe they have an important role to play in professionalizing the industry and are, in fact, doing so.

To examine the debate on professionalization closely, a starting point is to reflect upon what makes a profession:

A profession is a disciplined group of individuals who adhere to ethical standards and who hold themselves out as, and are accepted by the public as possessing special knowledge and skills in a widely recognised body of learning derived from research, education and training at a high level, and who are prepared to apply this knowledge and exercise these skills in the interest of others. It is inherent in the definition of a profession that a code of ethics governs the activities of each profession. Such codes require behaviour and practice beyond the personal moral obligations of an individual. They define and demand high standards of behaviour in respect to the services provided to the public and in dealing with professional colleagues. Further, these codes are enforced by the profession and are acknowledged and accepted by the community. (Professions Australia, 2018)

And, from a similar source, what makes a professional:

A professional is a member of a profession. Professionals are governed by codes of ethics, and profess commitment to competence, integrity and morality, altruism, and the promotion of the public good within their expert domain. Professionals are accountable to those served and to society. (Professional Standards Councils, 2018)

These quotes, albeit lengthy, capture the overall requirements of a profession and a professional. In essence, we can reduce these quotes to the following characteristics, shown in Table 6.

Table 6. Characteristics of a profession and a professional

Profession	Professional
Specialized knowledge	Honest
Formal qualifications	Integrious
Best practice materials	Accountable
Research	Self-regulating
Accreditation	Credible
Supervision	Ethical
Code of ethics	Confidential

Using these characteristics and reviewing the activities of the certification bodies discussed in this chapter, many (if not all) of the bodies, have met, or are striving to meet, all of those characteristics. Following on from this, because of the emphasis on codes of ethics and indeed, the expectations of both individuals within the information security industry and the people they work for, a very high percentage of individuals within the information security industry hold themselves to the characteristics listed in Table 6 as well.

However, despite meeting many of the characteristics mentioned above, many information security certifications are not regulated by formal education bodies or regulators. This results in the certifications having no academic standing, as they are not mapped to national academic frameworks, such as England's Regulated Qualifications Framework (OfQual, 2015 and 2016) or regional frameworks, such as the European Qualifications Framework (EQF; CEDEFOP, 2008), nor can they be compared to recognized academic qualifications, such as undergraduate and postgraduate degrees. In the information security industry, the lack of inclusion in these educational frameworks does not limit the effectiveness and importance of information security certifications but this lack of inclusion does hinder widespread understanding outside of the industry and hinders acceptance of the certification bodies as representing a profession and certificate holders as professionals.

VALUE AND BENEFIT OF CERTIFICATION

As can be seen from the above, most (if not all) certifications require an individual (or their employer) to expend time, money and effort to both gain the certification and to then maintain it. Individuals wishing to obtain certifications can spend considerable sums, with costs of about GBP5,000 for face-to-face training, examination fees and supporting material not uncommon. Individuals also have to make time to study, prepare and then sit the examination, usually while carrying out their day job.

So, why make the investment? Individual professional certifications provide an indication of an individual's knowledge and/or skills measured by some form of independent assessment. They provide a method by which an individual can assess and demonstrate their progress, their level of knowledge and their level of skill – or, in other words, their competence, or a demonstrated ability to apply knowledge, skills and attitudes for achieving observable results (CEN 2014).

The benefit of holding a certification is both tangible and intangible. Tangible benefits include:

- **Better Remuneration:** For example, the Global Information Security Workforce Study (Frost and Sullivan, 2015) states that the holder of a CISSP can expect to receive a salary premium of 35% compared to non-CISSP holders for the same role
- **Better Opportunities:** Holders of certifications are more likely to be considered for roles at all levels and at the more senior levels, a certification is a prerequisite for selection. They may also be offered unadvertised roles as well, or the certification may allow them to pursue particular roles or careers
- **Better Networking:** Many of the organizations involved are membership organizations, so gaining the certification allows an individual to widen their circle of knowledgeable and helpful individuals
- **Better Access to Education:** Most (if not all) of the organizations mentioned in the chapter provide a range of member benefits, including continuing education, webcasts, tutorials, resources and events.

The intangible benefits include:

- **Greater Industry Recognition:** A number of the certifications discussed here are well known and respected globally and hence don't require explanation or justification
- **Greater Impact:** Possession of a certification places the individual above someone who doesn't possess a certification as there is an assumption of greater insight, knowledge, expertise and experience ("you know what you are doing") of the certified individual
- **Higher Prestige:** Because many of the certifications are perceived to be difficult to obtain (and many are in reality), possession of one or more certifications marks an individual out amongst peers
- **Greater Respect:** The individual gains a measure of respect because people know how difficult it is to get the certification; they respect the effort and determination of the individual
- **Better Moral Compass:** Because certifications usually require the individual to agree to code of ethics, the individual may be seen as more trustworthy, more altruistic and to have an ethical approach to the work they do.

The Cybersecurity Credentials Collaborative has published a presentation outlining the value of certification (Cybersecurity Credentials Collaborative, 2015b). This insider view lists the following value propositions for certification:

1. confidence in competency and quality of work
2. tool for hiring managers
3. contribute to career success
4. establishment of ethical bonds.

From an organizational viewpoint, the same source list these value propositions from an organizational perspective:

-   Certification preparation leads to confidence. Well-trained IT professionals are more confident that the skills they possess are appropriate and useful for their responsibilities.
-   Validation reliably attests to the level of knowledge. Certified employees can be relied on to perform at a higher level and have more domain knowledge than untrained employees.
-   Execution is the performance of important business activities. Certified employees can be expected to perform assigned tasks more consistently, increasing reliability and overall organizational execution.

Despite the value of certification, many individuals find it difficult to decide which certification is best for them. Each of the certification bodies (naturally) touts the advantages and benefits associated with their certification(s); many magazines, training organizations and blogs have frequently updated "best/top/best-paying five/ten cybersecurity certifications/qualifications" articles; and if the individual has peers or friends in the industry, then their advice will often be tempered by the experience they have and the certifications they hold. Often, the best advice for an individual is to research the certifications thoroughly, take time to understand what they offer to the individual (at that time) and then, using all the facts gathered, decide.

MISUSE AND ABUSE

Certifications, because of the value and benefit they bring, along with professional recognition and even prestige, are highly prized. It doesn't take much thought to realize that the certifications can be misused and abused.

Obvious methods are to simply lie about the possession of certifications – adding particular certifications to an individual's CV for example – to gain an advantage in a job selection or increase the daily rate that can be charged. All the bodies are alert to this and expend considerable effort to stop such practices.

More subtle is to add terms such as "Master" or "Lead" to the title of the certification, implying greater knowledge, more experience or even a high passing grade. The terms are then used to justify higher fees, differentiate education opportunities and even offer examination guarantees. As discussed above, a number of these certifications only have one level and so these designations are both meaningless and misleading. However, for new entrants looking for education and guidance, these terms are taken at face value and may lead the new entrants to spend more time and money that is necessary to gain the education they want.

The use of digital badging for example can assist in reducing both types of misrepresentation, as can legal action. However, legal action can be slow and expensive and often means that these misrepresentations can continue until the legal process is exhausted. It should be stressed that these occurrences are few and far between, but they do exist, and individuals and organizations should be aware of these and the actions that are taken.

Perhaps the greatest misuse of certifications is what your author calls "shorthand". Shorthand encompasses the use of certifications to screen candidates and/or where a certification is added to a job description, regardless of the suitability of the certification to the job described. The former, screening candidates, makes the possession of one or more certifications the minimum requirement. Thus, regardless of expertise, experience, attitude or aptitude, suitable candidates may be rejected out of hand or stopped from applying for a particular role. This can reduce the pool of candidates dramatically and may actually not be beneficial to the hiring organization. Well known examples of the latter are where a certification requiring five or more years' experience is required for an entry-level or junior post requiring between none and two years' experience. The use of the certification drives away individuals who do not possess the certification (typically the right candidates) and also more experienced candidates who see the role as unsuitable (a step back perhaps) and who also infer that the hiring organization does not understand what it wants or what it is trying to accomplish. Unfortunately, many HR functions and recruitment consultancies are guilty of both of these types of shorthand, often because the individuals in those functions or consultancies do not understand the certifications in detail.

There is also the "groupthink" factor to address. If a security team is made up of individuals who all possess the same qualifications and/or certifications, then there is a possibility that the group will look at issues, problems, challenges and information security operations from one particular perspective. Whilst this may promote consistency and stability of approach, it may mean that certain approaches, creative thinking and activities are missed or downplayed, which may lower the overall security status of an organization and make it more vulnerable to an event or incident.

Finally, certification training is an attractive revenue opportunity. The certification bodies cannot necessarily meet the demand for courses (even moving online), so a "grey market" of unauthorized instructors and training organizations exist. These typically offer certification education at a discount compared to authorized providers, may use previous versions of education material and typically do not use authorized instructors. Grey market providers split the certification industry: one on hand, they are competition and offer a less than premium product and experience, perhaps tarnishing the certification's brand; on the other, they are often found in areas where no authorized providers exist, expend time and resource to advertise and attract individuals and provide a route to membership for individuals who cannot afford the authorized providers.

FUTURE TRENDS

In the near future, certification will continue to play a major role in the industry. With demand for individuals to work in information security and a documented global skills shortage (Center for Cyber Safety and Education 2017), certifications may actually become more important. The certification bodies will play an important role in the professionalization of information security, as they provide an objective measure of knowledge, sometimes skill, and a code of ethics and behavior to hold individuals to account.

Certification bodies are regularly enjoined to create new certifications in the field and examples being proposed certifications in fields such as the Internet of Things and Artificial Intelligence, alongside updating their current certifications. It is likely that new certifications will emerge, or current certifications will expand their coverage of these new technologies.

The rise of university education in cybersecurity at all levels can be seen as a challenge to certification, as more individuals enter the industry with formal qualifications. Entry-level certificates may lose their value and hence market share, whilst intermediate and senior level certifications will hold or increase their value, benefit and market share. Certification bodies will work hard to increase the value and benefits their certifications offer.

CONCLUSION

Certification and certification bodies have had and continue to have a significant impact on both individuals working in information security and on the information security industry itself. Certifications fulfil a number of roles for individuals and within the industry, and their importance shows no sign of diminishing in the near future.

Despite their differing genesis, philosophies and perspectives, information security certifications possess marked similarities, in terms of knowledge domains, experience and maintenance. Whilst the multiplicity and variety of information security certifications may be confusing to the uninitiated or outside observer, it reflects an industry that is growing and developing in real time. This multiplicity of certifications also reflects the range of roles, knowledge, skills and importance of information security in today's world and the varied approaches to protecting information.

Interestingly, given the scale and impact of these certifications, your author has seen very little academic research carried out into the various aspects of certification discussed here. As a final conclusion, your author would draw the readers' attention to this fact and encourage research into this topic.

REFERENCES

Australia, P. (2018). *What is a Profession?* Retrieved from http://www.professions.com.au/defineprofession.html

BCS. (2014). *Membership can make the difference.* Retrieved from https://www.bcs.org/upload/pdf/membership-difference.pdf

BCS. (2017). *BCS Foundation Certificate in Information Security Management Principles Syllabus Version 8.2 March 2017.* Retrieved from https://certifications.bcs.org/upload/pdf/infosec-ismp-syllabus.pdf

CEDEFOP. (2008). *European qualifications framework (EQF).* Retrieved from http://www.cedefop.europa.eu/en/events-and-projects/projects/european-qualifications-framework-eqf

CEN. (2014). *European e-Competence Framework 3.0, A common European Framework for ICT Professionals in all industry sectors.* CWA 16234:2014 Part 1.

Center for Cyber Safety and Education. (2017). *Global Information Security Workforce Study*. Retrieved from https://iamcybersafe.org/GISWS/

Cloud Security Alliance. (2011). *Certificate of Cloud Security Knowledge*. Retrieved from https://cloud-securityalliance.org/education/ccsk/#_overview

Cloud Security Alliance. (2017a). *Security Guidance for Critical Areas of Focus in Cloud Computing v4.0*. Retrieved from https://cloudsecurityalliance.org/download/security-guidance-v4/

Cloud Security Alliance. (2017b). *Cloud Controls Matrix v3.0.1 (9-1-17 Update)*. Retrieved from https://cloudsecurityalliance.org/download/cloud-controls-matrix-v3-0-1/

Collins. (2018). *Free Online Dictionary*. Retrieved from https://www.collinsdictionary.com/dictionary/english/certification

CompTIA. (2016). *CompTIA Security+ Certification Exam Objectives EXAM NUMBER: SY0-401*. Retrieved from https://certification.comptia.org/docs/default-source/exam-objectives/comptia-security-sy0-401.pdf

CompTIA. (2018). *IT Certification Roadmap*. Retrieved from https://certification.comptia.org/docs/default-source/downloadablefiles/it-certification-roadmap.pdf

CompTIA. (n.d.). *Continuing Education (CE) Activities Chart*. Retrieved from https://certification.comptia.org/docs/default-source/downloadablefiles/comptia-continuing-education-activity-chart.pdf

Council, E. C. (2017). *CEH Candidate Handbook v2.2*. Retrieved from https://cert.eccouncil.org/images/doc/CEH-Handbook-v2.2.pdf

Council, E. C. (2018a). *What are the five CCISO Domains?* Retrieved https://ciso.eccouncil.org/cciso-certification/ciso-faq/#four

Council, E. C. (2018b). *CEH Exam Blueprint v2.0*. Retrieved from https://cert.eccouncil.org/images/doc/CEH-Exam-Blueprint-v2.0.pdf

CREST. (2016). *Professional Qualifications*. Retrieved from http://www.crest-approved.org/examinations/index.html

CREST. (2017). *CREST Examinations*. Retrieved from https://www.crest-approved.org/wp-content/uploads/Exams-Overview.pdf

Cyber, S. N. (2018). *35 Cybersecurity Jobs*. Retrieved from https://www.cybersn.com/products/35-job-categories.html

Cybersecurity Credentials Collaborative. (2015a). *A Unified Principles of Professional Ethics in Cyber Security*. Retrieved from http://www.cybersecuritycc.org/

Cybersecurity Credentials Collaborative. (2015b). *Why certification* matters. Retrieved from http://www.cybersecuritycc.org/C3_Value_of_IT_Certification_2015.pdf

Davis, Adrian (2017). Presentation given to University of Manchester students

ENISA. (2009). *Cloud Computing Risk Assessment*. Retrieved from https://www.enisa.europa.eu/publications/cloud-computing-risk-assessment

Frost and Sullivan. (2015). *The 2015 (ISC)² Global Information Security Workforce Study*. Retrieved from https://iamcybersafe.org/wp-content/uploads/2017/01/FrostSullivan-ISC%C2%B2-Global-Information-Security-Workforce-Study-2015.pdf

GIAC. (2016). *GIAC certificate brochure*. Retrieved from https://www.giac.org/media/about/cert-brochure.pdf

GIAC. (2018). *GIAC Certification Renewal: Guidelines and Requirements*. Retrieved from https://www.giac.org/certifications/renewal

IISP (Institute of Information Security Professionals). (2018a). *Membership Levels*. Retrieved from https://www.iisp.org/iisp/Membership/Individuals/Membership_Levels/iispv2/Membership/Membership_Levels2.aspx

IISP (Institute of Information Security Professionals) (2018b). *Skills framework, version 2.2, IISP, March 2018*. IISP.

Infosec Institute. (2018). *CIA Triad*. Retrieved from https://resources.infosecinstitute.com/cia-triad/#gref

ISACA. (2012). *COBIT 5*. Retrieved from http://www.isaca.org/cobit/pages/default.aspx

ISACA. (2015). *CSX Practitioner Certification*. Retrieved from https://cybersecurity.isaca.org/csx-certifications/csx-practitioner-certification#0-about-this-certification

ISACA. (2017). *Job Practice Areas 2017* Retrieved from http://www.isaca.org/Certification/CISM-Certified-Information-Security-Manager/Job-Practice-Areas/Pages/default.aspx

ISACA. (2017). *ISACA Annual report*. Retrieved from http://www.isaca.org/About-ISACA/annual-report/Pages/default.aspx

ISACA. (2018a). *How to Report and Earn CPE*. Retrieved from http://www.isaca.org/Certification/Additional-Resources/Pages/How-to-Earn-CPE.aspx

ISACA. (2018b). *The CISA Certification*. Retrieved from http://www.isaca.org/Certification/CISA-Certified-Information-Systems-Auditor/Documents/ISACA_CISA_40th_Anniversary_Infographic_0618.pdf

(ISC)². (2015). *CCSP Certification Exam Outline, effective date April 2015*. Retrieved from https://www.isc2.org/-/media/ISC2/Certifications/Exam-Outlines/CCSP-Exam-Outline.ashx

(ISC)². (2017). *2017 Annual report*. Retrieved from https://www.isc2.org/-/media/ISC2/Data-Privacy-and-Security-Briefings/2018/2017AnnualReport.ashx

(ISC)². (2018). *CISSP Certification Exam Outline, effective date April 2018*. Retrieved from https://www.isc2.org/-/media/ISC2/Certifications/CISSP/CISSP-Exam-Outline-121417--Final.ashx

(ISC)². (2018). *History of (ISC)²*. Retrieved from https://www.isc2.org/About

ISO. (2017). *ISO/IEC 27021:2017 Information technology -- Security techniques -- Competence requirements for information security management systems professionals*. Retrieved from https://www.iso.org/standard/61003.html

NCSC. (2016). *About the certified professional scheme*. Retrieved from https://www.ncsc.gov.uk/articles/about-certified-professional-scheme

Ofqual (2015). *Regulated Qualifications Framework: a postcard*. Retrieved from https://www.gov.uk/government/publications/regulated-qualifications-framework-a-postcard

Ofqual (2016). *Awarding organisations: understanding our regulatory requirements*. Retrieved from https://www.gov.uk/guidance/awarding-organisations-understanding-our-regulatory-requirements

Parker, D. B. (1998). *Fighting Computer Crime*. New York, NY: John Wiley & Sons.

Professional Standards Councils. (2018). *What is a Profession?* Retrieved from https://www.psc.gov.au/what-is-a-profession

SANS. (2018). *Information Security Training Winter/Spring 2018 Course Catalogue*. Retrieved from https://www.sans.org/media/security-training/course-catalog-2018.pdf

Security, O. (2018a). *Offensive Security Certified Professional*. Retrieved from https://www.offensive-security.com/information-security-certifications/oscp-offensive-security-certified-professional/

Security, O. (2018b). *Penetration Testing with Kali Linux*. Retrieved from https://www.offensive-security.com/documentation/penetration-testing-with-kali.pdf

Wikipedia. (2018). *List of computer security certifications*. Retrieved from https://en.wikipedia.org/wiki/List_of_computer_security_certifications

ENDNOTE

[1] The term "information security" is used throughout the text, rather than "cybersecurity", as many certifications in this space are referred to as "information security certifications".

This research was previously published in Cybersecurity Education for Awareness and Compliance; pages 222-248, copyright year 2019 by Information Science Reference (an imprint of IGI Global).

Chapter 6
Certifications in Cybersecurity Workforce Development:
A Case Study

Ping Wang

https://orcid.org/0000-0003-0193-2873
Robert Morris University, USA

Hubert D'Cruze
University of Maryland, USA

ABSTRACT

The workforce demand for cybersecurity professionals has been substantial and fast growing. Qualified cybersecurity professionals with appropriate knowledge, skills, and abilities for various tasks and job roles are needed to perform the challenging work of defending the cyber space. The certified information systems security professional (CISSP) certification is a globally recognized premier cybersecurity credential and validation of qualifications. This case study analyzes the CISSP certification requirements, domains and objectives and attempts to map them to the cybersecurity industry competencies and the US national cybersecurity workforce framework (NCWF). This research is an extended study with full mapping of all CISSP domain areas to the knowledge, skills, and abilities in NCWF. The extended study aims to discover the in-depth value and role of reputable certifications such as CISSP in competency development for cybersecurity workforce. This article also discusses the value and implications of the CISSP certification on cybersecurity education and training.

1. INTRODUCTION

There has been a significant workforce gap and a fast-growing industry demand for qualified cybersecurity professionals globally and in the United States. According to the (ISC)[2] Cybersecurity Workforce Study, the shortage of cybersecurity professionals is close to three million globally and about half a million in North America and the majority of the companies surveyed reported concerns of moderate or extreme

DOI: 10.4018/978-1-6684-3554-0.ch006

risk of cybersecurity attacks due to the shortage of dedicated cybersecurity staff ((ISC)[2], 2018c). An information security analyst is only one of the career titles in the cybersecurity profession. The latest career outlook published by the United States Labor Department Bureau of Labor Statistics shows that the employment of information security analysts is projected to grow 28 percent from 2016 to 2026, much faster and with better pay than the average for all occupations (US Labor Department BLS, 2018).

Education, training, and professional certifications are common solutions for alleviating shortage of professional staff. However, a recent study shows that top universities in the United States were failing at cybersecurity education with a lack of cybersecurity requirements for graduates and a slow change in curriculum and courses (White, 2016). The national Centers of Academic Excellence in Cyber Defense Education (CAE-CDE) designation program jointly sponsored by the US National Security Agency (NSA) and Department of Homeland Security (DHS) has been a reputable standard for certifying and maintaining high quality of cybersecurity education with rigorous requirements for program evaluation and assessment of cybersecurity knowledge units. However, only less than 300 (or about four percent) of the all colleges and universities in the U.S. have achieved the CAE-CDE designation status so far (Wang, Dawson, & Williams, 2018).

Recognizing the need to develop more and qualified cybersecurity professionals to meet the workforce demand, the U.S. National Initiative for Cybersecurity Education (NICE) recently published the NICE Cybersecurity Workforce Framework (NCWF SP800-181), which specifies cybersecurity professional categories, tasks, job roles as well as knowledge, skills, and abilities (KSAs) needed for cybersecurity jobs (NICE, 2017). These KSAs are also mapped to the cybersecurity knowledge units (KUs) for college and university programs with CAE-CDE designations. An initial effort to map the KSAs with limited cybersecurity certification domains was conducted by Wang and D'Cruze (2019).

Professional certifications are an important supplemental credential system to help select talents and guide the training and development of cybersecurity workforce. In hiring information security analysts, for example, many employers prefer their candidates to have some relevant professional certification in the field, such as Certified Information Systems Security Professional (CISSP) in addition to a minimum of a bachelor's degree in order to validate the knowledge and best practices required for the job (US Labor Department BLS, 2018). Ideally, the certification process used for developing and selecting qualified professionals in the cybersecurity field should incorporate the job tasks and KSAs specified in the NCWF as well.

There are many different types of certifications for the cybersecurity field with various levels of requirements and rigor. The CISSP (Certified Information Systems Security Professional) certification stands out as a challenging but popular vendor neutral certification choice coveted by cybersecurity professionals and employers. Studies show CISSP as a top cybersecurity credential sought after and most valued by employers (Brown, 2019; (ISC)[2], 2017b; ISCN, 2018; Wierschem, Zhang, & Johnston, 2010). This study is motivated by the urgent need and research efforts for viable solutions to the shortage of cybersecurity talent and by the recent study on the CISSP certification by Wang and D'Cruze (2019).

Based on the recent and initial KSA mapping by Wang and D'Cruze (2019), this paper reviews and evaluates the rigorous requirements of the CISSP certification and continues to explore the significant value and benchmark role of the CISSP certification in developing and maintaining cybersecurity workforce competencies with substantial and extended mapping data. This paper will reveal the value and limitations of the CISSP certification and contribute a thorough mapping of all the CISSP knowledge domains and objectives to the model of competencies of the US cybersecurity industry and knowledge, skills, and abilities (KSAs) in the NICE cybersecurity workforce framework (NCWF). The goal of this extended study is to uncover and recognize the in-depth value of the CISSP certification process and its domains and objectives to the cybersecurity workforce development and implications to cybersecurity education and training.

2. BACKGROUND

A professional certification should be a process of independent verification of one's expertise of a certain level in a particular professional area and should require meaningful steps to examine one's knowledge, skills, and expertise before the certification designation is issued by the independent organization (Martinez, 2000). There are many organizations that provide certifications for professionals in the computing and information technology areas. These certifying organizations include industry vendors, such as Cisco Systems, Microsoft, Oracle, IBM, Amazon, and vendor neutral or vendor independent organizations, such as CompTIA, (ISC)², EC-Council, ISACA, GIAC. There should be three critical components included in a professional certification process: (1) An exam-based test for candidates to demonstrate mastery of a common body of knowledge in the area; (2) commitment and adherence to a code of ethical conduct for the professional community; and (3) Mandatory continuing education or professional development (Martinez, 2000). In addition, more rigorous and reputable professional certifications require certain minimum amount of relevant and verifiable professional experience for certification whereas some other and less rigorous certifications only recommend but not require such experience.

Professional certifications in computing and information technology (IT) areas that include Cybersecurity not only benefit employers in improving human resources, work productivity and employee performance but also give a competitive advantage to employees in financial compensation and future career and professional development and training (CompTIA, 2015; Global Knowledge, 2018; Martinez, 2000). Here are the important findings presented in the 2018 IT Skills and Salary Report published by Global Knowledge: (1) About 90% of IT professionals globally hold at least one certification, which is an increase of 3% over 2017; (2) The average salary of certified IT staff in the U.S. and Canada is $15,913 or 22% more than non-certified peers, and in the Asia-Pacific region, certified IT professionals make 45% more than their non-certified peers; and (3) Professionals with cybersecurity certifications have significantly higher average salaries; In North America, for example, the average salary of security-certified professionals is $101,083, or about 15% more than the average of all certified IT professionals (Global Knowledge, 2018). In addition, professional certifications and validation of technical skills will add a competitive edge for career advancement and leadership opportunities (Aufman & Wang, 2019).

Professional certifications help to alleviate the persistent shortage of supply of qualified cybersecurity professionals, which causes increased risks of cyberattacks and decreased productivity and revenue. Research shows that the shortage of cybersecurity professionals continues to leave companies and organizations vulnerable and is now the number one job concern among those working in the field ((ISC)², 2018c). A recent industry survey shows that 63% of organizations have reported a shortage of IT staff dedicated to cybersecurity and nearly 60% of the companies surveyed say they are at risk of cybersecurity attacks due to the shortage ((ISC)², 2018c). According to the latest data from Privacy Rights Clearinghouse (PRC), a nonprofit consumer education and advocacy organization, there have been a total of 9,002 data breach cases known to the public since 2005 with a total of 11,587,118,203 records breached. The cybersecurity attacks can be costly with negative impact to the corporate revenue and bottom line. The average direct financial cost of a typical data breach is $3.86 million according to the 2018 study report by IBM Security and Ponemon Institute (Ponemon Institute, 2018). Additionally, there are various hard-to-measure cost factors including hidden and indirect costs, such as damage to corporate reputation and loss of customer confidence as a result of the data breach (Agrafiotis et al., 2018; Anderson et al., 2012).

In terms of solutions, 95% of IT industry leaders surveyed believe that certifications add value of increasing productivity and closing skillset gap, especially in Cybersecurity, which often requires further education and training; accordingly, cybersecurity certifications hold the top spots for IT salaries in the last three years (Global Knowledge, 2018). For organizations to reach the maximum effectiveness of certifications in Cybersecurity, the certification domains and objectives should have substantial match with the competencies and knowledge, skills, and abilities (KSAs) for the cybersecurity industry, such as the Industry-wide Technical Competencies and the Workplace Competencies in the Cybersecurity Industry Model published by the U.S. Department of Labor and the specific KSAs in the NICE cybersecurity workforce framework (NCWF) (NICE, 2017; US Department of Labor, 2014). Research on the information security practitioners in the United Kingdom shows similar positive sentiment and motivation for licensing and certification as a path to professionalization (Reece & Stahl, 2015).

Professional certifications are usually intended to be a supplemental validation of formal education and training and a professional motivation or requirement for further professional development, including continued education and training. Therefore, the knowledge and skill domains and objectives of professional certifications should have substantial reflection or coverage of the education and training programs and learning outcomes in a particular field. Research shows that professional certifications can be used as a valuable guidance in designing and maintaining a vibrant cybersecurity curriculum as both professional certifications in Cybersecurity and cybersecurity curriculum and courses need to incorporate the important factors of cyber threat landscape, changing technology, workforce needs, industry standards, and government regulations (Knapp, Maurer, & Plachkinova, 2017). In addition, the curriculum and course learning outcomes and activities should support the educational and professional and career goals of the students (Wang, 2018).

The next section of the paper will propose and explain a model of professional certifications in Cybersecurity in relation to the cybersecurity workforce demands and cybersecurity education and training curriculum design.

3. MODEL

Professional certifications are designed to meet the industry and workforce demands of a particular field. The industry needs for workforce development and validation are the main reason for a certain certification to exist. The certification domains and objectives should address the specific professional qualifications, technical and non-technical competencies, and specific knowledge, skills, and abilities (KSAs) required for successful performance of a certain profession. For a certification to be valuable and reputable, it should be mapped to industry standards at a national or international level. In addition, professional certifications should be designed to motivate and incorporate continued education and training for professionals to maintain the currency of their KSAs in the field as technical fields such as cybersecurity change and develop rapidly. Based on these assumptions, this paper adopts the theoretical model of professional certifications by Wang and D'Cruze (2019) as presented in Figure 1 below.

Industry and workforce demands are the original driving force for professional certifications. Certifications help employers fill open positions and close skills gap as education and training are not sufficient (CompTIA, 2015; Global Knowledge, 2018). The industry and workforce demand, such as those in IT and Cybersecurity areas, are reflected in the specific professional competencies and KSAs. For example, the Cybersecurity Competency Model published by US Department of Labor includes not only the basic personal effectiveness competencies and common academic and workplace competencies often acquired through formal education and training but also more specialized industry-wide technical competencies and industry-sector areas, such as cybersecurity technology, incident detection and response, and protection and defense against cyber threats (US Department of Labor, 2014). In addition, the NICE Cybersecurity Workforce Framework (NCWF) presents similar and more comprehensive and detailed work roles and tasks as well as specific attributes of KSAs for each task in the cybersecurity industry (NICE, 2017).

Figure 1. Certification model (Wang & D'Cruze, 2019)

In addition to work experience and education and training, professional certifications are an important means of validating and updating employees' competencies and KSAs needed for successful performance the industry. Accordingly, professional certification domains and objectives should and often do reflect the workforce skillset needs of the industry. Therefore, mapping the certification objectives to the industry competencies and KSAs is an important measure of the validity and value of the professional certification. A reputable cybersecurity certification for the U.S. cyber workforce should map with and reflect some or most of the professional KSAs identified and described in the NICE Cybersecurity Workforce Framework (NCWF).

The certification domains and objectives in the proposed model also serve to inform and shape relevant education and training programs in terms program curriculum and course design. Studies on cybersecurity education have shown that incorporating important content areas and objectives from top professional certifications, such as CISSP in cybersecurity certificaiton, is found to be valuable to the design and maintenance of a regular college degree curriculum in Cybersecurity (Hentea, Dhillon, & Dhillon, 2006; Knapp, Maurer, & Plachkinova, 2017; Sharma et al., 2013).

4. CASE STUDY: CISSP

This paper uses the case study methodology to discover and illustrate the value and benchmark role of professional certifications in developing and validating workforce qualifications for the cybersecurity industry. The case study focuses on exposing the features of the CISSP (Certified Information Systems Security Professional) certification. Relationships between cybersecurity industry competencies and workforce KSAs will be discussed in relation to the CISSP certification requirements, domains and objectives.

CISSP is a cybersecurity professional certification credential issued by International Information Systems Security Certification Consortium, better known as (ISC)^2, which is a global non-profit membership association for information security and cybersecurity professionals and leaders. The CISSP certification program has been in existence since 1994. To qualify for the certification, a candidate must pass a comprehensive exam, have minimum relevant work experience, endorsement from a CISSP-certified professional, and agree to the (ISC)^2 Code of Ethics ((ISC)^2, 2018b; (ISC)^2, 2018d).

The CISSP certification exam is a 6-hour traditional linear exam currently offered in eight different languages with the passing grade of 700 out of 100 points. The exam evaluates and validates the candidate's professional knowledge and expertise across the following eight cybersecurity domains in the CISSP Common Body of Knowledge (CBK):

Domain 1. Security and Risk Management
Domain 2. Asset Security
Domain 3. Security Architecture and Engineering
Domain 4. Communication and Network Security
Domain 5. Identity and Access Management (IAM)
Domain 6. Security Assessment and Testing
Domain 7. Security Operations
Domain 8. Software Development Security ((ISC)^2, 2018b; (ISC)^2, 2018a).

Passing the exam is not sufficient for the CISSP certification. The candidate must have at least five years of verifiable paid work experience in at least two of the eight domains of the CISSP CBK. The candidate also needs a formal and signed endorsement from a CISSP-certified professional who can attest to the candidate's professional experience. In addition, the candidate must subscribe to and fully support the following (ISC)^2 Code of Ethics in order to qualify for the CISSP certification:

- Protect society, the common good, necessary public trust and confidence, and the infrastructure.
- Act honorably, honestly, justly, responsibly, and legally.
- Provide diligent and competent service to principles.
- Advance and protect the profession ((ISC)^2, 2018b).

The CISSP certification program has been a positive response to help alleviate the workforce shortage and improve quality standard of professional skillsets for the cybersecurity industry. So far, over 140,000 professionals around the world have obtained the CISSP certification, and CISSP was ranked as the security credential most valued by employers by a margin of 3 to 1 in a recent cybersecurity trends report ((ISC)^2, 2017b; (ISC)^2, 2018d). The high ratings of the CISSP certification by employers in the cybersecurity industry not only confirm the professional popularity and workforce relevancy of the certification process. In fact, the CISSP was the first certification in the information security field to meet the requirements of ISO/IEC Standard 17024, which requires confirmation and validation of the relevancy of exam content areas (Knapp, Maurer, & Plachkinova, 2017). The high demand and popularity of the CISSP certification may also be attributed to the fact that it is the most comprehensive vendor-neutral certification covering most of the information security domains (Haqaf & Koyuncu, 2018). The CISSP certification process is a very rigorous one, including a difficult, comprehensive and lengthy (traditionally 6-hour long) exam. Even though the passing rate of the CISSP exam is never released, it is widely assumed that it is well below 50% (Lee, 2018). In addition to passing the exam, a verification of relevant 5-year professional work experience and an ethical endorsement by a certified CISSP professional are required for certification, which are not a requirement for most other certifications. Thus, the rigorous certification and maintenance process and requirements help to establish its outstanding quality and reputation and help to explain why not every applicant of the certification is able to obtain it.

The domains of expertise and objectives of the CISSP certification closely match the functional areas and technical competencies for the cybersecurity industry. The ideal target audience for CISSP are high-level experienced security practitioners, manager and executives, including the following positions with knowledge and expertise in a wide array of cybersecurity practices and principles ((ISC)^2, 2018b):

- Chief information security officer
- Chief information officer
- Secure acquisition
- IT director/manager
- Security systems engineer
- Security analyst
- Security manager
- Security auditor
- Security architect
- Security consultant

The majority of Chief Information Security Officers (CISO), a key cybersecurity practitioner and leader position, hold or pursue the CISSP certification in reality (Karanja & Rosso, 2017).

These security positions are demanded for the industry-sector functional areas listed in the Cybersecurity Industry Model published by the US Department of Labor (US Labor Department, 2014). The specific industry-sector functional areas in the model that can be addressed by the CISSP target positions include the following (US Labor Department, 2014):

- Secure acquisition
- Secure software engineering
- Systems security architecture
- Systems security analysis
- Enterprise network defense analysis
- Network defense infrastructure support
- Strategic planning & policy development
- Security program management
- Security risk management

In addition, the domain areas and objectives in the CISSP exam include coverage of the following industry-wide technical competencies and corresponding critical work functions and associated knowledge, skills, and abilities (KSAs) listed in the US Labor Department Cybersecurity Industry Model (US Labor Department, 2014; (ISC)², 2018a):

- Cybersecurity technology
- Information assurance
- Risk management
- Incident detection
- Incident response and remediation

The CISSP knowledge domains and objectives also have substantial coverage of the specific cybersecurity knowledge, skills, and abilities (KSAs) published in the NICE Cybersecurity Workforce Framework (NCWF). The appendix shows a complete mapping between CISSP domains of expertise and exam objectives and NCWF KSAs [5, 16]. The complete mapping is a special contribution of this study that connects all CISSP domain objectives to the specific KSAs in NCWF. The content of each of the mapped KSAs is in the NCWF publication.

The challenging rigor and high quality of CISSP is also bolstered by the certification renewal and maintenance requirements. Maintenance of the CISSP certification requires continuous education, learning, and professional development. Each certification cycle is only valid for three years, during which the annual minimum number of Continuing Professional Education (CPE) credits must be earned, documented and submitted. To actively maintain and renew the CISSP certification, the certification holder must earn at least 40 CPE credits per year that are subject to auditing. The CPE credits can be earned through cybersecurity related education and training courses, research and publications, unique service contributions to the cybersecurity community, and general professional development activities ((ISC)², 2017a).

5. FINDINGS AND DISCUSSIONS

This study finds that industry and workforce demand for qualified and skilled talent are the driving force behind professional certifications that are expected to serve as independent validation of professional qualifications. The CISSP case study in this paper reveals the outstanding features of this certification in meeting the industry and workforce demands for the cybersecurity even though it is not a replacement for a comprehensive college education. The unique mappings between CISSP domain objectives and the industry-sector and technical competencies as well as specific knowledge, skills, and abilities (KSAs) for the cybersecurity industry indicate a strong correlation between CISSP domain objectives and the cybersecurity professional competencies and KSAs. The rigorous annual CPE requirement for maintaining the CISSP certification also positively motivates cybersecurity professionals towards further education and training in the field.

The market value of the CISSP certification further reinforces its significant benchmark role in cybersecurity workforce development. A recent independent study comparing CISSP certification holders and non-holders of the certification in Europe also finds that CISSP certification holders add more accreditation value to employers and are more attractive to industry recruiters (Aijala, 2018). In addition, the recent research reports on global IT and cybersecurity workforce skills and salaries have shown that CISSP certification is not only found to be "the most valued security credential" by the overwhelming majority of the employers but also holds the top spot in average global salary ((ISC)², 2017b; Global Knowledge, 2018; (ISC)², 2018d). The rigorous exam, mandatory work experience and ethical compliance, as well as strict professional development requirement are all contributing factors to the strong value and credibility of the CISSP certification.

The rigor of the CISSP certification and its benchmark value to cybersecurity workforce development can be effectively incorporated into cybersecurity education and training programs and their curricula. There has been a gap between university programs and the cybersecurity workforce demands. "The increased demand for cybersecurity professionals is relatively new, and universities are still unable to respond to this demand by incorporating it in their curricula" (IEEE Cyber Security, 2018). Research shows that CISSP certification domains and objectives can be effectively integrated into an undergraduate cybersecurity curriculum with 100% coverage of the entire CISSP CBK domains in nine different cybersecurity courses (Knapp, Maurer, & Plachkinova, 2017).

The proposed model and study in this paper shows significant value and a benchmark role of the CISSP certification in cybersecurity workforce development. The adoption of the certification domain objectives can be useful to educational programs and curricula. However, it should be emphasized that even the most rigorous professional certifications such as CISSP are a valuable supplement to but not a replacement of formal long-term education in the field.

6. CONCLUSION

This extended study focuses on the important value and benchmark role of cybersecurity certifications in addressing workforce shortage and development of the cybersecurity industry with substantial new data in mapping of certification domains and objectives with the knowledge, skills and abilities expected for the cybersecurity industry. This research adopts a robust certification model that describes the close correlations between industry and workforce demands, professional competencies and KSAs, certification domains and objectives, and education and training curriculum and outcomes. The extended case study of CISSP certification for the cybersecurity industry is used to illustrate the model and the correlations. The study finds that CISSP certification is a rigorous, comprehensive and reputable credential highly valued by the cybersecurity industry and workforce. However, it should be recognized that certifications, including CISSP, are not a replacement of a well-rounded college education. Unlike a 4-year comprehensive college education with progressively sequenced course work, a professional certification such as CISSP is limited to a specialized area based on existing knowledge, skills, and abilities.

This study has contributed valuable and thorough mappings between CISSP certification domain objectives and industry-sector and technical competencies and KSAs for specific work roles and tasks defined in the NICE cybersecurity workforce framework (NCWF). This paper is an important follow-up and extended study of the previous research by Wang and D'Cruze (2019), which only presented the mapping between CISSP Domain 1 objectives and KSAs in the NCWF. This study contributes complete and specific mappings between all CISSP domains and objectives with cybersecurity knowledge, skills and abilities in NCWF. Such detailed mappings will be very valuable to credential evaluation and validation for targeted industry recruiting and to the design of college and university cybersecurity program curriculum and course learning outcomes.

The topic of the CISSP certification has been an established area of academic research with 207 articles published in 122 different journals since 1995 and has substantial potential for future research (Brown, 2019). With the fast growth of cybersecurity and workforce demand, more research is expected to address the potential of professional certifications in the cybersecurity field. A possible follow up topic for further study is on the integration of cybersecurity certifications with undergraduate or graduate educational programs in cybersecurity.

REFERENCES

Agrafiotis, I., Nurse, J. R. C., Goldsmith, M., Creese, S., & Upton, D. (2018). A taxonomy of cyber-harms: Defining the impacts of cyber-attacks and understanding how they propagate. *Journal of Cybersecurity*, *4*(1), 1–15. doi:10.1093/cybsec/tyy006

Aijala, T. (2018). CISSP certification – accreditation value for employees and recruiters. Retrieved from http://www.theseus.fi/handle/10024/148953

Anderson, R., Barton, C., Böhme, R., Clayton, R., van Eeten, M., Levi, M., & Savage, S. (2012). Measuring the cost of cybercrime. *Proceedings of Workshop on Economics of Information Security (WEIS 2012),* Berlin, Germany, June (pp. 1-31). Academic Press.

Aufman, S., & Wang, P. (2019). Discovering student interest and talent in graduate cybersecurity education. In S. Latifi (Ed.), *Information Technology - New Generations (ITNG 2019)* (pp. 77–83). Cham: Springer; . doi:10.1007/978-3-030-14070-0_12

Brown, R. (2019, June). The contribution of the CISSP (Certified Information Systems Security Professional) to higher education research. *Information Systems Education Journal*, *17*(3), 50–54.

CompTIA. (2015). Reasons Why Employers Look for IT Certifications. Retrieved from https://certification.comptia.org/why-certify/professionals/5-reasons-employers-look-for-it-certifications

Cyber Security, I. E. E. E. (2017). The Institute: The Cybersecurity Talent Shortage Is Here, and It's a Big Threat to Companies. Retrieved from https://cybersecurity.ieee.org/blog/2017/04/13/the-institute-the-cybersecurity-talentshortage-is-here-and-its-a-big-threat-to-companies/

Global Knowledge. (2018). 2018 IT Skills and Salary Report. Retrieved from https://www.globalknowledge.com/us-en/content/salary-report/it-skills-and-salary-report/

Haqaf, H., & Koyuncu, M. (2018). Understanding key skills for information security managers. *International Journal of Information Management*, *43*, 165–172. doi:10.1016/j.ijinfomgt.2018.07.013

Hentea, M., Dhillon, H. S., & Dhillon, M. (2006). Towards changes in information security education. *Journal of Information Technology Education*, *5*, 221–233. doi:10.28945/244

Information Security Careers Network (ISCN). (2018). What are the Best Cyber Security Certifications to have in 2019? (List of the Top 10). Retrieved from https://www.infosec-careers.com/2018/07/16/the-best-cyber-security-certifications-in-2019/

(ISC)². (2017a). (ISC)² Continuing Professional Education (CPE) Handbook. Retrieved from https://www.isc2.org/-/media/ISC2/Certifications/CPE/

(ISC)². (2017b). Cybersecurity Trends: 2017 Spotlight Report. Retrieved from https://www.isc2.org

(ISC)². (2018a). CISSP Certification Exam Outline. Retrieved from https://www.isc2.org/-/media/ISC2/Certifications/Exam-Outlines/CISSP-Exam-Outline-2018-v718

(ISC)². (2018b). CISSP – The World's Premier Cybersecurity Certification. Retrieved from https://www.isc2.org/Certifications/CISSP

(ISC)². (2018c). Cybersecurity Professionals Focus on Developing New Skills as Workforce Gap Widens:

(ISC)². (2018d). The Ultimate Guide to the CISSP. Retrieved from https://www.isc2.org/Certifications/Ultimate-Guides/CISSP

(ISC)² Cybersecurity Workforce Study 2018. (2018). Retrieved from https://www.isc2.org/research

Karanja, E., & Rosso, M. A. (2017). The chief information security officer: An exploratory study. *Journal of International Technology and Information Management*, *26*(2), 23–46.

Knapp, K. J., Maurer, C., & Plachkinova, M. (2017). Maintaining a cybersecurity curriculum: Professional certifications as valuable guidance. *Journal of Information Systems Education*, *28*(2), 101–114.

Lee, J. (2018). Why you failed the CISSP exam. *CyberVista*. Retrieved from https://www.cybervista.net/you-studied-you-didnt-pass-cissp-exam-why/

Martinez, A. (2000). *Get certified & get ahead* (3rd ed.). New York, NY: Computing McGraw-Hill.

NICE (National Initiative for Cybersecurity Education). (2017, August). NICE Cybersecurity Workforce Framework (SP800-181). Retrieved from https://csrc.nist.gov/publications/detail/sp/800-181/final

Ponemon Institute. (2018). 2018 Cost of data breach study: Global overview. Retrieved from https://www.ibm.com/security/data-breach

PRC (Privacy Rights Clearinghouse). (2019, July 12). Data breaches. Retrieved from https://www.privacyrights.org/data-breaches

Reece, R. P., & Stahl, B. C. (2015). The professionalization of information security: Perspectives of UK practitioners. *Computers & Security*, *48*, 182–195. doi:10.1016/j.cose.2014.10.007

Sharma, A., Murphy, M. C., Rosso, M. A., & Grant, D. (2013). Developing an undergraduate information systems security track. *Information Systems Education Journal*, *11*(4), 10–17.

US Department of Labor. (2014). Cybersecurity Industry Model. Retrieved from www.doleta.gov

US Labor Department BLS (Bureau of Labor Statistics). (2018). Retrieved from https://www.bls.gov/ooh/computer-and-information-technology/information-security-analysts.htm

Wang, P. (2018). Designing a doctoral level cybersecurity course. *Issues in Information Systems*, *19*(1), 192–202.

Wang, P., & D'Cruze, H. (2019). Cybersecurity certification: Certified Information Systems Security Professional (CISSP). In S. Latifi (Ed.), *Information Technology - New Generations (ITNG 2019)* (pp. 69–75). Cham: Springer; . doi:10.1007/978-3-030-14070-0_11

Wang, P., Dawson, M., & Williams, K. L. (2018). Improving cyber defense education through national standard alignment: Case studies. *International Journal of Hyperconnectivity and the Internet of Things*, *2*(1), 12–28. doi:10.4018/IJHIoT.2018010102

White, S. K. (2016, April 25). Top U.S. universities failing at cybersecurity education. *CIO*. Retrieved from https://www.cio.com/article/3060813/it-skills-training/top-u-s-universities-failing-at-cybersecurity-education.html

Wierschem, D., Zhang, G., & Johnston, C. R. (2010). Information technology certification value: An initial response from employers. *Journal of International Technology and Information Management*, *19*(4), 89–108.

This research was previously published in the International Journal of Hyperconnectivity and the Internet of Things (IJHIoT), 3(2); pages 38-57, copyright year 2019 by IGI Publishing (an imprint of IGI Global).

APPENDIX

Table 1. Domain 1

Domain 1: Security and Risk Management	Knowledge (K) ID	Skill (S) ID	Ability (A) ID
1.1 Understand and apply concepts of confidentiality, integrity and availability	K0001, K0003, K004, K0005, K0019, K0037, K0038, K0044, K0168, K0203, K0260, K0262, K0295	S0006, S00367	A0094, A0119, A0123
1.2 Evaluate and apply security governance principles	K0002, K0003, K0005, K0026, K0044, K0048, K0070, K0168, K0203, K0262, K0267	S0034, S0367	A0033, A0094, A0111, A0119, A0123, A0170
1.3 Determine compliance requirements	K0003, K0004, K0027, K0028, K0037, K0038, K0040, K0048, K0049, K0054, K0168, K0169, K0260, K0261, K0262, K0267, K0624	S0034, S0367	A0033, A0094, A0111, A0123, A0170
1.4 Understand legal and regulatory issues that pertain to information security in a global context	K0003, K0004, K0019, K0037, K0038, K0040, K0048, K0049, K0054, K0059, K0126, K0146, K0169, K0199, K0267, K0322	S0034, S0367	A0033, A0077, A0090, A0094, A0111, A0117, A0118, A0119, A0123, A0170
1.5 Understand, adhere to, and promote professional ethics	K0003, K0206	S0367	A0123
1.6 Develop, document, and implement security policy, standards, procedures, and guidelines	K0002, K0003, K0004, K0005, K0006, K0013, K0019, K0027, K0048, K0059, K0070, K0146, K0168, K0179, K0199, K0203, K0267, K0264	S0034, S0367	A0033, A0094, A0111, A0117, A0118, A0119, A0123
1.7 Identify, analyze, and prioritize Business Continuity (BC) requirements	K0006, K0026, K0032, K0037, K0041, K0042	S0032	A0119
1.8 Contribute to and enforce personnel security policies and procedures	K0003, K0004, K0038, K0039, K0044, K0072, K0146, K0151, K0204, K0208, K0217, K0220, K0243, K0239, K0245, K0246, K0250, K0252, K0287, K0615, K0628	S0018, S0027, S0064, S0066, S0070, S0086, S0102, S0166, S0296, S0354, S0367	A0004, A0013, A0015, A0018, A0019, A0022, A0024, A0027, A0028, A0032, A0033, A0054, A0057, A0070, A0094, A0110, A0111, A0171
1.9 Understand and apply risk management concepts	K0005, K0006, K0013, K0019, K0027, K0028, K0037, K0038, K0040, K0044, K0048, K0049, K0054, K0059, K0070, K0084, K0089, K0101, K0126, K0146, K0168, K0169, K0170, K0179, K0199, K0203, K0260, K0261, K0262, K0267, K0295, K0322, K0342, K0622, K0624	S0001, S0006, S0027, S0034, S0038, S0078, S0097, S0100, S0111, S0112, S0115, S0120, S0124, S0128, S0134, S0136, S0137, S0171, S0238, S0367	A0028, A0033, A0077, A0090, A0094, A0111, A0117, A0118, A0119, A0123, A0170
1.10 Understand and apply threat modeling concepts and methodologies	K0005, K0006, K0021, K0033, K0034, K0041, K0042, K0046, K0058, K0062, K0070, K0106, K0157, K0161, K0162, K0167, K0177, K0179, K0180, K0198, K0199, K0203, K0221, K0230, K0259, K0287, K0288, K0332, K0565, K0624	S0003, S0025, S0044, S0047, S0052, S0077, S0078, S0079, S0080, S0081, S0120, S0136, S0137, S0139, S0156, S0167, S0173, S0236, S0365	A0010, A0015, A0066, A0121, A0123, A0128, A0159

continues on following page

Domain 1: Security and Risk Management	Knowledge (K) ID	Skill (S) ID	Ability (A) ID
1.11 Apply risk-based management concepts to the supply chain	K0001, K0002, K0005, K0013, K0019, K0038, K0048, K0049, K0054, K0057, K0065, K0103, K0122, K0126, K0147, K0148, K0149, K0154, K0165, K0169, K0179, K0195, K0214, K0263, K0264, K0296, K0297, K0298, K0322, K0506, K0527, K0530, K0621, K0623	S0022, S0170, S0171, S0331, S0368, S0373	A0009, A0077, A0090, A0111 A0120, A0132 A0133, A0134, A0135
1.12 Establish and maintain a security awareness, education, and training program	K0040, K0054, K0059, K0124, K0204, K0208, K0215, K0217, K0218, K0220, K0226, K0239, K0245, K0246, K0250, K0252, K0287, K0313, K0319, K0628	S0001, S0004, S0006, S0018, S0027, S0051 S0052, S0053, S0055 S0056, S0057, S0060, S0064, S0070, S0073, S0075, S0076, S0081, S0084, S0086, S0097, S0098, S0100, S0101, S0121, S0131, S0156, S0184, S0270, S0271, S0281, S0293, S0301, S0356, S0358	A0013, A0014, A0015, A0016, A0017, A0018 A0019, A0020 A0022, A0023 A0024, A0032 A0055, A0057 A0058, A0063 A0066, A0070 A0083, A0089 A0105, A0106 A0112, A0114 A0117, A0118 A0119, A0171

Table 2. Domain 2

CISSP Domain		NCWF KSA IDs	
Domain 2:	Knowledge (K) ID	Skill (S) ID	Ability (A) ID
Asset Security			
2.1 Identify and classify information and assets	K0020, K0021, K0022, K0023, K0025, K0069, K0083, K0095, K0097, K0197, K0420	S0002, S0013, S0028, S0029, S0035, S0037, S0042, S0045, S0089, S0119, S0126, S0127, S0202	A0035, A0041, A0176
2.2 Determine and maintain information and asset ownership	K0003, K0004, K0027, K0038, K0040, K0054, K0059, K0083, K0101, K0260, K0262, K0295, K0382, K0454, K0521	S0002, S0034, S0367, SO238, SO304, SO305, SO325, S0336, S0339, S0304, S0316, S0336	A0078, A0170, A0070, A0078
2.3 Protect privacy	K0001, K0003, K0004, K0025, K0065, K0066, K0168, K0162, K0615, K0277, K0278, K0615	S0126, S0127, S0354, S0355,	A0041, A0066, A0033, A0110, A0111, A0112, A0113, A0115, A0125
2.4 Ensure appropriate asset retention	K0001, K0002, K0003, K0004, K0005, K0009, K0038, K0044, K0060, K0083, K0097, K0361, K0482, K0496, K0503, K0516, K0618, K0619	S0068, S0112, S0304, S0347, S0369	A0033, A0130, A0137, A0094 A0095, A0096, A0097
2.5 Determine data security controls	K0001, K0003, K0005, K0014, K0017, K0020, K0021, K0022, K0023, K0024, K0038, K0083, K0095, K0097, K0128, K0133, K0152, K0182, K0193, K0195, K0197, K0202, K0210, K0260, K0261, K0262, K0277, K0285, K0305, K0364, K0394, K0420, K0567	S0002, S0013, S0021, S0029, S0042, S0045, S0068, S0091, S0106, S0113, S0126, S0127, S0178, S0181, S0202, S0217, S0286, S0369	A0003, A0005, A0026, A0029, A0030, A0040, A0084, A0176
2.6 Establish information and asset handling requirements	K0003, K0004, K0005, K0018, K0038, K0045, K0047, K0083, K0120, K0152, K0190, K0260, K0262, K0277, K0285, K0305, K0361, K0417, K0427, K0482, K0496, K0503, K0618, K0619,	S0034, S0059, S0193, S0112, S0138, S0218, S0219, S0261. S0286, S0304, S0345, S0347, S0369	A0013, A0078, A0083, A0110, A0130, A0134, A0146, A0153, A0159, A0160

Table 3. Domain 3

CISSP Domain		NCWF KSA IDs	
Domain 3:	**Knowledge (K) ID**	**Skill (S) ID**	**Ability (A) ID**
Security Architecture and Engineering			
3.1 Implement and manage engineering processes using secure design principles	K0001, K0002, K0003, K0004, K0005, K0006, K0009, K0019, K0045, K0059, K0067, K0075, K0076, K0080, K0082, K0086, K0090, K0102, K0126, K0171, K0172, K0174, K0175, K0176, K0179, K0183, K0202, K0209, K0267, K0268, K0269, K0271, K0280, K0288, K0296, K0297, K0310, K0314, K0321, K0333, K0342, K0499	S0002, S0005, S0021, S0022, S0036, S0052, S0116, S0122, S0135, S0140, S0141, S0148, S0172, S0270, S0365	A0001, A0018, A0019, A0023, A0049, A0061, A0121, A0122, A0142, A0143, A0144, A0150, A0151, A0152, A0170
3.2 Understand the fundamental concepts of security models	K0007, K0044, K0081, K0087, K0114, K0180, K0198, K0199, K0202, K0203, K0211, K0213, K0221, K0230, K0258, K0260, K0261, K0262, K0288, K0295	S0029, S0050, S0073, S0136, S0139, S0236, S0297, S0365, S0367	A0032, A0121, A0123
3.3 Select controls based upon systems security requirements	K0001, K0002, K0003, K0004, K0005, K0006, K0007, K0009, K0011, K0013, K0018, K0019, K0018, K0021, K0024, K0026, K0027, K0028, K0033, K0037, K0038, K0049, K0054, K0056, K0059, K0061, K0065, K0070, K0089, K0100, K0101, K0114, K0126, K0146, K0148, K0158, K0169, K0170, K0179, K0199, K0203, K0260, K0261, K0262, K0267, K0287, K0322, K0341, K0377, K0488, K0537, K0617, K0622, K0624	S0001, S0006, S0007, S0023, S0027, S0031, S0034, S0038, S0073, S0078, S0097, S0120, S0124, S0135, S0137, S0138, S0141, S0145, S0147, S0152, S0171, S0172, S0236, S0238, S0240, S0241, S0242, S0279, S0280, S0307, S0367, S0374	A0001, A0015, A0036, A0040, A0056, A0069, A0092, A0093, A0094, A0111, A0116, A0119, A0123, A0124, A0143, A0148, A0152, A0153, A0154, A0157, A0170
3.4 Understand security capabilities of information systems (e.g., memory protection, Trusted	K0008, K0049, K0190, K0114, K0277, K0264, K0285, K0305, K0417, K0427, K0487, K0561,	S0001, S0062, S0059, S0076, S0138	A0001, A0015, A0123
3.5 Assess and mitigate the vulnerabilities of security architectures, designs, and solution	K0005, K0009, K0013, K0019, K0023, K0024, K0040, K0063, K0070, K0076, K0077, K0078, K0095, K0106, K0147, K0193, K0197, K0202, K0230, K0272, K0277, K0283, K0289, K0296, K0314, K0339, K0363, K0364, K0373, K0375, K0394, K0402, K0419, K0420, K0421, K0440,	S0001, S0042, S0045, S0073, S0078, S0081, S0137, S0151, S0153, S0154, S0155, S0157, S0164, S0167, S0170, S0220, S0242, S0269, S0275, S0286, S0288, S0292, S0305, S0365,	A0001, A0015, A0052, A0092, A0121, A0149, A0155, A0176
elements			
3.6 Assess and mitigate vulnerabilities in web-based systems	K0001, K0010, K0011, K0029, K0046, K0050, K0056, K0061, K0094, K0099, K0104, K0105, K0131, K0135, K0136, K0160, K0165, K0167, K0177, K0179, K0205, K0221, K0371, K0388, K0392, K0393, K0398, K0417, K0444, K0452, K0536, K0565, K0624	S0006, S0007, S0025, S0077, S0079, S0084, S0101, S0137, S0141, S0196, S0197, S0198, S0258	A0001, A0046, A0048, A0052, A0063, A0065, A0172, A0173, A0174, A0123

continues on following page

CISSP Domain	NCWF KSA IDs		
Domain 3:	**Knowledge (K) ID**	**Skill (S) ID**	**Ability (A) ID**
3.7 Assess and mitigate vulnerabilities in mobile systems	K0070, K0269, K0274, K0283, K0438, K0614	S0001, S0015, S0016, S0033, S0036, S0075, S0071, S0075, S0078, S0085	A0002, A0033, A0163, A0164, A0165, A0166, A0167, A0168, A0177
3.8 Assess and mitigate vulnerabilities in embedded devices	K0005, K0008, K0009, K0030, K0322	S0001, S0003, S0006, S0058,	A0001, A0052
3.9 Apply cryptography	K0001, K0002, K0003, K0004, K0005, K0006, K0015, K0018, K0019, K0044, K0201, K0203, K0211, K0277, K0285, K0305, K0427	S0006, S0027, S0047, S0059, S0089, S0138, S0139, S0298, S0367	A0123, A0163, A0164, A0165, A0166, A0167, A0168, A0177
3.10 Apply security principles to site and facility design	K0001, K0002, K0003, K0005, K0091, K0618, K0619	S0068, S0208, S0256	A0050, A0051, A0052, A0092, A0097, A0126, A0144, A0148, A0149, A0153
3.11 Implement site and facility security controls	K0021, K0022, K0023, K0024, K0038, K0083, K0097, K0109, K0118, K0125, K0133, K0152, K0155, K0156, K0182, K0193, K0195, K0197, K0210, K0251, K0419, K0420, K0622,	S0002, S0042, S0068, S0133, S0143, S0144, S0151, S0153, S0154, S0155, S0157, S0275, S0286, S0340	A0001, A0005, A0052, A0176

Table 4. Domain 4

CISSP Domain	NCWF KSA IDs		
Domain 4:	**Knowledge (K) ID**	**Skill (S) ID**	**Ability (A) ID**
Communication and Network Security			
4.1 Implement secure design principles in network architectures	K0001, K0034, K0061, K0108, K0174, K0179, K0221, K0231, K0255, K0274, K0332, K0375, K0388, K0417, K0428, K0442, K0470, K0471, K0491, K0500, K0555, K0565, K0600, K0614	S0046, S0056, S0057, S0168, S0178, S0182, S0236	A0048, A0172
4.2 Secure network components	K0001, K0005, K0007, K0010, K0011, K0013, K0029, K0033, K0038, K0046, K0049, K0050, K0053, K0061, K0071, K0074, K0076, K0088, K0093, K0104, K0108, K0109, K0111, K0113, K0114, K0135, K0136, K0137, K0138, K0159, K0160, K0179, K0180, K0200, K0201, K0224, K0230, K0237, K0283, K0296, K0324, K0332, K0405, K0472, K0473, K0488, K0622, K0625, K0630	S0004, S0007, S0025, S0035, S0039, S0040, S0041, S0056, S0058, S0076, S0077, S0079, S0084, S0120, S0137, S0142, S0150, S0159, S0162, S0170, S0192, S0206, S0280, S0365	A0025, A0034 A0052, A0055, A0058, A0059, A0062, A0063, A0065, A0121, A0122, A0128, A0159
4.3 Implement secure communication channels according to design	K0071, K0097, K0104, K0108, K0130, K0136, K0159, K0189, K0247, K0269, K0272, K0274, K0356, K0388, K0417, K0431, K0444, K0446, K0491, K0609, K0610	S0059, S0073, S0077, S0225, S0297	A0032, A0063, A0082

Table 5. Domain 5

CISSP Domain	NCWF KSA IDs		
Domain 5:	Knowledge (K) ID	Skill (S) ID	Ability (A) ID
Identity and Access Management (IAM)			
5.1 Control physical and logical access to assets	K0005, K0007, K0009, K0056, K0073, K0074, K0276, K0537	S0001, S0073, S0022, S0031, S0034, S0038, S0077, S0097, S0120, S0138, S0141, S0145, S0147, S0225, S0297	A0032, A0063, A0082, A0085, A0092, A0154
5.2 Manage identification and authentication of people, devices, and services	K0007, K0033, K0044, K0056, K0071, K0114, K0158, K0177, K0202, K0247, K0275, K0276, K0284, K0336, K0398, K0452, K0487, K0488, K0537, K0561	S0007, S0031, S0067, S0073, S0077, S0121, S0225, S0297, S0367	A0038, A0048, A0049, A0052, A0059, A0083, A0085, A0107, A0123, A0154, A0155
5.3 Integrate identity as a third-party service	K0028, K0037, K0044, K0194, K0230, K0283, K0483	S0034, S0043, S0073, S0313, S0365, S0367	A0119, A0123, A0121, A0151
5.4 Implement and manage authorization mechanisms	K0007, K0033, K0037, K0065, K0158, K0537, K0598	S0007, S0031, S0034, S0367	A0001, A0002, A0006, A0013, A0015, A0033, A0034, A0037, A0049, A0062, A0064, A0106, A0111, A0138, A0141, A0143
5.5 Manage the identity and access provisioning lifecycle	K0007, K0033, K0049, K0050, K0053, K0056, K0064, K0065, K0071, K0077, K0088, K0100, K0103, K0104, K0105, K0114, K0117, K0130, K0158, K0167, K0177, K0179, K0197, K0247, K0289, K0318, K0332, K0336, K0383, K0488, K0521, K0537, K0562	S0007, S0016, S0031, S0033, S0043, S0073, S0076, S0111, S0143, S0144, S0151, S0153, S0154, S0155, S0157, S0158, S0214, S0304, S0305, S0313	A0025, A0027, A0034, A0055, A0062, A0074, A0088, A0123, A0124

Table 6. Domain 6

CISSP Domain	NCWF KSA IDs		
Domain 6:	Knowledge (K) ID	Skill (S) ID	Ability (A) ID
Security Assessment and Testing			
6.1 Design and validate assessment, test, and audit strategies	K0003, K0004, K0005, K0091, K0157, K0168, K0202, K0315, K0317, K0363, K0377, K0599, K0600, K0614	S0015, S0026 S0047, S0048 S0082, S0085 S0167, S0192	A0026, A0033, A0034, A0040, A0110, A0112, A0141, A0142, A0143, A0167
6.2 Conduct security control testing	K0013, K0132, K0229, K0290, K0342, K0362, K0363, K0367, K0402, K0440, K0529, K0536, K0629	S0001, S0025, S0038, S0039, S0040, S0042, S0044, S0051, S0052, S0083, S0120, S0121, S0130, S0137, S0149, S0167, S0242, S0257, S0270	A0001, A0015, A0044, A0092, A0127, A0128, A0149, A0155, A0176
6.3 Collect security process data (e.g., technical and administrative)	K0008, K0021, K0026, K0053, K0064, K0146, K0180, K0210, K0265, K0311, K0316, K0373, K0589	S0032, S0038, S0042, S0150, S0157, S0201, S0312, S0317, S0322, S0354, S0368	A0006, A0038, A0062, A0117, A0126, A0136, A0176
6.4 Analyze test output and generate report	K0003, K0098, K0107, K0315, K0317, K0354, K0355, K0384, K0451, K0462, K0468, K0572	S0003, S0037, S0115, S0210, S0302, S0344, S0370	A0013, A0014, A0078, A0085, A0102, A0132, A0133, A0135, A0136, A0137, A0140, A0150, A0155, A0156, A0159, A0166, A0167
6.5 Conduct or facilitate security audits	K0001, K0002, K0003, K0004, K0005, K0006, K0043, K0047, K0048, K0072, K0090, K0120, K0126, K0148, K0154, K0165, K0169, K0198, K0200, K0202, K0235, K0257, K0270, K0363, K0523, K0536	S0001, S0011, S0012, S0013, S0014, S0015, S0038, S0085, S0104, S0132, S0134, S0137, S0143, S0192, S0195, S0372	A0015, A0056, A0167,

Table 7. Domain 7

CISSP Domain	NCWF KSA IDs		
Domain 7:	**Knowledge (K) ID**	**Skill (S) ID**	**Ability (A) ID**
Security Operations			
7.1 Understand and support investigations	K0013, K0017, K0042, K0046, K0064, K0075, K0098, K0107, K0110, K0118, K0120, K0122, K0123, K0125, K0128, K0129, K0131, K0133, K0134, K0142, K0143, K0145, K0155, K0156, K0167, K0180, K0182, K0184, K0185, K0188, K0206, K0209, K0251, K0268, K0301, K0304, K0315, K0318, K0324, K0334, K0339, K0342, K0353, K0354, K0355, K0362, K0364, K0382, K0383, K0384, K0386, K0387, K0388, K0389, K0390, K0391, K0394, K0404, K0409, K0427, K0428, K0433, K0451, K0462, K0468, K0469, K0492, K0503, K0536, K0558, K0570, K0571, K0573	S0003, S0046, S0047, S0051, S0054, S0065, S0068, S0069, S0071, S0075, S0081, S0087, S0088, S0120, S0133, S0173, S0187, S0243, S0267, S0270, S0276, S0279, S0289, S0295, S0324, S0325, S0327, S0339, S0346, S0352, S0353, S0370, S0372	A0005, A0019 A0043, A0086 A0099, A0100, A0102, A0145, A0160
7.2 Understand requirements for investigation types	K0003, K0041, K0042, K0043, K0054, K0107, K0122, K0125, K0133, K0150, K0155, K0168, K0187, K0222, K0260, K0261, K0262, K0267, K0287, K0288, K0314, K0317, K0351, K0410, K0411, K0447, K0449, K0524, K0615	S0054, S0078, S0215, S0240, S0263	A0033, A0046, A0094, A0110, A0113
7.3 Conduct logging and monitoring activities	K0046, K0054, K0070, K0106, K0132, K0144, K0160, K0161, K0162, K0177, K0180, K0189, K0191, K0202, K0229, K0234, K0259, K0292, K0305, K0317, K0322, K0324, K0362, K0408, K0440, K0472, K0479, K0480, K0488, K0616, K0620	S0003, S0020, S0025, S0042, S0079, S0084, S0087, S0090, S0096, S0109, S0120, S0124, S0131, S0136, S0149, S0155, S0192, S0206, S0258	A0010, A0015, A0092, A0093, A0094, A0107, A0116, A0127, A0128, A0173, A0174, A0176
7.4 Securely provisioning resources	K0011, K0035, K0073, K0083, K0097, K0104, K0130, K0132, K0189, K0194, K0230, K0275, K0283, K0332, K0361, K0393, K0491, K0516, K0531, K0609, K0610, K0618, K0619	S0073, S0074, S0076, S0112, S0144, S0151, S0153, S0154, S0157, S0168, S0170, S0178, S0206, S0207, S0208, S0304, S0321, S0345, S0347, S0365, S0369	A0001, A0052, A0121, A0126, A0130, A0137, A0151, A0172
7.5 Understand and apply foundational security operations concepts	K0020, K0021, K0022, K0024, K0025, K0038, K0054, K0083, K0177, K0182, K0202, K0210, K0266, K0271, K0305, K0332, K0384, K0509, K0537, K0579, K0585, K0608, K0616, K0620, K0622	S0002, S0042, S0043, S0063, S0068, S0086, S0087, S0090, S0121, S0123, S0146, S0155, S0168, S0258, S0355, S0362	A0035, A0045, A0046, A0097, A0127, A0146, A0164, A0172, A0176
7.6 Apply resource protection techniques	K0011, K0021, K0060, K0073, K0074, K0077, K0080, K0097, K0108, K0122, K0152, K0167, K0178, K0193, K0210, K0212, K0224, K0239, K0246, K0271, K0278, K0296, K0318, K0373, K0397, K0406, K0417, K0491, K0530, K0531, K0537, K0608, K0618, K0619, K0625	S0016, S0024, S0042, S0065, S0075, S0083, S0089, S0148, S0158, S0206, S0298	A0049, A0052, A0126, A0152, A0175, A0176
7.7 Conduct incident management	K0021, K0041, K0042, K0046, K0054, K0107, K0150, K0230, K0292, K0315, K0317, K0324, K0354, K0451, K0462, K0472, K0527	S0025, S0037, S0054, S0080, S0084, S0157, S0192, S0365	A0025, A0037, A0113, A0121, A0128, A0166

continues on following page

CISSP Domain	NCWF KSA IDs		
Domain 7:	**Knowledge (K) ID**	**Skill (S) ID**	**Ability (A) ID**
7.8 Operate and maintain detective and preventative measures	K0040, K0046, K0049, K0054, K0132, K0188, K0189, K0191, K0229, K0259, K0312, K0324, K0352, K0363, K0392, K0405, K0452, K0472, K0473, K0479, K0480, K0487, K0488, K0516, K0536, K0561, K0629, K0630	S0003, S0025, S0054, S0076, S0079, S0083, S0084, S0087, S0120, S0121, S0131, S0149, S0170, S0187, S0192, S0280, S0371	A0010, A0128, A0149, A0176
7.9 Implement and support patch and vulnerability management	K0005, K0009, K0013, K0040, K0070, K0074, K0079, K0106, K0115, K0147, K0177, K0178, K0234, K0309, K0314, K0339, K0351, K0373, K0375, K0440, K0467, K0481, K0507, K0522, K0523, K0530, K0536, K0538, K0554, K0569, K0625	S0001, S0003, S0078, S0081, S0083, S0137, S0167, S0206, S0220, S0242, S0269, S0293, S0334, S0362	A0001, A0015, A0033, A0092, A0093, A0155,
7.10 Understand and participate in change management processes	K0008, K0011, K0032, K0073, K0074, K0108, K0121, K0149, K0154, K0180, K0194, K0200, K0214, K0217, K0231, K0263, K0264, K0271, K0275, K0276, K0284, K0292, K0296, K0299, K0429, K0516, K0517, K0527, K0534, K0537, K0585, K0586, K0588, K0608	S0027, S0041, S0055, S0136, S0143, S0170, S0192, S0227, S0243, S0262, S0356	A0009, A0052, A0133, A0135, A0137, A0147, A0149, A0154, A0173
7.11 Implement recovery strategies	K0021, K0026, K0032, K0038, K0044, K0053, K0078, K0089, K0097, K0109, K0114, K0149, K0153, K0210, K0211, K0229, K0287, K0289, K0295, K0299, K0323, K0361, K0373, K0605, K0622	S0002, S0006, S0027, S0032, S0039, S0042, S0083, S0150, S0157, S0158, S0201, S0244, S0367	A0084, A0123, A0176
7.12 Implement Disaster Recovery (DR) processes	K0002, K0010, K0021, K0026, K0037, K0054, K0091, K0093, K0108, K0113, K0136, K0165, K0170, K0204, K0209, K0210, K0215, K0226, K0239, K0243, K0245, K0250, K0252, K0269, K0272, K0290, K0317, K0342, K0396, K0417, K0431, K0438, K0446, K0459, K0528, K0539, K0540, K0550, K0556, K0560, K0601, K0614, K0630	S0015, S0021, S0026, S0030, S0032, S0048, S0061, S0077, S0080, S0104, S0107, S0112, S0115, S0135, S0150, S0157, S0171, S0177, S0182, S0201, S0213, S0224, S0225, S0243, S0262, S0282	A0006, A0026, A0030, A0040, A0063, A0177, A0171
7.13 Test Disaster Recovery Plans (DRP)	K0001, K0002, K0003, K0004, K0005, K0006, K0021, K0026, K0033, K0034, K0041, K0042, K0046, K0058, K0062, K0070, K0106, K0157, K0161, K0162, K0167, K0177, K0179, K0221, K0230, K0259, K0287, K0332, K0565, K0624	S0003, S0032, S0047, S0077, S0078, S0079, S0080, S0173, S0365, S0150, S0151, S0157, S0201	A0121, A0128
7.14 Participate in Business Continuity (BC) planning and exercises	K0008, K0026, K0146, K0316, K0586	S0100, S0354	A0085, A0111, A0117, A0121, A0128, A0136, A0139
7.15 Implement and manage physical security	K0015, K0018, K0019, K0024, K0035, K0036, K0040, K0044, K0049, K0052, K0056, K0060, K0061, K0063, K0075, K0082, K0093, K0102, K0179, K0180, K0200, K0203, K0227, K0260, K0261, K0262, K0263, K0266, K0267, K0275, K0276, K0281, K0284, K0285, K0287, K0290, K0297, K0322, K0333, K0339, K0487, K0561	S0024, S0027, S0031, S0036, S0060, S0141, S0147, S0167, S0192, S0357, S0367	A0006, A0015, A0048, A0049, A0113, A0123, A0124, A0131, A0142, A0149, A0153, A0156 A0157, A0158, A0170, A0172

continues on following page

CISSP Domain	NCWF KSA IDs		
Domain 7:	**Knowledge (K) ID**	**Skill (S) ID**	**Ability (A) ID**
7.16 Address personnel safety and security concerns	K0008, K0021, K0025, K0026, K0027, K0037, K0040, K0041, K0042, K0044, K0049, K0071, K0097, K0147, K0149, K0150, K0151, K0155, K0156, K0165, K0167, K0190, K0195, K0210, K0211, K0260, K0261, K0262, K0263, K0264, K0265, K0276, K0277, K0294, K0295, K0297, K0298, K0299, K0308, K0341, K0455, K0487, K0499, K0523, K0530	S0001, S0022, S0097, S0116, S0141, S0145, S0152, S0167, S0357	A0001, A0006, A0015, A0048, A0113, A0153, A0156, A0157, A0174, A0176

Table 8. Domain 8

CISSP Domain	NCWF KSA IDs		
Domain 8: Software Development Security	**Knowledge (K) ID**	**Skill (S) ID**	**Ability (A) ID**
8.1 Understand and integrate security in the Software Development Life Cycle (SDLC)	K0003, K0039, K0045, K0075, K0081, K0090, K0112, K0121, K0147, K0203, K0242, K0276, K0298, K0299, K0455	S0001, S0031, S0036, S0083, S0097, S0116, S0139, S0141, S0145, S0357	A0001, A0015, A0021, A0039, A0123, A0129, A0142, A0143, A0144, A0149, A0150, A0151, A0152, A0155, A0161
8.2 Identify and apply security controls in development environments	K0031, K0039, K0073, K0079, K0080, K0081, K0082, K0087, K0090, K0140, K0152, K0153, K0175, K0178, K0212, K0246, K0275, K0325, K0373, K0380, K0406, K0475, K0530, K0576, K0618, K0625	S0014, S0016, S0024, S0058, S0060, S0076, S0083, S0087, S0088, S0090, S0095, S0158, S0172, S0174, S0203, S0245	A0007, A0036, A0044, A0152
8.3 Assess the effectiveness of software security	K0002, K0048, K0147, K0149, K0165, K0202, K0214, K0229, K0263, K0264, K0297, K0298, K0363, K0452, K0527, K0623, K0624	S0022, S0085, S0121, S0149, S0171, S0192, S0331	A0133, A0135, A0137, A0140, A0149, A0167, A0173
8.4 Assess security impact of acquired software	K0039, K0079, K0080, K0081, K0082, K0087, K0090, K0152, K0153, K0175, K0178, K0212, K0246, K0373, K0406, K0491, K0530, K0531, K0625	S0014, S0016, S0024, S0058, S0076, S0083, S0245, S0292	A0047, A0161
8.5 Define and apply secure coding guidelines and standards	K0005, K0009, K0016, K0068, K0070, K0106, K0147, K0178, K0339, K0372, K0373, K0375, K0396, K0440, K0523	S0001, S0060, S0078, S0081, S0137, S0167, S0239, S0242, S0266, S0269	A0010, A0015, A0044, A0047, A0056, A0092, A0142, A0149, A0152, A0155

Chapter 7
Cyber Security Competency Model Based on Learning Theories and Learning Continuum Hierarchy

Winfred Yaokumah
https://orcid.org/0000-0001-7756-1832
Pentecost University College, Ghana

ABSTRACT

There is an urgent need for transformative changes in cyber security awareness and training programs to produce individuals and the workforce that can deal with business risks emanating from the prevailing and emerging cyber-attacks. This chapter proposes a cyber security competency model that integrates learning theories (cognitive, affective, and psychomotor), learning continuum hierarchy (awareness and training), and cyber security domain knowledge. Employing literature search of scholarly and practitioner works, together with cyber security standards from governmental and non-governmental organizations, the chapter integrates cyber security domain knowledge, learning theories, and learning continuum hierarchy to design a model of cyber security competencies suitable for use in educating individuals and the general workforce. This theoretical-based approach to designing cyber security awareness and training programs will produce skillful individuals and workforce that can mitigate cyber-attacks in the global business environment.

INTRODUCTION

Cyber security is a global concern owing to the increasing reliance on the Internet (Dahbur, Bashabsheh, & Bashabsheh, 2017). It is one of the most serious economic and national security challenges faced by governments (Moskal, 2015), developed and developing nations (Stoddart, 2016), and public and the private businesses (Gunzel, 2017). National and international businesses are at risk as the Internet facilitates both business transactions and cyber-attacks across geographical boundaries. Cyber threats

DOI: 10.4018/978-1-6684-3554-0.ch007

come from numerous sources, including hostile governments, terrorist groups, disgruntled employees, and malicious intruders (Nunez, 2017). The attacks can range from stealing of employees' personal information (Office of Personnel Management, 2015) to attacks on critical infrastructure such as derailment of passenger trains, contamination of water supplies, and shutting down of power grid (Palmer, 2014).

Dealing with cybercrime becomes necessary because of the high cost of cybercrime on the societies, governments, and individuals (Wiederhold, 2014). For instance, the loss of revenue due to cyber attacks is estimated at US$240,000 per day among business organizations and can be more than US$100,000 per hour for retailers (Hui, Kim, & Wang, 2017; Neustar 2012). The Center for Strategic and International Studies estimates that an average annual cost of cybercrime to the global economy is $400 billion (McAfee, 2014); whereas Eubanks (2017) predicts that an average approximate cost of cybercrime will reach US$6 trillion by 2021.

Cyber threats pose danger to national security, financial security, and undermine individuals' privacy. Cyber security has become a top national priority (Proclamation 9508, 2016). It is an important institutional and community responsibility that requires an effective partnership between institutions and the entire community (Oblinger, 2015), including individuals and the general workforce. Thus, to effectively deal with cyber attacks, action is needed at national and global levels requiring individuals, society, and private businesses to better understand and to deal with cyber threats (Stoddart, 2016). The workforce and individuals need competencies and skills, including behavioural, management, and technical expertise to handle cyber attacks in the dynamic cyber threats environment (Singapore Increases Cyber security Training for Youths, 2014).

However, there seems to be a problem of inadequate knowledge and skill among individuals and the general workforce as to how to appropriately maintain cyber safety and respond to cyber attacks. Individuals and the current workforce apparently lack how to effectively apply cyber security measures. According to Russell (2017), public awareness of cyber threats is growing. However, evidence suggests that there are rapid increases in cyber related crimes in the recent years. For example, Global Economic Crime Survey records a high rise of cybercrime from 4th to 2nd position on the global economic crimes list (Global Economic Crime Survey, 2016).

Therefore, there is an urgent need for transformative changes in the current cyber security education to produce individuals and workforce to deal with business risks emanating from the prevailing and emerging cyber attacks. These changes are necessary because of the multifaceted nature of cyber security, the scope of cyber attacks and activities, and the targets of cyber attacks (businesses, government, individual users, and ICT service providers).

Cyber security awareness and training underpinned by relevant learning theories are needed for individuals in the society and the workforce to produce people that are capable of mitigating the current and future cyber attacks (Moskal, 2015). Thus, there will be improvement in cyber security if the individuals and the workforce are aware and properly trained to apply necessary safeguards to deal with issues related to digital privacy and security (Rohrer & Hom, 2017).

The purpose of this chapter is to propose a Cyber Security Competency Model for the current workforce and individuals aimed at developing cyber security knowledge and skills needed to address current global cyber security labor shortage (ITU, 2017). The study includes adding learning theories to cyber security body of knowledge and the learning continuum hierarchy (awareness and training) to support cyber security instructional design and development activities. Efforts at strengthening cyber defences warrant a solid theoretical research foundation (Ortiz & Reinerman-Jones, 2015). However, too often, theory and practice are separated from one another in training programs (ACM, 2014). A cyber security domain knowledge that is underpinned by learning theories (Bloom, 1956; Krathwohl, Bloom, & Masia, 1973; Simpson, 1972), mapped to learning continuum hierarchy will have greater impact. The proposed model will provide a reference and an understanding of how educators should design and manage cyber security awareness and training programs.

In order to achieve the purpose of this chapter, a review of literature of prior practitioner and scholarly works was conducted. The review examines contents of cyber security awareness and training programs from international standards (ISO/IEC 27032, 2012; NIST Special Publication 800-16, 2003), professional training institutes and manuals (Laudon & Traver, 2014; QS TopUniversities, 2018; Sans Technology Institute, 2018), and governmental cyber awareness campaigns (Proclamation 9648, 2017; Proclamation 9508, 2016), and scholarly works (Abawajy, 2014; Affisco, 2017; Poboroniuc et al., 2017; Porter (2016).

The cyber security domain areas relating to cyber security awareness and training were classified using a simple sorting tool to ascertain the number of occurrences of common themes. The themes with higher scores were used to illustrate the matching of learning continuum hierarchy and the learning theories (cognitive, psychomotor, and affective).

BACKGROUND

Cyber Attack Targets and Threats Environment

The literature discusses cyber threats and their influence on businesses, governments, individuals, and other stakeholders. Australian Cyber Security Centre Threat Report (ACSC, 2017) classifies the targets for cyber attacks into four: Businesses, Governments, Home users, and ICT Providers. The Australian Cyber Security Centre is an important Australian Government initiative to ensure that Australian cyber networks are amongst the hardest in the world to compromise (ACSC, 2017). Figure 1 shows the targets of cyber attacks. Among others, businesses are targets for trade secrets, personal sensitive information, and client information. Governments are targeted for national security information, communications among politicians, and for sensitive legal documents. Home users or individuals are the target of cyber attacks with respect with individual's banking information and personal identifiable information, while ICT providers' networks are targeted for clients' data.

A recent study finds that 24% of cyber attacks target banks, 23% target telecommunications companies, while 20% target financial services organizations (Hui, Kim, & Wang, 2017). Cyber related offences are of many forms, including malware and ransom ware infection, misuse of personal data (Bergmann et al., 2017), advanced persistent threats, social engineering attacks, insider threats, attacks on network assets (Happa & Goldsmith, 2017), and distributed denial of service (DDOS) attacks. For example, a survey of IT professionals from 38 countries finds 50% of the respondents having experienced business disruptions due to DDOS attacks (Kaspersky Lab 2015). According to Hui, Kim, and Wang (2017), the motives for cybercrime consist of disrupting business operations (28%), distracting the business to make way for main attacks to take place (18%), holding the companies to ransom (17%), and political motivations (11%).

Figure 1. Targets of cyber attacks

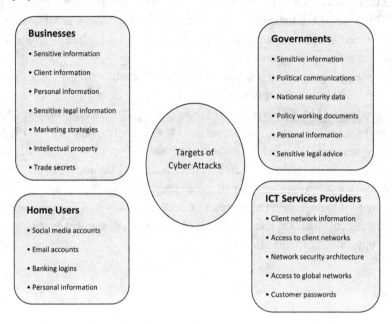

Business Risk and Cyber Security Labor Landscape

A major risk that businesses across all sectors are facing today is the threat of cyber-attacks (Russell, 2017). Cyber violence and the antidote to cybercrime are fast becoming a global concern for businesses (Hanewald, 2008). Recent years have witnessed cyber attacks on businesses, government agencies, schools, hospitals, and critical public infrastructure, threatening public safety and national security (Proclamation 9648, 2017). Engle (2017) predicts that cyber security threats will represent the third highest risk businesses will face in 2018. Therefore, cyber security concerns are shared responsibilities (Proclamation 9508, 2016) requiring individuals in the society, general workforce, and cyber security professionals to promote cyber security education to defend the cyberspace (McDuffie & Piotrowski, 2014).

Currently, there is an increasing demand for cyber security workforce (Yang & Wen, 2017). Cyber security and safety are seriously challenged by shortages of skilled cyber security personnel (VanDerwerken & Ubell, 2011), trained cyber security workforce, and knowledgeable cyber security individuals who use the cyberspace for their everyday activities. There are currently 2 million shortages of cyber security personnel worldwide (Bell, 2016). According to the U.S. Bureau of Labor Statistics, there is a growing need for cyber security personnel and it is expected that by 2022 information security analyst jobs would grow by 37 percent (Patel, 2014).

Bell (2016) emphasizes that having the workforce with the skills and experience in cyber security is the most critical for business success. Organizations should provide cyber security training for their entire workforce to avoid cyber vulnerabilities. Locasto et al. (2011) suggest training of new information security workers through education rather than mass certification of the existing cyber security workforce. The need to develop cyber security talent from within the organization is important (Bell, 2016). Teaching both technical and societal aspects of cyber security is of critical importance (Vishik

& Heisel, 2015). This may begin from developing fundamental skills and knowledge for individuals and general workforce.

Thus, the problem of a cyber security labor shortage should be tackled not only by producing technical professionals to handle cyber crime because cyber safety involves individuals, businesses, society, and governments. For example, individuals interact with businesses and government information systems in the cyber space and need to know how to safely navigate the cyber space. Additionally, the workforce who are professionals from different disciplines are unable to actively keep themselves updated with the latest information related to cyber security (Tan Kar & Ramaiah, 2007). This makes them vulnerable to cyber attacks, thereby putting their organizations at risk. Hence, collective awareness and training of all peoples will improve resilience to cyber threats (Proclamation 9648, 2017).

Addressing Cyber Security Labor Shortage

Information security program developed and run by training and educational institutions can contribute immensely to making organizational environment more secure and efficient (DePaolis and Williford; 2015; Eyadat, 2015; Bicak, Liu, & Murphy, 2015). Cyber security awareness and training play a major role in mitigating cyber attacks. Security awareness is a primary pillar of security for any organization to avoid major security breaches (Dahbur, Bashabsheh, & Bashabsheh, 2017). For instance, Porter (2016) notes the importance public education in mitigating cyber deception.nMcCrohan, Engel, and Harvey (2010) examine the impact of cyber threat education and awareness intervention on changes in user security behavior and find that when users are educated of the threats and trained about proper security practices, their behaviors can enhance online security for themselves and the firms where they are employed.

Abawajy (2014) also finds that information security awareness using combined delivery methods of text-based, game-based and video-based are needed in security awareness programs. Information sharing can strengthen the maturity of cyber security program (Korte, 2017). Consequently, Affisco (2017) suggests expanding of cyber security learning in the business programs. Security programs, among others, should address modern technical needs of the individuals, workforce, industry, and academics (Poboroniuc et al., 2017).

MAIN FOCUS OF THE CHAPTER

The proposed Cyber Security Competency Model provides learning strategies for individuals and the workforce who will help reduce business risks emanating from cyber attacks. The model is composed of three components: Learning continuum hierarchy, cyber security domain knowledge, and learning theories. In the following sections, the chapter discusses and establishes the relationships among the components.

Component 1: Learning Continuum Hierarchy

This section describes the stages of learning (awareness, training, and education) referred to as the learning continuum hierarchy (NIST Special Publication 800-16, 2003). Learning is a continuum, which starts with awareness, builds on to training, and evolves into education (NIST Special Publication 800-16, 2003). The first and the lowest level (Stage 1) of learning continuum hierarchy is *awareness*. At this level, users need to know about how cyber security affects them, their work, their home, and which methods to use to defend themselves against the threats. Awareness stage aims at allowing individuals to recognize IT security concerns and respond accordingly (NIST Special Publication 800-16, 2003). Cyber security awareness seeks to focus an individual's attention on security issues. The second level (Stage 2) of the learning continuum hierarchy is *training*.

Training strives to produce relevant and needed skills and competencies within an area of practice. Training is learning by doing, which is a well-planned program to develop specific skills and knowledge (Surbhi, 2015). Training aims at improving the performance, productivity, and competency of learners (Surbhi, 2015). The third level (Stage 3) is *education*. Education is a means of learning which develops an individual's sense of reasoning, understanding, judgement and intellectual abilities (Surbhi, 2015). It aims at delivering knowledge about facts, events, values, beliefs, general concepts, and principles (Surbhi, 2015).

Table 1. Stages of cyber security learning continuum

Stages of Learning	Learning Continuum	Focus/Objective	Target Group
Stage 1	Awareness	• Knowledge of a situation or fact • Focus attention on an issue • Change behaviour • Reinforce best practices	Users of IT Systems (Individuals in the Society)
Stage 2	Training	• Inculcate specific skills • Develop specific skills • Practical application • Hands-on experience • Narrow • Job experience • Short term • Present job • Improve performance and productivity • How to do specific task	General Workforce
Stage 3	Education	• Produces theoretical knowledge • Theoretical oriented • Develop a sense of reasoning and judgement • Teaches general concepts • Wide • Comparatively long term • Future job • General concepts	IT Professionals and Related Discipline

Component 2: Cyber Security Domain Knowledge

A review of literature reveals several themes that form cyber security domain knowledge in terms of security training and awareness. Secondary data were gathered from scholarly sources, practitioner sources, training manuals and programs in cyber security (Laudon & Traver, 2014; Sans Technology Institute, 2018), and international governmental and non-governmental organizations (ISO/IEC 27032, 2012; NIST Special Publication 800-50, 2003) championing cyber security. ISO/IEC 27032:2012 is an international standard that provides guidance for improving the state of cyber security. The standard describes cyber security practices and the roles of stakeholders in the cyberspace, guideline for resolving common cyber security issues, and a framework for stakeholders to collaborate to resolve cyber security issues (ISO/IEC 27032, 2012).

The standard identifies the following major domains: (a) Information security, (b) Network security, (c) Internet security, and (d) Critical information infrastructure protection. In addition, NIST Special Publication 800-50 (2003) provides a list of cyber security awareness themes. Sans Technology Institute is a major professional cyber security training provider and provides in-depth cyber security training contents. About 175 items were retrieved from the literature search. The core competencies associated with cyber security training and awareness themes were grouped using a simple sorting program and manual inspection of similar themes. The number of occurrences of each theme were derived and presented in Table 2.

Table 2. Cyber security training and awareness themes

Cyber Security Training and Awareness Theme	N
Malware	15
Phishing	12
Hacking	9
Spoofing	8
Pharming	3
Identity fraud	17
Denial-of-Service (DOS)	5
Sniffing	3
Password protection	9
Email protecting	11
Data backup	9
Incident response	7
Handheld device security	13
Encryption	5
System patches	4
Software licensing	2
Access control	6
Privacy protecting	8
File sharing	10
Social engineering	12
Shoulder surfing	7

N=175 (N= number of occurrence of similar themes)

Component 3: Learning Theories

Theories are organized and systematic articulation of a set of statements in a particular discipline or subject area, communicated in a meaningful way that describe, explain, predict, and prescribe conditions under which some phenomena occur (Ingelse, 1997). Learning theories are often used when designing educational, training, and learning processes (Bloom, et al. 1956). Here, the chapter employs three learning theories (cognitive, affective, and psychomotor) to explain cyber security awareness and training program development. The choice of the three theories is as a result of their various focuses that fall in line with the core cyber security controls (technical, administrative, and physical).

Figure 2 shows the three learning theories and their sub domains. Cognitive domain is mental skills often referred to knowledge (Bloom, 1956) and is more closely related to technical control. Affective domain is the growth in feelings or emotional area often known as attitude or self (Krathwohl, Bloom, & Masia, 1973), which is closely linked to the administrative control. The psychomotor domain is the manual or physical skills, generally referred to as skills (Simpson, 1972), which is also related to the physical control.

Figure 2. Learning theories (three domains of learning)

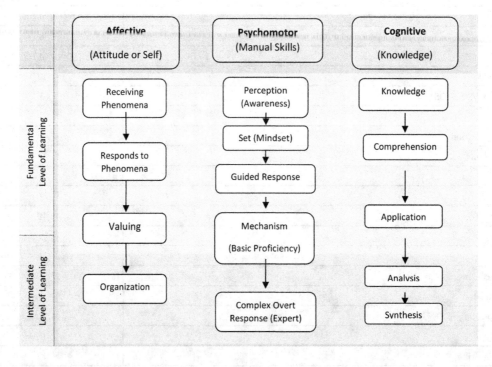

Cognitive Theory

This is mental skills often referred to as knowledge (Bloom, 1956). The cognitive domain involves knowledge and the development of intellectual skills (Bloom, 1956; Anderson et al., 2000). This comprises of recall or recognition of specific facts, procedural patterns, and concepts that serve in the development of intellectual abilities and skills. There are six major categories (remembering, understanding, applying, analyzing, evaluating, and creating) of cognitive processes. The categories can be thought of as degrees of difficulties. That is, the first one must normally be mastered before the next one can occur.

In chronological order, *remembering* involves recall or retrieval of previously learned information. *Understanding* involves comprehension of the meaning and interpretation of instructions and problems (Anderson et al., 2000). This stage helps the learner to state a problem in one's own words. *Applying* involves the use of a concept in a new situation. For example, applying what was learned in the classroom in novel situation at the work place. *Analyzing* involves separation of information or concepts into component parts so that its organizational structure may be understood.

It includes drawing distinction between facts and inferences (Anderson et al., 2000). *Evaluating* makes judgments about the value of ideas or information. Lastly, *creating* builds a structure or pattern from diverse elements and puts parts together to form a whole, with emphasis on creating a new meaning or structure.

Psychomotor Theory

This is the manual or physical skills, generally referred to as skills (Simpson, 1972). The psychomotor domain includes physical movement, coordination, and use of the motor-skill areas (Simpson, 1972). Development of these skills requires practice and is measured in terms of speed, precision, distance, procedures, or techniques in execution (Simpson, 1972). Thus, psychomotor skills rage from manual tasks, such as fixing a computer component, to more complex tasks, such as operating a complex piece of machinery. Psychomotor has seven constructs (perception, set, guided response, mechanism, complex overt response, adaptation, and origination). *Perception* (awareness) gives the individual the ability to use sensory cues to guide motor activity (Simpson, 1972). This ranges from sensory stimulation, through cue selection, to translation. *Set* (mindset) makes individuals ready to act. It includes mental, physical, and emotional sets.

These three sets are dispositions that predetermine a person's response to different situations sometimes called mindsets (Simpson, 1972). *Guided Response* is the early stages in learning a complex skill that includes imitation and trial and error. At this stage adequacy of performance is achieved by practicing. *Mechanism* (basic proficiency) is the intermediate stage in learning a complex skill. Learned responses have become habitual and tasks can be performed with some confidence and proficiency.

In addition, *Complex Overt Response* (expert) is the skilful performance of motor acts that involves complex movement patterns (Simpson, 1972). *Proficiency* indicates by a quick, accurate, and highly coordinated performance, requiring a minimum of energy (Simpson, 1972). This category includes performing without hesitation – an automatic performance. *Adaptation* skills are well developed and the individual can modify movement patterns to fit special requirements. Lastly, *Origination* is the creating of new movement patterns to fit a particular situation or specific problem (Simpson, 1972). At this stage, learning outcomes emphasize creativity based upon highly developed skills.

Affective Theory

This is the growth in feelings or emotional area often known as attitude or self (Krathwohl, Bloom, & Masia, 1973). Affective domain has five constructs (receiving phenomena, responds to phenomena, valuing, organization, and internalizes values). *Receiving Phenomena* is the awareness, willingness to hear, selected attention. *Responds to Phenomena* is an active participation on the part of the learners (Krathwohl, Bloom, & Masia, 1973). The learner attends and reacts to a particular phenomenon. Learning outcomes may emphasize compliance in responding, willingness to respond, or satisfaction in responding. *Valuing* is the worth or value a person attaches to a particular object, phenomenon, or behaviour (Krathwohl, Bloom, & Masia, 1973).

This ranges from simple acceptance to the more complex state of commitment. Valuing is based on the internalization of a set of specified values, while clues to these values are expressed in the learner's overt behavior which is often identifiable. *Organization* organizes values into priorities by contrasting different values, resolving conflicts between them, and creating a unique value system (Krathwohl, Bloom, & Masia, 1973). Here, the emphasis is on comparing, relating, and synthesizing values. Finally, *Internalizes Values* (characterization) is a value system that controls behaviour (Krathwohl, Bloom, & Masia, 1973). The behavior is pervasive, consistent and predictable, which are the most important characteristics of the learner.

SOLUTIONS AND RECOMMENDATIONS

Proposed Cyber Security Competency Model

The section presents the basic components of the proposed Cyber Security Competency Model (see Figure 3). This is followed by the detailed Cyber Security Competency Model (see Table 3). The model integrates all the components (Learning Continuum Hierarchy, Cyber Security Domain Knowledge, and Learning Theories) presented in the previous sections. Figure 3 shows the major parts of the model by mapping the Learning Continuum Hierarchy (awareness & training) to Cyber Security Domain Knowledge and Learning Theories in order to achieve cyber security awareness and training objectives. In its basic form, the model suggests that the foundation of getting the desired result from cyber security efforts depends on the following theoretical perspectives:

1. Changing perception and building user's interest (affective theory – such as valuing and internalizing values.
2. Recognizing the threats (cognition theory – such as knowledge and comprehension).
3. Employing practical techniques and methods (psychomotor theory – such as perception and mindset).

Firstly, affective theory can be used to build users' interest in cyber security because users tend to retain facts better when they are personally identified with or use the information personally. Secondly, users are more inclined to follow procedures they have good understanding of. Therefore, cognitive theory (knowledge, comprehension) should form the foundation of user's recognition of threats and attacks. Thirdly, psychomotor theory of makes users adept to practically deal with cyber attacks.

The detailed model (see Table 3) has two cyber security competency levels: Level 1 (Cyber Security Awareness for individuals and general public) and Level 2 (Cyber Security Training for the general workforce. The third level, which is outside the scope of this chapter, addresses Cyber Security education for IT technical and professional workers.

Figure 3. Basic components of cyber security competency model for individuals and general workforce

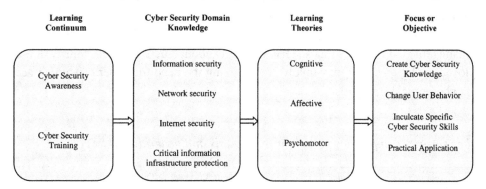

Level 1: Cyber Security Awareness for Individuals and General Public

This cyber security awareness level of competency mainly focuses on individuals and the general public. The model suggests that cyber security awareness will encourage safe usage habits, change user perceptions of cyber security, inform users about how to recognize potential cyber threats and attacks, and educate users about cyber security techniques to be used to mitigate cyber threats. *At the awareness level, remembering, understanding,* and *applying* of *cognitive theory can be linked to cyber security themes.* For example, at the *remembering* level individuals will be made to describe or recall the types of malware. At the *understanding* stage individuals can explain the steps involved in scanning malware. Also at the *applying* stage the individual will be expected to follow cyber security best practices to mitigate identity fraud and phishing attacks. *Psychomotor theory can also be used to explain individual awareness of cyber safety.*

For instance, cyber security awareness at the *perception* (awareness) stage, individuals can learn to physically protect their mobile devices. At the *set* (mindset) stage, individuals may show desire to learn a new process, such as how to use antimalware to scan viruses on their mobile devices. *Guided response* makes individuals, for example, to follow instructions to configure anti-virus software or assemble a portable computing device. Also, *mechanism* (basic proficiency) enables individuals to use personal computers or repair a computer. Also, affective theory can be applied to cyber security awareness. For example, *receiving phenomena* can explain individuals' listening and remembering of cyber security awareness messages on hacking, password protection and identity theft. *Responds to phenomena* involves compliance with cyber safety rules and practicing them.

Level 2: Cyber Security Training for the General Workforce

This cyber security training level of competency mainly focuses on the general workforce. Cognitive theory again explains how the workforce should be trained to mitigate cyber attacks. For example, at the *analyzing* stage the workforce is able to analyze the performance of a laptop computer and deploy security patches. At the *evaluating* stage, the workforce will justify the choice of anti-malware or encryption method. Additonally, at the training stage, psychomotor theory can explain the workforce's ability to deal with cyber attacks. For instance, *complex overt response* (expert) makes individuals to response quickly to cyber incidents.

Moreover, the *adaptation* stage underpins individuals' ability to modify email protection instructions to meet the current needs of dynamic cyber environment. Moreover, affective theory explains the effectiveness of cyber security training. For example, an employee's valuing of cyber security measure will inform management on matters that she feels strongly about (such as cyber security non-compliance among employees). *Organization* may involve recognizing the need for cyber privacy or acceptance of professional cyber ethical standards.

Table 3. Cyber security competency model for individuals and general workforce

Cyber Security Competency Level	Component 1 Cyber Security Learning Hierarchy	Component 2 Awareness and Training Themes	Component 3: Learning Theories			Focus/Objective
			Cognitive Domain	Affective Domain	Psychomotor Domain	
Level 1 (Every Individual/ General Public)	Cyber Security Awareness	Malware Spoofing Phishing Hacking Identity fraud Shoulder surfing Protect mobile device Password protection	Knowledge Comprehension Application	Receiving phenomena Responding to phenomena	Perception Set (Mindset) Guided response Mechanism	Knowledge of a situation or fact Focus attention on an issue Change user behavior Reinforce best practices
Level 2 (General Workforce)	Cyber Security Training	Encryption Data backup System patches Privacy protecting Email protection Identity fraud Handheld device security Incident response Ethical standards	Comprehension Application Analysis Synthesis	Responding to phenomena Valuing Organize values into priorities	Guided response Mechanism Complex response Adaptation	Inculcate specific skills Develop specific skills Practical application Hands-on experience On-the-job experience Improve performance and productivity Perform specific task

Recommendations

Cyber security is a global phenomenon that requires attention of governments, businesses, service providers, and individuals. Several stakeholders are needed to help improve cyber security and business risks, decrease cyber security risks, and reduce cyber security labor shortages. The role of international organizations, the role of governments to establish cyber security community training centers and to embark on awareness programs, and the role of the businesses community and training institutions to undertake research and develop instructional manuals. Weiser and Conn (2017) suggest that to avoid data breaches there is the need to integrate cyber security into business curriculum.

At the global level, international organizations and governments should lead the way of sponsoring cyber security awareness, training, and education programs in both developed and developing nations. There is an urgent need for the government and training institutions to establish several training centers to train individuals and the current workforce, including workers from both government agencies and private companies. There is the need for government grants and private companies' investment in cyber security education. As there is insufficient number of available courses in the cyber security related area in colleges (Namin, Hewett, & Inan, 2014), educators should promote cyber security education by introducing new course modules (Namin, Hewett, & Inan, 2015). Thus, there is also the need to support cyber security researchers and educators who are developing the skills, tools, and workforce required for a safer technology future (Proclamation 9335, 2015).

While there is a general shortage of cyber security skills, the cyber security instructors at training centers and faculty teaching at colleges should be thoroughly trained through workshops so that they can be more competent in developing cyber security programs to train the workforce. These workshops should focus on theoretical basis of cyber security to practical application of measures to curb cyber attacks. The cyber security competency model proposed in this chapter can be a reference point. Development of learning centers, community of practice, and online learning portals will be effective means of cyber security education (Pittman & Pike, 2016). International organizations, governments, and businesses should support cyber security training and research centres. When grants are available, individuals and the workforce will be encourage to undertake training in cyber security, leading to reduction in cyber security business risks and vulnerabilities.

FUTURE RESEARCH DIRECTIONS

Research in cyber security is emerging. Because of the breadth and multi-disciplinary nature of cyber security, training and educational institutions are constantly attempting to improve curricula to address rapid changes in cyber crime environment and attack strategies. The current chapter addresses a model of cyber security awareness and training for individuals and the general workforce. However, two issues have not been adequately addressed in the chapter. First, there is an issue with the mapping cyber security domain knowledge to learning hierarchy (awareness and training). This is because some of the themes are overlapping. For instance, a topic on malware scanning may overlap, falling under awareness as well as training. In order to deal with this concern, future work will involve an empirical primary research to investigate this classification. Second, the proposed model is based on learning theories only. The study did not examine the theories behind individual cyber security topics, for example a topic on cryptography, penetration testing and compliance.

Future work will examine theoretical underpinning of each topic so as to provide better understanding of the topics (themes) when they are being taught. Thirdly, the current model addresses only individuals and the general workforce. Future work will focus on developing and designing cyber security curricula, based on sound theories, for IT professionals and cyber security personnel.

CONCLUSION

This chapter propose cyber security competency model to be use in cyber security awareness and training programs for individuals and the general workforce. The model combined three learning models with cyber security awareness and training domain knowledge identified in the literature. The three theories have different theoretical perspectives. Combining theories in training and awareness programs is important. However, too often, theory and practice are separated from one another in training programs (ACM, 2014). A cyber security domain knowledge that is underpinned by learning theories, mapped to learning continuum hierarchy (awareness and training) is important. It will enable individuals and the workforce to effectively deal with cyber vulnerabilities and attacks within their domain.

Virtually everybody uses the cyberspace. Therefore, depending on only few individuals (cyber professional) to protect cyber space and curb cyber crime can be challenging. Accordingly, this chapter proposed a holistic approach to learning that involves individuals (every individual that uses the cyber space) and the general workforce. Teaching cyber security at the two stages of learning (awareness and training) that includes the theoretical domains of learning (cognitive, affective, and psychomotor) and mapped to appropriate cyber security domain knowledge is expected to have a greater impact on cyber workforce development. Moreover, the proposed cyber security competency model provided a reference and an understanding of how educators and trainers should manage cyber security awareness and training programs to prepare individuals and the workforce to minimize cyber security risks.

REFERENCES

Abawajy, J. (2014). User preference of cyber security awareness delivery methods. *Behaviour & Information Technology*, *33*(3), 236–247. doi:10.1080/0144929X.2012.708787

ACM. (2014). Toward Curricular Guidelines for Cybersecurity. Report of a Workshop on Cybersecurity Education and Training. *Proceedings of the 45th ACM technical symposium on Computer Science education*. doi: 10.1145/2538862.2538990

Affisco, J. F. (2017). Expanding cyber security learning in the business curriculum. *Proceedings for the Northeast Region Decision Sciences Institute (NEDSI)*, 420-435.

Australian Cyber Security Centre ACSC. (2017). *ACSC threat report 2017*. Retrieved on August 4, 2017, from: https://www.acsc.gov.au/publications/ACSC_Threat_Report_2017.pdf

Bell, R. (2016). Cybersecurity: It's mission critical for business. *Workforce*, *95*(10), 12.

Bicak, A., Liu, M., & Murphy, D. (2015). Cybersecurity curriculum development: Introducing specialties in a graduate program. *Information Systems Education Journal*, *13*(3), 99–110.

Chowdhury, W. (2015). Are warnings from online users effective?: An experimental study of malware warnings influencing cyber behaviour. *International Journal of Cyber Behavior, Psychology and Learning*, *5*(2), 44–58. doi:10.4018/IJCBPL.2015040104

Dahbur, K., Bashabsheh, Z., & Bashabsheh, D. (2017). Assessment of security awareness: A Qualitative and quantitative study. *International Management Review*, *13*(1), 37–58.

DePaolis, K., & Williford, A. (2015). The nature and prevalence of cyber victimization among elementary school children. *Child and Youth Care Forum*, *44*(3), 377–393. doi:10.100710566-014-9292-8

Engle, P. (2017). Key business risks for 2018. *Industrial Engineer: IE*, *49*(12), 20.

Eyadat, M. S. (2015). Higher education administrators roles in fortification of information security program. *Journal of Academic Administration in Higher Education*, *11*(2), 61–68.

Gunzel, J. A. (2017). Tackling the cyber threat: The impact of the DOD'S network penetration reporting and contracting for cloud services rule on DOD contractor cybersecurity. *Public Contract Law Journal*, *46*(3), 687–712.

Hanewald, R. (2008). Confronting the pedagogical challenge of cyber safety. *Australian Journal of Teacher Education*, *33*(3). doi:10.14221/ajte.2008v33n3.1

Ingelse, K. (1997). *Theoretical frameworks. Northern Arizona University NAU OTLE Faculty Studio*. Retrieved on June 2, 2017, from: http://www.ljemail.org/reference/ReferencesPapers.aspx?ReferenceID=799515

ISO27032 (ISO 27032). (n.d.). *Guidelines for cybersecurity information technology -- Security techniques -- Guidelines for cybersecurity*. Retrieved on August 15, 2017, from: https://www.iso.org/standard/44375.html

ITU. (2017). *Global Cybersecurity Index 2017*. Retrieved on December 22, 2017, from: https://www.itu.int/en/ITU-D/Cybersecurity/Pages/GCI-2017.aspx

Korte, J. (2017). Mitigating cyber risks through information sharing. *Journal of Payments Strategy & Systems*, *11*(3), 203–214.

Laudon, K. C., & Traver, C. G. (2014). *E-Commerce – Business, Technology, and Society* (10th ed.). Upper Saddle River, NJ: Pearson Education, Inc.

Leung, L. (2015). A panel study on the effects of social media use and internet connectedness on academic performance and social support. *International Journal of Cyber Behavior, Psychology and Learning*, *5*(1), 1–16. doi:10.4018/ijcbpl.2015010101

Locasto, M. E., Ghosh, A. K., Jajodia, S., & Stavrou, A. (2011). Virtual extension the ephemeral legion: Producing an expert cyber-security work force from thin air. *Communications of the ACM*, *54*(1), 129–131. doi:10.1145/1866739.1866764

McCrohan, K. F., Engel, K., & Harvey, J. W. (2010). Influence of awareness and training on cyber security. *Journal of Internet Commerce*, *9*(1), 23–41. doi:10.1080/15332861.2010.487415

McDuffie, E. L., & Piotrowski, V. P. (2014). The Future of Cybersecurity Education. *Computer*, *47*(8), 67-69. doi:10.1109/MC.2014.224

MIT. (2013). *Cyber security and human psychology*. Retrieved on November 11, 2015, from: http://cybersecurity.mit.edu/2013/11/cyber-security-and-humanpsychology

Moskal, E. J. (2015). A model for establishing a cybersecurity center of excellence. *Information Systems Education Journal*, *13*(6), 97–108.

Namin, A. S., Hewett, R., & Inan, F. A. (2014). Building Cyber Security Instructional Plans Through Faculty Development Program. *Annual International Conference On Infocomm Technologies In Competitive Strategies*, 91-100. doi:10.5176/2251-2195_CSEIT14.22

Namin, A. S., Hewett, R., & Inan, F. A. (2015). Faculty Development Programs on Cybersecurity for Community Colleges. *Annual International Conference On Computer Science Education: Innovation & Technology*, 19-28. doi:10.5176/2251-2195_CSEIT15.9

NIST. (2014). *NIST Cybersecurity Framework*. Retrieved on May 19, 2017, from: https://www.nist.gov/sites/default/files/documents/cyberframework/cybersecurity-framework-021214.pdf

Nunez, K. A. (2017). Negotiating in and around critical infrastructure vulnerabilities: Why the department of defense should use its other transaction authority in the new age of cyber attacks. *Public Contract Law Journal*, *46*(3), 663–685.

Office of Personnel Management (OPM). (2015). *Notify employees of cybersecurity incident*. Retrieved on July 3, 2017, from: https://www.opm.gov/news/releases/2015/06/opm-to-notify-employees-of-cybersecurity-incident

Ortiz, E. C., & Reinerman-Jones, L. (2015). Theoretical Foundations for Developing Cybersecurity Training. Lecture Notes in Computer Science, 9179, 480-487. doi:10.1007/978-3-319-21067-4_49

Palmer, R. K. (2014). *Critical Infrastructure: Legislative Factors for Preventing*. Retrieved on October 7, 2016, from: http://archive.defense.gov/transcripts/transcript.aspx? transcript-id=5136

Parry, M. (2009). Community Colleges Mobilize to Train Cybersecurity Workers. *The Chronicle of Higher Education*, 14.

Patel, P. (2014). Defense against the dark arts (of Cyberspace) universities are offering graduate degrees in cybersecurity. *IEEE Spectrum*, *51*(6), 26. doi:10.1109/MSPEC.2014.6821610

Pittman, J. M., & Pike, R. E. (2016). An observational study of peer learning for high school students at a cybersecurity camp. *Information Systems Education Journal*, *14*(3), 4–13.

Poboroniuc, M. S., Naaji, A., Ligusova, J., Grout, I., Popescu, D., Ward, T., & Jackson, N. (2017). ICT security curriculum or how to respond to current global challenges. *World Journal on Educational Technology*, *9*(1), 40–49.

Porter, C. (2016). Toward practical cyber counter deception. *Journal of International Affairs*, *70*(1), 161–174.

Prichard, J. J., MacDonald, L. E., & Hunt, L. (2004). Cyber terrorism: A study of the extent of coverage in computer security textbooks. *Journal of Information Technology Education*, 3279–3289.

Proclamation 9335. (2015). Proclamation 9335--National Cybersecurity Awareness Month, 2015. *Daily Compilation Of Presidential Documents*, 1-2.

Proclamation 9508. (2016). National Cybersecurity Awareness Month, 2016. *Daily Compilation of Presidential Documents*, 1-2.

Proclamation 9648. (2017). National Cybersecurity Awareness Month, 2017. *Daily Compilation Of Presidential Documents*, 1-2.

QS TopUniversities. (2018). *QS World University Rankings by Subject 2016 - Computer Science & Information Systems*. Retrieved on February 2, 2018, from: https://www.topuniversities.com/university-rankings/university-subject-rankings/2016/computer-science-information-systems

Rohrer, K. K., & Hom, N. (2017). Where do we start with cybersecurity? *Strategic Finance*, 62-63.

Ruiz, R., Winter, R., Kil Jin Brandini, P., & Amatte, F. (2017). The leakage of passwords from home banking sites: A threat to global cyber security? *Journal of Payments Strategy & Systems*, *11*(2), 174–186.

Russell, G. (2017). Resisting the persistent threat of cyber-attacks. *Computer Fraud & Security*, *2017*(12), 7–11. doi:10.1016/S1361-3723(17)30107-0

Sans Technology Institute. (2018). *Master's Degrees - Information Security*. Retrieved on April 2, 2018, from: https://www.sans.edu/academics/degrees/msise

Singapore Increases Cybersecurity Training for Youths. (2014). *Information Management Journal*, *48*(1), 17.

Stoddart, K. (2016). UK cyber security and critical national infrastructure protection. *International Affairs*, *92*(5), 1079–1105. doi:10.1111/1468-2346.12706

Surbhi, S. (2015). *Difference Between Training and Education*. Retrieved on September 22, 2017, from: https://keydifferences.com/difference-between-training-and-education.html

Tan Kar, P., & Ramaiah, C. K. (2007). Awareness of cyber laws in young Singaporeans. *DESIDOC Bulletin of Information Technology*, *27*(6), 41–53. doi:10.14429/djlit.27.6.144

Vishik, C., & Heisel, M. (2015). *Cybersecurity Education snapshot for workforce development in the EU Network and Information Security (NIS) Platform*. Retrieved on January 6, 2017, from: https://resilience.enisa.europa.eu/nis-platform/shared-documents/wg3-documents/cybersecurity-education-snapshot-for-workforce-development-in-the-eu/view

Weiser, M., & Conn, C. (2017). Into the Breach: Integrating Cybersecurity into the Business Curriculum. *Bized*, *16*(1), 36–41.

Wiederhold, B. K. (2014). The role of psychology in enhancing cybersecurity. *Cyberpsychology, Behavior, and Social Networking*, *17*(2). doi:10.1089/cyber.2014.1502 PMID:24592869

Yang, S. C., & Wen, B. (2017). Toward a cybersecurity curriculum model for undergraduate business schools: A survey of AACSB-accredited institutions in the United States. *Journal of Education for Business*, *92*(1), 1–8. doi:10.1080/08832323.2016.1261790

KEY TERMS AND DEFINITIONS

Cyber Competency: The ability, skill, and knowledge by individuals to protect themselves and their organization's cyberspace.

Denial of Service (DoS): This happens when hackers flood a server with useless traffic to inundate and overwhelm the network, often degrading the server's performance and causing it to shut down with the intent of damaging the organization's reputation and customer relationships.

Hacking: An intentional disruption, defacing, or even destroying an information resources normally carried out on the internet.

Identity Fraud: This is an unauthorized use of another person's personally identifiable information, such as social security, driver's license, credit card numbers, user names, and passwords for illegal financial benefit.

Pharming: This involves redirecting a web link to an address different from the intended one, with the fake site appearing as the intended destination.

Phishing: A deceptive normally online attempt by an attacker to obtain user's confidential information for financial gain.

Sniffing: This is a program that monitors information travelling over a network, enabling hackers to steal proprietary and sensitive information from anywhere on a network.

Spoofing: This occurs when hackers attempt to hide their true identities or misrepresent themselves by using fake e-mail addresses or masquerading as someone else.

This research was previously published in Global Cyber Security Labor Shortage and International Business Risk; pages 94-110, copyright year 2019 by Business Science Reference (an imprint of IGI Global).

Chapter 8

Online Calling Cards and Professional Profiles in Cybersecurity From Social Media

Shalin Hai-Jew

https://orcid.org/0000-0002-8863-0175

Kansas State University, USA

ABSTRACT

Demand is very high for people to work in various cybersecurity professions and ceteris paribus that demand may well continue into the near term. While there are more formal trails for employment, such as higher-educational pathways, performance in cybersecurity competitions, participation in professional conferences, and social media presentations may all offer less conventional paths into cybersecurity hiring. Through a convenience sample across a number of social media platforms and bottom-up coding, this work explores some aspects of cybersecurity professional profiles ("calling cards") available on the open Social Web and what may be learned about respective skills and capabilities from these glimmers of the person(s) behind the profiles. These profiles are assessed based on a 2x2 axis with focuses on (1) target skills and (2) personhood attributes. From these analyses, some tentative insights are shared about the cybersecurity calling cards and how informative they may be for recruitment and retention of cybersecurity workers.

INTRODUCTION

George Smiley: "The more identities a man has, the more they express the person they conceal." -- John Le Carré in Tinker Tailor Soldier Spy (1974, 2012)

DOI: 10.4018/978-1-6684-3554-0.ch008

"Cybersecurity," defined as "a set of techniques used to protect the integrity of networks, programs and data from attack, damage or unauthorized access" ("What is cybersecurity?" n.d.), encompasses a broad range of professional positions and skill sets. At present, there is a lack of a consensus definition about what actually constitutes a cybersecurity professional. One researcher writes:

… a literature review confirms there is no standard definition of a cybersecurity worker, associated skills, or educational requirements. The cybersecurity workforce to which we speak in this report consists of those who self-identify as cyber or security specialists as well as those who build and maintain the nation's critical infrastructure. (Wilson & Ali, 2011, p. 15) (note: original source italics)

There are some definitions from the environment. A Department of Homeland Security secretary defined cybersecurity professionals as those in charge of "… cyber risk and strategic analysis; cyber incident response; vulnerability detection and assessment; intelligence and investigation; and network and systems engineering" (Krebs, 2009, as cited in Wilson & Ali, 2011, p. 16). In terms of secure software development, there are designers, developers, and testers (Shumba, et al., 2013, p. 4). A perusal of job sites today includes a wide range of roles. In one schematic, authors mentioned red team members (who serve as network attackers to help companies strengthen their defenses), blue team members, systems administrators, computer network defense analysts, computer programmers, targeting analysts, security engineers, computer network defense forensic analysts, collection operators, and exploitation analysts (Campbell, O'Rourke, & Bunting, 2015, p. 722). According to another source, the most in-demand cybersecurity jobs include the following three, in descending order: 1) penetration testers, 2) cybersecurity engineers, and 3) CISOs (chief information security officers), according to Mondo, a company providing technical staffing (Rayome, 2017). There have been calls for as-yet uncreated positions, such as for "cyber diplomats" to work at the nation-state level to ensure there may be clearer understandings of each other's uses of cyberspace and to help with the resolution of cyber-related issues that may arise (Maller, 2013). With the advent of the Internet of Things (IoT), with cyber tools used in homes, healthcare, cars, and other spaces, the need for professionals in cybersecurity will expand further.

Currently, there is serious planning and work to try to secure the IoT (Ahlmeyer & Chircu, 2016). Additionally, for all the mentions of full-time employees, there are also interns, "gig workers" or "temps," and others who fill cybersecurity positions. In addition, with regards to cybersecurity, there is the formal job market, the freelance, and the informal black job market. Broadly, professional roles in cybersecurity may be understood in broad categories: leadership / management, policy, legal, technology, research and development, and education and training. In some cases, there may be crossover among these categories.

The cybersecurity market is projected to be a US$170 billion industry by 2020 (Morgan, 2016). In 2016, some 209,000 cybersecurity jobs in the U.S. were unfilled (Morgan, 2016), and this number is expected to rise to "6 million globally by 2019, according to the CEO of Symantec (Morgan, 2016). Organizationally, labor shortages mean that some functionalities are simply not addressed, and current staff tend to be over-worked and potentially under-attentive; also, there are pressures on wages (Wright, 2015). A number of efforts are ongoing to address the workforce shortfall in this critical and dynamic area, particularly with the onboarding of more cyber with the Internet of Things (IoT).

With the popularization of cyber, in early years, individuals with "hacker" skills were in high demand, and while the field has formalized to some degree (with internships, competitions, growing technical certifications, undergraduate and graduate degrees, post-graduate studies, cyber defense competitions, and formal modeling of cyber jobs and cybersecurity workforce frameworks), there is still room for talented self-taught mavericks (white-hats) and others, in part because the field is so "hot" and the demands so high…and in part because the threat landscape is so dynamic and difficult to anticipate. This work examines the making of online cybersecurity "calling cards" by those in the field—at early, mid, and late careers—on a range of social media platform types.

To explore cybersecurity profile-making on the Social Web, three interrelated hypotheses are explored in this work. The hypotheses read:

Hypothesis 1: A way to simplify and summarize people's professional cybersecurity profiles is on two general dimensions: (1) target skills and (2) personhood attributes.

Hypothesis 2: People (individually and collectively) create cybersecurity "calling cards" on the Social Web that may be partially informative of their (1) target skills and (2) personhood attributes [related to cybersecurity work].

Hypothesis 2a: Various categories of social media offer different insights and levels of informativeness about the target individual.

Hypothesis 2b: Online cybersecurity "calling cards" inform approaches in cybersecurity talent-scouting, head-hunting and recruitment, professional transitioning, interview and test setups, and other work-based designs.

Hypothesis 3: There are (in)effective ways to design and communicate cybersecurity calling cards.

Hypothesis 3a: A calling card that is more aligned between "saying" and "doing" would be more convincing. (This refers to the difference between "cheap talk" and "costly signaling.")

Hypothesis 3b: A calling card focused on "social benefits" will be more effective than those based on commercial interests.

Figure 1 depicts a simplified cybersecurity employment sequence and how an online calling card may inform the process at various stages, from head-hunting to interviews and testing to a hiring decision to the actual assigned work and teaming (all within the proper constraints of employment law and ethical practices) to employee retention and development. Every aspect of this sequence is important. The cybersecurity shortfall, in both public and private industry, highlights the need to also retain talent in this space (Nissen & Tick, 2017).

Figure 1. Simplified cybersecurity employment sequence

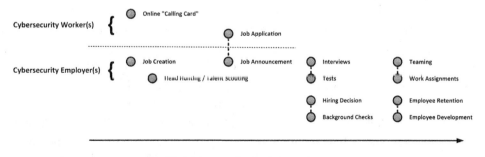

Simplified Cybersecurity Employment Sequence

What follows is a review of the relevant literature. Then, a convenience sample of individuals in various phases (early, mid, and late) of their cybersecurity careers are mapped. To simplify, the general somewhat-arbitrary cut-offs are as follows: early careers (0 – 14 years), mid-careers (15 – 29 years), and late / mature careers (30 – 50 years). In the early career category, two females and one male—all Americans—were studied; in the mid-careers, seven males were studied (and these hailed from three different countries); in the late careers, a male and a female, both Americans, were studied. The author tried to capture individuals who were demographically diverse—by age (20s to 70s), gender (both female and male), backgrounds (educational background from high school-educated to college educated, work in public and private industries, expertise in a range of aspects of cybersecurity, and others). The studied individuals were from three different nationalities: U.S., Russian, and Finland. A broader mix would have been preferable, but there were other limitations in terms of shared information across a range of social media platforms and data modalities.

Delimitations

While a broad (and disparate) range of social media data types are explored, not every leading or popular branded social media service in that class was used. The companies running the respective sites tend to be Western-based, and most of the information was collected in English (and Spanish). The sampling was a slice-in-time sampling over a period of a few weeks in October, 2017. This means that messaging which was erased would not be captured (in the way that it would if continuous monitoring were applied, such as through Google Alerts). Additionally, studying a dozen individuals at varying points in their cybersecurity careers is by definition limited and based on convenience sampling.

Pseudonymous accounts, which are not uncommon, are not included. These accounts may be sussed out through computational link analysis (such as through Paterva's Maltego, with an open-source and a commercial version) but then needs to be explored to validate account ownership. If that can be established with some certainty, then some insights may be assertable from these accounts. This research did not pursue pseudonymous accounts linked to the target individuals.

This approach is not scalable unless it is automated, with scraped data, such as with the help of tools that capture open-source intelligence. (On the commercial software market, there are some tools that seem able to collect partial information, but this author has not found any tools that enable a comprehensive capture of such data across the range of social media platforms and sites listed here. There are also challenges with targeting individuals with common names, without sufficient disambiguation.) Nonetheless, this approach is not applicable in a large-scale way given the need for human attention and analytics.

In addition, the same data points may be interpreted in different ways as pros or cons. For example, what should one make of a cybersecurity professional who is eliciting funds on a crowd-sharing site for a new company or the development of a new training or a new office? Is this elicitation for funds a sign of positive initiative? Is this request a sign of negative financial health for the individual? How a data point is interpreted in relation to the target individual and to the professional cybersecurity context will have repercussions. This reality brings us to an important: how should an online "calling card" be used?

This ego mapping approach maybe should only be used to general assessment and possible "tagging" for later exploration and more in-depth research (with verified factual data). In this work, the individuals will not be identified to a name because the analyses are non-definitive and incomplete, with limited (partial) and noisy (not impartial) data in the wild. Additionally, while "telling" details are important, those that could identify the studied subject to personally identifiable information (PII) were also omitted.

The purpose of this research is to see how this mapping of online "calling cards" in cybersecurity may be conducted, albeit not to directly profile individuals (with the attendant risks of inaccuracy and stereotyping and discrimination). For example, what if a potential cybersecurity recruit has objectionable politics? What if the potential hire spent some time as a black-hat? Or had leaked some privy data to journalists? Or is unlikeable? Or is litigious? What if there are unexplained gaps in a work history? What if the target individual has a few instances of flaming others online and getting into social kerfuffles?

Employment law also has safeguards in place for job applicants, and this data should be understood and applied in fair and legal- and policy-based contexts. In addition, people with impressive skill sets are often given more leeway to have some personal quirks, and the opposite is also sometimes true, that a person with a lot of social skills and political cover can get away with having less technical talent. A "big tent" approach makes sense for this field albeit without causing unnecessary risk. How people's characteristics are framed can affect whether a set of facts is read one way or another.

The value here, though, is that profiling egos (individuals and entities) across the Web and Internet may provide insights to capabilities and character, particularly in work that can be sensitive—with malice (and acting on malice) and with non-malicious ineptitude (causing harm unintentionally) and inefficacy. With the high costs of recruitment and retaining, using publicly available information may prove advantageous. Finally, the mention of technologies here does not suggest endorsement.

REVIEW OF THE LITERATURE

The efforts to make cybersecurity more appealing as a field are occurring in a multi-pronged manner. There is strategic messaging that such work is "heroic":

The key feature, whether it be self-sacrifice, protection, intelligence, creativity, or skill, is that the individual stands out from the crowd in a manner that goes beyond normal expectations and is highly appreciated by others. (Nugent & Collar, 2015, p. 1)

Another team noted the need to build cybersecurity work so that it is rewarding (Parker, Winslow, & Tetrick, 2016). There have been endeavors to reach out to freshman students to test for interest in information technology, using gamification elements; even if the students enter other fields, the exposure to information technologies make them more hire-able (Cunha, Winders, Rowe, & Cornel, 2016). Community colleges are positioned to provide the necessary trainings and certifications for cybersecurity professionals (Koermer, 2014), as are universities and some entities in private industry.

The personnel recruitment challenge does not only involve a general shortfall, but there is a need for more women and minorities in cybersecurity roles, in light of Bureau of Labor Statistics reporting that "12% of Cybersecurity specialists were women, 10% African American, and 15% Latino, though the numbers were so small for some job titles that the figures were found to be unreliable" (Shumba, et al., 2013, p. 2).

Recruitment efforts for under-represented populations into cybersecurity work includes ensuring neutral non-genderized language in the field, sharing cybersecurity information in a culturally sensitive manner, establishing mentor networks, holding conferences in cybersecurity for those in high school and college, setting up diverse speakers bureaus for K-20 audiences, supporting the development of educational programs, making scholarships available, and others (Shumba, et al., 2013, pp. 9 - 10).

Another endeavor involves retraining people from other careers to retrain and work in cybersecurity (Shumba, et al., 2013, p. 10). Another researcher suggests the importance of "taking advantage of the window of opportunity, allowing individuals interested in moving into the cybersecurity field to do so via education and training" (Vogel, 2016, p. 34). The human resources supply chain (aka pipeline) for cybersecurity extends from "pre-kindergarten through university, certifications, training, and other life-long learning opportunities" (Wilson & Ali, 2011, p. 18).

Some of the demographic disparities in representation in the cybersecurity field are attributed to preparation in the Science, Technology, Engineering, and Math (STEM) subjects, which are "strongly correlated with their race, ethnicity, and gender with a gap that grows worse with age" (Shumba, et al., 2013, p. 3). Individuals fall out of the STEM pipeline as they progress in their formal education, in the U.S.

From the earliest days of childhood learning, learners acquire knowledge and skills that may coalesce into an individual who can effective engage cyber. To meet this challenge, there are efforts on a number of fronts: policy, educational, recruitment, technological, and others. Currently, while there are new bac-calaureate and graduate degrees for cybersecurity, there are opportunities for those who have not followed a formalized educational and training and career path. There is some room for self-definition and innova-tion, and those who can prove their skills in action (such as in cybersecurity competitions) may have a place in the field (Balaish, 2017). In a sense, the field may continuously have space for nonconventional thinkers because cyberattacks are constantly evolving, complex, mixed-modal, pernicious, and elusive.

Within the cybersecurity profession, the culture is to be "perfectly paranoid" (Rose, 2012), with their suspicions sufficiently and sensitively tuned in order to protect against compromises and "pwning" ("player owning" or being defeated and humiliated) by adversaries. They have to think both technically and socially, since both are channels through which cybersecurity compromises occur. As an extension of this caution, most do not over-share online because they know that whatever information they leak can be harnessed as a come-on, as spear-phishing, and as misrepresentations to compromise themselves or others (such as using personal information to pretend to be a friend or colleague of the individual in order to inveigle others into sharing private information). There is a leeriness in the culture against showboating, and the skepticism of people's claims runs deep: extraordinary claims require extraordinary evidence (an assertion attributed to Carl Sagan).

When people make claims in widely accessible and public online spaces, though, they trigger oth-ers' interest and self-appointed detective work. They inspire others to check their record for all testable propositions, so that an actual record may be "locked down" in some parts and potentially disproved in others. Social networks may be mapped, and declared / formalized and undeclared / informal / ad hoc relationships may be observed and documented. In the same way as public information may draw interest, and so will online "calling cards". The way a calling card is used here is in both the sense of a business card and as a unique professional "signature."

In the cybersecurity field, there are two main foci: (1) target skills and (2) personhood attributions. The "target skills" are those that serve a person well in the professional role: understandings of technolo-gies, understandings of people, applied logic, precision, clear written communications, and others. The desirable "personhood attributes" are aspects of character, trustworthiness, soft skills (like interpersonal communications), grit, and others. The ethical soundness is a concern even from early days, with one research team noting: "The sensitive and confidential nature of cybersecurity requires trainees to not only be exceptional students, but to also be ethically sound individuals" (Cunha, Winders, Rowe, & Cornel, 2016, p. 26). These concepts are expressed in a 2x2 axis in Figure 2. A by-the-book recruitment

Figure 2. Employment recruitment in cybersecurity: Target skills and personhood attributes (a 2 x 2 axis)

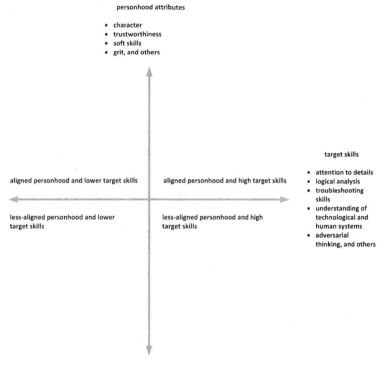

Employment Recruitment in Cybersecurity: Target Skills and Personhood Attributes
(a 2 x 2 axis)

of cybersecurity professionals would be at the top right quadrant, for candidates with high target skills and "aligned" (to the field or domain) personhood characteristics.

In 2013, a committee of experts was brought together to consider whether it would be a good idea to professionalize cybersecurity and formalize a workforce development path ("Professionalizing the Nation's Cybersecurity Workforce? Criteria for Decisionmaking," 2013, p. ix), and one of their conclusions was that premature professionalizing the space might be counterproductive (p. 28). One of their main conclusions: "Because cybersecurity is not solely a technical endeavor, a wide range of backgrounds and skills will be needed in an effective national cybersecurity workforce" (pp. 24 – 25). A few years after this initial report was released, another researcher observed the importance of diverse skills in cybersecurity:

Cybersecurity is a contest of competence. Vulnerabilities are limitless because they emanate from constantly expanding human intellect, imagination, and ingenuity. The mission of the cyber defender is therefore continually shifting; best practice heuristics have a near zero half-life as every day brings new attack vectors, exploitation techniques, or exfiltration targets. (Tobey, 2015, p. 32)

Professionals have already started work in defining the desirable characteristics and aptitudes for work in cybersecurity. The National Initiative for Cybersecurity Education (NICE) has announced goals of addressing the shortage of skilled cybersecurity workers in the U.S. NICE proposed a framework to conceptualize cybersecurity work, including the following: securely provision, operate and maintain, protect and defend, investigate, collect and operate, analyze, and oversee and govern ("NICE Cybersecurity Workforce Framework," 2017).The actions are high level and general ones that apply to a range of needs within the field. Saner, Campbell, and Bunting (2015) had conceptualized the NICE framework as follows:

- **Securely Provision:** IA (information assurance) compliance, system requirements planning
- **Operate and Maintain:** Data admin, network services
- **Protect and Defend:** CND (certified network defender) analysis, incident response
- **Investigate:** Digital forensics, investigation
- **Collect and Operate:** Collection operations, cyber operations, cyber operations planning
- **Analyze Threat:** Analysis, exploitation analysis, all-source intelligence
- **Oversight and Development:** Legal advice, education, ISSO, CISO (Slide 15).

There have been certain certifications in cybersecurity, such as the Certified Information Systems Security Professional (CISSP certification), but these are for particular contexts and particular professional roles. Using certifications, which are specific to domains in lieu of actual professional performance indicators, requires supervisors to:

…rely almost exclusively on professional certifications that are designed to assess possession of domain knowledge, not the skill or ability to perform under pressure. In an attempt to fill the knowledge-skill gap with competent recruits, the already overtaxed cybersecurity staff must spend considerable time designing and overseeing "gauntlets" through which prospective new talent must pass to demonstrate their ability to meet current and projected job demands. This "expert eyes" approach is costly, error-prone, and can only succeed in organizations that have previously been successful in attracting top level talent, creating a Matthew Effect: those rich with talent can recruit the best, while those in greatest need are incapable of improving their ability to accurately assess vulnerability or respond to an attack. (Tobey, 2015, p. 31)

Because of the demands of the field, "general-intelligence" is an important element given the need for "real-time or deliberate performance, and proactive or reactive actions" (Campbell, O'Rourke, & Bunting, 2015, p. 721); "non-cognitive attributes" are critical as well (p. 722). Likewise, cybersecurity work requires technical expertise as well as non-technical (Hoffman, Burley, & Toregas, 2012, p. 33). Given the ranges of work in cybersecurity, the respective roles require different "technical skills, temperaments…(and) cognitive abilities" (Campbell, O'Rourke, & Bunting, 2015, p. 721), and early work has gone into the Cyber Aptitude Talent Assessment (CATA), with definition of some desirable aptitudes for the work. The expected "knowledge, skills and abilities" (KSAs) vary depending on the workplace contexts and conditions, without fully defined consensus-accepted requirements. Those working in the cybersecurity field also need to be aware of the laws under which they work (Appazov, 2014).

Cybersecurity professionals also must work in a high pressure and ambiguous environment, which is sometimes somewhat emulated in cybersecurity competitions to find individuals with dispositional aptitudes. A four-year study of cyber defense competitions found that competitors need accurate situational awareness in order to respond effectively in the simulated critical incidents events, particularly the following steps:

1. Establish vignettes (or scenarios) that define situated expertise in job roles;

2.   Detail the goals and objective metrics that determine successful performance;

3.   Identify responsibilities by job role necessary to achieve the objectives;

4.   Detail the tasks, methods, and tools along with how competence may differ by level of expertise or by the difficulty of achieving that level of expertise. (Tobey, 2015, p. 32)

Necessary skills for members of Computer Security Incident Response Teams (CSIRTS) include the need to have "investigative skills, a desire to acquire new knowledge and share this knowledge with others, the ability to problem-solve, curiosity, and attention to detail" (Chen, Shore, Zaccaro, Dalal, Tetrick, & Gorab, 2014, p. 65). They also need social skills in order to share information with others and to collaborate (p. 65), and they have to be able to "detect patterns in routine material or data" (p. 65). Cybersecurity expertise has to be adaptive, and it is not about learning heuristics or rules. As a case in point, multiple works point to the growing complexity of cybersecurity, including the harnessing of machine learning (Fraley & Cannady, 2017) and artificial intelligence (Moore, 2017). Certainly, novel research is required to advance the field.

Soft skills are critical in cybersecurity (Schirf & Serapiglia, 2016). In another study, researchers surveyed cybersecurity competition participants to try to identify what factors enable cybersecurity competitions to convince participants "to pursue a future career in cybersecurity," and they found that those who "displayed higher self-efficacy, rational decision-making style, and more investigative interests were more likely to declare an interest in a career in cybersecurity after the competition" (Bashir, Wee, Memon, & Guo, 2017, p. 153). Cybersecurity competitions also convey "useful skills" particularly in "reverse engineering and analytic skills" to those already working in cybersecurity (Wee, Bashir, & Memon, 2016).

A number of works address how to build effective educational paths for cybersecurity workers. One authoring team argues for the importance of bringing together "educators, career professionals, employers, and policymakers" in a "holistic" way to address the design (Hoffman, Burley, & Toregas, 2012, p. 33). Another team interviewed learners in a cybersecurity course to understand what their takeaways were (Bell, Sayre, & Vasserman, 2014). There are opportunities to learn from others' development experiences. A game was created for middle- and high-school students to learn more about cybersecurity, so the recruitment for possible future cybersecurity learners and professionals begins early (Stumbaugh, 2016). There have been some early studies of best practices in cybersecurity education and training for learner efficacy (Beuran, Chinen, Tan, & Shinoda, 2016).

CYBERSECURITY "CALLING CARDS" ON THE OPEN AND SOCIAL WEB

While the culture in cybersecurity is to lie low and to target messaging to intended recipients instead of the broad public, there are also countervailing needs to reach out to the public to notify them of cybersecurity risks and data breaches. There is a need to refresh the talent pool with newcomers. There are needs to reach out to policymakers to ensure that proper policies and sufficient funding are put into place to support the work. Any professional who wants to engage the idea space has to go public to some degree, and with the amount of competition in the attention economy, he or she had better be quite savvy or hire others to advance a concept or practice or attitude.

Strategic messaging to the public, particularly in this Social Age, may be a central part of the cybersecurity skill set. There are many who work in cybersecurity who have created online profiles across a range of social media and other sites, including the following:

1. Employment sites (online job boards)
2. Social sharing sites (microblogging, social networking)
3. Information sharing sites (news sharing sites, crowd-sourced encyclopedia sites, informal information sharing sites)
4. Social image sharing sites
5. Social video sharing sites
6. Social code-sharing sites
7. Academic publishing (subscription-based and open-access)
8. Academic research sharing sites
9. Open education / training sites (massive open online course or MOOC platforms, digital learning object repositories / referatories)
10. Crowd-based fund-raising sites

The above categories of sites are not generally for simple one-directional broadcast usages, such as single-to-many. Rather, these are used interactively—in two-way narrowcast interactions, multi-way narrowcast interactions (such as in groups), and many to many interchanges. The types of interactions may include the following: commenting, emails, video replies, digital data sharing, and others.

It is possible to make some simple assumptions about what information might be available from the respective sites (Table 1). By cobbling multimodal data (text, imagery, audio, video, and others) from these respective sites, it is possible to create targeted profiles or electronic dossier of people working in cybersecurity. These profiles are complementary to formal mass media and official government records (including court records and business filings), both of which are quite widely available online. The reason why mass media reportage and official government records were not included in this work is that they are not part of a direct shaping of a personal professional "calling card," although those formal streams of somewhat verified data are informative and will certainly be checked formally for employment purposes into sensitive positions.

Mass media reportage is available on the Open Web, and many government records are available on the Deep Web (through services such as pipl.com). Criminal records can be found fairly easily through open searches, which can nullify people's strategic hiding behaviors (by hiring services to create links that appear on the top few pages of a search engine search and to "bury" derogatory information further in).

From an original list of about 20 individuals in cybersecurity with presence on social media, the list was culled based on the requirements in Table 2: those with at least representations online in five digital modalities; those with presences on at least five social media and information platform types; a time measure of digital contents; both self-descriptions and other-descriptions (of them); and research background / innovations in the field.

As the target individuals were explored, other names arose which would have enriched the research, but it was important to work with a reasonable convenience sample. Because of these requirements, there is a tendency to select individuals who tend to be more mid-career and late-career. However, for this work, there was representation from across the career spectrum (Figure 3).

Table 1. Social sharing site types...and possible available information for individual cybersecurity dossiers

Social Media Site Types	Possible Available Information for Individual Cybersecurity Dossiers
employment sites	• full curriculum vitae (CVs) or résumés (with formal education, formal trainings, job histories, awards, conference presentations, publications, and others), recommendation letters, transcripts, professional bios, photos, and others • expected wages
social networking and sharing sites	• **Microblogging Sites:** Electronic social networks, messaging, connections to events, areas of interest, and personality indicators (through messaging and shared digital contents, among others) • **Social Networking Sites:** Electronic social networks, family, friends, group membership, level of activity, and personality indicators
information sharing sites	• **Social News Sharing Sites:** Political interests, opinions, thinking about social issues • **Crowd-Sourced Encyclopedia Sites:** Third-party provided information as well as self-provided "objective" information • **Informal Information Sharing Sites:** Ads, desired connections, desired job situations, and others
social image sharing sites	• **Image-Sharing Sites:** Hobbies of interest, photography skill level, (public) group memberships, and others • **On Web and Internet:** Appearance
social video sharing sites	• **Own Channel:** Self-representations • **Others' Channels:** Presentations at conferences
social code sharing sites	• **Social Coding:** Types of coding languages, skill level, projects-of-interest (with attendant implied values), collaborations, messaging, personality indicators
academic publishing sites	• **Publications and Publishers, Subscription Databases, Open-Access Sites and Databases:** Reputation of work, impact metrics, logical reasoning, knowledge base, research methodologies, research areas of interest, and others
academic research sharing sites	• **Research Sharing Sites:** Profile, publications, treatment of others, announcements of own continuing and unpublished research
open education / training sites	• **Massive Open Online Courses:** Knowledge and skills, organization skills, treatment of learners and colleagues, humor, personality, tech savvy, professional standing, and others • **Digital Learning Object Repositories / Referatories:** Knowledge and skills, technical skills, areas of expertise, and others
crowd-based fund-raising sites	• **Calls for Support:** Projects and endeavors that individuals and groups want funding support for

Another way to measure renown online is to use mass-scale search data captured over extended time. Google Correlate explorations were run on the dozen individuals selected to see if they were of sufficient reputation that Google Searches of their names would bring up some cybersecurity correlates. In this exploration, only three of the 12 names had correlations with cybersecurity terms. One was a long-time cybersecurity blogger with multiple books to his name, another a hacker who spent jail time for his exploits before turning "white-hat," and a third was a high-profile hacker who was turned by the FBI but still spent jail time. In order to appear on Google Correlate, it would seem that the individuals would have to be recognized widely in mass media as well as social media. One of the screenshots shows a redacted version of this search for correlations over mass-scale search data and extended time (Figure 4).

The respective identities of the individuals are hidden per the reasons in the "delimitations" section earlier. While the author strove to keep identities secret, there may be sufficient information to engage in a light parlor game of guessing identities. Table 3 shows the various social media platform types on which each of the dozen individuals profiled had presences.

Table 2. Prerequisites for the selection of target individuals for the across-social media profiling

Requirements	Details	Main Rationales
1. A range of digital modalities (at least 5):	code, text, imagery, photos, figures, audio, video, and others	diversity of data modality types
2. Presences on > 5 social media and information platforms	employment sites; social networking and sharing sites (microblogging sites, social networking sites); information sharing sites (social news sharing sites, crowd-sourced encyclopedia sites, informal information sharing sites); social image sharing sites; social video sharing sites; social code sharing sites; academic publishing sites; academic research sharing sites; open education / training sites; crowd-based fund-raising sites	diversity of social media presences (across social media platforms)
3. A time measure of digital contents	several years: 0 to 4 years > 5 years > 10 years	years of information collection
4. Self-description and other-description	self-description other-description	points of view
5. Personal and professional representations and data	personal representation: hobbies, personality, family, friends, and others other representation: family representation of the target individual, friend representation of the target individual, colleague representation of the target individual, and others	multi-dimensional representations
6. Research background / innovations	research background innovations (including patented ones) contributions to the field	some earned level of claim to fame

Figure 3. Target Cybersecurity Professionals from the Career Phase Spectrum

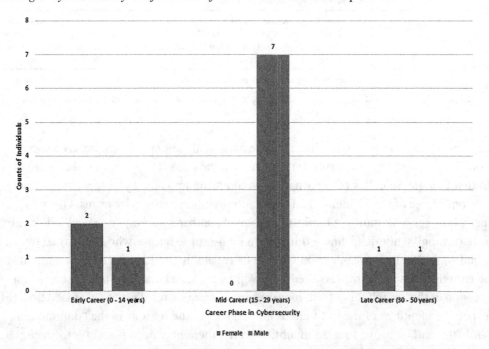

Figure 4. A cybersecurity guru's name and correlational Google searches month-to-month over extended time (2004 – 2017)

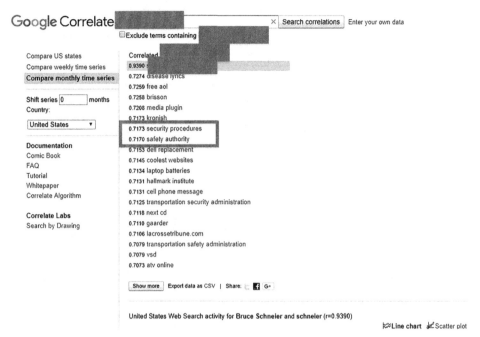

Figure 5 refers to theorized intended and unintended audiences for a cybersecurity calling card or profile. The concentric circles convey that a person's professional and online calling card may be distributed to a wide range of individuals in terms of the targeted audiences: self, family and friends, colleagues, employers and potential employers, clients and potential clients, professionals in the field, niche and mass media (and social media), and there are unintended audience members (including adversaries, malicious actors, and competitors). Depending on the objectives of the communicators (whether the target individual or those communicating about the target individual), varying concentric circles may be more important than others even if they are further away from the original center.

The way to understand this visual depiction is that a person communicates a calling card to himself or herself because ego and self-perception are important for self-efficacy. The social performance for family and friends is understandable because of the need for social value among those emotionally close to the individual. Then, there are professional audiences to whom a person may want to demonstrate expertise and personhood, for instrumental means (jobs, invitations to conferences, and others) and for professional affirmation. While unintended publics are listed outside of the circles, these adversaries can exist at any level of the circles.

Additionally, it may be difficult to understand first, second, and third order effects from the release of information (although some impacts may be assumed, albeit with varying levels of accuracy/inaccuracy). For example, an individual may communicate something about a difficult-to-identify "zero day" in a particular app used on a particular device. If the individual is highly credible, that may set off a spate of speculations; change the value of related company stocks; spark others' research in this area; result in some members of the general public in choosing to go with competitor apps or different competitor devices, and so on. There may be illogical and unintended effects, such as hackers trying to exploit the vulnerability before a patch is available, for example.

Table 3. Vetting potential targets by threshold presences on social media platform types

	1	2	3	4	5	6	7	8	9	10
	Employment Sites	Social Networking and Sharing Sites	Information Sharing Sites	Social Image Sharing Sites	Social Video Sharing Sites	Social Code Sharing Sites	Academic Publishing Sites	Academic Research Sharing Sites	Open Education / Training Sites	Crowd-Based Fund-Raising Sites
Early-Career (0 – 14)										
Target1	0	1	0	1	1	0	1	1	0	0
Target2	0	1 (but limited)	0	1	1	1 (mentions but not directly sharing code)	0	1 (cited by others)	0	0
Target12	0	1	0	1	1	1 (mention but not directly sharing code)	1 (cited by others)	0	0	0
Mid-Career (15 – 29)										
Target3	0	1	0	1	1	1 (for a software security course)	1	1 (cited by others)	1	0
Target4	0	(but private)	0	1	1 (including at Blackhat) and others	1 (cited by others)	1	1 (with co-authorship)	1	0
Target8	0	1	0	1	1	1 (related to his software company's code)	1	1 (cited by others)	1	0
Target7	0	1	0	1	1	1 (cited by others)	1	1 (as a research subject)	1	0
Target10	0	1	0	1	1	1 (cited by others using the platform)	1	1 (as part of a presentation)	1	0
Target9	0	1	0	1	1 (and keynotes)	1 (cited by others but not sharing direct code on platform)	1 (sometimes first author, sometimes back of the list)	1 (cited by others)	1	0
Late-Career (30 – 50)										
Target5	0	0	0	1	1 (even a TED talk)	1 (cited by others but not directly sharing code)	1	1 (a direct member with a high readership over 4,000 and 10,000 citations)	1	0
Target6	0	1	0	1	1	1 (encryption algorithm)	1	1 (cited by others)	1	0

Online calling cards are part of strategic signaling, and they are assumed to meet the needs of the target individual over time. Early in a career, these may show the job hunter's capabilities. Over time, postings by more established members may change up people's interests and directions in a field and attract newcomers.

Figure 5. Theorized target audiences for online "calling cards" in the cybersecurity job market: intended and unintended publics

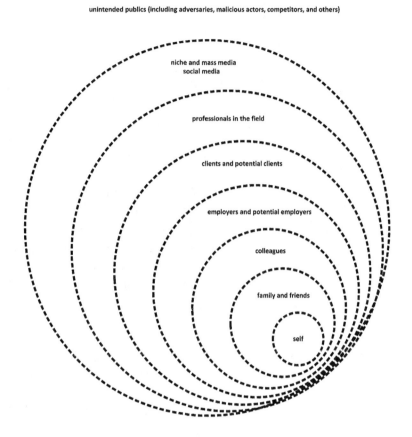

**Theorized Target Audiences for Online "Calling Cards" in the Cybersecurity Job Market:
Intended and Unintended Publics**

The profiles are not to be read as fully accurate portrayals but rather as both self-representations and other-representations of the individuals. The idea is that people generally do not have full cognitive controls at play, so they will be leaking data. People may have shared a CV or resume on a job-sharing site early in their careers, but maybe not used it again for years and forgot to delete the information. Or a mid-career individual may have participated in a professional conference that captured slideshows, video, and still images of an individual—as part of the conference. There are all sorts of data remaining online after various events and endeavors. Depending on the sourcing of the information, those who are viewing the calling cards can make some partially-informed inferences about the individual, his / her skills, and his / her personality—with varying levels of confidence. Sometimes, what people choose not to share, what they stay silent about, may be a "tell" as well, albeit a potentially quite ambiguous one.

A resulting dossier might include the target individual's name and demographics (e.g., age, nationality, gender, race / ethnicity, and others), their targeted skills (e.g., formal trainings, informal trainings, capabilities, research work and interests, and other areas of speciality), and personhood attributes (e.g., psychometrics from remote reads). There may also be a space for interesting details and leads for further research. Such details may not be necessarily net positives or net negatives, and these details may or may not be revelatory about how they may perform in a professional context. To be fair, biasing information may be hidden from hiring committees so as not to sway impressions. A blank dossier may look something like the following in Table 4.

Table 4. A sample resulting "dossier" table

Individual Name and Demographics	Targeted Skills	Personhood Attributes

Because online exploration through manual means is effortful, it may help to visualize a sequence of decisions in exploring cybersecurity calling cards, beginning with identification of a target individual and ending with a go or no-go decision about whether to reach out to the individual (in the context of a recruitment). Figure 6, a decision tree, addresses this sequence in more detail. Essentially, if a person's identity is verified to an actual person and the person shows some of the requisite skills and aligned personhood, the decision is to advance. If there are shortcomings in the skill set or red flags, those may be explored further, and if verified, the process stops.

Figure 6. Go or no-go in the mapping of cybersecurity calling cards online

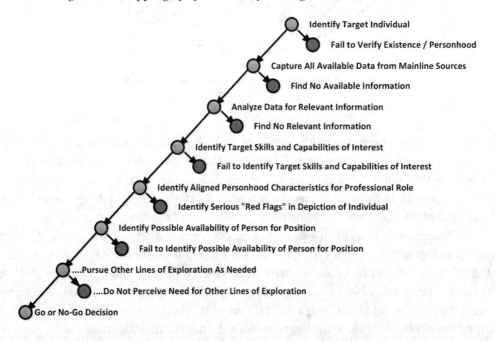

Go or No-Go in the Mapping of Cybersecurity Calling Cards Online

A CALLING: TARGET12

To convey a sense of how this might work, Target12's "calling card" will be shared here, but it will be partially masked. Target12 is a female cybersecurity professional who started out in penetration testing and has evolved into a leadership and supervisory capacity, in a Fortune 500 company. Her "calling card" draws from the following: social networking and sharing sites (2), social image sharing sites (4), social video sharing sites (5), social code sharing sites (6) albeit as a mention and not a sharer, and academic publishing sites (7) albeit as a citation, and not an author). A Google Search of her name in quotation marks brings out about 1,900 results.

On the bing web search engine (by Microsoft Corporation), it produces 2,800 results. Interestingly, images linked to her name show hundreds of people but only a few of those are the subject. Her story is a compelling one, aligning with a popular movie, *Girl with a Dragon Tattoo*. On a microblogging site, she shares a passion for a dangerous sport involving jumping off cliffs, and with only seconds to correct mistakes or risk-all. In a talk, she relates her interest in this sport with her high-risk work in cybersecurity. On her microblogging site, she has almost 2,000 microblogging messages and approximately 3,200 followers; she generously follows some 759 others. She engages a number of themes with her followers (Figure 7).

Figure 7. Autoextracted themes from Target12's tweetstream on Twitter

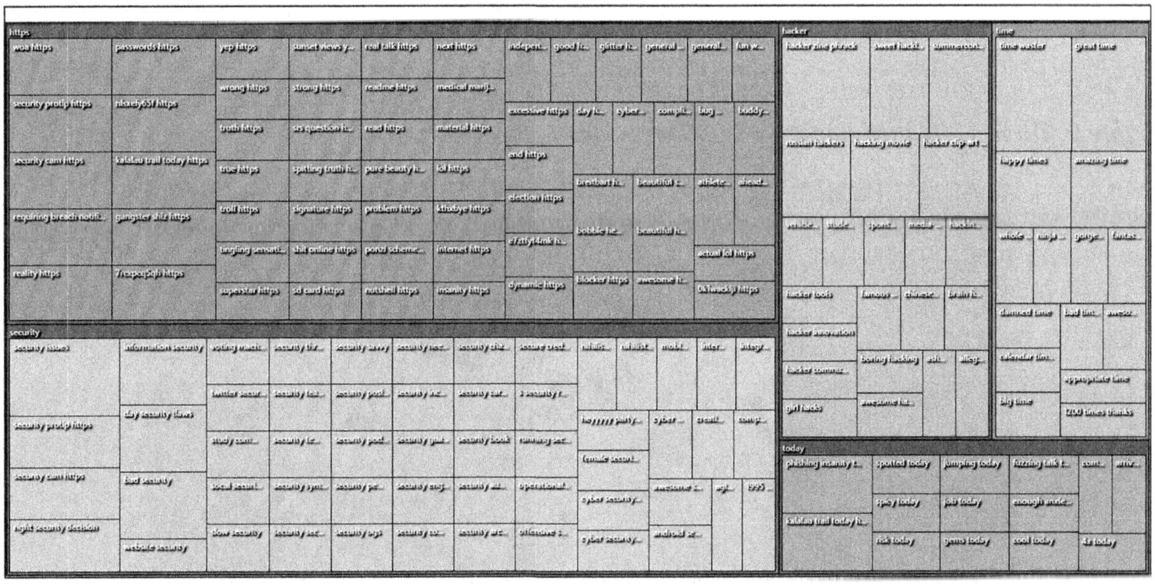

Her Tweetstreams engage particular individuals and do not seem to engage hashtag networks (Figure 8). For this word cloud, no words were put on the stopwords list.

The location of her social network is global, if the microblogging site is an indicator (Figure 9).

An automated sentiment analysis the messaging on her network shows the following: a balance between sentiment categories (Figure 10), which bucks the trend of the group statistics (See the Appendix.)

Figure 8. A word cloud from Target12's Tweetstream on Twitter

Figure 9. Target12 Twitter map from 1,750 messages

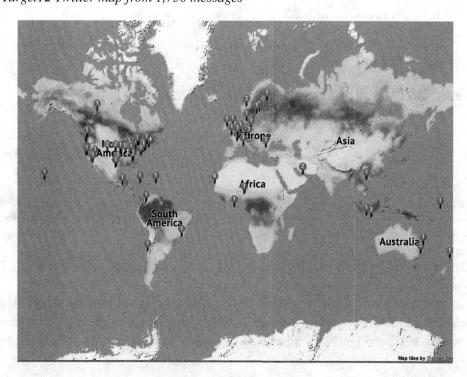

Figure 10. Sentiment analysis of Target12's microblogging site on Twitter

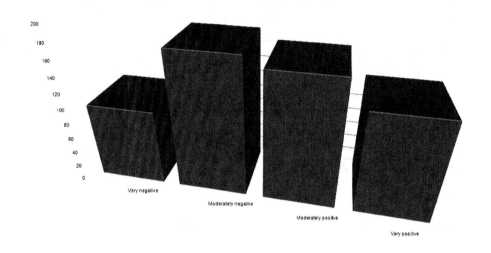

Figure 11. A followership sociogram of one target social media account on Twitter

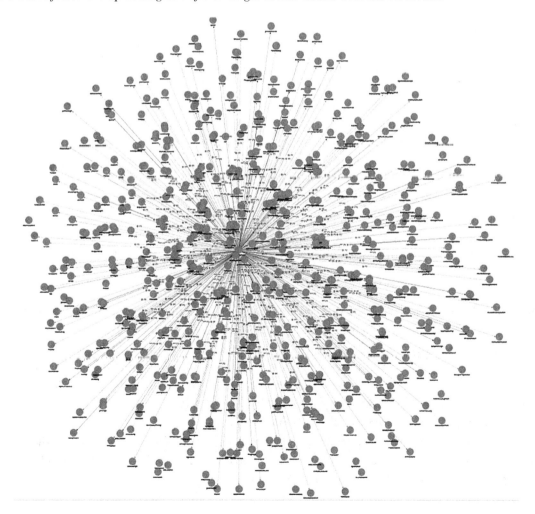

Target12's sociogram from the microblogging site shows the social accounts whom she follows, and if a person is known by the company he or she keeps (including online), this may be informative (Figure 11).

On the social code sharing site, she is cited but does not share code directly herself. Likewise, she is mentioned in academic publishing (such as via Google Scholar), but she does not seem to have published academic research herself, or to have co-authored research with others (yet). Her path seems to be more of a corporate one, with corporations often managing their own in-house publishing channels and discouraging publishing outside because of valid fears of loss of intellectual property.

She does not have a presence in open education, and there was also no sign of her in the crowd-based funding site analyzed. If a full dossier were to be worked up from her data, she might come onscreen as a person with serious technology and person skills, and a motivating personal story of trauma and over-coming. In her talks, she models a clear sense of ethics and laws affecting the field.

DISCUSSION

The main hypothesis explored were as follows:

Hypothesis 1: A way to simplify and summarize people's professional cybersecurity profiles is on two general dimensions: (1) target skills and (2) personhood attributes.

Hypothesis 2: People (individually and collectively) create cybersecurity "calling cards" on the Social Web that may be partially informative of their (1) target skills and (2) personhood attributes [related to cybersecurity work].

Hypothesis 2a: Various categories of social media offer different insights and levels of informativeness about the target individual.

Hypothesis 2b: Online cybersecurity "calling cards" inform approaches in cybersecurity talent-scouting, head-hunting and recruitment, professional transitioning, interview and test setups, and other work-based designs.

Hypothesis 3: There are (in)effective ways to design and communicate cybersecurity calling cards.

Hypothesis 3a: A calling card that is more aligned between "saying" and "doing" would be more convincing. (This refers to the difference between "cheap talk" and "costly signaling.")

Hypothesis 3b: A calling card focused on "social benefits" will be more effective than those based on commercial interests.

With regards to Hypothesis 1, the two dimensions of target skills and personhood attributes were fairly useful in offering a simplified parsimonious approach to defining, generally, two areas of focus for personnel in cybersecurity. The 2x2 axis shared is sufficiently broad to enable the inclusion of various types of relevant information. The second hypothesis was also borne out—that there are cybersecurity calling cards built over social media platforms. The different platform types do offer different types of information at the individual level.

Employment sites provide a sense of the skills that individual cybersecurity practitioners are interested in sharing. These seem to attract people who are just starting out in cybersecurity or are in their careers and wanting to transition. These do not seem to attract the top-caliber individuals in the field. In the gig or temp space, though, there are people from early, mid, and late career phases.

Social networking and sharing sites provide a sense of individuals' interests, their professional events, and how they engage others—such as on microblogging sites. In the culture of microblogging, those who participate had better have some real knowledge; otherwise, they will be called out and publicly shamed. On social networking sites, people who socialize appear (depending on how they use the sites).

In terms of information sharing, news sharing sites show what issues a person cares about particularly in terms of news appearing in mass media. Crowd-sourced encyclopedia sites offer more of an objective sense of people's achievements; those who create their own pages about themselves often have those pages removed by the crowd-sourced encyclopedia administrators and editors. Informal information sharing sites tend to be used as free classified ads, and these may be helpful for general job announcements, but these do not tend to have scope for individual profiles. In terms of social image sharing sites, it is possible to understand the interests of the cybersecurity professional as well as their social groups (around photographic interests). In terms of cybersecurity, the images often show people at conferences presenting from a slidedeck or standing behind computers demo-ing exploits.

Social video sharing sites can be highly informative of cybersecurity professionals, not only in how they instantiate physically, but in terms of areas of knowledge and skill specialty, and also sometimes about how they engage an audience (in interactive and non-interactive sessions). In addition, video sharing sites can shed light on individuals' hobbies and outside-interests. These may also be used in social ways to show the individual interacting with family and friends, and others. On video sharing sites, the presenters at public conferences do not have control over who is videotaping, usually, or how the videos will be framed and introduced.

Social code-sharing sites can shed light on the individual's development skills, their willingness to work on others' open-source projects, and their professional interests (assuming that the coding relates to the professional work of the individual). Academic publishing databases provide a sense of the academic and research chops of the target individual and how others regard them (from author and publication and article influence metrics, from publication reputations, from topics, and so on). Given that publications are peer reviewed, the work has to meet professional standards in the domain. A Google Scholar search can highlight author presence, and there are various verification protocols for author names, which are helpful if the individuals do not have unique disambiguated names.

In terms of academic research sharing sites, it is possible to ascertain how "friendly" a researcher is with colleagues and peers online, how closely they adhere to intellectual property rules, how revealing they are of ongoing projects, and so on. These seem to attract more of the junior cybersecurity professions who are actively wooing an audience and making a reputation.

In terms of open education and trainings available on the open web, it is possible to explore capabilities of the target individual because these show the person's teaching chops and something about their areas of specialty and how they approach their field.

Crowd-funding sites may be informative about what a target wants, how he or she conceptualizes the work, how he or she budgets, and so on—if they actually use such sites (and some do). While "technology" is not a common category on crowd-based fundraising sites, there are hundreds of results with "cybersecurity" as the search term in one popular site explored recently.

The cybersecurity information that may be found on the prior categories of social media platforms seems to be fairly limited. These are lagging indicators of innovations because there are no reasons to offer the finer details about innovations. If there are discovered vulnerabilities that require broad public attention, the information is about how to deal with the vulnerability (if a solution is available). People do not go online to leak competitive advantage.

Figure 12 provides an overview of the relative informational value from the respective social site types in terms of this research.

Figure 12. Relative informational value of respective social media platform types in cybersecurity profiling of individuals

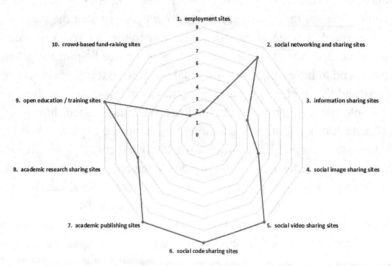

In terms of the media platform categories explored here, these were more informative of (1) target skills than (2) personhood attributes (Figure 13). This may be because of the type of information that this researcher extracted from the respective platforms, or it may be because of the nature of the topic domain that emphasizes informational value over performative egocentrism. This is not to say that eccentricity is not encouraged because there is a trope in cybersecurity that intellect and talent often manifest in part as unusual personality traits.

The third hypothesis suggests that some types of messaging in cybersecurity calling cards are more effective than others. Certainly, in reviewing a dozen samples of real-world calling cards, the individual's credibility was heightened with a closing of the say-do gap, where individual assertions were borne out by their colleagues, their publically available work output, their work histories, and other details. Also, the focus on social benefits in the sharing of cybersecurity information vs. commercial interests made the messaging more compelling.

Setting a Baseline

The same technologies may be used to set a baseline for understanding cybersecurity calling cards. Once created, a baseline can give a sense of where an individual lies along a "normal curve" in terms of how common their calling cards are as compared to others and whether they may be outliers. In some ways, the respective social media platform types may be more effective for group-level insights than individual level ones. For example, job sites may give a sense of what is available job-wise, but these sites do not enable access to curriculum vitae (CV) and resumes, unless one is a verified employer.

Figure 13. Relative informativeness of social media categories for (1) target skills and (2) personhood attributes

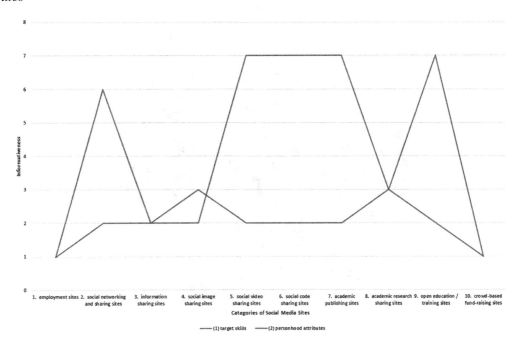

Additionally, the people who seem to post CVs and resumes on job sites are those who are just graduating, who just may have lost a job, and those in transition points in their lives. Also, crowd-funding sites show group-level patterns than insights about individuals (although in one recent skim of some 528 records on one well known site, one of the requestors was a named head of a cybersecurity company). A recent perusal showed a range of asks for moneys related to "cybersecurity" projects on a crowd funding site for the following: tuition costs, school travel, IT certifications, development of an ethical hacking cybersecurity online training, conference trips, planned class action lawsuits, and others. The range of values for the asks was from US$20 to "US$1.0 million."

Some asks included budgets, some as specific as chair mats for a home office. The projects proposed ranged from very new ones to ones that had been around for a number of years. Some of the projects had been removed even though the top-level title and related image were still findable in a search. In terms of the categories in which the cybersecurity projects were, they were in "Education," "Business," and "Other." There was not a direct category for "Technology," for example. These appeals, to generalize, focused on emotions as well as ideals. Some made identity appeals, with individuals showing photos of themselves and their families, along with biographical appeals as military veterans, as youth, as single parents. Some involved shared videos as well to humanize the individuals behind the request. Some included links to other websites.

Other asks seemed to promise a return on investment, with some back-of-the-napkin math and a paragraph-or-two length of business plans. Many of the requests conclude with a request that the reader forward their message to others, to try to spark a run of interest and financial support. The asks seemed difficult, with more than half of the observed requests earning less than US$0 towards their goals. To capture a sense of these financial requests, over 60 profiles were captured and 14,000 words, to create

Figure 14. Themes in cybersecurity-based asks for funding on a crowd-funding site

Figure 14, a word cloud of the requestor-written texts. Note the appeals for help in promoting a cybersecurity agenda by promoting efforts in study, training development, and entrepreneurship, among others.

A computational analysis of the extracted texts in Linguistic Inquiry and Word Count (LIWC, pronounced as "luke") to capture features of the writing show a few things. First, the writing tends to be fairly analytical, scoring at the 84th percentile, and this aligns with practices in the cybersecurity field. The Clout score is fairly high, indicating that the writers are making the crowd-funding ask sometimes from a position of confidence. The Authentic score is fairly low, indicating that the writing does not offer much in the way of actual personal sharing or revelation. Finally, the Tone is fairly high, showing a positive sentiment (anything over 50 is positive, in that score) as part of the sell.

Another way to thin-slice and analyze the cybersecurity profiles is to consider the following applied concepts:

1. The messenger is the message.
    a. How does the person "instantiate" online?
    b. What is communicated about values and point-of-view?
    c. What is communicated about the treatment of others? The positioning of the self in relation to others?
    d. What is the attitude communicated about relating with authority and The Man?
2. The message is the message.
    a. What do the various multimodal expressions communicate?
    b. What is the level of tech savvy in the communicating of the messages? The dependencies behind the message?
3. The documented actions (and capabilities) are the message.

      a.   What do digital left-behinds show about capability from reverse or backwards engineering?

      b.   What do the documented skills reveal (based on dependencies—for method and for technologies)?

4.   The social is the message.

      a.   Who does the target individual socialize with, and what are the reasons for those connections?

      b.   How long do relationships last?

      c.   What is the quality of the observed interrelationships?

Figure 15. Computational text analysis of crowd-funding appeals for cybersecurity projects

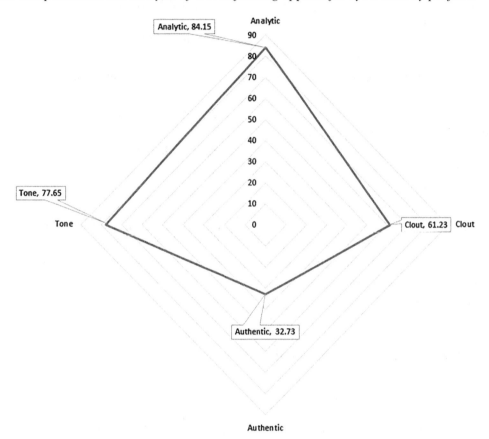

So while this scraped online information is maybe taken at the level of anecdotal, these are not without analytical value, even if not everything is run to ground.

Critical Thinking Questions

After the capture of the relevant data and their analysis, it is helpful to apply some questions.

- How well does the focal individual's targeted skills and personhood attributes align with the target role?

- ○ Does the target individual show indicators of talent in the domain and professional performance in the field?
- ○ Does the target individual show consistent and sustained performance and not just showy one-offs?
- ○ Does the target individual show growth potential in terms of demonstrating interest in the field and interest in growing in the field?
- ○ Does the target individual assess themselves accurately and with an openness for self-improvement?
- ○ If they do not align, are there other positions for which that profile might fit better?
- Does the target individual show self-awareness in their self-depictions? Why or why not?
- Does the target individual's "calling card" align with the verifiable facts? Or is there a say-do (talk-action, for-show/for-real, fronting/actual) gap?
- In a person's calling card, is there a typical signal:noise ratio, or is there more of the latter than the former? If so, why? (Are there signs of manipulations and deceptions? Ego-based fluffery?)
- Does the target individual's calling card align with (informed) others' senses of them? Where do these apparently align, and where do they not align?
  - ○ Is there "social proof" around the interpretation of the target individual? (Does a larger part of the population align around the target individual's self-image?)
  - ○ How does the target individual handle critics and detractors (the so-called "haters" on social media)? Do they engage (clash) substantively and constructively or not?
- What information is shared in the calling card, and what information is not shared? How may such "silences" be understood fairly and accurately?
- If there are professed individual and professional ethics, does the target individual have the strength of character and skill to live the ethics?
- Does the resulting dossier from the online "calling cards" give a sense of a complete and holistic person, or are there disparate elements? In totality, what do the calling cards communicate?

Handling Negative Counter-Messaging

For individuals who have a public-facing identity and persona, they have had to address the headwinds not only of self-portrayal in public spaces (while maintaining privacy and security). They have had to socially position and perform for targeted audiences, but also have much of the same data viewed by others whom they are not directly targeting. Those with online calling cards have to address adversaries and critics. For those professionally consuming cybersecurity online calling cards, how should they handle counter messaging about the individual?

Again, it is important to consider the following:

- How credible is the adversarial source(s)?
- What does the source want in making the assertions known?
- If there are multiple detractors, what are the sources asserting? Is there a common theme?
- Do these critiques exist over time? Or do these seem to be a one-off?
- Are the criticisms about one-off mistakes or continuing problems with character and personality?
- What does the evidence suggest about the validity or invalidity of the negative assertions?

- How does the target individual respond to detractors? Is there respect or professionalism in the messaging?

Testing the Validity of the "Cybersecurity Calling Card" Assessment

So how accurate are cybersecurity calling cards in terms of the hired individuals? There is not a direct way to test this unless the initial cybersecurity calling cards are included in the employee dossier…and then the individual's supervisory assessments, employment file, and other elements are studied over time, through the lifetime employment of the individual. This may be in the purview of the Human Resources / Personnel department.

Another way to assess this is to go backwards in time. An individual may have his / her personnel file assessed and a retroactive cybersecurity calling card recreated from the residua on the archived Internet and various social media platforms. A team may individually assess the cybersecurity calling cards, and those assessments may be compared against the actual individual's performance in the real. How productive were they? How creative? How pro-social and collaborative? What did they actually contribute to the field over their years of employment?

Technologies Used

Some of the sites used in this work include the following: Google Correlate, LinkedIn, Twitter, Facebook, Reddit, Wikipedia, Craigslist, Flickr, Google Images, YouTube, GitHub, ResearchGate, SlideShare, Coursera, Google Scholar, GoFundMe, and others. In terms of subscription-based academic databases, there were too many to list. Tools used to capture information include Flickr Downloadr, Picture Downloader Professional (on Chrome), NVivo 11 Plus's NCapture, Gadwin PrintScreen, and others.

Software used to analyze data included MS Excel, NVivo 11 Plus, Linguistic Inquiry and Word Count (LIWC), and Network Overview, Discovery and Exploration for Excel (NodeXL). The visualizations in this work were created using the data analytics software suites as well as MS Visio and Adobe Photoshop. The author has no formal tie to any of the makers of the listed technologies.

FUTURE RESEARCH DIRECTIONS

This work involved information shared as open-source intelligence (OSINT) in the clear and collecting these as "calling cards" in the cybersecurity domain. One way to extend this work is to bring into play other social media platform categories and more exemplars of sites within the existing ten categories offered here. For example, online and augmented in-world game spaces and applications ("apps"), virtual worlds, and other such spaces may be revelatory.

Based on this work, making inferences from people's communications can be inexact, tentative, and provisional. This is so even with the inclusion of big data analytics, close-in reads of small data, multimodal data analysis, and other approaches common in social media analysis. There may be more efficient ways to get to more informative "calling cards," such as by going past paywalls for individual information, engaging with the target through social media, or even making contact and requesting closed-source data from the target. The acceptable "range of motions" depend on the law, workplace policies, resources, and interests.

It would be helpful to create (in)validation methods for the assessment of such "calling cards." What exactly is revelatory, and what exactly is noise? What introduces accuracy / inaccuracy in such assessments, and to what degree? The author offered some ideas in the Discussion area, but there are other ways to approach this as well. The online professional "calling cards" approach may be transferable outside of cybersecurity. This can be another exploratory track.

CONCLUSION

This study showed that cybersecurity "calling cards" do exist on the Web and Internet, and they may be made somewhat coherent by collecting data across a range of social media platform types. These calling cards may be used to capture insights' of others (1) targeted skills and (2) personhood attributes, albeit more of the first than the latter. In terms of the intentionality behind the "calling cards," those did not seem too difficult to infer, although more work would be helpful in validating / invalidating those interpretations. (Common motivations seem to be as follows: public education, policy-making, promoting the field of cybersecurity, showing technical skills and exploits, and others.) One byproduct of this work is the observation that those working in cybersecurity would benefit from developing their skills at intercommunications, coalition-building, expressivity, and leadership—both in real-space and online, as part of their work.

As to whether there are effective or ineffective ways to design and communicate cybersecurity calling cards, that would depend on how the messages are received by those who would make use of the information, such as for recruitment, interviews, hiring, work assignments, retention, and other decisions. As noted earlier, control over what is communicated is important since widely available open-source information can be mis-used and applied adversarially as well. A dominated strategy in "calling card" development would be to give away advantage.

Finally, this work does not suggest that there are not many other ways to identify talent. As noted, this field already starts head-hunting among teenagers with national-level competitions and money incentives. In universities, professors with ties to particular corporations will funnel their talented students to apply for various internships, summer placements, and other opportunities; they will "head hunt" for the corporations. Massive open online course (MOOC) platforms enable head-hunters to have access to some of their best learners to pull from a global pool of potential talent.

Cybersecurity calling cards are just an additional facet to consider when scouting for highly skilled and intelligent individuals for important cybersecurity jobs. These calling cards do not replace any of the regular aspects of the employment process: the multiple interviews, the work demonstrations, the tests, the background checks, and so on; however, they do provide another surface to identify critical talent.

ACKNOWLEDGMENT

This is for R. Max.

REFERENCES

Ahlmeyer, M., & Chircu, A. M. (2016). Securing the Internet of Things: A review. *Issues in Information Systems*, *17*(IV), 21–28.

Appazov, A. (2014). Legal aspects of cybersecurity. *Justitsministeriet*. Retrieved on May 9, 2017, from: http://justitsministeriet.dk/sites/default/files/media/Arbejdsomraader/Forskning/Forskningspuljen/Legal_Aspects_of_Cybersecurity.pdf

Balaish, T. (2017, Aug. 21). Cyber Soldiers: White-hat hackers. *CBSN*. Retrieved on December 22, 2017, from: https://www.cbsnews.com/news/cyber-soldiers-cbsn-on-assignment/

Bashir, M., Wee, C., Memon, N., & Guo, B. (2017). Profiling cybersecurity competition participants: Self-efficacy, decision-making and interests predict effectiveness of competitions as a recruitment tool. *Computers & Security*, *65*, 153–165. doi:10.1016/j.cose.2016.10.007

Bell, S., Sayre, E., & Vasserman, E. (2014). *A longitudinal study of students in an introductory cybersecurity course. Proceedings of the 121*st *ASEE Annual Conference & Exposition*.

Beuran, R., Chinen, K., Tan, Y., & Shinoda, Y. (2016, Oct. 14). *Towards effective cybersecurity education and training*. Technical report. Japan Advanced Institute of Science and Technology (JAIST). Retrieved on November 11, 2017, from: https://www.jaist.ac.jp/~razvan/publications/effective_cybersecurity.pdf

Campbell, S. G., O'Rourke, P., & Bunting, M. F. (2015). Identifying dimensions of cyber aptitude: The design of the cyber aptitude and talent assessment. *Proceedings of the Human Factors and Ergonomics Society 59*th *Annual Meeting*, 721 – 725.

Chen, T. R., Shore, D. B., Zaccaro, S. J., Dalal, R. S., Tetrick, L. E., & Gorab, A. K. (2014). An organizational psychology perspective to examining computer security incident response teams. *IEEE Security and Privacy*, *12*(5), 61–67. doi:10.1109/MSP.2014.85

Cunha, S., Winders, W., Rowe, D. C., & Cornel, C. (2016). The untrustables: How underclassmen evolved our approach to student red-teaming. *Proceedings of the 17*th *Annual Conference on Information Technology Education*, 26 – 30.

Cybersecurity Workforce Framework, N. I. C. E. (2017, Oct. 19). National Initiative for Cybersecurity Education (NICE) of NIST (National Institute of Standards and Technology), U.S. Department of Commerce. Retrieved on December 2, 2017, from: https://www.nist.gov/itl/applied-cybersecurity/nice/resources/nice-cybersecurity-workforce-framework

Fraley, J. B., & Cannady, J. (2017). *The promise of machine learning in cybersecurity*. IEEE. doi:10,1109/SECON.2017.7925283

Hoffman, L. J., Burley, D. L., & Toregas, C. (2012). Holistically building the cybersecurity workforce. *IEEE Security and Privacy*, *10*(2), 33–39. doi:10.1109/MSP.2011.181

Koermer, K. A. (2014). Anne Arundel Community College: At the Epicenter of Cybersecurity. In A. M. Kress & G. E. de los Santos (Eds.), *The Role of Community Colleges in Regional Economic Prosperity* (pp. 2–5). League for Innovation in the Community College.

Le Carré, J. (1974). Tinker Tailor Soldier Spy. New York: Penguin Books.

Maller, T. (2013, Oct. 3.) *Enhancing the cyber diplomacy arsenal. Blogs of War.* Working Paper presented at China-U.S. Cooperation & Disagreement Management with a Vision of a New Type of Relations, by the China Institute of International Studies. Retrieved on June 2, 2017, from: https://blogsofwar.com/tara-maller-enhancing-the-cyberdiplomacy-arsenal/

Moore, K. (2017, Jan. 3). Artificial intelligence to the rescue: The race against cyber crime is lost without AI. *Spark Cognition.* Retrieved on September 11, 2017, from: https://sparkcognition.com/2017/01/race-cyber-crime-lost-without-ai/

Morgan, S. (2016, Jan. 2). One million cybersecurity job openings in 2016. *Forbes.*

Nissen, M. E., & Tick, S. L. (2017). Four key steps to retaining talent in the information warfare community. *CHIPS: The Department of the Navy's Information Technology Magazine.* Retrieved on August 19, 2017, from: http://hdl.handle.net/10945/55716

Nugent, P. D., & Collar, E. (2015, April). Where is the cybersecurity hero? Practical recommendations for making cybersecurity heroism more visible in organizations. *International Journal of Computer Science and Information Security, 13*(4), 1–5.

Parker, S. K., Winslow, C. J., & Tetrick, L. E. (2016). Designing meaningful, healthy, and high performing work in cybersecurity. In S. Zaccaro, L. Tetrick, & R. Dahl (Eds.), The Psychosocial Dynamics of Cyber Security. New York: Taylor & Francis/Routledge.

Professionalizing the nation's cybersecurity workforce: Criteria for decision-making. (2013). The National Academies Press. Retrieved on October 7, 2017, from: https://www.nap.edu/catalog/18446/professionalizing-the-nations-cybersecurity-workforce-criteria-for-decision-making

Rayome, A.D. (2017, July 17). The *3 most in-demand cybersecurity jobs of 2017.* TechRepublic.

Rose, S. (2012, Sept. 20). NSC 2012 Shyama Rose 2. *YouTube.* Retrieved on August 4, 2017, from: https://www.youtube.com/watch?v=vtKmbN0SaRg&ab_channel=ArniMarHardarson

Saner, L.D.S., & Bunting, M.F. (2015). *Cyber Aptitude and Talent Assessment. Slideshow.* Academic Press.

Saxenian, A. (1996). Regional Advantage: Culture and Competition in Silicon Valley and Route 128. Cambridge, MA: Harvard University Press.

Schirf, E., & Serapiglia, A. (2016). Identifying the real technology skills gap: A qualitative look across disciplines. In *Proceedings of the EDSIG Conference.* Las Vegas, NV: Systems & Computing Academic Professionals (ISCAP).

Shumba, R., Ferguson-Boucher, K., Sweedyk, E., Taylor, C., Franklin, G., Turner, C., . . . Hall, L. (2013). Cybersecurity, women and minorities: Findings and recommendations from a preliminary investigation. *Proceedings of the ITiCSE working group reports conference on innovation and technology in computer science education—working group reports.*

Stumbaugh, K. (2016, May). *The social startup game: Creating an educational cybersecurity game and collecting empirical data* (Unpublished honor's thesis). Ball State University, Muncie, IN.

Tobey, D. H. (2015). A vignette-based method for improving cybersecurity talent management through cyber defense competition design. *Proceedings of the SIGMIS-CPR'* 15, 31–39. 10.1145/2751957.2751963

Vogel, R. (2016). Closing the cybersecurity skills gap. *Salus Journal, 4*(2), 32–46.

Wee, C., Bashir, M., & Memon, N. (2016). The cybersecurity competition experience: Perceptions from cybersecurity workers. *SOUPS 2016: Twelfth Symposium on Usable Privacy and Security*. Retrieved on May 21, 2017, from: https://www.usenix.org/system/files/conference/soups2016/wsiw16_paper_wee.pdf

What is cybersecurity? A definition of cybersecurity. (n.d.) *Cyberpedia*. Palo Alto Networks. Retrieved on January 21, 2018, from: https://www.paloaltonetworks.com/cyberpedia/what-is-cyber-security

Wilson, A., & Ali, A. (2011). The biggest threat to the U.S. digital infrastructure: The cyber security workforce supply chain. *Proceedings of the Academy for Studies in Business, 3*(2), 15 – 20.

Wright, M.A. (2015, Oct.). Improving cybersecurity workforce capacity and capability: Addressing the education-to-workforce disparity. *ISSA Journal*, 14 – 20.

KEY TERMS AND DEFINITIONS

Academic Publishing Sites: Sites on which recognized and respected publishers share peer-reviewed academic research by professional researchers.

Academic Research Sharing Sites: Sites that enable people to create persistent accounts through which they may share copyright-released works, identify co-authors, and connect with other researchers (in order to increase their readership).

Autocode: Using computers to label or "code" information (in this case, textual).

Calling Card: A business card, a unique and individual signature of a person based on how he or she acts or performs in a context.

Crowd-Based Fundraising Sites: Websites set up to enable people to request funds for particular endeavors and for the broad public to decide whether or not to fund the endeavor and to comment (the site may act in an escrow capacity as well).

Cybersecurity: The protection of digital information and related technologies against misuse, unauthorized access, or any form of compromise.

Deep Web: A term that refers to database information hosted on the web and dynamically generated; this database information is not directly found by traditional search engines traversing http-based web pages but which are inter-actable through other methods and portals. (This is not to be confused with the Dark Web, a term which describes online spaces accessible through anonymized access where people may engage various black markets and illicit goods and services.)

Employment Sites: Sites that bring together potential employers with potential employees.

Information Sharing Sites: Sites designed for people to interact around information—its creation, its commenting (such as around news), its sharing, and other aims (including commerce, relating, house-hunting, and other aims).

Microblogging Site: An application enabling the sharing of short text messages, imagery, and short video snippets.

Online Calling Card: A professional profile left online by an individual and his/her associates to convey relevant skills and personhood.

Open Educational/Training Sites: A general category of sites that enable open learning such as massive open online course (MOOC) sites, digital learning object repositories, digital learning object referatories, and other site types.

Social Code Sharing Site: Sites that enable people to share various types of computer code and to share projects on which others may collaborate.

Social Image Sharing Sites: Sites that enable the sharing of image sets and the creation of distributed groups with shared interests.

Social Sharing Sites: A category of sites that enable people to create persistent identities from which they may interact to targeted populations and broadly, with both private and public channels; these sites include microblogging and social networking sites and others.

Social Video Sharing Sites: Sites that enable people to share self-created videos with others (through both private and public channels).

This research was previously published in Global Cyber Security Labor Shortage and International Business Risk; pages 149-186, copyright year 2019 by Business Science Reference (an imprint of IGI Global).

APPENDIX

The same profiling approach can be applied to small groups and to an entire domain (assuming one has the resources and the time to achieve this.) Nine of the 12 individuals identified for this work had accounts on Twitter. The @ ("at" symbol) refers to social accounts with whom the focal individuals interacted, and the #hashtags ("pound sign" or "hashtag") refer to campaigns and labeled themes in the messaging. In Figure 16, the "http" and "https" were added to stopwords list. Based on a Tweet set including retweets from all nine members, the resulting word cloud may be seen at Figure 16.

Figure 16. @Accounts and #Hashtag campaigns from Tweetstreams of combined cybersecurity professionals' accounts on Twitter

A group sentiment analysis may be seen in Figure 17. Sentiments tend to trend towards the moderately negative in terms of cybersecurity messaging among these individuals.

Autocoded group discussion topics may be seen in Figure 18.

In Figure 19, the main topics of discussion are listed in descending order in a Pareto chart. Note that the topics are one-grams generally.

It is possible to explore the text messages by URL. It is also possible to generate interactive word trees to listen in on the specific messages being shared around particular topics (Figure 20).

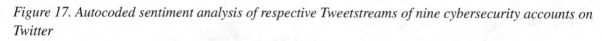

Figure 17. Autocoded sentiment analysis of respective Tweetstreams of nine cybersecurity accounts on Twitter

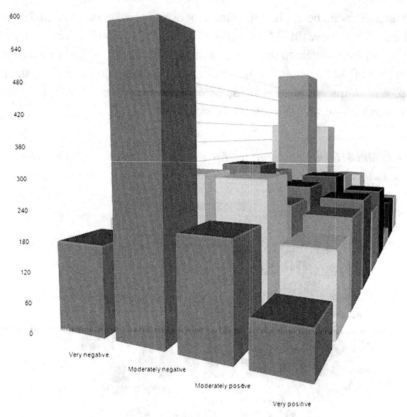

Figure 18. Autocoded themes from one cybersecurity expert's Tweetstream on Twitter

Figure 19. Descending list of auto-extracted topics from one Tweetstream of a targeted cybersecurity individual

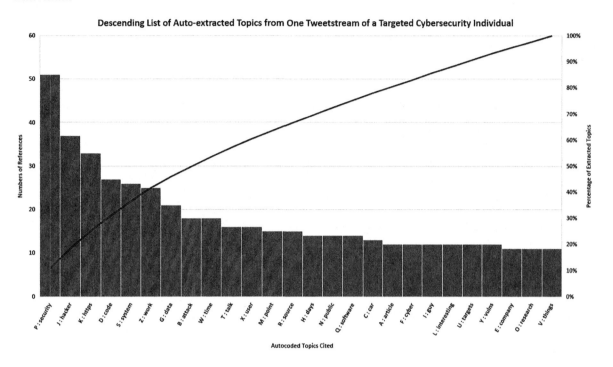

Figure 20. A comprehensive word tree of "stuxnet"

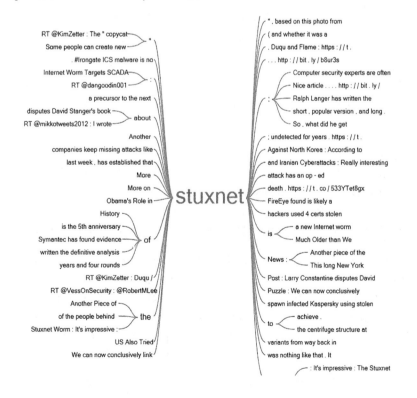

Four maps of the respective networks of four of the social accounts are drawn here, and all have global constituencies in their networks (Figure 21). There are many Twitter accounts that are merely regional, with networks clustered in one city or state, for example, in which case the maps would be zoomed in ones to particular geographical locales. For the owners of these accounts, there are announced or declared home locales for the accounts.

Figure 21. Geographical maps of Twitter followers for four targets from three nationalities

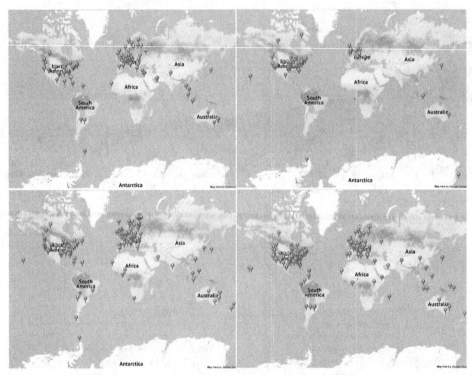

Geographical Maps of Twitter Followers for Four Targets from Three Nationalities

The Tweet locales may also be shared if the person sharing the message agrees to allow the app to capture and share the location as latitude and longitude data. [Part of profiling may involve geographical locations. For example, innovations in an industry are partially predicted by the locational context, which enables people from disparate fields to interact and learn from each other (Saxenian, 1994, 1996). In other cases, the locale may be misleading and uninformative by offering noise instead of signal.]

Another way to understand cybersecurity professionals is how they engage around a particular topic, such as on microblogging sites. Based on textual similarity in messaging, small clusters of communicators may be computationally extracted. In Figures 22 and 23, #cybersecurity hashtag networks were identified from Twitter, and the results may be seen in the first figure as a ring lattice graph and the same data as a 3D cluster diagram in the latter. (In the latter, both the proximity of the respective social nodes and the sizes of the nodes are relevant because the size represents the node's in-degree and out-degree, or amount of information exchange and connectivity with other nodes.)

Figure 22. #cybersecurity hashtag network on Twitter and who is talking with whom (in a ring lattice graph)

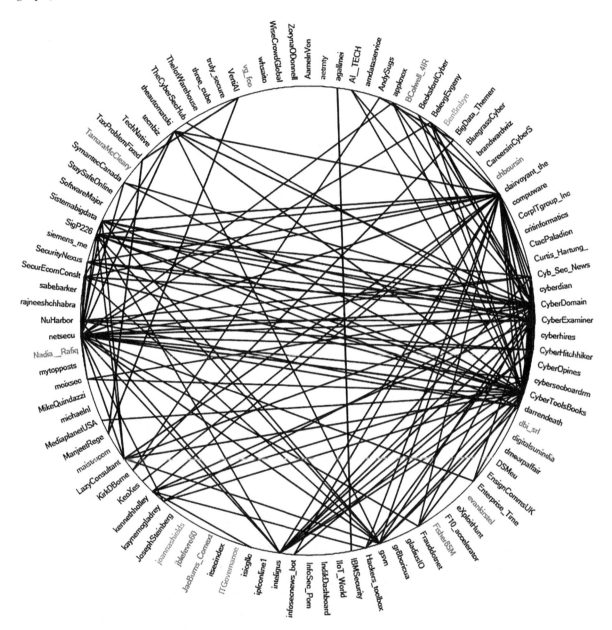

A #cybersec hashtag network was extracted using a different tool, and from this, related groups and clusters of conversationalists were extracted using network analysis (Figure 24). Motifs, small patterned clusters, may also be extracted. The clusters were extracted with the Clauset-Newman-Moore algorithm, and 196 groups were extracted. The graph in Figure 24 is laid out using the "packed rectangles" layout and the Harel-Koren Fast Multiscale layout algorithm for clusters. One inference in network analysis stems from the adage that a person may be known by the company he or she keeps.

Figure 23. #cybersecurity hashtag network on Twitter and who is talking with whom (in a 3d cluster diagram)

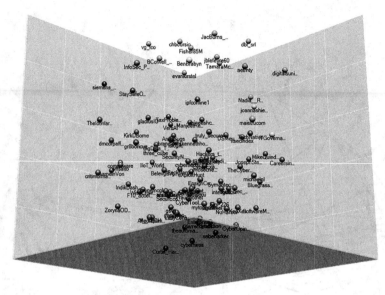

Figure 24. #cybersecurity hashtag network on Twitter and groups

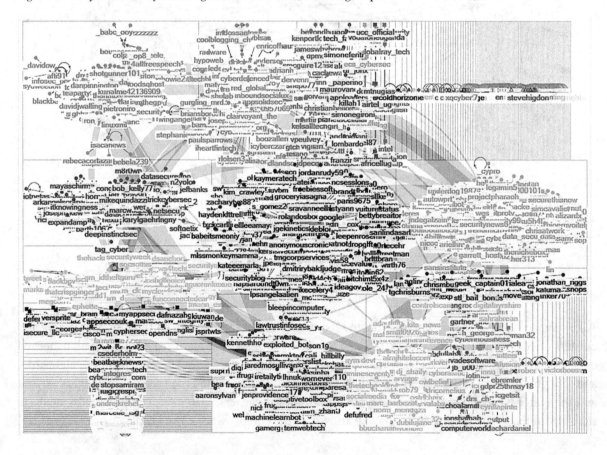

The graph metrics table related to Figure 24 follows. This shows that a network with 1,353 vertices (social accounts) was identified discussing #cybersec, and there were 1,663 unique edges (relationships based on replying). The largest cluster has 177 social accounts, and the largest ego network has 102 social accounts. The diameter of this #hashtag network is 10, which means the longest distance between any two most-distant nodes is 10 hops. The average geodesic distance is 4 hops.

Table 5. #cybersec hashtag network on Twitter

Graph Metric	**Value**
Graph Type	Directed
Vertices	1353
Unique Edges	1663
Edges With Duplicates	2432
Total Edges	4095
Self-Loops	1491
Reciprocated Vertex Pair Ratio	0.007874016
Reciprocated Edge Ratio	0.015625
Connected Components	177
Single-Vertex Connected Components	102
Maximum Vertices in a Connected Component	1016
Maximum Edges in a Connected Component	3658
Maximum Geodesic Distance (Diameter)	10
Average Geodesic Distance	4.151887
Graph Density	0.000979633
Modularity	Not Applicable
NodeXL Version	1.0.1.336

Chapter 9
Opinions of the Software and Supply Chain Assurance Forum on Education, Training, and Certifications

Beatrix Boyens
Adaptive Management Concepts, USA

ABSTRACT

This article provides an overview of discussions held at the Software and Supply Chain Assurance (SSCA) forum held May 1-2, 2018, in McLean, Virginia. The two-day event focused on education and training for software assurance (SwA) and Cyber-Supply Chain Risk Management (C-SCRM). Attendees discussed questions such as "What are some challenges facing industry, academia, and government organizations in this area?" "Who needs education or training?" "What needs to be taught?" and "What strategies do or do not work?" Discussions related to the current environment, hiring and retaining qualified employees, defining roles and responsibilities, and the knowledge, skills, and abilities (KSAs) that are most in-demand.

1. INTRODUCTION

On May 1-2, 2018, 118 persons representing industry (64), government (45), and academia (12)[1]gathered in McLean, Virginia, to discuss education, training, and certifications for software assurance (SwA) and Cyber-Supply Chain Risk Management (C-SCRM). Because the events are held under Chatham House rule (Chatham House, N.D.), no attributions are made in this paper.

The event was part of a regular series titled the Software and Supply Chain Assurance (SSCA) Forums, held 2-3 times/year, as a venue for participants from around the world to learn about and discuss software and supply chain risks, mitigation strategies, tools, and any gaps related to the people, processes, or technologies involved. These forums are co-led by the U.S. National Institute of Standards and Technology (NIST), the Department of Homeland Security (DHS), the Department of Defense (DoD),

DOI: 10.4018/978-1-6684-3554-0.ch009

and the Government Services Agency (GSA). The Software Engineering Institute based in Pittsburgh, Pennsylvania, helped co-lead the May 2018 event.

The goal of the event was to identify what knowledge, skills, and abilities (KSAs) should be taught in formal education and training programs and relevant opportunities or roadblocks. This paper contains an overview of the event to provide information useful for the design or use of education, training, or certifications, as well as to provide insight into the opinions of SwA and C-SCRM experts. Portions of the event which did not directly tie into education and training, while valuable, are out of scope of this paper. This paper is intended to provide an overview of the discussions from the forum; any opinions, recommendations, or suggestions included in this paper are based on attendees' comments and do not necessarily reflect the opinions of the authors or the sponsoring organizations.

2. BACKGROUND

The Online Trust Alliance (2018) found that the number of cybersecurity incidents doubled from 82,000 in 2016 to nearly 160,000 in 2017. Many of these incidents highlighted risks associated with software and/or supply chain management. High-profile incidents have helped highlight the importance of software assurance (SwA) and cyber-supply chain risk management (C-SCRM).

For this paper, C-SCRM is loosely defined as a discipline located at the intersection of supply chain management and cybersecurity. It covers the entire life cycle of information or operations technology (IT/OT) and often overlaps or includes disciplines like third-party risk management, logistics, and quality control. SwA is a closely related, more focused, and mature discipline concentrated on ensuring a level of confidence that software is free from vulnerabilities. Cybersecurity generally denotes the protection of technologies and processes related to the creation, transmission, modification, analysis, and control of data or information. For the purposes of this paper, the term cybersecurity is inclusive of C-SCRM and SwA.

Along with the steady increase of cybersecurity-related incidents, there has been steady growth in the reported cybersecurity skills gap. In 2015, it was estimated that there would be a global shortage of 1.5 million workers by 2020; in 2017, the shortage estimate increased to 1.8 million by 2022 (Frost & Sullivan, 2017, p. 3). Specializations such as SwA and C-SCRM have an even greater shortage. A study by Burning Glass Technologies (2015) found that cybersecurity-related job postings increased 91 percent from 2010 to 2014 (p.3) and that hybrid jobs (such as cyber-supply chain risk management) took roughly 17 percent longer to fill than other cybersecurity job openings (p. 11). The main reasons for the shortage were reported as qualified personnel were difficult to find and job requirements were not understood by leadership (Frost & Sullivan, 2017, p. 4).

3. WHY THERE IS A SWA/C-SCRM PROBLEM

More than one attendee commented that software has evolved significantly since the 1960s. According to one participant, the Orange Book, one of the first cybersecurity guidelines, never looked at software. Software was viewed as simple logic that was added on to hardware. Today, software is ubiquitous. As a result, society is moving from an area of information-only risk to more severe impacts, including direct physical harm to people.

Similarly, supply chain threats that used to be considered a fringe risk, now represent a core problem for many organizations. The use of counterfeits, poor-quality code, the intentional or unintentional insertion of malware, and a lack of cybersecurity in service vendors are some examples of supply chain risks that have become commonplace. Organizations regularly use outsourced software, hardware, and services, and consumers do not consider the impact of outsourcing decisions.

Language barriers were a recurring theme throughout the event. The use of different terminologies can create artificial divides. For example, Information and Communication Technology (ICT) and Industrial Control Systems (ICS) rely on the same or very similar technology. However, according to one attendee, because some groups use the term ICT, and others use the term ICS, they do not talk to each other. To address this kind of communication challenge, a common lexicon and common definitions of IT and cybersecurity-related terms are needed to enable more effective conversations about education and training.

The human aspect of cybersecurity, meaning users and decision makers, was acknowledged to be a challenge. An analysis of aviation incidents was described which concluded that over 70 percent of incidents were attributable to human factors such as poor judgement and diverted attention (Bureau of Air Safety Investigation, 1996). It was suggested that, if a similar analysis was done for cybersecurity, the percentage would be at least the same, if not greater.

Attendees also noted a general culture of reactivity, lack of collaboration, and prejudice as a significant barrier. Some stated that cybersecurity is often viewed as tedious; a few attendees stated that people simply do not care. The increase in cybersecurity incidents was attributed at least in part to a lack of interest from senior executives, middle-level managers, and information technology (IT) professionals, and by extension, students and teachers.

Attendees expressed concern that many people do not view SwA or C-SCRM as part of IT, cybersecurity, or business. An analogy was given of the medical field, where it took hundreds of years to learn that washing hands would help prevent death – they only fully realized this when they washed their hands between every patient. It was noted that modern society is still in the early stages of a cultural shift towards improved security, but there is no concerted effort and only a "tiny proportion" of people are being reached through education and training efforts.

The discussion touched on behavioral economics: i.e., how to incentivize people to do what is necessary to be more secure. One attendee stated that there is always going to be "a problem [in SwA and C-SCRM] until there is a way to give somebody credit for doing cyber well." After a lively discussion regarding the role of legislation and the power of market forces, attendees agreed that any incentive strategy must both reward good behavior and penalize bad outcomes. It should focus on incentivizing organizations to be more secure, which will lead them to hire and heed the advice of skilled employees, which in turn will incentivize education and training institutions to produce knowledgeable students.

There was some disagreement with this notion of incentivizing organizations. Does the projected shortage of people able to fill open SwA and C-SCRM positions indicate that organizations are already incentivized? Attendees concluded that it appears there is a disconnect between what organizations want, what they actually need, and what education and training institutions provide.

4. RECRUITING AND RETAINING

One area of concern with broad implications was the difficulty of education, government, and industry institutions in recruiting and retaining students or employees. Some attendees argued that many organizations do not effectively make use of the individuals that could be trained, either when recruiting or with existing employees. Challenges were grouped into three main categories: unfounded cultural assumptions, a lack of appropriate environment, and misuse of requirements.

4.1. Cultural Assumptions

Attendees lamented that organizations often stereotype people with SwA skills, assuming they are all "socially inept, cyber-punk teenagers with a love of sugary drinks." This is not necessarily true and has discounted many qualified candidates. Attendees indicated that the lack of interest by organizations for retraining / reskilling their employees to have cybersecurity skills is one example of bias that impacts the ability of an organization to have the workforce it needs. In order to avoid meritocracy or institutional bias, organizations – educational, industry, or government - must explicitly make a concerted effort to attract and retain people who are different in how they think and their backgrounds, promoting diversity in skills. Attendees expressed desire for a framework that enables this goal.

4.2. Environment

Providing an appropriate workplace environment was viewed as a critical factor in retaining people with cybersecurity skill sets, both for employment and in education/training. Many organizations use negative enforcement (e.g., employee clawbacks), but many believed that promoting the value proposition is more effective. Although money is a consideration, many cybersecurity professionals value experience, the mission of an organization, or job perks that can offset a low salary. Students often value these same perks and, anecdotally, will be more likely to value a similarly structured educational environment. Although it is important to note the previous comment about not type-casting or making assumptions about what students or employees want or need, some of the perks that can be attractive to employees and students include:

- The ability to work independently or with self-organized teams as the situation demands;
- The opportunity to work with and learn from highly respected individuals;
- Self-selected training opportunities;
- A culture of acceptance and belonging;
- State-of-the-art equipment;
- Toys (such as drones, different types of computers, etc.) that they can dissect;
- A space where they can experiment and collaborate (akin to a garage);
- A security net that allows the ability to "play" and potentially fail;
- Rewards in the form of money, toys, goods ("swag"), or an opportunity;
- Being around people with similar (non-cybersecurity-related) interests and hobbies;
- Short-duration tasks;
- Competition.

Attendees repeatedly highlighted that students want to learn real-world skills with hands-on, active learning. Training should be actionable, reasonable, and effective. Because soft skills are in great demand, attendees noted that educational institutions can train or reinforce such skills in the classrooms using collaborative environments or tangential groups with a mixture of skill sets. Team processes should allow individuals to track their individual work and how it is included into the delivery of a product.

4.3. Education and Certification Requirements

One of the challenges noted that had broad consensus was that employer requirements when describing vacancies or positions are inconsistent, unfounded, and unreasonable. For example, employers often misunderstand and misuse certification and education requirements. Job descriptions for entry-level positions show that there are many employers looking for somebody to perform entry-level work, but the education and certification requirements do not match an entry-level person; somebody with all the requirements of the job posting would not accept entry-level pay. This led to a discussion on the role of certifications and educational degrees.

In most cases, certifications and degrees do not guarantee that a candidate can perform cybersecurity tasks desired by an organization. Attendees highlighted how organizations must require that candidates demonstrate their skills instead of trusting the implications of a resume or any certificate they may have. Unfortunately, in the jobs market, there are many employers who default to relying on education and certificates as requirements to be considered for a job. Many organizations copy what others require instead of determining their own needs, or they rely on the same position descriptions multiple times. These methods add to the challenges to fill openings when the number of certificate holders is less than the number of vacancies listed. This is further exasperated by the fact that many of the certificate holders already have jobs and are not seeking to fill vacant positions.

Attendees stated that it is important for hiring organizations to focus more on the KSAs needed to perform the tasks to be completed and not to rely solely on education and certification requirements. Education and certification providers need to better align their offerings with the competencies needed by organizations, and better communicate to employers that their students can join the workforce with competencies that allow them to perform cybersecurity work. Two resources were mentioned to enable this kind of approach: The National Initiative for Cybersecurity Education [NICE] Workforce Framework (2017) and work by Hayden (2017).

5. THE ROLE OF EDUCATION AND TRAINING

It is quite possible to purchase a computer and learn how to program or modify a network without any formal cybersecurity education or training. In fact, attendees stated that the trend is towards allowing anyone to develop or use software technologies. One participant told a story about reviewing code written by students with no formal, but a lot of informal, training. The code was functional but did not pass any security tests. The attendees' conclusion was that coding securely does not come naturally. Computer science education and training should be directed towards improving the quality of products being developed, bought, and used.

To this end, attendees agreed that there is no single education or training solution. Education generally focuses on theory and can build a foundation for future advancements; training helps apply that theory into practice. Formal education is useful for the long term, but not for the short term. Training programs allow workers to move into or increase their role in the cyber field in the short term. According to a study by Stack Overflow (2018), colleges and universities can reach 63 percent of the software engineering community. It was unclear how many people training efforts could reach, but attendees generally agreed that the potential of both education and training programs was not being reached.

5.1. Challenges

It was mentioned that relatively few institutions teach SwA. It appeared that attendees collectively felt that SwA would not be taught until students demanded it be taught, and that students wouldn't demand it until hiring organizations required it. However, there is not a broad recognition of the need for SwA, so the demand signal is not strong. Even if there was "the greatest course around," students would not attend.

Participants suggested that building a quality curriculum and presenting the value of that curriculum to employers is one way to attract student demand. Distance learning, it was mentioned, especially struggles with motivating students, but one representative found that quality was less of a motivator than availability. Many organizations have agreements with schools and training institutions, and one person mentioned that when organizations sponsor a seat in a course, the students become very motivated.

One question posed to the attendees was, "Where are [education and training institutes] getting [their] SwA expertise?" Attendees lamented that many educational institutes do not have faculty capable of effectively teaching SwA / C-SCRM. It was unclear whether training organizations face similar challenges, but many universities rely on adjuncts. Adjuncts are usually retirees whose knowledge may be out of date, or industry/government employees who do not have a lot of time to devote to effective teaching. Unfortunately, adjuncts are often paid very little, with few to no benefits, which makes attracting quality instructors very difficult.

There are not enough instructors who understand security. Those who teach programming often don't understand safe coding practices. It was indicated that a part of the problem is academia typically does not like change. They do not change curricula easily or quickly. Tenured faculty often do not want to update their courses and may be uncomfortable with teaching security. A similar challenge can be seen with training organizations that rely on a broad consensus for curriculum development, changes to that curriculum are slow.

5.2. Curricula Design

Effectiveness of education and training programs is inseparably linked to curricula design. During the event, three main qualities surfaced that anecdotally make SwA/C-SCRM-related curricula effective: they focus on foundations, they seamlessly integrate cybersecurity concepts into lessons, and they focus on real-world applications. Attendees discussed curricula guidelines and how to know what to teach.

One attendee claimed that, by the time a student completes a four-year program, half of what they learned is outdated. Several attendees strongly asserted that teaching the foundational underpinnings of computer science enables students to apply their knowledge broadly and prepares them for future developments. Attendees stated how much of today's technology, such as the Internet or AI, relies on principles which have been around for decades. One participant observed that when he was teaching networking for telecommunications, every year there would be a "new" technology, but when he pulled back the layers, it was always the same core concept of a packet-switched network. Although it had a new name, the principles were the same.

Attendees generally agreed that there is a need for cybersecurity modules which can be adopted directly into mainstream curriculum. They complained about the difficulty involved with understanding and integrating curricula. One also lamented a lack of curriculum and resources such as a cyber range for educational institutions to share.

Recently, the Joint Task Force on Cybersecurity Education (2017) and the Task Group on Information Technology Curricula (2017) developed curricular guidelines that incorporate SwA and C-SCRM. There was also an Accreditation Board for Engineering and Technology (ABET) cybersecurity curriculum proposed in 2017. Attendees expressed concern with computer science curricula that teaches security as a separate course. The common view was that security principles should always be discussed; whenever an instructor teaches coding, they should be teaching secure coding.

One attendee remarked, with some agreement, that all students should be taught the ethical imperative of following secure practices. Unfortunately, when ethics is mentioned in computer security, it is usually restricted to laws and regulations. Instead, ethics should focus on the potential impact of students' risk decisions. One participant recommended the establishment of an "oath of responsibility."

Several attendees mentioned using collaborative, hands-on labs and projects that reflect real-world situations. These kinds of activities best reflect how students will be expected to function in the workforce. An instructor mentioned that his part-time students (typically employed) especially want to see how a lesson can be applied. However, one attendee cautioned that the ability to apply skills in one space may or may not apply in another domain; making good decisions for building an airplane may not translate to making good decisions on a business network.

Several attendees professed that there are no one-size-fits-all criteria. While all students should have some level of cybersecurity awareness, education and training institutions need to work with industry to identify what specific competencies should be taught more in-depth. Participants reiterated the importance of connecting curriculum with the "real world." A constant stream of feedback from local businesses and professionals was identified as key. Using graduate committees with representatives from industry, government, and academia can help provide this feedback.

6. KNOWLEDGE, SKILLS AND ABILITIES

There was consensus that there is a misunderstanding of what cybersecurity jobs, including SwA and C-SCRM jobs, entail. One person described his organization, which has three types of employees who do the same thing, but with completely different job descriptions. A consolidated and internationally recognized standard ontology of job titles, roles, and responsibilities was repeatedly mentioned as a need.

The NICE (2017) Workforce Framework (aka the NICE Framework) categorizes and describes cybersecurity KSAs and tasks in terms of 52 work roles; this framework includes in its Securely Provision category the areas C-SCRM and SwA. It was brought up that, while extremely useful, the framework is not yet an internationally accepted standard, meaning it has no weight to enforce adoption. In addition, the NICE Framework, an initial effort to describes cybersecurity work, needs to expand to include competencies, concepts of proficiency, and needs to be updated periodically to address emerging cybersecurity challenges. There was a demonstration that showed how one could use a <u>DHS database</u> to search for KSAs and tasks in the NICE Framework.

Much of the event focused on identifying what KSAs the attendees felt should be taught in formal education and training programs. Participants were asked to consider KSAs needed in cybersecurity, software development, and C-SCRM work roles. Although KSAs needed would differ depending on the tasks within specific roles and responsibilities that a student would eventually be hired to perform, some general opinions emerged which are discussed in this section.

6.1. IT/Cybersecurity Professionals

Attendees discussed that the role of cybersecurity professional is so broad as to be almost indefinable. Software engineers, hardware developers, network architects, and many more are involved in cybersecurity, as seen in the NICE Framework. Although Burning-Glass Technologies (2015) uses the terms "cyber" and "cyber-enabled" to differentiate between roles where cybersecurity is a core vs. a secondary focus, here was discussion about how every role in an organization is likely "cyber-enabled,"as most if not all use technology to some degree.

There are some skills, however, that are specific to the cybersecurity domain. Niche skills such as penetration testing were mentioned as valuable. Attendees stated that a network engineer or software developer should have an understanding of penetration testing so that they can better design their systems. Further discussion concluded that all IT professionals should have an awareness of cybersecurity concepts, but that the level of understanding or skill needed would differ depending on that professional's role in an organization.

6.1.1. Soft Skills

Interestingly, participants nearly unanimously proclaimed that soft skills were critical to success in their own careers. The ability to communicate was uniformly asserted as the most valuable skill anyone in these field could possess. Attendees specifically highlighted the ability to communicate across organizational boundaries about technical issues and the ability to bring different types of people together to collaborate, work out problems, and share ideas.

There was a slight disagreement about whether bottom-line workers such as programmers need soft skills. Some said that their coders are not people they would put in front of an executive. Others noted that not every programmer will want leadership positions that require those kinds of soft skills. In the end, it was agreed that communication is critical, but the means of communication may differ. Even technical employees need to be able to explain what they have done, but this communication may be done electronically. Many employees who are very shy in person are very good at collaborating with each other using electronic means, and they do so naturally.

Industry representatives seemed to agree that they would generally rather hire somebody with soft skills but lacking in technical skills versus somebody with strong technical skills but weak soft skills. One complained that prospective employees want to dazzle with their technical brilliance, but they don't know how to communicate that brilliance. Many stated they have a process for training new hires in technical skills, but not soft skills. An attendee from an academic background stated that educational institutes often don't focus on soft skills until upper levels. In some institutes, soft skills are looked down on and isolated to liberal arts majors. This is an area of opportunity, but one that is seldom recognized. Many view soft skills as innate, but the attendees emphatically stated that soft skills can, and should, be trained.

6.1.2. Risk Management

Attendees indicated that all IT and cybersecurity professionals, including SwA and C-SCRM professionals, should have KSAs related to risk management. Key points mentioned were the ability to assess and manage risk in the context of organizational or business goals. While one person's conceptual understanding of risk will never be identical to another's, there should be some consensus within an organization of what is and is not acceptable. It was argued that students should be taught how their decisions can impact the cybersecurity risk of an organization and how to make risk-based decisions.

The majority of KSAs that attendees mentioned should be taught referenced vulnerabilities. People in development or operational positions should have a general knowledge of common mistakes (i.e., vulnerabilities or weaknesses) related to their field(s) and know the countermeasures to those weaknesses and the trade-offs of different countermeasures. Attendees noted the need for the ability to assess vulnerability reports and understand their importance. The ability to recognize or find vulnerabilities was repeatedly mentioned as a needed skill many IT professionals currently lack.

Threats were another focus area. Attendees mentioned that the ability to think like an adversary is important. It was mentioned that more education and training courses are needed, teaching students how to hack a system or network in order to show students how it's done. However, attendees clarified that most students or employees need only a general awareness of how adversaries operate; the ability to develop a custom exploit, for example, may be less important than the ability to understand how custom exploits are created.

Other suggestions included focusing on prevention, detection, and recovering. Attendees stated that students should be taught to apply the earliest practical prevention methods, but that prevention isn't enough. Regarding software maintenance, developers need to learn of a vulnerability, update, test, and field to production faster than an attacker – within hours or days, not the current standard of months or years.

6.1.3. Tools and Technology

Attendees discussed the need to understand both technology and the roles tools and technology play in cybersecurity. It was mentioned that students need to know the kinds of tools available to them, as well as the underlying theories behind various technologies. Examples of tools and technology discussed included: compilers with vulnerability checkers, machine learning algorithms, cyber-physical or Internet of Things devices, and assessment questionnaires. Tools and technologies can be used to automate cybersecurity, reduce costs, enable continuous monitoring, and support programmers or cybersecurity experts. Yet, if a user doesn't know what the tool is capable of, how it works, what its limits are, and what capabilities it provides, the usefulness of the tool will be limited.

Many issues arise when people rely too heavily on tools. An example was given of the standardized third-party assessment questionnaire; it can provide indicators that there may be a concern, but a knowledgeable analyst is needed to interpret the results to decide if there really is a concern or not, and then a decision is needed about what to do about the concern. Without such an analyst, decisions could be made to the detriment of the organization. Tools should be used as a feedback loop, but the operator of the tool must be able to interpret results, use data, make appropriate risk-based decisions, and solve the problems that the tool discovers.

6.2. Software Developers

The field of system and software developers was compared to some of the more traditional engineering disciplines; software development applies knowledge to solve human problems and involves trade-offs. It is a quickly evolving discipline that requires lifelong learning in order for a practitioner to stay relevant.

Much of the discussion on software developers focused on the need to impress upon them their role in society from an ethics standpoint. Upon graduation, many Canadian-trained and some U.S.-trained engineers receive a ring that is intended to serve as a reminder to the engineer of their ethical obligations. The ring is often associated with the first Quebec Bridge, which collapsed in 1907, killing seventy-five construction workers. Several attendees declared that "software is today's bridge." Software and systems engineers must understand the impact their decisions can have and be held accountable, especially as we move to a world where, more and more, IT systems can cause physical harm.

Continuing the thread, the fact that secure software engineering is a separate discipline from software engineering was cited as strange. One attendee stated, "We don't have 'don't-fall-down' bridge engineers, just engineers who build bridges that don't fall down." Security needs to be an integral part of any IT or cyber role, and it needs to be integrated early – not only as a reaction to a bad scan or report. Attendees generally agreed that all software development should be taught as secure software development.

Attendees listed numerous KSAs that they felt software developers should understand. These generally fell into six areas:

- The foundational underpinnings and general nature of software, including math, logic, the purpose of software, and how software and software development has changed throughout history;
- Secure coding techniques, including secure coding standards, develops processes, and the ability to provide quality assurance cases;
- Architecture and design, including least privilege, secure design principles, dataflow mapping, key hardening mechanisms to counter "vulnerabilities left over," whitelisting, stack interface layers, and system awareness;
- Analysis and testing, including different types of test/analysis tools, negative testing, high test coverage, operational assessments, library decomposition, data distillation and analysis, and system function assessments;
- Context, including understanding how code is likely going to be used, alternative use-cases, and the consequences of design trade-offs;
- Machine learning and other state-of-the-art tools, including an understanding of how vulnerable commonly used algorithms are.

6.3. Cross-Domain

Multiple times, attendees mentioned the need for employees with a diverse set of skills. In fact, industry representatives implied that they would be much more inclined to hire a student with a mixed background rather than somebody who specialized in only one field. For example, a hospital hiring a programmer

would chose somebody with less experience in programming but had a background in hospital administration over somebody who had only ever done programming.

Attendees mentioned several specialties and KSAs that they look for or that are needed to supplement
the cybersecurity/SwA realm:

- **Hardware:** To better align software with hardware capabilities and needs;
- **Business:** To enable communication and make better risk decisions;
- **Project Management:** To better support development efforts;
- **Quality:** To bring lessons-learned from the quality community and to enable communication with
  quality experts;
- **Humanities:** To better understand customer needs, enable communication with customers, and
  understand human decision-making processes to build better tools or systems.

Industry-specific skills were also mentioned. Many organizations desire cybersecurity professionals
with a background in their industry, but many organizations do not consider retraining / reskilling their
own workforce to meet that need. Valued employees with outdated skills, but the appropriate industry
background, are let go while the organization searches for somebody with the skill set and background
they need. Attendees suggested that organizations should instead focus on retraining valued employees
to have the cybersecurity skills they need.

6.3.1. Cyber Supply Chain Risk Management

Cyber supply chain risk management is in itself a cross-domain field, overlapping with logistics, cybersecurity, and other fields. This is a new discipline that is implemented in organizations in a variety
of ways. It appears that there is not currently a single, clearly defined C-SCRM role; defining such a
role is a challenge. Attendees were asked what, if any, KSAs were unique to the C-SCRM field. While
some KSAs were mentioned that C-SCRM professionals would need, none were unique, but instead
represented an overlap of other disciplines.

The majority of KSAs mentioned were related to the complexity of the supply chain. Multiple times,
attendees mentioned the need for an understanding of the complexities of the software supply chain.
Understanding traditional supply chains or hardware supply chains does not provide the background
necessary to understand the challenges associated with software supply chains. Those in a C-SCRM
position should understand concepts such as indirect supply, how to manage suspect but unavoidable
components (e.g., using mitigating controls), and developing a chain of trust.

Government and industry representatives stated that people with software and supply chain knowledge
need to be in place during every phase of the system development life cycle (SDLC), but especially in
the design and test phases. It was suggested that a body of knowledge could be built from NIST Special
Publication (SP) 800-161, *Supply Chain Risk Management Practices for Federal Information Systems
and Organizations* and the Department of Defense Instruction number 5200.44, *Protection of Mission
Critical Functions to Achieve Trusted Systems and Networks (TSN).*

6.4. "Everyone"

One question asked was "What does 'everybody' need to know about SwA/C-SCRM?" Answers roughly fell into three categories: collaboration, risk awareness, and process control.

Collaboration was the dominant ability described as critical to SwA and C-SCRM. Attendees mentioned that everybody – cyber professionals or others – needs the ability to collaborate. Specific collaboration skills mentioned were the ability to ask good questions, knowing when and who to ask, how to constructively point out or discover problems, how to blend business with technology cultures and language, how to work in a diverse team environment, and leadership skills.

Some questions that attendees wished people would ask more included, "Where does this technology come from?", "Who built it?", and "What's inside the box." One attendee noted that good questions can be formed using the five w's (who, what, when, where, and why). It was also stated that people need to learn to defer to expertise regarding these questions, instead of deferring to management or rank.

An awareness of risk was also highlighted as something everybody should know, but how much awareness and about what was disputed. Attendees desired everybody to have an appreciation for SwA/C-SCRM concerns, preferably in being informed and "smart" about threats. Some highlighted understanding the impact of insecure software in general. One mentioned the ability to make risk-based decisions, but another observed that the attendees may be unique when it comes to understanding risk, calling it a "special kind of paranoia." There was some agreement that everybody should be able to do after-action reviews, analyze impacts, and identify mitigation strategies.

In a similar vein, some comments regarding what everybody should know dealt with inventory or process control, or an understanding of what they have and how it is used. Comments included, "What data do they use/have?", "What do [they] do with the data under [their] stewardship?", "Where is the processing being done?", "What tools are out there?", "What are the limits of tools?", and "What is their individual contribution?" from a system-level perspective.

6.4.1. General Users

Users were a major concern. An example was given of public-switched telephones – the most the typical user knew of these phones is that they picked it up and there was a dial tone. Yet, there was a lot behind that phone to make it work than most users never knew. There are millions of people using software who have never taken a course on programming. This causes a lack of understanding about how fragile software can be, of the need for updates, or the need to buy from reputable sellers.

Many attendees complained that users often pass incomplete or inadequate requirements through the procurement process, expecting developers to "magically" fix or deliver whatever they need. Then, they ask for something late in the development process that they "didn't know they needed." Users expect more functionality than developers can handle; they expect guarantees on security and quality that are impossible to provide.

A question posed to the audience was, "What do we tell the healthcare professionals or others about what they need to know about [C-SCRM]?" Attendees mostly agreed that users need to be able to articulate needs so that procurement personnel can act to support that need. Also, users need to understand their role in the community and the impact their decisions can have on security and safety.

6.5. Other Personnel

6.5.1. Senior Leadership

Senior leadership drive the culture of an organization. They are responsible for making security a part of the organization's everyday activities by setting requirements for software assurance to be a factor in acquisition and procurement. Without those requirements, nothing will change. The C-suite (e.g., Chief Information Officer, Chief Technology Officer, Chief Security Officer) of an organization creates the demand for security, which then drives the demand for appropriate education and training. Multiple attendees identified getting executive leader support as the most important priority.

Attendees mentioned that executive leaders have been taking more notice of the C-SCRM issue and having conversations about it. They also noted that the opinions of cybersecurity professionals are given more weight than in the past. The greatest concern regarding educating and engaging leadership revolved around the content of the message. Several indicated that case studies were an extremely useful tool. Some mentioned that messages about the cost of insecurity, including the use of news stories, was not useful as they did not provide actionable information. Executives need case studies that promote the idea that it is cheaper and better to build security in; attendees noted that these types of case studies are very difficult to find.

6.5.2. Project/Middle Managers

Middle managers and project managers were identified as key roadblocks. One attendee described situations where newly graduated cybersecurity students were unable to apply what they learned because their immediate supervisors didn't understand the concepts and did not see the value. Leadership was mentioned as fundamental to providing guidance and oversight, ensuring adherence to SwA/C-SCRM standards.

Overall, it was agreed that program/project managers must be engaged and held accountable. Managers in charge of a development project must "own" the system development life cycle and be held responsible for the quality or trustworthiness of that system. To do this effectively, program managers may need specialized training in software engineering best practices and principles. They need to know about cybersecurity in general, but probably require more oversight experience than hands-on (i.e., programming) experience.

6.5.3. Acquisitions

There was some disagreement as to the role of the acquisition community. It was mentioned that in the U.K., C-SCRM is a procurement challenge and so the responsibility for ensuring that acquisitions meet the appropriate risk tolerance levels lies with the acquisition community. In the U.S., C-SCRM is a cybersecurity concern, and the acquisition community is not expected to understand the risks. As a result, the ultimate responsibility lies with the end user or system owner. Because of this, the level of education or training that acquisition personnel need was left unanswered.

Some attendees recommended that acquisitions personnel should be trained to seek advice from cybersecurity professionals when making purchasing decisions. One attendee noted that metrics should be used in such a way as to clearly place the responsibility for ensuring secure practices with programs and business units, not acquisitions personnel. Several attendees, however, agreed with the statement that the acquisition community needs to be more proactive and informed about cybersecurity and C-SCRM issues. It was agreed that more communication between acquisition personnel, cybersecurity personnel, and the end user/system owner was needed. There also seemed to be agreement that people acquiring technology need to know what questions to ask. One concrete example given was that, throughout the supply chain, there needs to be a way to express that "This piece of software can do this much damage." In that way, a buyer can make informed decisions about the software they use.

7. CONCLUSION

According to comments made by attendees at the Software and Supply Chain Assurance Forum, SwA and C-SCRM both strive to attain greater security in the IT systems we use, and a greater understanding of how that security is attained. While there was some disagreement during the forum as to who "owns" these goals, attendees generally recognized that a shared solution is necessary. With the growing ubiquity of technology, every discipline that is involved in the creation, maintenance, use, or destruction of that technology must also be involved in protecting it. It was stated multiple times that industry alone cannot solve the problem, and neither can the government alone.

Attendees stated that the largest challenge in this space appears to be that employers do not understand their own needs, misuse education and training requirements, and do not have processes in place to effectively attract, retain, train, and retrain qualified employees. Similarly, some education and training institutions do not sufficiently consider the needs of employers, and thus produce candidates whose KSAs are outdated. Attendees suggested that organizations should work with educational institutions to identify the skills that are needed, so that the education and training institutions can produce candidates with those skills.

A common theme throughout the event was how SwA and cybersecurity KSAs should be taught as part of regular computer engineering, IT, or similar curricula. Many attendees recommended that "Security" should be an integral part of IT. It was noted that cross-domain KSAs such as those needed for C-SCRM may best be obtained through retraining of the existing workforce and by promoting cybersecurity awareness for every organizational role. However, attendees were careful to highlight that overuse of any one solution could be detrimental, and that a quality cybersecurity workforce will include people from diverse education, training, employment, and cultural backgrounds.

REFERENCES

Accreditation Board for Engineering and Technology (ABET). (2017). ABET seeks feedback on proposed accreditation criteria for cybersecurity engineering academic programs. Retrieved from http://www.abet.org/abet-seeks-feedback-on-proposed-accreditation-criteria-for-cybersecurity-engineering-academic-programs/

Bureau of Air Safety Regulation (BASI). (1996). *Human factors in fatal aircraft accidents.* Civic Square ACT, Australia. Retrieved from https://www.atsb.gov.au/media/28363/sir199604_001.pdf

Burning Glass Technologies. (2015). Job market intelligence: cybersecurity jobs, 2015. Retrieved from https://www.burning-glass.com/wp-content/uploads/Cybersecurity_Jobs_Report_2015.pdf

Chatham House. (n.d.). Chatham house rule. Retrieved from https://www.chathamhouse.org/chatham-house-rule

Frost & Sullivan. (2017). *2017 Global information security workforce study.* Retrieved from https://iamcybersafe.org/wp-content/uploads/2017/06/Europe-GISWS-Report.pdf

Hayden, L. (2016). *People centric security: Transforming your enterprise security culture.* McGraw-Hill Education. Retrieved from http://lancehayden.net/culture/

Joint Task Force on Cybersecurity Education. (2017). *Cybersecurity curricula 2017: Curriculum guidelines for post-secondary degree programs in cybersecurity.* Computing Curricula Series. Retrieved from https://cybered.hosting.acm.org/wp-content/uploads/2018/02/newcover_csec2017.pdf

National Initiative for Cybersecurity Education (NICE). (2017). *NICE cybersecurity workforce framework.* National Institute of Standards and Technology. Retrieved from https://www.nist.gov/itl/applied-cybersecurity/nice/resources/nice-cybersecurity-workforce-framework

Online Trust Alliance. (2018). *Cyber incident & breach trends report.* The Internet Society. Retrieved from https://otalliance.org/system/files/files/initiative/documents/ota_cyber_incident_trends_report_jan2018.pdf

Stack Overflow. (2018). *Developer survey results 2018.* Retrieved from https://insights.stackoverflow.com/survey/2018/

Task Group on Information Technology Curricula. (2017). *Information technology curricula 2017: Curriculum guidelines for baccalaureate degree programs in information technology.* ACM. Retrieved from https://www.acm.org/binaries/content/assets/education/curricula-recommendations/it2017.pdf

ENDNOTE

[1]   Some attendees represented more than one group; two did not provide their affiliations.

This research was previously published in the International Journal of Systems and Software Security and Protection (IJSSSP), 9(2); pages 1-13, copyright year 2018 by IGI Publishing (an imprint of IGI Global).

Chapter 10
A Cybersecurity Skills Framework

Peter James Fischer
Institute of Information Security Professionals, UK

ABSTRACT

This chapter traces the evolution of cybersecurity skills requirements and development over the past 40 years, from the early days of computer security (Compusec) to the present day. The development of cybersecurity skills is traced from an initial focus upon national security and confidentiality through to the current recognition as business driver. The main part of the chapter concentrates on the development of a specific skills framework from the Institute of Information Security Professionals. Originally conceived in 2006 and initially used for purposes of membership accreditation, the IISP Skills Framework has since been used extensively by commerce, industry, government and academia in the UK and more widely. Version 2 of the framework was published in 2016, and the chapter discussion outlines both the original structure and the notable changes in the later release. These developments collectively illustrate the ongoing recognition of cybersecurity skills, as well as the evolution of the skills themselves.

INTRODUCTION

The content of this chapter is based on the evolving requirement for identifiable, specific and measurable skills in cybersecurity disciplines to enable organizations to identify the range and blend of skill sets they require to secure their business and to gain assurance that the individuals employed to deliver the required cybersecurity services are competent to the required level. As a corollary to this, individual cybersecurity professionals need to be able to measure themselves against an appropriate subset of cybersecurity skills in order to deliver effective cybersecurity services to their employer or customer.

The Institute of Information Security Professionals (IISP) Skills Framework was developed to identify the range of cybersecurity skills needed in the modern business world and provide some criteria against which practitioners could measure the level of their skill. It is used as the main focus for describing cybersecurity skills and knowledge. However, it should be recognized that other frameworks have been developed and are in common use, most notably those developed by ISC[2] and ISACA. In

DOI: 10.4018/978-1-6684-3554-0.ch010

terms of knowledge, the Cyber Security Body of Knowledge (CyBOK) Project sponsored by the UK National Cyber Security Centre (NCSC) will enhance further the knowledge standards and criteria for cybersecurity professionals.

However, it was felt that it would be useful to provide some historical perspective on the development of, and the need for, cybersecurity skills over the past 40 years or so. In doing so, the modern term 'cybersecurity' has been used throughout, although different terms were used at the time, including Computer Security (Compusec), Data Security, Information Security (Infosec) and Information Assurance (IA). There is a strong UK focus in the text, but reference is made to seminal work in the USA and also within Europe which has influenced and contributed to the UK positions.

BACKGROUND

In this section, we cover cybersecurity perspectives from the 1970s to the early 2000s, showing the changes in skill requirements.

The Early Days: Confidentiality Is King

Research by David Bell and Leonard LaPadula in the 1970s, building on work by Ware (1967), resulted in the Bell–LaPadula Security Model (Bell and LaPadula, 1973; Bell and LaPadula, 1976). This was used as a basis for the US Trusted Computer Security Evaluation Criteria (TCSEC), commonly referred to as 'The Orange Book'. TCSEC was issued by the US National Computer Security Center (NCSC) in 1983 and published as a Department of Defense Standard in 1985. Its focus was unashamedly the protection of confidentiality, based on national security classifications and labels and, as such, became the benchmark for government security in both the UK and US during the late 1980s.

TCSEC utilized four categories of security functionality and assurance (DoD 1985):

D: Minimal protection, reserved for products which had failed evaluation at a higher level
C: Discretionary Protection (C1 and C2)
B: Mandatory Protection (B1, B2 and B3)
A: Verified Protection (A1)

The rigor of the development and evaluation processes were linked to the functionality levels, i.e. C1 systems possessed relatively limited security functionality and assurance, whereas A1 systems possessed finely-defined security functionality combined with rigorous standards for development and evaluation, including formal methods.

A range of supporting standards and guides were published by the US National Computer Security Center (NCSC) during the period 1988-1995. These were published with covers in different colors and were known as the 'Rainbow Series'. Arguably, the most notable of these were the Trusted Network Interpretation (TNI) and the Trusted Database Interpretation (TDI) published with red and purple covers respectively, although the color purple was also used for guides on the procurement of trusted systems.

Under the regime of TCSEC and the Rainbow Series, the need for cybersecurity skills, as defined in the IISP Skills Framework, was restricted more or less to Security Architecture, Secure Development and Security Evaluation plus, on the user side, Security Policy and Standards. There was little scope for either risk assessment or risk management and government security authorities tended to mandate compliance, with little regard for business requirements.

Around the same time there were integrity models such as Biba (1975), Clark-Wilson (1987) and Brewer-Nash (1989), but these tended to be the inverse of the Bell-LaPadula model and had little influence on development and implementation, given the confidentiality focus of government organizations. Consequently, they had little influence on the need for cybersecurity skills.

By the late 1980s, security practitioners, in Europe at least, were finding TCSEC constraining. Efforts to extend the criteria to cover networking and related areas were not entirely satisfactory, and the close linkage between functionality and assurance did not meet many business models, for example the need for C2 functionality and B1 assurance or vice-versa. Also, TCSEC evaluations were funded by the US Government and therefore not available to non-US developers. As a result, the European Commission, recognizing that national evaluation criteria had been developed and were being used in the UK, and evaluation criteria were being developed by France, Germany and the Netherlands, brought the contributors together to develop a single, European set of security evaluation criteria, the Information Technology Security Evaluation Criteria (ITSEC), published in 1990.

The success of ITSEC caused a degree of consternation in the US as it meant that they had lost their pre-eminent position in cybersecurity as recognized at that time. After a brief flirtation with a draft Federal Criteria, the US authorities met with the European Commission and an agreement was made to join forces on developing a Common Criteria. Canada had also developed its own Canadian Trusted Computer Product Evaluation Criteria (CTCPEC), but also joined the Common Criteria initiative. Common Criteria was underpinned by the Common Criteria Recognition Arrangement (CCRA) under which nations recognized evaluations certified by other nations. Common Criteria was incorporated as an ISO standard (ISO15408) in 1999.

However, the focus remained on confidentiality and the flawed view that cybersecurity could be delivered primarily through the use of evaluated products and systems. Moreover, the credibility of the scheme was undermined by the insistence that products and systems should be re-evaluated following every change, i.e. patches should not be applied to products until they had been re-evaluated – a time-consuming and costly process which did not recognize the timescales of technical refresh.

In terms of cybersecurity skills, the focus during this period focused strongly on Security Architecture, Secure Software Development, Security Evaluation, Policy and Standards. Threat and risk assessment and analysis, which has formed the foundation for cybersecurity in the UK over the past 20 years, was the preserve of the few in the 1980s and early 1990s. Given the strong government focus, threat intelligence and assessment were the preserve of the Intelligence Agencies, and risk assessment was often simplistically based on the security classification of the data and the security clearances of the users. Computer security audit was in its infancy and not highly valued. Penetration testing as a specialism was non-existent, although the evaluators in the two UK Evaluation Facilities (EFs) at Logica and Admiral conducted some effective penetration testing work in the late 1980s, outside the constraints of TCSEC. Integrity and Availability were viewed by senior management as IT project and management issues, not cybersecurity.

It should be recognized that some excellent research into the wider aspects of cybersecurity was being undertaken in academia, especially in the USA, throughout this period, but this was not cascading into the organizational profile of cybersecurity.

Intervention by Business and Commerce

In the mid-1990s business and commerce began to recognize the importance of cybersecurity in terms of the protection of their business interests. This was driven to a large extent by the development of the Internet as a global communications mechanism and exacerbated by the fact that it was designed with no reference to security. The continuous growth of the Internet as a global communications mechanism has continued to fuel the evolution of threats.

This intervention from business brought a much broader perspective to the subject of cybersecurity. No longer was it tightly focused on the confidentiality of classified government information, but included a host of supporting controls and functions, including governance, policies, compliance with legal and regulatory requirements, risk assessment and management, and ongoing security management. This broader approach was re-enforced by high profile corporate financial governance issues such as those uncovered by the Enron scandal in 2001, which led to the bankruptcy of the Enron Corporation, the effective dissolution of Arthur Andersen as an audit and accountancy partnership and the Sarbanes-Oxley Act of 2002, commonly referred to as SOX. As a consequence, the cybersecurity skills requirements profile became much richer and broader.

The Institute of Information Security Professionals (IISP)

It was against this background that a few luminaries in the field of cybersecurity recognized that the subject was becoming too important to continue as a marginal interest group under the umbrella of other professional bodies but needed to become a profession in its own right. Hence, in 2006 the Institute of Information Security Professionals (IISP) was born.

From the outset it was decided that professional membership of the Institute must be based on a combination of knowledge and practical, real-world experience. Whilst other professional bodies were prepared to accept candidates for Associate Membership based solely on academic qualifications, the IISP believed that practical experience in applying the knowledge and understanding was critical to the recognition of professional status. The problem with this approach was how individuals applying for professional membership of the Institute could express their skills and capabilities, and how the Institute could assess and validate those claims. Thus, the need for a Skills Framework was identified.

AN OVERVIEW OF THE IISP SKILLS FRAMEWORK

The IISP Skills Framework[1] was originally developed by a group led by Bob Coles of Royal Bank of Scotland and Chris Ensor of CESG[2]. The main purpose of this was to define the cybersecurity skills extant at the time in order to support the assessment of each individual's knowledge, understanding and competence profile for assessment for professional membership on the Institute.

The Framework is structured as a series of Security Disciplines, representing broad areas of security provision in which skills may be needed, each of which is then broken down into a number of Skills Groups, representing more focused areas of particular activity in which individuals may then develop knowledge and experience. Recognizing that these may be needed and developed to differing degrees in different contexts, the framework also defines a number of Skill Levels at which each skill can exist.

Security Disciplines and Skills Groups

Skills Group definitions were deliberately kept at a high level in recognition of the fact that cybersecurity disciples and skills were evolving at a significant pace, and maintenance of a Skills Framework containing highly-specific definitions would be onerous to maintain and would become outdated quickly.

Version 1 of the Skills Framework defined 35 Skills across 11 Security Disciplines. Of these Security Disciplines, 9 (A-I) were categorized as "technical skills" and the remaining two (J-K) as "soft skills". In version 2, these were reduced to 33 Skills in 10 Security Disciplines, as summarized in Table 1 (noting that Discipline G, which was present in version 1 of the framework, is no longer used).

Skill Levels

There were four Skills Levels defined in version 1 of the IISP Skills Framework, these Awareness, Basic Application, Skillful Application and Expert. However, over several years of using these in practice, it was considered by many that four levels did not meet either the real-world scenarios of job roles or personal development within corporate organizations. Some had introduced Level 3- and Level 3+ to address is issue. There were also concerns regarding a single Skill Level (1) covering the wide waterfront of awareness, knowledge and understanding.

To address these concerns, six Skill Levels were introduced in version 2.0. Initially, all six level descriptors were mapped against the National Occupational Standards (NOS) for Cyber Security, developed by e-Skills UK. However, practical use of version 2.0, especially in developing the IISP Knowledge Framework, indicated that the NOS descriptions at Levels 1 and 2 did not reflect the usage of these levels. Consequently, these descriptors were revised to reflect Bloom's taxonomy in versions 2.1 onward, and the specifics of each level are presented in Table 2.

Use of these levels in practice both within the IISP (for assessment for membership) and a range of corporates (for job definitions, personal development, etc.) indicates that these levels better reflect the real world of cybersecurity professionalism.

To aid understanding of how the levels come together for specific Security Disciplines and Skills Groups, Table 3 illustrates the application in the context of the Threat Intelligence, Assessment and Threat Modelling skill group within the discipline of Threat Assessment and Information Risk Management.

EVOLUTION OF SECURITY DISCIPLINES AND SKILLS

Although originally developed for use in assessing applications for membership of the Institute, the Skills Framework was used by commerce and industry, in the form of IISP Corporate Members, for internal staff management and development purposes. It was used to:

- Define the skills requirements for specific roles and job families;
- Performance assessment;
- Staff personal development; and
- Corporate cybersecurity training and education strategies.

Table 1. Breakdown of security disciplines showing subordinate skill groups

Security Discipline	Skills Groups
A - Information Security Governance and Management Capable of determining, establishing and maintaining appropriate governance of (including processes, roles, awareness strategies, legal environment and responsibilities), delivery of (including polices, standards and guidelines), and cost-effective solutions (including impact of third parties) for information security within a given organization).	A1 – Governance A2 – Policy and Standards A3 – Information Security Strategy A4 – Innovation and Business Improvement A5 – Behavioural Change A6 – Legal & Regulatory Environment and Compliance A7 – Third Party Management
B - Threat Assessment and Information Risk Management Capable of articulating the different forms of threat to, and vulnerabilities of, information systems and assets. Comprehending and managing the risks relating to information systems and assets.	B1 – Threat Intelligence, Assessment and Threat Modelling B2 – Risk Assessment B3 – Information Risk Management
C - Implementing Secure Systems Comprehends the common technical security controls available to prevent, detect and recover from security incidents and to mitigate risk. Capable of articulating security architectures relating to business needs and commercial product development that can be realized using available tools, products, standards and protocols, delivering systems assured to have met their security profile using accepted methods	C1 – Enterprise Security Architecture C2 – Technical Security Architecture C3 – Secure Development
D - Assurance: Audit, Compliance and Testing Develops and applies standards and strategies for verifying that measures taken mitigate identified risks. Capable of defining and implementing the processes and techniques used in verifying compliance against security policies, standards, legal and regulatory requirements.	D1 – Internal and Statutory Audit D2 – Compliance Monitoring and Controls Testing D3 – Security Evaluation and Functionality Testing D4 – Penetration Testing
E - Operational Security Management Capable of managing all aspects of a security program, including reacting to new threats and vulnerabilities, secure operational and service delivery consistent with security polices, standards and procedures, and handling security incidents of all types according to common principles and practices, consistent with legal constraints and obligations.	E1 – Secure Operations Management E2 – Secure Operations and Service Delivery
F - Incident Management, Investigation and Digital Forensics Capable of managing or investigating an information security incident at all levels, including the use of digital forensic techniques.	F1 – Intrusion Detection and Analysis F2 – Incident Management, Incident Investigation and Response F3 – Forensics
H - Business Resilience Capable of defining the need for, and of implementing processes for establishing business continuity.	H1 – Business Continuity and Disaster Recovery Planning H2 – Business Continuity and Disaster Recovery Management H3 – Cyber Resilience
I - Information Security Research Original investigation in order to gain knowledge and understanding relating to information security, including the invention and generation of ideas, performances and artefacts where these lead to new or substantially improved insights; and the use of existing knowledge in experimental development to produce new or substantially improved devices, products and processes.	I1 – Research I2 – Applied Research
J - Management, Leadership, Business and Communications Recognizes the importance of wider communication and interpersonal skills in order to enable the effective communication and integration of cybersecurity within an organizational context.	J1 – Management, Leadership and Influence J2 – Business Skills J3 – Communication and Knowledge Sharing
K - Contributions to the Information Security Profession and Professional Development Recognizes the need for ongoing development of cybersecurity practitioners, and their potential to contribute to the wider community and profession.	K1 – Contributions to the Community K2 – Contributions to the IS Profession K3 – Professional Development

Table 2. The skill level definitions in version 2.2 of the IISP skills framework

Level	Title	Description	
		Knowledge	**Practice**
1	Knowledge	Has acquired and can demonstrate basic knowledge associated with the skill, e.g. through training or self-tuition.	N/A
2	Knowledge and Understanding	Has acquired and can demonstrate the basic knowledge associated with the skill, for example has attended a training course or completed an academic module in the skill. Understands how the skill should be applied.	Can explain the principles of the skill and how it should be applied. This might include experience of applying the skill to basic tasks in a training or academic environment, for example through participation in syndicate exercises, undertaking practical exercises in using the skill, and/or passing a test or examination. Should be aware of recent developments in the skill.
3	Practitioner (Apply)	Has acquired a good understanding of the knowledge associated with the skill and understands how the skill should be applied.	Has experience of applying the skill to a variety of basic tasks. Can work as an effective member of a team. Contributes ideas in the application of the skill. Demonstrates awareness of recent developments in the skill. Has experience of training potential and actual IS practitioners in the basics of the skill. Demonstrates awareness of recent developments in the skill.
4	Senior Practitioner (Enable)	Has acquired a deep understanding of the knowledge associated with the skill. Understands how the skill should be applied.	Has experience of applying the skill to a variety of tasks, including some complex tasks under supervision. Contributes ideas in the application of the skill. Demonstrates awareness of recent developments in the skill. Contributes ideas for technical development and new areas for application of the skill. Has experience of training IS professionals in the skill above an introductory level. Demonstrates awareness of recent developments in the skill. Contributes ideas for technical development and new areas for application of the skill.
5	Principal Practitioner (Advise)	Has acquired a deep understanding of the knowledge associated with the skill. Understands how the skill should be applied across a number of projects in different client environments and/or within a large corporate organization.	Has experience of applying the skill to a variety of complex tasks. Demonstrates significant personal responsibility or autonomy, with little need for escalation. Contributes ideas in the application of the skill. Demonstrates awareness of recent developments in the skill. Contributes ideas for technical development and new areas for application of the skill and contributes to public discussion/debate on the skill. Has effective leadership and management skills. Has experience of training IS professionals in the skill at an advanced level or as a university lecturer. Demonstrates awareness of recent developments in the skill. Contributes ideas for technical development and new areas for application of the skill.
6	Expert/Lead Practitioner (Initiate, Enable, Ensure)	As for Level 5.	Has oversight responsibility for overall application of the skill across a range of customers or within a large corporate organization, often reporting at Board level. Recognized as a Subject Matter Expert within a large organization. Has experience of applying the skill in circumstances without precedence. Proposes, conducts, and/or leads innovative work to enhance the skill. Is approached to provide keynote presentations or papers on the skill. Develops and leads programs of advanced training in the skill. A Professor or Senior Lecturer contributing sessions on the skill at MSc level.

Table 3. An example of a skills group definition and the skills at different levels

Skills Group	Principles	Example Skills
B1 – Threat Intelligence, Assessment and Threat Modelling	Assesses and validates information on current and potential Cyber and Information Security threats to the business, analyzing trends and highlighting information security issues relevant to the organization, including Security Analytics for Big Data. Processes, collates and exploits data, taking into account its relevance and reliability to develop and maintain 'situational awareness'. Predicts and prioritizes threats to an organization and their methods of attack. Analyses the significance and implication of processed intelligence to identify significant trends, potential threat agents and their capabilities. Predicts and prioritizes threats to an organization and their methods of attack. Uses human factor analysis in the assessment of threats. Uses threat intelligence to develop attack trees. Prepares and disseminates intelligence reports providing threat indicators and warnings	**Level 1:** Can describe the concepts and principles of threat intelligence, modelling and assessment.
		Level 2: Can explain the principles of threat intelligence, modelling and assessment. This might include experience of applying threat intelligence, modelling and assessment principles in a training or academic environment, for example through participation in syndicate exercises, undertaking practical exercises, and/or passing a test or examination.
		Level 3: Undertakes/assesses routine threat intelligence/modelling tasks or threat assessments under supervision.
		Level 4: Undertakes/assesses routine threat intelligence/modelling tasks or threat assessments without close supervision. Undertakes complex threat intelligence tasks or threat assessments under supervision.
		Level 5: Undertakes/assesses complex threat intelligence/modelling tasks or threat assessments without supervision. Manages threat intelligence/assessment teams.
		Level 6: Leads corporate threat intelligence processes, reporting to the Board.

There were also various examples of wider adoption. For instance, the Framework was adopted by CESG, the UK National Technical Authority for Information Assurance, as the basis for the CESG Certified IA Professional (CCP) Scheme and also for developing the criteria for approved cybersecurity degree programs. Meanwhile, it was also used by e-Skills UK to produce the standards for cybersecurity apprenticeships. As can be deduced from this, the Skills Framework has proven to have had a valid role in the definition of cybersecurity skills requirements for job roles and families in the workplace, and in training and education.

However, whilst version 1 of the Skills Framework (with a few minor changes) remained the *de facto* standard for cybersecurity skills definition for 10 years, over this period specific issues were reported back to the IISP. While the high-level definitions enabled users to 'shoe-horn' evolving skills into the Framework, this was becoming increasingly difficult. Also, as previously mentioned, the constraints of the four Skill Levels were becoming increasingly problematic. As such, in 2015, the IISP Board commissioned a study to assess whether there was a requirement for a fundamental review of the Skills Framework, The conclusion from that study was that, whilst the Framework remained largely fit for purpose, it would benefit from a full review to assess and address the issues reported by users and issues identified by the Board, specifically the desire to attract more members from academia and the need to re-focus the membership application process better to reflect and serve the cybersecurity profession.

The review of the Skills Framework involved in-depth consultation with business (conducted with the IISP Corporate Members), internally within the IISP (e.g. with IISP Assessors and Interviewers), CREST (a not-for profit organization representing the technical information security industry), and with CESG as the (then) National Technical Authority for Information Assurance. Consideration was given to the Skills Framework for the Information Age (SFIA – see www.sfia-online.org) – a framework developed and maintained by the SFIA Foundation to match the skills of the workforce to the needs of the business - but it was felt that the two frameworks were complementary rather than identical in that SFIA focuses on levels of responsibility and authority, whereas the Skills Framework focuses on technical knowledge, understanding and experience. Many IISP Corporate Members use both, but in different contexts.

This section examines the notable changes that were made to the Skills Framework, in terms of the top-level Security Disciplines and (more particularly) the underlying Skills Groups in the years since the 2006. In doing so, it serves to illustrate the evolving recognition of cybersecurity skills and how they integrate together.

Security Discipline A: Information Security Governance

In 2006, as today, effective cybersecurity within an organization depended on commitment from the top, demonstrated by an effective governance and management regime, involving definition (and acceptance) of ownership, clear lines of delegated authority, and with cybersecurity policies, standards and practices supporting the business and ensuring compliance with legal and regulatory requirements. Consequently, Security Discipline A – Information Security Management came first.

The changes were subtle. First of all, the Security Discipline title was changed to *Information Security Governance and Management* to re-enforce the point that management supports and is driven by governance (the original wording was felt to imply that somehow governance was subordinate to management).

The title of Skill A5 was changed to *Behavioural Change* and the criteria amended to reflect the increased awareness within organizations that training courses and awareness campaigns were not enough in themselves but need to be supported by mechanisms to measure changes in security attitudes and culture. Several organizations have introduced mechanisms to assess the security culture within the organization, e.g. by running exercises to assess the response to false malicious emails and assessing the results.

The title of Skill A6 was changed to add *Compliance* to reflect the increasing requirement on organizations to monitor and maintain records of compliance with legal and regulatory instruments.

A number of observations can be made based upon the experience of using these Skills Groups in practice:

- **A1 - Governance:** In practice, the IISP has found that most cybersecurity professionals operate at project/program level with respect to governance, i.e. Skill Level 3-4. A few, mainly CISOs and Principal Consultants operating at Board level have the involvement at corporate level required for Skill Level 5-6.
- **A2 - Policy and Standards:** Early assessment against this Skill Group found that much of the evidence concentrated on Her Majesty's Government (HMG) standards published by the Cabinet Office, e.g. the Security Policy Framework and constituent documents such as the CESG Infosec Standards. However, as cybersecurity in the private sector became more mature, the focus switched to ISO/IEC 27001 and compliance checks against the controls specified in the Statement of Applicability. Experience in assessing applicants for membership of the IISP indicates that initial gap analyses against ISO/IEC 27001 uncover the absence of essential policies covering issues such as acceptable use, use of removable media and associated disciplinary policies.
- **A3 - Information Security Strategy:** The main foci of this Skill Group are: the balancing of cost against security risk for the business; and balancing technical and non-technical controls to achieve a cost-effective solution. Here again, there is a tension between cybersecurity profes-

sionals working in the public sector, where security rules tend to be more prescriptive, and in the private sector where there is usually more flexibility to take into account business drivers. However, this gap has lessened over time, especially outside the HMG 'High Threat Club', i.e. those Government Departments processing large volumes of highly-classified information marked SECRET and TOP SECRET.

- **A4 - Innovation and Business Improvement:** This Skill Group concentrates on 'security as an enabler', i.e. how security could improve the business. An example would be hardening a web service so that it can support online services rather than just brochure-ware. In practice, this Skill Group has tended to focus on resolving conflicts between the business and security in order that business benefits can be delivered securely. An example of this would be the resolution of a situation whereby the CIO wishes to authorize the use of BYOD without considering the cybersecurity risks involved and the options for addressing at least some of the security concerns. This Skill Group also addresses the use of cybersecurity products, the analysis of their efficacy and management overheads, and making recommendations based on cost/benefit analysis principles.

- **A5 – Behavioural Change:** This Skill Group originally focused on the identification of cybersecurity training needs within an organization, gaining management commitment to training and the development and delivery of training programs. Initially, practitioners in this Skill Group concentrated on the development and delivery of formal training to individuals with cybersecurity responsibilities, progressing to cover user training involving other methods such as CBT. In response to feedback from IISP Corporate members on common practice, the criteria were extended to cover behavioral analysis, security culture management programs, with the application of analysis of human factors.

- **A6 - Legal & Regulatory Environment and Compliance:** This is a very broad Skill Group addressing a wide range of legal and regulatory instruments. In recent years, the focus of expertise has been the Data Protection Act 1998, with the General Data Protection Regulation (GDPR) taking center stage more recently. Experience of assessing applicants for membership of the IISP has shown that many cybersecurity professionals need knowledge and understanding of legislation in other countries when working for multi-national organizations, and of specific regulatory requirements such as those applying to the nuclear and oil and gas industries, and in the financial sector.

- **A7 - Third Party Management:** The importance of this Skill Group has increased over the years, with more and more organizations outsourcing functions not deemed to be core business and working more closely with partners. In practice, within this Skill Group, cybersecurity professionals tend to work with corporate legal and contractual authorities to ensure that security risk management is adequately covered in contracts and partnership agreements, in conducting compliance checks against those requirements, and assisting the third-party organizations in resolving any issues identified.

Security Discipline B: Threat Assessment and Information Risk Management

Moving on from governance and management, the next Security Discipline is Information Risk Management, as this should underpin the whole ethos of cybersecurity within an organization. Cybersecurity policies, strategies and controls need to be firmly grounded on a foundation of risk management, taking into account the business drivers and constraints.

Risk assessment and management are often considered to be core disciplines in the cybersecurity profession. Not only are these core skills in their own right – e.g. the majority of cybersecurity consultants consider them to be their main business – but risk assessment and management knowledge and expertise are crucial components for a range of cybersecurity job families including security architects, penetration testers, system security managers, Security Operations Center (SOC) staff and incident managers.

Security Discipline B originally contained two Skill Groups: Risk Assessment and Risk Management. However, several IISP Corporate Members suggested that this did not adequately reflect the growing importance of Threat Intelligence in their risk management processes. Consequently, the Discipline was expanded to 3 Skill Groups: Threat Intelligence, Assessment and Threat Modelling; Risk Assessment; and Risk Management.

The associated observations from practical use in these cases are as follows:

- **B1 - Threat Intelligence, Assessment and Threat Modelling**: Reflects the increasing importance of Threat Intelligence and associated disciplines, especially within large corporate organizations. It covers activities such as:
  - Assessing and validating information from several sources on current and potential Cyber and Information Security threats to the business.
  - Analyzing trends and highlighting Information Security issues relevant to the
  - organization, including Security Analytics for Big Data.
  - Processing data, taking into account its relevance and reliability to develop and maintain 'situational awareness'.
  - Predicting and prioritizing threats to an organization and their methods of attack.
  - Analyzing intelligence to identify significant trends, potential threat agents and their capabilities.
  - Predicting and prioritizing threats to an organization and their methods of attack.
  - Using human factor analysis in the assessment of threats.
  - Using threat intelligence to develop attack trees.
  - Preparing and disseminating intelligence reports providing threat indicators and warnings.
  - Providing input to the development of scenarios for Red Team testing.
- **B2 - Risk Assessment:** Common practice within this Skill Group tended to concentrate on HMG Infosec Standard 1&2 (IS1&2) in the public sector, and ISO/IEC 27005, ISO/IEC 31000 and risk assessment methodologies such as the Information Security Forum IRAM2 in the private sector. Since IS1&2 was withdrawn as an HMG Standard, there has been much convergence of practice within the cybersecurity community towards bespoke risk assessment approaches based on ISO/IEC 27005 and modifications to one of the standard risk assessment methodologies, including IS1&2. The IISP continues to find that a few Government Departments, most notably the Ministry of Defence, continue to use IS1&2.
- **B3 - Risk Management:** Practice in this Skills Group typically includes the development of risk registers and risk treatment plans. Risk management needs to take into account the risk appetite of the organization, the organization's risk tolerance for a particular activity – which might be different from the risk appetite, and an understanding of how risk management could support the taking of opportunities by the business. Examples of opportunities during the life of version 1 of the IISP Skills Framework included several examples of moving into online sales and services.

Security Discipline C: Implementing Secure Systems

The focus here is defining effective security architectures for systems and networks and developing secure products which can then be incorporated into systems and networks. The Discipline originally contained two Skill Groups: Security Architecture and Secure Development. This was based on the view in 2006, which was heavily influenced by the culture of previous years, i.e. secure systems and networks are built from secure products. In consultation with practicing security architects, the definitions were changed to moderate the focus on secure products and to separate Security Architecture into two Skills Groups – Enterprise Security Architecture and Technical Security Architecture. Although it was recognized that there was significant overlap between the two, it was felt that some architects tended to concentrate on enterprise level aspects and others on the technical detail closer to design and development.

- **C1 - Enterprise Secure Architecture:** Although there can be a significant skill overlap between Enterprise and Technical security architects, it was felt important to separate the two, if only to stress the corporate business and risk drivers for security architecture at the enterprise level. The skills profile of the Enterprise Security Architect therefore focuses on using organizational security requirements in the development of Enterprise Information Security Architectures, interpreting security policies and threat/risk profiles to develop secure architectural solutions that mitigate the risks, conform to legislation and regulations, and relate to business needs.
- **C2 - Technical Secure Architecture:** Whilst many of the skill definitions for the Technical Security Architect replicate those of the Enterprise Architect, the skills focus is more on:
    - The development of Computer, Network and Storage Security Architectures, incorporating hosting, infrastructure applications and cloud-based solutions.
    - Applying security architecture principles to networks, IT systems, Control Systems (e.g. SCADA, ICS), infrastructures and products.
    - Devising standard solutions that address requirements delivering specific security functionality.
    - Maintaining awareness of the security advantages and vulnerabilities of common products and technologies.
- **C3 - Secure Development:** This focuses on the design, development and implementation of secure systems and products using appropriate standards and practices, including verifying that the security criteria are met. Whilst in 2006 this Skill Group was targeted largely at the development of secure products, this has changed over the years and was expanded to cover secure systems development. Nevertheless, concerns remain over the quality and robustness of all software, not just security software, and the IISP is working with the Trustworthy Software Foundation and the Information Assurance Advisory Council (IAAC) to raise awareness of this issue.

Security Discipline D: Assurance: Audit, Compliance, and Testing

This is the Security Discipline where the most significant changes between versions 1 and 2 of the Framework have occurred. In 2006, this Security Discipline was entitled *Information Assurance Methodologies and Testing* and contained two Skills Groups, Information Assurance Methodologies and Security Testing. Largely as a result of representations from IISP Corporate Members, this was changed radically in version 2. The arguments were:

- Security Methodologies were no longer viewed as a skill in themselves, but needed to be recognized as an important factor in each of the skills, e.g. risk assessment methodologies should be addressed under Skill Group B2, Secure Architecture methodologies under C1/C2, etc.
- Organizations, especially at Board level viewed skills like audit, compliance and testing as essentially part of the corporate security assurance process, so it was felt that these should be incorporated in the same Security Discipline.
- As a result of the increase in compliance monitoring and testing since 2006, it was felt that this should be recognized by separating these functions from traditional audit as the practices, training and qualifications were significantly different. Both were covered by a single Skill Group in version 1 which, it was felt, led to confusion and conflict.
- The testing of security functionality should be separated from penetration testing, as the knowledge and skills requirements were significantly different.

As a result, Security Discipline D was renamed as *Assurance: Audit, Compliance and Testing*, and divided into four Skill Groups: Internal and Statutory Audit; Compliance Monitoring and Controls Testing; Security Evaluation and Functionality Testing; and Penetration Testing. The related observations from experience here are as follows:

- **D1 - Internal and Statutory Audit:** During the life of version 1 of the framework, compliance monitoring became an increasingly important tool in the corporate security armory. Whilst there had been a tendency to 'shoe-horn' these skills under the Security Audit Skill Group, this resulted in some confusion and a degree of conflict between professional auditors and compliance monitors. As a result, it was decided to split these into two separate Skill Groups.
- **D2 - Compliance Monitoring and Controls Testing:** As indicated above, this Skill Group covers compliance monitoring against recognized standards such as ISO/IEC27001, the Payment Card Industry Data Security Standard, the HMG Information Assurance Maturity Model (IAMM), and also against legal and regulatory instruments.
- **D3 - Security Evaluation and Functionality Testing:** In version 1, security evaluation, security functionality testing and penetration testing (but not vulnerability assessment) were covered by a single Skill Group. In recognition of the different knowledge and skill requirements between these two Skill Groups, it was decided to move security evaluation and functionality testing to a separate Skill Group in version 2. In practice, the IISP has found that security evaluation skills are applied mainly against secure products. Since the demise of the CESG (formerly CSIA) Claims Tested Mark (CCTM) scheme and the marginalization of Common Criteria (ISO/IEC 15408), security functionality testing has concentrated on systems. The scope of such testing tends to be equally split between confidentiality and availability requirements.
- **D4 - Penetration Testing:** For purposes of consistency, and to reflect common practice, the technical vulnerability assessment skill has been transferred from Operational Security Management in version 1 to become part of the D4 Skill Group in version 2.

Security Discipline E: Operational Security Management

It has been argued that this particular Security Discipline is covered by the Information Technology Infrastructure Library (ITIL). Whilst this is largely true, it is important to recognize the importance of cybersecurity professionalism in this area. Consequently, those elements of operational IT management which are directly relevant to security were included in version 1 of the Skills Framework and have been retained in version 2.

There were three Skill Groups in version 1, but these were reduced to two. The Group removed was *Vulnerability Assessment*, with the majority of the skill definitions being transferred to Skill Group F1, e.g. monitoring, reviewing and filtering external vulnerability reports and analyzing internal problem reports. The removal of this Skill Group also removed a source of confusion regarding technical vulnerability assessment, which is more properly included in Skill Group D4 as it is closely related to penetration testing.

Security Discipline F: Intrusion and Incident Management, Investigation and Forensics

In version 1 of the Skills Framework this Security Discipline was entitled *Incident Management* and contained three Skill Groups – Incident Management, Investigation and Forensics. In version 2 it was renamed as *Intrusion and Incident Management, Investigation and Forensics*. It still contains three Skill Groups, but the first 2 have been changed significantly:

- **F1 - Intrusion Detection and Analysis:** This Skill Group was introduced to reflect the increase in Security Operations Center and Security Incident and Event Management (SIEM) systems since 2006. It recognizes the skill sets needed to identify potential intrusion or other anomalous behavior, the use of security analytics to monitor and filter external vulnerability reports, and the production of targeted warning material.
- **F2 - Incident Management, Incident Investigation and Response**: In version 1, Incident Management and Incident Investigation were listed as separate Skill Groups. This caused some confusion as the skills sets and activities were inextricably linked. Under version 2 this Skill Group covers managing and investigating incidents as well as responding, which is of equal importance. This reflects common practice in the real world.

Security Discipline G

The only Skill Group (Audit and Review) in this Security Discipline was relocated to Security Discipline D. It is retained it as a blank discipline in order to ensure comparability and avoid confusion amongst parties referring across both versions of the framework.

Security Discipline H: Business Resilience

As with Security Discipline E, there are arguments that this is a separate set of professional skills covered by other organizations. However, the same counter-arguments apply. In version 1 of the Skills Framework the Discipline was named *Business Continuity Management* with 2 Skill Groups – *Business Continuity Planning (H1)* and *Business Continuity Management*. It was renamed in Version 2 as *Business Resilience* and a third Skill Group was added following representations from stakeholders to cover the need to address cybersecurity resilience in implementation and operations:

- **H3 - Cyber Resilience:** Whilst this largely replicated in other Security Disciplines (especially B, C, E and F), it was felt important to bring cybersecurity resilience issues into the corporate business continuity and disaster recovery processes.

There is also an additional element in this Skill Group and that is putting in place mechanisms to manage the fallout from serious security breaches. It is not just about recovering processing capability, but also about managing the interaction with individuals (customers and/or staff members) whose personal information has been compromised. Activities include: engagement with the Information Commissioner's Office (ICO); deciding what follow-up action would be appropriate (e.g. legal assistance with identity theft); setting up and briefing a help desk to deal with enquiries from individuals affected by the breach. The issue of obtaining and managing cybersecurity insurance to cover such circumstances is also covered in this Skill Group.

Security Discipline I

This Security Discipline was named *Information Systems Research* in version 1, but changed to correctly reflect its focus in version 2. It originally contained three Skill Groups – *Research, Academic Research, and Applied Research* – but these were reduced to two to reflect the confusion by many stakeholders between the, admittedly rather vague, definitions.

- **I1 - Research:** This Skill Group covers, for example:
  - Conducting original investigation to gain knowledge and understanding relating to cybersecurity.
  - Defining research goals.
  - Writing/presenting papers on the results of research.
  - Contributing to the development of an organization's Information Security research policy.
  - Developing new or improved cybersecurity models or theories including new cryptographic algorithms.
  - In cybersecurity, using existing knowledge to produce new or improved devices, products and processes or to improve understanding of behavioral response to security controls.
- **I2 - Applied Research:** By contrast, this group covers aspects such as:
  - Vulnerability Research and Discovery, leading to the development of exploits, reverse engineering and researching mitigation bypasses.
  - Cryptographic research leading to the assessment of existing algorithms.

Security Discipline J: Management, Leadership, Business, and Communications

There was an argument in favor of removing the J Security discipline from the Skills Framework on the basis that these skills should be covered under each of the individual skills in the Framework. However, stakeholders argued strongly in favor of retaining a subset of the original seven Skill Groups as they were considered important to the effective use of the Framework. Indeed, this is an area of increasing importance. There have been cases where senior managers have stated that it is easier to teach cybersecurity skills to business experts than teach business knowledge and understanding to cybersecurity specialists.

Whilst one can understand the dilemma, it really is not that easy, and cybersecurity professionals need to recognize business drivers and not just follow the security mantras. There have been several examples whereby individuals with long experience and a strong reputation in the standards and policy areas have moved into the "real world", often the financial sector and had a rude awakening by realizing that implementation of standard policies, principles and practices was not as easy as they thought.

- **J1 - Management, Leadership and Influence:** This Skill Group concentrates on working with and managing teams, exercising leadership in promoting cybersecurity and interfacing effectively with management.
- **J2 - Business Skills:** To a great extent, this Skill Group replicates the content of A3 and A4 (Information Security Strategy and Innovation & Business Improvement). Corporate stakeholders felt strongly that it should be included specifically as a soft skill to reinforce the point that cybersecurity needs to recognize and take account of business opportunities and drivers.
- **J3 - Communication and Knowledge Sharing:** Recognizes the importance of good communications skills, written and verbal, for a cybersecurity professional, and also the need for cybersecurity professionals to share knowledge, mentor and educate those that they work with.

Security Discipline K: Contributions to the Information Security Community and Professional Development

This final Discipline covers Contributions to the Community, Contributions to the Profession, and Professional Development. The focus of these Skill Groups is self-explanatory, the change in version 2 separated contributions to the community from those to the profession.

CONTINUING DEVELOPMENT AND MOVING FORWARD

Whilst the IISP skills framework remained stable and relevant for 10 years, there is no doubt that cybersecurity challenges and the need for new or more refined skills were expanding at an increasing pace. This was largely due to the rise of cybercrime (such as ransomware), fraudulent activity, the impact of breaches involving personal information and, possibly to a lesser extent, concerns over national state activity in the cyber arena. Cybersecurity issues are now taken seriously at corporate Board level, and this resulted in two further significant changes to the IISP Skills Framework as it moved towards version 2.3:

- **D4 – Penetration Testing:** Penetration testing has proved to be a growth industry over the past 10+ years and continues to provide an important assurance. However, it is recognized that, in the current hostile cyber environment, penetration testing, i.e. testing against known public domain vulnerabilities, is not enough. In the past year or so a requirement for extensive testing and attack exercises using scenarios based on threat intelligence has evolved. These activities are commonly categorized as red, blue, purple and white teaming:
  - Red Teaming exercises mimic an attack against an organization using scenarios developed from (often independently provided) threat intelligence to evaluate the effectiveness of its security defenses, including people and processes.

- ○ Blue Teaming describes the operation of an organization's internal security team to detect and respond to Red Team activities.
- ○ Purple Teaming describes an arrangement whereby experience Red Teamers are embedded into the Blue Team to assist and mentor.
- ○ White Teaming describes a non-intrusive method of assessing the ability of an organization to resist attack, although the IISP has found no evidence from applicants for membership of this approach being used in anger.

The knowledge and skill requirements involved in these activities will be more extensive that those traditionally assigned to penetration testers, or Security Operations Center (SOC) staff for that matter.

- **H3 - Cyber Resilience:** The whole issue of managing cybersecurity breaches has escalated and is now, rightly, considered seriously at Board level. The cost, impact on the business, and resource overheads of managing and recovering from an incident are a serious concern, and issues which most companies and corporations are ill-equipped to cope with. The UK Data Protection Act 2018, which embodies the standards published in the EU General Data Protection Regulation, has raised the bar regarding breaches involving personal information, and it is only a matter of time before the Information Commissioner's Office serves heavy fines for breaches. The issue of cyber breach insurance has also moved on, with many major insurance companies and large consultancy firms now offering security breach management services.

The IISP Skills Framework has proven itself to be a valuable tool in assessing cybersecurity skills for a range of purposes including personal development, the definition skill requirements of job roles, job families and professional membership. It has also been used effectively in the definition of cybersecurity skills requirements for academic qualifications and apprenticeship schemes.

Many of the specific uses of version 1 of the Framework are described earlier in this chapter. Version 2 has been used by Qufaro (see qufaro.uk) to underpin its Extended Project Qualification coursework and qualification, an AS-level qualification aimed at bridging the gap between school curricula at GCSE level and degree programs. The IISP will be working with Qufaro to assist in the development of Level 3 apprenticeship criteria (as opposed to the Level 4 and higher apprenticeship criteria currently in place). It also hopes to work with the London Institute of Banking and Finance who are seeking to introduce an apprenticeship scheme with a specific focus on cybersecurity in banking and finance.

Even so, the Skills Framework cannot stand still. Issues such as red/blue/purple and white teaming (Skill D4) and security breach management (Skill H3) mentioned earlier in this chapter are not adequately addressed in Version 2.2 of the IISP Skills Framework. Action is in hand to address these issues in version 2.3. There are also the evolving security issues surrounding the Internet of Things (IoT) which will no doubt have an impact of the IISP Skills Framework, as well as the IISP Knowledge Framework and Common Body of Knowledge work mentioned below.

Also, it must be recognized that the strength of the IISP Skills Framework is also its weakness. The skills definitions within the Framework are deliberately set at a high level to minimize the need for constant change, although changes will still be required to reflect new technologies and specialisms, perhaps more so than in the past as the pace of change seems to be increasing. As with all high-level definitions, their interpretation is subjective and can result in inconsistency. It is also true that knowledge, understanding and expertise in a specific skill can be relevant to several Skill Groups. An example is

Cryptography, which falls to a greater or lesser extent under all the Skill Groups in Security Disciplines A, C, D and F, and in Skill Groups B3, E2 and H3.

All of this points to the need for a Common Body of Knowledge (CBK) for the cybersecurity profession, and in the UK context this was recognized by both the IISP and NCSC in 2016, albeit with different requirements and priorities.

The IISP sees the priority and a baseline set of knowledge and understanding which represents the baseline for anyone wishing to call themselves a cybersecurity professional. This recognizes the issue that a number of self-professed cybersecurity professionals have a deep and expert knowledge in certain skill areas, bit little or no broad knowledge across the cybersecurity skill spectrum. From the IISP perspective, this is a little like a neurological consultant having no knowledge of physiology. Consequently, the priority for the IISP, driven by its Corporate members, was to develop a body of knowledge covering Level 1, and edging into Level 2, across Security Disciplines A through H.

Meanwhile, the NCSC, given its position as the UK National Technical Authority for cybersecurity, felt that a comprehensive body of knowledge was needed, covering not just the baseline criteria, but also the specialist technical areas against which Subject Matter Experts could be trained and assessed. Whilst the IISP continued to work with the NCSC on the resulting CyBOK project (www.cybok.org), it took the initiative in developing a Knowledge Framework to meet its own priorities, primarily the development of a baseline framework of knowledge and understanding across the whole cyber skills waterfront. Version 1 of the Knowledge Framework was published in 2017, but (as with CyBOK) the level of detail means that changes in technology, threats and attack vectors will require a constant review and update process in order to ensure that currency is maintained in later years.

CONCLUSION

Cybersecurity, then called Computer Security, first came to prominence as a study and career specialism in the 1980s. For many years the skills requirements remained limited for a number of reasons including: limited threats; limited networking capability; and the focus on the confidentiality of classified information.

This changed in the late 1990s when industry and commerce began to take a real interest; a factor in this being the evolution of the Internet as a global communications medium. This led to the development of commercial standards, and the cybersecurity skill sets expanded significantly to address the whole range of confidentiality, integrity and availability issues. This trend accelerated in the new millennium, with the growth of cybercrime, fraud and much-publicized corporate financial governance failures. This was reflected, amongst other things, in the growth of the penetration testing industry, SIEM technology and the development of Security Operations Centers (SOCs) and, later, the evolution of Threat Intelligence as a major plank in corporate cybersecurity strategies.

By 2018, the increasing frequency and sophistication of attacks by cyber criminals, and the financial and reputational damage caused by compromises of personal information have raised the profile of cybersecurity to Board level. This is reflected by penetration testing being complemented by, and in some cases replaced by teaming exercises simulating attacks based on scenarios developed from threat intelligence. The growing concerns of the security of control systems, the Internet of Things (IoT) and the evolving disciplines in Artificial Intelligence (AI) – which could be a force for good and bad – are issues that the profession will need to get to grips with.

Whilst the IISP Skills Framework has maintained its position as the basis of cyber skills definition and categorization, it has been recognized that these high-level definitions, although important, are not sufficient in themselves. As a result, the IISP has developed a Knowledge Framework to complement the Skills Framework by providing baseline definitions of knowledge and understanding of cybersecurity skills sufficient for an entry level to the profession. At the same time, the NCSC has let a contract to academia to develop a comprehensive Cyber Security Body of Knowledge covering the whole range of Skill Levels, not just Levels 1 and 2.

The challenge facing the profession, and the bodies with professional responsibilities, is to maintain and expand the frameworks and bodies of knowledge to reflect adequately the skills requirements to meet and manage threats, which are evolving at an ever-increasing rate.

REFERENCES

Bell, D. E., & LaPadula, L. J. (1973). Secure Computer Systems: Mathematical Foundations. In Secure Computer Systems: Mathematical Foundations (MTR–2547, Vol. 1). The MITRE Corporation. (ESD–TR–73–278–I)

Bell, D. E., & LaPadula, L. J. (1976). Secure Computer System: Unified Exposition and Multics Interpretation. MTR–2997. The MITRE Corporation. (ESD–TR–75–306). doi:10.21236/ADA023588

Biba, K. J. (1975). *Integrity Considerations for Secure Computer Systems*. The MITRE Corporation.

Brewer, D. F. C., & Nash, M. J. (1989) The Chinese Wall Security Policy. *Proceedings of IEEE Symposium on Security and Privacy*.

Clark, D. D., & Wilson, D. R. (1987). A comparison of Commercial and Military Computer Security Policies. *Proceedings of the 1987 IEEE Symposium on Research in Security and Privacy*, 184-193. 10.1109/SP.1987.10001

DoD. (1985). *DoD Trusted Computer Security Evaluation Criteria (DoD 5200.28-STD)*. US Department of Defense Computer Security Center.

Ware, W. H. (Ed.). (1967). *Security Controls for Computer Systems: Report of Defense Science Board Task Force of Computer Security*. RAND Corporation for the Office of the Secretary of Defense.

KEY TERMS AND DEFINITIONS

Cyber Resilience: The ability of an organization to deliver continuously the intended outcome despite adverse cyber events, including the ability to respond holistically to adverse cyber events and to restore regular delivery mechanisms.

Penetration Testing: The assessment of an IT system, infrastructure, or application to identify public domain vulnerabilities and assess the risk of these being exploited.

Security Discipline: A collection of skill groups with a common high-level focus (e.g., governance, assurance, etc.).

Security Evaluation: The assessment and testing of an IT product or system against specified security claims using an established methodology such as Common Criteria (ISO15408).

Skill (Skill Group): The definition of a skill of group of skills against which a cyber security practitioner can be assessed.

Skill Level: A scale of six (formerly four) levels defining the level of knowledge, understanding, and practical competence in a cyber security skill.

Skills Framework: A framework of cyber security skills developed and maintained by the Institute of Information Security Professionals.

Threat Intelligence: The collection of intelligence related to cyber security threats to an organization. Sources include open source intelligence, social media intelligence, and the dark web.

Vulnerability Assessment: The assessment of an IT system, infrastructure, or application to identify potential public domain vulnerabilities. Vulnerability assessment differs from penetration testing in that no attempt is made to exploit the identified vulnerabilities.

ENDNOTES

[1]   A copy of the current version of the Skills Framework can be required via the IISP's website at www.iisp.org.

[2]   CESG, formerly the Communications-Electronics Security Group, is the UK government's National Technical Authority for Information Assurance and is part of the National Cyber Security Centre.

This research was previously published in Cybersecurity Education for Awareness and Compliance; pages 202-221, copyright year 2019 by Information Science Reference (an imprint of IGI Global).

Chapter 11
Why One Should Learn Ethical Hacking

Sunita Vikrant Dhavale
Defence Institute of Advanced Technology, India

ABSTRACT

This chapter presents the importance of learning hacking techniques by each and every person dealing with cyber operations. The chapter explains various basic terminologies used in the ethical hacking domain and also provides step-by-step instructions for setting up an ethical hacking lab. The chapter also reveals the legal issues with the ethical hacking domain by providing details of existing cyber laws, acts, and regulations framed by various countries in order to deal with the harmful hacking activities and cybercrimes.

INTRODUCTION

"If you know your enemies and know yourself, you will not be imperiled in a hundred battles... if you do not know your enemies nor yourself, you will be imperiled in every single battle"; was quoted precisely by the famous Chinese military General Sun Tzu (Sun Tzu, 2018). Studying attackers and their attack techniques will definitely help us in building effective defense posture for our systems and networks in the cyber space.

As of the most recent reported period, the number of internet users worldwide has increased to 3.58 billion. Access to the internet by users becomes unavoidable with the advent of technological developments and numerous advantages like easy data sharing, collaborative working style, flexibility, low cost, easy access, availability of different cloud computing models, online storage models, social networking, shopping, browsing publicly available data/information etc. As each and every individual or organization/institute has gained a greater online presence, cyber security has become a vital topic of concern (Singer & Allan, 2014). Many individual activities continue to evolve in the cyber space and this increased dependence on cyberspace can escalate vulnerability in one's information assets. The threats from hackers, spies, terrorists, and criminal organizations against our information assets are undeniable. Recently a

DOI: 10.4018/978-1-6684-3554-0.ch011

massive ransom waremalware attack hit many critical servers across the globe including countries like Russia, Ukraine, Romania, the Netherlands, Norway, France, Spain, Britain, US, Australia and India. The attackers used social engineering tools and techniques successfully to exploit these systems by luring the innocent users to download popular tax accounting package or to visit a local news site (Jessica, 2018). The attackers were successful to extort money from some of the computer users. If we don't prepare our self against these attacks in time, the serious consequences like identity theft, theft of sensitive/proprietary information/trade secrets or loss of reputation/credibility in the market; may result. A single malicious attempt can bring down any reputed organization or financial institution to a halt, by causing a great damage may be costing in millions of dollars per hour.

One cannot protect his information assets if he doesn't know how attackers think and what techniques attackers use to exploit systems. Hence, learning offensive security techniques like Ethical Hacking is becoming a need of future cyber security world. Ethical hacking knowledge base can be used for testing/improving network and system security posture of organization. One can identify the security risks and vulnerabilities in a network with the help of ethical hacking knowledge base. There is a need for each individual and institute to learn hacking tools and techniques which are used by these dangerous hackers and to create a cyber-security team including Ethical hacking professionals in order to test their systems effectively (UKEssays, 2018). It's always good to know in prior, if there is any means to gain access to our stored sensitive data; before getting it exploited by the wrong persons. This will help us in protecting our valuable data from getting into wrong hands in this connected cyber world (Arce, & McGraw, 2004).

Before starting, one should keep in mind that there is a difference between learning ethical hacking subject and other traditional network security subjects. In general, traditional system and network security (Bishop, 2004) educational domain generally focus on the topics like network defense, firewalls, intrusion prevention systems (IPS), Intrusion Detection Systems (IDS), Antivirus techniques, Security Policies, Computer Security etc. (Bishop, 2002). while; Ethical Hacking domain focus on attacking the secure or unsecure networks and systems, sniffing transmitted data, password cracking, social engineering attacks, malware generation and all means that can exploit a network and system defense perimeter. Hence the learning approach of ethical hacking subject will be totally different from that of other network security related subjects. The offensive nature of ethical hacking subject makes it different.

Also, traditional cyber security education is based on bottom-up approach where security topics are taught separately in an isolated context, with little effort to link these topics together. Top-down and case-driven (TDCD) teaching model (Cai, & Arney, 2017) can be adopted for teaching offensive cyber security which allows learner to follow the footprints of hackers during the case analysis in order to gain practical experience along with the detailed study on how exploitation of different security mechanisms and weakest links can be achieved by attacker. The case analysis can be based on real-world cyber breaches like the Target Corporation breach, the Anthem Inc. Breach etc. Such case-study based cyber security course teaching models (Cai, 2016) will help one to gain a holistic view of security and to apply multiple defensive techniques in complex contexts by observing the flow of attack and its impact.

BASIC TERMINOLOGIES

Before exploring ethical hacking domain, we would need to know a few basic terms and what they mean.

Asset

Anything which is valuable to an organization is termed as an asset. It can be hardware, software, people or data. Information or organizational data is considered as a highly valuable asset as any damage/theft to it may bring sudden financial or credibility loss to an organization. Information or data may exist in various forms like records in database, documents, network packets, memory space, print jobs etc. Further, data may present in different phases like Data at rest (e.g. data recorded in storage media), Data in transit (e.g. network packets transmitted between two communicating nodes on public/private network) and Data in use (e.g. data in resident memory or cache operated by any running process in system). Our aim should be to protect sensitive data which may exist in any of these forms and phases.

Vulnerability

Vulnerability is a weakness in the security system that can be exploited to cause harm to organizational assets. A system without any authentication mechanism is vulnerable to unauthorized data modification or deletion. A system with un-updated antivirus package is vulnerable to newly created malware infections.

Threat

Threat is a possible danger or menace that would harm organizational assets. Threats may exist due to external hackers, criminals, terrorists, malicious or untrained insiders, natural disasters, competitors etc. The intense of threat can be controlled by fixing or minimizing vulnerabilities in the system. There is a threat to intercept, modify, or fabricate the data in an unauthorized way or to make it unavailable to authorized person.

Attack

Attack is an action or attempt carried out against organizational assets with the intention of doing harm. It may be an attempt to disclose, alter, destroy, and steal sensitive information or to gain unauthorized access to the system. An attack exploits vulnerabilities in the system. If a new attack can exploit a system before a security patch is released for a given application/software being used by the users, then it is called as a zero-day attack.

Risk

Risk is the likelihood that some event will occur by exploiting system vulnerabilities that can cause harm to an asset. The likelihood that a threat will use a vulnerability to cause harm creates a risk. It is difficult to identify or eliminate all risks. There always exists some remaining risk which is called as residual risk.

CIA Triad

CIA triad, also known as Confidentiality, integrity and availability, is a model designed to guide implementation of policies for information security management within an organization. Confidentiality refers to an assurance that the information is disclosed to the authorized users only in order to prevent any unauthorized viewing/copying/printing of data. Sometimes confidentiality is also known as secrecy or privacy. Integrity refers to an assurance that the information is modified by the authorized users only in order to prevent any unauthorized modification or tampering of data. Availability refers to an assurance that the information and services are delivered to the authorized users only, whenever they needed. Ensuring availability involves preventing service disruptions due to power outages, hardware failures, system upgrades, and denial-of-service attacks etc.

Authenticity

It is property or characteristic of system which ensures the quality of being genuine. An entity is authentic if it is what it claims to be.

Non-Repudiation

It is a property of system that guarantees that the sender of message cannot later deny having sent the message and that the recipient cannot deny having received that message. Both authenticity and integrity serves as pre-requisites for non-repudiation property as it becomes necessary to prove that only the sender could have sent the message and nobody else could have altered it in transit.

Authentication

Authentication is a process that is used to confirm that a claimed characteristic of an entity is actually correct. It generally involves a way of identifying a user for e.g. if the credentials like username and passwords entered by the user match, then authentication process becomes successful and the system will grant user the access to the system resources.

Authorization

Authorization is the process that determines what access rights the authenticated user has for the given system. It enforces the policies for authenticated users regarding which actions are allowed by user on accessible resources, which services are permitted for the user etc. Usually, authorization occurs after successful authentication.

Accountability

Accounting is a process which makes the user accountable for his actions carried on the available resources once he is authenticated by the system and authorized to carry out certain activities on the resources. Audit trails and system logs will help system to manage accountability.

Information Security Management

Information security management is a procedure which involves the identification of an organization's assets, development and implementation of security policies and procedures in order to protect these assets. It aims to ensure the confidentiality, integrity and availability of an organization's information.

Information Security Policy

Information Security Policy is a set of rules enacted by an organization to ensure that all users accessing organizational resources abide by the described rules in order to protect the resources. Generally it is properly documented, authorized by the approval of top management and ensured to be read by all users.

Hacking

Hacking means intentional exploitation of vulnerabilities that exist in the system or network. When this hacking happens with the permission of authority then it is called as ethical hacking. Here, always remember the word "prior permission of authority or owner of system" is very critical requirement. For e.g. if someone without any prior permission uses his skills to exploit the system first and later informs the authority/owner about the vulnerabilities found during the exploitation event is not considered as a part of ethical hacking and may result into legal actions against that hacker.

Hacker

A person who utilizes hacking techniques in order to exploit the vulnerabilities that exist in the system or network is called as a Hacker (Surgey, 2007). We can categorize a hacker into different types based on their motives and skills (Hackers Online Club, 2018; Thomas, Low & Burmeister, 2018).

1.   Black Hat Hacker

A black hat hacker, also known as cracker is one who breaks in the system or network security without the owner's permission or knowledge for malicious or destructive purpose like financial gain, revenge etc. He uses his hacking skills for purely offensive purpose like destroying or stealing classified data. He may be involved in cyber-crimes like espionage, spreading malware, identity theft etc. Most of the time, black hat hackers try to target victims located in other countries in order to avoid any violation of the laws of their own country. They may use multiple freely available proxy servers to hide their actual location. Prosecuting these Black Hats is difficult if their own country is not willing to act against them.

2.   White Hat Hacker

White Hat Hacker, also known as ethical hacker/ Penetration Tester, is an information security expert, who uses hacking and penetration testing techniques with the prior legal permission from the owner of the system for ensuring the security of an organization's security systems (Slayton, 2018). He uses his hacking skills for defensive purpose like enhancing the security posture of an organization. They can be part of organization's information security team. They carryout penetration testing and vulnerability assessment for their organization with proper permission and authority. Recently there is a huge rise in requirement of such skilled security professionals by reputed organizations and hence, opting career as an ethical hacker has become lucrative one.

3.   Grey Hat Hacker

Grey hat hacker is one who uses his hacking skills sometimes for defensive and good cause but sometimes for purely offensive and bad motive. He will try to discover the system vulnerabilities without the owner's permission or knowledge. Sometimes, he may report the discovered vulnerabilities to the owner or sometimes he may publicize the discovered vulnerabilities. He may sometimes violate ethical standards, but does not have the malicious intent typical of a black hat hacker.

4. Suicide Hacker

Suicide hacker is one who uses his hacking skills to exploit critical systems without the owner's permission or knowledge and without bothering about any strong consequences like long term jail, legal sanctions or any punishments. They are like suicide bombers, not worried about their activities and sacrifice their life for an attack.

5. Script Kiddie

A Script Kiddie is a non-professional hacker who doesn't have much knowledge of programming, computers and hacking techniques. He may use different open source hacking tools or scripts or programs developed by others for carrying out security attack in order to impress people or gain credit in cyber community.

6. Spy Hacker

Spy hacker is one who is employed by our competitor to reveal our trade secrets. He may be an insider who can take advantage of his assigned privileges to hack our system or network.

7. Cyber Terrorist

A Cyber Terrorist is a one who breaks into and damages the computer system or network for religious or political beliefs to create mass disruptions.

8. State Sponsored Hacker

State sponsored hacker is one who is employed by the government to gain access to top-secret information of other governments and enemy countries.

9. Hacktivist

A hacktivist is one who uses his hacking skills against government organizations in order to bring some social changes or to promote political agenda mostly by defacing government websites. He may relate his unethical tasks to the freedom of speech, human rights, or freedom of information movements.

Previously hackers were largely unfunded, unorganized and work individually but now they are largely funded, state sponsored and work in a team. Hence, the attack vector also changed from simple Denial of Service (DOS)/web defacement attacks to information theft/Distributed DOS attacks not only targeting large companies but each and every individual.

Vulnerability Assessment

A vulnerability assessment is used to evaluate the security settings of an information system, which may include the evaluation of security patches applied tithe system, or evaluation of missing security controls in the system. One can also use automated tools for discovering potential vulnerabilities. Here, full exploitation of systems and services is not generally in scope and resulted actionable reports may include identified and prioritized list of vulnerabilities along with detail mitigation strategies such as applying missing patches, or correcting insecure system configurations.

Penetration Testing

Penetration testing is the methodology used by testers within approved guidelines to attempt to circumvent the protection offered by existing systems security features. It can assess the technical, administrative, and operational settings and controls of a system. The target system administrators and his team may or may not know that a penetration test is taking place. Vulnerability assessment focuses on finding vulnerabilities in the system while penetration testing focuses on exploiting those vulnerabilities in order to determine whether unauthorized access or other malicious activity is possible. A typical goal could be to access the contents of the customer database on the internal network, or to modify a record in an HR system. Rules of Engagement/ agreements/Scope of Engagement are formed in order to decide what pen tester can do or cannot do (Thomas, Low & Burmeister, 2018). The deliverable for a penetration test generally includes a report that elaborate the penetration act carried out to breach the security (e.g. how the sensitive records in the customer database was changed without any authorization). A non-disclosure agreement (NDA) is also signed by pen tester to maintain confidentiality of critical findings. The risk of accidentally causing unintentional attacks like disruption of critical services/corruption of sensitive data is higher compared to vulnerability assessment procedures. Also the skill requirements of a penetration tester are higher compared to that of a person carrying out vulnerability analysis.

Penetration Testing can be (Intelisecure, 2018):

1.   **Black Box:** In this case, the tester will have no idea about the system to be tested and hence, he closely represent a hacker attempting to gain unauthorized access to a system;
2.   **White Box:** Here, a tester will be provided with whole range of information about the internal details of the program of a system such as Schema, Source code, OS details, IP address, etc., and hence, he closely represent a malicious insider (may be part of system administration team) having enough access to the system, and;
3.   **Grey Box:** Here, the tester usually provided with partial or limited information about the internal details of the program of a system. It can be considered as an attack by an external hacker who had gained illegitimate access to an organization's network infrastructure documents.

Penetration Testing can also be: 1) Announced penetration testing which attempts to compromise systems on the client's network with the full cooperation and knowledge of the IT staff. This type of testing examines the existing security infrastructure for possible vulnerabilities but fails to provide realistic scenario about organizational security or; 2) Unannounced penetration testing which is carried out secretly in order to give a measure of preparedness in situations when no one is expecting an attack to occur. Unannounced penetration tests are the more powerful option from an analysis point of view since they simulate the kinds of real world conditions in which attackers are not exactly likely to make their sudden intrusion attempts known.

Red Team

Red Team usually simulates a potential adversary or Black Hat Hacker for reliable assessment of defensive capabilities of an organizational information system security controls. Red Teams attack an organization through technical attacks that use offensive hacking/penetration test tools, social engineering attacks like phishing, and/or physical attacks like dumpster diving. This team can expose existing security weaknesses before real criminals may take advantage of them. Mostly, the target organizations staff will not know a Red Team Exercise is being conducted (Pierluigi, 2016).

Blue Team

Blue Team is usually trained and expected to detect, to oppose and to weaken the Red Team's efforts. Their activities may include accessing and interpreting system log data, gathering threat intelligence information, performing network traffic and data flow analysis etc. This team sees the Red Team's activities as an opportunity to understand potential attacker's tactics, techniques, and procedures (Pierluigi, 2016).

Social Engineering

Social Engineering refers to an attack vector that relies heavily on human interaction and often involves tricking users or administrators into breaking normal security procedures. It includes techniques like trying to get helpdesk analysts to reset user account passwords or have end users reveal their passwords in order to gain unauthorized access to the system accounts. Social engineering techniques also include phishing and spear phishing attacks in order to steal user credentials. Phishing attacks use authentic looking, but fake, emails from reputed corporations, banks, and customer support staff or tricks users to click on fake malicious hyperlinks in order to install malicious code on their machines without their knowledge. Spear Phishing is a form of phishing in which the target users are specifically identified.

Dumpster Diving

Dumpster Diving, also known as trashing refers to collecting lucrative information through company dumpsters/garbage cans in order to understanding the target. This information could be system configurations and settings, network diagrams, software versions, hardware components, user names, passwords, company phone books, organizational charts, memos, company policy manuals, calendars of meetings, events and vacations, system manuals, printouts of sensitive data or login names and passwords, printouts of source code, disks and tapes, company letterhead and memo forms etc. This information enables a hacker to extract names/contact details/designations of employees to whom he may target or impersonate. The policy manuals may show hackers, thesecurity posture of the organization while calendars may tell hackers which employees are out of town at a particular time.

HACKING PHASES

According to the EC-Council's Certified Ethical Hacker Course (EC-COUNCIL, 2018), Hacking involves following five phases: Reconnaissance, Scanning, Gaining Access, Maintaining Access, and Covering Tracks as shown in Figure 1.

Figure 1. Ethical Hacking Phases

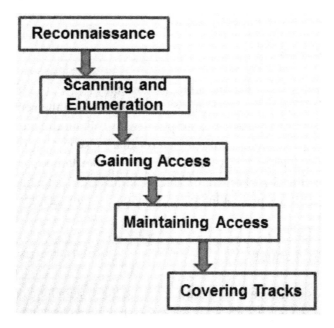

Phase 1: Reconnaissance

In reconnaissance phase, a hacker tries to gather as much as the information possible about a target or victim organization prior to launching any attack. This phase may take longer time. The study may include getting knowledge about target's client, business, employees, operations, networks, systems, assets using various available information sources like Internet, public records, news releases, Social engineering, Dumpster diving, Domain name services and any other non-intrusive network scanning methods (TOM, 2008). Reconnaissance can be passive which involves no direct interaction with the target like Internet searching or can be active which involves direct interaction with the target like Social engineering, telephone calls to help desk etc. During this phase an ethical hacker will be able to discover the potential threats imposed on the organization due to the freely available organizational data in public domain (like number of employees, product details, employee names, email ids, telephone numbers, project names, research details, recruitments, specialization, company's financial condition or market value etc.) as well as due to weakness exerted by insider's behavior at various times (like insiders revealing their system credentials/passwords/sensitive company data to unknown fake telephone calls, un-properly disposed sensitive documents in trash bin, employees visiting fake websites/downloading malicious softwares/opening spam emails etc.).

Phase 2: Scanning

In this phase, hacker scans the network for specific information after analyzing the information gathered from the previous phase. He may scan perimeter and internal network devices looking for vulnerabilities like open ports, open services, applications and operating systems versions, firewall rules, weak protection systems, network equipment device types, system uptime using different hacking tools like dialers, port scanners, ping tools, nmap tool etc. During this phase an ethical hacker will be able to discover the potential threats imposed on the organization due to any single leftover entry point which can be exploited by an attacker.

Phase 3: Gaining Access

In this phase, hacker gains access to the operating systems and applications on systems present in the internal network in order to either extract sensitive information or use the network as a launch site for attacks against other targets. He may try to escalate privileges to obtain complete control of the systems. During this process, he will try to compromise all intermediate systems. During this phase, he will use hacking tools like password cracker, Denial of Services (DOS) attack tools, session hijacking methods etc. During this phase, an ethical hacker will be able to discover the potential threats imposed on the organization due to vulnerabilities present in OS, application, system security policies and authentication systems.

Phase 4: Maintaining Access

In this phase, a hacker tries to maintain the gained access to the system long enough to accomplish his motives. He tries to retain the ownership of the hacked system using hacking tools like creating backdoors, maintaining rootkits, Trojans etc. He may continue to extract/damage sensitive information or use the network as a launch site for attacks against other targets. During this phase, an ethical hacker will be able to discover the potential threats imposed on the organization due to vulnerabilities present in various intrusion detection systems.

Phase 5: Covering Tracks

In this phase, a hacker tries to hide any evidences for the malicious acts carried by him in order to evade from any detection. He tries to delete any evidences, overwrite server, system, and application log files to hide his identity and activities using hacking tools like malicious scripts, tunneling, steganography etc. During this phase, an ethical hacker will be able to discover the potential threats imposed on the organization due to vulnerabilities present in intrusion detection systems, audit log creation, audit log maintenance and security.

At the end of all phases, an ethical hacker can generate report including the result of hacking activities carried out against target systems and networks; which will help their organization to strengthen security posture in order to prevent hackers from gaining organization's sensitive data. Organization will also get the idea on how much time, cost and effort they should invest for protecting their information assets.

LEGAL ISSUES INVOLVED IN HACKING (WILK, 2016)

As ethical hackers always use their hacking skills for security assessment of their organization with the permission of concerned authorities, ethical hacking is completely legal. It is expected that a person working as an ethical hacker should have strong work ethics and should be committed to organization security policies. Any person working as a hacker should keep this in mind that any unauthorized access to the computer systems without owner consent is always considered as a serious crime. He or she should be aware of following existing laws, regulations and standards against cyber-attacks from different countries, before acquiring knowledge about hacking tools or before carrying out any hacking activity. Along with these government regulations, most of the cyber/information security related certification courses and training programs like International Information Systems Security Certification Consortium, or (ISC)2 Certified Information Systems Security Professional (CISSP) (David & Mike, 2016), EC-Council's Certified Ethical Hacker (CEH), System Administration, Networking and Security (Sans, 2005) Institute Global Information Assurance Certifications (GIAC) etc. mandate their students to give the declaration stating that they will strictly adhere the ethical guidelines and code of conduct; else rejection/revocation of earned certification along with penalty may be enforced (Slayton, 2018).The emphasis on ethics within ethical hacker community needs to be constantly addressed in order strictly inculcate the ethical behavior within the ethical hacker community.

Also, there is a dilemma when teaching offensive techniques to the learners as these techniques can be misused by immature students and involves legal issues (Zouheir & Walid, 2013). To reduce the educator's liabilities toward teaching ethical hacking, teaching these techniques should be accompanied by a basic discussion of legal implications and ethics (Mink, & Freiling, 2006). Learners should be aware of the legal implications and the ethics of ethical hacking. One should understand that the aim of teaching offensive techniques is to improve the defensive techniques and to implement the appropriate security solutions.

The Computer Misuse Act 1990

This Act of the UK Parliament recognizes a computer crime or hacking activity as a criminal offence. Many other countries including Canada and the Republic of Ireland have considered this act when subsequently drafting their own information security laws.

Computer Fraud and Abuse Act (CFAA) 1986

This Act of USA is an amendment to existing computer fraud law (18 U.S.C. § 1030), which had been included in the Comprehensive Crime Control Act of 1984. Accessing a computer without authorization is considered as federal crime by this act (Charles, 2014).

USA Patriot Act 2001 (King, 2003)

This Act of USA is included for Uniting and Strengthening America by Providing Appropriate Tools Required to Intercept and Obstruct Terrorism. This Act exists to deter and punish terrorist acts in the United States and around the world, to enhance law enforcement investigatory tools. This act allows employers/law agencies to review employee communications, including e-mail and Internet activity although non-job related electronic communications are private in nature.

Identity Theft and Assumption Deterrence Act (ITADA)

This law specifies broad definition of identity theft including misuse of different forms of information, including name, Social Security number, account number, password, or other information linked to an individual other than the one providing it (Crescenzo, 2009). ITADA includes penalties for violation of these laws for e.g. some offenses can result in prison terms up to three years, however if the criminal obtains more than $1,000 in goods or services during a one-year period through violating this law, they can be imprisoned for as long as 15 years (ITADA, 2018).

Electronics Communications Privacy Act (ECPA)

This act by the United States extends government restrictions on wire taps from telephone calls to include transmissions of electronic data by computer (18 U.S.C. § 2510 et seq. It sets down more stringent requirements for search (Faganel & Bratina, 2012). It protects wire, oral, and electronic communications while those communications are being made, are in transit, and when they are stored on computers. The Act applies to email, telephone conversations, and data stored electronically (U.S. Department of Justice, 2013)

Information Technology Act, ITA-2000 (VATS, 2016)

ITA-2000 Act of the Indian Parliament is the primary law in India dealing with cybercrime and electronic commerce. It includes many amendments penalizing different cybercrimes like sending of offensive messages, financial crimes, sale of illegal articles, pornography, online gambling, intellectual property crime, e-mail, spoofing, forgery, cyber defamation, cyber stalking, unauthorized access to computer system, theft of information contained in the electronic form, e-mail bombing, physically damaging the computer system, cyber terrorism and voyeurism etc. It also provides the law authorities power of interception or monitoring or decryption of any information through any computer resource (Dhawesh, 2011).

Cyber Intelligence Sharing and Protection Act (CISPA)

This act Directs the federal government to provide for the real-time sharing of actionable, situational cyber threat information between all designated federal cyber operations centers to enable integrated actions to protect, prevent, mitigate, respond to, and recover from cyber incidents. It allows technology and manufacturing companies like Google and Facebook to share Internet traffic including private data about their customers to the U.S. government (congress.gov, 2015).

Gramm–Leach–Bliley Act of 1999 (GLBA)

This Act of USA is also known as the Financial Services Modernization Act of 1999 and protects the privacy and controls the ways that financial institutions deal with the private information of individuals (GLBA, 2018).It requires financial institutions or companies that offer consumers financial products or services like loans, financial or investment advice, or insurance to disclose their information-sharing practices to their customers and to safeguard sensitive data.

Sarbanes–Oxley Act of 2002 (SOX)

This Act of USA mandates publicly traded companies to assess the effectiveness of their internal controls for financial reporting. It protects investors from the possibility of fraudulent accounting activities by corporations. The SOX Act mandated strict reforms to improve financial disclosures from corporations and prevent accounting fraud (SOX, 2018).

FISMA (Federal Information Security Management Act)

This United States Federal law defines a comprehensive framework to protect government information, operations and assets against natural or man-made threats. It codifies the Department of Homeland Security's role in administering the implementation of information security policies for federal Executive Branch civilian agencies, overseeing agencies' compliance with those policies, and assisting Management and Budget's (OMB) in developing those policies (Homeland Security, 2014).

Health Insurance Portability and Accountability Act (HIPAA) of 1996

This Act by the U.S. Department of Health and Human Services developed to address privacy standards with regard to medical information (OMOGBADEGUN, 2006). It requires the adoption of standards for electronic health care transactions. It mandates health care and insurance provider companies to safeguard the security and privacy of health data including individually identifiable patient's health information (HPS, 2018).

Digital Millennium Copyright Act (DMCA)

This United States copyright law implements two 1996 treaties of the World Intellectual Property Organization (WIPO). It criminalizes production and dissemination of technology, devices, or services intended to evade measures that control access to copyrighted works (Qiong, 2003). It sets the penalties for copyright infringement on the Internet (DMCA, 2018).

Payment Card Industry Data Security Standard (PCI DSS)

This standard is applicable to companies of any size that accept credit card payments (Liu, Xiao, Chen, Ozdemir, Dodle, & Singh, 2010). It mandates all such companies store, process and transmits cardholder data securely with a PCI compliant hosting provider (PCIDSS, 2018). It covers technical and operational practices for system components included in or connected to environments with cardholder data. The compliance of merchants or service providers to the PCI DSS is assessed by PCI Qualified Security Assessors (QSAs). PCI DSS requires an organization to: 1) maintain secure network by using secure firewall configuration and avoiding usage of default passwords; 2) protect cardholder data by implementing different security measures including strong encryption techniques; 3) manage vulnerability by updating antivirus regularly and using secure applications only; 4) implement strong access controls via need to know policy, assigning unique IDs, restricting physical access etc.; 5) Monitor and test network regularly, and; 6) maintain information security policy (Liu, Xiao, Chen, Ozdemir, Dodle, & Singh, 2010).

ISO/IEC 27002

This information security standard, titled Information technology – Security techniques – Code of practice for information security management is published by the International Organization for Standardization (ISO) and by the International Electro-technical Commission (IEC).This standard provides best practice recommendations on information security management for use by those responsible for initiating, implementing or maintaining information security management systems (ISMS) (Sussy, Wilber, Milagros, & Carlos, 2015). In order to protect the information, this standard specifies many control objectives related to various security domains like asset management, information security policies, organization of information security, supplier relations, cryptography, physical security, human resource security, operations security, communications security, incident management, business continuity management, compliance, system acquisition development and maintenance (ISO/IEC 27002:2013, 2018).

The US National Institute of Standards and Technology (NIST)

This is a non regulatory federal agency within the U.S. Department of Commerce. The NIST Computer Security Division develops standards, metrics, tests and validation programs as well as publishes standards and guidelines to increase secure IT planning, implementation, management and operation. NIST is also the custodian of the US Federal Information Processing Standard publications (FIPS). NIST SP800-115 (Technical Guide to Information Security Testing and Assessment)- provide guidelines for organizations on planning and conducting technical information security testing and assessments, analyzing findings.

Federal Financial Institutions Examination Council's (FFIEC)

This council, formal U.S. government interagency body composed of five banking regulators provides security guidelines for auditors which specify the requirements for online banking security (FFIEC, 2018).

Internet Society (ISOC)

ISOC is a professional membership society with more than 100 organizations which supports and promotes the development of the Internet as a global technical infrastructure by facilitating the open development of standards, protocols, administration, and the technical infrastructure of the Internet. ISOC also hosts the Requests for Comments (RFCs) which includes the Official Internet Protocol Standards and the RFC-2196 Site Security Handbook (ISOC, 2018).

Information Security Forum (ISF)

ISF is a global nonprofit organization of several hundred leading organizations in financial services, manufacturing, telecommunications, consumer goods, government, and other areas. ISF is dedicated to investigating, clarifying and resolving key issues in information security and risk management, by developing best practice methodologies, processes and solutions that meet the business needs of their members (ISF, 2018).

Open Source Security Testing Methodology Manual (OSTTMM)

This peer-reviewed formalized methodology from Institute for Security and Open Methodologies (ISECOM) concentrated on improving the quality of enterprise security as well as provides guidance regarding methodology and strategy of penetration testers. It covers topics like Competitive Intelligence Review, Internet Security, Communication Security, Physical Security, Wireless Security etc. (Pete, 2018)

Control Objects for Information and Related Technology (COBIT)

COBIT (Sussy, Wilber, Milagros, & Carlos, 2015) security standard by the Information Systems Audit and Control Association (ISACA) and the IT Governance Institute (ITGI), is an IT governance framework and supporting toolset that allows managers to bridge the gap between control requirements, technical issues and business risks (ISACA, 2018). COBIT enables clear policy development, good practice, and emphasizes regulatory compliance by categorizing control objectives into domains: Planning and organization, Acquisition and implementation, Delivery and support, Monitoring and evaluation. Each domain contains specific control objectives. This standard helps security architects figure out and plan minimum security requirements for their organizations (ISACA, 2018).

Open Information Systems Security Group (OISSG)

OISSG is an independent and non-profit organization with vision to spread information security awareness by hosting an environment where security enthusiasts from all over globe share and build knowledge. It also defines an Information Systems Security Assessment Framework (ISSAF)which can model the internal control requirements for information security (OISSG, 2018).

Open Web Application Security Project (OWASP)

OWASP is worldwide not-for-profit charitable organization focused on improving the security of software. It issues software tools and knowledge-based documentation on application security (OWASP, 2018). It enables various organizations to develop, purchase, and maintain applications and APIs that can be trusted (Rafique, Humayun, Hamid, Abbas, Akhtar & Iqbal, 2015). Every year, it declares the OWASP Top Ten list containing 10 most dangerous current web application security flaws, along with effective methods of dealing with those flaws. In 2017, SQL/LDAP Injections, Broken Authentication and sensitive data exposure risks stood as top most application security risks (OWASP, 2018).

Web Application Security Consortium (WASC)

WASC is nonprofit consortium made up of an international group of experts, industry practitioners, and organizational representatives who produce open source and widely agreed upon best-practice security standards for the World Wide Web. It facilitates the exchange of ideas and organizes several industry projectsto assist with the challenges presented by web application security (WASC, 2018).

Information Systems Security Association (ISSA)

ISSA is a nonprofit organization, which focuses on promoting security and education within the field of Information Technology (ISSA, 2018). It provides educational forums, publications, and peer interaction opportunities that enhance the knowledge, skill, and professional growth of its members. It mandates its members to adhere to a code of ethics, which includes: 1) Performing professional duties in accordance with all applicable laws and the highest ethical principles, with diligence and honesty; 2) Promoting generally accepted information security current best practices and Standards, and; 3) Maintaining appropriate confidentiality of proprietary /sensitive information encountered in the course of professional activities and many more.

INTERNET ACTIVITIES BOARD (IAB)

IAB is a committee of the Internet Engineering Task Force and an advisory body of the Internet Society. In RFC 1087 (Request for Comment) draft, it has declared following activities which purposely: 1) seeks to gain unauthorized access to the resources of the Internet; 2) disrupts the intended use of the Internet Ethical Standards; 3) wastes resources; 4) destroys the integrity of computer-based information, and/or; 5) compromises the privacy of users as an unethical and unacceptable (IAB, 2018) in order to enforce proper use of the resources of the Internet.

INSTITUTE OF ELECTRICAL AND ELECTRONICS ENGINEERS (IEEE)

IEEE, a nonprofit association mandates its members to adhere to a set of standards (IEEE, 2018) like: 1) To accept responsibility in making decisions consistent with the safety, health and welfare of the public, and to disclose promptly factors that might endanger the public or the environment; 2) To be honest and realistic in stating claims or estimates based on available data; 3) To improve the understanding of technology, its appropriate application, and potential consequences; 4) To maintain and improve our technical competence and to undertake technological tasks for others only if qualified by training or experience, or after full disclosure of pertinent limitations, and; 5) To seek, accept, and offer honest criticism of technical work, to acknowledge and correct errors, and to credit properly the contributions of others and many more.

ORGANIZATION FOR ECONOMIC COOPERATION AND DEVELOPMENT (OECD)

OECD, an intergovernmental economic organization with 35 member countries, provides the following guidelines for protection of personal data that crosses national borders (OECD, 2018):

1. **Collection Limitation Principle:** There should be limits to the collection of personal data and any such data should be obtained by lawful and fair means and, where appropriate, with the knowledge or consent of the data subject;

2. **Data Quality Principle:** Personal data should be relevant to the purposes for which they are to be used, and, to the extent necessary for those purposes, should be accurate, complete and kept up-to-date;

3. **Purpose Specification Principle:** The purposes for which personal data are collected should be specified not later than at the time of data collection and the subsequent use limited to the fulfillment of those purposes or such others as are not incompatible with those purposes and as are specified on each occasion of change of purpose;

4. **Use Limitation Principle:** Personal data should not be disclosed, made available or otherwise used for purposes other than those specified in accordance with Paragraph 9 except: With the consent of the data subject/By the authority of law;

5. **Security Safeguards Principle:** Personal data should be protected by reasonable security safeguards against such risks as loss or unauthorized access, destruction, use, modification or disclosure of data;

6. **Openness Principle:** There should be a general policy of openness about developments, practices and policies with respect to personal data;

7. **Individual Participation Principle:** An individual should have the right to obtain from a data controller, or otherwise, confirmation of whether or not the data controller has data relating to him, and;

8. **Accountability Principle:** A data controller should be accountable for complying with measures which give effect to the principles stated above.

SETTING UP YOUR ETHICAL HACKING LAB

Now, there is question, once a person learns ethical hacking skill, where he should practice and test them without any legal problem? So here is first advice, setup your own ethical lab using virtual machine manager and apply your attack scenarios on your guest VM operating systems. This is the safest option and explained in detail in next section.

NSF sponsored projects such as SEED (Wenliang, 2011) offers lab environment setup at http://www.cis.syr.edu/~wedu/seed/lab_env.html. The project offers a free SEED prebuilt VM image that can be used with both VMware and Virtual Box. It requires no physical lab space and all the lab activities can be carried out on learners' machine. Cloud-based virtual lab platforms such as EDURange (Richard, Stefan, James, Jens & Erik, 2015) and DETERlab (Peter, Peterson & Peter, 2010) can also be utilized for large scale security related education. They offer dynamic, flexible cyber-security scenarios through which learner can gain analysis skills along with toolsets and specific attacks.

Next, there are some freely available vulnerable websites that can be used for practicing ones hacking skills safely. These open source web applications/wargames help security enthusiasts, developers and students to discover and to prevent web vulnerabilities (Checkmark, 2018). They are:

1. bWAPP - Buggy Web Application (http://www.itsecgames.com/);
2. DVIA- Damn Vulnerable iOS App (http://www.damnvulnerableiosapp.com);
3. Game of Hacks (http://www.gameofhacks.com/);
4. Google Gruyere (http://www.google-gruyere.appspot.com/);
5. HackThis!! (https://www.hackthis.co.uk/);

6.   Hellbound Hackers (https://www.hellboundhackers.org/);
7.   McAfee HacMe Sites (https://www.mcafee.com/us/downloads/free-tools/index.aspx);
8.   Mutillidae (https://www.owasp.org/index.php/Category:OWASP_Mutillidae);
9.   OverTheWire (http://www.overthewire.org/wargames/);
10. OWASP Juice Shop Project (https://www.owasp.org/index.php/OWASP_Juice_Shop_Project);
11. Perrugia (https://www.sourceforge.net/projects/peruggia/);
12. Root Me (https://www.root-me.org/);
13. Vicnum (http://www.vicnum.ciphertechs.com/);
14. Hackademic (https://www.github.com/Hackademic/hackademic);
15. Hack This Site (http://www.HackThisSite.org);
16. SlaveHack (http://www.slavehack.com);
17. Hackxor (http://www.hackxor.sourceforge.net/cgi-bin/index.pl);
18. BodgeIt Store (https://www.github.com/psiinon/bodgeit), and;
19. SmashTheStack (http://www.smashthestack.org) and many more may exist.

Besides this, there are lots of CTFs (capture the flag) competitions held, where hackers can demonstrate their skills. Some of the wellknown CTFs are DEFCON CTF, picoCTF, Ghost in the Shellcode, ROOTCON Campus Tour CTF, ROOTCON CTF, CSAW CTF, HSCTF, UCSBiCTF, Infosec Institute CTF, Embedded Security CTF, DefCamp CTF, HITCON CTF, Trend Micro CTF Asia Pacific & Japan and many more…(http://resources.infosecinstitute.com/tools-of-trade-and-resources-to-prepare-in-a-hacker-ctf-competition-or-challenge/#gref). One can also register to Bug bounty platforms like Bugcrowd (https://www.bugcrowd.com/), HackerOne (https://www.hackerone.com/), Synack (https://www.synack.com/), Crowdcurity (https://www.producthunt.com/posts/crowdcurity) and earn money to find the bugs in registered applications.

Instructions to Setup Your Lab

In order to practice the attack experiments carried out in this book, you need to setup your lab. Due to legal consequences discussed earlier, we should always keep in mind that we cannot test a network or system that does not belong to us. There is no need to purchase costly equipment's like switches, servers or other networking components. You will need only following things to setup your ethical hacking lab.

A laptop with core i5 processor, at least 4GB RAM 500GB Hard disk with windows 7 professional preloaded.

Connection to internet (wired/wireless) for downloading required softwares

Oracle Virtual Box virtual manager (You can use VMware Player instead of Virtual Box)

Windows Server 2008 as VM

Windows 7 as VM

Windows XP as VM

Kali Linux as VM

We will see now step by step procedure to configure your lab.

Try to connect your laptop to existing LAN. You may have wired or wireless connection.

Go to command prompt. Type cmd in search tab and press enter key.

Confirm the IP (Internet Protocol) address of your machine and default gateway/router by entering command ipconfig/all as shown in Figure 2.

Figure 2. Output of ipconfig command

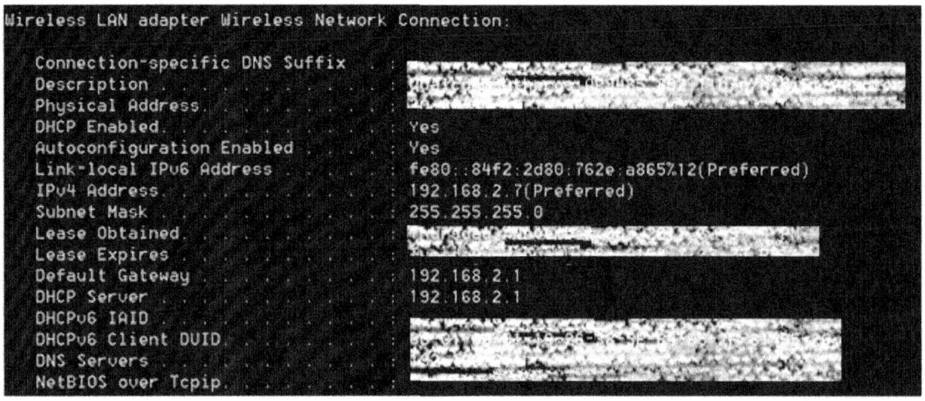

Once you note down IP address of default gateway (say here 192.168.2.1), disable the DHCP (Dynamic Host Control Protocol) server on your router and enable static IP addressing scheme. Set new static IP address (say here 192.168.2.7) for your host machine and check the connectivity by ping 192.168.2.1 command as shown in Figure 3. Also check internet connectivity by either browsing internet or use ping google.com.

Figure 3. Output of ping gateway

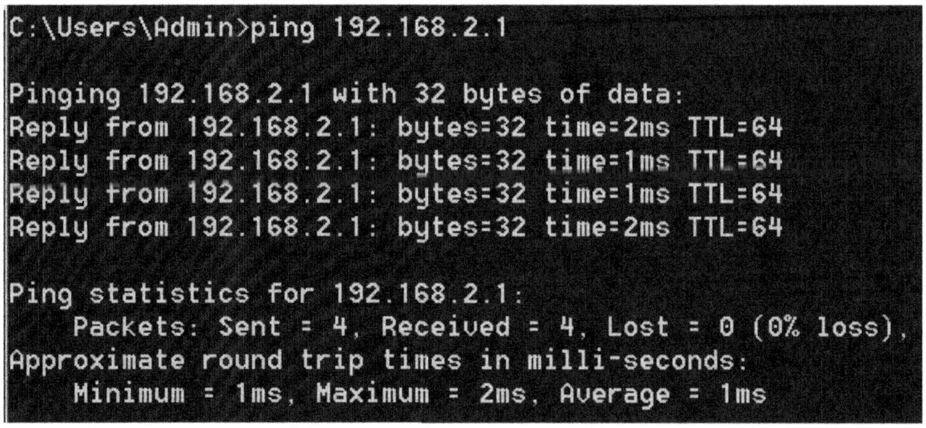

Set Up OracleVirtual Box on Your Host Machine

Before starting, we should know that virtualization is useful for: 1) running multiple operating systems simultaneously without having to reboot to use it; 2) testing software before implementing on real server; 3)Virtual Box feature called "snapshots", one can save a particular state of a virtual machine and revert back to that state if necessary, and; 4) can significantly reduce hardware and electricity costs. Oracle Virtual Box is a powerful x86 and AMD64/Intel64 virtualization product runs on Windows, Linux, Macintosh, and Solaris hosts and supports a large number of guest operating systems including but not limited to Windows (NT 4.0, 2000, XP, Server 2003, Vista, Windows 7, Windows 8, Windows 10), DOS/Windows 3.x, Linux (2.4, 2.6, 3.x and 4.x), Solaris and OpenSolaris, OS/2 etc. (Virtualbox, 2018). Virtual Box consists of following components:

1. **Host Operating System (Host OS):** The operating system of the physical computer on which Virtual Box was installed;

2. **Guest Operating System (Guest OS):** The operating system that is running inside the virtual machine;

3. **Virtual Machine (VM):** The special environment that Virtual Box creates for guest operating system while it is running. Hence, the guest operating system runs "in" a VM. Normally, a VM will be shown as a window on desktop of our laptop. VM determine hardware settings like how much memory the VM should have, what hard disks Virtual Box should virtualize through which container files, what CDs are mounted, state information like whether the VM is currently running, saved, its snapshots etc.

4. **Guest Additions:** Special software packages which are shipped with Virtual Box but designed to be installed inside a VM to improve performance of the guest OS and to add extra features like automatic adjustment of video resolutions, seamless windows, accelerated 3D graphics and more shared folders etc. Here, shared folder allows us to access files from the host system from within a guest machine (Virtualbox, 2018).

Now download Oracle Virtual Box latest version for host operating system (here it is windows 7, 64bit OS) from oracle official website link http://www.oracle.com/technetwork/server-storage/virtualbox/downloads/index.htmlas shown in Figure 4.

Figure 4. Downloading Oracle VM Virtual Box Installer

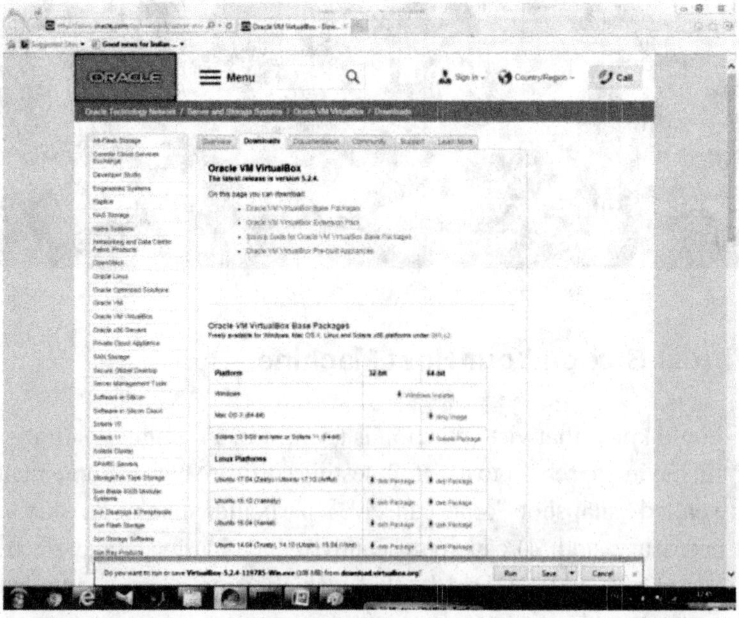

Now run the downloaded installer file and follow the instructions. After installation, start Oracle VM Virtual Box (WIKI, 2018) as shown in Figure 5.

Figure 5. Run Downloaded Oracle VM Virtual Box Installer

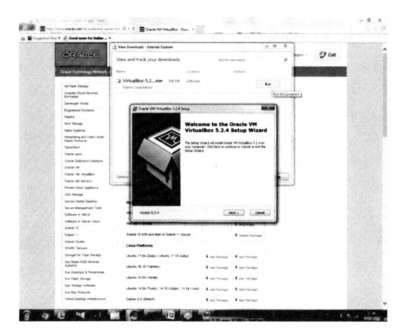

Virtual Box from Oracle is available for free from the developer's website. Make sure that you download the correct version for your operating system. Virtual Box allows us to create virtual computers within our laptop, enabling us to run multiple operating systems without dealing with dual booting or hardware configurations. During installation, the application asks for any modification needed to change the way the features are installed, click next as shown in Figure 6. Before clicking next, you can view disk usage requirements i.e. only 236MB is sufficient for the installation of package, as shown in Figure 7.

Next, the dialog box asking features to be enabled pops up, ensure all options are selected by default and click next tab as shown in Figure 8.

Next the dialog box warning about temporarily resetting the network interface may appear, click next tab as shown in Figure 9. Click install tab, when next dialog box asking ready to install appears as shown in Figure 10. Then, installation will start and take couple of minutes as shown in Figure 11.

Next, the dialog box asking installation of some additional USB drivers may appear, click next tab as shown in Figure 12. Finally installation complete dialog box will appear as shown in Figure 13. Clicking Finish tab will open the virtual box as shown in Figure 14.

Before using, install Oracle VM VirtualBox Extension Pack to get added functionality like the virtual USB 2.0 (EHCI) device, VirtualBox Remote Desktop Protocol (VRDP) support, Host webcam passthrough, Intel PXE boot ROM and Experimental support for PCI passthrough on Linux hosts. Navigate back to: https://www.virtualbox.org/wiki/Downloads in web browser and download the latest Oracle VM VirtualBox Extension Pack as shown in Figure 15. Once downloaded, double-click the file to install it as shown in Figure 16. Agree to the End User License Agreement when prompted as shown in Figure 17, then installation starts as shown in Figure 18. After couple of seconds, installation finished dialog box appears as shown in Figure 19.

Now the Oracle VM VirtualBox is ready for creating VMs and adding the guest operating systems that we need for our experimentation.

Figure 6. Oracle VM Virtual Box Installer dialog Box

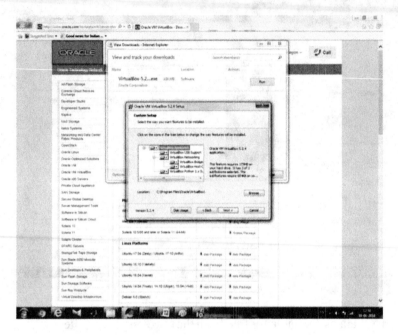

Figure 7. Oracle VM VirtualBox Disk space Requirements

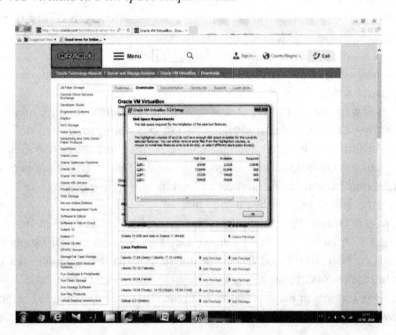

Figure 8. Oracle VM VirtualBox Installer dialog Box for Feature

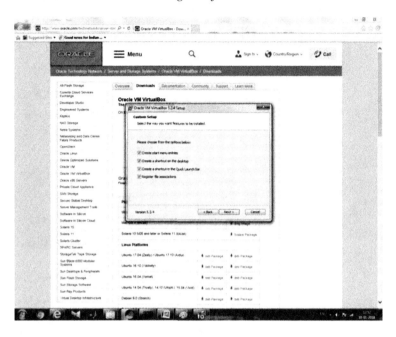

Figure 9. Oracle VM VirtualBox Installer dialog Box Displaying Warning

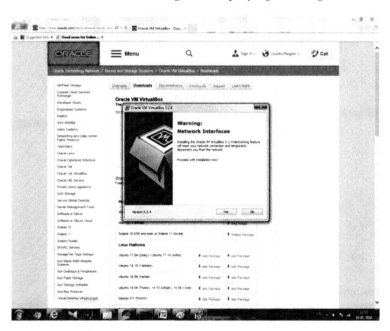

Before creating any virtual machine you will need to download corresponding .iso file. For our lab, we will need to download .iso files for Windows Server 2008 VM, Windows 7 VM, Windows XP VM and Kali Linux VM from Microsoft official website: http://www.microsoft.com and https://www.kali. org/ respectively. Once you downloaded these VMs, go to Oracle VM VirtualBox application and create virtual machines.

Figure 10. Oracle VM VirtualBox Installer dialog Box Displaying Ready to Install

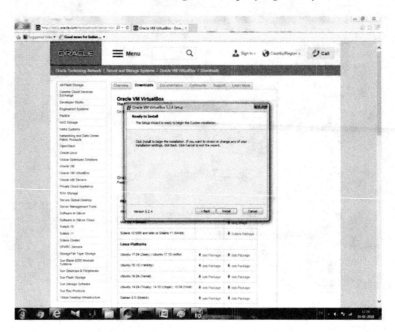

Figure 11. Oracle VM VirtualBox Installation

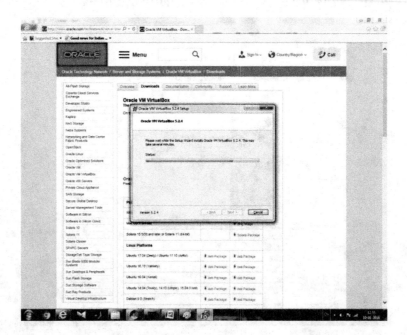

Figure 12. VirtualBox USB Driver Installation

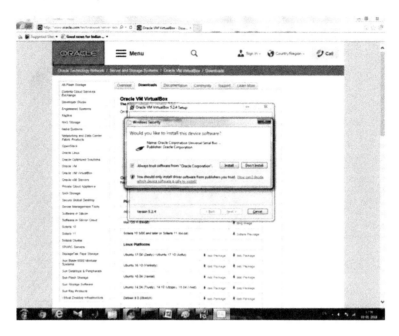

Figure 13. VirtualBox Installation-Completion

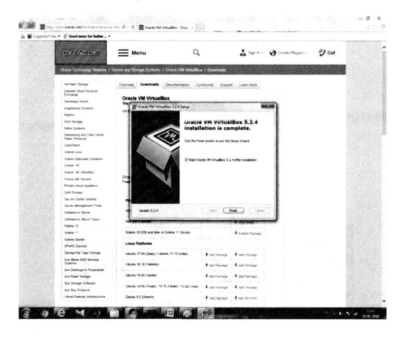

Figure 14. Oracle VM VirtualBox Manager

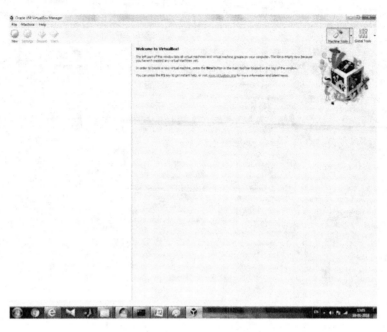

Figure 15. Oracle VM VirtualBox Extension Pack

Figure 16. Oracle VM VirtualBox Extension Pack Install

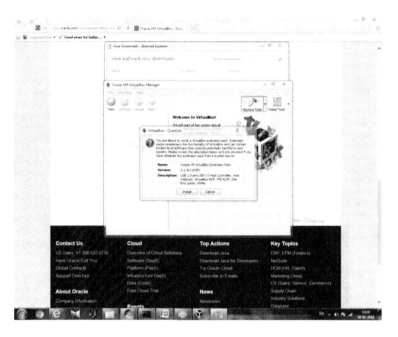

Figure 17. Oracle VM VirtualBox Extension Pack License

Figure 18. Oracle VM VirtualBox Extension Pack Installation Process

Figure 19. Oracle VM VirtualBox Extension Pack Installation Process Complete

Creating Virtual Machine

First download the latest Kali Linux image from site: https://www.kali.org/downloads/ as shown in Figure 20.

Figure 20. Kali Linux .iso image Download

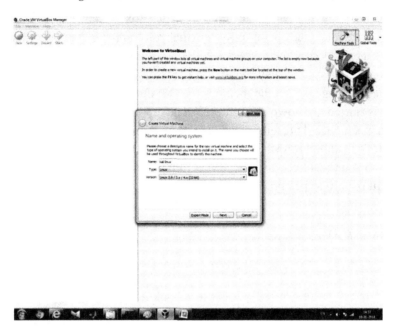

Then go to Oracle VM VirtualBox Manager interface and click on the "New" button at the top of the VirtualBox Manager window. A wizard will pop up to guide you through setting up a new virtual machine (VM) as shown in Figure 21. If VirtualBox is only showing 32 bit versions in the Version list make sure that your host OS is 64-bits, Intel Virtualization Technology and VT-d are both enabled in the BIOS, and the Hyper-V platform is disabled in your Windows Feature list.

Figure 21. Create new VM for Kali Linux

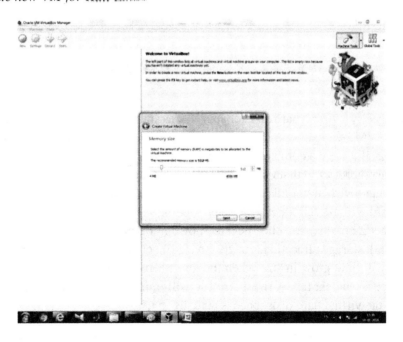

The wizard will ask name, type and version to create a VMas shown in Figure 21. The VM name entered here will later be shown in the VM list of the VirtualBox Manager window, and it will be used for the VM's files on disk. Select the operating system that you want to install later (here, choose Linuxas we want to use kali Linux). Depending on our selection, VirtualBox will enable or disable certain VM settings that guest operating system may require. It is therefore recommended to always set it to the correct value. On the next page, select the memory (RAM) that VirtualBox should allocate every time the virtual machine is started as shown in Figure 22. The amount of memory given here will be taken away from your host machine and presented to the guest operating system, which will report this size as the (virtual) computer's installed RAM. Select this setting carefully! The memory you give to the VM will not be available to your host OS while the VM is running, so specify as much as your guest OS and your applications will require to run properly.

Figure 22. Memory Size for VM

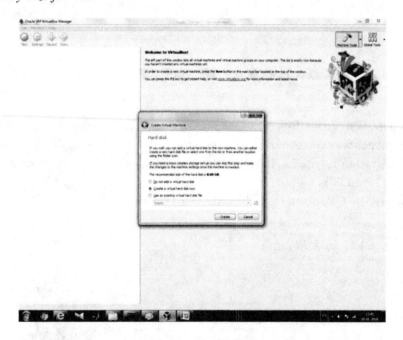

Next, you must specify a virtual hard disk for your VM as shown in Figure 23. VirtualBox can provide hard disk space to a VM by creating a large image file on real hard disk, whose contents VirtualBox presents to the VM as if it were a complete hard disk. This file represents an entire hard disk and it can be copied/used for another host with another VirtualBox installation.

Here, select "create a virtual harddisk now", to create a new, empty virtual hard disk and click on create tab. The wizard will ask harddisk type, select option VDI if the downloaded VM file is .iso file (else chose from other 2 options) and click next as shown in Figure 24.

The wizard will ask storage allocation type for image file created as shown in Figure 25. A dynamically allocated file will only grow in size when the guest actually stores data on its virtual hard disk, hence select it and click on next tab. A fixed-size file will immediately occupy the file specified, even if only a fraction of the virtual hard disk space is actually in use.

Figure 23. Virtual Hard Disk for VM

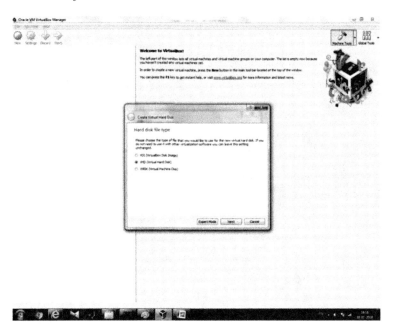

Figure 24. Virtual Hard Disk Type for VM

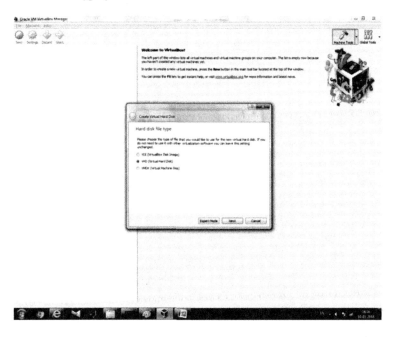

Next, the wizard will ask file location and size before creating VDI file as shown in Figure 26, click create, by accepting default values.

After clicking on "Create", new virtual machine will be created and can be seen in the list on the left side of the Manager window, as shown in Figure 27.

Figure 25. Virtual Hard Disk Dynamic Allocation for VM

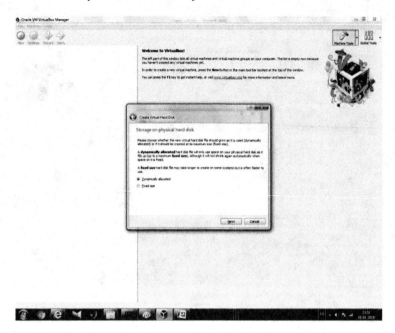

Figure 26. Virtual Hard Disk File Locations and Size for VM

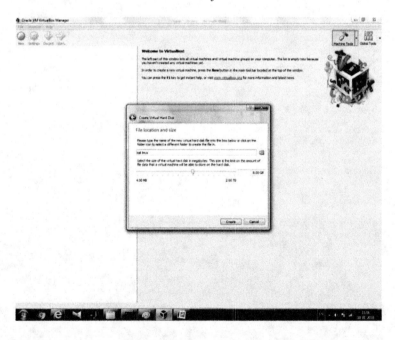

Now we have to configure it for kali Linux guest operating system. Click on settings tab and select storage setting in the dialog box as shown in Figure 28. Click on Empty tab will enable selection of virtual optical disk on right side. Click on that circle enables you to select the .iso file downloaded for kali Linux VM setup as shown in Figure 29. Select the .iso file and click on open.

Figure 27. VM Created

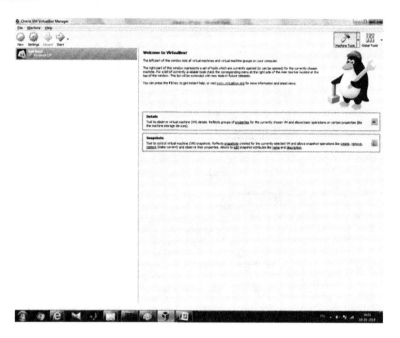

Figure 28. Configure Guest OS in created VM

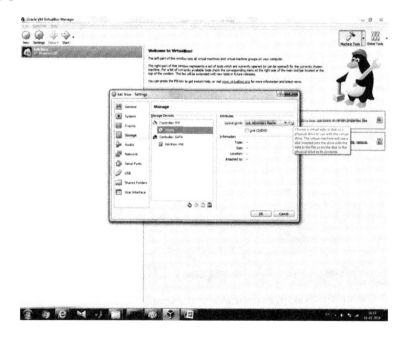

To start a virtual machine, either double click on its entry in the list within the Manager window or select its entry in the list in the Manager window it and press the "Start" button at the top or for virtual machines created with Virtual Box or right click and start as shown in Figure 30.

Figure 29. Select Kali Linux .isofile for created VM

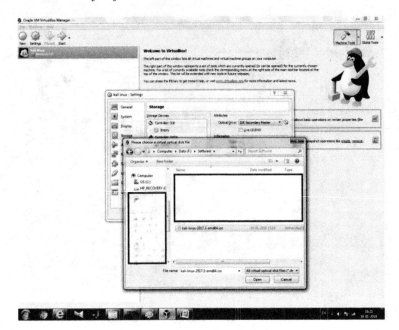

Figure 30. Start SelectedVM

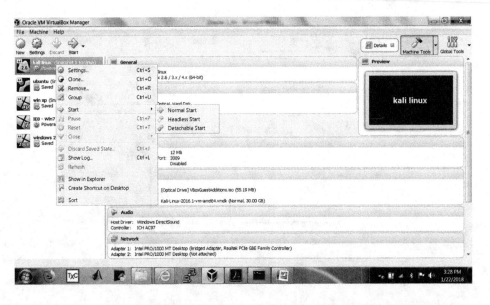

This opens up a new window, and the selected virtual machine will boot up. When a VM gets started for the first time, another wizard will pop up to help you select an installation medium. Since the VM is created empty, it would otherwise behave just like a real computer with no operating system installed: it will do nothing and display an error message that no bootable operating system was found (Virtualbox, 2018).

In the same way try to create VMs and install different guest for different OS required like win2008 server, windows 7 VM etc.

In case if .OVA file is provided by Microsoft for creating windows 7 VM, then carry out following steps into Oracle VM VirtualBox to import that file:

Select File>Import Appliance.

In the Appliance Import Wizard, click Choose as shown in Figure 31.

Browse to the.ova file, select it, and click Continue.

Select Reinitialize the MAC address of all network cards and click Import.

Figure 31. Creating VM if .ova file

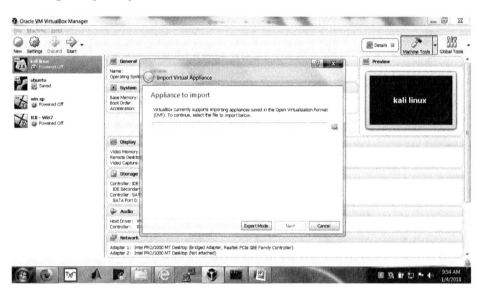

Configuring Different Virtual Machines

After creating VMs and installing of guest OS, you need to install the Guest Additions for each VM. For seamless keyboard and mouse operation, VirtualBox Guest Additions provides a set of tools and device drivers for guest systems. First, activate the mouse in the VM by clicking inside it. In order to return the ownership of keyboard/mouse back to the host operating system, press a special host key (By default, this is the right Control key) on the keyboard. The VirtualBox Guest Additions for all supported guest operating systems are provided as a single CD-ROM image file which is called VBoxGuestAdditions. iso. This image file is located in the installation directory of VirtualBox as shown in Figure 32. To install the Guest Additions for a particular VM, mount this ISO file in VM as a virtual CD-ROM and install from there. Installing Guest Additions will also automatically adjust the screen resolution of the guest OS and enables to shared folders/files of host system from within the guest system. Guest Additions also enables automatic mounting of shared folders as soon as a user logs into the guest OS.

Operating systems like windows reserve certain key combinations (e.g. Ctrl+Alt+Delete) for initiating special actions like reboot. But pressing the same may reboot your host instead of causing desired action to guest VM. Hence, in order to send these key combinations to the guest OS in the VM, use the items in the "Input" ® "Keyboard" menu of the VM or use special key combinations with the Host key (for e.g. Host key + Del to send Ctrl+Alt+Del to reboot the guest).

When you click on the "Close" button of your virtual machine window as shown in Figure 33, VirtualBox allows you to "save" or "power off" the VM. Saving the machine state option, freezes the VM by completely saving its state to local disk and when we start the VM again later, the VM continues exactly where it was left off.

Figure 32. Install VM Guest Additions

Figure 33. Closing VM

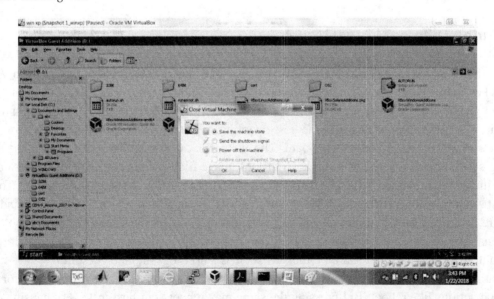

With snapshots feature, we can save a particular state of a virtual machine for later use and we can revert to that state at any time. This feature allows us testing software or other configurations. We can also create a full or a linked copy of an existing VM, in order to experiment with a VM configuration, or to backup a VM. VirtualBox can also import and export virtual machines in the industry-standard Open Virtualization Format (OVF), which can be used to distribute disk images together with configuration settings. Appliances in OVF format can appear in two variants: 1) VMDK format (Disk image files VDI, VMDK, VHD, HDD) and a textual description file in an XML dialect with an .ovfextensionor, and; 2) a single archive file, typically with an .ova extension which use a variant of the TAR archive format.

Next the network settings play important role for getting connectivity to all guest OS as shown in Figure 34.

Figure 34. Network Setting for VM

PCNet FAST III is the default and supported by nearly all operating systems out of the box while the Intel PRO/1000 MT Desktop type works with Windows Vista and later versions. The selected networking adapters can be separately configured to operate in one of the following modes as shown in Figure 35.

1. **Not Attached:** This mode is used to inform a guest OS that no network connection is available;
2. **Network Address Translation (NAT):** In this mode, VMs cannot interact with each other as well as they are unreachable from the outside internet unless port forwarding technique is used. This mode offers secure configuration while testing any malware inside any VM;
3. **NAT Network:** This is similar to that of NAT mode except that it allows all VMs to interact with each other and with internet;
4. **Bridged Networking:** This mode is useful for ethical hacking lab setup as it allows all VMs to interact with each other as well as with external networks. The VMs are also reachable from the outside internet. Hence this setting allows running servers in a guest. VirtualBoxexchanges network

packets directly through the installed network card circumventing host operating system's network stack;

5. **Internal Networking:** Used to create a different kind of software-based network which is visible to selected virtual machines, but not to applications running on the host or to the outside world;

6. **Host-Only Networking:** This can be used to create a network containing the host and a set of virtual machines, without the need for the host's physical network interface. Instead, a virtual network interface (similar to a loopback interface) is created on the host, providing connectivity among virtual machines and the host, and;

7. **Generic Networking Mode:** This mode is rarely used and allows the user to select a driver which can be included with VirtualBox or be distributed in an extension pack.

Figure 35. Network Modes for VM Network Adapter

For our lab, we will use bridged mode so that all VMs can talk to each other and host OS and also browse the internet. Bridging to a wireless interface is difficult and need to handle differently from bridging to a wired interface, because most wireless adapters do not support promiscuous mode. Here, we have used the wired interface for our experimentation.

Set static IP address for all VMs. Each system should able to ping each other as well as to the live hosts like google.com on internet. Also make sure the web browsers installed in the corresponding VMs can access any live standard websites like google.com. Keep any one directory (say D:\SharedItems) shared through all these VMs and check if it is accessible via all VMs. You can map this directory permanently as a network drive (Say I:).

Now your lab is ready for further experimentation.

CONCLUSION

In recent decades, there has been incredible growth in the usage of various internet applications by users. With the use of internet, we should prepare our self against undeniable cyber attacks from malicious hackers. This suggests for effective cyber secure interactions, we need to learn and understand hacker's methods and techniques. Hence there is a need to create an ethical hacking knowledge base for cyber threat awareness and prevention. A person having knowledge of the enemy's technique can better defend his own network.

This chapter has revealed the importance of learning hacking techniques by individual dealing with cyber operations. The chapter explains various basic terminologies, instructions for setting up ethical hacking lab in order to carry out the attacks mentioned in further chapters of this book. The chapter also explains the different phases of ethical hacking that any cyber user reading this book should know before starting any attack experiments. The chapter also reveals the legal issues with the hacking by providing different laws, acts and regulations governing the hacking activity and cyber crimes. Although, both technology advancements in security controls and law together play a crucial role against cyber attacks, there is no silver bullet that will solve the upcoming cyber threats by the smart hackers. This shows a need to find alternative ways like recruiting ethical hacking professionals and utilizing hacking tools/ techniques for efficient safeguarding of our systems and networks.

Finally, it is important to note that for an ethical hacker it is always mandatory and crucial to take authorized permission or consent of the system owner before carrying out any hacking activity.

REFERENCES

Arce, I., & McGraw, G. (2004). Why attacking systems is a good idea. *IEEE Security and Privacy, 2*(4), 17–19. doi:10.1109/MSP.2004.46

Bishop, M. (2002) *Computer Security. Art and Science*. Addison-Wesley Professional.

Bishop, M. (2004). *Introduction to Computer Security*. Addison-Wesley Professional.

Bratus, S. (2007). What Hackers Learn that the Rest of us don't: Notes on Hacker Curriculum. *IEEE Security and Privacy, 5*(4), 72–75. doi:10.1109/MSP.2007.101

Cai, Y. (2016). Designing A New Cyber Security Course by Dissecting Recent Cyber Breaches. *USENIX Summit for Educators in System Administration (SESA)*.

Cai, Y., & Arney, T. (2017). Cybersecurity Should be Taught Top-Down and Case-Driven. *ACM Proceedings of the 18th Annual Conference on Information Technology Education (SIGITE 17)*, 103-108.

Charles, D. (2014). *Cybercrime: An Overview of the Federal Computer Fraud and Abuse Statute and Related Federal Criminal Laws*. Congressional Research Service. Available from: https://fas.org/sgp/crs/misc/97-1025.pdf

Checkmark. (2018). *15 Vulnerable Sites To (Legally) Practice Your Hacking Skills*. Available from: https://www.checkmarx.com/2015/04/16/15-vulnerable-sites-to-legally-practice-your-hacking-skills/

congress.gov. (2015). *H.R.234 - Cyber Intelligence Sharing and Protection Act*. Available from: https://www.congress.gov/bill/114th-congress/house-bill/234

Crescenzo, D. G. (2009). On the Statistical Dependency of Identity Theft on Demographics. In Lecture Notes in Computer Science: Vol. 5661. Protecting Persons While Protecting the People. Springer.

David, S., & Mike, C. (2016). CISSP Official (ISC)2 Practice Tests (2nd ed.). SYBEX.

Dhawesh, P. (2011). *Cyber Crimes and The Law*. Available from https://www.legalindia.com/cyber-crimes-and-the-law

DMCA. (2018). *Digital Millennium Copyright Act*. Available from: http://www.dmca.com

Du, W. (2011). SEED: Hands-on lab exercises for computer security education. *IEEE Security and Privacy*, 9(5), 70–73. doi:10.1109/MSP.2011.139

EC Council. (2018). *Certified Ethical Hacking Certification*. Available from: https://www.eccouncil.org/programs/certified-ethical-hacker-ceh

Faganel, A., & Bratina, D. (2012). Data Mining and Privacy Protection. In Cyber Crime: Concepts, Methodologies, Tools and Applications (pp. 154-174). Hershey, PA: IGI Global. doi:10.4018/978-1-61350-323-2.ch111

FFIEC. (2018). *Federal Financial Institutions Examination Council's (FFIEC)*. Available from: https://www.ffiec.gov

GLBA. (2018). *Gramm-Leach-Bliley Act*. Available from: https://www.ftc.gov/tips-advice/business-center/privacy-and-security/gramm-leach-bliley-act

Hackersonlineclub. (2018). *Hackers Types*. Available from: http://hackersonlineclub.com/hackers-types

Homeland Security. (2014). *Federal Information Security Modernization Act*. Available from: https://www.dhs.gov/fisma

HPS. (2018). *Health Information Privacy: Health Insurance Portability and Accountability Act of 1996*. Available from: https://www.hhs.gov/hipaa

ISACA. (2018). *COBIT 5*. Available from: http://www.isaca.org/cobit/pages/default.aspx

ISF. (2018). *Internet Security Form*. Available from https://www.securityforum.org/about

ISOC. (2018). *About Internet Society*. Available from: https://www.internetsociety.org

ISO/IEC 27002:2013. (2018). *ISO/IEC 27000 family - Information security management systems*. Available from: https://www.iso.org/isoiec-27001-information-security.html

ITADA. (2018). *The Identity Theft and Assumption Deterrence Act of 1998*. Available from:https://www.thebalance.com/the-identity-theft-and-assumption-deterrence-act-of-1998-1947482

Jessica, H. (2018). *Cyber attack: What's going on with the latest ransomware virus?* Available from:http://www.abc.net.au/news/2017-06-28/whats-going-on-with-the-latest-cyber-attack/8658332

King. (2003). *Electronic Monitoring to Promote National Security Impacts Workplace Privacy*. Academic Press.

King, N. J. (2003). Article. *Employee Responsibilities and Rights Journal, 15*(3), 127–147. doi:10.1023/A:1024713424863

Liu, J., Xiao, Y., Chen, H., Ozdemir, S., Dodle, S., & Singh, V. (2010). A Survey of Payment Card Industry Data Security Standard. IEEE Communications Surveys & Tutorials, 12(3), 287-303. doi:10.1109/SURV.2010.031810.00083

Mink, M., & Freiling, F. C. (2006). Is attack better than defense? Teaching information security the right way. *Proc. of the 3rd Annual Conference on Information Security Curriculum Development*, 44-48. 10.1145/1231047.1231056

OISSG. (2018). *Open Information Systems Security Group*. Available from: http://www.oissg.org

Omogbadegun, Z. O. (2006). Security in Healthcare Information Systems. *ITI 4th International Conference on Information & Communications Technology*, 1-2. doi: 10.1109/ITICT.2006.358263

OWASP. (2018). *Open Web Application Security Project*. Available from: https://www.owasp.org/index.php/Main_Page

PCIDSS. (2018). *Payment Card Industry Data Security Standard*. Available from:https://www.pcisecuritystandards.org

Pete, H. (2018). *Open Source Security Testing Methodology Manual (OSSTMM)*. Available from: www.isecom.org/research

Peter, A., Peterson, & Peter, L. (2010). Security Exercises for the Online Classroom with Deter. *Proceedings of the 3rd International Conference on Cyber Security Experimentation and Test*, 1–8.

Pierluigi, P. (2016). *Cyber Security: Red Team, Blue Team and Purple Team*. Available from: http://securityaffairs.co/wordpress/49624/hacking/cyber-red-team-blue-team.html

Qiong, L., Reihaneh, S., & Nicholas, P. S. (2003). Digital Rights Management for Content Distribution. *Australasian Information Security Workshop 2003 (AISW2003)*.

Richard, W., Stefan, B., James, S., Jens, M., & Erik, N. (2015). Teaching Cyber-security Analysis Skills in the Cloud. *Proceedings of the 46th ACM Technical Symposium on Computer Science Education*, 332–337.

Singer, P. W., & Allan, F. (2014). Cybersecurity and Cyberwar: What Everyone Needs to Know. Oxford University Press.

Slayton, R. (2018). Certifying Ethical Hackers. *ACM SIGCAS Computers and Society, 47*(4), 145-150.

SOX. (2018). *The Sarbanes-Oxley Act*. Available from: http://www.soxlaw.com

Sun Tzu. (2018). *The Art of War*. Available from: https://en.wikiquote.org/wiki/Sun_Tzu

Sussy, B., Wilber, C., Milagros, L., & Carlos, M. (2015). ISO/IEC 27001 implementation in public organizations: A case study. *2015 10th Iberian Conference on Information Systems and Technologies (CISTI)*, 1-6. doi: 10.1109/CISTI.2015.7170355

Thomas, G., Low, G., & Burmeister, O. (2018). "Who Was That Masked Man?": System Penetrations - Friend or Foe? In Cyber Weaponry: Issues and Implications of Digital Arms (pp. 113-123). Springer.

Tom, O. (2008). *The five phases of a successful network penetration.* Available from: https://www.techrepublic.com/blog/it-security/the-five-phases-of-a-successful-network-penetration/

UK Essays. (2018). *Importance of Ethical Hacking.* Available from:https://www.ukessays.com/essays/information-systems/importance-of-ethical-hacking.php

U.S. Department of Justice. (2013). *Electronic Communications Privacy Act of 1986 (ECPA), 18 U.S.C. § 2510-22.* Available from:https://it.ojp.gov/PrivacyLiberty/authorities/statutes/1285

Vats, P. (2016). A Comprehensive Review of Cyber Terrorism in the Current Scenario. *2016 Second International Innovative Applications of Computational Intelligence on Power, Energy and Controls with their Impact on Humanity (CIPECH),* 277-281. doi:10.1109/CIPECH.2016.7918782

WASC. (2018). *Web Application Security Consortium.* Available from: http://www.webappsec.org/

Wiki. (2018). *How to Install VirtualBox.* Available from: https://www.wikihow.com/Install-VirtualBox

Wilk, A. (2016). Cyber Security Education and Law. *IEEE International Conference on Software Science, Technology and Engineering (SWSTE),* 94-103. doi: 10.1109/SWSTE.2016.21

Zouheir, T., & Walid, I. (2013). Teaching ethical hacking in information security curriculum: A case study. *Proceedings of the 2013 IEEE Global Engineering Education Conference (EDUCON).*

This research was previously published in Constructing an Ethical Hacking Knowledge Base for Threat Awareness and Prevention; pages 1-43, copyright year 2019 by Information Science Reference (an imprint of IGI Global).

Chapter 12
Teaching Offensive Lab Skills:
How to Make It Worth the Risk?

Zouheir Trabelsi
UAE University, UAE

Margaret McCoey
La Salle University, USA

Yang Wang
La Salle University, USA

ABSTRACT

This chapter identifies and discusses the learning outcomes to be achieved because of hands-on lab exercises using ethical hacking. It discusses the ethical implications associated with including such labs in the information security curriculum. The discussion is informed by analyses of log data on student malicious activities, and the results of student surveys. The examination of student behavior after acquiring hands-on offensive skills shows that there is potentially a high risk of using these skills in an inappropriate and illegal manner. While acknowledging the risk and the ethical problems associated with teaching ethical hacking, it strongly recommends that information security curricula should opt for a teaching approach that offers students both offensive hands-on lab exercises coupled with ethical practices related to the techniques. The authors propose steps to offer a comprehensive information security program while at the same time minimizing the risk of inappropriate student behavior and reducing institutional liability in that respect and increasing the ethical views and practices related to ethical hacking.

INTRODUCTION

The importance of experimental learning has long been recognized in the learning theory literature (Denning, 2003). Despite the fact many graduate and undergraduate courses in information security still offer a limited number of hands-on laboratory exercises as part of the curriculum the need to use a theory and practice-oriented approach in information security education is seen as paramount (Chiou

DOI: 10.4018/978-1-6684-3554-0.ch012

& Li Lin, 2007). A program that covers only the theoretical aspects of information security may not prepare students well for overcoming the difficulties associated with the efficient protection of complex computer systems and information assets. Furthermore, a learning environment that does not give the students an opportunity to experiment and practice with security technologies does not equip them with the skills and knowledge required for doing research and development in the computer security field. The introduction of information security courses aimed at offering a practice-oriented component have been well received by students (Hartley, 2015). However, review of literature acknowledges the issues of the ethical dilemma associated with these components (Hartley, 2015; Pike, 2013; Wang, McCoey, & Zou, 2018). Some programs enhance their offerings by adding a practice-oriented component that includes laboratory exercises (labs) based on defensive information security techniques (Hill, Carver, Jr., Humphries, & Pooch, 2001; Special Report on Forensic Examination of Digital Evidence, 2004; Vigna, 2003). However, many academics and industry practitioners feel that to defend a system one needs a good knowledge of the attacks a system may face (Arce & McGraw, 2004). Students who understand how attacks are designed and launched will be better prepared for opportunities as security administrators than those without such skills (Logan & Clarkson, 2005). As a result, interest in incorporating labs on offensive techniques originally developed by hackers has grown significantly (Brutus, Shubina & Locasto, 2010; Damon, Dale, Land & Weiss, 2012; Ledin, 2011; Trabelsi & Al Ketbi, 2013; Trabelsi, 2011; Yuan & Zhong, 2008) and teaching [ethical] hacking techniques has become a vital component of programs that aim to produce competent information security professionals (Dornseif, Gärtner, Holz, & Mink, 2005; Mink & Freiling, 2006).

Adding hacking activities to the information security curriculum raises a variety of ethical and legal issues. By using log data as well as data gathered through student surveys, it investigates the ethical implications of offering hands-on lab exercises on attack techniques in information security education. It emphasizes teaching offensive techniques that are central to better understanding a hacker's thinking and the ways in which security systems fail in these situations. Moreover, hands-on labs using attack strategies allow students to experiment with common attack techniques and consequently allow them to implement the appropriate security solutions and protect more efficiently the confidentiality, integrity, and availability of computer systems, networks, resources, and data. This research proposes measures that schools and educators can take to develop successful and problem free information security programs while reducing their legal liabilities, preventing student misconduct, and teaching students to behave responsibly.

The work is organized as follows: Section 2 presents the motivation for teaching offensive techniques. Section 3 presents case of teaching offensive techniques in hands-on lab exercises and the expected learning outcomes resulting from this learning and teaching approach. Sections 4 and 5 discuss the risks arising from teaching offensive techniques in an academic environment, the associated ethical concerns, and the emerging liability issues. Section 6 includes a framework for teaching these techniques Finally, Section 7 summarizes the results and conclusion.

OFFENSIVE SKILLS: WHY SHOULD THEY BE TAUGHT?

Teaching offensive skills brings a group of benefits to information security education. First, a good knowledge of offensive skills provides a perspective from the attackers' view, which better prepares students with mindsets for preventing future attacks. Second, the exposed security vulnerabilities of a target system under attack lead to deeper understanding of the security mechanism for the system. Last but not the least, it is worth noting that students are interested in skills that are offensive in nature, as found in a recent survey that we conducted.

In this anonymous student survey (Table 1), feedback from 40 students enrolled in our information security program were collected to reveal the students' interests in offensive labs, and the questions and results from the survey are presented below.

Table 1. Students' view of learning from offensive labs

Questions	Responses
Q1. Are you interested with learning offensive security skills?	• Strongly interested: **93%** • Interested: **5%** • No opinion: **1%** • Not interested: **1%**
Q2. Compared to labs that are designed in a defensive manner and those in offensive manner, which ones are more interesting to you?	• Labs designed in defensive manner are more interesting to you: **10%** • Labs designed in offensive manner are more interesting to you: **88%** • I don't know: **2%**
Q3. (Assume that we can classify the group of labs of a semester as either offensive and defensive ones:) given the list of labs that we completed in this semester, rank your interests about those labs from high to low. (This question could more precisely reveal their interests in offensive labs)	• Offensive labs: **Very High** • Defensive labs: **Middle**
Q4. (Assume that we can classify the group of labs of a semester as either offensive and defensive ones) given the list of labs that we completed in this semester, rank those labs from high to low based on the amount of knowledge that you learned. (This question could more precisely understand their learning outcome to see whether offensive labs lead to more understanding of the subject.)	• Offensive labs allow you to acquire more about the area of information and network security: **High**. • Bothe offensive and defensive labs together allow you to acquire more about the area of information and network security: **Very High.** • Defensive labs allow you to acquire more about the area of information and network security: **Middle.**

From the first question, it is evident that the majority of the students acknowledged that they are very highly interested in labs with offensive skills. The second question further confirmed that most students preferred labs with offensive skills. From the other two questions, one can see that the labs only with defensive skills are the least favored by the students. In conclusion, this survey reveals that students are motivated with more interests in labs with offensive skills.

STRATEGIES TO TEACH OFFENSIVE SKILLS

The overall purpose of applying a hands-on approach to teaching information security is to provide students with an opportunity to complement the theoretical knowledge with operational experience by using offensive and defensive techniques. The laboratory exercises developed for such a course need to be relevant to the course curriculum and need to be compatible with the existing laboratory environment so that their set up is affordable. Furthermore, the exercises need to be sufficiently simple in order to fit in with the time allocated for the lab and portable so that they can be easily and implemented in different operating system environments using different hardware and software platforms.

From each laboratory exercise students learn how to perform a specific attack, and how to prevent malicious hosts from performing it successfully. The learning objective is included in the laboratory exercise manual that also contains descriptions of the attack and the corresponding security solutions. While students would have already covered the information security aspects of each attack in the lecture class, the laboratory exercise begins with summarizing the theoretical concepts related to the attack under consideration. Next students are asked to perform the exercise tasks within the lab time frame. They are given instructions about how to set up and configure an isolated laboratory network, how to generate the attack, and how to implement and test appropriate defensive solutions. Normally students work in small groups of three to four. Each group's isolated network may include one victim host and two or three malicious hosts used to generate the attack traffic.

Several outcomes are expected because of using the teaching and learning approach described above. First students will be able to develop some of the "soft" skills required for information security graduates, including communication and persuasion skills especially when using social engineering techniques. Leadership and teamwork will be also developed since students work in teams and gain a chance to act as team leaders and members. Students will also acquire a sense of accomplishment when they successfully break into a system, and a sense of pride when they successfully defend a system. They learn a valuable lesson in persistence and the ability to work within a time constraint on a specific set of objectives.

Second students will deepen their understanding of information security as they become aware of the technology's weaknesses and vulnerabilities, and that often it is the users of the technology who need to take appropriate corrective actions depending on the situation and circumstances. Students will become more motivated as they will be proactively involved in the entire attack and defend process, culminating with a presentation of each team's results and observations to their peers and the instructor.

Finally, adoption of the approach allows students to understand the hacker's thought process. Hence, students will be prepared to combat the hacker's activities more efficiently. Although the offensive hands-on lab exercises will be done in a controlled environment, the university could also benefit by permitting students to complete a network survey of the university's network implementation and conduct network and system vulnerability assessments. This would be done within a specified set of strict guidelines so that no unintentional harm is done to the university network infrastructure and servers. This will help the university to strengthen its network security implementation while providing an experiential learning opportunity for the information security students.

Table 2 shows the results of an anonymous questionnaire that was administered to 110 students enrolled in the information security program and who participated in a majority of the hands-on lab exercises that demonstrated the attack techniques. The objective of the questionnaire was to collect the students' feedback regarding the lab exercises. The results of the questionnaire showed that more than 85% of all students believed the exercises to be useful and helped them better understand the underlying theoretical concepts associated with the lab attacks. The questionnaire also revealed that 87% of the students were interested in similar exercises in other information security classes, and 86% would strongly recommend the lab exercises to other students. Hence, it is expected that offensive hands-on lab exercises will have a positive impact on the students' performance in achieving the course outcomes, because the exercises allow students to better anatomize the attacks and assimilate the concepts learned from the lecture.

Table 2. Student feedback

Questions	Responses			
	Strongly Agree	**Agree**	**Neutral**	**Disagree**
Do you think the lab exercises are easy to follow and straightforward?	82%	10%	5%	3%
Do you feel you better anatomize the attacks and assimilate the concepts learned from the lectures after performing the lab exercises?	85%	13%	1%	1%
Do you feel you understand hackers' thinking ways and the ways in which security systems fails better after performing the lab exercises?	84%	7%	5%	4%
How likely are you to recommend the lab exercises to others?	86%	11%	2%	1%
Would you like to see similar lab exercises offered in all information security classes?	87%	8%	4%	1%
Lab exercises helped me to learn how to apply security principles and tools in practice.	80%	10%	4%	6%

RISKS AND OUTCOMES RELATED TO OFFENSIVE LABS

Students who have acquired hands-on skills using offensive techniques may attempt to use these attack skills in an irresponsible, inappropriate and illegal manner to perform malicious activities. Such students may represent a serious threat to the academic environment as well as to the society. For example, using the learned DoS attacks, students may attempt to crash the university servers. Alternatively, using the learned sniffing attack, they may attempt to collect confidential and sensitive information about the university's users (e.g. faculty members). Finally, they may use this information for additional malicious activities such as accessing the mailboxes or the university's Learning Management System (LMS) to change exam grades.

To support this claim, we attempted to analyze the log files generated by our university's intrusion detection sensors (IDSs) before and after practicing two offensive hands lab exercises on sniffing and DoS attacks. The analysis results confirmed the concern dealing with unethical use of these skills. In fact, the university IDSs' log files showed clearly a significant increase in the average number of sniffing hosts detected during the few days following the sniffing hands-on lab exercise practice (Figure 1). Similarly, the log files showed clearly a significant increase in the average number of DoS attacks detected during the few days following the DoS hands-on lab exercise practice (Figure 2). The detected DoS attacks were targeting the main university servers, namely the web, email, DNS and DHCP servers.

In addition, most types of DoS attacks detected by the university's IDSs just after performing the lab exercises are similar to the ones tested during the class offensive hands-on lab exercises on DoS attacks, namely the TCP SYN flood, UDP flood, Land, Teardrop, and Smurf DoS attacks (Figure 3).

Moreover, anonymous student surveys were conducted to probe the students' behavior after executing offensive hands-on lab exercises. The surveys' results showed that most of the students acknowledged that they had tried the learned attack techniques outside the isolated network laboratory environment. Tables 3 and 4 show the result of the surveys conducted over the last three years on about 110 students enrolled in our information security program. In Table 3, the results of the questionnaire showed that about 88% of all students who answered the questionnaire tried to sniff the university network traffic. The questionnaire also revealed that 70% of the students were targeting faculty members as their victim while sniffing the university network. Fortunately, most of the students (72%) did not have malicious intention since their main objective behind their sniffing activities was just for fun and show of power. In Table 4, the results of the questionnaire showed that most of the students (85%) acknowledged that they had tried the learned DoS attacks outside the isolated network laboratory environment. The university's Web and Email servers were the main targets for these students. About 70% of the students attempted to attack these two servers. Fortunately, 89% of the surveyed students said that they did not have malicious intention while attacking the aforementioned university servers and the main objective of their attack activities was again just for fun and show of power. A review of the responses indicates that the students' major objective is fun and show of power. This is reflected by the fact that a review of the attack numbers after about 20 days returns to "normal" levels.

Figure 1. Evolution of the number of sniffing hosts detected by the university's IDSs before and after the sniffing hands-on lab exercise practice

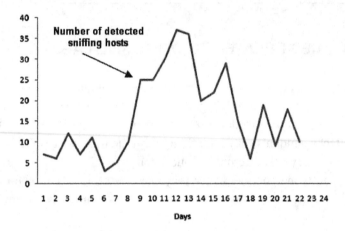

Figure 2. Evolution of the number of DoS attacks detected by the university's IDSs before and after the DoS hands-on lab exercise practice

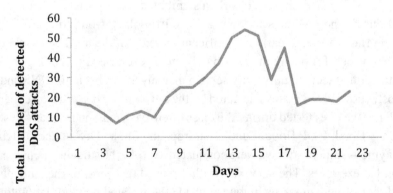

Figure 3. Types and percentages of DoS attacks detected by the university's IDSs after experimenting the hands-on lab exercise on DoS attacks

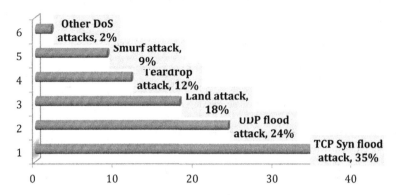

Table 3. Survey results of sniffing hands-on lab exercise

Number of Surveyed Students: 110	Survey Results
After the hands-on lab exercise practice on sniffing attack, did you try to sniff the University network?	• 88% of the students said "Yes" • 10% of the students said "No" • 2% abstained
If yes, who were your main target users while sniffing the University network?	• Faculty members as your target (70%) • Students as your target (20%) • Staff members as your target (5%) • All of them (5%)
If yes, what were your main objectives behind your sniffing activities in the University network?	• For fun (72%) • Collect user logins and passwords (15%) • Spy and watch network user activities (8%) • Other malicious activities (5%)
If yes, did you succeed to capture logins and passwords?	• 89% of the students said "Yes" • 9% of the students said "No" • 2% abstained
If yes, did you succeed to access the University's systems using the capture logins and passwords (such as the Backboard system)?	• 61% of the students said "Yes" • 35% of the students said "No" • 4% abstained
If yes, did you succeed to access users' mailboxes using the capture logins and passwords?	• 65% of the students said "Yes" • 33% of the students said "No" • 2% abstained
If yes, did you succeed to capture other confidential and sensitive information?	• 82% of the students said "Yes" • 17% of the students said "No" • 1% abstained

Table 4. Survey results of DoS attack hands-on lab exercise

Number of Surveyed Students: 110	Survey Results
After the hands-on lab exercises practices, did you experiment the DoS attacks outside the isolated network laboratory environment?	• 85% of the students said "Yes" • 12% of the students said "No" • 3% abstained
If yes, what were your main target systems?	• University Web servers (56%) • University Email servers (14%) • Other university servers (9%) • Outside systems (21%)
What were the objectives of the attacks?	• For fun (89%) • Attempting to slow down the target systems (11%)

In a survey that was conducted recently, we further confirmed that a few important issues are raised in teaching offensive skills. The survey results are presented in Table 5.

Table 5. Students' motivation for using offensive skills

Questions	Responses
Q1. (anonymous) Will you apply the offensive skills that you learned to real-life after class?	Yes, I will try: **83%** No, I will not try: **15%** I don't know: **2%**
Q2. If your answer is yes for Q1, will you investigate the legal/ethical outcome of your attack before you launch?	Yes, I will try to investigate: **20%** No, I will not try to investigate: **76%** I don't know: **4%**
Q3. What is your purpose of applying your attack: rank the following motivations: a. for fun b. show off my skill c. test the learned knowledge c. cause actual damage to the target system d. others: ___ (please provide)	a. For fun: **45%** b. Show off my skill: **27%** c. Test the learned knowledge: **15%** d. Cause actual damage to the target system: **10%** e. Others: **3%**
Q4. If you know there is a serious legal/ethical consequence due to your attack, will you still launch it?	No, I will not still launch it: **87%** Yes, I will still launch it: **12%** I don't know: **1%**

First, based on Q1 of the survey, it is surprising that a large majority of the students tend to apply the offensive skills in real life. This poses a potential serious technical challenge to targets such as the university web server. This issue needs to be addressed as part of the lab exercises. Second, based on Q2 and Q3, over 70% of the students will not investigate the legal or ethical outcome of their attacks on their own, even though only 10% of the students have a real intention to break the target system. Their ignorance on the legal and ethical outcomes indicates a critical gap that must be filled in teaching offensive skills. Last but not the least, Q4 of the survey does shed light on addressing the above issues: if proper legal and ethical education is included, only a small portion (i.e., 12%) of the students will still attempt on the attack. In the next section, we further elaborate on the ethical, legal and liability concerns in teaching offensive techniques and propose the countermeasures.

MITIGATING ETHICAL, LEGAL AND LIABILITY RISKS

The use of a teaching approach that is based on offering extensive offensive hacking hands-on lab exercises in information security curricula raises a variety of ethical and legal issues. The data collected from the university IDSs' log files and the students' survey results support the belief that some irresponsible or malicious students will attempt to experiment using the learned attacks outside the isolated network laboratory environment, in inappropriate and illegal ways. This also supports the concern of many security educators, who feel that teaching offensive techniques is unethical and are concerned that teaching dangerous skills to immature and unqualified students may be socially irresponsible. The schools and instructors stress they should not take on the responsibility of teaching new hackers. In addition, the misuse of information security expertise is serious and can result in criminal prosecution, bad publicity, personal injury, cyber bullying, and termination of educational programs, along with many other numerous negative outcomes. In addition, unmonitored offensive hands-on lab exercises may be a breach of the university's technology policy and of the law. Hence, students may threaten their careers, hurt others, and put their institution's entire academic information security program at risk. Consequently, both schools and educators may be held liable for the actions of the students. The study in Cook, et al discusses in detail the problem of misuse of the information security skills and provides detail of real-world incidents involving students (Cook T., Conti G., and Raymond D., 2012). In Damon, et al, there is a discussion of the ethical and legal concerns regarding the teaching of offensive techniques in the academic environment Damon, E., Dale J., Land N., and Weiss, R., 2012). In Logan and Clarkson, there is additional discussion on curricular issues surrounding ethical hacking (Logan, P. and Clarkson, A., 2005 .

Other sources claim that teaching offensive techniques yields better security professionals than teaching defensive techniques alone (Arce & McGraw, 2004; Arnet & Schmidt, 2005; Dornseif, Gärtner, Holz & Mink, 2005; Mink & Freiling, 2006; Vigna, 2003). We also believe that the argument that is against offering offensive hands-on lab exercises is flawed. In fact, ethical hacking techniques are central to better understanding ways in which security systems fail, and consequently are a critical component of a computer security curriculum. The trend towards penetration testing in corporate businesses shows that offensive techniques can be used to increase the level of security for an enterprise. It is questionable if students who have a poor understanding of attack techniques will be able to implement appropriate security solutions efficiently to protect the confidentiality, integrity, and availability of computer systems, networks, resources, and data. Not studying and applying these types of techniques, tactics, and methodologies from attackers will leave large gaps in the knowledge base of graduates (Brutus, Shubina & Locasto, 2010; Ledin, 2011). Hence, students trained in offensive techniques must not necessarily become malicious hackers, but rather can become talented security professionals.

In addition, we believe that, even though students may attempt to perform attack activities outside the isolated laboratory networks, their activities can be tolerated. The surveys' results (Tables 3 and 4 above) show that fortunately most of the students do not have general malicious intentions. The main objective behind their attack activities is just for fun and show of power. Secondly, the teaching of offensive techniques along with hands-on lab exercises yields better security professionals than teaching defensive techniques alone.

We agree that offensive techniques should not be taught in a standalone fashion. Every course in IT security should be accompanied by a discussion of legal, ethical and liability implications and standards. The survey results in Hill, et al show that 75% of the security faculty members agree that their schools should include an ethics course in the information security curriculum (Hill, Carver, Jr., Humphries & Pooch, 2001). A similar number of faculty members acknowledge that ethics should be part of every course in the information security curriculum. Hence, students should be educated on their ethical responsibilities. Ethical behavior is a mandatory part of information security curricula. Schools offering information security programs should develop and implement policies, procedures and guidelines to educate students on the consequences of unethical and malicious activities. Labs and curricula need to emphasis legal implications of these types of activities that are outside the isolated network laboratory environment. Student education becomes the solution to mitigate the risks associated with using offensive hands-on lab exercises for teaching information security.

FRAMEWORK FOR TEACHING ETHICAL HACKING COURSES

There are many concerns with teaching ethical hacking techniques. By including offensive hands-on labs in information technology programs, students improve analysis skills and improve defensive techniques for securing computers, networks and data. Educators must ensure that offensive labs are offered in isolated network environments. The emphasis is on the implementation of the hack and strategies to prevent and/or reduce the damage.

Programs must reduce liability and strive to prevent student misconduct by emphasizing responsible student behavior. Students need a context related justification for the need to be exposed to dangerous hacking techniques and tools (Hill, Carver, Jr., Humphries & Pooch, 2001), along with guidelines for ethical use of the tools. Schools may even choose to dedicate an entire course to "ethical hacking" (Epstein, 2006; Livermore, 2007; Logan & Clarkson, 2005). Furthermore, students need to be educated on the negative effects of malicious actions, including awareness of the legal implications of attack activities conducted outside the isolated laboratory network environment.

Practical administrative and technical steps include:

1. **Prepare the Environment**: An environment that allows the exploration and safe testing of hacking techniques should be provided to students. These are usually in the form of laboratories with isolated networks that do not communicate with the institution's main network. The objective here is to minimize the risk of any form of abuse of the skills learned by the students (Caltagirone, Ortman, Melton, Manz, King & Oman, 2006). Educators will need to inform the students of the legal statutes regarding the use of any hacking tools and techniques. This should be done throughout the course providing the lab exercises.

2. **Require Selective Student Enrollment**: Institutions should consider requiring a background check on students before admitting them to check for any criminal, unstable, or malicious history (Logan & Clarkson, 2005). The schools involved may also require applicants take and pass a psychological assessment before allowing them to apply for any courses. If such a background or psychological check cannot be applied, an ethics course should be a mandatory pre-requisite for any future information security courses. Enrolling students with a history of criminal activity or psychological activity poses a risk on not only the information security program, but also the entire institution.

3. **Institute a Mandatory Code of Conduct**: Students registering for courses in the information security field should be required to sign a code of conduct during that time. This form should detail how a student should behave while at the institution, as well as the consequences of unacceptable behavior that would break the code. With the code of conduct in place, the institution may forbid students from testing attack techniques learned in practical exercises outside of the lab's isolated network. A few examples of items in a code of conduct are the following:
   a. Resources should not be used to perform activities that may disrupt international peace and security.
   b. Resources should not be used to interfere in the internal affairs of other parties, or with the goal of undermining political, economic, or social stability.
   c. The courses taught are meant to develop confidence-building measures meant to decrease the likelihood of any misunderstanding and the risk of conflict.

4. **Educate Students on Ethical and Professional Behavior:** Usually, upon entering an academic institution, students are given orientation sessions or introductory courses. This should be taken

as an opportunity to communicate with the student population and discuss the boundaries between ethical and unethical behavior, also mentioning any local and international regulations related to such behavior.

5. **Create Awareness Programs:** Alongside the orientation session and introductory courses in an information security program, students will need constant reminders of the consequences of partaking in malicious activities. The faculty involved should dedicate at least one lesson in each semester to warn students of the risks of performing these activities outside of the dedicated laboratories. An example of a subject that would be covered in this lesson are the punishments that not only the university, but also the nation, has set for partaking in malicious activities outside of the lab, such as fines or jail time. It is imperative that the students are made aware of the legal implications of performing these attacks outside of the dedicated laboratory, as it may demotivate them from applying the skills learned in an external network.

6. **Accompany Each Lab of Offensive Nature With Components on the Legal/Ethical Consequence:** Other than providing education on legal/ethical education as individual modules in the information security education, it is also vital to provide clarification on the legal/ethical consequences with each lab to provide students a timely and detailed per-instance education.

7. **Monitor the Network:** Monitoring the network can help administrators keep track of the activities of the network's users. In an institution, this can allow administrators to detect when users are attempting malicious activities, especially students. Network monitoring allows the administrators responsible for the institution's network to create reports of the traffic passing through the network. The typical traffic that passes can be observed in order to ensure that the network is being managed and secured in the appropriate manner. Any attempted actions that are considered suspicious, even something as innocent as trying to ping another machine, can also be noted down and observed to detect patterns and prevent any possible impending attacks. Observing the type of traffic that passes through a network helps administrators prepare for the inevitable.

8. **Filter and Inspect Student Network Traffic:** Schools would need to filter and inspect students' network traffic and activities within the university network using intrusion detection systems and firewalls to ensure that key servers and systems are protected from potential malicious activities and traffic.

9. **Register the MAC Addresses of Student Devices:** Monitoring the network can be made simpler by also recording the devices that each student uses on the institution's network. Schools may ask students to provide the MAC addresses of their personal laptops and mobile devices to help computer forensics and specialists identify/eliminate the devices that initiated attacks (Special Report on Forensic Examination of Digital Evidence, 2004). A student's name or ID can be associated with a device's MAC address, helping administrators identify who is partaking in malicious activities so that they can be confronted. Having a form of identification to match a device's MAC address can also determine if the party involved is also in the information security program.

10. **Perform Penetration Testing on the Institution's Network:** Any organization that has a large network needs to perform penetration testing to ensure that the network is not vulnerable to attacks. The malicious activities taught to information security students are performed in an isolated laboratory and should not occur outside of the course involved. The institution's network will need to be properly protected to ensure that any students that attempt these attacks outside of the course's dedicated labs are not successful in doing so. The institution should consider hiring a third party to perform the penetration test, in case the administrators in charge of setting up the network left any

vulnerabilities behind, some of which they may not know. Network security is constantly updating, due to the constant and rapid development of exploits for any system. The laboratory networks dedicated to teaching these skills should also be tested to ensure that no traffic is leaked into the institution's external network. Mixing networks poses a great risk, even if it is unintentional. The lab's network should be secured properly to prevent any conflicts.

Despite the risks associated with offensive hands-on lab exercises and the view of some educators that offering such exercises is unethical (Harris, J., 2004), we are convinced that denying computer security students' practical application for defending against hacking restricts their development as security specialists. In fact, if students have not experimented with real hacking they may not be able to design and implement architecturally sound and efficient security solutions as to thwart future attacks, especially with the quickly evolving threats.

CONCLUSION

Students must understand a hacker's thought process and anatomize offensive techniques to defend networks and computer systems, and while at the same time strengthening their security skills. This work discussed several expected learning outcomes that can be achieved by a teaching approach based on offensive hands-on lab exercises. Using log data from students' malicious activities and students' surveys results; it discussed the ethical implications associated with offering offensive hands-on lab exercises, as well as the risks of producing malicious graduates with hacking skills. However, the results concluded that the ethical concerns of teaching students "hacking" are dwarfed by the need for knowledgeable, competent, and experienced computer security professionals in industry and government. The results proposed steps that schools and educators may take to reduce liabilities and provide a successful, problem-free information security program.

The work suggests inclusion of curricula to incorporate offensive techniques to teach security and include the following components:

1. **Review of Acceptable Use Policy for the Institution:** Beginning a course in offensive hacking should include a review of the acceptable use policy for the institution. Guidelines in the policy include acceptable use of university resources and use of protocols. Students are expected to understand and conform to the policy.
2. **Develop a Usage Agreement and Contract for the Course:** Courses in ethical hacking require students to test and develop skills which can be used to attack credible areas of the institution. The faculty in coordination with the institution's IT department and security officer should consider developing an agreement and contract that details permitted actions within the confines of learning and consequences for using these actions for illegal activities.
3. **Require Students Sign the Agreement:** Students participating in the security course should be required to review the contract for ethical hacking within the course. Students should be required to sign the contract attesting to understanding of the expectations and the restrictions for using these skills.
4. **Provide a Discussion With the Institution IT Security Director on the Consequences Related to Breach of Contract:** The discussion of the course contract should include an open discussion

with the institution IT Security director related to the consequences related to using these offensive skills for unethical or illegal purposes.

5. **Develop a Component on the Legal and Ethical Issues and Consequences for Using the Skills Outside the Lab Experience:** The offensive lab modules should include activities tied directly to the ethical and legal discussions related to the use these skills. The discussions need to expand to consequences related to using offensive skills for activities that extend beyond the institution prevue. Sample cases related to legal responses for using these types of skills illegally provide a basis for this type of discussion.

Student perception of learning from offensive and defensive labs tied to learning security strategy shows student's preference for offensive learning (Wang, McCoey & Zou, 2018). A survey of CIOs (Pike, 2013) indicates the need to include these types of ethical hacking skills to prepare students for the careers in cybersecurity. The survey expands on the need to mitigate the legal and ethical risks tied to this style and pedagogy (Pike, 2013). A curriculum that teaches ethical hacking needs to address both the offensive skills while enforcing mitigation of the ethical and legal risks tied to teaching these skills. Discussion of ethical and legal issues in collaboration with case studies tied to the skillset develops these values and prepare future cybersecurity professionals.

REFERENCES

Arce, I., & McGraw, G. (2004). Guest editors' introduction: Why attacking systems is a good idea. *IEEE Security and Privacy, 2*(4), 17–19. doi:10.1109/MSP.2004.46

Arnet, K. P., & Schmidt, M. B. (2005, August). Busting the ghost in the machine. *Communications of the ACM, 48*(8), 92–95. doi:10.1145/1076211.1076246

Bishop, M. (1997). The state of infosec education in academia: Present and future directions. *Proceedings of the National Colloquium on Information System Security Education*, 19–33.

Brutus, S., Shubina, A., & Locasto, M. (2010). Teaching Principles of the Hacker Curriculum to Undergraduates. *Proceedings of the 41st ACM technical symposium on Computer science education, ACM SIGCSE*, 122-126.

Caltagirone, S., Ortman, P., Melton, S., Manz, D., King, K., & Oman, P. (2006). Design and Implementation of a Multi-Use Attack-Defend Computer Security Lab. *Proceedings of the 39th Annual Hawaii International Conference on System Sciences - HICSS.* 10.1109/HICSS.2006.115

Chen, Li, & Lin. (2007). Combining Theory with Practice in Information Security Education. *Proc. 11th Colloquium for Information Systems Security Education*, 28-35.

Cook, T., Conti, G., & Raymond, D. (2012). When Good Ninjas Turn bad: Preventing Your Students from becoming the Threat. Proceedings of the 16th Colloquium for Information System Security Education, 61-67.

Damon, E., Dale, J., Land, N., & Weiss, R. (2012). Hands-on Denial of Service Lab Exercices Using Slowloris and RUDY. *Proceedings of the 2012 Information Security Curriculum Development Conference*, 21-29.

Denning, P. J. (2003). Great principles of computing. *Communications of the ACM*, *46*(11), 15–20. doi:10.1145/948383.948400

Dornseif, M., Gärtner, F. C., Holz, T., & Mink, M. (2005). *An Offensive Approach to Teaching Information Security: "Aachen Summer School Applied IT Security"*. Technical Report AIB-2005-02, RWTH Aachen.

Epstein, R. G. (2006). An ethics and security course for students in computer science and information technology. *Proceedings of the 37th SIGCSE Technical Symposium on Computer Scienece Education*, 535-537. 10.1145/1121341.1121506

Frincke, D. (2003). Who watches the security educators? *IEEE Security and Privacy*, *1*(3), 56–58. doi:10.1109/MSECP.2003.1203223

Harris, J. (2004). Maintaining ethical standards for computer security curriculum. In *InfoSecCD '04: Proceedings of the 1st Annual Conference on Information Security Curriculum Development* (pp. 46-48). New York, NY: ACM Press. 10.1145/1059524.1059534

Hartley, R. D. (2015). Ethical hacking pedagogy: An analysis and overview of teaching students to hack. *Journal of International Technology and Information Management*, *24*(4), 95.

Hill, J. M., Carver, C. A., Jr., Humphries, J. W., & Pooch, U. W. (2001). Using an isolated network laboratory to teach advanced networks and security*Proceedings of the 32nd SIGCSE Technical Symposium on Computer Science Education*, 36–40.

Ledin, G. Jr. (2011). The growing harm of not teaching malware. *Communications of the ACM*, *54*(2), 32–34. doi:10.1145/1897816.1897832

Livermore, J. (2007). What are Faculty Attitudes toward Teaching Ethical Hacking and Penetration Testing? *Proceedings of the 11th Colloquium for Information Systems Security Education*, 111-116.

Livermore, J. A. (2011). Screening IA Students for Criminal background. *Proceedings of the 15th Colloquim for Informaion System Security Education*, 81-86.

Logan, P., & Clarkson, A. (2005). Teaching Students to Hack: Curriculum Issues in Information Security. *Proceedings of the 36th SIGCSE Technical Symposium on Computer Science, ACM SIGCSE*, 157-161.

Mink, M., & Freiling, F. C. (2006). Is Attack Better Than Defense? Teaching Information Security the Right Way. *Proceedings of the 3rd annual conference on Information security curriculum development, InfoSecCD'06*, 44-48. 10.1145/1231047.1231056

Mullins, P., Wolfe, J., Fry, M., Wynters, E., Calhoun, W., Montante, R., & Oblitey, W. (2002). Panel on integrating security concepts into existing computer courses. *Proceedings of the 33rd SIGCSE Technical Symposium on Computing Education*, 365-366.

Pike, R. E. (2013). The "ethics" of teaching ethical hacking. *Journal of International Technology and Information Management*, *22*(4), 67.

Special Report on Forensic Examination of Digital Evidence: A Guide for Law Enforcement. (2004). U.S. Department of Justice, National Institute of Justice.

Trabelsi, Z. (2011). Hands-on lab exercises implementation of DoS and MiM attacks using ARP cache poisoning. *Proceedings of the 2011 Information Security Curriculum Development Conference*, 74-83.

Trabelsi, Z., & Al Ketbi, L. (2013). Using Network Packet Generators and Snort Rules for Teaching Denial of Service Attacks. *Proceedings of the 18th Annual Conference on Innovation and Technology in Computer Science Education (ITiCSE 2013)*, 285-290.

Vigna, G. (2003). Teaching hands-on network security: Testbeds and live exercises. *Journal of Information Warfare, 2*(3), 8–24.

Wang, Y., McCoey, M., & Zou, H. (2018). Developing an Undergraduate Course Curriculum on Information Security. *Proceedings of the 19th Annual SIG Conference on Information Technology Education.*

Yuan, D., & Zhong, J. (2008). A lab implementation of TCP SYN flood attack and defense. *Proceedings of the 9th ACM SIGITE Conference on Information Technology Education*, 57-58. 10.1145/1414558.1414575

This research was previously published in the Handbook of Research on Diverse Teaching Strategies for the Technology-Rich Classroom; pages 138-152, copyright year 2020 by Information Science Reference (an imprint of IGI Global).

Section 3
Curriculum and Program Development

Chapter 13
A Holistic View of Cybersecurity Education Requirements

Steven M. Furnell
University of Plymouth, UK and Edith Cowan University, Australia

Ismini Vasileiou
https://orcid.org/0000-0001-6174-3586
University of Plymouth, UK

ABSTRACT

This chapter sets the scene for the book as a whole, establishing the need for cybersecurity aware-ness, training, and education in order to enable us to understand and meet our security obligations. It begins by illustrating key elements that ought to form part of cybersecurity literacy and the questions to be asked when addressing the issue. It then examines the problems that have traditionally existed in terms of achieving awareness and education, both at the user level (in terms of lack of support) and the practitioner level (in terms of a skills shortage). The discussion highlights the importance of a holistic approach, covering both personal and workplace use, and addressing the spectrum from end-users through to cybersecurity specialists.

INTRODUCTION

From office applications to social media, from electronic business to global communications, the rise of information technology and the Internet has offered numerous benefits to individuals and organiza-tions alike. With all the positives to point at, it is sometimes easy (and certainly convenient) to forget the downside – namely that the technology that we now take for granted (and often depend upon) comes with associated risks. Systems can be attacked. They can fail. Data can be lost or exposed. Users themselves can be targeted. At the same time, cybersecurity is often assumed to be someone else's problem, with the consequence that the very parties that ought to have a stake in it end up distancing themselves from it instead. For example, end users frequently seem to assume that their employer, their Internet Service Provider, or some other party (*any* other party!) is taking care of their security needs. In reality of course,

DOI: 10.4018/978-1-6684-3554-0.ch013

they have a role to play as individuals, because no matter what steps may be taken elsewhere, there will be some threats that reach them directly. So, they will find themselves needing to make security-related decisions, and they clearly need a level of awareness and understanding in order to do so. Meanwhile, organizations may look at their employees and assume that they should already have acquired a level of general cybersecurity awareness from somewhere else. While this nicely excuses the organization from taking responsibility, it is often an entirely unrealistic stance. One of the key requirements is therefore for the various parties concerned to recognize their role and take ownership of it.

In fact, there is more to know at all levels of an organization, from the individuals who simply wish to use the technology, through to those that are tasked with providing the infrastructure and safeguards that enable them to do so securely. Indeed, a fundamental challenge is that we are not dealing with a one-size-fits-all situation. SETA needs exist at several levels, from users in personal settings, to users in a workplace context, and from technical specialists through to security professionals. As an illustration of how these levels may be split, and the requirements in each case, we can consider the following groupings:

- **Personal Users:** Need to understand how to protect their own data and use the associated technologies (devices and services) in a secure manner. They also need to be aware of why such protection is required.
- **Workplace Users:** Similar to the needs of personal users, other than the reason now relates to the need to protect workplace systems and data, in which they may not feel as directly invested.
- **Technical Specialists:** Refers to those responsible for designing, developing, implementing and running technology systems. There is a clear need for them to understand where security is required and how to deliver it.
- **Security Professionals:** Need a specific security skillset, which may be characterized and supported by specialist academic study and professional certifications.

These parties will develop and acquire their cybersecurity knowledge and skills in different ways and to different levels. Figure 1 presents a broad contrast between the paths that may be taken by general users versus those that become security professionals (noting that, for the cybersecurity professionals in particular, this is an illustration of a route rather than a prescription). For the former, one would hope that a general familiarity with cybersecurity issues would be developed during schooling, and then supported and supplemented by ongoing awareness-raising during any subsequent study and during their workplace life. This is intended to reflect that while they will not become in any way specialized in cybersecurity or technology more generally, they nonetheless need to have a credible understanding of the cybersecurity issues relating to them as individuals (and therefore require academia and employers to be playing their part in supporting this). Meanwhile, the path for security professionals is rather more focused. They would inherit the literacy and awareness aspects as lay users but would additionally be expected to have more specialized activities at each stage. For example, during schooling they may show a preference towards STEM (Science, Technology, Engineering and Mathematics) subjects, and then supplement this during higher education by opting for qualifications in subjects such as computer science or cybersecurity directly. Their workplace activity could then be supported by further specialized industry or professional certifications.

Figure 1. Contrasting the SETA pathways for general users versus cybersecurity specialists

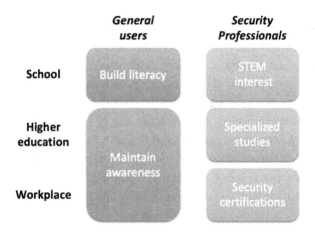

Of course, while this works from one perspective, it is certainly not a definitive view. In practice, there are numerous ways to cut this. For example, the need for awareness and the level of understanding required can also depend upon the individual's position within the organizational hierarchy, their responsibility for data and devices, and their role in the overall compliance structure. Taking their level within the organization as an example, typical staff members will inherit the needs of 'workplace users' in the previous list. Meanwhile, looking from a management perspective, local and departmental mangers will need to understand additional aspects in order to support them in making security-informed decisions in relation to people and processes for whom they are responsible. Meanwhile, at the leadership level of the organization, the understanding will need to reflect the relationship between security and issues such as business continuity and resilience, with the ability to factor security considerations into strategic planning. In parallel with this, an individual's responsibilities will help to inform any specific awareness or training that is needed in relation to the systems and data that they use or become responsible for. Finally, from the compliance perspective, the general staff require awareness and education in order to *be* security compliant, whereas the specialists require security understanding and skills in order to establish the framework that *enables* compliance (i.e. it is unlikely to be achieved if the organizations lacks staff with the knowledge and skills to put the right technologies and processes in place to support secure behaviors and practices).

Whichever way this issue is viewed, it ultimately leads to the questions of what needs to be done and the challenges that may be faced in doing it. This chapter consequently examines the situation in relation to supporting end-users, as well as in relation to the specialists needed to support cybersecurity. The discussion begins by considering what today's users need to know in terms of cybersecurity, and the extent to which they are supported to do so. This links to the impacts within the workplace context, and then broadens to consider the organization's needs more widely in terms of having appropriately skilled staff to define and manage their cybersecurity, alongside the general workforce being cyber-aware. In this sense, the chapter sets the scene on a range of topics that are explored more fully in later parts of the book.

CYBERSECURITY AWARENESS FOR END-USERS

Since the emergence of information technology, and particularly the widespread advent of personal computing in the late 1970s and early 1980s, there has been much reference to the need to foster and ensure *IT literacy* in our society. In more modern times, the parlance has become *digital literacy*, reflecting the fact that – for many people - IT has become embedded in virtually everything around them. Given the range of threats they are facing, it quickly becomes clear that citizens require *cybersecurity literacy* in order to safeguard themselves in their daily use of technologies and online services. As an example, some core areas of literacy are summarized in Table 1 (Furnell & Moore, 2014). For each topic there is an indication of what everyday users should understand and what they should be able to do as a consequence. Looking at the list, it is easy to see that many of the topics are unlikely to part of people's default knowledge and behavior, and so they need to learn the lessons from somewhere.

Table 1. Examples of baseline cybersecurity literacy

Topic	Users Should Understand ...	Users Should Be Able to ...
Authentication	The role of authentication in preventing unauthorized access.	Choose and use suitable passwords, and then follow good practice in terms of managing them.
Backup	The risks to systems and devices that may result in data loss, and the impact that such a loss may have for them.	Utilize appropriate means to backup their data and devices, and appreciate the need for these to be stored away from the original copies.
Malware protection	The potential impacts of malware and the possible routes for infection	Check that appropriate antivirus protection is installed and enabled.
Mobile devices	The risks that devices can face from both technical threats and the physical environment.	Employ available features for security and privacy, and take appropriate precautions to safeguard devices when on the move.
Privacy and data leakage	The sensitivity of different types of data, and the ways in which it could be misused (e.g. to support identity theft).	Configure privacy and access settings in contexts where personal data may be most readily shared (e.g. in social networks, between apps, or within cloud services), and make informed decisions about what to divulge.
Safe Internet access and web browsing	The existence of threats such as phishing, malicious sites, and unsafe downloads.	How to spot the signs of scams and social engineering, alongside recognizing the indicators that denote security and trustworthiness.
Secure networking	The risks posed by using unprotected or unknown networks.	Ensure that their own networks are protected, and make informed decisions about when it is safe to connect to others.
Software updates	The reason why software updates are released and the importance of patching vulnerabilities	Configure the system to handle updates in the most appropriate manner.

Such cybersecurity literacy is actually required in relation to both personal and workplace use, as we find ourselves confronted with related threats and vulnerabilities across a range of systems and devices, and in relation to both personal and workplace data. Some lessons are generic and span both contexts, whereas some are more specific to one or the other. For example, the core principles of selecting and safeguarding an appropriate password are the same regardless of where it is being used or what it is being used to protect. However, the specific rules and requirements (e.g. around length and composition) will often vary between systems. And so even at this level, ensuring the necessary knowledge and skills is a challenge. Users need to know what's expected of them, and they need to be equipped to do it. Additionally, there is also the small matter of getting them to accept that it's worth doing. Being able to reach that point requires action and support across a number of fronts.

In the context of their personal use, it is ultimately down to individuals to take a level of responsibility for themselves and to realize that it is in their own interest to do so. If they fail to understand the threats and take precautions it will primarily be their own systems and data that they are putting at risk as a result (although even here it is not *exclusively* a risk to themselves - for example, a personal system that has become malware-infected because the owner did not understand or accept the need to protect it may end up affecting *other* users on the network if it starts spewing out spam or phishing messages, or starts to try to launch attacks against them). Of course, an individual's personal practices are quite likely to influence their default behavior when dealing with systems and data in the workplace as well. However, in the workplace the implications of an unaware and non-compliant user are immediately more significant, as they are now occurring in a context that has the direct potential to affect others and to impact upon the organization itself. Equally, in this scenario, it ought to be more obviously in the interests (as well as within the control) of the employer to support the staff in doing the right thing.

All of this leads to the obvious question of how aware and prepared the end-users actually *are*. Do they understand the problems and have the skills to deal with them? Of course, there is no single answer to this, because the situation is likely to differ according to personal circumstances and the degree to which cybersecurity issues have been promoted to them. If the user is in a country where there has been a sustained public awareness campaign, or where service providers have been proactive in pushing the messages and providing solutions, then they are likely to be better positioned than those that have not received such support. However, even where public awareness campaigns exist, they cannot be relied upon to be having as much impact as we would like. For example, in the UK, the Get Safe Online initiative has existed since 2006 as a public / private sector partnership to promote online safety and security advice to personal users and businesses (supported by the government as well as leading organizations in banking, retail, technology and other sectors). More recently it has been joined by the Cyber Aware campaign, a cross-government initiative that aims to drive cybersecurity-related behavior change amongst small businesses and individuals. In spite of these laudable efforts, a recent study from the UK Home Office determined that a large proportion of the public (along with Small and Medium-sized Enterprises) were underestimating the risk of cybercrime and feeling powerless in terms of protecting themselves against it (Home Office 2018). This in turn does not paint a picture of a confident and cybersecurity-aware user community, even where efforts had ostensibly been made to support them (or at least to make such support available via web guidance and resources).

Meanwhile, as an illustration of the position of users in the workplace, we can consider some findings from EY's Global Information Security Survey. This is a long-standing annual survey series and so looking at findings over successive years enables patterns and trends to be observed. The responses are drawn from executive and management level participants across EY's operating regions of EMEIA (Europe, Middle East, India and Africa), the Americas, Asia-Pacific, and Japan, with an average of over 1,600 respondents per annum across the surveys considered here (EY, 2017; EY, 2018). As such, they represent a fair sample from which to form an impression of how things stand in relation to end-users, and unfortunately, as we see from Figure 2, this impression is not a good one. Respondents were asked to indicate the top areas of vulnerability that were leading to increased risk exposure and what is notably clear is that 'careless or unaware employees' was consistently rated as the topmost area throughout this period. Perhaps unsurprisingly then, EY's 2017-18 survey report concluded with a number of key actions that all organizations should consider, and clearly listed amongst them is the advice to 'Focus on education and awareness' with recommendation that they should: *establish an education and awareness program, ensuring all employees, contractors and third parties can identify a cyber attack and are aware of the role they play in defending your business* (EY, 2017). Such advice leads to the clear question of whether organizations are *taking* such actions.

Figure 2. Top-rated areas of cybersecurity vulnerability in organizations (EY, 2017; EY, 2018)

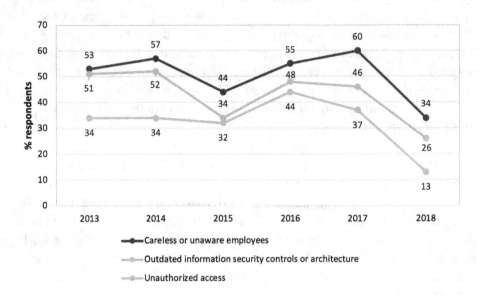

PROMOTING CYBERSECURITY IN THE WORKPLACE

The EY findings illustrate that organizations can find themselves with a problem. Regardless of the ups and downs of the specific figures, the undeniable message is that the employees represent the most significant area of vulnerability. Moreover, it is an aspect that is arguably preventable, to at least some degree. If the cause is employee unawareness, then supporting them in becoming aware ought to address the problem. In reality of course this is easier said than done, but organizations have at least *some* opportunity to influence their own fate in this area.

In terms of their staff community, they need to raise awareness, they need to educate them, and ideally, they need to build an overall cybersecurity culture. This latter point is somewhat aspirational and refers to security having become embedded within users' attitudes and activities. In this sense, it is the ultimate level of security-compliant behavior. Unfortunately, it is highly unlikely to be the norm, and most organizations are likely to find their staff operating across a spectrum of compliance levels, as illustrated in Figure 3 (Furnell & Thomson, 2009). These levels are briefly defined as below, with the first four reflecting different degrees of security compliance, while the remaining four then relate to non-compliant behavior:

- **Culture:** The ideal state, in which security is implicitly part of the user's natural behavior.
- **Commitment:** Security is not a natural part of behavior, but if provided with appropriate guidance/leadership then users accept the need for it and make an associated effort.
- **Obedience:** Users may not fully understand or buy into the principles but can be made to comply via appropriate authority (i.e. implying a greater level of enforcement than simply providing guidance).
- **Awareness:** Users are aware of their role in information security but are not necessarily fully complying with the associated practices or behavior as yet.
- **Ignorance:** Users remain unaware of security issues and so may introduce inadvertent adverse effects.
- **Apathy:** Users are aware of their role in protecting information assets but are not motivated to adhere to good information security practices.
- **Resistance:** Users work against security, through factors such as laziness and disregard for known procedures.
- **Disobedience:** Users actively work against security, with insider abusers intentionally breaking the rules and circumventing controls.

Figure 3. Compliance and non-compliance behavior within an organization
(Furnell & Thomson, 2009)

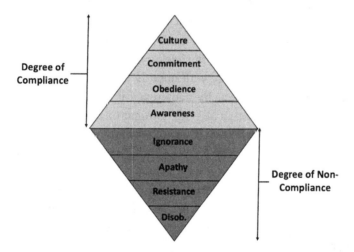

A key point to recognize is that where staff are actually positioned within these levels will be closely linked to the efforts that the organization has made in terms of SETA-related activities. By default, the distribution is likely to be similar to that depicted in the Figure, with the majority of staff positioned within the middle categories, and relatively few staff at the extremes. Clearly, the objective of an effective SETA strategy would be to get as many staff into the higher levels as possible (albeit recognizing that those in the Disobedience category are unlikely to be reached via this route, and ought to be dealt with via disciplinary processes instead). Unfortunately, although it is a widely *recognized* issue, the extent to which cybersecurity education is actually *addressed* can at best be described as variable. Indeed, while organizations may readily see evidence of the need for it, following this up with action does not always appear to come naturally.

An Ongoing Lack of Provision

A look back at survey findings over many years suggests that lack of awareness is a long-standing and well-established problem. Consider, for example, the following selection of statistics taken from a range of past survey findings amongst UK organizations[1], each basically suggesting that only a third of organizations were making SETA provision:

- KPMG's Information Security Survey in 1998 found that 31% of organizations had security education and training programs (KPMG, 1998)
- In the Audit Commission's 2001 survey of IT abuse, 34% of the public and private sector respondents indicated that they had any form of computer security awareness training (Audit Commission, 2001)
- In its 2006 information security breaches survey, the Department of Trade and Industry found that an average of 35% of businesses utilized ongoing security training (DTI, 2006)

Of course, one may try to excuse these cases, because they were from many years ago when the role of technology was less prominent than it is today. However, aside from the fact that it *was* actually a problem even then, jumping forward to more recent findings unfortunately suggests little change. For example, looking at the UK's more recent Cyber Security Breaches Survey, we find that on average only 20% of the 1,500+ respondents indicated that their staff had attended "internal or external training, or seminars or conferences on cybersecurity in the last 12 months" (DCMS, 2018) – a picture that is also essentially unchanged from two prior years of the study (with the likelihood of provision increasing the larger the organization concerned). Moreover, the question is very broad and so positive answers could actually cover some quite dissimilar options, with notably differing impacts. For example, a member of the IT team having attended a cybersecurity conference is unlikely to have any direct effect upon general staff awareness, whereas an internal all-staff seminar on cybersecurity principles and practices would likely have a very positive effect. However, both scenarios would score a positive response to the question, and hence contribute to the 20% result overall. A more direct insight into the provision for employees in general came from a further question asking which types of staff had attended training. This revealed that while three quarters of directors or senior managers had attended or received training, only a quarter of general staff had done so. As such, the overall results portray a situation where only a minority of organizations are offering training, and then only a minority of those are doing so in a manner that reaches the general user community.

Of course, with the varying interpretations of what might be meant by training, there is arguably doubt about the accuracy of this picture. Organizations *could* still be doing things that help to promote security awareness, but without it falling into a class of activity that they would regard as 'training'. On this basis, it is worth looking at the responses to a further question from the same survey series, in which respondents were asked whether they were undertaking actions from the UK National Cyber Security Centre's *10 Steps to Cyber Security* (which have been advocated to UK businesses since 2012). One of these steps is 'User Education and Awareness', which is described as follows:

Users have a critical role to play in their organisation's security and so it's important that security rules and the technology provided enable users to do their job as well as help keep the organisation secure.

This can be supported by a systematic delivery of awareness programmes and training that deliver security expertise as well helping to establish a security-conscious culture. (NCSC, 2015)

Figure 4 presents the claimed level of adoption by the Cyber Security Breaches Survey respondents, with the responses for the other nine steps also included for context. It is particularly notable that attention towards education and awareness is not only in the minority but is being omitted by organizations that clearly *have* addressed other aspects of security. It is also notable that the steps tending to receive greater attention are those of a technical nature, where it is perhaps possible to automate or buy a product/tool that claims to do the job. Dealing with people does not fall as neatly into this category, and so related controls may assume a lower priority – not because they are less important, but because they are more difficult to do.

Figure 4. Attention towards the 10 Steps to Cyber Security (DCMS, 2018)

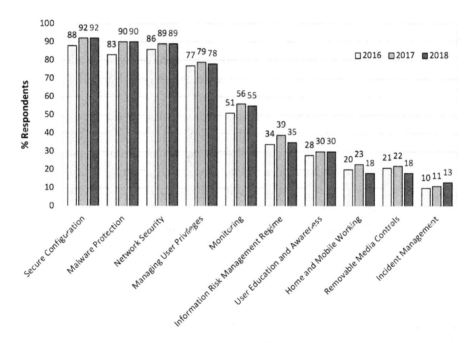

So, considering the results here, with 30% claiming to offer education and awareness, it is clear that the result is essentially no different to those previously listed above, from 10-20 years ago. Indeed, as a broad generalization, one might suggest that looking at almost any survey from any year is likely to reveal that no more than around a third of organizations are giving attention to SETA issues.

This all serves to raise the question of whether the lack of provision is simply because organizations are facing few problems, and do not feel they need it. Unfortunately, it takes little effort to disprove this theory. For a start, we have already seen the EY results showing unawares as a key area of perceived vulnerability. We can add to this from the Cyber Security Breaches Survey, where respondents cited both human error and lack of staff awareness as notable factors in their *most disruptive* breaches. Furthermore, looking at what respondents then did in the wake of such breaches, it becomes apparent that additional staff training or communications was one of the most prominent responses (it was actually the topmost response in 2017, from 28% of organizations, and second place in 2018 at 18%, just behind installing, changing or updating anti-malware protection at 22%). So, many of the organizations that had revealed a lack of awareness-raising were also suffering as a consequence and were only then making efforts to address the issue.

So, based on the above, a rather unfortunate picture appears to emerge – one of the main areas of vulnerability appears to center around people and their lack of security awareness, and yet the majority of organizations appear to persist in overlooking security awareness and education as an area for attention. Thus, while some commentators have dismissed security awareness as *a waste of time* (Schneier, 2013), it would seem naïve to think that the findings were not connected in some way!

Security Education: More Than Just a Policy

These days we are generally okay at pushing the message that security is important. Indeed, it would be relatively rare to find someone – at home or in the workplace - that does not know that it is something they *ought* to be concerned about. To that level then, awareness has been raised. Unfortunately, this does not get us very far in terms of something actually being done about it. Establishing cybersecurity as something of significance should be just the starting point, but risks being the end of the journey if users feel they cannot do it or do not feel the need to bother.

In the personal or home context, the user often has a choice about what to protect and to what level (e.g. whether to password-protect their device in the first place), whereas in the business setting they are more often going to be working at the behest of what the organization has prescribed. However, in either scenario, they still need to understand *what* they supposed to do, *how* to do it, and ideally *why* they ought to be doing it. Indeed, these questions potentially need to be addressed for any cybersecurity issue that we believe users should be aware of. Table 2 presents them in the order that they would most usefully be tackled, and explains the rationale behind each of them.

A bugbear in the provision of many security controls is that we will all too readily set rules and write policies, but then forget the need to support the people that are expected to abide by them. These people need more than just policies to be quoted at them; they need to be guided on how they are supposed to comply. Indeed, the distinction between *policy* and *guidance* is important, and is often a fundamental area in which the human aspect of cybersecurity falls down. Organizations are often good at setting policies, but typically less proficient following them up with meaningful support. Taking a somewhat cynical view, one might often suspect that this is because they need to be seen to have a policy in place in order to comply with expectations (or even regulations), and so by doing so they have ticked the box for compliance purposes. Additionally, by having a policy, there is something that staff can be held accountable against if an incident or breach occurs. Of course, while this may cover things from the perspective of the business, it's hardly fair from the perspective of those expected to follow the policy if they are expected to do so without further support.

Sometimes organizations may even be challenged to appreciate the distinction between policy and guidance in practical terms. So, as a brief illustration, let's consider a simplified example of the difference that might exist in relation to the theme of user authentication:

Table 2. Key questions when promoting cybersecurity to users

Issue	Related Questions	Rationale
Why	Why does this matter and why should I care?	Arguably the most fundamental issue, as it justifies why the issue matters and provides the foundation for the individual to buy into the subsequent points. If we have elected to make the individual aware of an issue, then we ought to ensure that they understand why.
Who	Whose concern is this? Is it something that I have a role in handling, or is someone else covering it for me? Do I just need to *know* about it, or do I have to *do* something?	The user needs to be clear on the role that they are expected to have in relation to the issue (again it will make them more attentive to absorbing later aspects of precisely what they then need to do as a consequence). There are, of course, some issues that users need to be aware of, even though no further action is required from them, and if a given issue is entirely for someone else to handle, then they can step out at this point, having been made aware that it exists and why it matters.
What	What am I supposed to do?	Having established that they have a role to play, the individual needs to know what it is. This is typically conveyed in the form of *policy*.
How	How do I do what I am supposed to do?	The obvious accompaniment to the previous issue, but often overlooked or under-supported. Conveyed to the individual in the form of *guidance*.
When / Where	When and where is it relevant? Does it apply all the time and to all systems?	Also covered as part of the *guidance* aspect, this is a further refinement that addresses the scenarios in which the security issue would be expected to be encountered. It should also cover whether there are any exception cases (e.g. situations where the desired practice cannot be followed due to technical limitations, or emergency scenarios where less secure alternatives are permitted).

- **Policy:** Your device should be protected with suitable user authentication.
- **Guidance:** You should choose a password that is at least 10 characters long, and which includes letters, numbers and symbols. You should avoid using dictionary words or personal information that others may know about you.

Now, we could likely argue about many of the specifics here (including whether passwords are an appropriate form of protection in the first place!), and it is acknowledged that the guidance is not anywhere near comprehensive enough (e.g. nothing is mentioned about writing the password down and not sharing it with others, and we could further quibble about whether 10 characters is long enough or whether the user ought to be explicitly asked to use both upper and lower-case letters)! However, the point is hopefully already clear that policy and guidance are not the same thing. Policy raises awareness, while guidance aids understanding.

As an aside, there is also the potential to address another 'why' question here for the user. It is all very well telling them that they need to use at least 10 characters, and to avoid dictionary words, but the guidance could become more *explanatory* if it also indicated why this mattered (which, in case you are wondering, is primarily to reduce the vulnerability to compromise by password cracking tools that many attackers would be likely to use). Of course, some users might be suitably convinced simply on the basis of being told to do it, but for others the explanation will help them to make sense of it, and thereby improve the likelihood of their later acceptance and compliance.

What should be fairly readily apparent from the above is that none of this comes naturally. Cybersecurity is not an area in which people tend to be pre-equipped with the necessary knowledge and skills. They are not born with it, and historically they have not got much exposure to it through prior schooling. So, if we want people to know about it and practice it, then we need some way to get their attention and tell them. This, to differing degrees, is the role of cybersecurity awareness, training and education, and it provides the backdrop not only for this chapter, but in large part for the remainder of the book as a whole.

WHAT GOOD LOOKS LIKE

One question that possibly remains in the mind at this point is what are we seeking to achieve and what does a good approach look like? Is a more effective approach to SETA going to deliver any benefit? With this in mind, it is relevant to characterize what we should expect from a more effective approach to SETA issues. And, in short, it ought to be more compliant behavior from users, and a corresponding reduction in related security incidents.

As previously mentioned, cybersecurity awareness and education are often criticized as ineffective or even dismissed as a waste of time. And indeed, they *can* be – but it rather depends on how you do it. SETA is not just a question of repeatedly pushing a security policy at staff and annually testing them on it. Repeatedly telling people the same thing is not education. If they did not understand or agree with it the first time, then simply going around the track again is unlikely to have the desired effect. Similarly, achieving security compliance is not intended to be just box-ticking. We want to foster a cybersecurity mindset and culture that becomes embedded across the organization and the individuals within it.

The authors' own prior work has argued for a more personalized approach to SETA provision, which takes account of the individual circumstances of the learners concerned (Vasileiou and Furnell, 2019). Figure 5 presents the contrast between this and the traditional one-size-fits-all approach. While the left of the diagram depicts the typical provision, the righthand side suggests an approach that is tailored based upon factors specific to the individual concerned and denoting various factors that may influence both the SETA provision that is needed and the manner in which it may be best presented. For example, an individual's role within the organization will directly inform some of the aspects of security that they need to know about (perhaps emphasizing specific systems or data that they will come into contact with over and above the norm). Meanwhile, if we can take account of the individual's prior knowledge and existing predisposition towards dealing with security, then this could help frame the way that messages are targeted toward them. For instance, the way that we address someone who is risk averse and tends to be policy-compliant would ideally differ from the way in which we might approach someone who is security-resistant and risk tolerant (Pattinson and Anderson, 2005). Similarly, it may be helpful to recognize that people learn in different ways, and so presenting the materials in a manner matched to their preferred style could deliver better results. As an example, Fleming (2006) proposes the VARK (Visual, Aural, Read/write and Kinaesthetic) model, reflecting four sensory modalities that may be used for learning information (e.g. looking at diagrams rather than reading texts, or doing practical tasks rather than simply listening to presentation-style delivery). Finally, different people may face barriers to learning in terms of threshold concepts and troublesome knowledge that need to be understood, integrated and overcome before they are in a position to me make sense of other aspects (e.g. this could well be the case in a cybersecurity context if individuals are unfamiliar or uncomfortable with some of the surrounding IT knowledge that tends to underpin why security is required).

Figure 5. Traditional and proposed modes of SETA provision
(Vasileiou and Furnell, 2019)

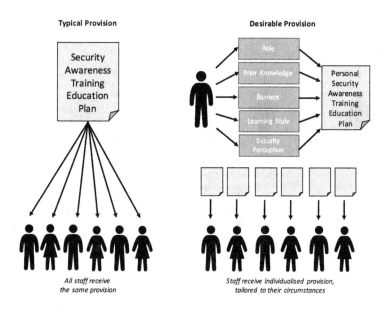

Of course, while this is easy to present in a diagram, it is far harder to achieve in practice. Enacting this approach would require information gathering in order to profile the individual needs and circumstances of each user. However, the associated effort here has the potential to deliver a far more tailored SETA experience, which ought to yield better results in terms of acceptance, understanding and compliance. Indeed, it is possible to go even further than this. For example, the ISF (2014) suggest that people/employees can be our strongest control, but simply delivering a training programme is not enough and that any security awareness training needs to target behaviour change by engaging people at personal level and setting realistic expectations. Linked to this, Gabriel and Furnell (2011) and Beris et al. (2015) both suggest the notion of security champions, where certain individuals are identified to lead a peer-learning approach, which aims to foster a community of good practice amongst colleagues within the workplace environment. This in turn aligns with Boud and Middleton (2003), who identify that learning in workplaces can take an informal format, encompassing a diverse range of people to work with. If the champions are well-selected and appropriately regarded amongst their peers, then they are well placed to guide and influence others towards the desired direction. The conceptual integration of this idea with the personalized plans is depicted in Figure 6, albeit recognizing that this represents more of an aspiration than a reality in the majority of cases.

SPECIALIST CYBERSECURITY SKILLS FOR THE ORGANIZATION

Unfortunately, the requirement for cybersecurity education and training does not end with the users. It is also key for organizations in terms of supporting those responsible for implementing and running the security the protects everyone else. Security will not manage and direct itself, and if SETA provision is to be made for staff, then someone needs to lead and deliver it. And more generally, there needs to

Figure 6. Incorporating peer learning and security champions
(Vasileiou and Furnell, 2019)

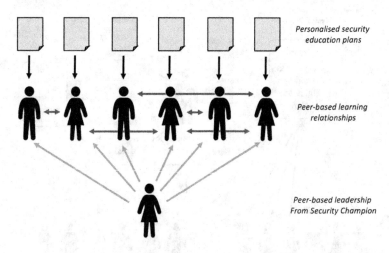

be appropriate people to handle the selection, deployment and management of other security controls as well. In order to do this, organizations need to have enough people with the right skills to do what is required. However, this is again an area in which many have historically been challenged, and there are actually two dimensions to this problem. Firstly, organizations need to realize that they *need* cybersecurity expertise to support them, and secondly, they need to be able to *find* it.

The realization aspect basically means recognizing and allocating cybersecurity responsibilities and putting the right people into roles. This may sound obvious, but there is ample evidence to show that it does not always happen. A common problem is that security is perceived to be an 'IT thing' and so the responsibilities are simply landed upon general IT staff to deal with. However, there is no guarantee that they will have any familiarity or interest in the area, risking the situation where security becomes half a job done badly (which in turn means that a credible level of security is unlikely to be achieved). What is actually needed is for security to be handled by people who understand the concept, the technologies and processes involved, and its relationship to the business, and have the skills and experience to enact it.

Looking again at the surveys considered in the earlier section, the UK Cyber Security Breaches Survey indicates that 70% of the 1,500 businesses surveyed agreed or tended to agree that the people dealing with cybersecurity in their organization had "the right cyber security skills and knowledge to do this job effectively". Although this is clear the majority, it this leaves almost a third of them in varying degrees of uncertainty or disagreement. Meanwhile, looking at the EY survey, only 8% of the respondents believe that their information security function *fully* meets the organization's needs, while more than a quarter directly indicate that the needs are not met, or that the function needs to be improved. A common cause of these gaps is found to be a shortage of skills to do the job, with 30% of respondents citing this as a reason. And so, in short, a lack of skills emerges as a common theme from both of the surveys.

This is turn leads to the question of why the organizations have a shortfall. Is it because they have not hired the right people, or because they could not find the right people to hire? The likely answer is a combination of both, and even if they have got themselves to the point of realizing that security-specific expertise is needed, organizations can find themselves challenged in terms of both a shortage of skilled practitioners in the market, as well as knowing what qualifications or certifications they should be looking for to match the skills they need.

While Table 1 summarized some areas of baseline cybersecurity literacy for the lay user, the skills needed from security practitioners need to go significantly beyond this. Unfortunately, one aspect resulting from an overall lack of security education is a lack of professionals skilled to handle and support it. This in turn causes knock-on problems for organizations wishing to address security concerns without the capability to do so. Indeed, the situation in the professional context is also challenging, and recent years have consistently provided evidence to indicate not only a skills shortage, but a significant level of shortfall. The following provide some examples of related forecasts, and while the specific numbers vary, the overall picture is essentially consistent (i.e. the industry is facing a situation of long-term under-supply):

- **2013:** The UK's National Audit Office suggested that it could take up to 20 years to bridge the cyber-skills gap (NAO, 2013).
- **2015:** Frost and Sullivan and (ISC)[2] concluded that there would be a global shortfall of around 1.5 million security practitioners by 2020 (Frost and Sullivan, 2015).
- **2016:** Foote Partners predicted that while global demand for cybersecurity talent would rise to six million by 2019, there would be a shortfall of 1.5 million professionals to fill the positions (Schneiderman, 2016).

This shortage of skilled practitioners has a resulting impact. For example, global findings from Intel Security and the Centre for Strategic and International Studies (CSIS) suggested that more than 80% of organizations considered there to be a shortage of cybersecurity skills, with almost three quarters suggesting that direct and measurable damage occurred as a consequence (Correa, 2016). Meanwhile, findings from Kaspersky Lab (based upon surveying over 4,000 companies) suggested that organizations lacking security skills can end up spending at least three times as much to recover from security breaches (Kaspersky, 2016). Moreover, half of those surveyed indicated that they had seen a growth in wages due to the talent shortage of talent, with similar proportions suggesting that they had experienced the shortage themselves and needed more security specialists. Adding a direct experience of their own to the findings, Kaspersky Lab indicated that they typically needed to interview 40 people in order to hire one expert.

Unfortunately, the supply issue is not the only challenge. Knowing that we *need* skills and specialists is one thing but knowing how to *identify* them is another matter. As discussion elsewhere in the book explores more fully, there is a range of providers (including CompTIA, EC-Council, ISACA, (ISC)[2] and SANS to name just a few of the leading and most recognized names), and each offers a range of related certifications to choose from. However, as one might expect, the range is there for a reason, with different certification options being available to suit different security specializations and levels of experience. Indeed, looking at the marketplace as a whole, we find a potentially bewildering array of certifications, with a study by Tittel et al. (2017) revealing over one hundred distinct offerings available (with 70 general, vendor-neutral certifications, 24 related to forensics or anti-hacking, and 10 other specialized options). Adding academic qualifications into the mix as well potentially muddies the waters even further, and so it is important to know what we are looking for in terms of both coverage and the level of depth. For example, do we want someone with a holistic understanding who can manage the overall cybersecurity provision, or do we need someone with specific expertise to handle a particular task or element of the technology? The needs are quite different and so the supporting qualifications/certifications should be matched accordingly. Figure 7 presents a way of looking at things, in terms of the different focus that may be given and the types of skills that may be developed as a consequence.

Figure 7. Different levels of cybersecurity qualification and certification

The key thing to realize here is that it is not a question of any of these options being right or wrong – all can have a relevant part to play – but it *is* important to recognize that they are *different*. As such, a qualification acquired at one level is unlikely to offer a natural substitute for another. This goes back to organizations needing to know what they need, and the later sections on academic and professional perspectives will help to provide further clarity.

CONCLUSION

The overall message of this chapter, setting the scene for those that follow, is that SETA not only needs to be done, but needs to be done *well*. Unfortunately, there is no one-size-fits-all answer, and it requires action on several fronts. As such, like cybersecurity in general, it is not a simple problem to solve!

At the user level, there can currently be a great variance in who receives training and what they get trained in. Broadly speaking we need a better level of cybersecurity literacy coming through from general education in order to position people better for both workplace and personal use. At the organizational level, there is consequently a challenge to be faced in terms of ensuring an environment where the staff collectively operate within a coherent security culture. But the issue is wider than having a cybersecurity-aware workforce. It ideally needs people to be prepared prior to this, so that they are essentially cyber-ready by the time they get there. In this sense, it needs to be promoted in academic education – in schooling of the general populous in order to raise the baseline literacy early on, and then specifically in higher education for IT-related degrees (for the cybersecurity-specific skills).

Organizations can also suffer from a lack of specific cybersecurity expertise to set the agenda in the first place, and so this again depends upon support from academia to feed through appropriately qualified graduates, and from the profession more widely to support further skills development and certification. As such, cybersecurity needs to be promoted at the professional level. Indeed, it needs to be recognized *as* a profession, with the accompanying expectation for qualified and credible specialists to do the work.

The resulting situation is something of a jigsaw puzzle, and there are currently more pieces in some parts of the picture than others. However, recognition of the need is the first step towards addressing it, and the ultimate aim must be to ensure that cybersecurity awareness, training and education are appropriately provided all the way from general end-users through to cyber practitioners. The chapters that follow collectively draw upon both theoretical principles and practical experience in order to consider *what* must be done, and *how* to achieve it. The different sections suggest actions for different audiences, but collectively aim to enable an overall understanding of what is required and who can help us in trying to achieve it.

REFERENCES

Audit Commission. (2001). yourbusiness@risk – An Update on IT Abuse 2001. Audit Commission Publications.

Beris, O., Beautement, A., & Sasse, M. A. (2015). Employee rule breakers, excuse makers and security champions: Mapping the risk perceptions and emotions that drive security behaviors. *NSPW '15: Proceedings of the 2015 New Security Paradigms Workshop*, 73-84.

Boud, D., & Middleton, H. (2003). Learning from others at work: Communities of practice and informal learning. *Journal of Workplace Learning*, *15*(5), 194–202. doi:10.1108/13665620310483895

Correa, D. (2016). 82% of global IT pros admit to a shortage of cyber-security skills. *SC Magazine*. Retrieved from http://www.scmagazineuk.com/82-of-global-it-pros-admit-to-a-shortage-of-cyber-security-skills/article/512830

DCMS. (2018). Cyber Security Breaches Survey 2018. Main report. Department for Digital, Culture, Media & Sport.

DTI. (2006). *Information security breaches survey – technical report*. London, UK: Department of Trade and Industry.

EY. (2017). *Cybersecurity regained: preparing to face cyber attacks. 20th Global Information Security Survey 2017–18. EYG no. 06574-173Gbl*. EYGM Limited.

EY. (2018). *Is cybersecurity about more than protection? EY Global Information Security Survey 2018-19. EYG no. 011483-18Gbl*. EYGM Limited.

Fleming, N. D. (2006). *Teaching and learning styles: VARK strategies* (2nd ed.). Christchurch, New Zealand: Neil D Fleming.

Frost & Sullivan. (2015). *The 2015 (ISC)² Global Information Security Workforce Study*. Retrieved from https://iamcybersafe.org/wp-content/uploads/2017/01/FrostSullivan-ISC²-Global-Information-Security-Workforce-Study-2015.pdf

Furnell, S., & Moore, L. (2014). Security literacy: The missing link in today's online society? *Computer Fraud & Security, 2014*(May), 12–18. doi:10.1016/S1361-3723(14)70491-9

Furnell, S., & Thomson, K. (2009). From culture to disobedience: Recognising the varying user acceptance of IT security. *Computer Fraud & Security, 2009*(February), 5–10. doi:10.1016/S1361-3723(09)70019-3

Gabriel, T., & Furnell, S. (2011). Selecting Security Champions. *Computer Fraud & Security, 2011*(August), 8–12. doi:10.1016/S1361-3723(11)70082-3

Home Office. (2018). *A Call to Action: The Cyber Aware Perception Gap*. Retrieved from https://www.gov.uk/government/publications/cyber-aware-perception-gap-report

ISF. (2014). *From Promoting Awareness to Embedding Behaviours - Secure by choice, not by chance*. Information Security Forum. Retrieved from https://www.securityforum.org/uploads/2015/03/From-Promoting-Awareness-ES-2014_Marketing.pdf

Kaspersky. (2016). *Lack of Security Talent: An Unexpected Threat to Corporate Cybersafety*. IT Security Risks Special Report Series 2016, Kaspersky Lab. Retrieved from https://www.kaspersky.com/blog/security_risks_report_lack_of_security_talent/

KPMG. (1998). *Information Security Survey 1998*. London, UK: KPMG Information Risk Management.

NAO. (2013). *The UK cyber security strategy: Landscape review*. National Audit Office. Retrieved from https://www.nao.org.uk/report/the-uk-cyber-security-strategy-landscape-review

NCSC. (2015). *10 Steps: User Education and Awareness*. National Cyber Security Centre. Retrieved from https://www.ncsc.gov.uk/guidance/10-steps-user-education-and-awareness

Pattinson, M., & Anderson, G. (2005). Risk Communication, Risk Perception and Information Security. *Security Management, Integrity and Internal Control in Information Systems, Proceedings of IFIP TC-11 WG11.1 & WG11.5 Joint Working Conference*, 175-184.

Schneiderman, R. (2016). *Cyber Skills in High Demand Well Into The Future*. newswise. Retrieved from http://www.newswise.com/articles/view/660345/

Schneier, B. (2013). *On Security Awareness Training*. DARKReading. Retrieved from https://www.darkreading.com/risk/on-security-awareness-training/d/d-id/1139381

Tittel, E., Lemons, M., & Kyle, M. (2017). *Information security certifications: Introductory level*. TechTarget. Retrieved from http://searchsecurity.techtarget.com/tip/SearchSecuritycom-guide-to-information-security-certifications

Vasileiou, I., & Furnell, S. (2019). Personalising Security Education - Factors influencing individual awareness and compliance. In P. Mori, S. Furnell, & O. Camp (Eds.), *Information Systems Security and Privacy, Fourth International Conference, ICISSP 2018, Madeira, Portugal, January 22-24, 2018, Revised Selected Papers*. Communications in Computer and Information Science, Springer.

ENDNOTE

[1]   The situation is by no means unique to the UK but drawing upon past and present survey findings from the same region enables a level of consistency and continuity for comparison.

This research was previously published in Cybersecurity Education for Awareness and Compliance; pages 1-18, copyright year 2019 by Information Science Reference (an imprint of IGI Global).

Chapter 14
Developing the Social, Political, Economic, and Criminological Awareness of Cybersecurity Experts:
A Proposal and Discussion of Non-Technical Topics for Inclusion in Cybersecurity Education

Marcus Leaning
https://orcid.org/0000-0002-8985-2431
University of Winchester, UK

Udo Richard Averweg
eThekwini Municipality, South Africa

ABSTRACT

The global shortage in skilled labor for cybersecurity and the risk it presents to international business can only be solved by a significant increase in the number of skilled personnel. However, as the nature of risks proliferate and bifurcate the training of such, personnel must incorporate a broader understanding of contemporary and future risks. That is, while technical training is highly important, it is contended that future cybersecurity experts need to be aware of social, political, economic, and criminological issues. Towards this end, this chapter considers a number of exemplary issues that are considered worthy of inclusion in the development of future cybersecurity workers. Accordingly, an overview is given of the issues of the "dark side of the net" that cause problems for global cybersecurity and international business risk. The issues are discussed so that from these a skill set can be articulated which will attend to (and mitigate against) potential threats.

DOI: 10.4018/978-1-6684-3554-0.ch014

INTRODUCTION

The global shortage of skilled Information technology (IT) security staff presents a significant problem to business. Without qualified and skilled staff, ever increasing cybersecurity threats will make businesses untenable (Evans & Reeder, 2010). However, as explored in this collection there is currently a significant shortage of such qualified and skilled staff. This chapter is concerned with the education and training of such staff. However, despite a number of attempts (Hansche, 2006; Paulsen, McDuffie, Newhouse & Toth, 2012; Vinnakota, 2013; Kim, 2014; Beuran, Chinen, Tan, & Shinoda, 2016) definitions of what constitutes a trained IT security specialist are fairly fluid.

As Martin (2015) notes, there is not as yet a widely accepted structure or framework of skills. Indeed, there is a discrepancy between what different national governments and providers of education see as key areas of such an education (Henry, 2017). For the most part, staff and students willing to gain entry to the lucrative IT security workforce can choose from a very wide and heterogeneous educational market. Courses on offer tend to center upon two main approaches: first are courses that offer training at various levels in specific technological practices to detect and protect organizations from cyber-attacks.

Such training programs range from short upskilling in specific technologies through to full bachelors and masters level degrees in universities. Many of these courses, particularly at the sub-degree level, are accredited by brand leaders in the cybersecurity industry. Second are business and management courses which incorporate a component of cybersecurity. Such programs tend to seek to accord cybersecurity a significant role in management practices and advance the idea that individuals at all levels of an organization have a vital role to play in ensuring there is a robust defense to those wishing to attack it.

In this chapter, the authors contend that cybersecurity training has to-date neglected a significant aspect in its scope. Drawing upon ideas from cultural criminology it is asserted that those charged with defending against cyber threats should be cognoscente of a range of non-technical issues which relate to the reasons for attack. Also included are the wider social and cultural aspects of attacks such as the culture of those attacking understanding the political, economic and psychological motivations of attackers, the economics of the attacker's culture and the cultural norms of the attackers. Cultural criminologists have asserted that through such awareness those involved in defending an organization from external threats can better predict and mitigate future threats (Ferrell & Sanders, 1995; Jaishankar, 2011).

To address such issues, the authors assert that cybersecurity should incorporate a range of topics and issues currently outside of the accepted scope of training. Determining the scope of such topics and issues is problematic and the list of such areas will need to be continually revised as new aspects emerge and new social issues arise. Indeed, ensuring that cybersecurity personnel are as aware of contemporary social issues in security is as difficult as ensuring the technical skills are up-to-date. Mindful of this, the authors here identify four key areas in this chapter that will serve the contemporary and immediate future needs of cybersecurity personnel.

The objective of this chapter is to advance an outline of four areas the authors feel cybersecurity personnel need to consider: (1) the rationale for spam emails; (2) the reasons people hack; (3) the new economy of crypto currencies; and (4) the places of communication used by cyber criminals.

BACKGROUND

The first part of this chapter commences with a discussion of the activity of spam as this often serves as a gateway to and facilitator of many other forms of illicit behavior (Krebs, 2014). Spam refers to the mass sending of unsolicited messages - most typically emails. It is recognised by the authors that the term *spam* is also used to refer to other types of unsolicited communication, such as personal messaging, texting and communication on virtual forums. Spam accounts for a significant proportion of all email traffic and though the prosecution of key spam senders often has an impact upon the total volume, such actions tend to be short-lived and new spammers soon take their place. Spam email currently amounts to 86% of all email traffic (Robertson, 2016) though much spam is caught in the various filters on servers and email clients in organisations. Indeed, only approximately 30% of spam sent gets through the various filters (Stone-Gross, Stringhini, & Vigna, 2011).

Spam is sent so as to make some form of financial gain for the sender. As will be discussed below, the ways in which the financial benefit is achieved is varied but the main purpose is to induce some action on the part of the recipient that will facilitate the sender of the spam email obtaining benefit. Though much spam is sent from legitimate organisations as part of their marketing campaigns, a significant proportion of unsolicited email traffic is sent by or criminal or semi-legal activity and it is this aspect that is focused upon in this chapter. Krebs (2014) sees a strong link between criminally orientated, spam email and organised crime.

The second part of the chapter provides a discussion of hacking which is a topic that has attracted much attention in the popular press and media in general. Rarely a week goes by without a story appearing of how hackers have attacked a bank or financial institution (Collinson, 2017), stolen money from individuals (Jones, 2017), or even interfered with elections (Gilsinian & Calamuir, 2017). This section considers hacking and looks at some of the reasons people hack. Though hacking is a term of some longevity it has multiple common meanings. The word retains its original Anglo Saxon meaning for chopping wood but in more recent years it has been used to refer to the skilled but unorthodox use of a technology. For example, computer scientists often refer to a hack as a way of circumventing a problem or making a computer system do something that it was not originally designed to do.

The term has also been expanded to refer to small techniques used in everyday life to achieve goals (the term 'life hacking' is often used in this regard). Here the discussion is limited to the illicit use of or breaking into computers. Such activity is virtually as old as computers themselves. There is a rich history of examples of attacks upon and through computer systems and one may draw upon an early account to define what one is concerned with. Parker (1976) refers to 'system hackers' and defines the activity they engage in as computer abuse which refers to "any incident associated with computer technology in which a victim suffered or could have suffered loss and a perpetrator by intention made or could have made gain". Accordingly here the concern is with the ways in which computers and computer networks are attacked, penetrated without the sanctioned user's permission or against their interests.

The focus of the third part of the chapter is on bitcoin and crypto currencies. Such phenomena are currently very prominent in the news (see the use of bitcoin to facilitate payment for the 2017 international extortion 'wannacry' attack launched against the British National Health Service, FedEx, the German railway company Deutsche Bahn AG, the Spanish mobile phone and broadband provider. Telefonica and many other companies and organisations in 150 countries were involved in the unrelated vast increases in Bitcoin's value in the latter part of 2017). In this section, the focus is not upon the actual means of attack, but rather upon the means of payment, bitcoin as an example of cryptocurrencies. Here some of the key features of bitcoin and how it functions are discussed.

The fourth part of the chapter focuses on the online social environments of the dark use of the Internet. The dark net can be understood as a subset or category of the deep net. As such, one can demarcate the dark net from other forms of communication and data. For the purposes of this chapter, the dark net is identified as a specific section of the deep net that cannot be readily access through search engines. It is not a hidden part of the normal web, such as a secret Facebook group, but a specific approach to hiding information and making the identity of the users of that data difficult to identify. The methods by which the dark net can be reached and some of the available services that exist there, are described.

MAIN FOCUS OF THE CHAPTER

The Activity of Spam: Understanding It as A Social, Criminal, and Economic Action

The Spam Eco System

Spammers make use of a number of different campaign techniques to increase the success rate of spam emails. Spam email campaigns tend to be differentiated by the level of particularity of the email. At one end of the spectrum is the 'spear phishing' technique in which emails are crafted for particular people (information about the target is gained through web searching and 'social engineering' – contacting the organisation and using charm and simple lies obtaining information about the people and organisation). The information is then used to craft emails that are likely to get through spam filters and be opened and actioned by the intended targets. At the other end of the spectrum is the mass emails distributed to millions of people simultaneously. Such emails require the assistance and collaborative activity of computer system penetration experts and other types of hackers.

Central to the sending of mass spam emails are email lists which are the large lists of email addresses of potential recipients. Email lists can be composed in numerous ways, including the manual and automated gathering of emails from various sites and services. Email lists can also be purchased or rented through various legitimate services. Such lists can be specific and relate to key demographics and psychographics. Email lists are also sold by hackers who purposefully break into an organisation's central records (such as billing systems or customer databases) to steal email addresses (Spammer-X, 2004).

In some cases, such lists are highly valuable as the proportion of genuine, active email addresses to inactive or false ones tends to be very high. The sale of such lists and the contracting for the commission of thefts of specific lists of email addresses is conducted through various 'dark markets' – venues for the trading of illegal merchandise on the internet or through personal contacts.

Botnets

The sending of spam emails for illicit purposes cannot be done through usual email practices which would reveal the spammers identity and make them liable to prosecution and other forms of sanction. Accordingly, spammers often make use of what is termed botnets (robot network) or zombie armies: networks of private computers that have been infected with viruses (which were typically delivered by a spam email). The viruses on such computers operate often undetected and while allowing the legitimate user of the computer to carry on working causing the computer to carry out other tasks simultaneously (hence, the label *zombie*).

For spammers, the most common task is to transform the computers in the botnet into a device that can send and relay emails in a complex network (Stone-Gross et al., 2011). Such compromised computers are used to send and pass on spam emails and to replace details of the originating sender with a fake name. The growth, use and maintenance of botnet armies is a practice often conducted by acolyte hackers as it can be achieved through the use of 'off-the-shelf' hacking software packages. Such packages involve the hacker infecting private computers with a virus and then using a control application to launch email campaigns (or other activities such as a deliberate denial of service attacks on particular web sites or services) from the infected machines.

Types of Criminal Spam

One can broadly identify four main types of criminally-orientated, mass spam emails:

- The first type is emails that serve a marketing purpose for a product. In these emails the product is often 'real' – that is there is a definite product or service for sale though its effectiveness, fidelity or genuineness may vary. Examples of such emails include sales emails for various personal or sexual issues such as the 'enlargement' of various organs, adverts for pornography sites, adverts for illegal articles such narcotics, software or pirated media texts or adverts for cheap replica medicines and drugs (such emails are primarily targeted at citizens of countries with expensive private medical systems in which medicines would be out of the reach of most people. The emails do often offer medicines that are similar to those available in pharmacies but are produced outside of the legitimate supply chain and thus may not be as effective as the genuine drugs);

- A second common form of spam email are those emails termed advanced fee fraud and classified under the Nigerian Penal code as 419 violations. Such emails are varied and function by alerting the recipient to a possible large financial reward for their willingness to engage in a smaller transaction such as sending an 'advance fee'. Of course the larger financial reward will never materialise and the recipient may need to send more money. A variant of this approach is to send a spear fishing attack claiming to be from a friend of the recipient and that they have been robbed or lost a bag while abroad and need emergency cash sent to them;

- A third approach involves attacking the recipient's computer. This form of spam will often contain a link or a file which will install a virus upon the recipient's computer. The viruses can serve a number of functions. The least serious involves using the computer as part of a botnet army to send out further emails to others. A similar use is for the recipient's computer to be used in a distributed denial of service attack against a web host or other computer. Both such activities will involve slowing the host computer down but not damaging it so much that the recipient will want to have the decline in function investigated and remedied as to do so would involve the virus being removed. More severe are viruses that disable the host's computer and demand a ransom fee payable to the sender in exchange for a code that will unlock the computer. Failure to provide the fee within a short period of time will result in an increase in the fee and eventually encrypting of all the information on the computer. Viruses are also used to secure personal details from host computers that can be used in identity theft; and

- • A fourth approach involves the recipient being sent what appears to be an email from their bank or other service (such as PayPal) requesting they log in to their account using the link provided – in some instances the email will seek to cause alarm in the recipient so as to encourage rapid action. The linked bank login page is a fake and the user will provide their login details to the fraudster. The details can then be used to steal money and other identity fraud activities.

Many organisations have software filters and rigorous user guidelines to prevent spam emails and hacking incursions. However, skilled spammers and hackers can circumvent such systems with original and cunning tricks. One of the authors of this chapter fell victim to an attack; this involved the use of a spam email that contained the header 'printer malfunction' and was spoofed so as to appear to emanating from the 'ITHelpDesk'. Unfortunately the spam email arrived moments after a document had been sent to print. The author concluded that something had gone wrong with the printing (the printer was in a room on another floor and so could not be checked) and it was an automated response from the networked printer.

The email contained a link which was said to lead to the printer queue – however, upon clicking the link it installed a virus. Remedying the situation involve having the computer reformatted and the user account frozen (and passwords on all internal accounts changed) until it could be determined that no further damage could occur. This resulted in significant inconvenience to the user and a delay of nearly two days. This then had an impact on other parts of the organisation for which time dependent tasks were pending. Even though the user was mindful of the many ways spammers and hackers work, the serendipitous timing plus a brief lack of thoroughness resulted in significant time wastage, inconvenience and a cost to the organisation.

While spam emails are relatively inexpensive to the sender, they can prove to be a costly business risk to an organisation. Spam emails invariably 'rob' organisations of valuable lost productive time when employees attempt to determine the legitimacy (and resultant deletion) of such emails. Furthermore there is also the cost of extra storage space which has been purchased for spam emails that have been quarantined until they are automatically purged. Accordingly, for organisations, a continuous promotion of anti-spam awareness raising activities (such as an organisation's intranet) alongside rigorous technical means of spam defence is advocated. Such technical defence mechanisms for mitigating the resultant damage of spam in an organisation, should include plans and implementation schedules drawn up by reputable anti-spam consultants.

The Activities of Hacking: Identifying the Economic, Political, and Mischievous Rationales for Hacking

The Identity of Hackers

Despite the media stereotype of all hackers being disgruntled youth, there is little that unites hackers beyond their interest in computing. The perpetrators of hacking do not constitute any form of traditional community apart from their interest in the activity itself. Contemporary hackers come from different societies and countries; have different political persuasions; are of different ages, social classes and educational levels. There is no common value system and notwithstanding the selective cultural construction of the ethical hacker, the understanding of and adherence to appropriate behaviour by hackers is varied to say the least.

The Reasons for Hacking

Given the heterogeneity of hackers it is not surprising that the reasons people engage in hacking are very varied. It is asserted that the reason people hack can be understood in three broad categories. These categories have been derived from reports and accounts of hacking within academic and popular literature (for example, see Décary-Hétu & Dupont (2013); Turgeman-Goldschmidt (2005; 2008) and Mitnick & Simon (2009)). Furthermore, hackers may well conduct different hacks for different reasons; that is they may hack two organisations for completely different reasons. The three broad categories that people hack are:

- **Economic Reasons for Hacking:** Hacking for economic reasons can be considered to be those activities that are conducted for financial gain and there are two sub-categories to consider here. First are criminal activities. These are hacks perpetrated to financially enrich the hacker or its organisation. Such activities are increasingly conducted by organised crime syndicates in systematic and complex crimes. The execution of these crimes often utilise other nefarious aspects of the dark net such as spamming and in particular the 'spear fishing' techniques discussed in the next sub-section and bitcoin or other digital currencies to be explored in the next main section. The nature of these crimes is varied but typically involves: stealing money from financial systems such as bank accounts and money transfer systems (Singh, 2015); stealing information either to order (Samani & Paget, 2015) or to sell on data markets (for example, credit card and account holder details stolen from retailers are sold on the dark web (McFarland, Paget, & Samani, 2016)), extorting money through the encrypting computers (see the successful attack on Calgary University in 2016, for example (Marotte, 2016)) and threatening to bring down computers using distributed denial of service attacks (for example, Russon (2016) details attacks made on small business in the United Kingdom and South Africa) and data or revealing personal and incriminating information (O'Neil, 2016)). In addition to the hacking of computers for nefarious purposes there are also numerous companies that offer the service of penetration testing; they attempt to break into computer systems to test the security systems in place for a fee;
- **Political Reasons for Hacking:** The second category relates to what may be termed political reasons for hacking. Here there are two further sub-divisions. First are those who hack so as to seek redress for what they perceive to be a political injustice. These groups deploy hacking skills to further the political aims of particular groups or political parties or to challenge and damage other political groups, agencies and governments. Such groups often operate under the portmanteau of 'hacktivist' – an activist who hacks. A contemporary example of such a group would be the hackers collective Anonymous which has attacked various targets it perceives as being oppositional to it political stance. Anonymous emerged out of the Occupy movement and shares many of the political concerns as Occupy (Goode, 2015). Second are those who hack on behalf of a government against either domestic or foreign targets. Examples of this include governments attacking foreign companies such as North Korea attacking Sony in revenge for releasing the film 'The Interview' – a satirical film about a planned assignation of North Korean Supreme Leader Kim Jong-Un (Sherr & Rosenblatt, 2014) and Israel's involvement in developing the StuxNet virus that was used to disabled a nuclear reactor in Iran (Lindsay, 2013); and
- **Personal and Social Reasons for Hacking:** The third main reasons for hacking may be considered social reasons. These relate to an individual's personal circumstances, beliefs and interests.

One may sub-divide the category into three sub-divisions: the first relates to personal interests and includes reasons such as mischief, the desire to vandalise websites for pleasure, the thrill of trespass in systems without permission and the fame and reputation amongst peers (Taylor, 1999). The second sub-division relates to individuals seeking redress against others for perceived slights. Here attention turns to inflicting cyber-mediated harm to another. There have been numerous conflicts between hackers and authority within groups is enforced through hackers attacking each other and 'doxing' (obtaining and releasing personal information about someone) (Sammons & Cross, 2016). The third sub-division concerns disgruntled employees who seek redress for a perceived work-based grievance. Such 'inside jobs' pose a serious problem for organisations as the attacks subvert the defences developed to counter normal externally originating attacks. Furthermore in certain instances it is the very people who are responsible for establishing and maintaining the defences who commit the attacks.

The rationale for hacking attacks is varied and complicated but cognisance of it may well afford organisations opportunity to address potential reasons for hacking through skilled use of public relations - that is due to the varied reasons for hacking which may include non-financial and even political and social reasons, some attacks may be dissuaded by addressing the public face of the organisation rather than technological means.

The Economic Systems: Alternative Currencies

Bitcoin and Crypto Currencies: A New Form of Money

Bitcoin is the most successful of a series of alternative currencies that make use of advances in computing and cryptography – the science of codes and codes. Bitcoins exist solely in the digital realm and there is not physical manifestation of them (though there have been several instances where pseudo coins have been produced bearing the bitcoin logo). Bitcoin was launched through an academic-styled paper published on October 31, 2008 (Nakamoto, 2008a) and was announced on a cryptography mailing list (Nakamoto, 2008b). The author of the paper and the post to the mailing list was listed as Satoshi Nakamoto though this has proven to be a pseudonym (the real identity of Satoshi Nakamoto is a hotly debated topic. An Australian, Craig Wright has made claim to the identity though this has yet to be fully proven (O'Hagan, 2016)).

What distinguishes cryptocurrencies and Bitcoin from other forms of currency, as well as its solely virtual nature, is its use of block chain database technology. Currency is ordinarily transferable between individuals and companies. If the money exists in a material form, such as cash, then ownership is transferred by giving the other person(s) our notes and coins. They then possess the value of the money that the notes and coins depict. They can avail themselves of this value by spending the money for other goods and services. Over the past few years the manner in which one transfers ownership of money has gradually changed and now for any large transaction and many small amounts, one uses electronic means and record the transfer of ownership of money on centralised registers. Indeed, according to some estimates upwards of 92% of the money in the world does not exist in a physical form but is recorded on lists and registers which note legal ownership. Many of these central registers are held by banks and similar financial organisations.

Banks keep records of how much money one has with them, credit card and loan companies record how much one owes them. Thus one's relative wealth is held not in our physical hands but in (often) electronic records. One's money is stored in a bank and they lend it out to other users or to other organisations who then loan it to other users themselves. Thus banks serve as a third party, someone who is trusted and who can record one's wealth in their books. To provide this service, banks make money by charging interest on the money loaned to other people. This is the money provided to them by users and they sometimes (but not always) pay users interest on this money. The difference between the two rates of interest is how banks make their money, they lend it for more than they pay for it. Bitcoin offers an alternative in that users can transfer money between themselves without recourse to a trusted third party. This direct form of transfer is conducted using the block chain database technology.

Prior to the application of block chain technology, there were systems by which money could be directly transferred between users through electronic means. However, without recourse to a centralised register, such as a bank, to police the transaction there was always the very real risk that fraud could occur. The block chain technology offers a decentralised register of transactions which is distributed all over the world. There is no single ownership or storage of records by a third party, rather bitcoin operates by having its register widely distributed.

Block Chain Technology

Block chains are a form of database that make use of the principles of cryptography to produce a record that cannot be changed but can be easily verified. The block chain is a distributed database which records a list of actions or changes made. These changes are stored in a list of discrete sequential, records or 'blocks'. Blocks have two particular features that greatly add to the security of block chains. First, blocks are time stamped at their moment of creation – they carry their exact time of their production within them. Second, each new block on the chain is created with an inherent link to the preceding block. Therefore if someone wanted to alter a block they would have to then alter all subsequent blocks in the chain. These two features mean that once a block has been created it cannot be altered though the information can be easily verified.

Virtual Wallets

When a user wishes to make a transaction they send Bitcoins from their 'virtual wallet' to another virtual wallet. The transaction is then recorded onto the block chain. Simply stated, virtual wallets are a means to store Bitcoins. They are pieces of client software that contain a secure folder on a computer (or in cloud storage) in which to store the digital credentials or the private keys used in public key encryption systems of Bitcoin to produce Bitcoin addresses for transactions. The wallets either contain or access a copy of the block chain and consult it to determine how many Bitcoins are in a user's wallet and whether they have enough to complete the proposed transaction. Bitcoins can also be stored with an exchange or custodian or can be stored entirely off line in what is termed a vault – a file storage system that cannot be accessed through the internet (Villasenor, 2014). This is typically accomplished through either having a computer that is not connected to any form of network that is connected to the internet or through a removable device that stores the Bitcoins until their need arises.

To transfer money to someone's wallet they will provide you with an address, this is a list of between 26-35 numbers and letters. The address is created by the bitcoin client and it is advised that each address is used only once with a new one being created for each transaction. As an example of what an address looks like, bitcoinwiki (2017) offers the following example of an address 3J98t1WpEZ73C-NmQviecrnyiWrnqRhWNLy. This address is then entered as the destination of the transaction. From an external viewpoint this address carries no information as to the identity of the recipient. Though it may be possible to see what transactions have been made to that address, it is impossible to deduce to whom the address actually belongs without additional information.

Once a transaction has been initiated, the instruction is broadcast to all computers on the internet running the distributed Bitcoin software. The transaction is recorded on the block chain by being written into a new block. This writing of a new block or recordkeeping activity is referred to by the disingenuous term 'mining'. It is a long and complex process that requires significant computing power and 'know-how'. This is also referred to as a proof of work and serves as a further security measure – the creation of a block takes significant effort. Once a broadcast of the transaction is made on the Bitcoin network, 'miners' can choose to complete the work. The first miner who completes the work is rewarded with new Bitcoins themselves but also transaction fees. These fees are small rewards that those initiating the transaction offer so that their transactions are mined. Users who do not offer such rewards may find their transactions take longer to be written to the block chain and be finalised.

Advantages of Bitcoin for 'Dark Net' Residents

As detailed above, Bitcoin provides a means by which wealth can be sent to someone without any knowledge of who that person actually is. Accordingly, Bitcoin has provided a completely anonymous, untraceable and covert system for passing money. As the identity of the recipients and senders of money cannot be traced, money passed around through the Bitcoin system cannot be monitored by governments or law enforcement agencies. Transactions can take place that involve illegal activity. There have been numerous instances of this occurring on various fora and play a significant part in facilitating economic activity on the dark net.

Ransomware attacks are likely to get worse in the future so companies and organisations will require enhanced security to protect themselves from such cyber-attacks. The recent attacks underscore the fact that any vulnerabilities will be exploited by hackers and criminals. Even as computing advances provide more secure security software, such vulnerabilities will not simply 'go away'. Companies and organisations will need to proactively avoid the bite of bytes.

The Online Social Environments of the Dark Use of the Net: Reaching the Dark Net and Available Services

The dark net can be understood as a subset or category of the deep net. As such the dark net can be demarcated from other forms of communication and data. For the purposes of this chapter, the dark net is identified as a specific section of the deep net that cannot be readily access through search engines. It is not a hidden part of the normal web, such as a secret Facebook group but a specific approach to hiding information and making the identity of the users of that data difficult to identify. The methods are now described by which the dark net can be reached and some of the forums that exist there.

Reaching the Dark Net: TOR

Dark net web sites are typically accessed using TOR (The Onion Router) – a technology that involves covering network traffic with layers of encryption and then routing the data through multiple network pathways which continually shift.

The TOR technology allows users to visit web pages anonymously and to circumvent attempts to restrict access to particular sites. It is used by dissidents, journalists and others who wish to communicate anonymously for fear of having their messages intercepted by state agencies. As well as being used in the United States of America, Europe, South Africa and other democracies, TOR is used by anti-government actors such as human rights activists in countries such as the People's Republic of China, the Syrian Arab Republic and Iran. TOR was developed by the United States (US) Naval Research Laboratory and was released under a free license in 2004 and then received backing from the Electronic Freedom Foundation. Because TOR is used by numerous anti-systemic groups which the US government has an interest in supporting, it continues to be in part funded (about 60%) by the US State Department and US Department of Defense (Greenwald, 2013).

TOR operates by having numerous computers functioning as nodes. These nodes can relay traffic between them. Once information is sent to the TOR network it is relayed across numerous nodes on its way to its destination. Traffic that is intercepted on the network is heavily encrypted multiple times. Moreover, the data has had both its origin and destination information removed and so is very difficult to trace.

From a client perspective, the TOR system is a browser that can be installed upon any Mac, PC or Linux machine – indeed the browser is a version of the *Firefox* browser. Once the TOR Browser Bundle has been downloaded and installed, the user enters addresses as they would any other web page. However, sites on the TOR network are not reachable via a normal browser and the addresses are constituted differently from normal web addresses and make use of a special top level domain – onion. TOR addresses consist of a string of 16 (seemingly) random numbers and letters with the suffix onion/.

For example, http://4u3ptawty2mn53bz.onion/ (this is a fake address). The actual address is the hash produced by public key encryption when the hidden service to which it points is initially established. Due to the various sites and services available on the dark net / TOR system being unindexed and unsearchable using normal web searching technologies, alternative systems have evolved. There are various search engines for the dark web (only reachable using the TOR browser) and a number of hidden wikis.

Available Services

The services available on the dark net can be grouped into a number of different categories, such as markets, sharing media files, and communication and community:

- **Markets:** There are numerous market places offering a vast array of services and goods. Historically one of the most famous dark net systems was the *Silk Road* – a site launched in February 2011 that was most famous for selling illegal narcotics. The site allowed users to buy and sell virtually any item but was best known for selling drugs in exchange for bitcoins. Allied sites such as *Armoury* sold guns and other weapons.

The *Silk Road* was closed down in October, 2013 after the Federal Bureau of Investigation seized control and impounded all the bitcoins in members *Silk Road* wallets (members had to load bitcoins onto a site specific wallet to purchase or sell items) (Clark, 2013). Following its closure and prosecutions of a number of the operators (who all worked under the pseudonym of the *Dread Pirate Roberts* (the name of the figure-head pirate who was role played by different people in the film *The Princess Bride*)) the *Silk Road* re-emerged as the *Silk Road 2* and then once that had also been closed down (in 2014).

A *Silk Road 3* emerged during 2016 but was unconnected to the original and seemed to have been established to defraud users. As with other market places the *Silk Road* allowed users to buy or sell virtually any goods anonymously.

In addition to the selling of illegal drugs there are also market places for stolen credit card numbers, stolen goods, fake passports, guns and weapons, counterfeit money, hacking software, stolen software and other media content. Services such as the laundering of Bitcoins, hacking and even assassination (though there has been considerable scepticism about whether this service was ever real or simply scams) are also proffered for sale on various market places. *AphaBay* and *Hansa* are both examples of such markets.

Markets on the dark web are unregulated and there is little recourse for buyers and sellers who are deceived. One innovation to remedy the problem of untrustworthy traders and vendors is the use of reviews in a similar way to other more legitimate web markets. Thus purchasers of drugs, fake passports and guns are able to offer a review of the service they receive and thus advise other customers of the reliability of the service;

- **Sharing Media Files:** There are numerous sites for the sharing of media files. These include commercial films and television series that have been stolen or illegally copied, large quantities of various forms of pornography and software. Such sites make use of various additional technologies and practices to share files. These include bit torrents and sharing systems such as virtual private networks that use TOR technology to allow users to share files without risk of interception.

The system *OnionShare* was developed after investigative journalist Glenn Greenwald's partner, David Miranda, was detained at Heathrow Airport under suspicion for transporting 58,000 documents (on a USB pen drive) which he had gained from Edward Snowden. Micah Lee, a staff developer with Greenwald's organisation, developed the system so that documents could be transferred without possible interference from third party agents (Crawford, 2014). Similarly Wiki leaks, the site established by Julian Assange to facilitate the release of government documents, can be found on the dark net; and

- **Communication and Community:** In addition to the commercial exchange and sharing of information, the dark net facilitates various forms of communicative spaces such as forums, blogs and secure email services. The secure email services draw heavily upon privacy and encryption software and a number of email systems are available.

SOLUTIONS AND RECOMMENDATIONS

As noted such topics need to be subject to continual revision and renewal as the political economic and social reasons for hacking are far from stable. As fast as technology changes (for example, the three-tier application architecture is obsolete and no longer meets the needs of modern applications in organisations

(Thomas & Gupta, 2016)), so do the reasons for its misuse and organisations need to be 'fleet of foot' to attend to such changes. Such changes will include the effective management of user single sign-ons and the proliferation of cookies. However, while the specificity of the training cybersecurity personnel needs to be continually updated, the authors assert that such training should incorporate aspects of social, political and economic awareness. As other areas of technological education such as engineering have indicated (Crawley, Malmqvist, Östlund, & Brodeur, 2007), for training to be effective for the 21st century it needs to accommodate a human and social aspect as well. Accordingly it is advocated that cybersecurity education incorporates a degree of social, political and economic awareness.

FUTURE RESEARCH DIRECTIONS

As has happened in other forms of practice where technology intersects with social action, future provision of the training and development of cybersecurity personnel may do well to include the development of specific non-technical roles. Technology may not be the only knowledge base required for the successful deterrence of cybersecurity attacks and future cybersecurity personnel and management may well need to broaden their understanding of the reasons and means of execution of various cybersecurity threats. Accordingly one future area for research is the development of greater sociological and cultural criminological investigation into hacking, deep net forums, the economics of spam and the use of crypto currencies to facilitate nefarious activity.

CONCLUSION

It is reiterated how the current labour shortage in cybersecurity experts necessitates the development of skilled workers and it is argued, however, that as well as the technical skills needed such workers will also need cognisance of a range of social, political and economic factors. It is contended that the four broad areas of attention covered here provide a sample of some of the social, political, economic and criminological issues of which current and future cybersecurity workers must be aware.

ACKNOWLEDGMENT

This research received no specific grant from any funding agency in the public, commercial or not-for-profit sectors. Some of this text appeared in a four-part article series in the *Journal of the Southern Africa Institute of Management Services (SAIMAS)*. Permission was granted by the Editor of SAIMAS to reuse this text.

REFERENCES

Beuran, R., Chinen, K.-I., Tan, Y., & Shinoda, Y. (2016). *Towards Effective Cybersecurity Education and Training*. School of Information Science, Japan Advanced Institute of Science and Technology. Retrieved on August 9, 2017, from: https://dspace.jaist.ac.jp/dspace/bitstream/10119/13769/1/IS-RR-2016-003.pdf

bitcoinwiki. (2017). *Address*. Retrieved on December 4, 2017, from: https://en.bitcoin.it/wiki/Address

Clark, L. (2013). *A guide to the Silk Road shutdown*. Wired. Retrieved on June 2, 2017, from: http://www.wired.co.uk/article/silk-road-guide

Collinson, P. (2017). Lloyds bank accounts targeted in huge cybercrime attack. *The Guardian*.

Crawley, E. F., Malmqvist, J. S., Östlund, S., & Brodeur, D. R. (2007). *Introduction. In Rethinking Engineering Education: The CDIO Approach* (pp. 1–5). Boston, MA: Springer US.

Décary-Hétu, D., & Dupont, B. (2013). Reputation in a dark network of online criminals. *Global Crime*, *14*(2-3), 175–196. doi:10.1080/17440572.2013.801015

Evans, K., & Reeder, F. (2010). *A Human Capital Crisis in Cybersecurity: Technical Proficiency Matters*. Center for Strategic & International Studies.

Ferrell, J., & Sanders, C. (1995). *Cultural Criminology*. Boston: Northeastern University Press.

Gilsinian, K., & Calamuir, K. (2017). *Did Putin Direct Russian Hacking? And Other Big Questions*. *The Atlantic*. Washington, DC: Atlantic Media Company.

Goode, L. (2015). Anonymous and the Political Ethos of Hacktivism. *Popular Communication*, *13*(1), 74–86. doi:10.1080/15405702.2014.978000

Greenwald, G. (2013). NSA and GCHQ target Tor network that protects anonymity of web users. *The Guardian*. Retricved on May 9, 2017, from: https://www.theguardian.com/world/2013/oct/04/nsa-gchq-attack-tor-network-encryption

Hansche, S. (2006). Designing a Security Awareness Program: Part 1. *Information Systems Security*, *9*(6), 1–9. doi:10.1201/1086/43298.9.6.20010102/30985.4

Henry, A. P. (2017). *Mastering the Cyber Security Skills Crisis: Realigning Educational outcomes to Industry Requirements*. ACCS Discussion Paper No. 4, Canberra, Australia: UNSW.

Jaishankar, K. (2011). *Cyber Criminology: Exploring Internet Crimes and Criminal Behavior*. CRC Press. doi:10.1201/b10718

Jones, R. (2017). I thought I'd bought my first home, but I lost £67,000 in a conveyancing scam. *The Guardian*.

Kim, E.-B. (2014). Recommendations for information security awareness training for college students. *Information Management & Computer Security*, *22*(1), 115–126. doi:10.1108/IMCS-01-2013-0005

Krebs, B. (2014). *Spam Nation: The Inside Story of Organized Cybercrime-from Global Epidemic to Your Front Door*. Sourcebooks.

Lindsay, J. R. (2013). StuxNet and the Limits of Cyber Warfare. *Security Studies*, *22*(3), 365–404. doi:10.1080/09636412.2013.816122

Marotte, B. (2016). Digital hostage. *The Globe and Mail*. Retrieved on September 2, 2017, from: http://www.theglobeandmail.com/news/national/how-the-university-of-calgary-hack-wentdown/article30358657/

Martin, K. M. (2015). Cyber Security Education, Qualifications and Training. *Engineering & Technology Reference*. The Institution of Engineering and Technology. Retrieved on February 22, 2016, from: https://pure.royalholloway.ac.uk/portal/files/25218802/IETEducationTraining.pdf

McFarland, C., Paget, R., & Samani, F. (2016). *The hidden data economy. Mcaffee report*. Intel Security.

Mitnick, K. D., & Simon, W. L. (2009). *The Art of Intrusion: The Real Stories Behind the Exploits of Hackers, Intruders and Deceivers*. Wiley.

Nakamoto, S. (2008a). *Bitcoin: A Peer-to-Peer Electronic Cash System*. Retrieved on December 1, 2017, from: https://bitcoin.org/bitcoin.pdf

Nakamoto, S. (2008b). *Bitcoin P2P e-cash paper*. Retrieved on December 1, 2017, from: http://article.gmane.org/gmane.comp.encryption.general/12588/

O'Hagan, A. (2016). The Satoshi Affair. *London EReview of Books*, *38*(13), 7–28.

O'Neil, S. (2016). *The Skype sex scam - a fortune built on shame*. Retrieved on December 2, 2017, from: http://www.bbc.co.uk/news/magazine-37735369

Parker, D. B. (1976). *Crime by computer*. London: Scribner.

Paulsen, C., McDuffie, E., Newhouse, W., & Toth, P. (2012). NICE: Creating a Cybersecurity workforce and aware public. *IEEE Security & Privacy*10(3), 76 79.

Robertson, J. (2016). E-Mail Spam Goes Artisanal. *Bloomberg Technology 2016*.

Russon, M. A. (2016). 'Armada Collective' hackers to launch bitcoin-extorting DDoS attacks on unwitting victims. *International Business Times*. Retrieved on December 2, 2017, from: http://www.ibtimes.co.uk/armada-collective-hackers-launch-bitcoin-extorting-ddos-attacks-unwitting-victims-1579789

Samani, R., & Paget, F. (2015). *Cybercrime exposed: Cybercrime-as-a-service*. Corporate white paper. Santa Clara, CA: McAfee Labs.

Sammons, J., & Cross, M. (2016). *The Basics of Cyber Safety: Computer and Mobile Device Safety Made Easy*. Elsevier Science.

Sherr, I., & Rosenblatt, S. (2014). Sony and the rise of state-sponsored hacking. *CNET*. Retrieved on February 3, 2017, from: https://www.cnet.com/uk/news/sony-and-the-rise-of-state-sponsored-hacking/

Singh, N. (2015). Online frauds in banks with phishing. *Journal of Internet Banking and Commerce*.

Spammer-X, S. X. (2004). *Inside the SPAM Cartel: By Spammer-X*. Elsevier Science.

Stone-Gross, B., Holz, T., Stringhini, G., & Vigna, G. (2011). The Underground Economy of Spam: A Botmaster's Perspective of Coordinating Large-Scale Spam Campaigns. *LEET*, *11*, 4–4.

Taylor, P. A. (1999). *Hackers: Crime in the Digital Sublime*. Routledge. doi:10.4324/9780203201503

Thomas, A., & Gupta, A. (2016). *Retire the Three-Tier Application Architecture to Move Toward Digital Business*. Gartner, Inc., G00308298.

Turgeman-Goldschmidt, O. (2005). Hackers' accounts: Hacking as a social entertainment. *Social Science Computer Review*, *23*(1), 8–23. doi:10.1177/0894439304271529

Turgeman-Goldschmidt, O. (2008). Meanings that hackers assign to their being a hacker. *International Journal of Cyber Criminology*, *2*(2), 382.

Villasenor, J. (2014). Secure Bitcoin Storage: A Q&A With Three Bitcoin Company CEOs. *Forbes*. Retrieved on December 19, 2017, from: https://www.forbes.com/sites/johnvillasenor/2014/04/26/secure-bitcoin-storage-a-qa-with-three-bitcoin-company-ceos/#1e36c2815cdd

Vinnakota, T. (2013). *A cybernetics paradigms framework for cyberspace: Key lens to cybersecurity*. Yogyakarta, Indonesia: Computational Intelligence and Cybernetics.

ADDITIONAL READING

Bartlett, J. (2014). *The Dark Net*. London: Random House.

Chertoff, M., & Simon, T. (2015). The Impact of the Dark Web on Internet Governance and Cyber Security. *The Global Commission on Internet Governance*. GCIG Paper No. 6. Retrieved on July 3, 2017, from: https://www.cigionline.org/publications/impact-dark-web-internet-governance-and-cyber-security

Crawford, D. (2014). *Onionshare: the 100 percent darknet file sharing app*. Retrieved on July 3, 2017, from: https://www.bestvpn.com/onionshare-the-100-percent-darknet-file-sharing-app/

Dutt, V., Ahn, Y. S., & Gonzalez, C. (2013). Cyber situation awareness modeling: Detection of cyber attacks with instance-based learning theory. *Human Factors: The Journal of the Human Factors and Ergonomics Society*, *55*(3), 605–618. doi:10.1177/0018720812464045 PMID:23829034

Keizer, G. (2010). Is StuxNet the 'best' malware ever? *InfoWorld*. Retrieved on August 1, 2017, from: http://www.infoworld.com/print/137598

Kelley, C. M., Hong, K. W., Mayhorn, C. B., & Murphy-Hill, E. (2012). Something Smells Phishy: Exploring Definitions, Consequences, and Reactions to Phishing. *Proceedings of the Human Factors and Ergonomics Society Annual Meeting*, *56*(1), 2108–2112. doi:10.1177/1071181312561447

Langner, R. (2011). StuxNet: Dissecting a Cyberwarfare Weapon. *Security & Privacy, IEEE*, *9*(3), 49–51. doi:10.1109/MSP.2011.67

O'Brien, D., Budish, R., Faris, R., Gasser, U., & Tiffany, L. (2016, 26 September). *Privacy and Cybersecurity Research Briefing*. Berkman Klein Center Research Publication No. 2016-17.

KEY TERMS AND DEFINITIONS

Block Chain: A digitized, decentralized, public ledger of all cryptocurrency transactions.

Cookie: A small piece of data sent from a website and stored on the user's computer by the user's web browser while the user is browsing.

Crypto Currency: A digital asset designed to work as a medium of exchange. It uses cryptography to secure its transactions to control the creation of additional units and to verify the transfer of assets.

Distributed Denial of Service Attack: A cyber-attack where the perpetrator seeks to make a machine (or network resource unavailable) to its intended users by temporarily or indefinitely disrupting services of a host connected to the internet.

Hacking: An attempt to exploit a computer system or a private network inside a computer.

Keylogging: The action of recording (sometimes covertly) the keys struck on a keyboard, so that the person using the keyboard is unaware that their actions are being monitored.

Ransomware: A type of malicious software from cryptovirology that threatens to publish the victim's data or perpetually block access to it unless a ransom is paid.

Spam: Unsolicited bulk email or junk mail.

This research was previously published in Global Cyber Security Labor Shortage and International Business Risk; pages 77-93, copyright year 2019 by Business Science Reference (an imprint of IGI Global).

Chapter 15
Cybersecurity Curricular Guidelines

Matt Bishop
University of California – Davis, USA

Diana Burley
The George Washington University, USA

Lynn A. Futcher
Nelson Mandela University, South Africa

ABSTRACT

The Cybersecurity Curricular Guidelines, a joint effort of the ACM, IEEE Computer Society, AIS SIGSAC, and IFIP WG 11.8, were created to provide developers of cybersecurity curricula with guidelines for material to include. The curricular guidelines have eight knowledge areas, broken down into knowledge units and topics. Underlying cross-cutting concepts provide linkages among the knowledge areas. Disciplinary lenses enable the developer to emphasize the knowledge units appropriate to the goals of the developed curricula. Each knowledge area also includes a list of essential concepts that all curricula should cover to an appropriate depth. The guidelines can be linked to workforce frameworks and certification criteria as well as academic curricula.

INTRODUCTION

The urgency of securing our information infrastructure is clear from the numerous compromises of personal data as well as from compromises of commercial and government information. A key part of this is securing the computing infrastructure, which consists of networks and computers in their various guises – the Internet, personal computers, laptops, servers, "smart" devices such as phones and sensors connected to the Internet — as well as the policies, procedures, and user and administrator interfaces controlling those components

DOI: 10.4018/978-1-6684-3554-0.ch015

Other chapters in this book cover the nature of threats, how the associated risks affect the proper handling of data and systems, and examples of notable compromises and their effects. The number and rate of compromises demonstrate that cybersecurity has not yet been fully integrated into the development, deployment, operation, and retirement of computing and network systems. Academic institutions are introducing courses and programs to teach students about cybersecurity. The topics covered, and the depth to which they are covered, vary greatly; thus, students who graduate from different cybersecurity programs may have very different skills and abilities. And as these programs are introduced, what to cover and to what depth it should be covered are among the primary considerations in the development of the curriculum.

There is no universally agreed upon cybersecurity curriculum, and indeed there cannot be. The security needs of a military organization, a commercial firm, a hospital, and an academic institution are often distinct. For example, a commercial firm may prize integrity above other security properties to ensure its products are not tampered with as they are developed and go to market. A military organization treats confidentiality and integrity as the most important properties, as it must protect plans and disposition of troops and ensure only authorized changes by authorized people occur. A hospital must protect both, because a failure in integrity could result in the death of a patient, and a violation of confidentiality could result in a large fine and multiple lawsuits. Thus, no one curriculum can encompass all cybersecurity needs. So rather than a standard curriculum, a set of guidelines will enable institutions introducing new cybersecurity programs to select those areas of cybersecurity most relevant to the needs of their constituents (such as typical employers of their students), and emphasize those while covering the other topics in less depth. Institutions with existing programs can also use guidelines to determine whether their curriculum covers the material appropriate for their needs, as different cybersecurity curricula will emphasize different aspects of security.

The effectiveness of guidelines has been shown by the impact of the Software Engineering Body of Knowledge's (Bourque & Fairley, 2014) effect on software engineering education (Ludi & Collofello, 2001; Fairley, Bourque, & Keppler, 2014; Alarifi, Zarour, Alomar, Alkshaikh, & Alsaleh, 2016). It has changed how software engineering programs are developed and evaluated.

In September 2015, the Association for Computing Machinery (ACM) Education Board, the IEEE Computer Society, the Association for Information Systems Special Interest Group on Information Security and Privacy, and the International Federation for Information Processing's Technical Committee on Information Security Education collaborated to launch the CSEC2017 Joint Task Force on Cybersecurity Education (JTF).

For 28 months, the JTF engaged with the cybersecurity community through presentations and discussions at U.S. and international conferences and workshops. Members of an Industrial Advisory Board ensured that the resulting work included input from industries; members of a Global Advisory Board provided input from educators and professionals from around the world. In all, more than 325 people from 35 countries and 6 continents contributed to the development of the cybersecurity guidelines.

The first version of the Cybersecurity Curricular Guidelines (CSEC2017) (Joint Task Force on Cybersecurity Education, 2017) was completed in December 2017. This chapter discusses those guidelines, their use, and their future.

BACKGROUND

Before 2000, cybersecurity was generally considered of little interest in most, but not all, academic institutions. During the first decade of the 21st century, interest in cybersecurity as an academic area of research and education picked up considerably as the lack of security in our systems and infrastructure resulted in successful large-scale attacks and effects. Funding increased, and research and technology grew. In 2013, the ACM included it in its computer science curricular guidelines (Joint Task Force on Computer Curricula, 2013). In 2014, the Cyber Education Project (CEP) began to develop curriculum guidelines for "cyber science" programs. A logical outgrowth of this was the idea of developing curricular guidelines for cybersecurity; this led to the establishment of the JTF, and the development of CSEC2017.

A variety of efforts have examined what students need to know in cybersecurity. For example, the U.S. National Initiative for Cybersecurity Education (NICE) has developed a Cybersecurity Workforce Framework (NCWF) (Newhouse, Keith, Scribner, & Witte, 2016) that presents the knowledge, skills, and abilities that enable workers to carry out specific tasks, and relates those tasks to work roles. The knowledge, skills, and abilities are general, such as "Knowledge of secure coding techniques" (K0140; Newhouse, Keith, Scribner, & Witte, 2016, p. 110), "Skill in conducting application vulnerability assessments (S0137; Newhouse, Keith, Scribner, & Witte, 2016, p. 80), and "Ability to apply cybersecurity and privacy principles to organizational requirements (relevant to confidentiality, integrity, availability, authentication, non-repudiation)" (A0123; Newhouse, Keith, Scribner, & Witte, 2016, p. 91). So the NIST NICE Framework would be good for people whose goal is to be able to satisfy the requirements of a specific cybersecurity work role, but they do not encompass the breadth that an academic program covers. Further, it does not provide guidance for those who are not working in the cybersecurity area, such as students of law, political science, medicine, and other disciplines. Curricular guidance for academic institutions must also provide guidance for curricula for these students. Thus, the NIST NICE Framework complements CSEC2017, and indeed some tasks may suggest specific exercises that may be incorporated as part of a cybersecurity curriculum. This is discussed in the section about workforce frameworks.

The ACM Computer Science Curricula 2013 provides curricular guidelines for undergraduate degree programs in computer science. Information assurance and security is one of 18 knowledge areas in the guidelines, and like CSEC2017 parts of it are distributed throughout the other knowledge areas. So it is much less detailed than CSEC2017, and it organizes KUs based on other computer science disciplines and not as intrinsic parts of cybersecurity. The ACM Information Technology Curricula 2017 (Task Group on Information Technology Curricula, 2017) includes Cybersecurity Principles as an essential IT domain, and Cybersecurity Emerging Challenges as a supplemental IT domain. The Cybersecurity Principles domain is essentially a cybersecurity core, with subdomains at a high level, and some of the subdomains augment other domains. The Cybersecurity Emerging Challenges domain speaks to topics that are rapidly changing, and so supplements the other domain. The two Curricula provided a basis for much of the CSEC2017 development in its early stages.

The US NSA/DHS Knowledge Units (KUs) for Centers of Academic Excellence in Cyber Defense (CAE-CD) provide a basis for determining whether a program meets the requirements for being designated a CAE-CD. These KUs focus on educating cybersecurity workers. It provides specific outcomes for each KU, and schools can map the outcomes of their classes to these to demonstrate they satisfy the requirements for that designation. CSEC2017 has different goals. It allows flexibility in the development of curricula for what is to be covered in different fields, and is not tied to any designation. Conklin and Bishop (2018) provide a detailed comparison.

Many curricula for cybersecurity are available to meet specific objectives. The (ISC)[2] Common Body of Knowledge (International Information Systems Security Certification Consortium, 2018) prepares students for the CISSP exam. The ISACA Online Courses on Cybersecurity also speaks to certifications (ISACA, 2018). The IEEE Cyber Security Program's goals (IEEE, 2018) are to help businesses improve their practices. These are curricula, specific to their goals, and as such can provide insight and ideas for exercises to academic educators. As noted above, CSEC2017 has different goals. It is a set of guidelines rather than a prescriptive curriculum.

CYBERSECURITY

The term "cybersecurity professional" has many meanings. Cybersecurity professionals secure systems at corporations. They develop policies and plans to handle successful attacks, and to track unsuccessful ones. They work with legislators to write laws affecting the use and misuse of technology. Cybersecurity professionals can be found in almost all fields, performing a wide variety of jobs. As a result, people have different opinions of what a cybersecurity professional should know, and what skills and abilities they could have.

Given that the term "cybersecurity" has many different meanings, this is not surprising. Thus, a large number of educational programs and curricula fall under this term. Some organizations, such as NIST, have developed frameworks for the knowledge, skills, and abilities required for specific cybersecurity jobs. But these frameworks speak to specific jobs and not an education program in cybersecurity.

Cybersecurity is a discipline that touches many other disciplines, just as mathematics, which is found in the disciplines of physics, chemistry, and other physical sciences and social science disciplines. Any definition of cybersecurity should acknowledge these influences, and accept that it is "cross-disciplinary".

The Joint Task Force defined cybersecurity as:

A computing-based discipline involving technology, people, information, and processes to enable assured operations. It involves the creation, operation, analysis, and testing of secure computer systems. It is an interdisciplinary course of study, including aspects of law, policy, human factors, ethics, and risk management in the context of adversaries. (Joint Task Force on Cybersecurity Education, 2017, p. 10)

This formed the underpinning of the material in the guidelines.

THE CSEC2017 FRAMEWORK

The CSEC2017 framework begins with a model having three parts. The knowledge areas describe the subject matter relating to the discipline of cybersecurity. The cross-cutting concepts underlie multiple knowledge areas, providing interconnections among those areas. The disciplinary lenses show the content of the discipline of cybersecurity appropriate for that lens. These combine to produce a cohesive thought model that underlies the curricular guidelines. Figure 1 shows the model.

Figure 1. CSEC Thought Model
(Joint Task Force on Cybersecurity Education, 2017, p. 20)

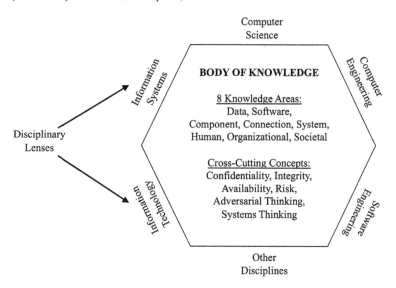

Basis for the Guidelines

The basis for the guidelines themselves drew on five bases.

First, a cybersecurity education program is based upon core knowledge and skills. These underlie all aspects of cybersecurity, and all ways in which cybersecurity manifests itself across other disciplines. The particular understanding of cybersecurity may color the interpretation of the knowledge, and the use of skills. For example, confidentiality may encompass protecting data from being revealed to an adversary in one realm. In the guise of privacy, it may simply allow those to whom the information refers to control its distribution and use. But in both realms, a basic understanding of confidentiality is critical to the application of cybersecurity principles and mechanisms.

Next, cybersecurity has a computing-based foundation. This is an acknowledgement of the prefix "cyber". Computers and their infrastructure, including networks, are the focus of cybersecurity. The information to be protected is stored on those systems. The resources to be protected are controlled by those systems. For example, contact lists are stored on smartphones, and those must be protected against corruption and, usually, disclosure. Medical devices such as pacemakers must have their control programs be both assured and secured against unauthorized changes or interference. This assumption includes interactions between people, procedures, and computing systems. How computers are used affects how they are secured, and if policies and procedures provide inadequate or misguided security properties, then the computing system will be vulnerable.

Third, a good cybersecurity education program should enable students to undertake many different types of jobs in many different areas. The precise knowledge, skills, and abilities for each job will depend both on the nature of the job and the environment in which the employee works. As these differ among different employers and organizations, a graduate of a general cybersecurity program will need to learn the specific tasks expected, and how to work in the organization's political, legal, social, and human environment. The cybersecurity education program cannot teach these unless the program has as its specific goal the training of employees for that particular organization. But the program can teach the students so they are flexible and can quickly learn what specialized knowledge they need for a job in a given organization. Thus, the cybersecurity education program should teach concepts applicable to a broad range of cybersecurity expertise.

Conversely, cybersecurity education guidelines are flexible so programs can tailor their curriculum to specialized needs. For example, a legislator need not know the details of a cryptosystem, but she should know what cryptography is, how it works in a general sense, and – perhaps most important – what its limits are and how it can be compromised. A developer of medical systems need not know the details of cybersecurity theory, but must understand the need to provide mechanisms to enable process separation and protection of user data. If the goal of the program is to train a network analyst to use a Big System firewall, then the program should focus on those aspects of cybersecurity relevant to the configuration and use of that firewall and not, for example, stray into multilevel integrity policy enforcement by operating systems.

Finally, ethical issues are inherent in cybersecurity, and a cybersecurity education program should emphasize the ethical obligations and responsibilities that designing, implementing, and administering security measures entails. A good example is the adding of "back doors" to cryptographic mechanisms so trusted people can decipher any traffic using those mechanisms, or requiring that cryptographic keys be escrowed for that purpose. The former fails because of the difficulty in distinguishing legitimate requests from illegitimate ones, in light of the insider threat. The latter also may be unreasonable if the effect is the same as a "back door". But key escrow may be reasonable, for example if the mechanism is used for an organization's business data; should the user become unavailable, the organization needs a way to recover its data. Students and practitioners of cybersecurity need to apply ethics to their tasks to determine how best to do them, or indeed whether they should be done.

The Model

Knowledge areas (KAs) describe the subject matter of cybersecurity. They provide a tool for understanding or exploring cybersecurity ideas. Further, the material in the area can be learned in varying levels of detail and understanding.

The KAs are composed of knowledge units (KUs), which group multiple related topics. The topics are specific guidelines for the curricular content of the knowledge unit. The KAs are:

- Data Security;
- Software Security;
- Component Security;
- Connection Security;
- System Security;
- Human Security;
- Organizational Security; and
- Societal Security.

The KUs and topics may overlap different KAs. As an example, consider the design of a library that reads packets from a network and processes them. The library is privileged, and it must ensure that the contents of the packets are read properly and protected. Thus, this falls into the topics of using security features (restricting privileges) and encapsulating structures and modules in the implementation KU of the Software Security KA. It is also a composition of components, because the library interface ties the system and network together. Thus, that aspect of the design falls under the network traffic topic of the network defense KU of the Connection Security KA.

Learning outcomes would be tied into the topics in the KUs. With one exception, learning outcomes are not present in CSEC2017. The topics presented are simply examples of material the KU is to cover. Further the specific learning outcomes depend on the use to which the knowledge is to be put – that is, upon the disciplinary lens through which the topic is viewed, and upon the goals of the curriculum or program using the curricular guidelines. How best to incorporate them is a discussion for the future.

Cross-cutting concepts unify ideas underlying the KAs, and provide a framework for making connections among them. They span most, if not all, of the KAs, and are fundamental to students' understanding of core ideas, regardless of the discipline or program they are studying. This provides a coherent view of cybersecurity, and also reinforces the mindset of each of the knowledge units.

The KAs are common to all cybersecurity. However, the approach to teaching and learning the material in the KAs, and the depth to which they and the ancillary skills must be mastered, depends on how that knowledge will be used. A lawyer would be expected to understand much of the material in the Organizational, Societal, and Human Security KAs, and only a little from the other three KAs. Contrariwise, a software engineer would be expected to know much of the material in the Data, Component, Connection, System, and especially Software Security KAs, and only a minimal amount from the other three KAs. And a system designer would emphasize the Component, Connection and Systems Security KAs, while learning the basics about Organizational, Human, and Societal Security and more about Data and Software Security. Thus, the "view" of the KAs differs, depending on discipline.

CSEC2017 is designed to help with the development of a course, a curriculum, or a training program. As this development proceeds, the topics must be instantiated with specific material appropriate for that course. The content will undoubtedly change over the lifetime of the program as newer material becomes available. For example, the description of the topic "Logical data access controls" in the access control KU of the Data Security KA lists 9 example access controls such as access control lists, mandatory access control, role based access control, and attribute-based access control. But a class on Android security will cover the Android access control mechanism in this topic, even though it is not explicitly listed in the description. As the Android phone does not provide many of the types of access control such as attribute-based access control, the course would not cover that even though it is listed explicitly in the description of that topic. Similarly, a course on cryptography would discuss the GCM mode as a mode of operation for block ciphers, which is in the symmetric (private key ciphers) topic of the cryptography KU in the Data Security KA, even though GCM is nowhere mentioned explicitly. These examples emphasize that the curricular guidance identifies topics that a cybersecurity curriculum might include. The curriculum developer must supply the specific contents for those topics because the developer knows the goals of the class, the needs of the students, and the resources available, and so can tailor how each topic is covered, and what is used to cover it.

Many topics also overlap a number of different KUs and KAs, because each KU and KA presents a different view of the topics. Take privacy as an example. In the Data Security KA, it appears in the Legal Issues KU because of the need to understand the conditions under which there is a right to privacy of data; the Secure Communication Protocols KU, in the guise of privacy-reserving protocols; and in the Data Privacy KU, which focuses on how the law views privacy in a variety of uses of data. In the Software Security KA, it is part of the learning outcomes of security requirements and an implicit part of the Design KU, because software developers must know how to use data anonymization techniques, and when not to record information, as part of the requirements analysis and software design. Privacy pervades the Human Security KA, being named explicitly in all but two KUs, and implicitly in those two. Privacy is part of the topic of identification and authentication (Identity Management KU) because identification information such as biometrics needs to be kept private. How users perceive risk to themselves includes a consideration of privacy, as does learning to identify phishing emails and unsafe web sites, and hence it is part of the Awareness and Understanding KU. It is explicitly named in the Social and Behavioral Privacy KU, the Personal Data Privacy and Security KU, and the Usable Security and Privacy KU. It is also a topic in the Security Governance and Policy KU of the Organizational Security KA because privacy is an element of those policies and governance procedures and requirements. In contrast to the technological orientiation of the topic in the Data Privacy KU in the Data Security KA, the non-technical view of privacy laws lies in the Cyber Law KU in the Societal Security KA. For obvious reasons, it is also its own KU in that KA.

Hardware security issues are another example of a topic that spans several KAs. Attacks such as Spectre and Meltdown (Kocher et al., 2018; Lipp et al., 2018), which deal with the interaction of software and hardware, fall into several KUs. The closest complete match would be component design security, a topic in the Component Design KU of the Component Security KA. Both take advantage of speculative execution in the chip. The best solutions are hardware-based, although some software-based mitigations have been proposed. Those software mitigations generally involve improving isolation, which falls under the topic of encapsulating structures and modules in the Implementation KU of the Software Security KA.

These examples show how CSEC2017 supports the view of the content presented for the same topic being different depending on the area being emphasized.

Knowledge Areas

The CSEC2017 task force assembled working groups to guide development of the KAs and their contents. Each working group developed the topics and KUs for a KA. The KAs, their KUs, topics, and essentials are shown in the Appendix. In order to provide a better understanding of the process followed for each KA, its related KUs, and topics, this section discusses the Software Security KA.

Example of Knowledge Areas Structure: The Software Security Knowledge Area

The Software Security KA focuses on the development and use of software that maintains the security of the information and systems it protects and is used on. Software is a key component of most systems currently in use. The security properties of the system, of the resources it protects, and of the information it holds rely on software to ensure those properties hold. As is well known, policies and procedures also determine the security of an entity, so how the software is designed, implemented, deployed, used, maintained and – at the end of life – decommissioned also bear on the security of both the software itself and what it protects. Directions for use must be clear and comprehensive, and the users must know what to do when something fails (even if they should simply call the vendor). Hence documentation also plays a role in software security. Ethical issues also abound; for example, when should vulnerabilities be announced, and to whom they should be reported. The purpose of the software may also raise ethical issues, and developers need to consider whether the software is to be used for malicious purposes (however those are defined). In light of this, ethical issues merit discussion in the context of software security.

The initial focus of the software security KA was the design principles. Several of the principles are from Saltzer's, Schroeder's, and Kaashoek's design principles (Saltzer & Schroeder, 1975; Saltzer & Kaashoek, 2009). The others come from principles of software engineering. The working group structured the resulting principles around three themes: simplicity, restriction, and methodology. These appeared in the final version, and are:

- KU: Fundamental Design Principles
  - Simplicity principles:
    - Economy of mechanism;
    - Minimize shared mechanisms; and
    - Least astonishment.
  - Restrictive principles:
    - Least privilege;
    - Fail-safe defaults;
    - Complete mediation;
    - Separation; and
    - Minimize trust.
  - Methodology principles:
    - Open design;
    - Layering;
    - Abstraction;
    - Modularity;
    - Complete linkage; and
    - Design for iteration.

Similar work led to six further KUs and their topics:

- KU: Design
  - Derivation of security requirements;
  - Specification of security requirements;
  - Software development lifecycle/security development lifecycle
  - Programming languages and type-safe languages.
- KU: Implementation
  - Validating input and checking its representation
  - Using APIs correctly;
  - Using security features;
  - Checking time and state relationships;
  - Handling exceptions and errors properly;
  - Programming robustly;
  - Encapsulating structures and modules; and
  - Taking environment into account.
- KU: Analysis and Testing
  - Static and dynamic analysis
  - Unit testing

- ○ Integration testing; and
- ○ Software testing.
- KU: Deployment and Maintenance
  - ○ Configuring
  - ○ Patching and the vulnerability lifecycle
  - ○ Checking environment
  - ○ DevOps
  - ○ Decommissioning/retiring
- KU: Documentation
  - ○ Installation documents
  - ○ User guides and manuals
  - ○ Assurance documentation; and
  - ○ Security documentation.
- KU: Ethics
  - ○ Ethical issues in software development
  - ○ Social aspects of software development
  - ○ Legal aspects of software development
  - ○ Vulnerability disclosure
  - ○ What, when, and why to test

These KUs cover the spectrum of software security, from conception (requirements analysis, specification) to deployment (decommissioning), and other critical aspects such as documentation and ethics. In the CSEC2017, each topic is augmented with curricular guidance. For example, the topic "Validating input and checking its representation," a topic in the KU Implementation, has as curricular guidance two items:

- Check bounds of buffers and values of integers to be sure they are in range, and
- Check inputs to make sure they are what is expected and will be processed/interpreted correctly.

The KUs in this knowledge area were validated by mapping the vulnerabilities of the OWASP Top 10 (OWASP, 2017), the MITRE/SANS Top 25 Programming Errors (Christey, 2011), and the design flaws identified in the IEEE Computer Society's Top 10 Security Design Flaws (Arce et al., 2015) against the KUs to ensure that all problems in those widely-used lists were covered. The Implementation KU topics are drawn from Tsipenyuk, Chess, and McGraw's taxonomy (2005). But the guidance does not identify any specific attacks that software developers should look for. Indeed, the topics, and their guidance, do not point out that cross-site scripting and injections fall into this group. Indeed, it does not present vulnerabilities from vulnerability lists, because those will change over time; indeed, cross-site scripting dropped from number 2 in the 2013 OWASP Top 10 list (OWASP, 2013) to number 7 in the 2017 OWASP Top 10 list (OWASP, 2017), and cross-site request forgery was dropped from the list. In a curriculum, these could be discussed to instantiate the topics. They make the subject matter come alive for the students. But for guidelines, the underlying problems creating those vulnerabilities is more important because the classes of vulnerabilities will continue to exist; only their instantiation, which those and other lists cover, will change.

Knowledge Areas as Curricular Guidance

The curricular guidance for topics sometimes presents specific protocols or instances as examples of what should be covered. Curricula that use other protocols or instances to teach the associated topics follow the guidelines, because the named protocols are simply intended as guidance. The topic "Application and transport layer protocols" in the KU Secure Communication Protocols of the Data Security KA identifies four protocols as examples (HTTP, HTTPS, SSH, and SSL/TLS). An instructor may choose not to discuss SSL, and add DNSSEC or SNMP to this list. This emphasizes the focus of the topics, and indeed of the CSEC2017: guidance, not prescription, for curricula.

Some of the KUs overlap KUs in other KAs. The Fundamental Design Principles KU of the Software Security KA overlaps a similar KU in the System Security KA, the Analysis and Testing KU overlaps with the Component Testing KU in the Component Security KA, and the Ethics KU overlaps with similar KUs in the Organizational Security KA and the Societal Security KA. But the emphasis on the material presented varies among the KAs. For example, Ethics in the Organizational Security KA focuses on laws, ethics, and compliance with regulatory and legal requirements, whereas in the Software Security KA, the emphasis is on the software itself and handling issues that arise from what the software is to do, how it does it, and how it is maintained and tested.

Essential Concepts

In addition to the KAs, KUs, and topics, each KA identifies a set of essential concepts and associated learning outcomes. These capture the content that every student of cybersecurity should know about that KA. The depth to which they should know these concepts and their application will vary among disciplines and programs, but every program should cover these essentials to some extent.

The Software Security KA identifies six essentials:

- Fundamental design principles including least privilege, open design, and abstraction;
- Security requirements and their role in design;
- Implementation issues;
- Static and dynamic testing;
- Configuring and patching; and
- Ethics, especially in development, testing and vulnerability disclosure.

In terms of Bloom's revised taxonomy (Committee for Computing Education in Community Colleges, 2000), the learning outcomes for each generally lie at the "understanding" and "applying" levels. Examples of these are:

- For the fundamental design principles, "discuss the implications of relying on open design or the secrecy of design for security";
- For security requirements, "explain why security requirements are important";
- For implementation issues, "explain why input validation and data sanitization are necessary";
- For static and dynamic testing, "discuss a problem that static testing cannot reveal";
- For configuring and patching, "discuss the need to update software to fix security vulnerabilities"; and

- For ethics, "discuss the ethical issues in disclosing vulnerabilities".

Each of these speak to the principles and concepts rather than specific instances. They can of course be tailored to specifics, but the goal of the essentials is to ensure that students learn key concepts at a high level, unless the discipline requires them to delve more deeply into that KA. Using the above as an example, a law student studying cyberlaw should be able to explain why "security through obscurity" is an inadequate defense by itself, but not necessarily how to combine it with other defenses – only that it should be. A software architect, of course, should know the latter as well as the former.

The learning outcomes are intended to apply across all disciplines. Hence they are oriented towards discussion and explanation rather than demonstration. For example, a law student studying cyberlaw should understand the limits of static testing, and hence be able to discuss a problem that static testing cannot reveal. However, for a software engineering student, this learning objective would be subsumed by another, specifically that the student be able to demonstrate the difference between static and dynamic testing (based on the topic static and dynamic testing, in the Analysis and Testing KU of the Software Security KA) by applying her knowledge to create a problem that static testing could not reveal.

Cross-Cutting Concepts

The cross-cutting concepts identify concepts underlying the KAs. The concepts are expressed in different ways in the different KAs, but they are present in most, if not all, of them.

The cross-cutting concepts are (Joint Task Force on Cybersecurity Education, 2017, p. 22):

- *Confidentiality*, or "rules that limit access to system data and information to authorized persons" (Joint Task Force on Cybersecurity Education, 2017, p. 22). Privacy is a form of confidentiality in which control of the data, and of the use of data, is emphasized.
- *Integrity*, or "assurance that the system, data, and information are accurate and trustworthy" (Joint Task Force on Cybersecurity Education, 2017, p. 22). This includes the level of assurance of the initial data as well as it being manipulated only by authorized users in authorized ways. It also includes the level of assurance that the hardware will work as expected.
- *Availability*, or "the data, information, and system are accessible" (Joint Task Force on Cybersecurity Education, 2017, p. 22). In practice, determining availability relies on quality of service requirements. Accessibility is not enough, as some uses may require specific levels of service rather than just being able to connect.
- *Risk*, or "the potential for gain or loss" (Joint Task Force on Cybersecurity Education, 2017, p. 22). Although often seen as undesirable, risk is an everyday phenomenon that businesses and organizations use to guide how they do their work.
- *Adversarial thinking*, a thought process "that considers the potential actions of the opposing force working against the desired result" (Joint Task Force on Cybersecurity Education, 2017, p. 22). It requires understanding what threats could compromise the system, resources, or data, and how they could happen. It is sometimes called "playing the role of the attacker."
- *Systems thinking*, a thought process "that considers the interplay between social and technical constraints to enable assured operations" (Joint Task Force on Cybersecurity Education, 2017, p. 22).

As an example, consider confidentiality. This property is defined by rules controlling the spread of information. It is a cross-cutting concept. It is foundational to the Data Security, Systems Security, and Organizational Security KAs. In the guise of privacy, it is a component of human security. And Societal Security combines components of all these KAs but with a different emphasis, and confidentiality is one of the properties that carries over.

Disciplinary Lenses

Although the KAs cover the knowledge of cybersecurity, and the cross-cutting concepts show their interrelationships, an observation made earlier is that different disciplines require different levels of knowledge and expertise of cybersecurity. The depth, approach, and specific knowledge from the KA depends upon how that knowledge will be used in that discipline. This aspect of the model uses the ACM computing disciplines to provide examples of differing views. These are:

- Computer science;
- Computer engineering;
- Information systems;
- Information technology;
- Software engineering; and
- Mixed disciplines.

As an example, a student of software engineering would focus on the Software Security KA and possibly the Data Security KA. The depth to which the KUs and topics in the Societal Security KA are explored depends upon the nature of the software engineering program. One that focused on medical devices, for example, would need to emphasize privacy and the laws controlling access to medical data, so the students understood the risks and could develop countermeasures. One that focused on web development would also focus on Connection Security as well as Component Security.

The mixed disciplines includes disciplines that require some knowledge of cybersecurity. As mentioned earlier, lawyers specializing in cyberlaw, or dealing with computer-controlled assets such as driverless automobiles, will need to know enough about cybersecurity to understand the technology sufficiently to develop and present their cases. Doctors will need to know enough to understand why many medical records systems use multifactor authentication rather than a simple password, and why all accesses are logged and audited. Health informaticians will need to understand how to position medical systems to minimize the threat of compromise – for example, by ensuring they are not connected to the Internet, or if they are that the network security measures are sufficient.

Summary

The framework of knowledge areas, crosscutting concepts, and disciplinary lenses provide comprehensive guidelines for developing cybersecurity programs and curricula. Through the disciplinary lenses, developers of those curricula can determine what to include, and at what depth, and with what view, to meet the needs of the users of their curricula. Those who have developed curricula can compare them to the KAs, KUs, and topics to determine how comprehensive their curricula are, and can add material as needed.

APPLICATIONS

As the threats increase, and new methods of attack are uncovered, the need for cybersecurity professionals grows. Programs to increase the number of cybersecurity workers are training many, but the organization (ISC)² estimates that by 2022, there will be a shortage of almost 2 million cybersecurity jobs (International Information Systems Security Certification Consortium, 2017). Students graduating from technical programs have the breadth and depth of knowledge needed to succeed, but often lack the experience or specific skills that their job would require. Students graduating from non-technical programs often lack the depth of understanding of cybersecurity concepts to be able to apply them in their jobs. Linking the CSEC2017 guidelines to the workforce would help guide prospective employees to curricula that would support the jobs they they are interested in. This linking would also support employers because they can link their job requirements to specific guidelines and topics, and from that to specific academic curricula or workforce frameworks.

Cybersecurity practices, a critical component in cybersecurity education, refers to the knowledge, skills, and abilities required to perform the duties that a job, or set of jobs, require (Joint Task Force on Cybersecurity Education, 2017, p. 80). The guidelines must be linked to workforce frameworks and professional practice.

Application Areas

This is done through application areas. *Application areas* are an organizing framework for competency levels for each practice (Joint Task Force on Cybersecurity Education, 2017, p. 80). They bridge the thought model to specific workforce frameworks and practices. By defining them, the bodies of knowledge for workforce frameworks and job requirements can be codified by mapping the appropriate application area back to the CSEC2017 framework. Then the codifiers can extract both core knowledge and cross-cutting concepts that are appropriate, and then view them through the appropriate disciplinary lens. The seven application areas mimic a system's life cycle, with supporting areas such as research added. The following descriptions give highlights of topics that people working in the application area need to know.

The *public policy* application area covers executive managers, members of boards of directors, legislators who write and pass laws about the development, deployment, and use of information systems, regulators who regulate those systems, and others who will develop public policy about those systems. They must understand how society and organizations use these systems, and how humans interact with them. This leads to an understanding of the advantages and drawbacks of rules and regulations governing the use of the systems. People working in this application area must also understand the basics of design because the design of the system affects how it is implemented, how it is used and how it can be used, and what it can and cannot do. Similarly, they must understand the risks that the public policy introduces. All this affects the cost of security in both financial and human terms, which are often the focus of people working in this application area.

People working in the *procurement* application area determine what is required to build a system, purchase the technology or have it designed and built, and hire the people who will work with it. They must understand how the systems and the people hired support the general goals of the organization as well as the specific purposes for which the information technology system was obtained and the people hired. This requires an understanding of risk management and business continuity, and from that what is required of people and infrastructure, and what policies, procedures, and processes will provide an appropriate level of security and assurance to ensure the specific and general goals are met.

Managers work in the *management* application area. They must understand business continuity issues, what laws, regulations, and policies must be complied with, and especially how to demonstrate that compliance. They need to know how changes to the system affect its use. They also will be the ones dealing with attacks and the consequences, and so must know how to handle incidents and how those incidents will affect the organization.

The *research* application area is composed of researchers who study cybersecurity. They need to know the foundations of cybersecurity, and beyond that understand topics in their area of research. A theoretician, for example, would need to know the details of formal models of access control. A researcher studying network security would need to know that such models exist, but would focus on how software-defined networking switches could be compromised.

This leads to the *software development* application area. Software must meet any operational requirements, including those determined by laws, regulations, plans, and environmental factors. Developers must design the software to do that, or recommend changes to the requirements. The implementation must satisfy the design and be robust (secure programming), so it must handle exceptions and errors including those arising from humans They must be able to gather assurance evidence to demonstrate assurance claims, and document the installation and use of the systems.

The *information technology security operations* application area deals with preserving the security of the system. The information security managers and personnel must understand how to translate the security requirements into procedures and configurations. They must ensure that identity and authorization management systems are installed, initialized, configured, and connected properly. They have to test the systems, infrastructure, and procedures, and analyze the results. Operations personnel must understand system maintenance under both normal conditions (patching and upgrading, for example) and abnormal conditions (incident handling and response, for example).

The *enterprise architecture* application area refers to the management of systems, operations, and information technology in the organization. This area spans the other six application areas, because policy drives the enterprise architecture; the architecture also drives procurement, management, and security operations. Software runs the infrastructure that supports the enterprise architecture, and research works out ways to improve the architecture or validate it. The enterprise architects must therefore understand elements of all these applications areas.

Workforce Frameworks

Many nations and groups have begun to develop frameworks describing the skills required to work successfully in the field of cybersecurity. As an example, the NIST NICE Cybersecurity Workforce Framework (NCWF) is intended to be comprehensive, providing a lexicon and taxonomy for cybersecurity work in all areas of employment. Other nations have similar efforts underway.

As an example of how academic institutions might link the curricular guidelines to the workforce framework, consider the NCWF. Figure 2 shows the general idea. Essentially, the list of topics in the workforce framework is linked to the list of KAs and KUs in CSEC2017 by topic and learning outcomes. As an example, in the NCWF, a software developer (work role ID SP-DEV-001) must know cybersecurity and privacy principles (K0004), which map into the Fundamental Design Principles KU in the software security KA. She must be able to analyze user needs and software requirements to assess the feasibility of the design (T0011), which maps into the design KU of the Software Security KA. She must be able to debug software (S0014), which covers elements of both the Implementation KU and the Analysis and Testing KU of the Software Security KA. Finally, they must be able to develop secure software using secure software development techniques (A0047),[1] which falls into a number of KUs, most especially the design KU (because it covers the security development life cycle) and the Deployment and Maintenance KU of the Software Security KA. The mapping of these to KUs in other KAs, and of the other knowledge, task, skill, and abilities requirements of the software developer job in the NCWF, is left as an exercise for the reader.

Figure 2. Linking the CSEC thought model and a workforce framework
(Adapted from Figure 4, Joint Task Force on Cybersecurity Education, 2017, p. 21)

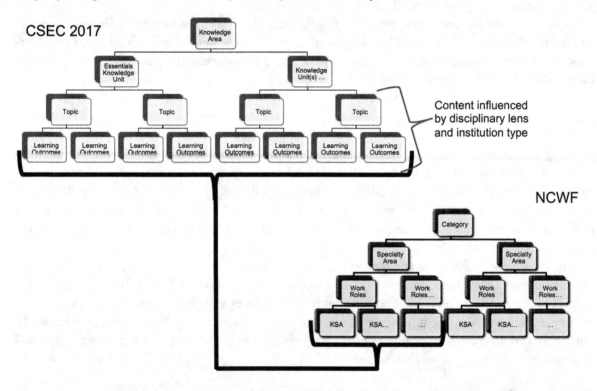

A similar approach is used for mapping courses and curricula to the CSEC2017 KAs and KUs. For example, an undergraduate course in computer security that presented the Fundamental Design Principles would map them to at least the Fundamental Design Principles KU in the Software Security KA, the Component Design KU of the Component Security KA, and the System Thinking KU of the System Security KA. Similarly, a course focusing on the application of the fundamental principles could look for the KUs that speak to those principles, and see whether the topics listed in those KUs are appropriate, or suggest others that are appropriate, for this course. This enables instructors to identify gaps. As an example, the cybersecurity program presented in the next chapter was developed with reference to the CSEC2017 guidelines.

Chapter 11 expands on workforce requirements, as certifications are intended to demonstrate competence of the holder. Thus, certifications and the CSEC2017 KUs and KAs can be mapped to one another, just as courses and the CSEC2017 KUs and KAs can.

To aid in this process, the CSEC2017 web site (Joint Task Force on Cybersecurity Education, 2017) has examples of these mappings, and templates with instructions on how to use the spread sheet provided on the web site to demonstrate the mapping. The JTF is encouraging people and groups to submit examples for their particular courses, curricula, and workforce framework. A subgroup of the task force will review them and assist the submitter in fixing any problems they find. The example will then be posted so others can work with it, or use it as a model for creating their own example.

As an example, CSEC2017 developers and industry partners such as Boeing and Intel are collaborating to map the curricular guidelines with specific professional requirements. The mapping process includes three phases. First, the industry partner identified a set of cybersecurity positions to map to the curricular guidance. For each position, the review team examined the detailed position descriptions for the knowledge, skills and abilities required to perform in the role; representative major tasks; typical education and experience requirements; and competencies. Next, the review team identified the CSEC2017 knowledge areas that included knowledge units and/or topics associated with the position requirements. Once the relevant content was identified, the position requirements were linked to CSEC2017 content through a series of mapping charts. These charts show the direct relationship between CSEC2017 recommended curricular content and specific professional requirements and provide a reference tool to facilitate communication between academic departments and their industry partners.

Each chart consists of a large box containing the job title and the key tasks for that job. In that box are sets of other boxes, one for each knowledge area relevant to the job. Within each box are the essential concepts and other KUs that are most relevant to the tasks the holder of the job will perform. The largest set, called the *primary* boxes, contains the KAs with most of the knowledge relevant to the job. The next set, called the *secondary* boxes, has KAs with a significant amount of knowledge for the job. The third set, called the *tertiary* boxes, represents KAs with more limited relevance. The third set may be omitted.

Burley and Lewis (2018) provide a detailed example of the mapping process and sample mapping charts for three positions in a major corporation. Consider the position of "incident response specialist," which in this organization performs the tasks of incident response activities, evidence collection, analysis, and determining the impact of the incident on resources; and incident reporting. The primary box contains the System Security KA, and all 8 essentials from that KA (holistic approach, security policy, authentication, access control, monitoring, recovery, testing, and documentation). The secondary box contains the Organizational Security KA, one essential (strategy and planning), and the Analytical Tools KU and the Business Continuity, Disaster Recovery, and Incident Management KU in that KA. The corporation can then look to academic programs that follow the curricular recommendations tied to those KAs, and academic programs that want to prepare students for this type of job should follow those recommendations as well.

CONCLUSION

The goal of the CSEC2017 is to provide guidelines to aid developers of workforce frameworks and cybersecurity curricula in ensuring their work is as comprehensive as possible with respect to their goals. This recognizes that cybersecurity is not a monolithic discipline; it is a discipline made up of parts of many other disciplines, and its contents change over time, with focus shifting to meet the needs of the cybersecurity practitioners and those they support.

CSEC2017 is a beginning. As the field evolves, new topics, and perhaps new KUs, will be added; others will be dropped. Sooner than that will be the addition of new curricular and workforce mappings contributed by the community. The process for doing so is being tested, and several curricula and course syllabi are already available. CSEC2017 is also being matched to other efforts. As noted above, it has been compared to the NSA/DHS Centers of Academic Excellence KUs (Conklin & Bishop, 2018). The British SecTech effort (Furnell et al., 2018) is also mapping their certification framework into the CSEC2017, and CSEC2017 is being used as the basis for postgraduate cybersecurity education in South Africa (von Solms & Futcher, 2018).

CSEC2017 can expand in directions beyond the workforce and academic mappings. Its flexibility makes it suitable for curricular guidance in the cybersecurity area for other disciplines. The disciplinary lens "mixed disciplines" refers to these other disciplines. However, the cybersecurity component of a legal education would be different than the cybersecurity component of an education in physics, art, and sociology. So adding disciplinary lenses tailored to specific non-technical disciplines will enhance the utility of CSEC2017. This will require the collaboration of educators and others in those fields, and will probably begin when curricula for those disciplines are added to the ones for technical disciplines.

Thus, the focus of CSEC2017 is not on how to teach cybersecurity, or what specific material should be taught. Instead, it provides a framework for instructors or developers of curricula to determine what they should teach, and how to teach it. Any curriculum evolves over time; and the guidelines will also change. The Joint Task Force invites readers, and anyone else, to participate by contributing exemplars for industry jobs, for both training and academic programs, and for courses. By doing so, they will contribute to improving the state of cybersecurity education.

AVAILABILITY

This chapter presented an overview of CSEC2017. For more details, the interested reader is referred to the most current version of CSEC2017, available at https://cybered.acm.org.

ACKNOWLEDGMENT

This chapter reports on work done by many people. The authors are members of the Joint Task Force; the others are Scott Buck (Intel Labs), Joseph J. Ekstrom (Brigham Young University), David Gibson (U.S. Air Force Academy), Elizabeth K. Hawthorne (Union County College), Siddharth Kaza (Towson University), Yair Levy (Nova Southeastern University), Herbert Mattord (Kennesaw State University), and Allen Parrish (U.S. Naval Academy). Other contributors, too numerous to name here, are listed in the CSEC2017 Final Report; we thank them for their work and assistance.

We also gratefully acknowledge the financial support of the U.S. National Science Foundation under Award 1623104 and the U.S. National Security Agency under Grant H98230-17-10219. Any opinions, findings, and conclusions or recommendations expressed in this material are those of the author(s) and do not necessarily reflect the views of the U.S. National Science Foundation or the U.S. National Security Agency.

Additional financial support was provided by the Intel Corporation, the Association for Computing Machinery (ACM), the IEEE Computer Society (IEEE-CS), and the Association for Information Systems Special Interest Group on Information Security and Privacy (AIS SIGSAC). We thank them for this.

REFERENCES

Alarifi, A., Zarour, M., Alomar, N., Alkshaikh, Z., & Alsaleh, M. (2016). SECDEP: Software Engineering curricula development and evaluation process using SWEBOK. *Information and Software Technology*, *74*, 114–126. doi:10.1016/j.infsof.2016.01.013

Arce, I., Clark-Fisher, K., Daswani, N., DelGrosso, J., Dhillon, D., Kern, C., … West, J. (2015). *Avoiding the top 10 software security design flaws*. Retrieved from https://www.computer.org/cms/CYBSI/docs/Top-10-Flaws.pdf

Bourque, P., & Fairley, R. E. (2014). *Guide to the Software Engineering Body of Knowledge Version 3.0*. Piscataway, NJ: IEEE.

Burley, D. L., & Lewis, A. H. Jr. (2018). CSEC2017 and Boeing: Linking Curricular Guidance to Professional Practice. *IEEE Computer*. (Manuscript submitted for publication)

Christey, S. (2011). *2011 CWE/SANS top 25 most dangerous software errors*. Retrieved from http://cwe.mitre.org/top25/

Committee for Computing Education in Community Colleges. (2000). *Bloom's revised taxonomy*. Retrieved from http://ccecc.acm.org/assessment/blooms

Conklin, W. A., & Bishop, M. (2018). Contrasting the CSEC 2017 and the CAE designation requirements. In *Proceedings of the 51ˢᵗ Hawaii International Conference on System Sciences* (pp 1–7). Manoa, HI: ScholarSpace. Retrieved from https://scholarspace.manoa.hawaii.edu/handle/10125/50194

Fairley, R. E., Bourque, P., & Keppler, J. (2014). The impact of SWEBOK Version 3 on software engineering education and training. In *Proceedings of the IEEE 27th Conference on Software Engineering Education and Training* (pp. 192–200). Klagenfurt, Austria: IEEE. 10.1109/CSEET.2014.6816804

Furnell, S., K, M., Piper, F., &Ensor, C. (2018). A National Certification Programme for Academic Degrees in Cyber Security. In *Proceedings of the 11ᵗʰ IFIP WG 11.8 World Conference on Information Security Education* (pp. 133–146). Poznan, Poland: IFIP. 10.1007/978-3-319-99734-6_11

IEEE. (2018). *Cyber Security Tools for Today's Environment*. Retrieved from https://forms1.ieee.org/Cyber-Security-Program.html

International Information Systems Security Certification Consortium. (2017). *(ISC)² cybersecurity workforce shortage continues to grow worldwide, to 1.8 million in five years*. Retrieved from https://www.isc2.org/News-and-Events/Press-Room/Posts/2017/02/13/Cybersecurity-Workforce-Shortage-Continues-to-Grow-Worldwide

International Information Systems Security Certification Consortium. (2018). *The (ISC)² CBK*. Retrieved from https://www.isc2.org/Certifications/CBK

ISACA. (2018). *Cybersecurity Fundamentals Online Course*. Retrieved from https://www.isaca.org/Education/on-demand-learning/Pages/cybersecurity-fundamentals-online-course.aspx

Joint Task Force on Computing Curricula. (2013). *Computer Science Curricula 2013: Curriculum Guidelines for Undergraduate Degree Programs in Computer Science*. New York, NY: ACM. Retrieved from https://www.acm.org/binaries/content/assets/education/cs2013_web_final.pdf

Joint Task Force on Cybersecurity Education. (2017). *Cybersecurity Curricula 2017*. New York: ACM. Retrieved from https://cybered.acm.org

Kocher, P., Genkin, D., Gruss, D., Haas, W., Hamburg, M., Lipp, M., . . . Yaroim, Y. (2018). *Spectre Attacks. Exploiting Speculative Execution*. Retrieved from https://arxiv.org/abs/1801.01203

LippM.SchwarzM.GrussD.PrescherT.HaasW.MangardS.HamburgM. (2018). *Meltdown*. Retrieved from https://arxiv.org/abs/1801.01207

Ludi, S., & Collofello, J. (2001). An analysis of the gap between the knowledge and skills learned in academic software engineering course projects and those required in real projects. In *Proceedings of the 31st Annual Frontiers in Education Conference* (pp. T2D-8–T2D-11). Reno, NV: Academic Press. 10.1109/FIE.2001.963881

Newhouse, W., Keith, S., Scribner, B., & Witte, G. (2017). *National initiative for cybersecurity education (NICE) cybersecurity workforce framework. NIST Special Publication 800-181*. Gaithersburg, MD: National Institute for Standards and Technology. doi:10.6028/NIST.SP.800-181

OWASP. (2013). *OWASP Top 10 – 2013: The ten most critical web application security risks*. Retrieved from https://www.owasp.org/images/f/f8/OWASP_Top_10_-_2013.pdf

OWASP. (2017). *OWASP Top 10 – 2017: The ten most critical web application security risks*. Retrieved from https://www.owasp.org/images/7/72/OWASP_Top_10-2017_%28en%29.pdf.pdf

Saltzer, J., & Kaashoek, M. (2009). *Principles of Computer System Design*. Burlington, VT: Morgan Kaufmann Publishers.

Saltzer, J., & Schroeder, M. (1975). The protection of information in computer systems. *Proceedings of the IEEE, 63*(9), 1278–1308. doi:10.1109/PROC.1975.9939

Task Group on Information Technology Curricula. (2017). *Information Technology Curricula 2017: Curriculum Guidelines for Baccalaureate Degree Programs in Information Technology*. New York: ACM. Retrieved from https://www.acm.org/binaries/content/assets/education/curricula-recommendations/it2017.pdf

Tsipenyuk, K., Chess, B., & McGraw, G. (2005). Seven pernicious kingdoms: A taxonomy of software security errors. *IEEE Security and Privacy*, *3*(6), 81–84. doi:10.1109/MSP.2005.159

Von Solms, S., & Futcher, L. (2018). Identifying the Cybersecurity Body of Knowledge for a Postgraduate Module in Systems Engineering. In *Proceedings of the 11th IFIP WG 11.8 World Conference on Information Security Education* (pp. 121–132). Poznan, Poland: IFIP. 10.1007/978-3-319-99734-6_10

ADDITIONAL READING

Anderson, L. W., & Krathwohl, D. R. (2001). *A taxonomy for learning, teaching, and assessing: A revision of Bloom's taxonomy of educational objectives*. New York, NY: Longman.

Bicak, A., Liu, X., & Murphy, D. (2015). Cybersecurity curriculum development: Introducing specialties in a graduate program. *Information Systems Education Journal*, *13*(3), 99–110.

Bishop, M., Burley, D., Buck, S., Ekstrom, J. J., Futcher, L., Gibson, D., ... Parrish, A. (2017). Cybersecurity curricular guidelines. In *Proceedings of the 2017 IFIP World Conference on Information Security Education: Information Security Education for a Global Digital Society* (pp. 3–13). doi: 10.1007/978-3-319-58553-6_1

Cooper, S., Nickell, C., Pérez, L., Oldfield, B., Brynielsson, J., Göcke, A. G., ... Wetzel, S. (2010). Towards information assurance (IA) curricular guidelines. In *Proceedings of the 15th Annual Conference on Innovation and Technology in Computer Science Education* (pp. 49–64). doi: 0.1145/1971681.1971686

Hoffman, L., Burley, D., & Toregas, C. (2012). Holistically building the cybersecurity workforce. *IEEE Security and Privacy*, *10*(2), 33–39. doi:10.1109/MSP.2011.181

McDuffie, E. L., & Piotrowski, V. P. (2014). The future of cybersecurity education. *Computer*, *47*(8), 67–69. doi:10.1109/MC.2014.224

KEY TERMS AND DEFINITIONS

Application Area: A structure linking academic curriculum to professional practice.

Cross-Cutting Concepts: Concepts that connect knowledge areas.

Cybersecurity: A computing-based discipline involving technology, people, information, and processes to enable assured operations. It involves the creation, operation, analysis, and testing of secure computer systems. It is an interdisciplinary course of study, including aspects of law, policy, human factors, ethics, and risk management in the context of adversaries.

Cybersecurity Practices: The combination of knowledge and skills required to perform in the field.

Disciplinary Lens: The view of a knowledge area, unit, or topic that focuses on those parts relevant to the discipline.

Discipline: A body of knowledge tied to a common theme.

Knowledge Area: A collection of critical knowledge forming a specialization within a discipline.

Knowledge Unit: A thematic grouping that encompasses multiple, related topics.

Workforce Framework: An organization of knowledge, skills, abilities, and competencies required to perform specific jobs or duties.

ENDNOTE

[1] A0047 states "according to secure software deployment methodologies, tools, and practices" (Newhouse, Keith, Scribner, & Witte, 2016, p. 89). From the context, it is clear the word "deployment" should be "development".

This research was previously published in Cybersecurity Education for Awareness and Compliance; pages 158-180, copyright year 2019 by Information Science Reference (an imprint of IGI Global).

APPENDIX

The Knowledge Areas

This appendix presents a description of each of the knowledge areas (except the Software Security KA, which is described in detail in the body of the paper).

- **Data Security KA:** The data security KA deals with the security of data when stored, when being processed, and when in transit.
- **Component Security KA:** The security of components making up a system have an effect on the security of a system. How that component is designed, fabricated, obtained, tested, integrated into the system, and maintained and disposed of when it reaches the end of its useful life affect the system's satisfying its desired security properties. This KA is concerned with all these aspects.
- **Connection Security KA:** Systems are made up of connected components, so the security of the connections affects the security of the system. The components interact through these connections. The connections can be short, as within a computer, or long, as in computer networks like the Internet. This KA focuses on the security of the connections between components, whether they be physical connections or logical connections.
- **System Security KA:** Understanding the security of a system requires more than understanding the security of its components and connections. It also requires understanding how these interact with one another, with the environment, and with users, policies, and procedures. Thus, the system must be viewed as a whole, and the system security KA does this.
- **Human Security KA:** Humans use and administer systems, and so need to ensure that the security properties of the systems, resources, and information they control hold. Thus, their actions are a critical component of computer and information security. The organizations and societies of which they are members impose both obligations and constraints within which they must act (or not act)
- **Organizational Security KA:** The extensive use of computer technology by organizations requires them to understand computer security. The aspects that are important vary with the goals of the organization, but certain generic attributes are common to all organizations. They are controlled by laws and regulations; they must manage people as well as equipment; and they handle sensitive data.
- **Societal Security KA:** Computer technology has had a profound impact on societies throughout the world. The Internet provides near-instantaneous communication among people and sites around the world. Previously private information about individuals can be derived by linking information in various databases. The law, policy, regulations, and ethics governing societies must take this information explosion, and the technology that supports it, into account.

Chapter 16
Developing Cyber Security Competences Through Simulation–Based Learning

Bistra Konstantinova Vassileva

https://orcid.org/0000-0002-5976-6807

University of Economics, Varna, Bulgaria

ABSTRACT

The importance of cyber security competences is growing both in practice and in academia during the last few years. This chapter provides a current overview of the existing body of the literature in the field of simulation-based learning and the key cyber security issues. The author's primary goal is to develop a methodological business-oriented and evidence-based learning framework which will provide students or trainees with the opportunity to develop practical skills in the field of cyber security issues through a virtual business simulator. The overall intention is to provide a coherent framework that makes use of active-based learning and gamification to support the active participation of students or trainees. To meet these goals, the Reference Framework for Applied Competences (REFRAC) is applied. Taking into account that in 2040 ICT and internet will be 'culturally invisible', cyber security competences will be a must for everyone. They will be critical both for personal and companies' survival in the turbulent and highly competitive digital environment.

INTRODUCTION

The importance of cyber security competences is growing both in practice and in academia during the last few years. This chapter provides a current overview of the existing body of the literature in the field of simulation-based learning and the key cyber security issues. The author's primary goal is to develop a methodological business-oriented and evidence-based learning framework which will provide students or trainees the opportunity to develop practical skills in the field of cyber security issues through a virtual business simulator. The overall intention is to provide a coherent framework that makes use

DOI: 10.4018/978-1-6684-3554-0.ch016

of active-based learning and gamification to support active participation of students or trainees in the learning process. To meet these goals, the Reference Framework for Applied Competences (REFRAC) is applied. Taking into account that in 2040 ICT and internet will be 'culturally invisible' (Manyika et al., 2015) cyber security competences will be a must for everyone. They will be critical both for personal and companies' survival in the turbulent and highly competitive digital environment. Research questions driving this chapter are as follows: 1/ to identify the key topics of cyber security which should be taken as mandatory topics during the training sessions; 2/ to evaluate the possibilities of simulation-based learning to be applied for cyber security issues, and 3/ to propose a methodological framework of simulation-based learning environment aimed at cyber security skills development.

BACKGROUND

This chapter begins with outline of the importance of cyber security issues, cyber security education and experience-based learning approach. The author's primary goal is to develop a methodological business-oriented and evidence-based learning environment which will provide students the opportunity to experience different professional skills, incl. cyber security competences. The overall intention is to offer a coherent framework that is student-oriented and makes use of active-based learning to encourage student active participation. A survey among students was conducted to support the identification of critical cyber security competences to be used in the background layer of the Reference Framework for Applied Competences (REFRAC).

Worldwide spending on on information security products and services is estimated to reach over $124 billion in 2019 (RSAC, 2019). Cyber security budgets have been on the rise for the past several years, increasing by 141% from 2010 to 2018. These numbers show the raising concern to the new challenges to legitimate businesses caused by the increasing activities of the cyber criminals. Cyber security is becoming a key business enabler and a vital tool to protect competitive advantage of companies (Buffomante, 2020:1). According to the World Economic Forum (WEF), the rising cyber interdependence of infrastructure networks is one of the world's top risk drivers. The WEF 2017 Global Risks Report found that cyberattacks, software glitches, and other factors could spark systemic failures that "cascade across networks and affect society in unanticipated ways" (WEF, 2017:7).

MAIN FOCUS OF THE CHAPTER

The Challenges of Cyber Security Landscape

Security is not a new concept but it is of vital importance nowadays when significant security incidents are a regular occurrence. Globalization and advances in technology have driven unprecedented increases in innovation, competitiveness, and economic growth. Critical infrastructure has become dependent on these enabling technologies for increased efficiency and new capabilities (NIST, 2014).

The key findings from The Global State of Information Security Survey 2018 done by KPMG (Castelli, Gabriel, Yates and Booth, 2020) show that massive cybersecurity breaches have become almost commonplace, regularly grabbing headlines that alarm consumers and leaders. Such strong dependence on ICT raises the following question to the academics in the field of economics and business: How well are we prepared to teach our students to be prepared to work in complex cyber threat landscape and highly competitive marketspace?

During the past decade the following four major drivers setting directions to security decision makers in organizations have been identified (Dias et al., 2017): government and industry-sector-specific regulations; standards and best practice models for IT security; business risks and security requirements of the business network that an organization has or wants to join; urgency to invent opportunities in the midst of security breakdowns that incur monetary damage, corporate liability, and loss of credibility. The additional reasons for paying attention on cyber security issues are rooted in the following market trends:

- increasing frequency and cost of security breaches;
- the speed of business activities in the post-economic-crisis world, incl. new product launches, M&A, market expansion, and introductions of new technologies;
- global accessibility of data due to high penetration rates and proliferation of mobile computing (use of internet, smartphones and tablets in combination with BYOD);
- continually complicated ecosystem of digitally connected entities;
- cloud based services, and third party data management and storage;
- open technology systems.

Therefore, cyber security is growing in complexity every day and requires continual refinement of the workforce's capacity for both skill and strategy (Tipton, 2014). The main results of research on cyber security are provided in Table 1.

The economic aspects of cyber security, addressing the specific risks and vulnerabilities of information technologies were investigated as well (Herzog, 2003; Baryshnikov, 2012; Bissell, Lasalle and Dal Cin, 2020). They became increasingly scrutinised, especially given the relatively open, standards driven character of most communication and data processing protocols (FireEye, 2020). According to Anderson (2008) the business impact of cyber security breaches can be classified into four broad categories. The first category is financial impact which results in loss of sales, loss of tangible assets, unforeseen costs, legal liabilities, and depressed share price. The operational impact includes loss of management control, loss of competitiveness, breach of operating standards. Customer-related impact stems from loss of customers or clients, loss of confidence, reputational damage, and delayed deliveries. Employee-related impact mainly results in reduction in staff morale and/or productivity. The above mentioned reasons explain why training on cyber security in the field of economics is needed. This conclusion is confirmed by the results of EY Global Information Security Survey 2018-19 and its implications for digital economy. Effective cyber security becomes increasingly complex to deliver which requires strategic business transformation especially toward the business ecosystem. Taking into account that many systems fail because their designers protect the wrong things, or protect the right things but in the wrong way (Anderson, 2008), we could assume that for an organization to be able to effectively manage the risks in its ecosystem, it needs to clearly define its limits, main components and critical business process which are vulnerable to security breaches. This corresponds to the more horizontal, strategic approach to cyber security in contrast to the vertical, technical approach.

Table 1. Attitudes toward cyber security: main reports and research findings

Title	Sample Size	Source	Most Important Findings
All hands on deck: Key cyber security considerations for 2020		https://home.kpmg/xx/en/home/insights/2020/03/key-cyber-security-considerations-for-2020.html	Six key cyber considerations: § Aligning business goals with security needs. § Digital trust and consumer authentication. § The evolving security team. § The next wave of regulation. § Cloud transformation and resilience. § Automating the security function.
2019 HIMSS Cybersecurity Survey	166	https://www.himss.org/himss-cybersecurity-survey	§ A pattern of cybersecurity threats and experiences is discernable across US healthcare organizations. § Many positive advances are occurring in healthcare cybersecurity practices. § Complacency with cybersecurity practices can put cybersecurity programs at risk. § Notable cybersecurity gaps exist in key areas of the healthcare ecosystem.
The Global State of Information Security Survey 2018	9500	https://www.pwc.com/us/en/services/consulting/cybersecurity/library/information-security-survey/strengthening-digital-society-against-cyber-shocks.html	§ 39% say they are very confident in their cyberattack attribution capabilities. § The frequency of organizations possessing an overall cybersecurity strategy is particularly high in Japan (72%) and Malaysia (74%). § Only 44% of the respondents say their corporate boards actively participate in their companies' overall security strategy. § 34% say their organizations plan to assess IoT risks across the business ecosystem. § Only half of respondents say their organizations conduct background checks. § Only 58% of respondents say they formally collaborate with others in their industry, including competitors, to improve security and reduce the potential for future risks.
The Global Risks Report 2017 12th Edition	745	http://www3.weforum.org/docs/GRR17_Report_web.pdf	§ The next global challenge: facing up to the importance of identity and community. § The risks associated with AI are considered the potential risks associated with letting greater decision-making powers move from humans to AI programs, as well as the debate about whether and how to prepare for the possible development of machines with greater general intelligence than humans. § Rising cyber dependency is determined as number 4 within the Top 5 Trends that determine global developments.
2015 HIMSS Cybersecurity Survey	297	https://www.hImss.org/2015-cybersecurity-survey	§ The most important problem is the breach of patient information. § The respondents'' organizations use an average of 11 different technologies to secure their environments. § 50% of respondents'' organizations have hired a full-time professional, such as a Chief Information Security Officer (CISO), to manage the information security functions. § 87% indicated that information security had increased as a business priority at their organizations over the past year. § Approximately 20 percent of these security incidents ultimately resulted in the loss of patient, financial or operational data. § Respondents were most likely to be concerned about phishing attacks, negligent insiders and advanced persistent threat (APT) attacks.
2015 Information Security Breaches Survey	664	https://www.pwc.co.uk/assets/pdf/2015-isbs-executive-summary-02.pdf	§ 90% of large organizations and 74% of small businesses had a security breach (81% and 74% increase respectively from year ago). § 59% of the respondents expect there will be more security incidents in the next year than last. § 69% of large organizations and 38% of small businesses were attacked by an unauthorised outsider in the last year (55% and 33% increase respectively from year ago). § 72% of large organizations and 63% of small businesses provide ongoing security awareness training to their staff (68% and 54% increase respectively from year ago). § 32% of respondents in 2015 haven't carried out any form of security risk assessment. § Despite the increase in staff awareness training, people are as likely to cause a breach as viruses and other types of malicious software.
Cyber security: Are consumer companies up to the challenge? (2014)	111	https://www.kpmg.com/BE/en/IssuesAndInsights/ArticlesPublications/Documents/Cyber-Security-Survey.pdf	§ Only 36% of the respondents indicated that their organization has a formal cyber incident response plan. § Nearly three-quarters of respondents rate their organization's cyber maturity level as average or below. § The majority of consumer companies are not yet considering how they will respond to a data breach before it occurs. § 44% of the respondents indicated that in their organization the CIO[1] is responsible for cyber security.
2014 Deloitte-NASCIO Cybersecurity Study	n.a.	https://www.nascio.org/publications/documents/Deloitte-NASCIO CybersecurityStudy_2014.pdf	§ Top five cyber security initiatives for 2014 include: 1/ risk assessments, 2/ training and awareness, 3/ data protection, 4/ continuous security events monitoring, 5/ incident response. § Lack of sufficient funding continues to be the #1 barrier since 2010. § Top 3 cyber concerns are as follows: 1/ malicious code (74.5% of respondents), 2/ hactivism (53.2% of respondents), and 3/ zero-day attacks (42.6% of respondents) § Top 5 cyber threats that the CISOs are more concerned with include: 1/ phishing and pharming; 2/ social engineering; 3/ increasing sophistication of threats; 4/ insecure code; 5/ mobile device threats.
EY's Global Information Security Survey 2014	1825	https://www.ey.com/Publication/vwLUAssets/EY-global-information-security-survey-2014/$FILE/EY-global-information-security-survey-2014.pdf	§ Organizations are lagging behind in establishing foundational cyber security. § The increased external thread is determined by cyber threats multiplying, disappearing perimeter, and growing attacking power of cyber criminals. § The increased internal pressures are defined by lack of agility, lack of budget, and lack of skills. § 56% of organizations say that it is unlikely or highly unlikely that their organization would be able to detect a sophisticated attack. § 36% of respondents do not have a threat intelligence program. § 58% of organizations do not have a role or department focused on emerging technologies and their impact on information security.

continues on following page

Table 1. Continued

Title	Sample Size	Source	Most Important Findings
15th Annual 2010/2011 Computer Crime and Security Survey	351	https://gatton.uky.edu/FACULTY/ PAYNE/ACC324/CSISurvey2010. pdf	§ 21.6% of the respondents indicate that they experienced targeted attacks, moreover, 3% experienced more than 10 targeted attacks. § The most common types of attacks are (in descending order measured by % of the respondents who answered positively) as follows: malware infection, phishing, laptop/mobile device theft, bots on network, denial of service, password sniffing, financial fraud, exploit of wireless network. § More than half of losses are not due to malicious insiders.

Source: Author's work

Recently the focus of cyber security research shifted to the role of people (wetware, liveware, meatware, humanware) (Harley, 2010) and especially to millenials-focused talent management presented in 2018 Deloitte-NASCIO Cybersecurity Study. A group of researchers and academics (Guzdial, 2015; Jurse and Mulej, 2011) emphasised the necessity to re-target the education from knowledge transfer to development of a mental models/mindsets which (1) make users vulnerable to cyber attacks, and (2) make management resistant to addressing cyber security issues (Harley, 2010).

Experience- and Simulation-Based Learning

In terms of education, there is increasing consensus (Berge and Verneil, 2002; OECD, 2014; Biggs and Tang, 2011) that beyond knowledge and skills training, learning process should emphasize on the following: (1) developing a mindset which is global; (2) working through a model of cross-cultural reconcilement; and (3) fostering relational skills. This involves, in the filed of cyber security education in the field of economics and business: (1) providing knowledge about cyber threat landscape and the assumptions which underlie intruding business practices and social engineering; (2) concentrating on the context of digital business and business ecosystems; (3) at the individual level, assessing the capabilities to recognize and to avoid cyber attacks. Under these conditions teaching is not merely a way of 'covering the curriculum' or transferring the knowledge directly from the 'expert' to the learner but a way of encouraging innovative thinking, creativity and responsibility for the decisions which are taken.

Research suggests that students must do more than just listen. They must read, write, discuss or be engaged in solving problems. Moreover, students must be engaged in such higher-order thinking tasks as analysis, synthesis, and evaluation, to be actively involved. Thus strategies promoting activities that involve students in doing things and thinking about what they are doing may be called active learning. Performing these activities especially in a team environment forces students to take a responsibility for their decisions.

The distinguishing feature of experience-based learning (or experiential learning) is that the experience of the learner occupies central place in all considerations of teaching and learning. This experience may comprise earlier events in the life of the learner, current life events, or those arising from the learner's participation in activities implemented by teachers and facilitators. A key element of experience-based learning is that learners analyse their experience by reflecting, evaluating and reconstructing it (sometimes individually, sometimes collectively, sometimes both) in order to draw meaning from it in the light of prior experience (Andresen, Boud and Cohen, 2001).

Simulation-based learning is a form of active and experience-based learning (or experiential learning). Its distinguishing feature is that the experience of the learner occupies central place in all considerations of teaching and learning. This experience may comprise earlier events in the life of the learner, current life events, or those arising from the learner's participation in activities implemented by teachers and facilitators. A key element of simulation-based learning is that learners analyse their experience by reflecting, evaluating and reconstructing it (sometimes individually, sometimes collectively, sometimes both) in order to draw meaning from it in the light of prior experience (Andresen, Boud and Cohen, 2001).

A group of authors (Darling, 1999; Shelton, 1999) proposed that the beginning of the twenty-first century could be called 'The Quantum Age' – time of changing paradigms, from Newton's mechanistic laws of classical physics to the theories of chaos and quantum mechanics. These authors suggest that new sciences provide the conceptual foundation for a new skill set for decision makers – a set of skills that can enable to view conflict from a new perspective, but also to respond to conflict in new ways. This paradigm shift affects the view point to conflicts and respectively to the skills required to deal with conflicts. Shelton and Darling (2004) use quantum theory in their research work as a metaphor for the development of a new set of skills aimed at decision makers, called quantum skills. The concept of quantum skills corresponds to the goals of simulation-based learning and will be used by the authors as a cornerstone of their methodological framework.

The Concept of Reference Framework of Applied Competences (REFRAC)

The concept of REFRAC was built on the assumption of education as a transformative process with its three particular outputs (knowledge, skills and values) which, when linked together, lead to sustainable competence development in any professional setting. None is independent of the others, and it is the interactions among these that leads to sustainability of learning within the profession and competence development. Each domain is, of course, a major field of professional enquiry and action, and its details and form vary from profession to profession.

Figure 1. REFRAC conceptual model
Source: Author's work

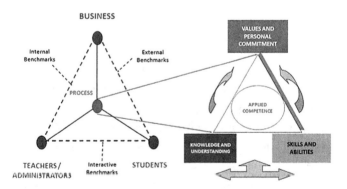

The perspectives on the learning process as a system (teachers and administrators, students, and audience such as policymakers, parents, communities) presented in Figure 1 have their own benefits and standings and also interact with one other continuously. The three major components of this transformative process (presented by the red spot in the middle of the pyramid on Figure 1) are (i) inputs to the educational system, (ii) the system itself, and (iii) the outputs to the system. The inputs to the educational system are the students, faculty and staff, funding, facilities and the university goals. They could be determined as human, physical, and financial resources. The system itself is created and controlled entirely by the elements that compose the system, regardless of the inputs, with some measurable points within; namely, personnel training, teaching methods, learning, advising, counseling, tutoring, evaluations, infrastructure, etc. The system outputs refer to the product that is generated within the system which include tangible outcomes, intangible outcomes and values.

The concept of REFRAC could be easily implemented to cyber security education. It corresponds perfectly to the ISF Security Model (Chaplin and Creasey, 2011) which is developed to support organizations in designing their approach to addressing information security and to give them a basis for identifying the key aspects of an information security programme. Research methodology (Figure 2) includes both qualitative and quantitative methods designed to meet the research goal to identify the critical points of cyber security competences within the background layer of the Reference Framework of Applied Competences (REFRAC).

Figure 2. REFRAC methodology
Source: Author's work

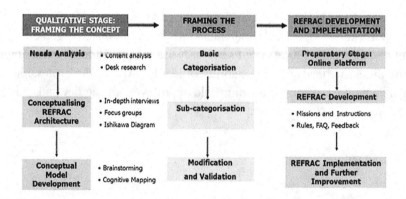

The qualitative study involved in-depth interviews with security and cyber security experts, focus group discussions with students, and content analysis to identify the key areas for cyber security capacity building. Five in-depth interviews with experts were conducted followed by two sessions of brainstorming. Two focus groups were undertaken with students. Content analysis was performed in specialised blogs and web posts. As a result a draft conceptual model in a form of Ishikawa diagram was constructed. The model has been "fine-tuned" during a series of workshops. The next step was a content analysis of information published in specialized blogs and web posts. The results showed quite diverse notions toward cyber security education. The most debatable issues covered declarative vs. procedural learning process, technical (computing) vs. non-technical education, traditional vs. interactive, passive vs. active, etc. The author decided that the context of the learning process is critical when the educational goal is to develop applied skills, especially cyber security skills. The students should be willing to explore which requires a combination between contextual and experience-based learning. Quantitative research included annual survey among students to evaluate their awareness and attitudes toward cyber security. The results were used to modify the anatomy of the knowledge areas of REFRAC (Figure 3) and content of the missions.

Figure 3. Anatomy of REFRAC
Source: Author's work

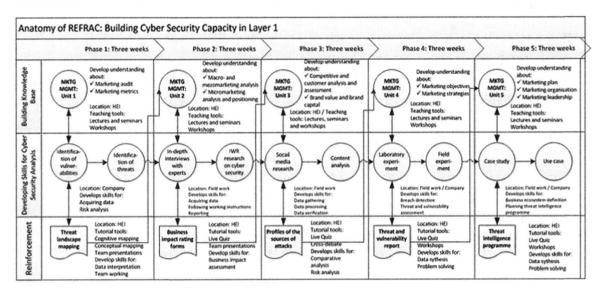

Mission (Figure 4) is defined as an assignment which requires a practical completion of a task or a sequence of tasks based on a certain knowledge. Its purpose is to crosswalk the skills and knowledge and to stimulate students to make grounded choices. Missions are accompanied by clear instructions and a feedback form. The feedback form is used for validation and it serves as an assessment tool thus providing transparency and creating a competitive environment among students (Vassileva, 2016).

Figure 4. Missions: the building blocks of REFRAC
Source: Author's work

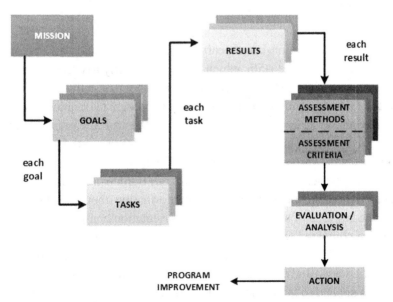

The mission-based methodology flows from the initial mission to the completion of the final mission. REFRAC methodology allows mission re-ordering which depends on planned and expected learning outcomes. REFRAC implementation requires a step-by-step approach. In the begininning of the process students/trainees should pass through initial training on how to read instructions (the core of the missions), how to follow instructions, and how to report the progress and accomplished results. The process itself (Figure 5) combines knowledge development, creativity stimulation, encouragement of innovative thinking, and intuition.

Figure 5. REFRAC simulation-based learning process
Source: Author's work

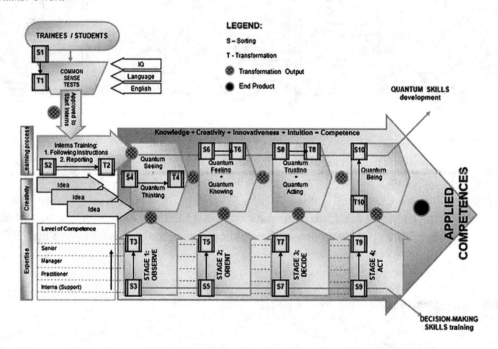

The focus of REFRAC simulation-based learning process is placed on developing the following three groups of skills. First, cognitive skills which require capability to cope with difficulties provoked by cyber security challenges. These skills are recognized as the main human capabilities, as it requires mental agility and tolerance for ambiguity or uncertainty to recognize or quickly adapt to the unknown. Second, decision-making skills, especially to understand the true areas of disagreement (conflict) which contribute to solving the right problems and manage the true needs of the parties. Third, tactical abilities. These skills as a background for quantum skills development could be achieved by applying the OODA (Observation – Orientation – Decision – Action) framework (Philip and Martin, 2009). Observation is the means by which one collects/registers information about the state of the external world and corresponds to the key area of structures/systems. Orientation comprises the internal processes by which observations are compared with prior knowledge and experience to update an understanding of the world. It corresponds to the key area of attitudes. Decision is the internal process by which various tentative solutions are assessed and one selected for action. Action is the process by which the internally constructed solution is applied to the world. It corresponds to the key area of behavior.

SOLUTIONS AND RECOMMENDATIONS

Based on results from conducted research and REFRAC methodology (Figure 3), the following structure and organization of course on cyber security is proposed. The first part of the course will include an introduction to cyber security as well as cyber hybrid warfare. In this section terms and definitions will compose the basic knowledge and terminology needed to understand the lectures. The course will in general, provide theory as well as recent publications and research in the field. The second part of the course will include a deep scanning of network security based on tools and examples taken from real scenarios which industrial decision makers in organizations had to face with. The third part of the course will involve a basic training of programming, mainly focuses on structured programming as well as object oriented. The students in this section will learn how to write software code. These pieces of code, are actually planned to be simple programs that can assist to evaluate and monitor malware that penetrates into the industrial's network. The fourth part of the course will be dedicated to security and encryption – description facilities which are common in many industries as well as academic institutions. The fifth part of the course will include a practical sessions on existing tools and models which are aimed to expose the student to cope with cyber attacks scenarios.

FUTURE RESEARCH DIRECTIONS

The proposed framework of applied competences (REFRAC) provide an opportunity for implementation of experience- and simulation-based learning in various scientific and business areas, incl. cyber security. Its main advantages include: 1/ stimulating creative and innovative (out-of-the-box) thinking, 2/ developing business-related skills at different levels (the basic level comprises business survival skills), 3/ stimulating entrepreneurial attitudes and activities of students. REFRAC could be used as a training tool to build cyber security competences and capacities. With a proper context (knowledge base, see top row in Figure 3), identity (valuable learning outcomes, see bottom row in Figure 3) and structure (flow of missions) REFRAC could contribute to the goals of the Standard of Good Practice for Information Security namely:

- Form basic skills for understanding and implementing the policies, standards and procedures for cyber security;
- Raise information security awareness;
- Form the basis of cyber security assessment;
- Develop specific cyber security arrangements.

When REFRAC is applied in a constant and systematic manner students can gain personal experience through engaging in various business and research activities related to various scientific fields and business areas. The main barriers during the process of REFFRAC implementation could be summarised as follows: 1/ Administrative barriers due to the restrictive internal rules of the HEI; 2/ Misunderstanding of the concept both from the management body of the HEI and lecturers /teachers. Such kind of activities require different type of management and high level of engagement of the teaching staff. 3/ Bureaucratic procedures embedded within the educational system which prolong the process of changes and modifications of teaching materials and the process of learning. 4/ Extremely low level of administrative flexibility.

CONCLUSION

The proposed REFRAC conceptual model provides an opportunity for implementation of simulation-based learning in cyber security area but the proposed methodology could be easily adapted to any AI topic, especially responsible AI, ethical considerations toward AI, etc. Facing the challenges of cyber threats, a combined methodology of training and education should be applied in order to: (1) develop cognitive skills; (2) provide situational knowledge; (3) stimulate critical thinking. Under these conditions teaching is not merely a way of "covering the curriculum" or transferring the knowledge directly from the 'expert' to the learner but a way of encouraging initiative, creativity and responsibility for the decisions which are taken. As a result, the competent graduates will possess diverse educational experiences, will be equipped with all required traditional and new skills, including or together with abilities from domain as cultural intelligence, cyber security and public diplomacy. This will require not just to modify our mindset but also to adapt fast to the changing dynamic environment at both individual and institutional level.

REFERENCES

Anderson, R. (2008). *Security Engineering: A Guide to Building Dependable Distributed Systems* (2nd ed.). Wiley Publishing, Inc.

Andresen, L., Boud, D., & Cohen, R. (2001). Experience-Based Learning. In G. Foley (Ed.), *Understanding Adult Education and Training* (2nd ed., pp. 225–239). Allen & Unwin.

Baryshnikov, Y. (2012). *IT security investment and Gordon-Loeb's 1/e rule*. WEIS paper.

Berge, Z., & Verneil, M. (2002). The increasing scope of training and development competency. *Benchmarking, 9*(1), 43–61. doi:10.1108/14635770210418579

Biggs, J., & Tang, C. (2011). Teaching For Quality Learning At University (4th ed.). New York: McGraw Hill Society for Research into Higher Education.

Bissell, K., Lasalle, R., & Dal Cin, P. (2020). *Innovate For Cyber Resilience*. Accenture.com. Available at: https://www.accenture.com/_acnmedia/PDF-116/Accenture-Cybersecurity-Report-2020.pdf

Buffomante, T. (2020). *All Hands On Deck: Key Cyber Security Considerations For 2020*. KPMG. Available at: https://home.kpmg/xx/en/home/insights/2020/03/key-cyber-security-considerations-for-2020.html

Castelli, C., Gabriel, B., Yates, J., & Booth, P. (2020). *Strengthening Digital Society Against Cyber Shocks*. PwC. Available at: https://www.pwc.com/us/en/services/consulting/cybersecurity/library/information-security-survey/strengthening-digital-society-against-cyber-shocks.html

Chaplin, M., & Creasey, J. (2011). *The 2011 Standard of Good Practice for Information Security*. Information Security Forum.

Contu, R., Canales, C., & Pingree, L. (2014). *Forecast: Information Security*. Worldwide, 2012-2018, 2Q14 Update. Gartner report, Gartner, Inc.

Darling, J. R. (1999). Organizational excellence and leadership strategies: Principles followed by top multinational executives. *Leadership and Organization Development Journal, 20*(6), 309–321. doi:10.1108/01437739910292625

Dias, J., Khanna, S., Paquette, C., Rohr, M., Seitz, B., Singla, A., Sood, R., & van Ouwerkerk, J. (2017). *Introducing The Next-Generation Operating Model.* Available at: https://www.mckinsey.com/~/media/mckinsey/business%20functions/mckinsey%20digital/our%20insights/introducing%20the%20next-generation%20operating%20model/introducing-the-next-gen-operating-model.ashx

FireEye. (2020). *Security Effectiveness 2020: Deep Dive Into Cyber Security Reality.* https://content.fireeye.com/security-effectiveness/rpt-security-effectiveness-2020-deep-dive-into-cyber-reality

Guzdial, M. (2015). *Using learning sciences to inform cyber security education.* Georgia Tech College of Computing. https://computinged.wordpress.com/2015/05/18/using-learning-sciences-to-inform-cyber-security-education/

Harley, D. (2010). *Re-floating the Titanic: dealing with social engineering attacks.* https://smallbluegreen-blog.files.wordpress.com/2010/04/eicar98.pdf

Herzog, P. (2003). *OSSTMM 2.1 Open-Source Security Testing Methodology Manual.* Institute for Security and Open Methodologies.

Jurse, M., & Mulej, M. (2011). The complexities of business school alignment with the emerging globalisation of business education. *Kybernetes, 40*(9/10), 1440–1458. doi:10.1108/03684921111169477

Manyika, J., Chui, M., Bisson, P., Woetzel, J., Dobbs, R., Bughin, J., & Aharon, D. (2015). *The Internet Of Things: Mapping The Value Beyond The Hype.* McKinsey Global Institute. Available at: https://www.mckinsey.com/business-functions/business-technology/our-insights/the-internet-of-things-the-value-of-digitizing-the-physical-world

NIST Roadmap for Improving Critical Infrastructure Cybersecurity. (2014). https://www.nist.gov/cyberframework/upload/roadmap-021214.pdf

OECD. (2014). *HEInnovate: Introduction to HEInnovate and its seven dimensions.* Available at: https://www.oecd.org/cfe/leed/HEInnovate-Introduction%20.pdf

Philp, W., & Martin, C. (2009). A philosophical approach to time in military knowledge management. *Journal of Knowledge Management, 13*(1), 171–183. doi:10.1108/13673270910931242

RSAC. (2019). *The Future of Companies and Cybersecurity Spending.* RSA Conference. Available at: https://www.rsaconference.com/industry-topics/blog/the-future-of-companies-and-cybersecurity-spending#:~:text=In%202019%2C%20worldwide%20spending%20on,to%20reach%20over%20%24124%20billion.&text=Spending%20on%20security%20services%20has%20reached%20%2464.2%20million%20in%202019

Shelton, C. (1999). *Quantum Leaps.* Butterworth-Heinemann.

Shelton, C., & Darling, J. (2004). From chaos to order: Exploring new frontiers in conflict management. *Organization Development Journal, 22*(3), 22–41.

Tipton, W.H. (2014). Cyber security education: remove the limits. *Information Week.* https://www.informationweek.com/government/cybersecurity/cyber-security-education-remove-the-limits/a/d-id/1306950

Vassileva, B. (2016). Increasing cyber security competences through mission-based learning. *Proceedings of the International Conference on Human Systems Integration Approach to Cyber Security*, 189-204.

World Economic Forum. (2017). *The Global Risks Report 2017 12ᵗʰ Edition.* Available at: http://www3.weforum.org/docs/GRR17_Report_web.pdf

ENDNOTE

[1]   CIO – Chief Information Officer.

This research was previously published in Responsible AI and Ethical Issues for Businesses and Governments; pages 148-163, copyright year 2021 by Engineering Science Reference (an imprint of IGI Global).

Chapter 17
Opportunities and Challenges of Cybersecurity for Undergraduate Information Systems Programs

Shouhong Wang
https://orcid.org/0000-0002-4634-8833
University of Massachusetts Dartmouth, Dartmouth, USA

Hai Wang
https://orcid.org/0000-0002-2860-1954
Saint Mary's University, Halifax, Canada

ABSTRACT

This article investigates the opportunities and challenges of cybersecurity for information systems (IS) programs and proposes a curriculum structure of cybersecurity track for IS programs. The study has collected data from eighty-two course websites of thirteen institutions at the graduate level and sixteen institutions at the undergraduate level as well as twenty descriptions of cybersecurity jobs posted on the internet. The collected qualitative data has been analyzed from the from the perspective of IS education. The findings indicate that the topics of cybersecurity management and essential cybersecurity technology are relevant to the IS discipline. The article suggests that these topics can be the components of two cybersecurity courses offered by IS programs to meet the demands and challenges of cybersecurity.

1. INTRODUCTION

Protection of information in business and government organizations in the global digital environment has become an urgent and current issue. The U.S. cybersecurity market size is estimated to grow from $1.8 billion in 2017 to $22 billion by 2022. ("Market Research Media," 2018). Given the increasing cyberattacks through the Internet, the need for highly trained cybersecurity professionals is acute. A

DOI: 10.4018/978-1-6684-3554-0.ch017

projected shortfall of cybersecurity professionals is significant (Nelson, 2016). U.S. News and World Report ranked a career in information security analysis eighth on its list of the 100 best jobs for 2015, and cybersecurity jobs are expected to grow at a rate of 36.5 percent annually through 2022 (South, 2015).

Given the increasing demand for the cybersecurity professionals across the world, it is clear to all disciplines related to information technology (IT) that strategic innovation of the IT curricula for cybersecurity is imperative. The information systems (IS) area in business education has expressed great concern about the stable low enrollments and career skills oriented undergraduate information systems curriculum (Harris et al., 2012; Khoo, 2012). The IS community has curriculum guidelines, IS 2010 (Topi et al. 2010), for undergraduate degree programs in IS and IT in general. The IS 2010 curriculum guidelines, established in a collaborative effort by ACM (The Association for Computing Machinery) and AIS (The Association for Information Systems), contain a set of model curricula for undergraduate degrees in IS. The IS 2010 curriculum guidelines are not directly linked to any degree structure in a specific environment but provide guidance regarding the core contents of the curriculum that should be present in various career tracks in the IS field. There is a wide range of adherence to the IS 2010 curriculum guidelines in business schools (Bell et al., 2013). As all aspects of the global computing field continue to face rapid and continuous changes, IS programs need to maintain currency of curricula to meet the dynamic needs of the job market of post-secondary IS/IT graduates. Whilst cybersecurity has been identified as one of the most serious challenges over the past several years (Agamba and Keengwe, 2012; Gill, 2016), the curriculum of cybersecurity in the IS discipline has not fully established yet. This study investigates how IS programs can contribute to cybersecurity education and how cybersecurity curriculum should be embedded in IS programs. The objective of the article is to propose a curriculum structure of cybersecurity track for IS programs to collaborate with other disciplines for cybersecurity education.

The rest of the paper is organized as follows. Section 2 is a review of literature of related work. Section 3 provides an overview of data collection through reviews of web documents related to cybersecurity education. The collection of qualitative data about cybersecurity programs and cybersecurity job requirements were used for this study. Section 4 describes the qualitative data analysis process used in this study. Section 5 presents the findings of the qualitative data analysis and recommendations. Section 6 discusses the limitations of the study. Finally, section 7 concludes the study.

2. LITERATURE REVIEW

Most studies of cybersecurity education emphasize on technical aspects of cybersecurity and suggest that operating systems, telecommunication, networking, cryptography, malware analysis, and computer forensics are important technical skills for cybersecurity students (Beznosov and Beznosova, 2007; Fulton et al., 2013; Trabelsi and McCoey, 2016). Given the board coverage of technical topics in cybersecurity, there is no standard set of learning outcomes associated with technical aspects of cybersecurity (Slusky and Partow-Navid, 2012). Some cybersecurity programs use professional certification standards (e.g., CISSP (Certified Information Systems Security Professional)), and others use curriculum guidelines (e.g., NSA (National Security Agency) and NHS (National Health Service)).

Research into cybersecurity has suggested that the process of cybersecurity requires much more than mere technical controls, and demands human-centered approaches (Noluxolo et al., 2017) and organizational development approaches (Stanciu & Tinca, 2017). From an organizational perspective, successful organizations typically have strong and reinforced cybersecurity policies and procedures, and set clear cybersecurity governance standards (Asllani et al., 2013). To protect information resources, the organization must allocate sufficient budgets and retain experienced cybersecurity personnel. User awareness of cybersecurity and social responsibility are important components of cybersecurity protection systems (D'Arcy et al., 2009). Research (Woszczynski and Green, 2017) has indicated that more than half potential topics for cybersecurity courses do not have heavy technical components.

To address organizational and social issues related to cybersecurity, many IS programs have launched new courses related to cybersecurity during the past several years (Cram and D'Arcy, 2016). Those courses of cybersecurity integrate basic technical components and managerial issues associated with cybersecurity (Yuan et al., 2017).

Overall, the number of papers on cybersecurity education in IS programs was limited. Few significant research papers on innovations of IS curriculum to meet cybersecurity job demands can be found in the literature.

3. COLLECTION OF DATA OF CYBERSECURITY PROGRAMS AND CYBERSECURITY JOB REQUIREMENTS

After a general literature review of cybersecurity education, a refined search for documents of cybersecurity programs and cybersecurity job requirements was conducted to collect data for this study. The tools used for the data collection were the ABI/INFORM Global database and Google Scholar. The ABI/INFORM database and Google Scholar cover the major academic journals in the areas of cybersecurity, information security, information systems, information technology, and information technology education.

3.1. A Review of Cybersecurity Programs and Courses

A recent survey report (Ponemon, 2014) presents experts' subjective ratings on educational institutions for cybersecurity in the US. However, the report does not provide detailed information about programs and courses offered at these institutions. To learn more about the structures and components of programs and courses of cybersecurity offered by higher educational institutions at the baccalaureate and master's levels, a review was conducted by collecting the available data on the Internet. The keywords used for the searches included "cybersecurity programs," "cybersecurity majors," "cybersecurity course," "cybersecurity concentration," "cybersecurity education," "information security majors," "information assurance," "information security course," "information security education," "information security concentration," and "information security programs". Many institutions offer cybersecurity programs or courses, but do not post detailed information about the programs or courses on the Internet. This study examined detailed information about cybersecurity programs or courses at thirteen institutions at the graduate level and sixteen institutions at the undergraduate level. The data of total eighty-two course web sites were collected during 2017 (see Appendix A) and were used for analysis.

3.2. A Review of Cybersecurity Job Requirements

The present data collection and analysis of cybersecurity job requirements follow the National Initiative for Cybersecurity Education (NICE) Workforce Framework (NICE 2018). The NICE framework provides a wide-ranging reference point for data collection and analysis for cybersecurity workforce education. To understand more about the applied job requirements for the cybersecurity workforce, a refined search was conducted to collect the available data on the Internet. The keywords used for the search included "cybersecurity jobs," "cybersecurity job requirements," "cybersecurity job opening," "cybersecurity position qualification," "information security jobs," "information security job require-ments," "information security job opening," and "information security position qualification". Twenty (20) informative descriptions of cybersecurity jobs were collected during 2017 (see Appendix B) and were used for analysis.

4. THE ANALYSIS OF QUALITATIVE DATA

4.1. Procedure of the Qualitative Data Analysis

This study is an induction process with the data triangulation tactic (Jick, 1979) which combines multiple sources of qualitative data to generate a generalized conclusion. Two MBA students as research assistants of this study collected the qualitative data described in the previous section. The two co-authors of this paper conducted a so-called Joint Analytical Process (JAP) (Wang and Wang, 2016) to conduct a qualita-tive data analysis. The reliability of qualitative analysis (Yin, 2003) is the key to meaningful qualitative data analysis. JAP can reduce risks of misinterpretation of qualitative data. In this study, JAP places the emphasis on identifying opportunities and challenges of cybersecurity education for IS programs. There were several JAP sessions for the entire qualitative analysis, and each of the JAP session had a specific task. A JAP session is a series of knowledge sharing meetings of the participants to discuss a case or an issue (cf. Dube and Pare, 2003). Each JAP session has iterative cycles of meetings. A JAP session could be virtual online meetings. JAP is different from brainstorming in that a JAP session must result in a consent conclusion among the participants. Before the first JAP session, the participants reviewed the entire set of collected qualitative data. In this study, the two co-authors were the participants. Figure 1 illustrates the qualitative data analysis process.

Figure 1. Process of qualitative data analysis

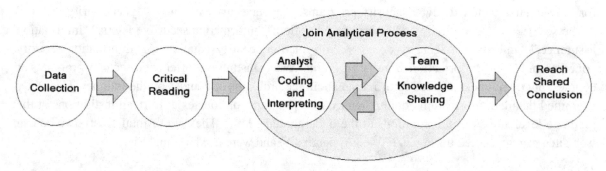

4.2. General Protocols of Qualitative Data Analysis

The first JAP session was to set a general guide for the analysis of multiple sources of qualitative data. A form of qualitative data analysis protocol (Yin, 2003) included the objective of analysis, specific questions for the analysis, and dictionary, as shown in Table 1.

Table 1. Outline of the protocol used in the qualitative data analysis

Protocol Sections	Protocol Components
1. Overview of the set of qualitative data	Objective: To identify opportunities and challenges of cybersecurity education for the IS discipline. Key issue: The body of knowledge of cybersecurity.
2. Questions	1. Given the fact that cybersecurity education offered by multiple disciplines, how is the curriculum of cybersecurity embedded in IS programs? 2. How can IS programs contribute to cybersecurity education? 3. What challenges is IS programs facing in cybersecurity education?
3. Dictionary	Terminology Synonyms

As this study did not make a priori hypothesis, the research questions are rather open to facts that emerge inductively from the data. Thus, the grounded approach (Glaser, 1992; Chesebro and Borisoff, 2007) to qualitative data analysis was applied.

4.3. The Qualitative Data Analysis Framework

Qualitative data analysis is more than the coding and sorting of qualitative data, and involves holistic understanding the context of data (Edwards et al., 2014). Qualitative data analysis retains contextual factors when researchers make conclusions on the basis not only of a commonly used research methodology, but also of the contexts and situations in which the study takes place (Chowdhury, 2015). The induction of this study in the present context of qualitative data analysis is to identify opportunities and challenges of cybersecurity education for IS programs through analyzing cybersecurity job requirements and cybersecurity programs. The qualitative data analysis framework is depicted in Figure 2. As illustrated in Figure 2, any item of cybersecurity job requirements is associated with the cybersecurity subjects and topics revealed in the qualitative data. If an item of job requirement does not have support by any education subject or topic (as illustrated by a shaded item in the sample data of job requirements in Figure 2), a new subject or topic of cybersecurity education is needed. If a subject or topic is not relevant to any job requirement (as illustrated by a shaded item in the sample data of cybersecurity subjects in Figure 2), it will not be considered in the subsequent analysis. Each of the relevant subjects or topics of cybersecurity education was then assigned to a category (e.g., a number ranging from 1 to 7) to indicate the extent of its relevance to the IS discipline on the basis of the IS 2010 curriculum guidelines (Topi et al., 2010).

Figure 2. The qualitative data analysis framework

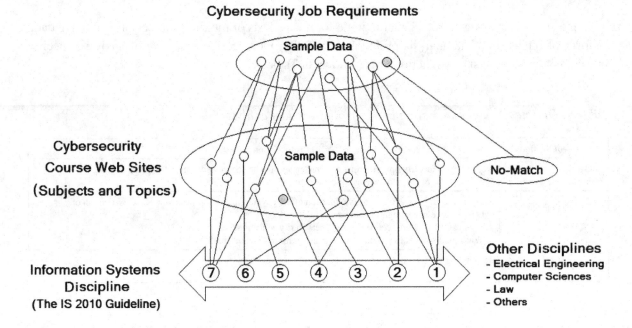

4.4. Coding

Coding has been applied as a tool to facilitate qualitative data analysis to discover the patterns of data and the relationships between sets of data (Miles and Huberman, 1994; Tashakkori and Teddlie, 1998; Kelle and Seidel, 1995; Straus and Corbin, 1998). There are many methods of coding (Saldana 2015). In the present qualitative analysis, the values coding method was applied. Each segment or item of cybersecurity job requirements and cybersecurity educational subjects was labeled with a "code" which was a keyword or a short phrase. A key word or short phrase can include sub-categories. For example, "network security" is a common term used in many places, but the contents and the technical depth of the subject depends on the context where the term is used. Thus, the code for "network security" can have sub-categories (e.g., communication protocol, firewall, network monitor, etc.) depending upon the contents and technical depth. The coded segments or items of cybersecurity job requirements and educational subjects were then related. Each applicable educational subject or topic was converted into an inferred value that indicated the relevance to the IS discipline. The coding process is illustrated in Figure 3.

To ensure the reliability of coding, the analysts exchanged general understanding of the research context and the overall qualitative data. The Cohen's Kappa Values were used to evaluate the inter-coder reliability of all the initial codes made by the individual analysts ($\kappa \geq 0.85$). The iterative data analysis process to define and revise the codes was carried out manually.

Figure 3. The coding process

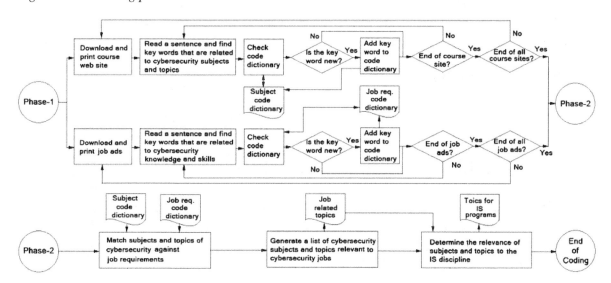

5. FINDINGS AND IMPLICATIONS

5.1. Overall Findings

Cybersecurity jobs demand a huge range of skills. On the managerial side, a large enterprise needs cybersecurity managers who are effective communicators with cybersecurity expertise and are able to prepare timely and accurate cybersecurity recommendations to internal and external stakeholders. The responsibilities for cybersecurity managers include development of cybersecurity procedures, analyses of threat and vulnerability, coordination of specific industry initiatives such as EPRI (Electric Power Research Institute) or government programs such as NCCIC (National Cybersecurity & Communications Integration Center), assessment of cybersecurity training and performance, and cost control.

On the technical side, the cybersecurity job market has created many job titles at different technical levels, including cybersecurity analysts, cybersecurity engineers, and cybersecurity technicians. The technical knowledge and skills needed for the cybersecurity jobs are related to all areas of IT, including cryptography and encryption, database and data storage, computer networks, wireless communications, computer operating systems, application software development, and others.

Cybersecurity is an interdisciplinary or a multi-disciplinary field that cuts across different but related fields – especially management, computer science, and computer engineering. The cybersecurity discipline in many higher education institutions has its independent identity. Nevertheless, the majority of cybersecurity programs are supported by the existing colleges or departments of engineering and colleges of business. Many cybersecurity programs have been designated by the NSA (National Security Agency) and DHS (Department of Homeland Security) as a center of academic excellence in cybersecurity education, and are offered at both undergraduate and graduate levels. Diversified curricula of cybersecurity address both technical and managerial issues. The boundary of cybersecurity curricula between the graduate level and the undergraduate level is not clear-cut. The introductory courses of cybersecurity cover all issues of cybersecurity in general, but do not elaborate technical subjects of cybersecurity. Many advanced cybersecurity courses address cybersecurity management for specific types of organizations or programs. Advanced technical courses offer particularized cybersecurity protection theories, techniques, and tools. In some technical hands-on courses, the instructors and industry experts collaborate to create exercises in emulate real-world hacking scenarios or to teach students skills of "white-hat" hackers.

5.2. Recommendations

The present qualitative data analysis indicates that the model of IT Security and Risk Management included in the IS 2010 Curriculum Guidelines (Topi et al., 2010, p. 411) as an IS elective course for IS programs is relevant to today's cybersecurity job market as well as cybersecurity education. The model catalog description, learning objectives, and selected topics for an introductory course of cybersecurity are still pertinent to today's IT environment. This IT Security and Risk Management course has its prerequisite IS 2010. IT Infrastructure (Topi et al., 2010, p. 396) which includes the essential body of knowledge about computer networks for cybersecurity. However, the data of cybersecurity job requirements and cybersecurity education have indicated that more advanced courses are needed for IS students to specialize cybersecurity. In the managerial aspect, a course of cybersecurity management can concentrate on organizational policies, plans, and industrial programs of cybersecurity. This managerial course has little overlap with other technical cybersecurity courses which are typically offered by faculties of computer science and computer engineering. In the technical aspect, a course of cybersecurity technologies can specialize cybersecurity techniques at various computing levels ranging from computer network layers to individual computers and from databases to web applications. To differentiate this course from other cybersecurity technical courses in computer science or computer engineering programs, this course focuses on techniques and applications of cybersecurity for organizations and their systems, instead of algorithms, theories, and cybersecurity software development. A cybersecurity track within an IS program can be implemented, as illustrated in Figure 4. Table 2 is a summary of specifications of the course descriptions, learning outcomes, and topics which are derived from the collected qualitative data.

Figure 4. Cybersecurity track in IS programs

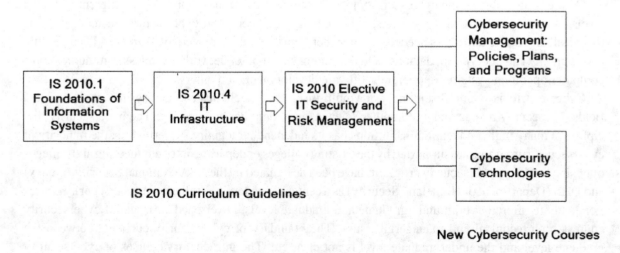

Table 2. Summary of specifications of two advanced cybersecurity courses

Course Description	Learning Outcomes	Topics
Cybersecurity Management: Policies, Plans, and Programs		
This course discusses cybersecurity management in various types of organizations including business enterprises, government, military, and industries. The course will address organizational strategies, procedures, standards, metrics and measures, and compliance practices for cybersecurity. Students will learn critical cybersecurity policies, plans, and programs that enable them to plan, develop, monitor, and evaluate cybersecurity operations.	Students will learn to 1. Describe cybersecurity in business enterprises. 2. Explain cybersecurity in government organizations. 3. Interpret cybersecurity in military. 4. Give examples of cybersecurity in various vulnerable industries. 5. Create, analyze, and maintain cybersecurity policies. 6. Create and implement cybersecurity plans. 7. Develop metrics and measures for organizations to monitor and evaluate cybersecurity operations. 8. Determine cybersecurity strategies for organizations to reduce vulnerabilities.	• Government and industrial cybersecurity programs • Cybersecurity in business enterprises • Cybersecurity in government organizations • Cybersecurity in military • Cybersecurity in vulnerable industries • Current cybersecurity issues • Cybersecurity regulations • Cybersecurity laws • Cybersecurity assessment models • Cybersecurity cases
Cybersecurity Technologies		
This course discusses cybersecurity technologies and applications. The focus of this course is on understanding cybersecurity concepts, encryption, authentication and authorization, intrusion detection and prevention, and cybersecurity disaster recovery. Students will learn cybersecurity techniques of protection of data, networks, and computers.	Students will learn to 1. Explain cybersecurity concepts and building blocks. 2. Describe authentication and authorization. 3. Give examples of encryption. 4. Use encryption techniques to protect data. 5. Defend storage devices and database. 6. Protect network firewalls, routers, and switches. 7. Secure wireless. 8. Develop secure Windows, Java, and mobile applications. 9. Design intrusion detection and prevention systems.	• Optimize authentication and authorization • Information right management and encryption • Defend data storage and databases • Protect network firewalls, routers, and switches • Secure VPN, wireless, and PBX infrastructure • Intrusion detection • Secure Windows applications • Secure Java applications • Secure mobile applications • Cybersecurity forensic analysis

5.3. Challenges of Cybersecurity Education for IS Programs and Suggestions

Cybersecurity education is an opportunity for IS programs, but also raises challenges for business schools to establish cybersecurity programs. Hiring PhD graduates in cybersecurity may not be a feasible option for the majority of IS programs given the shortage of PhD programs in cybersecurity for the time being. Accordingly, IS faculties need academic retraining in cybersecurity. The competence of the faculty must be adequate not only to teach the cybersecurity subjects but also to develop new curriculum and new teaching materials. Professional development and scholarly activities in cybersecurity are a joint obligation for the new track of cybersecurity. Collaboration with practitioners of cybersecurity and faculties of other academic disciplines is critical for the new track of cybersecurity.

Computer laboratory is another challenge for a new track of cybersecurity. The traditional open and public laboratories will not be sufficient for an advanced computer and network security course. Specialized laboratories with servers, routers, firewalls, and network emulators are needed to allow students to practice cybersecurity related laboratory exercises.

6. LIMITATIONS OF THE STUDY AND DISCUSSIONS

As a qualitative analysis of multiple sources based on the data of web documents and subjective understanding and interpretation, the study has its limitations. First, the sample qualitative data were obtained by limited searches. These sample qualitative data of cybersecurity education and job requirements on the Internet could be incomplete or contain errors. In addition, the sample qualitative data were collected from US-based information sources. Second, this study emphasizes on undergraduate IS programs that are guided the IS 2010 curriculum guidelines in business schools. Third, the coding and analyses of these qualitative data were certainly subject to biases or misinterpretations. Future studies are needed to improve the findings based on other independent studies.

Along with rapid changes of IT, the IS discipline is shifting its specialties faster than ever. The main stream of research in the IS discipline has been emphasizing behavioral aspects of IT/IS, but the education subjects, especially at the undergraduate level, have been relatively technical and have significant overlaps with computer science and computer engineering. Cybersecurity education is a multidisciplinary subject, and individual disciplines involved in cybersecurity education programs play distinctive roles. This study contributes to the field by providing an insight into the position of the IS discipline in cybersecurity education.

7. CONCLUSION

Cybersecurity has become a global urgent and current issue in the IT filed. Effective cybersecurity education involves multiple disciplines. Cybersecurity education is multidisciplinary, although it is too early to predict whether cybersecurity can become a transdisciplinary field. The IS discipline is one of the multiple disciplines involved in cybersecurity education. The study has examined cybersecurity programs or courses, requirements for cybersecurity jobs, and their relationships with the IS discipline. The qualitative data analysis reveals that there are needs for IS programs to formalize the curriculum structure to meet the global challenges of cybersecurity job requirements. Two advanced elective courses for cybersecurity have proposed by this study to enhance the IS curriculum guidelines. The availability of updated curriculum models for cybersecurity will enable IS programs to collaborate with other disciplines to develop the common body of knowledge of cybersecurity.

ACKNOWLEDGMENT

The constructive comments of two anonymous reviewers have contributed significantly to the revision of the paper.

REFERENCES

Agamba, J. J., & Keengwe, J. (2012). Pre-service teachers' perceptions of information assurance and cyber security. *International Journal of Information and Communication Technology Education*, 8(2), 94–101. doi:10.4018/jicte.2012040108

Asllani, A., White, C. S., & Ettkin, L. (2013). Viewing cybersecurity as a public good: The role of governments, businesses, and individuals, *Journal of Legal. Ethical and Regulatory Issues*, *16*(1), 7–14.

Bell, C. C., Mills, R. J., & Fadel, K. J. (2013). An analysis of undergraduate information systems (is) curriculum: Adherence to is 2010 curriculum guidelines. *Communications of the Association for Information Systems*, *32*, 2.

Beznosov, K., & Beznosova, O. (2007). On the imbalance of the security problem space and its expected consequences. *Information Management & Computer Security*, *15*(5), 420–431. doi:10.1108/09685220710831152

Chesebro, J. W., & Borisoff, D. J. (2007). What makes qualitative research qualitative? *Qualitative Research Reports in Communication*, *8*(1), 3–14. doi:10.1080/17459430701617846

Chowdhury, M. F. (2015). Coding, sorting and sifting of qualitative data analysis: Debates and discussion. *Quality & Quantity*, *49*(3), 1135–1143. doi:10.100711135-014-0039-2

Cram, W. A., & D'Arcy, J. (2016). Teaching information security in business schools: Current practices and a proposed direction for the future. *Communications of the Association for Information Systems*, *39*, 3. doi:10.17705/1CAIS.03903

D'Arcy, J., Hovav, A., & Galletta, D. (2009). User awareness of security countermeasures and its impact on information systems misuse: A deterrence approach. *Information Systems Research*, *20*(1), 79–98, 155, 157. doi:10.1287/isre.1070.0160

Dube, L., & Pare, G. (2003). Rigor in information positivist case research: Current practices, trends, and recommendations. *Management Information Systems Quarterly*, *27*(4), 597–635. doi:10.2307/30036550

Edwards, P., Mahoney, J. O., & Vincent, S. (Eds.). (2014). *Explaining Management and Organisation Using Critical Realism: A Practical Guide*. Oxford, UK: Oxford University Press. doi:10.1093/acprof:oso/9780199665525.001.0001

Yuan, X., Williams, K., Rorrer, A., Chu, B. T., Yang, L., Winters, K., ... & Yu, H. (2017). Faculty workshops for teaching information assurance through hands-on exercises and case studies. *Journal of Information Systems Education*, *8*(1), 11–19.

Fulton, E., Lawrence, C., & Clouse, S. (2013). White hats chasing black hats: Careers in it and the skills required to get there. *Journal of Information Systems Education*, *24*(1), 75–80.

Gill, G. (2016). Expanding joint vulnerability assessment branch, *Journal of Information Technology: Discussion Cases*, *5*, 1-14. Retrieved from http://www.jite.org/documents/DCVol05/V05-06-JVAB.pdf

Glaser, B. (1992). *Basics of Grounded Theory Analysis*. Mill Valley, CA: Sociology Press.

Harris, A. H., Greer, T. H., Morris, S. A., & Clark, W. J. (2012). Information systems job market late 1970's-early 2010's. *Journal of Computer Information Systems*, *53*(1), 72–79.

HP. (2014). *Ponemon 2014 Best Schools for Cybersecurity*. Ponemon Institute Research Report. Retrieved from http://www.hp.com/hpinfo/newsroom/press_kits/2014/RSAConference2014/Ponemon_2014_Best_Schools_Report.pdf

Jick, T. D. (1979). Mixing qualitative and qualitative methods: Triangulation in action. *Administrative Science Quarterly, 24*(4), 602–611. doi:10.2307/2392366

Kelle, K. U., & Seidel, J. (Eds.). (1995). *Computer Aided Qualitative Data Analysis: Theory, Methods, and Practice*. Thousand Oaks, CA: Sage.

Khoo, B. K. S. (2012). Towards a career skills oriented undergraduate information systems curriculum. *International Journal of Information and Communication Technology Education, 8*(2), 1–19. doi:10.4018/jicte.2012040101

Miles, M. B., & Huberman, A. M. (1994). *Qualitative Data Analysis: An expanded sourcebook*. Thousand Oakes, CA: Sage.

Nelson, P. (2016, August 12). Cybersecurity skills crisis creating vulnerabilities, *Network World*. Retrieved from http://www.networkworld.com/article/3106853/

NICE. (2018). National Initiative for Cybersecurity Education (NICE) Cybersecurity Workforce Framework. Retrieved from http://nvlpubs.nist.gov/nistpubs/SpecialPublications/NIST.SP.800-181.pdf

Noluxolo, G., von Solms, R., Grobler, M. M., & van Vuuren, J. J. (2017). A general morphological analysis: Delineating a cyber-security culture. *Information and Computer Security, 25*(3), 259–278. doi:10.1108/ICS-12-2015-0046

Saldana, J. (2015). *The Coding Manual for Qualitative Researchers* (3rd ed.). London, UK: Sage.

Slusky, L., & Partow-Navid, P. (2012). Teaching information assurance online. *The Review of Business Information Systems (Online), 16*(2), 53–66. doi:10.19030/rbis.v16i2.6892

South, J. R. (2015). Cybersecurity education: The growing pressure to fill one million jobs. *Security, 52*(11), 85–86.

Stanciu, V., & Tinca, A. (2017). Exploring cybercrime – realities and challenges. *Accounting and Management Information Systems, 16*(4), 610–632. doi:10.24818/jamis.2017.04009

Straus, A., & Corbin, J. (1998). *Basics of Qualitative Research: Techniques and Procedures for Developing Grounded Theory*. Thousand Oaks, CA: Sage.

Tashakkori, A., & Teddlie, C. (1998). *Mixed Methodology: Combining Qualitative and Quantitative Approaches*. Thousand Oaks, CA: Sage.

Topi, H., Valacich, J. S., Wright, R. T., Kaiser, K., Nunamaker, J. F. Jr, Sipior, J. C., & Vreede, G., J. d. (2010). IS 2010: Curriculum guidelines for undergraduate degree programs in information systems. *Communications of the Association for Information Systems, 26*, 18.

Trabelsi, Z., & McCoey, M. (2016). Ethical hacking in information security curricula. *International Journal of Information and Communication Technology Education, 12*(1), 1–10. doi:10.4018/IJICTE.2016010101

Wang, S., & Wang, H. (2016). A soft OR approach to fostering systems thinking: SODA maps plus Joint Analytical Process. *Decision Sciences Journal of Innovative Education, 14*(3), 337–356. doi:10.1111/dsji.12103

Woszczynski, A. B., & Green, A. (2017). Learning outcomes for cyber defense competitions. *Journal of Information Systems Education, 28*(1), 21–41.

Yin, R. K. (2003). *Case Study Research: Design and Methods* (3rd ed.). Thousand Oakes, CA: Sage.

This research was previously published in the International Journal of Information and Communication Technology Education (IJICTE), 15(2); pages 49-68, copyright year 2019 by IGI Publishing (an imprint of IGI Global).

APPENDIX A: SUMMARY OF CYBERSECURITY EDUCATION PROGRAMS AND COURSES

Table 3. Graduate level

	Institution	College/ Department/ Program	Course
1	Penn State University	College of Information Sciences and Technology/ M.S. in Information Sciences and Technology http://ist.psu.edu/education/degre	1. Network Security http://bulletins.psu.edu/graduate/courses/I/IST/451/201112SP 2. Information Security Management http://bulletins.psu.edu/graduate/courses/I/IST/456/201314FA 3. Network Management and Security http://bulletins.psu.edu/graduate/courses/I/IST/554
2	Boston University	Master of Criminal Justice concentration in Cybercrime Investigation & Cybersecurity http://www.bu.edu/online/programs/graduate-degree/master-criminal-justice/cybercrime-cybersecurity/	1. Cybercrime 2. IT Security Policies and Procedures
3	Iowa State University	College of Engineering/ The Department of Electrical and Computer Engineering http://catalog.iastate.edu/collegeofengineering/computerengineering/#courseinventory	1. Information System Security 2. Wireless Network Security
4	University of Maryland University College	College of Cybersecurity/ The Master of Science in Cybersecurity http://www.umuc.edu/academic-programs/masters-degrees/cybersecurity.cfm	1. Prevention and Protection Strategies in Cybersecurity http://www.umuc.edu/academic-programs/course-information.cfm?course=csec630 2. Cyberspace and Cybersecurity http://www.umuc.edu/academic-programs/course-information.cfm?course=ucsp615
5	Florida Institute of Technology	College of Engineering/ Master of Science in Information Assurance and Cybersecurity degree http://www.fit.edu/programs/8098/ms-information-assurance-cybersecurity#.VwNM6PkrJD8	1. Computer and Information Security 2. Secure Computer Systems and Organization 3. Secure Data Communications and Networks
6	Regis University	College of Computer and Engineering Science/ Information Assurance Degree Programs/Master of Science in Information Assurance http://informationassurance.regis.edu/ia-programs/ms-ia/courses?cmgfrm=https%3A%2F%2Fwww.google.com%2F	1. Certified Information Systems Security Professional https://www.isc2.org/cissp/default.aspx
7	Norwich University	Master of Science in Information Security & Assurance http://online.norwich.edu/degree-programs/masters/master-science-information-security-assurance/overview	1. Computer Security Incident Response Team Management 2. Cyber Crime
8	Maryville University	John E. Simon School of Business/ Master of Cyber Security- Online http://onlinesecurity.maryville.edu/lpap-mscs/?Access_Code=MVU-CS-SEO2&utm_campaign=MVU-CS-SEO2_	1. Critical Security Controls 2. Operating Systems/Application Security 3. Network and Wireless Security 4. Security Log Management and Analysis 5. Designing and Implementing Cloud Security http://catalog.maryville.edu/content.php?filter%5B27%5D=-1&filter%5B29%5D=&filter%5Bcourse_type%5D=-1&filter%5Bkeyword%5D=security&filter%5B32%5D=1&filter%5Bcpage%5D=1&cur_cat_oid=12&expand=&navoid=833&search_database=Filter#acalog_template_course_filter

continues on following page

	Institution	College/ Department/ Program	Course
9	The University of Alabama at Birmingham	School of Engineering/ The Master of Science in Electrical Engineering http://catalog.uab.edu/graduate/schoolofengineering/ electricalandcomputer/electricalengineering/#text	1. Introduction to Computer Networking 2. Experiments in Computer Networking
10	Baylor Business	Hankamer School of Business/ The Master of Information Systems program http://www.baylor.edu/business/msis/	1. Cyber Security Human Factors 2. Cyber Security Tech Factors https://www1.baylor.edu/scheduleofclasses/ Results.aspx?TermCC=20&Term=164&Colleg e=0&Prefix=ISEC&StartCN=5310&EndCN=5 346&Status=&Days=&Instructor=&IsMini=fal se&OnlineOnly=0&POTerm=
11	Brandeis University	Master of Science in Information Security http://www.brandeis.edu/gps/future-students/learn-about-our-programs/informationsecurity.html_	1. Information Security Management 2. Principles of Risk Management in IT Security 3. IT Security and Compliance 4. Network Security
12	DePaul University	College of Computing and Digital Media/ Master of Science - Concentration in Computer, Information and Network Security - Concentration in Network Security http://www.cdm.depaul.edu/academics/Pages/Current/ Requirements-MS-CINS-Computer-Security.aspx	1. Network security 2. Information Security Management 3. Foundations of Computer Security 4. Network Security II
13	University of Denver	College of Professional and continuing studies/ MS in Security Management with concentration in Information Security http://universitycollege.du.edu/smgt/degree/masters/ information-security-online/degreeid/431#courses	1. Security Concepts Overview 2. Business Function of Security 3. Integrated Security Systems 4. Threats in Security

APPENDIX B: SUMMARY OF CYBERSECURITY JOB REQUIREMENTS

Table 4. Undergraduate level

	Institution	College/ Department/ Program	Course
1	University of Maryland University College	College of Cyber Security/ Department of Cybersecurity management and policy http://www.umuc.edu/academic-programs/bachelors-degrees/cybersecurity-management-and-policy-major.cfm	1. Network Security 2. Cybersecurity processes and technologies 3. Cybersecurity in Business and Industry 4. Cybersecurity in Government Organizations 5. Cybersecurity Policy, Plans, and Programs 6. Advanced Information Systems Security 7. Practical Applications in Cybersecurity Management
		College of Cyber Security/ Department of Computer network and cybersecurity http://www.umuc.edu/academic-programs/bachelors-degrees/computer-networks-and-cybersecurity-major.cfm	1.Network Security 2.Current Trends and Projects in Computer Networks and Security 3.Advanced Information Systems Security
		College of Cyber Security/ Department of Software Development and Security http://www.umuc.edu/academic-programs/bachelors-degrees/software-development-and-security.cfm	1. Building Secure Web Applications 2. Database Security 3. Secure Software Engineering 4. Secure Programming in the Cloud 5. Mitigating Software Vulnerabilities

continues on following page

	Institution	College/ Department/ Program	Course
2	University of Massachusetts Lowell	Kennedy College of Sciences/ Department of Computer Science/ Bachelor of Science Degree in Information Technology http://continuinged.uml.edu/degrees/bs_informationtechnology.cfm	1.Introduction to information security 2.Network security
3	The University of Texas at San Antonio	College of Engineering/ Department of Electrical and Computer/ Bachelor of Science Degree in Computer Engineering http://engineering2.utsa.edu/undergraduate-studies/degrees-offered/bachelor-of-science-in-computer-engineering/	1. Unix and Network Security (CS 4353.)
		College of Sciences/ Department of Computer Science/ Bachelor of Science Degree in Computer Science http://catalog.utsa.edu/undergraduate/sciences/computerscience/#degreestext	1. Unix and Network Security (CS 4353) 2. Principles of Computer and Information Security
		College of Business/ Department of Information System and Cyber Security/ Bachelor of Business Administration Degree in Cyber Security http://catalog.utsa.edu/undergraduate/business/informationsystemscybersecurity/#cybersecurity	1.Network security 2. Information Assurance and Security 3. Web Application Security
4	Norwich University	Department of Continuing Studies/ Bachelor of Science in Cyber Security http://catalog.norwich.edu/onlineprogramscatalog/bachelorsdegrees/programsofstudy/bachelorofsciencecybersecurity/#text - Computer Forensics and Vulnerability Management Concentration - Information Warfare and Security Management Concentration	1. Cyber Law and Cybercrime 2. Cyber Investigation 3. Defense Information Warfare 4. National Security Policy
5	Mississippi State University	College of Aerospace Engineering/ Department of Computer Science and Engineering http://www.cse.msstate.edu/what-is-cs/	1. Cryptography and Network Security 2. Information and Computer Security
6	Syracuse University	College of Engineering and Computer Science/ Department of Electrical Engineering/ Bachelor of Science in Computer Engineering http://coursecatalog.syr.edu/preview_program.php?catoid=3&poid=1007&hl=%22computer+engineering%22&returnto=search	1. Introduction to Computer and Network Security
7	Carnegie Mellon University	College of Engineering/ Department of Electrical and Computer Engineering http://www.ece.cmu.edu/courses/course-homepages.html	1. Introduction to Computer and Network Security and Applied Cryptography 2. Introduction to Security and Policy 3. Introduction to Information Security 4. Introduction to Hardware Security 5. Network Security and Management 6. Special Topics in Security: Intrusion Tolerance 7. Introduction to Computer Security
8	University of Southern California	Viterbi School of Engineering/ Information Technology Program http://www.itp.usc.edu/courses/	1. From Hackers to CEOs; An Introduction to Information Security 2. Information Security Management 3. Web Application Security 4. Network Security
9	University of Pittsburgh	Kenneth P. Dietrich School of Arts and Sciences/ Department of Computer Science http://cs.pitt.edu/schedule/courses	1. Applied Cryptography and Network Security

continues on following page

	Institution	College/ Department/ Program	Course
10	West Chester University	College of Arts & Sciences/ Department of Computer Science/ Minor in Information Technology http://catalog.wcupa.edu/undergraduate/arts-sciences/ computer-science/information-technology-minor/	1. Computer Security
		College of Arts & Sciences/ Department of Computer Science/ Certificate in Computer Security http://catalog.wcupa.edu/undergraduate/arts-sciences/ computer-science/computer-security-certificate/	1. Computer Security 2. Computer Crime 3. Introduction to Cryptography
11	West Point- United State Military Academy	Department of Systems Engineering/ Systems and Decision Management- cyber Security Track http://www.westpoint.edu/se/SitePages/Systems%20 Management.aspx	1. Cyber Operations 2. Cyber Security Engineering
12	Bellevue University	College of Business/ BS Degree of Management Information Systems http://www.bellevue.edu/degrees/bachelor/management-information-systems-bs/	1. Information Security Management
13	Utah State University	Jon M. Huntsman School of Business/ MIS Department/ Bachelor of Science in Management Information System http://distance.usu.edu/MIS/	1. Security of Business Information Systems
14	Excelsior College	Business Degree/ Bachelor of Management Information Systems http://www.excelsior.edu/programs/business/business-management-information-systems-bachelor-degree	1. Overview of Computer Security 2. Network Security
15	Kennesaw State University	Coles College of Business/ Bachelor of Information Security Assurance http://coles.kennesaw.edu/programs/undergraduate/ information-security-assurance.php	1. Principles of Information Security 2. Network Security 3. Management of Information Security in a Global Environment 4. Perimeter Defense 5. Server Systems Security
16	Grand Canyon University	Colangelo College of Business/ Bachelor Of Science In Business Information Systems http://www.gcu.edu/degree-programs/bachelor-science-business-information-systems#degreeOverview	1. Platforms and Network Technologies Lecture and Lab 2. IT Project Management

(* All detailed descriptions of programs and courses are omitted in this document. All websites were accessed in November 2017)

Table 5. Cybersecurity job requirements

	Job Title and Web Site	Job Requirements
1	Cybersecurity Threat Detection Analyst https://secure.resumeware. net/gdns_rw/gdns_web/ job_detail.cfm?key=23711 2&ReferredId=158&referr ed_id=158_	- Bachelor's degree or equivalent experience. (Certification in Network or OS technology implementation required: MCSE, CCNA/ Certified information security professional preferred: GCIA, GCIH, CEH, CISSP, SSCP, etc.) - Requires 8-10 years of experience - Demonstrated experience with computer security or network technology (Unix/Windows OS, Cisco/Juniper Routing-Switching) experience in hands-on design/Implementation/Administration role required. - Demonstrated in-depth knowledge of TCP-IP protocol implementations for common network services. - Demonstrated capability to perform network packet analysis and anomaly detection. - Demonstrated experience with security products (IDS/IPS, Firewalls, ESM, etc.) is strongly desired - Demonstrated experience interfacing with customers in help desk or service desk environment strongly desired

continues on following page

	Job Title and Web Site	Job Requirements
2	Computer Network Defense (CND) Analyst https://www.nsa.gov/psp/applyonline/EMPLOYEE/HRMS/c/HRS_HRAM.HRS_CE.GBL?Page=HRS_CE_JOB_DTL&Action=A&JobOpeningId=1068279&SiteId=1&PostingSeq=1	- Entry is with a High School Diploma and 8 years of relevant experience, or an Associate's Degree and 6 years of relevant experience, or a Bachelor's Degree and 4 years of relevant experience, or a Master's Degree and 2 years of relevant experience or a Doctoral Degree. - Degree must be in Computer Science or related field (e.g., General Engineering, Computer Engineering, Electrical Engineering, System Engineering, Mathematics, Computer Forensics, Cyber Security, Information Technology, Information Assurance, Information Security, or Information Systems) - Relevant experience includes computer or information systems design/development, programming, information/cyber/network security, vulnerability analysis, penetration testing, computer forensics, information assurance, systems engineering, network and system administration, military training in a relevant area such as JCAC (Joint Cyber Analysis course), or related experience.
3	Cyber Security Analyst http://search.lockheedmartinjobs.com/ShowJob/Id/52080/Cyber%20Security	Basic Qualifications -Must have active Top Secret clearance and be able to obtain a TS/SCI clearance - Security+ certification - Familiarity with DIACAP or RMF certification and accreditation processes - Ability to adhere to guidance in the formulation of information security policies and standards. - Good oral and written communication skills Desired skills -Current TS or TS/SCI clearance -Experience working with USSTRATCOM, Air Force or any Unified Combatant Commands - ITIL certification - CISSP or CISM certification or equivalent - DIACAP or RMF certification and accreditation processes
4	Information Security Cyber Forensics Examiner https://sjobs.brassring.com/tgwebhost/jobdetails.aspx?jobId=268645&PartnerId=25999&SiteId=5373&Codes=IndeedOrg	1. Bachelor's degree in Computer Science or related field or equivalent education and related training 2. Broad knowledge of general IT with mastery of one or more of the following areas: operating systems, networking, computer programing, web development or database administration 3. Demonstrated advanced knowledge of cyber security operations with mastery of one or more of the following: attack surface management, Security Operations Center (SOC) operations, Intrusion Detection/Intrusion Prevention Systems (IDS/IPS), Security Information and Event Management (SIEM) use, threats (including Advanced Persistent Threat (APT), insider), vulnerabilities, and exploits; incident response, investigations and remediation 4. Experience with systems for automated threat intelligence sharing using industry standard protocols, such as Structured Threat Information Expression (STIX) and Trusted Automated Exchange of Indication Information (TAXII) 5. Advanced knowledge of processes, procedures and methods to research, analyze and disseminate threat intelligence information 6. Ongoing passion for learning about information security through self-education 7. Ability to lead and persuade individuals and large teams on ideas, concepts and opportunities 8. Consistent history of delivering on commitments 9. Critical thinking and problem solving skills 10. Knowledge of the incident handling procedures and intrusion analysis models 11. Ability to work independently with limited supervision 12. Proven communication skills, both written and verbal, to both business and technology audiences 13. Demonstrated proficiency in basic computer applications, such as Microsoft Office software products 14. Ability to travel, occasionally overnight
5	Cyber Security Administrator https://www.appone.com/maininforeq.asp?Ad=165285&R_ID=1170309&Refer=http://www.indeed.com/q-Cyber-Security-jobs.html&B_ID=44_	Bachelor's degree (B. A.) from four-year College or university; or three to five years related experience and/or training; or equivalent combination of education and experience. This may include server OS, network firewalls/routers, PCI, SecureWorks, and other experience/certifications

continues on following page

	Job Title and Web Site	Job Requirements
6	Information Security Program Manager https://swbc.wd1. myworkdayjobs.com/ en-US/swbccareers/ job/San-Antonio-TX/ Information-Security-Program-Manager_ R0000854-1_	- Bachelor's Degree in Information Security, Cybersecurity, Information Systems, or related. - Must have (4) years' experience in risk, program, policy, and training and education development. - Must have working knowledge of plan of action and milestones for security education and training development and production. - Skill in preparing responses to reviews and requests for information concerning information security matters. - Ability to interpret how standards and industry best practices apply to the company. - Experience reviewing and maintaining an organization's information security plan. - Must be able to use personal computer, general office equipment including copy machine and phone system. - Must be proficient with MS Word and Excel. - Candidate must demonstrate excellent writing and communication skills and his or her ability to work with teams and external stakeholders.
7	Cyber Security Engineer https://exelonjobs.ceco. com/psc/HRPC_TAM/ EMPLOYEE/HRMS/c/ HRS_HRAM.HRS_ CE.GBL?Page=HRS_CE_ JOB_DTL&Action=A&Job OpeningId=3017064&SiteI d=1&PostingSeq=1&HRS_ SUBSOURCE_ID=1226&	Minimum: -B. S. degree in engineering or related science or Professional Engineering Registration -Typically a minimum of 10 years of engineering experience and exceptional performance -Approval of VP Engineering required to obtain this classification Preferred: -Professional Engineering Registration, advanced technical degree or coursework
8	Security & Monitoring Technician http://jobs.jobvite.com/ careers/odyssey-reinsurance-company/job/oi1p2fwu	Minimum: 2 years' direct monitoring experience 2 years' experience with SCOM/SCCM Ability to work overtime as needed, including nights/weekends/holidays Active passport and the ability to travel overseas on short notice Preferred: 4 years' direct monitoring experience 2 years' experience in IT Security Experience with Exchange 2010 and associated applications software Experience with PowerShell
9	Cybersecurity and Information Security Manager http://www.careerbuilder. com/jobseeker/ jobs/jobdetails. aspx?APath=2.31.0.0.0&job_ did=JHS30S7697CSY9BR7 KJ&showNewJDP=yes&IPat h=ILKV0B	- Bachelor's degree in computer science, computer engineering, management information systems, related discipline or equivalent experience Strong experience with electronic document preservation and collection - General experience with archiving and search tools - Specific experience with Symantec Enterprise Vault, Symantec Classification Engine, Symantec Compliance Accelerator, Symantec Discovery Accelerator, Kazeon Search Appliance, Iron Mountain Discovery Assist is preferred - Functional understanding of SQL with the ability to write simple queries and Boolean search languages - General understanding of document archiving and disaster recovery strategies - Basic understanding of the Federal Rules of Civil Procedure

continues on following page

	Job Title and Web Site	Job Requirements
10	CyberSecurity Sr. Policy Analyst http://www.careerbuilder. com/jobseeker/ jobs/jobdetails. aspx?APath=2.31.0.0.0&job_ did=J3F22V61KBQ83VR65 DK&showNewJDP=yes&IP ath=ILKV0D	Minimum: - Bachelor's degree and 8+ years of professional experience with at least 3 years in information security, governance, compliance, risk management or similar discipline or in lieu of a degree a minimum of 12 years of related experience. - Demonstrated experience working with cross-functional teams. - Demonstrates good familiarity with security, privacy, and governance regulations and industry best practices such as Gramm-Leach-Bliley (GLBA), Sarbanes-Oxley (SOX), the Health Insurance Portability and Accountability Act (HIPAA), Payment Card Industry Data Security Standard (PCI), NIST SP800-53. - Excellent written and verbal communication skills. - Ability to communicate with senior management, peers, internal and external auditors and examiners, business partners and other security related agencies as required. - Ability to research and report on governance/compliance related topics using a variety of sources (ex: Internet, affiliate organizations, governmental agencies) and techniques. Preferred: - CISSP Certification helpful. - PMP Certification helpful. - A minimum of three (3) years supervisory / project management experience helpful.
11	Principal Cyber-security and Information Assurance Specialist http://www.careerbuilder. com/jobseeker/ jobs/jobdetails. aspx?APath=2.31.0.0.0&job_ did=J3J6JD63CRB7NBX3L QJ&showNewJDP=yes&IPat h=ILKV0E	Education: BS or BA degree in Computer Science, Information Systems or a Relevant Technical Discipline. Experience: At least ten (10) years of practical experience and either a broad background in numerous cybersecurity technologies/policy organizations or have deep background in a specific cyber technology such as Cross Domain Solutions, Multi-Level Security (MLS), Host Based Security Systems, Identity Management Solutions, Intrusion Detection/Prevention Systems, Public Key Infrastructure, Mobile Device Management, Wireless Security Solutions, Communications Security (COMSEC), Cryptography, or other emerging cyber technology solution; AND must meet current DoD 8570.01M training requirements.
12	CyberSecurity Sr Solutions Architect http://www.careerbuilder. com/jobseeker/ jobs/jobdetails. aspx?APath=2.31.0.0.0&job_ did=J3J2W474FL372Q6Y3 PW&showNewJDP=yes&Ith =ILKV0F	Minimum: Bachelor's degree and ten years Cybersecurity/Information Security experience or in lieu of a degree, 14 years of related experience. Strong knowledge of security technologies and architecture, including encryption, cloud network security design, security group configuration, intrusion detection, data loss prevention and application security. Knowledge of NIST standards and controls, NIST SP800-53r4. Demonstrated experience working with cross-functional teams. Strong written and verbal communication skills, particularly an ability to negotiate, influence and gain consensus. Ability to present complex information in a clear, concise manner. Ability to work individually as well as a member of a team. Ability to handle multiple tasks and work under time constraints in support of various projects. Working knowledge of Active Directory security. Working knowledge of project management methodology. Preferred: CISSP Certification CSSLP Certification
13	Sr. Cybersecurity Operations Engineer http://www.careerbuilder. com/jobseeker/ jobs/jobdetails. aspx?APath=2.31.0.0.0&job_ did=J3K17W72B22R5FPH WM2&showNewJDP=yes&I Path=ILKV0H	Bachelor's Degree and 5-7 years of experience or an equivalent combination of education and experience. Excellent written and verbal communication skills. Ability to explain technical concepts to technical or non-technical personnel. Ability to read, write, and interpret business and technical documents. Basic math functions, critical thinking and analytical skills. Must be able to work independently with minimal supervision. This position involves regular ambulating, sitting, hearing, and talking. May occasionally involve stooping, kneeling, or crouching. May involve close vision, color vision, depth perception, and focus adjustment. Involves use of hands and fingers for typing on keyboard and using a mouse. May be a need to move or lift items up to 50 pounds.

continues on following page

	Job Title and Web Site	Job Requirements
14	CyberSecurity Engineer http://www.careerbuilder. com/jobseeker/ jobs/jobdetails. aspx?APath=2.31.0.0.0&job_ did=J3L3HT5YZT57S6TBR WB&showNewJDP=yes&IP ath=ILKV0Q	7+ years of experience in an information security and risk management lead role supporting security programs or security engineering in complex enterprise environments, including 2 years of project or direct line management experience Strong skills in communication, presentation to senior executives You must demonstrate a high attention to detail that defines an execution plan Demonstrated ability mentor and guide project team members to meet the customer expectation Ability to develop project plans and create dashboards that demonstration performance and timelines Experience working with Security Authorization requirements, enhancing the security risk posture and analysis/reporting of IT security metrics Experience with enterprise security design and implementation Experience with providing guidance for data protection based on data sensitivity and associated business risk Knowledge of common Web vulnerabilities and experience guiding project teams throughout the remediation effort for discovered vulnerabilities Knowledge of best practices and standards for enterprise security architecture across one or more of the following areas: service-oriented architecture (SOA), enterprise service bus (ESB), business process management, Identity and Access management, collaboration tools, mobility, data analytics, and visualization Ability to effectively collaborate with senior CIO and CISO executives to identify requirements and drive compliance with approved standards Ability to think strategically and act tactically BA or BS degree in CS, Engineering, Information Systems, or a related technical field preferred; MA or MS degree in CS, Information Systems, or a related technical field a plus CISSP, GCIH, GPEN or other industry certifications Candidates must be able to work on-site at client sites located in Washington, D.C. or Alexandria, VA, and must be able to obtain a U.S. Federal government client badge and may be required to pass a government background investigation
15	Senior Consultant - Cybersecurity https://www.glassdoor.com/ Job/jobs.htm?suggestCount= 0&suggestChosen=false&cli ckSource=searchBtn&typed Keyword=cybersecurity&sc. keyword=cybersecurity&loc T=&locId=	3+ years' consultant experience performing and supervising IT Audits, Technology Risk Assessments, or IT internal control risk evaluation and reporting. Experience working within a team of consultants focused in IT Audit, Cybersecurity or risk management. Strong analytical and problem solving skills Outstanding time management and organization skills Superior attention to detail and conscientious quality of work product Professional demeanor with superior oral and written communication skills Bachelor's Degree in Accounting, Information Systems or similar discipline required Preferred Certifications: CISA, CPA, or CRISC
16	Network Security Analyst https://www.glassdoor.com/ Job/jobs.htm?suggestCount= 0&suggestChosen=false&cli ckSource=searchBtn&typed Keyword=cybersecurity&sc. keyword=cybersecurity&loc T=&locId=	- 7+ years experience in information security and networking systems - Bachelor's Degree required preferably in Computer Science or related field - Extensive knowledge of data security and access control systems, encryption and related matters; in-depth knowledge of information protection methodologies and concepts, such as identification and authentication, access control, inception and audit trails and system and network exploitation, attack pathologies and intrusion techniques, such as denial of services, Sync attack, malicious code, password cracking, etc.

continues on following page

	Job Title and Web Site	Job Requirements
17	Systems Engineer, Cybersecurity https://www.glassdoor.com/ Job/jobs.htm?suggestCount= 0&suggestChosen=false&cli ckSource=searchBtn&typed Keyword=cybersecurity&sc. keyword=cybersecurity&loc T=&locId=	- 5 years of experience in cybersecurity. (Manufacturer or reseller engineering experience preferred.) - Experience developing for desktop and/or mobile computing platforms - Knowledge of cybersecurity technologies and the use of cybersecurity resources - In-depth knowledge of UNIX, Linux and/or Windows Operating Systems - Experience with LDAP and/or Active Directory - Experience or exposure to work in Federal IT systems (Civ and/or DoD) - Basic working knowledge of virtualization and cloud technologies - Basic knowledge of big data and analytics platforms and concepts (Hadoop, MapReduce) - Experience with some or all of the following technologies is preferred: IPS, Network Access Control, SIEM, Data Loss Prevention, Encryption, Anti-virus - Working knowledge of standard cybersecurity or cybersecurity-related tools such as Nessus, nmap, Zap, Wireshark, Burp Suite, etc.) - Knowledge of and experience with Federal cybersecurity programs, laws, regulations, and standards, such as: - DOD HBSS program - NIST 800-53 - FIPS 140-2 - DIACAP/DIARMF - FedRAMP, FedRAMP+ - DHS CDM - FISMA
18	IT Cybersecurity Specialist https://www.glassdoor.com/ Job/jobs.htm?suggestCount= 0&suggestChosen=false&cli ckSource=searchBtn&typed Keyword=cybersecurity&sc. keyword=cybersecurity&loc T=&locId=	Bachelor's Degree in Computer Science, Information Systems or other related field, or equivalent work experience. 7-10 years of combined IT and security work experience with a broad range of exposure to systems analysis, application development, systems administration. 5 years' experience designing and deploying security solutions at the enterprise level. Requires in-depth knowledge of security issues, techniques and implications across all existing computer platforms. Requires Security Certification(s) (i.e., Certified Information Systems Security Professional (CISSP), or Certified Information Security Manage (CISM).
19	Lead - Cybersecurity Analyst https://www.glassdoor.com/ Job/jobs.htm?suggestCount= 0&suggestChosen=false&cli ckSource=searchBtn&typed Keyword=cybersecurity&sc. keyword=cybersecurity&loc T=&locId=	4-year university degree or equivalent experience required. Proven analytical skills with an acute attention to detail and persistence. Excellent communication skills (verbally and written). Understanding mobile/BYOD security controls and vulnerabilities Strong networking knowledge. CCNA/CCNP certification desired Ability to understand network traffic (e.g. PCAP output) Understanding of Information Security practices and methodologies. Relevant information security certifications (e.g. CISSP, CISM, GREM) recommended. Able to collaborate with peers to proactively determine indicators of compromise. Work independently, make decisions and multi-task effectively in a fast-paced dynamic environment. Good understanding of current malicious code practices and techniques. Keeps current with contemporary standards, practices, procedures and methods Team player Provides extraordinary service Furthers the First Republic Bank culture and values
20	Cybersecurity Engineer https://www.glassdoor.com/ Job/jobs.htm?suggestCount= 0&suggestChosen=false&cli ckSource=searchBtn&typed Keyword=cybersecurity&sc. keyword=cybersecurity&loc T=&locId=	Must have a minimum of 15 years of experience in INFOSEC or Cybersecurity Proficiency with MS Office, including Word, PowerPoint, Project, and Excel Must have the knowledge and skills to manage multiple projects, keep track of and identify new task or adjust existing task and expectations as the project evolves Must have proven social and interpersonal skills to coordinate with a team of professionals who are both technical and non-technical to keep everyone on task and progressing forward also ensure the team maintains a positive and collaborative relationship with external stakeholders Excellent writing, oral communication, and organizational skills. Ability to perform detailed work with little guidance and to interact in a positive manner with other government and industry personnel Bachelor's Degree in information management or computer science required Certified Information Systems Security Professional (CISSP) or equivalent is required.

(* All names of the hiring organizations and detailed job descriptions are omitted in this document. All websites were accessed in November 2017)

Chapter 18
Enhancing a SCRM Curriculum With Cybersecurity

Art Conklin

University of Houston, Houston, USA

Chris Bronk

University of Houston, Houston, USA

ABSTRACT

Supply chain-related curricula exist across many universities, with many including risk management as an important or focal element. With the rise of software-driven technology across the supply chain, how can firms manage the inherent risks associated with software as part of a procurement process? This article examines how to provide context appropriate cybersecurity exemplars in a model supply chain education program, bringing to light the issue of embedded risk in software acquisition. Through a series of specifically placed educational elements that provide targeted cybersecurity knowledge to students, the objective is to provide additional skill sets for future supply chain professionals to assist firms in including software related cybersecurity risk as a component in SCRM.

1. INTRODUCTION

In August 2017, Danish shipping conglomerate Møller Maersk reported that it had fallen victim to a catastrophic cyberattack on its enterprise computer systems and network. Months later, in a meeting of the World Economic Forum at Davos, Maersk chairman Jim Hageman Snabe offered gripping details of how the widespread cyber-attack referred to as *notPetya*, impacted the firm. It shut down computer operations at Maersk for at least 10 days at 76 ports around the world, and required remediation covering 45,000 PCs, 4,000 servers and over 2,500 applications (Allen 2018). Total costs associated with this event exceeded $300M US (a figure they cite in lost revenue) and clean-up costs. A similar attack befell Federal Express subsidiary TNT Express. The notPetya attack and its effects on these global logistics firms has cast light on the issues of cybersecurity risk to supply chains (Greenberg, 2018). Supply chain management is not immune to the cybersecurity issues found in other major industry verticals.

DOI: 10.4018/978-1-6684-3554-0.ch018

Supply chains are a ubiquitous attribute of business and their function or disruption can have significant impacts to the goods and services that the firms offer. Professionals in the supply chain field toil to obtain the required elements for business adhering to tight schedules and financial constraints. The field of supply chain risk management acknowledges the potential for disruption in the sourcing of materials, which must be incorporated into the overall business risk of the enterprise. With software now embedded in so many products and information technologies, cybersecurity risk from software must be incorporated into the supply chain risk equation. A significant challenge for the supply chain is how to determine, understand and manage the risk associated with software and information technology elements in the overall supply chain risk management process.

There have been a variety of efforts designed to raise awareness of software risk and supply chain issues with the intent to influence change in business practices (Ellison & Woody, 2010). One practical example is the U.S. Department of Homeland Security's Software Acquisition Working Group guidebook. It focuses on enhancing supply chain risk management throughout the software acquisition and purchasing process (Polydys & Wisseman, 2009). The US National Institute of Standards and Technology (NIST) published several relevant items on the issue of security and the supply chain (Boyens, Paulsen, Moorthy, Bartol, & Shankles, 2014; US National Institute of Standards and Technology (NIST), 2015).

The incorporation of cybersecurity risk into supply chain risk management curricula has ramifications for education and student preparation for careers in the field. The scope of cybersecurity and supply chain is very wide, and for this paper the focus is only on risk associated with software security. This paper examines the use of specific curriculum additions to include key points of software cybersecurity as part of a typical undergraduate program in Supply Chain and Logistics Technology. A series of targeted additions of software cybersecurity knowledge can be added to the curriculum for the purposes of improving understanding of the risks and mitigation methods associated with software security risks. Introducing software related cybersecurity risk into a supply chain education program is not a complete solution to the problem, but over time as more supply chain professionals are educated with an expanded knowledge base, the solutions will be easier to achieve. This is a long term first step in attacking this complex problem. This paper covers a set of points in series: first is an examination of what are the types of risks associated with cybersecurity and supply chain; next the notional curriculum elements of the education program are explained; and last a menu of the learning points and their placement is presented. It is worth noting that the curricular prescriptions offered here, like almost any involving cybersecurity, are a work in progress, and that the level of detail associated with the curriculum changes are still evolving.

Software is commonly a part of many large-scale integrated systems that are managed through an acquisition process focused on the whole as opposed to the individual elements. The approach suggested in this article, aimed at educating supply chain professionals toward cybersecurity risk associated with software applications is not a complete solution for large scale acquisition cybersecurity supply chain risks. It can clearly play a role in the examination of decomposition of specifications and procurement policies, but we are not proposing this as a complete solution to large scale acquisition risk issues.

2. BACKGROUND

The issue of software security and its inherent risk has been understood for a long time (Allen, Barnum, Ellison, McGraw, & Mead, 2008) (Boehm, 1991). Continued reduction in the cost of embedded computing has led to the inclusion of microprocessors and networking into a wide range of devices. The overall result is that software is embedded in more and more of the items being bought in today's marketplace. This leads to a concomitant increase in enterprise risk, due to software security risk embedded in the products being procured. This risk enters the enterprise as the devices become part of the value chain process, either as part of the business operations, or as part of the products being developed and sold.

The supply chain profession is a diverse set of jobs involved in the development, procurement, transportation, storage, and delivery of materials as part of an organization's operations. There are numerous certifications, jobs and professional societies associated with this field of work. There are education programs, both at the undergraduate and graduate level designed to prepare people for work in this professional area. This paper examines how targeted changes to the educational pipeline can better prepare future professionals to deal with cybersecurity risk associated with software acquisition whether as an item of procurement or software included in a larger item.

Understanding and being aware of the risks associated with software and its inherent vulnerabilities is part of a business's total risk management portfolio. Creating a specific awareness in the supply chain profession as to the nature, source and issues surrounding software security risks and how these risks are embedded in the very items being procured is important. This awareness is not just so that the purchasing agent at a firm can make determinations as to what software is being purchased in products and services, it goes more to the complete professional responsibility of the supply chain professional being involved in managing business risk. In an ideal world, the part of the business that specifies the requirements for a purchase would also be responsible for the risk inherent in the item being procured. In large enterprises, with extensive policies and procedures surrounding enterprise risk, these elements may be understood and properly managed. In smaller firms, this responsibility may be shouldered by a broader group of executives, including those involved in supply chain. Developing an understanding of the risks associated with software security in supply chain personnel enables them to be better partners in the shared risk management model, providing them with knowledge that can open discussions when the issues are missed by others in the business.

3. THE SUPPLY CHAIN SOFTWARE SECURITY PROBLEM

Understanding cybersecurity as a part of business processes and how cybersecurity risk issues can affect supply chain business processes is an important topic for supply chain professionals. The Maersk experience with notPetya, and the subsequent disruption of worldwide shipping, as well as the recent ransomware attack on Federal Express's subsidiary TNT Express, are all examples of cybersecurity risks in transportation firms that enable the operation of global supply chains (Chung, 2017). The cyberattacks on Maersk and TNT Express have served as a wake-up call in elevating awareness of cybersecurity issues in major supply chain facilitators, however, they are not the emphasis of this paper. As important as these examples are, their details are beyond the scope of this article as the focus here is on the subset of procurement of software containing items and the software security risks embedded in these items. These examples are relevant, for they illustrate that cybersecurity risks can have direct supply chain effects, and have significant economic impacts.

Cybersecurity knowledge related to software engineering can and should be incorporated into supply chain educational curriculum at the post-secondary level. The discipline needs educate students on the threats and opportunities associated with software-based cybersecurity risk as part of the supply chain process. The objective is not to make supply chain personnel security experts, but rather to raise awareness so that they understand the potential issues and so that they can raise the correct questions as part of their job duties and responsibilities in managing supply chain risk. Incorporating awareness of software security issues in the supply chain curriculum can no longer be avoided. Specifically, the risk equation associated with the purchasing of software and software containing systems needs to be understood by professionals entering the supply chain field.

3.1. Cybersecurity Risks

The list of cybersecurity related risks faced by contemporary firms would likely require a large book to enumerate and describe them (Conklin, White, Cothren, Davis, & Williams, 2018). There is also a literature on the process of secure software development (Conklin & Shoemaker, 2013; McGraw, 2006). Furthermore, there are detailed documents that fully describe the issues and corrective measures associated with software security risks (Goertzel et al., 2007). These topics are clearly beyond the required scope of this paper, so a few practical examples to describe risks associated with supply chain, and more specifically software are offered here. A typical discussion of supply chain risk includes such issues as:

- Counterfeiting
- Supply chain compromise or shadow
- Untrusted manufacturing lines
- Complex supplier issues
- End-of-life (EOL) components / assemblies
- Leaked tools, schematics / data
- Grey market problems

These all have analogues in the software world. Software development inherently involves complex supply chains in its own right. Software itself is a complex product and is frequently created by including other software from other supplies, creating unusual dependencies and often unknown internal supply chains (Ellison & Woody, 2010). Much software development practice could be considered a form of untrusted manufacturing line. This leads to questions of provenance, where did the code come from, what can it do, and why can we trust it? These are not simple questions to answer, and all go to the question of what risk am I inheriting when this particular piece of software in included into my product. Software can be viewed through the lens of a product, an item with specific characteristics, or through the lens of an output of a process that creates the product. Regardless of the lens, software has risks associated with it, and as a consequence of how it is developed.

At the core of software security issues is the fundamental issue of vulnerabilities. A vulnerability is an exploitable error in software that enables an adversary to perform functions neither intended nor desired by the design of the software. Software vulnerabilities have existed since the beginning of software, and common patterns have been identified. MITRE has developed a taxonomy of software security vulnerability-related issues including CVE, CWE, and other measures (R. A. Martin, 2007, 2008). There are also several standard, well-known enumerations of common software errors, such as the SANS Top 25 Software Errors (B. Martin, Brown, Paller, Kirby, & Christey, 2011), and the OWASP Top 10 Software Errors (OWASP Foundation, 2017). Vulnerabilities are challenging to eradicate as they are not necessarily all known when the software is created. Although proper coding methods and use of models listed above can reduce the instances of vulnerabilities, the complexity of software operations leads to errors and vulnerabilities that are discovered over time, over the life of the product. This complicates the risk equation in that risk will continue to increase over the useful life of the product.

A common issue when building a computer system with long life is ensuring that components needed for the maintenance of the deployed systems will be available across the lifecycle of a product. Dealing with end-of-life (EOL) issues has been a common problem associated with supply chains for decades. This some problem extends to software as software itself has a lifecycle. Software can become obsolete for several reasons; functional, technical, or logistical (Sandborn, 2007). Functional obsolescence is when system changes render the original software unable to properly function with regard to its intended purpose. An example of technical obsolescence is when licensing ends and/or updates are no longer available. Examples of logistical obsolescence include the incompatibility of distribution mechanisms, such as floppy disks or other media becoming unavailable.

While the complete list of security risks is longer, the previous examples are the first set of elements that were positioned in the model supply chain curriculum to assist graduates in understanding the key issues in software security as it applies to supply chain risk management. The issue of understanding where actual software components are sourced from and how to ensure that all components are under proper supply chain control is the first issue added to the curriculum. Understanding software lifecycles and how they fit into supply chain risk was the second, and details on how software can be defective was the last.

The security risks associated with software have become obvious thanks to a long record of significant cyberattacks. What is less understood is that many of these same risks can also be present in computer hardware purchases. Much of the electronic hardware used today is constructed with embedded controllers and software included as part of the device. Using a typical electronic device as an example, if it has any built-in intelligence, that is typically in the form of an embedded microprocessor, it will also require software to provide the instructions for it to operate. With low-cost Linux based computing hardware now carrying a device cost of less than $20, the capabilities of embedded microelectronic devices can be significant. With these capabilities comes risk, for the software package that is used is typically an older version of Linux operating system. While the software running a microelectronic device might have been current at the time of system design, by the time the device goes through the development process and is produced and sold, the software can be many revisions out of date. Keeping embedded software such as this up to date with to respect to security-related software revisions is a rarity. With so much computing now connected via homogenous networks, this ultimately results in purchasing networked devices that will be emplaced on a network with out of date vulnerable software, a major vector for system compromise by malicious parties. Creating an awareness that most electronic elements have some form of associated software and that the addition of the hardware element also brings software risks is important for supply chain professionals to understand. Again, the focus is on awareness, not a deep technical understanding of the details of specific vulnerabilities.

Supply chain students should be aware of how these vulnerabilities can impact overall enterprise supply chain risk. For this reason, awareness of a reasonable set of cybersecurity elements should be incorporated into the education for new practitioners entering the supply chain profession.

3.2. Notional Cybersecurity Curriculum for Supply Chain Education

Supply chain education programs exist in a wide range of educational venues, from community colleges to undergraduate programs, to graduate programs (U.S. News, 2018). These programs vary in focus and content, as well as location, some being technical and some managerial. While every university is different, and course names or content will vary, in the curriculum of each discipline, the overlap of delivered knowledge between institutions is typically very high. Math is math, independent of the institution. The same holds true for more specific degree plans such as supply chain and logistics management degrees. A typical supply chain curriculum covers topics such as procurement, inventory, and transportation (Lambert, 2008). One of the crosscutting themes of supply chain instruction is risk management. All activities have an element of risk, and how an activity is managed can have an effect on the level of commensurate risk. Keep inventory too lean, shortages can occur, increasing costs. Conversely, holding too much inventory has its own set of costs. Failures in procurement can result in an organization being unable to execute its value chain in producing product. Recent high profile failures in defense programs, stemming from software elements highlight the importance of software as a component in a system (Insinna, 2018). Fundamental in learning how to properly manage the supply chain is in gaining understanding of risk associated with the supply chain operation, and with elements going through the procurement process.

An example of specific courses that may be revised in a prospective cyber-infused curriculum are listed below. These courses are focused on developing the skillset of an entry-level supply chain professional, one with a bachelor's degree. The courses listed below represent offerings at a major US university, with the first digit indicating the class level (2 – sophomore, 3 – junior, and 4 – senior). These courses will be examined in the next section with regard to the injection of software security issues into the supply chain curriculum.

3.2.1. Introduction to Logistics Technology

Functions, processes and objectives of the logistics operation. Industrial distributor and its relationship to other channel members.

3.2.2. Distribution Channels

Organization and operations of distribution channels with emphasis on vendor evaluation, value analysis, complex pricing, promotional strategies, and execution issues.

3.2.3. Logistics Technology and Procurement

Capacity allocation, facility and flow design, retrieval mechanisms, and inventory control systems; impacts on service and cost performance.

3.2.4. Transportation Economics and Policy

History and effects of regulatory policies of carriers and shippers.

3.2.5. Procurement

Purchasing functions including vendor analysis, negotiations, value analysis, systems contracts, public purchasing, organization, personnel, policies, competitive bids, and ancillary functions.

3.2.6. Transportation Law

Regulatory and procedural requirements pertaining to domestic and international freight transportation.

3.2.7. Inventory and Materials Handling

Recognition and utilization of mechanical and automated handling systems, tools, and techniques required for the movement and storage of materials within a logistics operation.

3.2.8. Global Supply Chain

Relationships among international trade specialists, global distribution channels, and governments using international documentation, terms of trade, financial, and legal resources.

Each of these courses is 15 weeks long with a total of 45 hours of classroom time. There are many individual elements within each class, and the objective is to add specific cybersecurity-related content, sometimes as small as a bullet point on a slide up to a portion of a lecture, which bring relevant risk issues from software security to the student's attention. Although none of these classes has any module directly related to software, software security, or risk from embedded software, the context of the material opens the door for the use of these topics as examples, enabling a broadening and deepening of the material.

3.3. Incorporating Cybersecurity Knowledge into Supply Chain Curriculum

The idea driving this work was a question: What is the best method of incorporating content associated with software security risk and supply chain risk management into a typical supply chain curriculum? Two approaches were considered. The first was a creation of a dedicated module that covered all of the major cybersecurity issues for use in a single course. The second was a distributed application of the same material across multiple courses. The first method had one immediate glaring problem – where do you put it, and what do you take out to make room. The material required to sufficiently address cybersecurity added up to roughly half of a week's instructional time. This is a problem, as there is not that level of "available" time in the curriculum. In response, we approached the problem using the second method, dividing it up into smaller pieces scattered it across the courses. This allowed us the flexibility to put details where they contextually made sense with the topic addressed in the class. With cybersecurity risk applied across multiple classes, it is hoped that knowledge retention will be improved as well. To understand why it fits in this manner is also important, for just like packing rocks into a fixed size vessel, once you run out of room for the big rocks, you can always turn one or two more into sand and fit them in the remaining gap spaces. This increases the material and weight but fits the container. This was the approach that was adopted.

The first step in the education awareness project is exposing supply chain students to the prevalence of software within the items being procured, including software. But in the case of equipment or subassemblies, the use of embedded software as part of a product is often non-obvious, yet awareness is needed. Educating non-technical students on technical details is not the objective, rather simply increasing the awareness of how complex items can bring risk is the key lesson. This lesson sets the stage for software bill of material topics that will follow later.

When purchasing software or any item with a software component there are several issues previously identified that need to be addressed, such as elimination of vulnerabilities, managing the software lifecycle and dealing with the complexity of the software elements from a procurement perspective. One early approach to address software issues was the changing of procurement language to specifically include elements to address specific risks. A common element is to specify that known vulnerabilities are to be addressed by the supplier – don't buy software that has any of the commonly known vulnerabilities (Howard, 2009). While this can be accomplished by including model procurement language in contracts and purchase orders, the issue rests in how this operationally occurs. In large, multinational firms with significant resources and detailed processes and procedures, software procurement processes can automatically generate many of the desired requirements. But not all firms will have the large-scale systems designed to automate these types of requirements into purchasing documents. Nor can this be done by documents alone. The procurement process, driven by procurement specialists need to know what questions to ask and when to ask them if critical issues are to be identified and dealt with in the procurement process.

It is necessary to explain to the supply chain professional that the procurement of software possesses different issues than a simple part, such as a #10 hex nut in stainless steel with specific strength requirements. Parts are typically bought, with transfer of ownership to the procuring firm. Software is in many cases licensed for a specific use. As a result, we incorporated the licensing issues into the different law related lecture elements across the curriculum. This includes differences when the procurement moves into a global aspect, as license provisions from other countries may have their own set of peculiarities.

In addition to the issue of not specifically outright buying an item, software has a lifecycle as previously described. This lifecycle has its own set of issues, for instance how updates are handled or whether maintenance required to receive updates. While the topic of updating software is known by virtually every post-secondary student, the nuances of assuring that when software is procured, or how procurement includes the necessary clauses to ensure that software updates are automatically delivered to the organization are not well known. How to install the updates into the value chain associated with the software procurement is the organization's problem, however ensuring that the updates are included in the procurement and subsequent delivery to the correct department, this is a supply chain function. These concepts fit nicely into the *Logistics Technology & Procurement* course.

The concept that software is typically a complex item, comprised of other software components that may be created by other firms and programmers is readily known to computer scientists. Understanding that software is not a single item, but a collection of items, that work together, with each potentially having separate lineage, separate risks, is a key learning element in understanding the nature of embedded risk in software. This topic is brought into the context of *Distribution Channels*, where the idea of a software bill of materials (SBOM) is presented. The concept of a bill of material, enumerating the different elements of a complex part or assembly has already been introduced to students. The idea is then presented in light of security risks that have been recently experienced because of security failures of included components in an assembly. A software component may have third party libraries included as well. Obtaining the information as to what is included, down to version and patch level is important for the security team to assess risk that is incorporated from external sources (Landwehr & Valdes, 2017). The concept of software bill of materials is not new, but its importance in critical areas such as healthcare and critical infrastructure equipment is drawing attention to the issue (Beard, 2017). Educating the supply chain professional on this seemingly esoteric topic, as a needed risk mitigation element associated with complex items, will assist in the normalization of this as a mainstream item associated with procurement of any embedded software.

There are several ancillary issues that are included in criticality of a component and source of the component. Understanding that not all software components need the same level of scrutiny is an important risk management concept. Risk is context sensitive. It does not make sense to subject a software program being procured as an app on a mobile device with no connection to business information to the same security requirements as the software module that is an integral component of the firm's value chain. It is incumbent upon the supply chain personnel to understand the associated risk elements and draw the issue to the attention of management when critical components are being procured. The same scrutiny goes towards with respect to the source of software. Would you procure it from a vendor with which you have a long relationship, or an unknown entities GitHub page, or from a foreign country? Each of these has its own set of risks and applying that contextual risk management with respect to software procurement is an essential knowledge element for the supply chain professional to possess. When discussing legal regulations, the legal issues surrounding software rights and liabilities are introduced. When discussing global elements associated with supply chain, and the risks of other countries, software specific risks are also covered.

Another related issue with the complexity of software in terms of embedded components and the supply chain associated with those components is in the context of the lifetime of the software license and its use in the value chain of the organization. If the software is important to the functioning of the firm, what happens if the software vendor puts software to an end-of-life condition without offering a viable update path? Or consider a different scenario, but same ultimate concern: a software vendor ceases to remain in business. Because of the sole-source, proprietary nature of most software, an identical product can't necessarily be bought from another vendor. Thus, provisions to protect access to the software code may be needed. This is typically done through a process known as source code escrow, another legal element to consider as part of the procurement negotiations (Conklin & Shoemaker, 2013).

4. CONCLUSION

The issues of software security risk in supply chain management is a complex topic with many specific details. Attacking the issues associated with this problem will require multiple actions in an organization across multiple business processes. Here, we have examined one risk reduction action, that of using post-secondary supply chain education as a tool against accumulating unnecessary risk. The idea presented is not to make supply chain personnel security experts. That would be wasteful as the majority of a security professional's knowledge is not relevant in the tasks of a supply chain professional. The opposite case, complete ignorance of software security risks, is also an untenable situation for the enterprise. The best answer lies somewhere between these poles. The proposed curricula changes are being tested at a major university, although the ultimate effectiveness of this action will not be truly measurable until the students enter the workforce and make business decisions.

The concept proposed in this paper is the incorporation of specific pieces of software risk information within the context of the supply chain curriculum to provide contextual relevance to the student. This has been initiated with a limited set of security risk topics associated with software and based on results and student/graduate feedback the topic set will be improved in coming semesters. The process begins with increasing awareness regarding the inclusion of software in a wide range of procured items.

The curriculum expansion then progresses to cover a couple of key topics, including an understanding of vulnerabilities, and the complexity of software, and the inherent risks embedded in its creation. This culminates with the discussion of a software bill of materials, a risk reduction element that will continue to grow in importance.

This approach of embedding nuggets of cybersecurity knowledge into the supply chain curriculum will be reviewed with respect to effective coverage as measured by student responses on quizzes, exams, papers and other graded deliverables. The next step will be to examine student learning outcomes with respect to the material injected into the curriculum, making minor shifts as needed to result in effective learning.

The objective is not to completely solve the software security risk problem as it relates to supply chain, but rather to bring the issues into view and make them visible to the professionals best positioned to address them, the supply chain practitioners themselves. Adding the supply chain management professional to the ranks of those working to reduce risk is a welcome addition to any firm. Educating these professionals on the embedded risks associated with software makes them additional allies in the quest to improve risk management across the enterprise. Doing so through the use of examples, to drive both core supply chain principle learning and expand knowledge into relevant software security topics makes this a relatively painless method of improving both the supply chain process and ultimately software security.

REFERENCES

Allen, J. H., Barnum, S., Ellison, R. J., McGraw, G., & Mead, N. R. (2008). *Software security engineering: A Guide for Project managers*. Pearson/Addison-Wesley Professional.

Beard, D. (2017). Technical Tactics: Embedded Linux Software BOM. *Paper presented at the BSidesLV 2017*, Las Vegas, NV.

Boehm, B. W. (1991). Software risk management: Principles and practices. *IEEE Software*, 8(1), 32–41. doi:10.1109/52.62930

Boyens, J., Paulsen, C., Moorthy, R., Bartol, N., & Shankles, S. A. (2014). Supply chain risk management practices for federal information systems and organizations. *NIST Special Publication*, 800(161), 1.

Chung, J. J. (2017). Critical Infrastructure, Cybersecurity, and Market Failure. *Or. L. Rev.*, 96, 441.

Conklin, W. A., & Shoemaker, D. (2013). *CSSLP Certification All-in-one Exam Guide*. McGraw-Hill Education Group.

Conklin, W. A., White, G., Cothren, C., Davis, R., & Williams, D. (2018). *Principles of Computer Security: Security+ and Beyond* (5th ed.). McGraw-Hill Education Group.

Ellison, R. J., & Woody, C. (2010). Supply-chain risk management: Incorporating security into software development. *Paper presented at the 2010 43rd Hawaii International Conference on System Sciences (HICSS)*. 10.1109/HICSS.2010.355

Goertzel, K. M., Winograd, T., McKinley, H. L., Oh, L. J., Colon, M., McGibbon, T., & Vienneau, R. (2007). *Software security assurance: a State-of-Art Report (SAR)*. VA: Herndon. Retrieved from http://www.dtic.mil/dtic/tr/fulltext/u2/a472363.pdf doi:10.21236/ADA472363

Greenberg, A. (2018). The Untold Story of NotPetya, the Most Devastating Cyberattack in History. *WIRED*.

Howard, M. (2009). Improving software security by eliminating the CWE top 25 vulnerabilities. *IEEE Security and Privacy*, 7(3), 68–71. doi:10.1109/MSP.2009.69

Insinna, V. (2018). F-35 operational testing delayed until latest software delivers. *Defense News*. Retrieved from https://www.defensenews.com/air/2018/09/12/f-35-operational-testing-delayed-until-latest-software-delivers/

Lambert, D. M. (2008). *Supply chain management: processes, partnerships, performance*. Supply Chain Management Inst.

Landwehr, C. E., & Valdes, A. (2017). *Building Code for Power System Software Security*.

Martin, B., Brown, M., Paller, A., Kirby, D., & Christey, S. (2011). *2011 CWE/SANS top 25 most dangerous software errors*. Common Weakness Enumer.

Martin, R. A. (2007). *Making Security Measurable*. Bedford, MA: The MITRE Corporation. Retrieved from http://measurablesecurity.mitre.org/

Martin, R. A. (2008). Making security measurable and manageable. *Paper presented at the Military Communications Conference MILCOM 2008*. IEEE. 10.1109/MILCOM.2008.4753203

McGraw, G. (2006). *Software security: building security* (Vol. 1). Addison-Wesley Professional.

OWASP Foundation. (2017). OWASP Top 10 - 2017: The Ten Most Critical Web Application Security Risks.

Polydys, M. L., & Wisseman, S. (2009). Software Assurance in Acquisition: Mitigating Risks to the Enterprise. A Reference Guide for Security-Enhanced Software Acquisition and Outsourcing.

Sandborn, P. (2007). Software obsolescence-Complicating the part and technology obsolescence management problem. *IEEE Transactions on Components and Packaging Technologies*, 30(4), 886–888.

U.S. News. (2018, 2018). Best Undergraduate Supply Chain Management / Logistics Programs. Retrieved from https://www.usnews.com/best-colleges/rankings/business-supply-chain-management-logistics

US National Institute of Standards and Technology (NIST). (2015). *Best Practices in Cyber Supply Chain Risk Management*. Retrieved from https://csrc.nist.gov/CSRC/media/Projects/Supply-Chain-Risk-Management/documents/briefings/Workshop-Brief-on-Cyber-Supply-Chain-Best-Practices.pdf

This research was previously published in the International Journal of Systems and Software Security and Protection (IJSSSP), 9(2); pages 46-56, copyright year 2018 by IGI Publishing (an imprint of IGI Global).

Chapter 19

All the World's a Stage:
Achieving Deliberate Practice and Performance Improvement Through Story-Based Learning

Brian S. Grant

https://orcid.org/0000-0002-4375-7551

Raytheon Technologies, USA

EXECUTIVE SUMMARY

This chapter provides a case study where a systematic, organized method of storytelling, presented as the Story-based Learning model, is used to design a series of integrated and engaging activities for cybersecurity training (to protect computer systems and networks) that fosters deliberate practice and improves performance. To address the talent shortage in the global cybersecurity workforce, the client developed a blended curriculum designed to provide practical experience to prospective cybersecurity professionals. A key component of this curriculum was the capstone exercises, activities focused on application of the content introduced in the courseware. Essentially, this is a story of using stories, one of humanity's oldest technologies, to solve the problem of training and cultivating expertise in future cybersecurity personnel. Based on solid prior evidence supporting the use of stories to increase engagement and retention, this case study focuses on detailing the thought process used to reach this set of solutions, as captured by the Story-based Learning model.

ORGANIZATIONAL BACKGROUND

The client for this case study was a large global technology company with a long history of innovation and training, with capabilities and expertise built over decades. The client recently also cemented a specialization in providing cybersecurity solutions. Through my affiliation with a globally recognized learning center of excellence, I had the opportunity to support the client in developing the cybersecurity curriculum at the heart of this case study.

DOI: 10.4018/978-1-6684-3554-0.ch019

While there were countless individuals and groups involved in the strategic planning, analysis, design, development, and implementation of the cybersecurity training curriculum, this case study only mentions the areas most significant to this case study, categorized as follows:

- **Subject Matter Experts**: The team of Cybersecurity Subject Matter Experts (often abbreviated as SMEs) that supported all aspects of the cybersecurity curriculum development and delivery.
- **Analyst**: Individual who worked with the Subject Matter Experts to conduct an upfront work analysis, detailing the tasks and skills performed by cybersecurity professionals on a daily basis, as well as answering clarifying questions by Instructional Systems Designers during development.
- **Instructional Systems Designers**: The team of Instructional Systems Designers (often abbreviated as ISDs) that I worked with for this project. We worked with the Subject Matter Experts to develop the cybersecurity training, but the Instructional Systems Designers also provided each other unwavering support and fresh perspectives throughout the process.
- **Information Technology Infrastructure**: The team of Information Technology (often abbreviated as IT) Infrastructure personnel who configured the computer network infrastructure and environment to support the development and delivery of the cybersecurity curriculum, in particular the various lab exercises.

SETTING THE STAGE

Unfortunately, cybercrime is big business, to the tune of over $440 billion a year. Cybercriminals have grown increasingly more organized and aggressive, while the cybersecurity teams defending against such attacks have struggled to find qualified personnel. The fact remains that there continues to be a persistent talent shortage in the global cybersecurity workforce. One important reason for this dearth of qualified applicants was the past focus on hiring people with traditional technology degrees instead of "opening themselves up to applicants whose nontraditional background mean they could bring new ideas to the position and the challenge of improving cybersecurity" (Zadelhoff, 2017).

Recently, more companies have recognized that skills, knowledge, and willingness to learn can prove more vital than formal degrees. This turning point was a result of understanding that the characteristics critical to the success of cybersecurity professionals were not ones that taught in the classroom, including curiosity, problem solving, strong ethics, and risk management (Zadelhoff, 2017). When the prospective candidates start with these right characteristics, they are better positioned to complete a comprehensive cybersecurity training program that teaches the required technical and technological competencies, coupled with preparation to obtain recognized industry certifications. The client in this case study was one of these companies that recognized this attitude in closing the hiring gap in global cybersecurity professionals.

By embracing this attitude, the client sought to expand their role in providing broad-based, comprehensive cyber services. The learning solution at the heart of this case study was to develop a fully-functional, blended curriculum focused on providing practical experience to prospective cybersecurity professionals. The goal of the training program was to cultivate the new, and much needed, workforce required to secure the networks and systems of current and potential customers across the globe, including foreign governments, military, and large corporations.

This blended curriculum solution set offered a classroom-focused environment led by Instructors with the learners moving through the modules together as a group. This classroom also provided full access to the Web-based lab components, including the Capstone exercises placed at the end of each course of modules. The Capstone exercises were designed to provide learners the opportunity to demonstrate their ability to apply various skills learned throughout the earlier modules.

The focus of this case study will be on the development of the foundational and intermediate courses of training modules on the subject of cybersecurity, specifically the activities that provided learners with an introduction proficiency to the cybersecurity job roles of a general cyber analyst and operator. The development of the training for advanced job roles, along with leadership and executive-level training, will be outside the intended scope of this case study. In addition, it should be noted that while learners of this cybersecurity curriculum gained awareness and exposure to the full range of attack methods used by various external and internal threat actors, the orientation of the tools, methods, and skills taught in the curriculum was purely focused on reconnaissance and defense.

A critical component to the successful implementation of this defense-oriented curriculum involved the strategic placement of Capstone exercises at the end of a sequence of modules, but still conducted before the final testing preparation for obtaining corresponding certifications. Thus, these Capstone exercises served an integral role in reinforcing the knowledge, skill, and technologies introduced in their corresponding modules and reviewed through individual lab exercises embedded in the curriculum.

My specific challenge was to design these Capstone exercises. This involved creating a comprehensive set of interwoven activities in each Capstone exercise that provided the engaging deliberate practice experiences for key module objectives, resulting in the eustress (the positive stress that improves performance) that would lead learners toward proficiency, mastery of the skills, and eventual expertise. An additional challenge included integrating the various Capstone exercises into a coherent alignment that flows seamlessly as the learners advanced through the curriculum.

Solid evidence can be found in the literature involving the use of systematic deliberate practice to improve performance, as well as the important connections between increased engagement and improved learning. Deliberate practice produced the strong learning outcomes in both cognitive and psychomotor tasks, specifically by imparting the experience and performance required (Ericsson, Krampe, & Tesch-Römer, 1993). Likewise, clear evidence exists that using simulations, when coupled with deliberate practice, yielded better results than traditional educational approaches for complex activities such as medical and clinical training (McGaghie, 2011). I feel that these benefits can effectively map to the complex and mentally demanding work a cybersecurity professional performs.

Therefore, deliberate practice through simulations, such as those provided through hands-on scenarios, are important to providing the experience the learners need, specifically what Ericsson and his colleagues (1993) identified as the key aspects of developing elite performers: access to instruction and high levels of deliberate practice throughout development.

However, learners must also be actively engaged in the learning environment in order to encourage reflection, nurture emotional reactions, and convey credibility through relevance (Paulus, 2006). This can be done through the application of story, using a rich narrative to provide the substantial motivational benefits of self-efficacy, presence, interest, and perception (McQuiggan, 2008). And remember, these were precisely the desired characteristics for prospective learners starting their journey to become cybersecurity professionals. Furthermore, engagement appears to benefit new learners, such as entry-level cybersecurity learners, even more than experts (Carini, 2004), just as deliberate practice does (Ericsson et al, 1993).

The role of stories supporting retention of information has been well documented over the decades, even as early as the research by Bower and Clark, which clearly demonstrated how the use of narrative significantly increased recall (1969). This method was exemplified by competitive memory champion's use of narrative "memory palace" strategies, a method where one uses his/her mind to store imaginary visuals in a made-up location to aid in memory enhancement. However, this evidence only pointed to some deeper truths about the power that stories bring to the learning brain.

Neurobiology has unmistakably supported the theory that the evolution of our brains included a hard-wired fondness for stories, and that this story pathway may be accessed to motivate people, even in a business setting (Zak, 2014). Furthermore, there has been evidence that indicated the use of narrative-focused game-based environments does not, in fact, diminish learning. Instead, it showed a strong positive relationship between learning outcomes, in-game problem solving and increased engagement (Rowe, 2011).

Based on this solid foundation, I felt confident that using engaging, story-based scenarios would help achieve optimal learning. What I lacked was the map of how to effectively create such scenarios. Therefore, the goal of this case study is not to further underscore the consistent results in applying stories to learning, but to focus on a thread lacking in the literature: what repeatable process can be used to consistently create the rich narratives required to provide the necessary benefits to learners?

This case study proposes one such approach through the application of a Story-based Learning model that can be used to design and develop story-based scenarios, such as the Capstone exercises for the cybersecurity curriculum. The emphasis here is detailing the creative process utilized during the development phase of the foundational and intermediate curricula. The analysis of creative process will be expressed through the lens of the Story-based Learning model. Thus, this case study is as much about the building of the Story-based Learning approach as it is about the application of this approach in crafting engaging and learner-focused narrative concepts for training scenarios. It is a tale of using stories to tell the story of how such stories are made.

Figure 1.

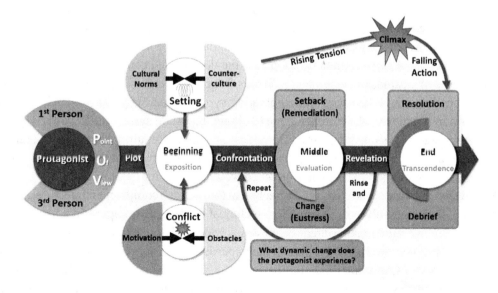

CASE DESCRIPTION AND TECHNOLOGY CONCERNS

There were two primary challenges in designing the Capstone exercises. First, they had to reinforce the crucial skills covered in the content. But they also had to engage the learners so they would perform the deliberate practice needed to reach proficiency. What would be the right balance between challenge and engagement, while still not becoming too academic? The key was in determining the best technologies to utilize.

Remember that the word *technology* does not refer merely to electronic hardware and software, as is so often used in our modern age. Instead, it derived from the Greek τέχνη (techne), which means "science of craft" and the word broadly referred to any capability offered by the practical application of knowledge to achieve an objective. We have embedded technology into machines that allowed for utilization of the technology without the user possessing detailed knowledge of the processes that enabled it. But even before that, some of our most profound technologies predate any mechanization. Just as the printing press was a radical new technology back in its day, so too were the ancient technologies profound in their prehistoric days, such as the invention of writing, the art of storytelling, and even the control of fire.

However, despite my awareness of using stories to optimize learning, I did not start the project with that solution in mind. Instead, as with any project, there was first an analysis of the challenge before determining the best technologies to solve it. In this case, to analyze the requirements for the Capstone exercises further, I had two paths to follow simultaneously, even while discoveries in one inevitably fed the other:

1. Which module objectives required capstone activities to reinforce them using purposeful and deliberate practice?
2. What framework for the delivery of these activities maximized learner engagement while providing the necessary alignment across the curriculum?

Thankfully, determining the required objectives was relatively straightforward due to the foresight of the Analyst and Subject Matter Experts having completed a comprehensive task analysis. Working with the Subject Matter Experts, I reviewed the existing analysis in order to identify a number of key tasks and skills that require reinforcement. And in subsequent meetings, we refined that list.

For example, when analyzing the foundational content for the first Capstone exercise, we determined that the ability to create a network map that depicted the devices and connections of a given computer environment was a critical task to reinforce, as it was frequently performed when identifying network structures. Meanwhile, the basic usage of the operating system Windows was also taught to ensure understanding of how to navigate the command line to obtain important system information. However, the ubiquity of the operating system did not translate to that knowledge requiring further deliberate practice outside module lab exercises. Instead of including the Windows topic into the Capstone exercise for reinforcement, the use of a job aid or other reference would suffice for that topic.

But other decisions were not so clear cut. Do technical topics, such computer architecture and scripting in programming languages, always outweigh less technical cybersecurity topics, like identifying threat actors and maintaining situational awareness? Given a wide variety of topics, we could not reinforce them all in the Capstone exercise, so I relied on the expertise of the Subject Matter Experts to help determine the right mix of Capstone topics. In this case, the Subject Matter Experts deemed some of the less technical topics as just as important to reinforce in the Capstone exercise as other technical ones.

This led to another question. How can we provide appropriate deliberate practice on softer skills and incorporate them seamlessly in with the technical ones?

To answer this, we had to consider the second path of analysis, the framework and method used to organize and deliver these Capstone activities; a framework that incorporated the interpersonal skill objectives, along with the technical ones, into a comprehensive and complete narrative that would engage the learners.

This is where the proposal for using story-based scenarios arose. As discussed earlier, this solution was a natural methodology to enabling deliberate practice. And, with my background as a writer and storyteller, I was confident that such an approach could be implement effectively. However, using a narrative method to address something as diverse and complicated as cybersecurity would still prove a leap of faith for some.

Can the narrative of a story convey both the mindset and technical skills required of a cybersecurity professional in an engaging manner?

I proposed that the answer was yes, if we created an immersive world for the story to unfold in. Then, we would place our learners, in the role as cybersecurity professionals, right at the heart of this detailed, relevant setting.

So, it was not without some irony that we could meet the challenge of designing cybersecurity Capstone exercises by using one of humanity's oldest technologies, storytelling, as a key component of the solution set. But to understand how this worked, to see how we could introduce entry-level learners to the mindset and workflow of a cybersecurity professional through a story, it would help to consult the Story-based Learning model.

The topics deemed important to reinforce in the Capstone exercises became our primary objectives for the story scenario. At this point we decided which Point of View (often abbreviated as POV) the learner would experience this story scenario through. Specifically, the point of view is the lens, or perspective, through which we chose to tell the story, the focus of the narrator conveying the narrative. There were a few options:

- 1st person – A commonly used method where the narrator was inside the story, and seen through the main character's perspective (using "I" or "we"):
  - 1st person example: "I am worried about learning the new computer application."
- 2nd person – A rarely used method where the narrator was outside the story but telling the tale to someone else, often the reader (using "you"):
  - 2nd person example: "You worry about learning the new computer application."
- 3rd person limited – A commonly used method where the narrator was outside the story, though it is told from the main character's limited perspective (using "he", "she", or "they")
  - 3rd person limited example: "She is worried about learning the new computer application."
- 3rd person omniscient – An uncommonly used variation of the 3rd person perspective where the story could view all character's thoughts (still using "he", "she", or "they")
  - 3rd person omniscient – "She is just as worried as her friend about learning the new computer application."

Figure 2.

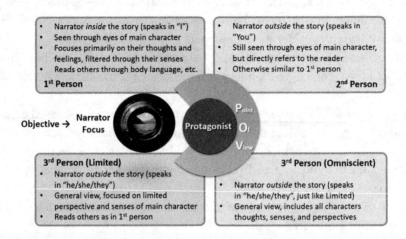

As illustrated by the figure, there were a wide variety of point of view options in the storytelling toolbox. However, for the intent and purpose of telling a training story scenario, the most commonly used narrative devices of 1st person and 3rd person limited were far superior for Story-based Learning scenario structures. Many people have found 2nd person uncomfortable as it is not the natural method used in daily conversation, and it could prove a difficult perspective to tell stories through. Likewise, 3rd person omniscient is often found too complex for the learner to keep track of. So, for these Capstone exercises we decided to pick from either 1st person or 3rd person limited.

In this case, the 1st person point of view perspective was the best choice strong choice for two main reasons. First, learner participation in the Capstone exercise was in a classroom setting, guided by an Instructor, even if they still access web-based materials. So, while the Instructor conveyed story information (explaining to them, "You will be assuming the role of…"), the scenario content itself would be best portrayed directly from the learner's perspective. The other reason that 1st person point of view worked best involved a clear understanding of who the main character, or protagonist, of the story would be: the learner themselves, placed into and assuming the role of a cybersecurity person, as opposed to viewing the story of a fictitious cybersecurity professional.

So, we realized that determining the story's protagonist, that is our main character, for the Capstone exercises was just as important as knowing the audience for the training itself, as it explained how the learners would be accessing the scenario. The main character protagonist, serving as the story's most prominent character, was placed at the center of the story, and typically provides the point of view perspective we focus on. We carefully considered the role that the protagonist has in the story, placing them in a decisive position that is relevant to the learners. Here, the learners would be assuming the role of a cybersecurity professional, such as an employee at a Security Operations Center (often abbreviated as SOC), a centralized unit that addresses organizational security issues. Therefore, it was the best choice for this scenario to align with a traditional "tabletop" roleplaying exercise, which is often conveyed through a 1st person point of view focus.

However, for other types of Story-based Learning scenarios, the requirements can drive different choices. In a purely Web-based delivery environment, I have found that providing the learner with a designated story character other than themselves often proved more effective. So, for a Web-based scenario, I often preferred using a 3rd person limited point of view over a 1st person point of view. The reason was that by purposefully separating the learner from the main character protagonist, it offered more of an observational experience.

Research in neuroscience has explained why this observational approach still works for learning, such that watching someone else perform actions can support the deliberate practice that learners need. Research points to the existence a mirror neuron network in the brain, a specialized set of neurons that fire not only when you perform an action, but when you observe someone else performing a similar action. The brain's mirror neuron network allowed for learning through both observation and through the experiences of others (Ramachandran, 2000). This mirror neuron network was also triggered when observing emotions (European Science Foundation, 2008). And further evidence has indicated that this mirror neuron system not only works for physical motor skills, but mental cognitive skill as well (Paas, 2008).

Based on these choices for the cybersecurity curriculum, the Subject Matter Experts and I were able to outline possible scenarios that string the objectives for a Capstone exercise together and place them in the best Point of View for the learners. In the case of the foundational Capstone, the early ideas outlined the learner as a Security Operations Center employee conducting an investigations of a fictitious university department. First, they created a visual network diagram of the department's computer network, a task they had done in an earlier lab exercise in the curriculum. But in the Capstone exercise, this task is placed in a larger context in both task and story. Next, the learner had to document potential vulnerabilities in that same network. Then, the learners were provided with fictional artifacts of content that they used to discern potential cyber threat actors and their motives. Then we confronted them with an incident that they had to respond to, analyzing logs to determine what happened, and then documenting remediation recommendations.

While this was a good start, we soon encountered a difficult technology problem.

CURRENT CHALLENGES FACING THE ORGANIZATION

The technology challenge we faced at this juncture was not about the use of the ancient art of storytelling, but instead the problem was with a more modern digital technology. It was a good plan to use the foundational Capstone exercise to provide the mindset and workflow of a cybersecurity professional, but that idea assumed that the learners would be able to utilize some digital software applications during the exercises. The problem was that the foundational courseware only has the learners utilize the most basic applications in a cybersecurity professional's software toolbox, and even then only at an introductory level. Furthermore, the primary orientation of the foundational cybersecurity tasks focused only on defensive postures, which limited our options for scenario activities.

This problem was not limited to the fundamentals courses, as the intermediate and later courseware would delve far deeper into the practical use of these industry-standard computer applications. For these more advanced courses, the question was how to create, spin up, and maintain the necessary equipment and virtual environments necessary to not only provide the learners fictitious systems and networks to probe, but also simulate the appropriate virtual machines that the learners would use to run these probing cybersecurity applications—all without interfering with each other as they work. This was definitely a thorny technological problem.

However, there was also a story obstacle to also overcome. We had to determine who in the scenario story was working against these learners as they confronted the activities that evaluated and reinforced their skills in deliberate practice? Could we use examples pulled from real-world threat actors? If so, were there issues with the rapidly changing landscape of cyber threats? If we could not, then what would make for an authentic formidable foe?

Figure 3.

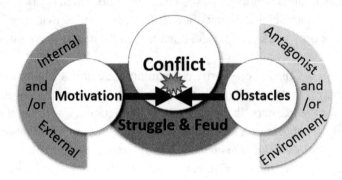

To understand the nature of this last problem, we needed to crack open the egg of conflict in the Story-based Learning model and see what sparks effective dramatic strife.

Good stories have typically thrived on conflict, serving as a story's oxygen and ignition. But physical danger was not the only means of achieving this needed struggle. At its source, conflict stemmed from pitting our protagonist's motivations (regardless of whether our main character was motivated by their own desires or driven by outside ones) against obstacles that must be overcome in order to achieve the goal. And these obstacles would either have occurred through the actions of an antagonist, someone who directly hampers the protagonist achieving their goal, through a physical or cultural environment that indirectly thwarts our protagonist, or both.

In this case, our cybersecurity professionals-in-training faced both forms of obstacles; first there were antagonists in the form of threat actors who aim to infiltrate or sabotage the learner's computer network systems. But there was also a hostile cyber environment, with the political and economic drama of countries hungry for information and a desire to expose and post secrets. We detailed these threats in order to provide the Capstone exercise the authenticity it needed to be relevant to the learners.

This led to further questions about the training scenarios. Where was all this conflict and drama taking place? In what countries was our story set? Could we use real countries, ripped from the headlines, as our primary locations? If not, what were our other options?

Using real countries for our Capstone exercises would lend authenticity, increasing the realism and gaining relevance through instant recognition of a real-world country. However, there was an important problem with this approach. Once we realized that many of the customers for this cybersecurity training would likely be foreign entities (governments, military, and large corporations), the option of using real-world countries would, at best, distract the learners with unnecessary knowledge and opinions they might bring with them about the country. At worst, casting of a country as a threat actor could accidently embarrass or even insult a potential client country.

Therefore, in this case, we needed to create a completely fictitious set of locations. Yes, this would require more upfront effort, but the benefits far outweighed the extra work. First, we could control every aspect of the content and deliver only what the learners needed to complete the exercise along with what was required to make it immersive enough. The trick was to provide an instructional environment that balanced engagement and streamlined learning by not overloading or distracting the learner. Also, not using real-world countries avoided any preconceived notions learners may have about those countries, which would also hamper the learners.

Our goal, and the goal to any story setting, was to drive the narrative and plot forward, and not derail it through either distraction or by burdening the pace with too much exposition, that is an information dump of too much story background. Instead, we wanted to provide enough realistic detail to suspend disbelief, while still offering clear tensions among the actors in the setting. Specifically, we could see what drives dramatic pressure when we cracked open the egg of setting in the Story-based Learning model.

Figure 4.

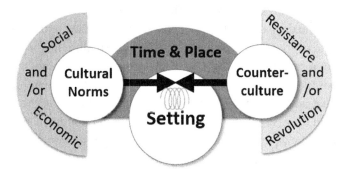

The tension of setting was caused by the interplay between clashing cultures. One group was based in the current cultural norms, which is the *status quo*, driven by social and/or economic motivations to maintain things as they are. The other group formed out of a counter-culture, which either silently or vocally react to the cultural norms of the status quo in hopes of changing the culture through resistance and/or revolution, as needed.

An interesting point about the dynamics of setting was that within any organizational group, the group that a story character may identify with, current norms or counter-culture, could change at any given moment in the story, and was purely based on their perception. In any given situational setting, both parties (the cultural norms group and the counter-culture group) believed they were in the right. Whether they were labelled as the hero or the villain, part of the empire or the rebels, depended on how the story is framed. And the character could also change allegiances, and align themselves with different group later in the story.

So, as the Story-based Learning model has illustrated, both the spark of conflict and the tension of setting were used to drive the drama of the story. These, along with the main character's point of view, were vital in feeding the plot as the design of our story began. However, the story could not finish its design until it has solved the challenges we still faced.

SOLUTIONS AND RECOMMENDATIONS

To recap, the challenges we needed to confront were as follows:

1. How do we enable the learners to participate in a Capstone exercise with only knowledge of cybersecurity fundamentals and an introductory exposure to cybersecurity applications?
2. Once the learners gain sufficient experience with the necessary computer applications through intermediate and more advanced training, how do we provide the necessary classroom infrastructure for the learners to conduct online deliberate practice sessions simultaneously?
3. Who are the antagonists serving as the cyber threat actors? Are they real-world agents or should they be fabricated?
4. What fictitious setting do we need to create? How can we make it realistic without overloading the learners?

To address the first problem, we had to think a little outside the box. While you could not teach cybersecurity without computers, networks, and applications, this does not necessarily mean that we had to throw our learners into the deep end of the pool right away. On the contrary, for fundamentals training, it was important not to overload the learner at first. The curriculum in question would eventually be many courses taught over a series of months. Our goal with this initial fundamental Capstone exercise was to lay the foundations for the learner to begin thinking like a cybersecurity professional, focused on emulating the mindset that an expert would use. What did they look for in the data? How did they see patterns? What actions did they take based on investigations and the information uncovered?

This mindset and workflow were not dependent on using computer systems to conduct. Instead, they could be delivered on paper, if the environment was still engaging enough. This means that the learner would receive a series of documents, either distributed in person or electronically, that would include artifacts from the fictional world setting that we created.

These artifacts—consisting of backgrounders, articles, posts, puzzles, and logs—will be covered in more depth shortly. But first, it should be noted that, in our case, this 'artifact-based' solution for the fundamental Capstone exercise had the added benefit of solving both the second challenge and an unforeseen and related scheduling issue.

As often happens in large-scale projects, intended schedules were subject to change. In this case, the client's first customer had a tight timeline for delivering the cybersecurity curriculum that required a very aggressive development cycle. This had the direct impact of leaving the development team with less time than originally hoped. This included condensing the time that the Information Technology Infrastructure team had for creating the computer network environment infrastructure that would be used by the learners in the classroom to conduct the online deliberate practice sessions during the lab and Capstone exercises.

But if we used a purely artifact-based approach for the fundamental Capstone exercise activities, we could delay the upfront need for this digital environment, and provide the Information Technology Infrastructure team more time to spin up the necessary solutions. While the computer network and virtual cyber environment that the Information Technology Infrastructure team did eventually create for the intermediate Capstone was truly innovative in its own right, and no less deserving of its own case study, that story was outside the scope of this case study's examination.

But this buffer time did not alleviate the need to tighten communications between the Instructional Systems Designer and the Information Technology Infrastructure teams in determining the network and system needs required for the intermediate and advanced Capstone and module lab exercises. To address this, I would highly recommend that someone is designated to serve as a liaison to the Information Technology Infrastructure group, as I did. This role did not exist at the start of our project, but was a best practice we learned and implemented. When we held regular meetings and adopting a single point of contact methodology, it optimized the communications between the teams about design needs and monitoring the progress in implementing them.

Next, we confronted our third challenge, which consisted of determining the antagonists in our story, that is the characters and/or environment that would play the role of cyber threat actors in these Capstone exercises. To recap, our main character, our protagonist, would encounter obstacles in achieving the goal, and it would be the antagonist, either person and/or environment, that would provide those obstacles. The question was which antagonist would be best for our story.

As we discussed, the lab exercises and the Capstone exercises embedded our learners as the protagonist, taking the central role in the roleplaying scenarios. We also knew that the political sensitivities of real-world customers required us to fabricate the settings and actors that drive our drama. This means that the learner's role as an employee of a national Security Operations Center (SOC) would have to be set in a fake country and that our learner would be pitted against fabricated enemies.

My early notes indicated that the Subject Matter Experts and I had an idea for focusing the fundamental Capstone exercise around a fictional public university. But since a public university was too large an organization for the fundamentals Capstone exercise, we narrowed the setting to something more manageable, and decided on creating a research-oriented department involved in cutting-edge medical device technology. Good, but where's the drama and inherent conflict in that? Who would oppose such a research department? Why? To get to the heart of these answers, we needed to take a step back and flesh out this fictitious world setting a bit more.

Through a series of brainstorming sessions, the Subject Matter Experts and I identified the characteristics of a respectable fabricated country, which here we refer to with the pseudonym of Country P, which served as the home to our main character's Security Operations Center. Country P was also where this fictional public university resided, and would be university department where the learner would map the computer network at the heart of our scenario.

We decided that Country P would be a first-world county with a strong economy founded on manufacturing, but developing a robust high-tech sector as well. By contrast, we decided that a good antagonist working against Country P would be a threat actor from a neighboring, rival country, in this case dubbed Country M. However, since there would often be more than one threat actor at work in cybersecurity, we decided to create another antagonist group, one not directly associated with any nation. We agreed that the rise in activists who used hacking to further their agendas, known in cybersecurity as hacktivists, would be a good third-party entity to serve as an antagonist against our learners in Country P. We dubbed this independent hacktivist organization Group V.

This was a strong start, as we now saw the outlines of potential conflict and dramatic tension. But what we were missing here were the details that defined the motivations of these antagonists opposing our main character protagonist. What kind of government does Country P employ? What are the economic and cyber capabilities of Country M? Who does Group V align themselves with?

I realized that a more formalized structure for collecting this background information is needed. In fact, I needed to create a document that would both capture this background on an entity, and this same document would be distributed to the learners as an artifact explaining the actors in the scenario. Such an artifact could also add realism and engagement, but had to balance providing enough information without giving too much.

First, I designed a template for this document that I called a backgrounder. I created a Country Backgrounder template for the likes of Country P and M to capture their socio-political and economic details. I searched for a standard set of attributes to consider, and found a public site that proved an indispensable resource: *the CIA World Factbook.*

I would highly recommend this site to anyone looking to create fictional countries, or to research existing ones in our world. While it offered a very comprehensive interface, I found it particularly helpful when I implemented the search as follows:

1. Begin by selecting a country to review from the dropdown menu on the homepage
2. Then, expand a section, like Economy
3. Choose a desired attribute, such as Industries or Import – Commodities
4. Select the icon across from the attribute name
5. This provides a field listing for that attribute and a full list of different countries for comparison

However, I must stress that if you were creating a fictional setting, never copy most of a single country's attributes completely. Instead, I found that when I mixed the attributes from different real-world countries together, the resulting fictional country felt more realistic and unique.

For example, in the background for Country P, we decided on a political mix of monarchy and democracy, perhaps more similar to the United Kingdom than the United States of America. But Country P's monarchy was still distinct from the UK's, as the king of Country P had reserved certain political powers. The backgrounder document also provided helpful information that could be used in scenario activities. It also conveyed subtle facts that added to the realism of the fake country, such as a fabricated flag, motto, and history. It also provided other details that not only added depth, such as allies and enemies in the region, but these details often provided hints and connections to future Capstone exercises.

Next, I designed a corresponding Actor Backgrounder template for the non-governmental entities. Using this backgrounder document, we fleshed out the information about the fictional university department in the scenario. For example, in this scenario we created a made-up engineering discipline involving nanotechnology, involving microscopic machines that can be programmed. This background detailed the cutting edge work our fictional university department performed in Country P, the goals of their research into this technology, and its potential applications.

By embedding such details into the backgrounder document, we laid the needed exposition information describing the plot for the fundamental Capstone exercise. The background for the university department explained their work in biomedical applications, their critical need for Rare Earth Elements (REEs), and the department's close ties to the government of Country P—all of which proved key plot points as the drama unfolds.

Figure 5.

THE WORLD FACTBOOK

Please select a country to view ⌄

| ⌂ | ABOUT | REFERENCES | APPENDICES | FAQs | CONTACT | THE WORLD FACTBOOK ARCHIVE |

FIELD LISTING :: INDUSTRIES

This entry provides a rank ordering of industries starting with the largest by value of annual output.

COUNTRY	INDUSTRIES
Afghanistan	small-scale production of bricks, textiles, soap, furniture, shoes, fertilizer, apparel, food products, non-alcoholic beverages, mineral water, cement; handwoven carpets; natural gas, coal, copper
Albania	food; footwear, apparel and clothing; lumber, oil, cement, chemicals, mining, basic metals, hydropower
Algeria	petroleum, natural gas, light industries, mining, electrical, petrochemical, food processing
American Samoa	tuna canneries (largely supplied by foreign fishing vessels), handicrafts
Andorra	tourism (particularly skiing), banking, timber, furniture
Angola	petroleum; diamonds, iron ore, phosphates, feldspar, bauxite, uranium, and gold; cement; basic metal products; fish processing; food processing, brewing, tobacco products, sugar; textiles; ship repair
Anguilla	tourism, boat building, offshore financial services
Antigua and Barbuda	tourism, construction, light manufacturing (clothing, alcohol, household appliances)
Argentina	food processing, motor vehicles, consumer durables, textiles, chemicals and petrochemicals, printing, metallurgy, steel
Armenia	brandy, mining, diamond processing, metal-cutting machine tools, forging and pressing machines, electric motors, knitted wear, hosiery, shoes, silk fabric, chemicals, trucks, instruments, microelectronics, jewelry, software, food processing
Aruba	tourism, petroleum transshipment facilities, banking
Australia	mining, industrial and transportation equipment, food processing, chemicals, steel
Austria	construction, machinery, vehicles and parts, food, metals, chemicals, lumber and paper, electronics, tourism
Azerbaijan	petroleum and petroleum products, natural gas, oilfield equipment; steel, iron ore; cement; chemicals and petrochemicals; textiles
Bahamas, The	tourism, banking, oil bunkering, maritime industries, transshipment and logistics, salt, aragonite, pharmaceuticals
Bahrain	petroleum processing and refining, aluminum smelting, iron pelletization, fertilizers, Islamic and offshore banking, insurance, ship repairing, tourism
Bangladesh	jute, cotton, garments, paper, leather, fertilizer, iron and steel, cement, petroleum products, tobacco, pharmaceuticals, ceramics, tea, salt, sugar, edible oils, soap and detergent, fabricated metal products, electricity, natural gas

In addition, we provided the learners with backgrounder documents on the potential threat actors relevant to this scenario, namely the neighboring rival of Country M, who used state-sponsored cyberattacks in order to achieve economic and political advantage. Simultaneously, Group V, the anonymous hacktivist group, stole unverified, but unfavorable information and then had it posted through another actor whose website was known for posting such leaked information. All of this was intriguing enough, but in order to enhance the realism and engagement, we designed the backgrounder document to appear like an official brief on the country or entity, and even enlisted the aid of a Graphic Artist to help craft unique country flags and logos for each actor.

These little details added much needed realism to the culture of these actors. And soon, even the Subject Matter Expert got into the act. Some wove the world setting and mythos into small activities and puzzles posed to the learners outside of the Capstone exercises. This not only further engaged the learners, but also continued to build on the world setting used in later Capstone exercises.

It wasn't long before we realize that this growing world setting needed a literal map that depicted how all these fictional countries related to one another. With the help of another Graphic Artist, we created a political map showing country boundaries and major cities overlaid onto a geographical map depicting important terrain such as mountains, rivers, and bodies of water.

I would like to advise anyone designing such a map to never underestimate how geographical and topological features—such as coastlines, mountains, lakes and rivers—can often dictate many of a country's and/or state's political borders. I found that using this organic approach provided a more natural and realistic layout.

However, while this map was made available as a resource for learners who desired a big picture, it was not presented up front to avoid overloading the learners with information. In fact, the sequence used to present the artifacts was quite important. In the fundamentals Capstone exercise, the two backgrounder documents on Country P and the university department were presented first, starting the plot of the training scenario's story, and providing the introductory exposition information to this fictional world.

Then we confronted the learner with their first challenge. Returning to the Story-based Learning model, we have moved past the beginning, where our conflict and setting converge to drive the plot forward. As the model suggested we should provide a first challenge and confrontation, which was actually an evaluation of the learner. Even if the scenario is structured where the learner observed the action through a separate designated character (remember our discussion of point of view for our main character), this evaluation was where the learner would be asked to control of the situation and decide what actions the main character should take. This way, it is always the learner that is evaluated on the knowledge and/or skills they have acquired.

In this case, the initial evaluation involved an important learning objective we determined back in our analysis: creating a map of a computer network, specifically the one for the university department in Country P. The learner practices this activity before during a module lab exercise, providing the required deliberate practice and immediate feedback that helped the learner succeed. Therefore, it was reasonable to expect the learner to meet this first Capstone exercise challenge, grow through the eustress and turn that positive stress into success and moving on to the next confrontation in the story.

As seen in the Story-based Learning model, there could be many cycles of confrontation, which has been denoted in the model as "Rinse and Repeat." This means that each time a learner encountered a confrontation, they need to be reset the learners before they attempt the failed confrontation again, and ensure a proper debrief or transition before moving onto the next confrontation. In the case of the Capstone exercises, a series of confrontations propelled the learner through the story as they also demonstrated mastery of the required knowledge and skills.

But how did we know that the learner successfully answered the confrontation questions, and completed the tasks that were set before them? In a complex exercise like the Capstone, we found there could be different interpretations of the information, such that different answers could also be partially correct. Therefore, we created a checklist answer sheet for the Instructors they would use to grade the learner's work. We detailed different point values for each part of the activity, and provided guidelines for Instructors for offering partial credit based on whether the Instructor felt the learner's work demonstrated the proper understanding of the problem, despite making small errors.

Therefore, after the initial confrontation the plot continued and we introduced the backgrounder documents for Country M, the rival neighbor of Country P, and Group V, the hacktivist group stealing secrets to further its own agenda. This background information served to set up the next confrontation and evaluation, where the learner had to identify potential threat actors (antagonists) and their motives in opposing Country P. To do this we created artifacts that displayed the increasing conflict in the form of imaginary news articles describing the increased tensions between Country P and Country M due to public accusations coupled with economic and political posturing.

Another artifact we provided was two blog posts by Group V, the first one described a leaked document from the university department in Country P, which painted a disturbing picture of what their new technology could be used for, while the second artifact turned the tables on Country M, describing embarrassing leaked emails. We wanted to make it clear that Group V was an agent of chaos, with no clear allegiance to any one country, but only to their misguided agenda of exposing "inconvenient truths."

This set the stage for the learner to confront their next evaluation in interpreting these artifacts and answering questions about potential threat actors and motives. This part of the Capstone exercise aligned with the goal of instilling a cybersecurity professional mindset in the learner, and we used artifacts like the news and blog postings to lend it more realism.

As indicated by the Story-based Learning model, this confrontation/evaluation cycle continues, as the protagonist, as well as our learner playing the main character, experience dynamic change and growth. Meanwhile, the story arc continues with further rising tensions and increased stakes for our protagonist. The next Capstone exercise activity catapulted the learners into the middle of an investigation of a cyber incident involving the stolen documents mentioned in the blog post artifact, but with the realization that the document's content had been altered by on of Country P's enemies before it was posted.

The learner was asked to continue the role as a member of the national Security Operations Center for Country P and set the task of analyzing a series of network activity log files. The log files provide a historical timeline of who did what on the network and are an important element in the investigation of the intrusion of how the documents were stolen, and by whom.

This led to the dramatic climax of our story for the fundamental Capstone exercise. As illustrated in the Story-based Learning model, the learner, as our main character protagonist, must transcend this final challenge and truly think like a cybersecurity professional. The participant had to utilize all acquired skills so far in order to answer key questions about what happened and offer remediation recommendations.

After the climax, the Instructor led the learners through the falling action phased of the story arc. They fulfilled this aspect of the Story-based Learning model by conducting a debrief discussion where we provided the resolution of the story and some closure by revealing some new evidence that showed what really happened. In this case, we created a final artifact in the form of a chat log revealing the archived messages between a graduate student in the university department and an unknown outside entity.

What happened was what is known as "phishing" a social engineering attack where someone outside the network entices someone inside to reveal information or provide access. So, the chat log showed that the graduate student was looking for some hardware and this unknown person, who was secretly working for the hacktivist organization Group V, enticed the grad student to log onto a fake website which captured his university login credentials. Using a password and access this outsider stole the documents, altered them, and had them posted on the Internet.

It was using this kind of rich narrative, built through dramatic conflict and a tension-filled setting, that we provided the engaging deliberate practice the learner needed to reinforce knowledge and skills while moving on to testing and certification. And this was the approach we followed in subsequent Capstone exercises.

For example, in the intermediate Capstone exercise, I built upon the setting first established in the fundamental Capstone exercise, by expanding the word and new actors. Expanding the world involved introducing Country J, as well as a new entity, Company T, which were actually named in the backgrounder documents as ideas for further growth of the story. Such attention to continuity and connection through the various Capstone exercises increased both their realism and engagement.

For instance, though Company T was mentioned only by name as a business partner for both Country P and their rival Country M in the foundational Capstone. Now in the intermediate Capstone, Company T plays a central role in the new story arc. We used the same process described earlier in this case study to flesh out this company, as well as the new Country J, and other needed actors to tell our story.

Once again our learners are the protagonists, our main characters assuming the role of a cybersecurity employee for Company T. This time the intriguing story involved typical computer network audits revealing a trail of deceit, insider threats, and even possible sabotage of Country P's water infrastructure through a potentially dangerous software vulnerability introduced by a subcontractor based in rival Country M, but hired by Company T.

All of this played out amidst the further escalation in rhetoric and actions between Country P and Country M, as captured in more news artifacts we created. The learners soon found out that Company T had contracts with both Country P and Country M, putting it in an awkward situation. And to make matters worse, we introduced a new hacking group, Group S, who is accused of performing recent cyberattacks on behalf of its close ally, the spy agency of Country M.

Again, we provided the evidence for this story again through artifacts, backgrounder documents, news articles, and other items electronically distributed to the learners. However, this time, we were able to utilize the computer network environments created by the Information Technology Infrastructure team so the learners could use real cybersecurity applications on virtual simulated networks during the intermediate course and its Capstone exercise.

The purpose of the depth and complexity of a rich narrative and world setting was to offer a highly engaging environment for the learner. And it proved quite successful. However, it was also an administrative nightmare for the Instructional Systems Designers to remember all of these narrative details, especially when designing courses in addition to the Capstone exercise.

My recommendation was to suggest one person serving as a "storyrunner," someone responsible for the tracking the continuity and consulting with Instructional Systems Designers and Subject Matter Experts on world setting questions as new material is developed. In our case, I assumed the role of storyrunner, which eventually became an official role, where the storyrunner Instructional Systems Designer was dedicated solely to designing the Capstone exercise, as well as integrating the story elements throughout the module content.

We also decided that another important lesson learned was to work on the key objectives for the Capstone exercise before development of the corresponding module content. This tightened the alignment of lab exercises with the Capstone exercise and avoided potential rework.

In closing, I cannot emphasize enough the importance of documenting details about the world setting. It was difficult for a single person to memorize all the nuances of countries, entities, and their intricate interactions. Furthermore, due to Human Resource staffing needs, the storyrunner for development of one phase of the curriculum may not be available for another, which necessitated a handoff to another Instructional Systems Designer. I recommended creating a document, or series of documents, which cataloged the various aspects of the world setting, especially those items that were important in the initial design decisions, but were not deemed relevant to provide to the learners.

As I worked through the designs of these complex scenarios, the outline of the Story-based Learning model continued to evolve and expand. What I discovered was that this model offered an organized and repeatable process that anyone can use to maximize character development to best serve the story, creating conflict that increased tension, and settings that propelled the narrative. Together, this can create engaging scenario stories that foster deliberate practice, learning to increased performance.

REFERENCES

Bower, G., & Clark, M. (1969). Narrative stories as mediators for serial learning. *Psychonomic Science*, *15*(4), 181–182. doi:10.3758/BF03332778

Carini, R. M., Kuh, G. D., & Klein, S. P. (2006). Student engagement and student learning: Testing the linkages. *Research in Higher Education*, *47*(1), 1–32. doi:10.100711162-005-8150-9

Ericsson, K. A., Krampe, R. T., & Tesch-Römer, C. (1993). The role of deliberate practice in the acquisition of expert performance. *Psychological Review*, *100*(3), 363–406. doi:10.1037/0033-295X.100.3.363

European Science Foundation. (2008). How mirror neurons allow us to learn and socialize by going through the motions in the head. *Science Daily*. Retrieved July 14, 2019 from https://www.sciencedaily.com/releases/2008/12/081219073047.htm

McGaghie, W., Issenberg, S., Cohen, E., Barsuk, J., & Wayne, D. (2011, June). Does simulation-based medical education with deliberate practice yield better results than traditional clinical education? A meta-analytic comparative review of the evidence. *Academic Medicine*, *86*(6), 706–711. doi:10.1097/ACM.0b013e318217e119 PMID:21512370

McQuiggan, S. W., Rowe, J. P., Lee, S., & Lester, J. C. (2008). Story-based learning: the impact of narrative on learning experiences and outcomes. In B. P. Woolf, E. Aïmeur, R. Nkambou, & S. Lajoie (Eds.), Lecture Notes in Computer Science: Vol. 5091. *Intelligent Tutoring Systems. ITS 2008*. Berlin: Springer. doi:10.1007/978-3-540-69132-7_56

Paulus, T. M., Horvitz, B., & Shi, M. (2006). 'Isn't it just like our situation?' Engagement and learning in an online story-based environment. *Education Tech Research*, *54*(4), 355–385. doi:10.100711423-006-9604-2

Ramachandran, V. S. (2000, June 29). Mirror neurons and imitation learning as the driving force behind "the great leap forward" in human evolution. *Edge Foundation, The Third Culture*. Retrieved July 14, 2019. https://www.edge.org/conversation/mirror-neurons-and-imitation-learning-as-the-driving-force-behind-the-great-leap-forward-in-human-evolution

Rowe, J., Shores, L., Mott, B., & Lester, J. (2011). Integrating learning, problem solving, and engagement in narrative-centered learning environments. *International Journal of Artificial Intelligence in Education, 21*(1-2), 115–133.

Zadelhoff, M. (2017). Cybersecurity has a serious talent shortage. Here's how to fix it. *Harvard Business Review, 5*. https://hbr.org/2017/05/cybersecurity-has-a-serious-talent-shortage-heres-how-to-fix-it

Zak, P. (2014). Why Your Brain Loves Good Storytelling. *Harvard Business Review, 10*. https://hbr.org/2014/10/why-your-brain-loves-good-storytelling

KEY TERMS AND DEFINITIONS

Capstone Exercise: A comprehensive set of scenario activities aligned to objectives designed to reinforce knowledge and skills at the end of a sequence of training.

Cybersecurity: Protecting digital networks and systems from unauthorized usage or disruption.

Deliberate Practice: The purposeful training experiences that reinforce motor and/or cognitive skills in an effort toward improving performance.

Engagement: The state of being mentally and/or emotionally invested in an event or occurrence.

Eustress: Physical or cognitive stress that is perceived as positive and beneficial, resulting in improved performance.

Scenario: A sequence of events taking place in a designed location involving predetermined characters, often engaged in a narrative structure.

Story-Based Learning: A systematic, learner-focused process for using narrative structures to increase engagement and foster deliberate practice.

Technology: Any capability offered someone by the practical application of knowledge to achieve an objective, or use of such capability embedded in something, such as a machine.

This research was previously published in Cases on Performance Improvement Innovation; pages 208-227, copyright year 2020 by Business Science Reference (an imprint of IGI Global).

APPENDIX: QUESTIONS

1. What are some benefits to utilizing a Story-based Learning approach for delivering scenario-based content and exercises? What are some possible negative in using this approach?
2. How does engagement translate into improved performance?
3. Can you provide some examples of how deliberate practice improved your performance?
4. What were some of the lessons learned conveyed in the case study? How could they prove helpful in your workplace?

Chapter 20
A Collaborative Cybersecurity Education Program

Teemu J. Tokola
University of Oulu, Finland

Thomas Schaberreiter
University of Vienna, Austria

Gerald Quirchmayr
University of Vienna, Austria

Ludwig Englbrecht
https://orcid.org/0000-0002-8546-3017
University of Regensburg, Germany

Günther Pernul
University of Regensburg, Germany

Sokratis K. Katsikas
https://orcid.org/0000-0003-2966-9683
Norwegian University of Science and Technology, Norway & Open University of Cyprus, Cyprus

Bart Preneel
Katholieke Universiteit Leuven, Belgium & imec, Belgium

Qiang Tang
Luxembourg Institute of Science and Technology, Luxembourg

ABSTRACT

This chapter presents an implementation of a cybersecurity education program. The program aims to address some issues identified in current cybersecurity teaching in higher education on a European level, like the fragmentation of cybersecurity expertise or resource shortage, resulting in few higher education institutions to offer full degree programs. As a result of the Erasmus+ strategic partnership project SecTech, the program tries to overcome those issues by introducing collaborative development to cybersecurity education. SecTech lays the foundations for a collaborative education program, like the definition of a clear content, module and delivery structure, and the appropriate tool support to facilitate collaboration and content reuse. Additional effort is required to achieve long-term success, including the creation of a community that drives the content creation and maintenance, as well as an independent governance structure to steer the project in the long-term. While the project focuses on European collaboration, a global community is envisioned.

DOI: 10.4018/978-1-6684-3554-0.ch020

THE NEED FOR COLLABORATIVE CYBERSECURITY EDUCATION

Given the mounting cyber threat levels Europe is faced with, a coordinated cybersecurity education effort becomes more urgent than ever. The malware waves hitting Europe in May 2017 and recent Europol reports (European Union Agency for Law Enforcement Cooperation (Europol), 2017) give a clear warning of the dangers lying ahead, ranging from criminal activities to often state sponsored theft of intellectual property and a rising possibility of cyber sabotage. It is against this background that building on the EU cybersecurity strategy (European Commission and High Representative of the European Union for Foreign Affairs and Security Policy, 2013), new legislation aimed at strengthening privacy protection (THE COUNCIL OF THE EUROPEAN UNION, 2016) – the General Data Protection Regulation (GDPR) - and securing IT-dependent critical infrastructures (THE EUROPEAN PARLIAMENT AND THE COUNCIL OF THE EUROPEAN UNION, 2016) – the directive on security of network and information systems (NIS) - was introduced. Both GDPR and NIS have come into effect in 2018. The obligations introduced by this legislation at European level have also increased the demand for cybersecurity experts in an already overstretched market. It is obvious that an increased supply of talent becomes an absolute necessity if Europe as a whole aspires to meet the high aims set in the legislation and in European and national cybersecurity strategies. However, a joint and well-coordinated European approach to education in this field is still missing. Given the variety and diversity of topics that need to be covered, comprising such diverse areas as information and communications technology, management and organization, law, economics, sociology, criminology and psychological issues, it becomes painstakingly clear that a wide range of expertise needs to be accessed to create a thorough curriculum. That is one major reason for comprehensive academic programs on cybersecurity and privacy being a rare exception.

In line with those developments the Erasmus+ strategic partnership project SecTech was formed by seven European higher education institutions (KU Leuven, Luxembourg Institute of Science and Technology, Norwegian University of Science and Technology, University of Oulu, University of Plymouth, University of Regensburg, and University of Vienna) to collaboratively develop a European cybersecurity curriculum. The core motivation of the Erasmus+ SecTech project is to provide a seed curriculum including ready to use on-line teaching materials to give European academic institutions a much better starting point for implementing and delivering a cybersecurity education program, either on their own or in cooperation with other institutions. The primary contributions this project is aimed at supporting are the integration of knowledge that is currently available across Europe, but today is hardly combined and far from being integrated, the introduction of a curriculum template, the provision of seed on-line course material that can serve as a core and finally the establishment of an on-line repository and cooperation platform that can serve as basis for a Europe wide joint educational effort. As the free sharing of the developed course materials is expected to have an essential impact, established open standards and systems such as Moodle and SCORM will form the technological basis.

With information and cybersecurity experts becoming an increasingly scarce resource, the pooling and sharing of teaching materials at a European level is expected to have a significant impact on enabling in a first step the participating universities and in a following expansion phase other tertiary level institutions to much easier offer credible cybersecurity degree programs and to incorporate modules or parts of modules in existing computer science and information systems programs. While in the course of the project we have not given specific focus on determining the advantages of such a curriculum for learners, one of the most obvious advantages is a more complete learning experience due to more extensive material and teaching expertise that would not be available at partner institutions without a collaborative curriculum.

The Erasmus+ SecTech project is therefore aimed at helping to provide a practicable way of countering the current shortage of teaching expertise in a field that is becoming strategic for the European economy and society through a Europe wide collaborative development and delivery approach. Given the current lack of experts, lecturers and the high cost of maintaining teaching resources, the integrative approach demonstrated by this project can serve as a basis for more effectively and efficiently developing the cybersecurity skills so urgently needed in the European economy. Having an on-line shareable, resource-backed European cybersecurity curriculum can consequently offer a way to finally change the situation in favor of substantially raising the levels of cybersecurity and privacy that can be offered, thereby making a significant contribution to reaching the goals laid out by the recent European legislation. In the long-term, and taking into account the global nature of cyberspace, the project partners see the work on a collaborative cybersecurity curriculum as a global challenge that should be driven by a global community.

CYBERSECURITY EDUCATION AS A MULTI-DISCIPLINARY CHALLENGE

Cybersecurity is an extremely complex problem that requires domain knowledge from many disciplines to allow cybersecurity experts and professionals to fully understand the dangers of cyberspace and to be able to develop and implement protection strategies for several use cases, for example, to provide cybersecurity in the personal, organizational or critical infrastructure context. With the dynamic and quickly evolving cybersecurity threat landscape as well as the multitude of application domains in mind, the challenge for cybersecurity education is to allow learners to develop sophisticated cybersecurity skills based on a multi-disciplinary understanding of the problem domain that is also able to keep up with ever-changing cybersecurity developments. The European Cyber Security Organisation (ECSO) highlights this issue and identifies in a recent position paper (European Cyber Security Organisation (ECSO), 2018) that the lack of sufficiently trained IT security specialists is a European-wide problem and highlights the need for a strong multi-disciplinary approach towards cybersecurity.

Besides the multi-disciplinary angle, a second requirement relating to curriculum development that specifically relates to the collaborative aspect of the SecTech project is that a curriculum does not only need to be multi-disciplinary by design, but also needs to be able to accommodate the different focus areas of education institutions and degree programs at those institutions, since the developed content should be reusable. While the areas that need to be covered may be similar, the focus on specific topics may shift depending if the degree program is, for example, technically or organizationally focused.

The goal of the SecTech curriculum is to rely on existing templates and guidelines used for the development of cybersecurity education programs that would fulfil the requirements identified above. To achieve this, various industry related standards and other cybersecurity curricula have been examined. At the first stage *CS2013*, the Computer Science Curricula 2013: Curriculum Guidelines for Undergraduate Degree Programs in Computer Science (Association for Computing Machinery (ACM) and IEEE Computer Society, 2013) and *IT2017*, the Information Technology Curricula 2017: Curriculum Guidelines for Baccalaureate Degree Programs in Information Technology (Association for Computing Machinery (ACM) and IEEE Computer Society, 2017) have been reviewed. In *CS2013* a curriculum guideline for undergraduate degree programs in computer science is presented. Within these guidelines the Body of

Knowledge is organized by 18 Knowledge Areas. Especially the Knowledge Area "Information Assurance and Security (IAS)" covers the field computer and network security and has been added due the high demand in this area. It is noteworthy that a relatively broad oriented curriculum for Computer Science already includes cybersecurity as an important part of the curriculum. The *IT2017* curriculum guidelines presents a framework which groups competencies in essential and supplemental IT domains. Thereby a specific cybersecurity domain is included as an essential IT domain and reaffirms the importance of cybersecurity in undergraduate degree programs.

Also the U.S. National Initiative for Cybersecurity Education (NICE) Cybersecurity Workforce Framework (Santos, 2016), the Guide to the Systems Engineering Body of Knowledge (Guide to the Systems Engineering Body of Knowledge (SEBok) v.1.9, 2018) and various national courses and degree programs focusing on IT and cybersecurity have been examined. While the above-mentioned standards and guidelines provide excellent recommendations for the contexts they were designed for, none of them provided adequate solutions to the requirements the project has identified for SecTech. The curriculum guidelines that have been selected as the template for the SecTech collaborative cybersecurity curriculum are the 2017 cybersecurity curricular guidelines (CSEC2017) (ACM, IEEE, AIS, IFIP, 2017), jointly developed by ACM, IEEE, the Association for Information Systems Special Interest Group on Security (AIS SIGSEC) and the International Federation for Information Processing Technical Committee on Information Security Education (IFIP).

As detailed in the previous chapter, the structure of CSEC2017 supports to a large extend the ideas of a multi-disciplinary and collaborative cybersecurity education program. The curriculum is grouped around a variety of knowledge areas and allows to look at those knowledge areas with both an institutional lens as well as a disciplinary lens in order to identify the concrete topics that are relevant for the degree program in a specific institution or profession and relate and integrate to the specific degree program covered at this institution. Specifically, this property was recognized as a key factor for the creation of a cybersecurity curriculum within the SecTech project. The CSEC2017 was developed to support academic institutions in creating their own cybersecurity curricula. The guideline represents a flexible model for designing a curriculum, and this flexibility enables users to develop a cybersecurity program tailored to their institution type. Different knowledge backgrounds of learners will be considered. For example, the thought model of CSEC2017 offers the possibility to look at the learning content from different perspectives and thereby to look at it in a different granular depth. Another aim of the CSEC2017 is to provide a guideline that allows IT security personnel to be as broadly and diversely specialized as possible.

For the intended development of a multi-disciplinary and flexible cybersecurity curriculum through the SecTech project, these knowledge areas could be used for the practical implementation of a curriculum for higher education. The knowledge areas specified in CSEC2017 are explained in Table 1. These knowledge areas were designed with a high flexibility in their adoption in mind. Depending on the institutional lens, disciplinary lens and topics, these knowledge areas allow to define the content of a curriculum in such a way that security programs can be created for different purposes. These could be programs designed for, amongst others, university degrees, polytechnic degrees, professional certifications. This feature was used for the development of the SecTech cybersecurity curriculum. For this purpose, the cybersecurity body of knowledge was determined by applying a mixed-disciplinary lens. The CSEC knowledge units (within the 8 knowledge areas) were evaluated by all SecTech project partners. The focus was on the development of a flexible and decentralized cybersecurity curriculum in which each partner can contribute its core competencies. However, just providing knowledge is not enough to equip students for real-life situations. It is an essential part of the ability to understand and adequately communicate information about cyber attacks and their defense within an organization. This is important to properly inform decision makers in the organization and to confirm the relevance for further initiatives in cybersecurity. This aspect of competence transfer was also taken into account in the development of the SecTech curriculum and has already been implemented through workshops organized by the project together with national partner organizations. The content developed within the project has been disseminated in lecture and workshop sessions to interested participants, ranging from university students to education professionals as well as industry and government representatives. The feedback from those workshops has in turn been used to further refine and develop the ideas of the SecTech curriculum and has strengthened the belief of the project partners that multi-disciplinarity is one of the core features of a modern cybersecurity curriculum.

The development of teaching programs in the field of cybersecurity has also found to be of great relevance by partner organizations on a national and international level. The goal is not only to combat the lack of trained employees in cybersecurity, but also to take up the fight against cybercrime with well-educated students in cybersecurity. For this purpose, the SecTech project aims to bundle the competences of seven European partner universities and research centers in a multi-disciplinary cybersecurity curriculum. The analysis of best practices presented here have led to a close alignment of the SecTech curriculum with the CSEC2017 guidelines. The knowledge areas Data Security, Software Security, Component Security, Connection Security, System Security, Human Security, Organizational Security and Societal Security have been identified and adopted as relevant topics. In addition to that the institutional lenses and the disciplinary lenses from the CSEC2017 guidelines provide a decisive advantage for the development of a curriculum that creates a multi-disciplinary understanding of cybersecurity.

DELIVERY STRATEGY

The need for and the benefit of high-quality European and international curricula is clear. The success of individual efforts, however, is not guaranteed. The quality of the material produced is certainly one measure of success, but the impact of the produced material and curriculum has definite measures: the amount of time saved in individual organizations thanks to the high-quality material, the improvement of teaching material quality and width of the topics covered, and most importantly the reach of the material across countries, institutions, students and time.

This impact is realized by the success of the curriculum delivery effort: the adoption of the curriculum and materials in different institutions, the engagement of the target audience, the future participation of current and new contributors of material and all similar measures of success in an international curriculum project are consequences of well-executed delivery activities.

An international collaboration on developing teaching materials on any subject matter that is evolving at a rapid pace poses a number of important challenges and risks. The risk scenarios themselves are quite clear: at the time of delivery, the material developed could lack depth or relevance, it might not reach the target audiences or it could fail to integrate into teaching organizations' curricula, and further, the risk exists that the material is not sufficiently maintained and loses relevance too quickly over the years, it is abandoned more than adopted and the invested effort ultimately is not worth the impact produced. Accounting for these risks in the content delivery is a key part of a curriculum process. If these are the risks, then what are the key areas in which to succeed and to counteract these risks? The key delivery activities are:

- Promoting adoption
- Retaining internal interest
- Retaining external interest

Table 1. The CSEC2017 knowledge areas

Knowledge Area	Description
Data Security	The knowledge area Data Security focuses on the protection of information processed and stored within information systems. In order to impart sufficient skills in this area, it is important that the application of mathematical and analytical algorithms is taught.
Software Security	Software Security is aimed at the development and the application of secure software. An essential focus is the protection of the information to be processed by an IT system. Fundamental aspects of secure software development are taught to the students. The different phases of software development (design, implementation, test, deployment and maintenance) with regard to security measures are considered.
Component Security	Not only the security of the software in use, but also the used hardware, is an important aspect for the development of a secure system. The knowledge area component security looks at the phases design, procurement, testing, analysis and maintenance within the life cycle of hardware components that are used in larger systems. The security-relevant preconditions and precautions of the supply chain are thereby considered.
Connection Security	Another important area of cybersecurity knowledge is connection security. The transmission of data via physical and logical connections needs to be studied. The intention of this area is to provide a profound basic knowledge in network technology and in communication between IT systems in order to manage risks along the transmission path.
System Security	The combination of individual components to build a larger system involves various IT security risks. The knowledge area system security provides a holistic view of the connected components and subsystems. Students are required to understand interactions and dependencies between the system components to identify security issues and to provide adequate countermeasures.
Human Security	The protection of an individual's personal data, both in private and professional environments, is covered by the knowledge area human security. This also includes the behavior of people in situations that are relevant to IT security, like for example security awareness or social engineering.
Organizational Security	Both public and private organizations can be a preferred target for cyber criminals. This may not only cause economic loss, it may also affect government functions. The knowledge area organizational security aims to impart competencies in the management of risks and to ensure their functionality.
Societal Security	The continuous integration of information systems into our daily lives inevitably involves the consideration of IT security aspects. Existing and absent protective mechanisms can have an influence on our society. The knowledge area societal security considers cybercrime, legislation, ethics, policy and privacy.

For promoting adoption of curricula and their modules, the curriculum process needs to have definitive answers to the question of why institutions should adopt the curriculum, provide effortless way of incorporating parts of the curriculum into the institutions own teaching activities and to make it effortless and enticing for teachers to use the materials and tools provided. Quality of the material and tools produced, credibility of the contributing community, compatibility with local curriculum features and international reference curricula all contribute to this.

While it can be said that development consortia in itself represent a group of stakeholders in the success of curriculum projects, both the initial contributing partners and future participants are asked for two key resources, time and effort, and expending these requires commitment to the success of the curriculum process. After all, once materials and curriculum details have been created, they need to be regularly maintained to retain the relevance and the interest in the material. Consequently, the contributing community needs to have the answers for the following questions: why should individual contributors keep their materials or the curriculum as a whole updated and why should new contributors join the community? In short, there needs to be benefits to the time and effort spent: the direct benefit of having the materials from other contributors available, the pull of the large external audience that have adopted the material and of course the societal impact of a successful campaign.

Similarly, retaining the interest of external organizations that have adopted the curriculum or parts thereof is a challenge with a definite set of questions to be answered. Why should organizations continue to use the material or adopt new parts? Why should new institutions start using the material provided? Does the curriculum cover enough topics to be relevant and interesting? Institutions tend to adopt new curricula, new course and module structures, new technological tools and implement new study programs - will the material and curriculum be a hindrance or even a benefit at that point? Will it easily live through these different types of changes?

In many ways the internal and external interest work in tandem: an external interest in the material will create the audience and consequently the demand for internal activities and keep the internal community motivated to contribute, and similarly a strong internal community of motivated, active domain experts and a good coverage of the curriculum will promote external interest and adoption of the material.

Consequently, a strong curriculum project will have a clear plan for promoting both adoption, internal and external interest, and a good understanding on the internal and external status of the project. Internally, the project needs to measure the dedication and activity of contributors, recruit new ones and keep existing ones active, and externally, the project needs to be able to measure the reach of the curriculum, and improve this reach to become relevant in the eyes of both contributors, funding organizations and students.

The SecTech project has a strong starting point for this work: the consortium represents a strong collection of excellent contributors with the areas of expertise and provided modules covering a wide area of reference curricula. The project is also working on creating a suitable representation between the course contents and the ACM reference curriculum: Figure 1 shows a draft version of how mapping between courses and curriculum topics are collected into an overview of how well different knowledge units of the reference curriculum are covered by the courses. Once the project concludes with all the planned modules ready, with the support of the dedicated consortium, the SecTech curriculum has a good chance of attracting a large external interest and consequently create a beneficial, upward spiral of both internal and external interest and dedication to the project.

COLLABORATIVE DEVELOPMENT: TAPPING INTO EXISTING EXPERTISE DISTRIBUTED ACROSS EUROPE

As pointed out in the ECSO position paper on the gaps in European cyber education and training (European Cyber Security Organisation (ECSO), 2018), cybersecurity education needs to be interdisciplinary covering a broad range of aspects well beyond purely technical ones. If one starts from the academic von Humboldt model of education based on research, one concludes that cybersecurity education should be based on large interdisciplinary research groups that cover all relevant aspects of cybersecurity. In very few universities such research teams are available. Even if one considers only the technical dimensions, there are currently a handful universities in Europe that cover all aspects of cybersecurity technology research. If one considers topics beyond core technical expertise such as usability of security, cybersecurity economics or organizational aspects of cybersecurity, the number of research groups in Europe is rather small.

Figure 1. Mapping of course contents to reference curriculum topics (upper table) and the derived overview of how well the knowledge units of the reference curriculum are covered by the developed courses (lower table).

Knowledge area	Knowledge unit	Topic	S	5	4	3	2	1	Introduction to cy 2	Introduction to C 1	Cryptography 2 1	Introduction to P 1	Privacy 2
Data Security	Secure Communication Protocols	Data link layer	0.00	0	0	0	0	0					
Data Security	Cryptanalysis	Classical attacks	0.25	0	0	1	0	0					
Data Security	Cryptanalysis	Side-channel attacks	0.50	0	0	2	0	0					
Data Security	Cryptanalysis	Attacks against private- key ciphers	0.00	0	0	0	0	0					
Data Security	Cryptanalysis	Attacks against public- key ciphers	0.00	0	0	0	0	0					
Data Security	Cryptanalysis	Algorithms for solving the Discrete Log Problem	0.00	0	0	0	0	0					
Data Security	Cryptanalysis	Attacks on RSA	0.00	0	0	0	0	0					
Data Security	Data Privacy	Overview	1.00	0	0	4	0	0					
Data Security	Information Storage Security	Disk and file encryption	0.25	0	0	1	0	0					
Data Security	Information Storage Security	Data erasure	0.00	0	0	0	0	0					
Data Security	Information Storage Security	Data masking	0.00	0	0	0	0	0					
Data Security	Information Storage Security	Database security											
Data Security	Information Storage Security	Data security law											
Software Security	Fundamental Principles	Least privilege											
Software Security	Fundamental Principles	Fail-safe defaults											
Software Security	Fundamental Principles	Complete mediation											
Software Security	Fundamental Principles	Separation											
Software Security	Fundamental Principles	Minimize trust											
Software Security	Fundamental Principles	Economy of mechanism											
Software Security	Fundamental Principles	Minimize common mechanism											

Knowledge area	Knowledge unit	# of topics	Coverage	1 2 3 4 5 6 7 8 9 10
Cyber Security Basics	Introduction to Cyber Security	1	25%	
Data Security	Cryptography	6	2%	
Data Security	Digital Forensics	10	13%	
Data Security	Digital Forensics	10	13%	
Data Security	Data Integrity and Authentication	4	9%	
Data Security	Access Control	4	13%	
Data Security	Secure Communication Protocols	5	15%	
Data Security	Cryptanalysis	6	13%	
Data Security	Data Privacy	1	100%	
Software Security	Fundamental Principles	14	0%	
Software Security	Design	4	6%	
Software Security	Implementation	8	19%	
Software Security	Analysis and testing	4	50%	
Software Security	Deployment and maintenance	5	10%	
Software Security	Documentation	4	0%	
Software Security	Ethics	5	28%	
Component security	Component Design	6	3%	
Component security	Component Procurement	3	17%	
Component security	Component Testing	2	50%	
Component security	Component Reverse Engineering	3	29%	
Connection security	Physical Media	4	0%	
Connection security	Physical Interfaces and Connectors	3	8%	

A second aspect is that collaboration with industry is essential to develop strong cybersecurity education programs, as there are clearly strong benefits in bringing together an academic approach with practical experience from industry. For several topics such as designing and operating Security Operating Centers (SOCs), configuring complex identity management systems, Common Criteria certification or large-scale malware filtering, expertise is concentrated in industry; this means that industry input in the cybersecurity education, for example by inviting guest lecturers, is essential for any state-of-the art cybersecurity program. The same holds mutatis mutandis for governance related expertise, and in particular national cybersecurity policies.

A third dimension are cultural differences among EU member states, which are reflected in the education programs in Europe. Even if the Bologna process has resulted in more integration in terms of names of degrees and credit systems, the fundamental vision on academic education is still very different across Europe. As an example, France and Belgium still believe in a broad basis for the engineering Bachelor education based on mathematics and science, followed by specialization during the Master's degree, while in The Netherlands and Germany engineering students can select their specialty (in a few universities even cybersecurity or information security) from the first Bachelor year onwards. Even if the education system would be the same, there are still cultural differences between EU member states. These differences are translated in their approach to cybersecurity, such as how to manage risks or how to define privacy and identity. As an example, some European countries have mandatory identity cards, while others have optional identity cards or none at all; similarly, some countries have central registers collecting information on their citizens, while others believe in distributed databases with various level of interlinking. In spite of having a common regulation governing the protection of personal data (the GDPR), the way the governments collect information about citizens is very different, and this is also reflected on how industry processes data. Of course, these cultural differences affect the level of maturity of the EU member states in terms of cybersecurity awareness. This can be deduced from the gaps between the publication dates of the national cybersecurity strategies across the EU or in the budgets of government agencies concerned with cybersecurity.

All these aspects clearly point towards the need for academic collaboration at a European level, or even collaboration at an international level beyond Europe. First, collaboration between universities is the only way that the required multi-disciplinary expertise can be entered into the cybersecurity education programs: this is essential to cover the seven knowledge areas discussed in Table 1 at a sufficient level of depth. Second, for industry input to cybersecurity education collaboration at European level is also essential: some of the expertise is only present at a few large industry players; in particular for smaller countries, the required expertise may not be present in the national industry. While the cultural diversity in Europe presents challenges, it is also opening opportunities: tackling a multi-dimensional and complex problem such as cybersecurity can greatly benefit from experts with various educational background, viewpoints and approaches. Ideally, this cultural diversity is already presented during the education programs so that the cybersecurity experts are aware of the challenges and opportunities brought by this diversity.

There are of course other reasons why education in cybersecurity can strongly benefit from European collaborations. Cybersecurity is by definition a problem that does not stop at the border: it is a global challenge that can only be addressed based on strong international collaboration. Moreover, in view of the scarcity of expertise in cybersecurity, there are strong benefits from developing a cybersecurity workforce at European level that is trained both with an understanding of cultural differences and with a view that surpasses national borders. The clear path towards creating such a workforce is to start from close collaboration between the Universities with expertise in cybersecurity. By bringing together their research and education expertise, their industry networks, and their understanding of cultural issues, they can together develop a more global and integrated approach to cybersecurity education that they could never create on their own and build the basis for the community able to develop and maintain a collaborative cybersecurity education program in the long-term.

CONTENT MODEL AND MODULE STRUCTURE

Delivering content in a varied environment creates challenges on their own. Despite the ECTS and Bologna processes, the reality remains that individual countries, institutions, faculties and even departments inside faculties can have drastically different practices and cultures with regards to courses and teaching. There is significant room for variation: the amount of ECTS credits that individual courses should have, the real amount of work one ECTS should incur on the student, individuality of the students' effort, the type and difficulty of that work, the situation of individual subject matters on the 3-year bachelor studies, 1 or 2-year master studies or post-graduate studies, the grading of student activities, the distribution of time between lectures, exercises and individual work etc.

Eradication of these differences and standardization of teaching activities across nations might be a worthwhile goal or perhaps not, but certainly it is not the prerequisite for a curriculum project whose main aim is to improve the quality and impact of teaching materials of a specific discipline. As a result, curriculum projects need to take these differences into account in order to improve the adaptability of the curriculum. In order to be applicable to various environments, the project outcome needs to provide ready answers to the issue of what difficulties may arise, and how local teachers can easily adapt the material and justify the adaptation to themselves and to administration. As discussed before, external interest is key to the impact of the project and also for retaining the interest of internal contributors, and as adaptability is a key factor in increasing adaptation, the details related to adaptability should be thoroughly thought out. The project has identified following curricula properties that cater adaptability and content reusability:

- small granularity of modules
- separation of practical and theoretical work
- adjustability of grading activities
- strong connection with reference curricula
- applicability to different disciplines (multi-disciplinarity)

The ECTS credit system provides the opportunity of creating courses of many different sizes, with ideally same amount of workload, with one ECTS credit corresponding to 25 to 30 hours of work. How much students should be able to cover during that time, and how much prior knowledge is required in order to manage in that time, however, is obviously left up to the course organizers. Individual institutions and countries might have different practices regarding the course sizes: some might opt to have 3 ECTS courses as the standard, with 5 ECTS left for advanced courses and 7 or 8 ECTS for project courses, some others might have smaller, and some even offer larger courses of 10 ECTS. To make the curriculum adaptable, the curriculum should have a small granularity and separation of theory and practice in order to fit into different schemes: from sufficiently small modules, individual institutions can build cybersecurity courses of desired ECTS workload and with desired distribution of practical and theoretical content. On the contrary, if the curriculum project tries to essentially lock an answer by having bigger units and a set distribution of theory and practice, individual institutions might find it impossible to fit the courses into their structures and practices. Whereas one could argue that such rigidity should not belong to contemporary teaching, from the perspective of international curricula there is no need to force that argument.

Similarly, module content should not lock the grading activities: when adapting modules to local environments, institutions should have the benefit of using a similar basis for assessment, while retaining control over how individual assessments affect the final grade from any learning activities. With different priorities with regards to content and on the scale from theory to practice, the modules should permit giving different weights to different activities for the purpose of grading.

For planning local adaptation, another issue is matching module contents with the plans of local curriculum planners: while module descriptions obviously are important in helping local institutions to choose appropriate content to complement their local teaching activities, defining the relationship of the modules and courses with regards to reference curricula such as the ACM curriculum is a key activity in module planning. Adapting organizations need to be able to clearly understand the content relationships to any reference curricula that they are working with.

Working with an international body of possible adopters of curriculum contents and individual modules, and with cybersecurity being increasingly a concern in a growing number of fields, planning of an international curriculum and designing content modules can no longer be done from just, for example, the engineering point of view. Being able to use the multi-disciplinary lenses, essentially asking the question of how this content should look like to representatives of a certain discipline, and whether the module can somehow serve that perspective, is a key part of making the modules adaptable to different institutions and disciplines.

The SecTech project participants represent a wide range of different expertise areas, institutions and academic traditions, and consequently the consortium has a good view on what should and could be provided in terms of module contents and arrangements. The consortium has settled on providing modules of 0.5, 1 or 2 ECTS credits to allow external organizations adapt modules of suitable size as either complete courses of any desired ECTS size or as parts of existing courses. Also, theory and practice has been divided into different modules to permit multi-disciplinarians to either include or exclude practical parts (for example programming) in disciplines where they are unnecessary. As an example, the modules on practical security testing provided by University of Oulu, Finland, provides a theoretical introduction of 1 ECTS and additionally practical 2 ECTS modules including programming exercises.

In order to facilitate the creation of individual modules, template module structures have been created for the SecTech project, with 0,5 and 1 ECTS theory modules and 1.5 and 2.0 ECTS modules with both practice and theory and 2.0 ECTS modules with project-oriented practical work, as shown in Figure 2 With these modules further subdivided to theoretical and practical parts and thus making it possible to adapt modules to interdisciplinary requirements, the module structure should be well-defined enough to create a feeling of common structure but at the same time flexible enough to be adaptable to local traditions and practices.

Figure 2. Overview of the teaching module templates employed by the SecTech project

LECTURE PACKAGE 1 ECTS		LECTURES AND EXERCISES 1,5 ECTS		LECTURES AND EXERCISES 2 ECTS		PROJECT PACKAGE 2 ECTS	
Component	ECTS	Component	ECTS	Component	ECTS	Component	ECTS
Introduction	0,5	Introduction	0,5	Introduction	0,5	Introduction	0,5
Lectures, preparatory work		Lectures, preparatory work		Lectures, preparatory work		Introduction to project, preparatory work	
Deepen the knowledge	0,5	Deepen the knowledge	0,5	Deepen the knowledge	0,5	Practical project	1,5
Lectures and associated work		Lectures and associated work		Lectures and associated work		40 hour practical project	
no practical exercise	0	Practical exercise		Workshop sessions and assignment			
		2-3 hour exercise and related preparatory and reporting work	0,5	A half-day workshop, preparatory work and exercise such as an essay	1		
Optional quizzes		Optional quizzes		Optional quizzes			
10 - 15 multiple choice questions for self-study.	0	10 - 15 multiple choice questions for self-study.	0	10 - 15 multiple choice questions for self-study.	0		
Total	1	Total	1,5	Total	2	Total	2

SUITABLE DELIVERY PLATFORMS

Recent years have seen a rapid change in the learning environment and the possibilities offered to learners by new education concepts enabled through technological advance. A prominent example for such an environment are MOOCs (Massive Open Online Courses) that provide on-line courses available to anyone who is interested in a topic, often free of charge. MOOC providers usually offer, besides the course material, interactive community support through on-line communication channels. MOOCs are enabled by technological advances that allow a completely virtual learning environment. In contrast, most higher education institutions still predominantly rely on traditional classroom education. This is a proven concept that still has many advantages over pure on-line courses, for example the development of social skills like team building, communication or interpersonal skills; and the possibility of a teacher to adjust to the individual needs of a learner (European Cyber Security Organisation (ECSO), 2018). Our implementation of a cybersecurity curriculum does not try to replace traditional classroom education, since the project partners are convinced that in the current form classroom education as it is realized nowadays in the majority of higher education institutions has advantages for a positive learning outcome in students that cannot be substituted by pure on-line education. Our intention is to supplement traditional education approaches in a meaningful way, in order to simplify processes that are complex or time consuming in traditional learning environments. Such processes may relate to course management and administration, which is traditionally a manual and labor-intensive task, but can be largely automated when integrated in the on-line learning environment. Furthermore, interactive learning environments help to improve the communication to other students, teachers and teaching assistants without the need to schedule specific and time-consuming appointments. A third advantage that is specifically interesting to our approach of a collaborative cybersecurity curriculum is the ability to develop and manage content and courses in a distributed and collaborative fashion. Collaborative authoring as well as the ability to share always up to date content are seen as a precondition for a European cybersecurity program that is developed by several independent higher education institutions.

At the core of each learning environment setup is the content that enables students to learn. In traditional classroom education, this content is usually a static set of slides presented to the learners by the teacher. Virtual environments allow for a different way of interaction by the students with the content, therefore providing opportunities to engage students in a dynamic way by embedding interactive elements, like for example quizzes, directly into the content. For a teacher, new possibilities for tracking the learning progress of students (completion, time, scores) is available. In order for this to work, the Advanced Distributed Learning Initiative (ADL) (The Advanced Distributed Learning Initiative, 2018) has proposed a standard that allows content to interact with learning management systems. The Shareable Content Object Reference Model (SCORM) or, in a recent evolution to overcome limitations of SCORM, the ExperienceAPI was developed. Those standards form the basis for most current virtual learning environment set-ups in their interaction with content, since they allow rich and dynamic content to be presented and integrated in the learning environment. Learning tool interoperability (LTI) by the IMS global learning consortium (IMS Global Learning Consortium, 2018) is another important standard in this context that allows content from an LTI provider (e.g. an authoring tool) to be integrated directly with one or more LTI consumers (e.g. a learning management system), including all the interactive features SCORM provides. One of the core advantages of LTI is that if the content is modified at provider side, the changes are immediately reflected at consumer side.

The project has identified that a basic virtual learning environment to support traditional classroom education, as well as the collaborative development and lecturing of content/courses in a European context, requires following basic tool set: An authoring tool that allows to create interactive and dynamic content according to, for example, the SCORM standard; a learning management system (LMS) that can host the content and provides a virtual environment for course management and administration, as well as a virtual classroom environment that can be used in addition to traditional classrooms. A virtual learning environment set-up should be as easy to use as possible. Ideally, all above described functionalities should be integrated in one single tool, however due to the different requirements posed such a tool may not exist. Alternatively, the set-up should aim for close integration of individual tools and ease of use for both students and teachers. A set-up that requires local install of software components should be avoided, and a web service based set-up should be favored. Access and rights management should be kept as simple as possible, one account that allows access to all services in the tool set should be aspired. In many cases tools are, even if developed by different organizations, tightly integrated with the central LMS system and may be configured to rely on the authentication credentials of the LMS. Our analysis has shown that there are many commercial as well as free and open source tools available that provide the functionalities of such a virtual learning environment. Our analysis has focused on setting up a completely free and open source learning environment and our experiences have shown that this goal can be achieved, and that large and active communities are driving the development of the chosen tool set.

The central role of a virtual learning environment is the LMS system. The concrete feature set varies between the implementations of different providers, but the basic feature of an LMS is to present activities (e.g. content) relating to a course and allow access to those activities according to the roles of the participants (e.g. teachers and students). LMS systems usually allow to facilitate communication among the course participants via mechanisms such as course specific forums, group chats or personal messages. A calendar functionality will allow to plan course activities and remind of upcoming deadlines. Regarding course administration, LMS systems usually allow to track the progress of students within course activities and allow teachers to derive grades based on those measures. The project has found Moodle (The Moodle project, 2018) to be the favored choice to fulfil our requirements for a collaborative cybersecurity curriculum. The deciding factor has been that Moodle has a long and active development history, the wide-spread use in learning institutions, and a very dynamic community that drives and supports the project.

Authoring tools are used to create learning content. The most widespread form of authoring tools is software able to create presentation slides. More recent authoring tools include the ability to create dynamic content, for example according to the SCORM/ExperienceAPI standards. Such authoring tools usually create content in HTML format, in order to integrate better with web based LMS tools, since no special software other than a web browser is required to display the content. While tools exist to convert traditional presentation slides to SCORM and HTML format, the project has identified Xerte online toolkits (XOT) (Xerte Online Toolkits, 2018) as a suitable authoring tool for our collaborative cybersecurity curriculum. Xerte is deployed as an on-line service, and allows integration and authentication using Moodle user accounts. Xerte allows to collaborate on content creation and allows to create content in SCORM compatible HTML5. Furthermore, configuration as an LTI provider is possible to allow direct integration with LMS systems.

The third class of virtual learning environment tool the project considers essential is a virtual classroom environment. While this functionality is not absolute necessary in an approach that tries to supplement and not replace traditional classroom education, a virtual classroom environment can be a convenient alternative to overcome for example scheduling issues or room shortage. A virtual classroom environment is a conferencing solution that allows similar activities than in a traditional classroom. A teacher is able to check student attendance, is able to present according to a slide set, and is able to visualize content via a blackboard/whiteboard. Teachers and students can communicate via various methods like audio, video or real-time chat. Most conferencing systems specifically developed for distance learning have other classroom specific features like for example the ability to group students in separate virtual rooms for group work. The project has identified BigBlueButton (BigBlueButton, 2018), a free and open source virtual classroom solution, to fulfil the requirements for a collaborative cybersecurity curriculum. BigBlueButton was chosen because of its large and active development community, as well as its ability to embed with LMS systems and authenticate participants according to their LMS credentials.

This Section provided an overview of the current state-of-the-art for virtual learning environments and have given examples of a set-up suited to the needs of a cybersecurity curriculum that is collaborative developed by several European higher education institutions, supporting traditional classroom education. This constitutes a basic set-up that does not take into account tool support for field specific activities (e.g. a code repository for programming exercises) but covers all the basic use cases of authoring and delivering content to students, managing courses and tracking results. The project partners have had positive experiences regarding the ease of use of those tools as well as the mostly seamless integration of tools developed by different communities. Especially initiatives like LTI support the concept of collaborative content development, since it allows seamless integration of content in LMS system of choice of the participating education institutions.

THE CONTENT AND MODULE STRUCTURE IN PRACTICE

To demonstrate how the SecTech content and module structure works in practice, an example of a SecTech module on Critical Infrastructure Security and Resilience is illustrated in this Section.

Various definitions exist for critical infrastructures and different methods for identifying critical infrastructures are being used by nations, reflecting different views on what constitutes a critical infrastructure. According to the Council Directive 2008/114/EC of 8 December 2008 on the identification and designation of European critical infrastructures and the assessment of the need to improve their protection, "Critical infrastructure means an asset, system or part thereof located in member states which is essential for the maintenance of vital societal functions, health, safety, security, economic or social well-being of people, and the disruption or destruction of which would have a significant impact in a member state as a result of the failure to maintain those functions" (THE EUROPEAN PARLIAMENT AND THE COUNCIL OF THE EUROPEAN UNION, 2008). Electric Power, electronic communications, water supply and sewage, transport, oil and gas, and banking are examples of industry sectors characterized as being critical infrastructures.

The subject of critical infrastructure security and resilience is interdisciplinary by nature and entails strategic, political, legal and technical aspects. Accordingly, this module aims to provide a holistic understanding of various approaches to critical infrastructure security and resilience, applicable to different sectors. It provides an introduction to the theoretical foundations; and of the techniques and methods used in critical infrastructure cybersecurity and resilience. It describes the concepts relevant to critical infrastructures and their cybersecurity; the elements of risk; models of critical infrastructures and ways of modelling interdependencies among them. It then focuses on particular aspects of critical infrastructures, namely cyber-physical systems; and industrial control systems and discusses issues, challenges, methods and techniques for their cybersecurity. The application of the methods and techniques discussed in the module to a number of critical infrastructures is demonstrated by means of case studies. The module is designed to promote subject-matter understanding, critical analysis of issues, and insight into the theory and application of cybersecurity methods and techniques.

The introductory part of the module (0.5 ECTS) consists of 1 - 1.5 h lecture units which give students an overview of the subject area. In general, no previous knowledge is required. Specifically, topics covered in this part are definitions of critical infrastructures and discussion of similarities and differences among them; examples of cybersecurity incidents that have involved and affected critical infrastructures, including some technical detail on how the relevant attacks were launched; statistics on the distribution of incidents per industry sector and per attack vector; the impact of cyber incidents; and the top vulnerabilities that have made these incidents possible. This discussion leads to making the point that the cybersecurity of critical infrastructures is primarily a human rather than a technology issue and should therefore be viewed in a structured and holistic manner that considers people, processes and technology. Such an approach is best implemented by means of national cybersecurity strategies and follows all phases of the NIST Framework for Improving Critical Infrastructure Cybersecurity (National Institute of Standards and Technology, 2018). This component also contains administrative information on the module.

A number of 2 - 3 h lecture units, each of 0.5 ECTS, which go deeper into the content of the introduction, each addressing one of the following topics or combinations thereof have been designed:

1. Threat actors and agents in critical infrastructures
2. Infrastructure modelling, robustness and dependencies
3. Cyber-physical systems and their security
4. Open research challenges in critical infrastructure security and resilience
5. Legislative impact of GDPR and NIS on critical infrastructure security

The unit on threat actors and agents in critical infrastructures discusses and analyses

- Assets, vulnerabilities, advanced persistent threats and threat agents in critical infrastructures
- Threat analysis, vulnerability assessment, likelihood estimation, impact assessment in critical infrastructures
- Risk aggregation and analysis in critical infrastructures
- Strategies and approaches for risk management in critical infrastructures.

The unit on infrastructure modelling, robustness and dependencies

- Introduces concepts of dependencies, interdependencies, and robustness in networks
- Discusses modelling approaches for critical (information) infrastructures at different levels of granularity and predictive power
- Presents model-based understanding of faults, robustness, and vulnerability to cascading faults in (infrastructure) networks
- Provides understanding into the network structure and dynamics in the design and construction of attacks

The unit on cyber-physical systems and their security

- Introduces cyber-physical systems and their distinctive characteristics
- Discusses attacks on cyber-physical systems and hybrid attacks
- Discusses and analyze security and privacy issues in the Internet of Things
- Discusses and analyses security and privacy issues in embedded systems
- Introduces and analyses moving target defense mechanisms for cyber-physical systems
- Reviews Intrusion Detection, Prevention, and Response Systems for cyber-physical systems

The unit on open research challenges in critical infrastructure security and resilience

- Reviews existing research agendas as they relate to critical infrastructure security and resilience
- Leverages the NIST cybersecurity framework (National Institute of Standards and Technology, 2018) to organize research challenges
- Extensively discusses and analyses open research challenges in these areas

The unit on legislative impact of GDPR and NIS on critical infrastructure security

- Reviews the General Data Protection Regulation and the Network and Information Security Directive
- Highlights provisions of the GDPR relevant to critical infrastructure security
- Leverages the Lloyd's emerging risks report 2017 (Lloyd's of London and Cyence, 2017) to identify and discuss the impact of the GDPR on areas where trouble can arise

A set of multiple-choice questions completes each 1.0 ECTS module. An example set of such questions for advanced persistent threats has been developed. Four possible answers are provided to the student, and more than one answers are sometimes correct. The system provides feedback to each student response stating whether the answer was correct or not. In the latter case, additional feedback including sources to consult is given.

For the 1.5 ECTS module, the learning content is further deepened through practical exercises. For this purpose, the students will receive clearly defined tasks. The working time of the students should be about 2 to 3 hours. It should be noted that the lecturer must find time for preparation, execution and wrap-up. The practical exercise requires the students to get prepared through reading list provided by the course lecturer. An example of such a practical exercise is the study of the 2015-2016 attacks against the Ukrainian power grid. The students will be expected to go through the provided reading list and analyze the incidents by mapping them to the ICS cyber kill chain (Assante & Lee, 2015). Another example is the US CERT Alert (TA18-074A) on "Russian Government Cyber Activity Targeting Energy and Other Critical Infrastructure Sectors" (US-CERT - United States Computer Emergency Readiness Team, 2018), which the students are invited to study and then answer questions on how the GDPR and the NIS would apply for taking preparatory measures to prevent the incidents and for notifying affected parties.

In the case of the 2.0 ECTS module, the above practical exercise is substituted by a half-day workshop conducted with the students. Ideally, this workshop is based on previously learned knowledge. The workshop session itself requires the students to get prepared through reading list provided by the course lecturer. After the course students will have to carry out an assignment on the selected topic, usually in the form of an essay. In our example, this can be implemented by means of a number of case studies on the applicability of the GDPR in various scenarios, such as the following:

- Personal data from EU used locally
- Personal data from EU used outside of the EU
- Personal data saved in a cloud based in the EU
- Personal data saved in a cloud based in the USA
- Personal data saved in a cloud based outside the OECD

CONCLUSION

Cybersecurity is becoming an increasingly important topic in the digital world. Through different types of attacks, cyber criminals are threatening our society and economy, for example by influencing the democratic process or by causing substantial economic losses. Such attacks can be driven by a variety of motivations, including financial, political or social aspects. The prevention and mitigation of cyber attacks and their effects have become an urgent and worldwide topic. From the history of the Internet and its associated technologies, it can be observed that security is often not an issue that is given the highest priority on a social level by the general population, or even at an organizational level in both the day to day operation of established or emerging businesses, and when bringing new technologies to the market. This makes it ultimately difficult to address security issues at a later stage. The SecTech project has observed that the education of cybersecurity professionals cannot keep up with the rapid change in the cybersecurity landscape and the education system is also not able to educate enough skilled graduates to cater to the current demand. In the European Union, the challenge also comes from the large number of member states and their imbalanced educational developments. While some higher education institutions are able to provide a high-quality five-year degree programs in cybersecurity, most higher education institutions do not have the resources or educational focus to provide dedicated cybersecurity degree programs - usually cybersecurity would be an add-on or specialization to existing degree programs in e.g. computer science or engineering, with a maximum of 2-year degree programs focused on cybersecurity. Driven by the digital single market strategy of the European Union, there is a great incentive to have a universal cybersecurity curriculum so that member states can have a common framework for cybersecurity education. With a common curriculum, it will become easier to cross-validate the academic degrees in different countries and facilitate the movement of talents in the job market. It also makes it easier for the employers to evaluate the job candidates regardless of where they have been educated in the EU.

In the Erasmus+ strategic partnership project SecTech, referring to the CSEC2017 cybersecurity curriculum guidelines, the project partners have collaboratively developed a distributed cybersecurity curriculum and associated seed lecture material that can be freely used by higher education institutions. It is our hope that the clear curriculum guideline and a focused content and module structure that was developed in SecTech helps to facilitate the development of a community of cybersecurity educators and professionals to provide, maintain and reuse content in the long-term, and to be able to fulfil all content requirements for a full cybersecurity program as laid out by CSEC2017 - even when looking through different institutional and disciplinary lenses. The tool support selected by SecTech, based on free and open source solutions, facilitates and supports collaborative content development and maintenance, and helps to deliver the content in a way that supports traditional classroom education, the most widely used form of teaching at higher education institutions. The SecTech content is designed to be freely available to project partners and collaborators. The possibilities of collaboration can range from simply using the provided lecture material, to utilizing recorded lectures or invited talks either locally or via virtual class-rooms. This may be particularly useful if a participating higher education institution lacks the teaching expertise in specific areas. For example, in Luxembourg, there is no expertise in software security and digital forensics, while strong expertise in those areas is available in Finland and Germany respectively. Furthermore, the joint effort will allow to develop content in new and emerging security topics more quickly and achieve a wide-spread availability of high-quality content in such areas at the same time.

While the project has been able to gain a good understanding of what is required to achieve a comprehensive cybersecurity education program for higher education, and how to best develop and deliver it in a collaborative way, there are some points that have not been addressed during the project that are important to ensure long-term sustainability. In the long-term it needs to be ensured that such a program can achieve freedom in terms of institutional governance and financing, and that it can build a community that is large enough to develop and maintain content in all the topics covered by the curriculum. Furthermore, a shift from European centric development to a global community needs to be achieved. The free and open-source software movement is an excellence example of how a free and open cybersecurity education program could be organized: Larger open source projects usually are divided in a foundation that is focused on the strategic planning as well as the fund raising for the project, while the project itself will lead the community-based development and maintenance efforts according to an appropriate management structure. A similar structure could be adopted for the SecTech curriculum development, for example by assigning dedicated maintainers to each of the identified knowledge areas or even knowledge units. A second aspect that was not covered by the SecTech project is multi-language support for lecture material. Many lecturers at higher education institutions, especially in the field of technology where many terms are only available in English language, already use a hybrid approach to teaching where the lecture material is English, and the presentations will be in the native language. However, depending on the cultural context or institutional policies, lecture material in native language may be required. In the long-term it is expected that SecTech will include multi-lingual support for lecture material. Furthermore, the SecTech project has only looked at the requirements for higher education. It is expected however that the knowledge that is to be disseminated to learners in different contexts like school education or professional education is the same or very similar to the knowledge relevant to higher education, but the requirements to content and module structure as well as the delivery strategy may be significantly different. In future, SecTech would like to look into ways to utilize the existing knowledge base to also address learners outside of higher education, for example by expanding on the concepts of institutional and disciplinary lenses to a much broader context.

Through the experiences gained in the SecTech project the partners are confident that a collaboratively developed cybersecurity program is a huge step forward in overcoming the current limitations in cybersecurity education. It was observed that due to advances in technological support there are nowadays few limitations regarding content creation and delivery in a collaborative set-up, and to increase reusability of content. However, more steps need to be taken to allow such a program to become self-sustainable, and to be able to produce and maintain high quality content in the long-term and on a global scale, which the project partners hope to achieve through the establishment of a community-based governance and management structure.

ACKNOWLEDGMENT

The SecTech project is funded by the European Union's Erasmus+ program as a strategic partnership in higher education with the grant number 2016-1-LU01-KA203-013834.

REFERENCES

ACM, IEEE, AIS, IFIP. (2017). Curriculum Guidelines for Post-Secondary Degree Programs in Cybersecurity. ACM.

Assante, M. J., & Lee, R. M. (2015). *The Industrial Control System Cyber Kill Chain*. Retrieved from SANS Institute InfoSec Reading Room: https://www.sans.org/reading-room/whitepapers/ICS/industrial-control-system-cyber-kill-chain-36297

Association for Computing Machinery (ACM) and IEEE Computer Society. (2013). *Computer Science Curricula 2013: Curriculum Guidelines for Undergraduate Degree Programs in Computer Science*. New York: ACM.

Association for Computing Machinery (ACM) and IEEE Computer Society. (2017). *Information Technology Curricula 2017: Curriculum Guidelines for Baccalaureate Degree Programs in Information Technology*. New York: ACM.

BigBlueButton. (2018, June). Retrieved from https://bigbluebutton.org/

European Commission and High Representative of the European Union for Foreign Affairs and Security Policy. (2013). *Cybersecurity Strategy of the European Union: An Open, Safe and Secure Cyberspace*. JOIN(2013) 1 final.

European Cyber Security Organisation (ECSO). (2018). *Position Paper: Gaps in European Cyber Education and Professional Training*. ECSO.

European Union Agency for Law Enforcement Cooperation (Europol). (2017). *Internet organised crime threat assessment (IOCTA) 2017*. Retrieved from https://www.europol.europa.eu/activities-services/main-reports

Guide to the Systems Engineering Body of Knowledge (SEBok) v.1.9. (2018, June). Retrieved from http://sebokwiki.org/wiki/Guide_to_the_Systems_Engineering_Body_of_Knowledge_(SEBOK)

IMS Global Learning Consortium. (2018, June). Retrieved from http://www.imsglobal.org/

Lloyd's of London and Cyence. (2017). *Emerging Risks Report 2017: Counting the cost - Cyber exposure decoded*. Retrieved from https://www.lloyds.com/~/media/files/news-and-insight/risk-insight/2017/cyence/emerging-risk-report-2017---counting-the-cost.pdf

National Institute of Standards and Technology. (2018, April). *Framework for Improving Critical Infrastructure Cybersecurity - Version 1.1*. Retrieved from https://www.nist.gov/publications/framework-improving-critical-infrastructure-cybersecurity-version-11

Santos, D. (2016). *National Initiative for Cybersecurity Education*. NICE.

The Advanced Distributed Learning Initiative. (2018, June). Retrieved from http://www.adlnet.gov/

The Council of the European Union. (2016). Regulation (EU) 2016/679 of the European Parliament And of the Council of 27 April 2016 on the protection of natural persons with regard to the processing of personal data and on the free movement of such data, and repealing Directive 95/46/EC. *Official Journal of the European Union, L, 119*(1).

The European Parliament and the Council of the European Union. (2008). Council Directive 2008/114/EC of 8 December 2008 on the identification and designation of European critical infrastructures and the assessment of the need to improve their protection. *Official Journal of the European Union, L, 345*(75).

The European Parliament and the Council of the European Union. (2016). Directive (EU) 2016/1148 of the European Parliament and of the Council of 6 July 2016 concerning measures for a high common level of security of network and information systems across the Union. *Official Journal of the European Union, L, 194*(1).

The Moodle project. (2018, June). Retrieved from https://moodle.org/

US-CERT - United States Computer Emergency Readiness Team. (2018). *Alert (TA18-074A) - Russian Government Cyber Activity Targeting Energy and Other Critical Infrastructure Sectors*. Retrieved from https://www.us-cert.gov/ncas/alerts/TA18-074A

Xerte Online Toolkits. (2018, June). Retrieved from https://www.xerte.org.uk

This research was previously published in Cybersecurity Education for Awareness and Compliance; pages 181-200, copyright year 2019 by Information Science Reference (an imprint of IGI Global).

Chapter 21
Techniques and Tools for Trainers and Practitioners

Melanie Oldham
Bob's Business, UK

Abigail McAlpine
Bob's Business, UK

ABSTRACT

If the material is to be delivered effectively, organizations need to understand the human side of cyber security training. In this chapter, the authors draw upon over a decade of experience in creating and adapting training and resources with the help of industry professionals and feedback from clients, which has led to a successful and highly acclaimed approach to cybersecurity education. The resulting discussion considers how to adopt the right approach to cybersecurity training for organizations, with training modules that cater to end users, and which are designed to ensure maximum retention of information by presenting short, humorous, animated scenarios that are relatable for the target audience.

INTRODUCTION

For organizations looking to meet compliance requirements or develop a security conscious workforce, this chapter can be used to provide insight into the different approaches to educating the workforce and the different tools and techniques to help develop an established awareness campaign. Understanding and assessing the needs of an organization is essential for the ongoing engagement of learners' interest in cybersecurity. While awareness campaigns are now becoming more commonplace in organizations many see the information as guidance rather than rules, some may even see it as a tick box exercise and cumbersome to integrate into staffs' roles, also possibly perceived as negatively affecting the performance in their tasks and activities.

DOI: 10.4018/978-1-6684-3554-0.ch021

As well as communicating the fundamental teachings of cybersecurity it is also necessary to understand how learners take in information. This chapter presents hints and tips on how to differentiate, plan and manage training sessions, courses and modules to best fit the organization's needs and those of its learners. This tactic allows more informed decisions about how to approach cybersecurity training and the benefits and problems with each tactic. Organizations can utilize combinations of different tactics to teach learners how to be safe and secure when engaging with the digital environment.

It is vital to provide factual and critical information when educating the workforce in the correct attitudes and behaviors to conduct within the organization. Cybersecurity training will also provide skills to navigate themselves more securely online with broader society. Adequate training is more than just providing the facts, and how to apply them, the most effective training changes how learners change their attitudes and behaviors in the long-term, it changes how the individuals engage with others online, their self-awareness and their ongoing interest in the education of cybersecurity. Cybersecurity awareness should not stop once a learner leaves an educational environment. Great training inspires and encourages learners to develop an inquisitive mind, not just for organization security but their personal security and those around them.

All organizations have the opportunity to become cyber secure; this is known as Cybersecurity Culture (CSC) which refers to people's behavior, knowledge, perceptions, attitudes, assumptions, norms and values interacting with technology and devices. Good CSC should encompass an understanding of the current culture within an organization and the gap before the ideal culture. The European Union Agency for Network and Information Security (ENISA) states that CSC should:

Encompasses familiar topics including cybersecurity awareness and information security frameworks but is broader in both scope and application, being a concern with making information security considerations an integral part of an employee's job, habits and conduct, embedding them in their day-to-day actions (ENISA, 2018).

This chapter provides practical help and support towards establishing the needs of learners and readers will be asked to consider, reflect and re-evaluate their teachings with feedback from learners. Whether organizations are at the start of the journey of educating their workforce, or part way through, and whether they are handling the training internally or externally, the chapter aims to provide the information required to create an efficient and effective learning plan.

WHY TEACH CYBERSECURITY ONLINE?

Learning is sometimes more useful as an isolated activity; many learners enjoy learning flexibly at their own pace, others prefer to learn in a social context. Using the courses provided by Bob's Business as an example, the aim is to combine the best of both, with online learning being accessible in the office or on the go. Training can be in a group environment, and post-training discussion is encouraged with extra learning re-enforcements and resources.

Although there is a now a recognized, established and growing need for cybersecurity training for organizations there is a fundamental lack of understanding of how to treat and educate workforces. An active CSC will drive changes in policy, procedures and everyday activities; the motives for different organizations to conduct cybersecurity training are different across the board. Cyber threat awareness campaigns are not sufficient to protect organizations and individuals from cyber threats independently. Cybersecurity awareness campaigns should be in tangent with business processes and everyday activities.

Humans are often the weakest link in cybersecurity; training should be sufficient and engaging enough for the workforce to feel that they work in an open and communicative organization and think that they know and understand how to raise cybersecurity threats in a positive environment that does not scrutinize employees for not spotting a warning earlier. Employees should not feel that they are unable to do their job and demonstrate cybersecurity awareness at the same time.

CSC should be adopted across the organization through all members of staff from top down. Security considerations should manifest themselves naturally in people's everyday activities, behaviors and attitudes as an integral part of an individual's role. CSC should be resilient but responsive to new threats and technologies; it should be implemented in new processes and procedures as time and tasks move forward.

Tools and practices must be tailored to the specific needs and circumstances of an organization. Matured and well-established CSC practices already implemented by organizations specifically cater to the different needs of their business, in some cases, the training should be individually tailored to the different audiences within their organization which helps provide a clear and structured approach to the development of a strong CSC.

Knowledge leadership ensures an evidence-based approach that builds CSC policies, programs and strategies tailored to the organization. The implementation of a secure CSC is to provide alignment with an organizations policies or daily processes. Bringing together a new approach to cybersecurity must be done in harmony with changes to organization policies as well as training. Maximizing the adoption of a new CSC requires support from all levels of an organization, core members of the workforce including management and senior management need to champion the change and push the tailoring of company-wide policies to support the training. Developing a robust cybersecurity culture requires repetitive ongoing engagement, this is not a simple on-off activity.

To successfully teach cybersecurity online training requires the adoption of many different training and education methods to provide open and flexible learning that suits the learners individual learning styles and supports the retention of information. The settings of a formal course where organizations must push employees into a meeting room or venue at the cost of their typical working day can be cast aside in favor of more adaptable online training. Training should be both initiated by management but also championed by them, CSC should be initiated at the top-level, mid-level and bottom-level of an organization.

An example drawn from the authors' own experience occurred during feedback discussion with a client organization regarding the success of a prior cybersecurity simulation course. The organization mentioned an authentic discussion caused because of the training. Specifically, one member of staff had posted in the organization's group messaging service that he had received a phishing email which directed him to the 'Think Before You Click' training course. The employee stated how doing the training was a waste of his time and he was too busy. His peers commented that his conduct was the reason for the training, as the exercise would not have launched without him interacting with a phishing email that could have been a scam. In this instance, his peers understood the need for the training and how vulnerable their organization was because of members of their organization not considering their attitudes and behaviors of engaging with the online environment and potential cybersecurity risks. The employee's dismissiveness reinforced the message that this training was needed as a result of employee conduct. It also created authentic conversations in the workplace that encouraged better cybersecurity awareness.

Successful CSC requires a complete change in mindset across an organization, regardless of which sector the organization sits in, its size or structure. Senior management often drives the culture change within organizations regarding cybersecurity, contextually with the introduction of stricter General Data Protection Regulation (GDPR) legislation many in senior management positions have taken note of the highly promoted fines for non-compliance with GDPR. This approach has forced a changing of goals, policies, objectives, processes, structures and management in an entire range of industries.

Technology opens the opportunity to upskill the standards of staff's cybersecurity knowledge to meet the needs of an organization to protect against the latest threats and vulnerabilities. For the best retention of information, learners need courses that are suited to their learning needs, not just the industry norms. Some employees may have a better understanding of the digital environment where others may have been within an organization before Internet use daily was the social norm. Cybersecurity courses must not assume a level of cybersecurity understanding. It is essential to assess needs for an organization before purchasing or creating cybersecurity training, while industry level training may meet the industry tick boxes, it may not meet the immediate knowledge, skill gaps and requirements of the learners or the organization.

One view of online courses is that they open the opportunity and ability for information access for all. It can be an opportunity to deliver existing course material online. However, this content would have to be adapted to support the alternative learning styles and needs. The discussion explains the need to assess the cybersecurity knowledge gaps of learners as well as the organization.

E-learning is often unsuccessful due to poor engagement rates, forcing learners to sit through hours of courses is not beneficial as learners struggle to take in the amount of information expected. E-learning can adopt the social benefits by rolling out company-wide campaigns that encourage communication and discussion that allows learners to discuss how the training can be utilized in their day to day role. A month by month approach is sufficient as it allows learners to absorb information at their pace while completing it in sync with the rest of the organization.

PREPARING TO TEACH ONLINE

Before developing cybersecurity training, organizations need to create an itinerary of needs to consider the correct methods to approach the training efficiently. These questions will help to design or purchase cybersecurity that will provide the best education and retention for the workforce:

- Why does your organization need cybersecurity training?
- What are the organizational risks?
- What makes an excellent training experience?
- What makes training stick?
- What reinforces learning?
- How to develop training that encourages ongoing conscious learning?
- What makes good engagement?
- Does it meet standards or legislation?

Once the organization has the answers to these questions, it should consider what would provide the opposite experience and then what would only provide an average experience. There are not necessarily right or wrong answers to these questions. This method is merely an opportunity to establish the expectations of training before considering the learning content.

There are many barriers created when training does not meet learners' levels of understanding, training can become tedious, patronizing or make learners feel insecure or stupid for their lack of knowledge. Pushing out training that is not catered to different learner levels can build a wall between learners and their understanding of the course and the lessons the training is communicating. This information is pivotal to understand and utilize in the event of a cybersecurity breach.

The authors' approach to cybersecurity training is an all-inclusive approach for every member of staff, no matter their level within the organization, no assumptions should be made on the level of understanding, and no learner should feel alienated or stupid because of the training. It also includes creation of bespoke training for organizations, as understanding how brand values and imagery function within an organization and communicate issues in a way that employees will understand and buy into is essential for many larger organizations. Learners should be provided with the skills to enable them to conduct themselves appropriately and safely inside and outside of the organization.

When delivering a training campaign to all learners, careful consideration should be made to understand the motivation for the training in the first place. Is the training simply a tick box exercise that names and shames individuals who later go onto fail when put under pressure, or alternatively is it a learning journey where individuals are given ample time, resources and support to learn how to prevent cybersecurity failures, what to do in the case of an attack and how to report it in line with legislation and organizational policies? Obviously, the latter is the more likely route to actually support the learner.

Creating a bespoke approach can require essential changes to branding, style and language changes to suit an organization, of course when creating a course with specific organizations in mind it becomes easier to add in exact details for contacts or where organization policies and procedures can be found.

Regulation can impose additional costs to an organization as the subsequent needs of designing, documenting and updating CSC policies, practices and responsibilities of organization can be cost heavy, the alternative consequence for ill preparation for a data breach or attack can be catastrophic.

The Directive on Security of Network and Information Systems (2016) and GDPR legislation state that those who fail to abide by security requirements entirely may result in fees or penalties for non-compliance. Reasonable care should be implemented to reinforce the importance of maintaining and updating policies within the organization. The structure should be enforced to remind individuals of the costs and personal responsibilities they must adhere to.

When planning a course, it requires careful consideration of disability access for all learners. The truth is that this is often something missed when organizations choose to build their training in-house, vitally missing the opportunity to train all employees equally. Good online courses adapt for a range of needs and provide the option of all learners to be:

- Independent and indiscriminate of any users of ICT
- Can match the needs of all audiences and learners
- Can help all learners reflect critically and evaluate their learning and training

Accessible training is not about providing special privileges to those with disabilities, it is about providing the equal opportunity and access to all learners to take in the same content in that benefits and supports them.

Through developing and researching learner needs across the years, the authors have developed and embraced the ways to make training more accessible and though often this requires extra design, feature building and testing, it has resulted in courses that are more engaging, interactive and retainable for learners.

Not making training accessible results in organizations identifying employees who would not be able to take the E-learning and provide a face-to-face alternative. Accessibility is not just for those who have disabilities, there are various barriers to the enjoyment and retention of information and adapting training to those with visual, audio or motor impairments adds to quality and value that is offered to learners, as employees learn in different ways.

The W3C has a published guide of recommendations for accessibility benchmarks for those developing online sites, programs or resources. The Web Content Accessibility Guidelines (WCAG) (Web Accessibility Initiative, 2018) not only provide great guidance for the inclusivity of content but also following these guidelines raise the levels of engagement across the board as there are less barriers for every learner.

The WCAG require courses to be screen reader compatible, and there are plenty of screen readers available on the market. The authors have encountered many organizations that require full reports of testing the courses for accessibility as a part of the educational tender and contract.

Long-term training should have a full breakdown of learning objectives and a summary of education that will be taught. Training should not be conducted in one session or a short amount of time. Not all learners can take in all the training at the same rate. It is essential to consider the amount of time that a piece of training will last for. It is important to consider readability metrics when writing cybersecurity training, communications and guidance. The comprehension of training for end-users can depend upon their understanding of the terminology and readability of the content (Alkhurayyif, 2017). When developing cybersecurity guidance, it is essential to consider the following points:

- Can the language in the course be simplified?
- Should additional steps be added to the instructions?
- Can the course be changed into an alternative format?

Considerations need to be made about how to introduce the material to the employees and get them used to the online course system. As learners get used to resources, it is then easy to gradually introduce language and concepts that are more difficult to memorize. The demographics of audiences change so training needs to be adapted to all needs.

At the end of the course, learners should be able to define and describe the critical vocabulary. Learners should know the ways to identify potential threats and understand the consequences of not identifying these threats. Finally, they should understand how to operate tactfully in the future by following or creating policies and procedures that deal with the specific topics covered in training. A final bonus of this training would be the ongoing learning of the student out of their interest and the transferal of the cybersecurity education into their personal lives.

Bloom's Taxonomy of Educational Objectives (Bloom, 1956) considers that many learners should be successful in their studies if provided with sufficient time and support. Bloom's Revised Taxonomy (Anderson, 2002) demonstrates an arrangement method theorizing that learners should be judged against clear objectives rather than competitive systems which categorize learners as successful or unsuccessful based on where their scores lie in comparison with others doing the same course. This approach means that the emphasis is on the learners understanding of a subject rather than their ability to memorize facts and figures.

Bloom's Revised Taxonomy (Anderson, 2002) categorizes taxonomies into three domains, 'Cognitive', 'Affective' and 'Psychomotor'. This theory has inspired decades of texts and educational theory about the levels of cognitive challenge with merely remember and reciting knowledge provided in courses being the lowest cognitive skill.

- **Remembering:** The ability to retrieve, recognize and recall information from the course. A simple quiz can prove this. Remembering what to do if a data breach occurs means that they know how to handle the situation, how to escalate and report it further.
- **Understanding:** The ability to construct meaning from the course and interpret, classify, summarize, compare or explain teachings from the course. Knowledge can be proven by the learner being able to show a full table of advantages and disadvantages. Do they appreciate the damage to reputation and impact a breach may have on the organization?
- **Applying:** The ability to use their knowledge such as in a defined situation or simulation. This ability can be confirmed by the learner being able to identify the appropriate methods to deal with possible cybersecurity scenarios. Do the learners take precaution? Do they lock their desktops and devices? Do they watch out for tailgaters? Are they building this into their normal daily activities?
- **Analyzing:** Can break material up into parts and understand how these parts interact with each other to provide an overall purpose. They can compare and ascertain how specific case studies are similar or dissimilar and why their results were different. Can they assess and analyze a situation? Do they click on links unthinkingly and in a rush? Can they identify cybersecurity vulnerabilities in their peer's behaviors?
- **Evaluating:** Can make judgements based on the information and standards provided. The learner should be able to create a model, table or method of comparison to understand how to support or disprove concepts and demonstrate findings. Are the learners able to identify issues that cause cybersecurity vulnerabilities by staff circumnavigating policies and procedures? Do systems need to be re-visited to become more cyber secure?
- **Creating:** Can put elements together to form a full concept of a topic, including the planning, generating of ideas and production. Learners should be able to provide a detailed plan of how the future of cybersecurity may be. Are they able to create a better cybersecurity culture? Are they able to develop security policies and procedures in future projects?

Learners can showcase all manners of cognitive skills listed in Bloom's taxonomy, some will only demonstrate one or two skills, but all learners should ultimately be encouraged to take an interest in cybersecurity as this will result in a behavioral change about any future cyber challenges or threats. Learning must be incremental, start simple and build confidence and increasing in complexity, consideration must be taken for learners' time to take the course and take in the information provided, from the research and experience of the authors, the full ideal course time should take between 8-12 minutes for optimum retention of information.

To assemble the perfect approach to company-wide adoption of new CSC policies and practices it is essential to consciously build commitment and champions of CSC from the different disciplines within the organization. It is also important to note that just because the technical team deal with the cybersecurity of the organization on a daily basis, they may not be the best communicators of the issues and challenges that cybersecurity creates.

Senior Management should be signaling support and ownership of the campaign for better CSC, by helping to embed the changes into organizational strategy. Cybersecurity enhancement should be an interest to senior management because of the fines and penalties for non-compliance with GDPR and the Data Protection Act from the ICO.

The IT Department or Tech Team should be able to offer and expand their expertise in the core competencies of CSC in an organization to implement and support cyber secure behavior and manage risk awareness. They are also key to developing a swift procedure, policy and response to how any incidents or breeches are handled and responded to. They should align IT and cybersecurity goals to the new legislation and provide a clear and concise breakdown of the expectations of individuals within an organization.

Human resources (HR) are essential to facilitate training, communications, awareness and in some cases to establish how staff should be monitored and handled in the case that an evaluation or disciplinary sanction need to be implemented. HR can also help to provide resources for incentives should the organization choose to do so for positive CSC relations.

Legal need to ensure that all policies and procedures meet and contribute to full compliance within the legislation the organization operates within. For example, legal obligations are not the same in different international countries, so consideration should be made for meeting international legislation. This includes the requirement that suppliers meet GDPR compliance. Legal are also responsible for making sure that expectations of employees are established and what monitoring/accountability should be managed in line with the law.

Marketing and Communications need to communicate a change in mindsets, perceptions and knowledge internally throughout the company, but they are also required to instill customer and business partner trust in the organization as the importance and relevance of CSC grows. The skill of these teams should be used to market cybersecurity in a way that is made attractive to all staff in a similar way they would market products and services.

There are many factors behind the successful adoption of a secure CSC program. How an organization accepts a behavioral change or adaptation, it is dependent on the workforce's collective beliefs, actions, values and attitudes towards cybersecurity. The CSC must work in tangent with everyday processes to avoid the possibility of employees circumnavigating the cybersecurity changes to the policy if they become cumbersome.

Upon starting Think Before You Click in 2015, one of the authors' biggest clients had a phishing rate of 43% in their initial baseline exercise. By 2018, this had decreased to 10.6%, a 75% reduction in phishing rate since the beginning of training. This clearly demonstrates the change in behavior that is promoted by phishing campaigns that focused heavily on communication, collaboration, trust and transparency.

The Internet allows the access to online courses; however, this does not mean that putting all learning materials online is sufficient for the learner. In face-to-face training, the trainer can teach learners through a combination of approaches and real-time feedback from the learners.

The use of alternative methods of teaching demands the course content adapts to a variety of learning styles and needs. Where some would assume that providing one course for many would limit the time-demands on trainers, it can result in higher demands and expectations to monitor and mentor learners through more stimulating instructional and supportive methods of training.

TOOLS AND TECHNIQUES

One of the problems facing Chief Information Security Officers (CISOs) is getting people to engage with an information security awareness campaign. Typically, engagement with E-learning is usually low if the course is made mandatory. This can be improved is by leveraging social influencing within an organization. Using the power of people to influence others to complete training because they want to be seen to be doing the right thing and following the herd.

By implementing companywide campaigns that include the whole organization (including the senior management team) it encourages ongoing social influencing. An effective way to achieve this is to run a campaign concentrating on one cybersecurity topic per month – for example: January - Perfect Passwords, February - Mastering Malware and supporting this with discussions on social forums.

It is important to use marketing techniques to help with companywide engagement. By delivering content in a way that attract people's attention whilst also delivering key messages in language and context that they understand, all of which is important to the success of an awareness campaign.

Another typical failing of in-house awareness campaigns, developed by the compliance or technical teams, is when training courses are in a language used by technical individuals. When course content is in a language that the majority of learners will not understand learners develop a fear of the unknown and therefore become more resistant to listen to the teachings of the course.

It is imperative that communication is at the heart of all information security training courses, what makes users more susceptible to information security threats are the very things that make them human: personality, emotions and motivations. It is impossible to understand what motivates and influences people if communication is poor or does not exist.

In the event of an information security breach organizations will want to encourage and ensure that the individual knows how to prevent putting themselves or the organization at risk, and that they know who to turn to for help and support to minimize the impact in the timely and effective manner. However, if individuals have a fear of those in technical positions and communication barriers exist then it is important to break these down.

The language and tone used should be inclusive, friendly and easy to understand. The more complicated it is, the more disengaged people become. The use of jargon and acronyms should be avoided, and messages should be kept simple and to the point. People learn more effectively when things are concise and in less than 10 minutes chunks.

Analogies and stories are a really effective way to help people to understand and have empathy with a given situation, if people can actually understand something, they are more likely to adopt measures to prevent the negative situations occurring.

One of the criticisms of information security is that it is a dry and quite dull subject it is important to consider where entertainment plays a part in education and the way that people absorb information. The more entertaining and humorous we find things the more we retain information that we are presented with. Making campaigns fun and engaging will consequently increase the retention rate of the information that is provided and enhance the overall experience.

Gamification is another really effective way of ensuring engagement and reinforcement of information. Humans are competitive by nature and strive to be the best. By introducing an element of gamification, where individuals are rewarded for their efforts and can see their progress in relation to their peers, can in turn increase their engagement.

Individuals also possess a fear of missing out (FOMO), so when competing for a title marketing can deliver an effective winners' campaign that will emphasize the importance of engaging with the training. It will also increase pressure amongst peers to compete with the opportunity to be rewarded or receive credit for completing training so that other individuals aspire to achieve the same accolade.

Interaction in training and education can be fundamental to fueling learning. Quizzes, questions and hotspot test learner's knowledge and provide instant recognition of their learning and newfound cybersecurity culture. How a learner takes in information relies on some factors.

Interaction fuels gratification – there are three forms:

1. Instant
2. Delayed
3. None

Instant validation of learning and knowledge helps the learner to retain information to pass on to others. This positive reinforcement for learners encourages them to positively recite and interact with the course content.

Simulated training exercises where users are presented with the impact of their actions at the point at which it occurs are more effective at changing behavior. This is because users are presented with the errors of their ways immediately and therefore can empathize. One way in which the authors have achieved this is that if simulated phishing emails have been delivered and recipients have clicked on the link, they are presented with an educational landing page highlighting the fraudulent and dangerous aspects of the email.

It's important when running simulations that adequate thought is given to the emotions the user may experience, and to avoid any negative reactions and ensure the success of the campaign. By providing individuals with an indication that the training exercise is going to happen and how to react in the event of such an incident and who is on hand to support this, again helps any organization to ensure an effective reaction in the event of a breach as there is barriers of fear and anxiety will be removed.

Simulations are a great way to conduct 'mock attacks' which take several forms, these can be conducted in a number of ways including smishing, phishing, vishing contact made with staff to test how individuals would deal with potential threats. This can also be applied offline with social engineering where individuals attempt to gain access to the office, computers or company files through malicious means. This approach tests whether staff adhere to correct procedures and policies regarding cybersecurity and also helps to identify any weaknesses. For example, if the office has a lot of outsourced staff and new faces, some members of staff are less likely to see new faces as a threat.

GENERAL CONSIDERATIONS

Learning is done by the learner; it is impossible to force them to learn no matter what teaching methods or tactics are utilized. The saying 'you can lead a horse to water, but you cannot make it drink' is the same as trying to teach employees something they have no interest in. However, there's an opportunity with cybersecurity to turn the tables on those who ordinarily tune out employment training

Cybersecurity is not just relevant at work; most people have a small level of understanding of the risks of the online environment for them at home. If organizations can get learners to see how a lack of cybersecurity awareness can put themselves, their friends and their family at risk it provides the opportunity to teach knowledge that sticks in their minds every time they go to click a link in an email, connect to public Wi-Fi or reply to an email from an unknown sender. It is easy to learn what is required or expected to tick boxes and memorize answers without developing a personal understanding of the subject, the key to cybersecurity training is to make it personal and that in turn makes it memorable. We need to let go of the idea of standing at the front of the room with a slideshow presentation and provide the opportunity for learners to learn in a way that benefits them.

Trainers and training can have an immediate and lifelong impact on learners, and the policies that an organization chooses to communicate through its training could have a lasting influence over the interest of those that participate.

Cybersecurity training should:

- Enable learners to reach their full potential
- Teach change right from the start
- Encourage ongoing interest in cybersecurity
- Make training enjoyable
- Encourage them to evaluate their habits at work and home
- Make training relatable

Most learners already work with new technologies such as smartphones, tablets and laptops. Applications open new opportunities to enhance the learning experience in a virtual learning environment.

Online courses mean that the role of the trainer changes entirely, the required knowledge for a course can be crowdsourced from a range of professionals in the industry to develop the best experience for learners. With bespoke or tailored online courses the role of the trainer can change significantly as more time is required to create, review and write content for the course.

It is essential to consider the design of the course and which learning aims and objectives need to be covered in the course. There is a subtle difference between goals, objectives and outcomes of a course. What is essential when developing a CSC course is a clear outline of what needs to be covered and how these points could be made in the most effective way for the learner to retain the information.

Learning aims, and objectives state a brief and basic idea of what level of education organizations want learners to achieve and what they should know by the end of the course. Specific interactive elements should be designed to support the learning of these key aims. The learning aims are likely to be very general summaries of a broader topic and bridging the knowledge gap between the two often requires a series of learning activities as stepping stones.

An excellent online course should not solely be theory or practical. Some courses only provide a combination approach in the way that they provide a method-based teaching course then conduct a quiz or test at the end. A good course should try to intertwine these approaches more effectively by utilizing these tactics throughout the course rather than separating the two into sections.

The theory may be demonstrated through rationale or demonstrative examples that discuss the various learning objectives or attributes that are necessary to meet the expectations of learners or the industry standards. Delivering these materials online require training providers to pick, plan and prepare appropriate course materials for the digital environment.

Technology drives the development of training delivery tools. The Internet as a delivery tool has some pros and cons which will be discussed later in this chapter. Consideration for structuring and pacing must be taken when building cybersecurity courses, long-winded sessions do not benefit learners, especially if learners spend a significant amount of time trying to figure out where they were the last time they were doing the training.

On paper, online training is more cost-effective, but considerations should be made about continuous expenses of making training more up to date and effective by putting potential cost savings into the tailoring content and courses to suit an organization.

Development of a successful CSC program within an organization requires full adoption across the board, the change in culture requires a nuanced approach with the support of influential employees and management as well as a sufficient training program. This education should shape norms, attitudes and behaviors within an organization.

Different departments within an organization compete for finite funds, allocation of financial and time resources into a CSC program need to be taken seriously as it is easy to waste resources on ineffective training.

Delivery costs such as making the course material and keeping it up-to-date, sometimes special software and licenses need to be purchased to create the course content. It is good to compare the costs of face-to-face training with online delivery, the latter of which could save substantial money but cost to host the training online. Venue costs in face to face delivery can add a significant sum to the total amount for the training.

Set-Up costs associated with setting up the training and collating the correct information about cybersecurity could be considered for those looking to build their training, the time cost and investment can be extensive. The development of training also requires a level of understanding of the subject or the purchasing of such information, certificates and education. When paying for trainer's organizations are paying to upskill employees with intellectual capital owned by the trainer. Trainers incur extra costs when needing to add or review and revise the courses to meet expectations and latest legislation such as GDPR (General Data Protection Regulation) or DPA 2018 (Data Protection Act).

Educational and training courses are a means of business and utilized for generating income. However, the standard of these courses is not necessarily the same across all suppliers; different trainers would break down resources and training into separate products.

If organizations wish to cut costs and corners with training, it is easy to provide large documents that explain all the essential information, but ultimately this does not adapt to the different learning types, and excessive clicking and scrolling will result in dissatisfaction from the learners, and the material will be ignored.

There are costs associated with providing a training service that is often absorbed by the trainers, such as materials costs, travel, accommodation, venues and course building. For the learner, there are often costs associated with training that is often left unconsidered.

Loss of working hours leaving them to catch up with their regular workload around their usual hours or catch up in overtime, stretching the workforce manhours to incorporate training can put extra stressors on employees and leave them vulnerable to burning out or making mistakes, training must not add too much stress on employees.

Organizations looking to build an interactive course internally will incur software or building costs; however, often it is far more beneficial to create bespoke training for the organization as it helps learners to imagine themselves in the same scenarios.

E-learning courses are a ready-made solution, but engagement stats are often low. To ensure an active adoption effort must be applied to create an implementation plan which will be adopted and supported by stakeholders and effectively communicated and executed. Face to face training tends to be more successful since it can separate the user from the working environment and the destructions of inbound communications and colleagues wanting attention. To compete learning must be engaging and immersive to eliminate distraction and keep the learner focused. However, blended learning allows the best of both opportunities, as it allows the learner to learn in an immersive way whilst the course content helps to reflect and allows discussion of subjects in a group environment.

There are benefits to any organization who are wishing to upskill their workforce with cybersecurity training. The online material in an Internet environment opens the opportunity to protect anyone from putting the organization at risk while also not at the significant cost of inflexibility.

It is feasible that there will be an increase in enrolment because of the courses being accessible online and on the go. If training is adequately developed and constructed course providers can provide instant feedback that help learners feel that their needs and opinions are satisfied and valued. The economic costs of breaches to an organization can encompass a range of financial and intellectual property costs as well as loss of reputation. Losses to an organization can take on multiple forms including the loss or compromise of confidential information, fines for personal data breaches, downtime of systems or services, disruptive costs to revenues, as well as damage the reputation and business.

Investment into developing better cybersecurity technology and practices can significantly reduce and prepare an organization against costs and losses; it also allows the opportunity to maintain and establish competitiveness by embracing security control that helps to alleviate the security risks of engaging with the online environment. Raising the immunity of the workforce to a security breach or infection can slow the spread of infection within an organization.

Learners are more connected to their phones, so they are more likely to complete the training in their own time willingly. If training is in a more comfortable format for learners, they are more likely to complete the training. The authors own experience has observed a trend in learners achieving their training before 9am, from 12pm to 2 pm (i.e. lunchtimes) and during weekends.

The structured nature of the training gives learners a view of the content as a professional in the industry would learn it, the ability to provide phishing simulations affords real-life experience which aids the learning experience. Online and flexible learning stimulates learners and promotes positive learning attitudes and behaviors towards education.

Online learning should provide the learners with the ability to login to learning at any time and provide feedback that can directly and positively affect the progression of the training programs. The ability to work on the course at any time convenient to the learner improves their motivation and ability to work on the training on the go. Bespoke training and tailored solutions allow for individualized instruction making it more relevant to the learner's environment.

Teaching spaces are not limited to online learning, it opens enrolment opportunities for more students to participate in learning the course content, and everyone receives the same experience every time, this means that any recognition for the course as an education or training leader such as awards and certification can be the same experience and training replicated for each learner.

Fundamental changes for an organization require evident involvement and responsibilities require everyone in the organization to foster a level of ownership of its success and motivation to commit to a change in CSC rather than simple tick box exercises to prove compliance. CSC is practical if all employees understand their role within it and the tools, skills and knowledge required for successful adoption. Learning should be done in a safe environment to prevent dismissive attitudes to CSC, dialogue should be encouraged to optimize learning. The opportunity to ask questions and receive responses that allow the reinforcement and motivations to be secured within the organization. Incentives can be created to align individuals closer to the new policies.

Cybersecurity extends beyond the workplace as employees can work on their own devices, travel from work and home and use some of the same identifying information in their personal and professional lives, education and utilization of this knowledge strengthen the organization's protection from cyber threats.

DEVELOPMENT AREAS

All teaching and training must consider learners, and learning styles dictate the relationships between education and learning. It is critical to understand the need to facilitate all learning styles so as not to alienate any learners. Some learners may find the use of computers scary or threatening and others may find it enjoyable and comfortable to utilize. Consideration must be made to explain how to make the most out of training and how to navigate the training for those who are less computer-literate.

Working through courses online can be a massive frustration for learners who face issues with the technology of the course if something goes wrong learners want to talk to people, not computers. It is essential that learners understand who they can contact if there is something wrong with the training. Recognition of progress is a positive reinforcement to learning, being able to promote new knowledge online can be a great way to reward hard work. The ability to encourage completed courses on LinkedIn and portfolios can be a great promotional tool for the training provider too.

Trainers who generate relatable concepts to aid learners in understanding and lead to positive learning experiences and outcomes. A good starting point for learners is a personal experience, learners who can relate to brilliant case studies or scenarios have a better chance of retaining information. This type of approach provides learners with the opportunity to self-reflect and analyze their actions in the workplace. By selecting scenarios that learners can relate to, the learning lasts long-term and can be seen and experienced in the learner's environment. Learners then adapt their cybersecurity education to their environment later. This approach is something that the authors have utilized in training courses, and it has helped learners to apply the skills demonstrated in courses in their real environments.

Stories are good because they create a visual picture; you are appealing to a human being, not a robot. Stories help to promote employee best practice with the relevant scenarios and advice. Learning material can help employees identify with the cybersecurity threats, they can also feature a response to threats and what measures and employee could take to prevent them from actualization. Stories can be communicated through online learning videos, posters, infographics and more.

Videos can communicate the correct response to cyber threats, but so can interactive tasks or gamification in online training. Games engage a learner to actively interact with the course, which facilitates participation with the training rather than watching a video play. Gamification can work as an online workshop that allows the learner to play around with different aspects of scenarios.

Accents, looks, prejudices all distract attention from the presenter rather than the content being told; cartoon characters work because people do not have the same prejudices against characters.

Cybersecurity training can be delivered in several online methods, as well as offline materials and hybrid learning. Hybrid learning provides an opportunity to raise the strength of CSC within an organization. The method of training should be delivered in the best way for the organization. Consultation of organizational resources should be made so that the implementation of the program is achievable.

Encouraging learners to reflect on their education is essential for them to develop their understanding of their habits, attitudes and behaviors. Change does not happen if participants cannot identify the questionable practices that may leave them vulnerable to exploitation or cyber threats.

Reflection enables learning to be more dynamic, it encourages critical thinking skills, to analyze their work and life situations and to imagine different scenarios and people these cybersecurity threats could exploit. This reflection helps to develop their skills and practice of the training they have been taught.

The privacy paradox (Barth & Jong, 2017) demonstrates major discrepancies between users and employees attitudes to cybersecurity and privacy and their actual behavior, mainly that whilst they may claim to be very concerned about their privacy they are very unlikely to take any actions to prevent or protect the disclosure of their personal data.

Simplifying layers of complexity in cybersecurity training is essential to communicate information and education to everyone; it is not productive to believe that all learners will understand the cyber risks, threats or consequences. Building on fundamental principles, some learners may realize the underlying cybersecurity concept, they may not know what they mean. When progressing from primary cybersecurity education to more complex concepts, it is best to lead learners through a story that links to their background so that they can relate it to their own life.

Some online courses or websites suffer the fatal flaw of inadequate or unclear navigation; this means that learners get frustrated or give up on learning due to difficulties in getting where they want to be. Not only is it essential to consider users understanding of how to navigate the learning platform but to track or beta test the learner's journey. Beta testing should be done by users who had no place in the design or development of the course for an accurate reflection of user experience. Explanations of how to navigate the learning platform should be readily available and explained to all learners.

Emails are a simple method of contacting everyone within an organization as they can deliver cybersecurity messaging directly to all members of staff, it also makes training more accessible at a later date so that staff can revisit the staff training portal. It is also easy to track click through rates of staff who take the training and can further help identify risks associated with attitudes and behaviors of staff within an organization. It can also be beneficial to ensure that access to training is found on the organization's intranet.

Training is often created by techies or legislation people. However, the best people to design courses are the marketing team who are great at communication; cybersecurity should be marketed internally,

Teaching cybersecurity courses online can be a perfect medium, a variety of strengths. The Internet is a vast area for growth and exposure for courses; material can be designed instructional to meet the needs of learners best. Humans can control and interact with the program themselves providing opportunities to interact kinesthetically. However, this has some failings as it requires learners to have reasonable access to the Internet to stream content, there can be the possibility of technology errors that lead to courses not being completed.

Adopting courses to the digital environment can be difficult for trainers who need to alter their teaching style, Course and training providers also need to boost or utilize their credibility and reputation as a provider of quality cybersecurity training.

LEARNING REINFORCEMENTS AND RESOURCES

Selecting and developing resources to provide stimulating context and structure to the learning experience fosters strong reinforcement to the learning objectives.

With each of the resources it is critical to consider the following points:

- How firmly does this resource support the key learning objectives?
- Is the language meeting learners reading ages?
- Is the design clear to navigate?
- Have you had others beta test or review the resources?
- Are the questions used to make learners consider the key learning points?
- Does it cater to a broad range of learners?

The more entertaining or funny it is, the more memorable the training is likely to be. Communication awareness training allows fast reactions rather than barriers. IT team need to be approachable and referenced in communications. To support more extensive and continuous learning, it is beneficial to bring cybersecurity back to the forefront of the workforce minds. Encourage members of the workforce to bring business cases to report on.

Reinforcement of training includes carrying out research into cybercrime and cybersecurity in the sector with reports, news articles and statistics about the organization's own industry. Managing cybersecurity risk projects, a robust unified approach to CSC. Behavioral change to develop cyber secure culture is not something that happens overnight. It is something that happens with continued reinforcement and it is therefore imperative that operational procedures and policies have information security at its center. Providing guidance, tools and advice on how to react in the event of an incident and the best practice behavior will benefit the organization immensely.

Reinforcement of key messaging via digital and physical resources such as posters, screen displays, floors stickers and web banners are effective in aiding cognitive recognition if the design, text and tone of voice are consistent, as the human brain subconsciously recognises and pieces together common aspects. Meanwhile, another method of reinforcement is to have the IT department collect evidence of log files presenting successful or unsuccessful attacks upon the organization. These should highlight the potential damage these attacks could present to the organization. This acts as a feedback tool to influence the next line of defense against security issues.

The adoption of a new CSC extends beyond a simple 'Cybersecurity Awareness' campaign. Learners should understand a clear concept of how they will be assessed on a regular basis. This concept may change how they approach cybersecurity risks as they become more alert to any potential examinations. There are however some assessments in cybersecurity that can be done best with a level of deception. This approach is not only practical to assess how high the cybersecurity risk is to an organization but also a learning opportunity for individuals who fall foul of the tests.

Monitoring and target setting, many online courses focus entirely on the outcomes of the end of course tests and quizzes. However, in cybersecurity, the real test comes when utilized in the right situations and learners keeping this education at the front of their mind when dealing with the potential cyber threats.

Activities and outcomes also fall under the greater umbrella of assessment as they are closely intertwined and should be considered in the broader evaluation of the cybersecurity course.

- **Activities:** What will learners do? What tasks will they interact with? Are there interactive knowledge checks or assessments?
- **Outcomes:** What questions will they be able to answer? What knowledge will they have a result of the cybersecurity training?
- **Assessment Criteria:** What are the key criteria points that will let trainers know that learners have taken information in? To what extent?

The best activities are easy to describe, use prompts to help learners understand the tasks, aid learning the critical points of the training and use a combination of stories, analogy, mystery and common interest and help learners to sustain interest in the discipline.

Evaluate learning with short summaries which help learners to remember key points. Users are presented with an oversaturation of information on so many varying forms of media that it has reduced the amount of time that they will concentrate on any one given thing; therefore, it's important the key messaging to be short sharp in order for the user not to be switched off. Recapping the key points from the lesson help to reflect on learning and summarize the courses.

Determining the need for a stronger CSC can be difficult as building a strong business case for the training relies on staff to be honest in relating the aspects of their attitudes, awareness and behavior when interacting with the online environment. IBM conducted a Cybersecurity Intelligence Index report which exposed that 95% of cybersecurity breaches are due to human error (Powers, 2018). Perceptions of staff in regard to cybersecurity can be quite problematic as even a positive attitude towards cybersecurity in organizations has related to risky cybersecurity behaviors (Hadlington, 2017) both attentional and motor impulsivity were both significant positive predictors of risky cybersecurity behaviors.

However, it is not a probable that individuals will be honest or understand the terminology used in self-completion questionnaires, there are a number of bias with self-reporting including the motive of providing desirable responses or misunderstanding of causality.

In research conducted on over 1,000 members of organizations just over half of the respondents (58%) stated that they were aware of security threats and the risk they pose to corporate information, whilst 39% of the respondents thought that it was the company's responsibility to protect data (Muncaster, 2017).

Almost two-thirds of the same respondents (62%) stated that they thought their behavior had a low to moderate impact on the corporation's security and just under half of the respondents (48%) claimed they were not bothered about their corporate security policy as they did not believe it affected their role (Muncaster, 2017).

There are seven core dimensions of security culture using the Security CLTRe Framework (da Veiga, 2010) and these can be used to measure the human factors that contribute to CSC.

1. Behaviors
2. Attitudes
3. Cognitions
4. Compliance
5. Communication
6. Norms
7. Responsibilities

The benefit to creating a business case for online CSC training is that it helps provide insight to the current cybersecurity weaknesses within an organization and it also enables key insights into any patterns of behavior within certain areas of the business. This approach also helps to provide a starting point for key metrics of improvement after implementation of the training. Pre and post measurements would be ascertained to prove a need for the training and the success of the program.

Commonly it is a combination of behavior or attitudes towards CSC that can cause the most human factor damage to an organization. By selecting metrics on attitudes and behaviors it becomes easier to understand and overcome the causal effect on the success of CSC programs and allow the future modification of the training to combat any issues that arise. Creating a report on the current CSC situation allows the reflection of specific contextual or situational security issues, it can also help to identify stronger and weaker groups or department within an organization or identify any patterns that may emerge.

CONCLUSION

There are many benefits to a business or organization getting involved in initiatives to build cybersecurity skills. These include providing individuals and employees with the skills and capabilities to identify and manage a cybersecurity risk effectively. This will benefit the organization as the financial cost to the business can be extremely high and the cost in consumer confidence can cripple a business. Investment into these skills are both essential and cost effective for organizations.

This also provides organizations the opportunity to prioritize, influence and reward employees for developing cybersecurity skills, knowledge and experience that they may pass on to others. It can also help to inspire a more diverse range of talented cybersecurity specialists within the business and beyond and finally it will increase awareness of the career opportunities that are offered, and loyalty to those organization, amongst those wishing to recruit and retain staff (HM Government, 2018).

After the points covered in this chapter, it may seem obvious that implementing a positive change to strengthen CSC in organizations to a sufficient cyber secure workforce would be beneficial to any organization. However, understandably all departments within an organization are competing for funding from a limited fund of financial resources. Some may be required to develop a strong business case for funding the input into CSC.

Recommendations for the successful adoption of a secure CSC is to:

- Secure at all levels of an organization – a full commitment to CSC is essential for the successful adoption across the business, this includes higher levels of the organization who are expected to champion the new cybersecurity policy.
- Implement a CSC plan and policy across the organization that provides a guide for anyone within an organization to follow
- To show successful metrics of companywide adoption and overcome any barriers is essential to assess where the organization currently sits in respect of its CSC and build a report centered around the implementation, goals, success criteria and target audience of the training. This will help provide the measurement of impact.
- Draw upon guidance provided by the industry blogs, resources and white papers.

The manner of communicate with learners and organizations requires a specific understanding of who are learners might be and what the organization want to achieve. Communicating training effectively does not just mean what is said about cybersecurity training but how it is presented. It is the language used, the construction of sentences, the sound of the delivery, and the personality of the trainers all have an influence.

If organizations engage effectively and positively with staff regarding cybersecurity education, then in the event of a breach they are more likely to understand that the organization is a safe environment in which they can report the incident, enabling a quicker response that can minimize the damage done.

REFERENCES

Alkhurayyif, Y. &. (2017). Evaluating Readability as a Factor in Information Security Policies. *International Journal of Trend in Research and Development*, 54-64.

Anderson, L. W. (2002). *Revising Bloom's taxonomy*. Ohio State University.

Barth, S., & Jong, M. D. (2017). The privacy paradox – Investigating discrepancies between expressed privacy concerns and actual online behavior – A systematic literature review. *Telematics and Informatics, 34*(7), 1038–1058. doi:10.1016/j.tele.2017.04.013

Bloom, B. S. (1956). *Taxonomy of educational objectives*. New York: Longmans, Green.

da Veiga, A., & Eloff, J. H. P. (2010). A framework and assessment instrument for information security culture. *Computers & Security, 29*(2), 196–207. doi:10.1016/j.cose.2009.09.002

ENISA. (2018). *Cyber Security Culture In Organisations*. Retrieved from ENISA: https://www.enisa.europa.eu/publications/cyber-security-culture-in-organisations/at_download/fullReport

Government, H. M. (2018). *Cyber Security Skills: A guide for business*. Retrieved from HM Government: https://assets.publishing.service.gov.uk/government/uploads/system/uploads/attachment_data/file/386248/bis-14-1276-cyber-security-skills-a-guide-for-business.pdf

Hadlington, L. (2017). Human factors in cybersecurity; examining the link between Internet addiction, impulsivity, attitudes towards cybersecurity, and risky cyber security behaviours. *Heliyon (London)*, 00346.

Muncaster, P. (2017). Cisco: Complacency and Ignorance Make Staff Major Security Threat. *Infosecurity Magazine*. Retrieved from https://www.infosecurity-magazine.com/news/complacency-and-low-awareness/

Powers, C. (2018). *Are hackers targeting your industry? Find out in the 2015 Cybersecurity Intelligence Index*. Retrieved from IBM: https://www.ibm.com/developerworks/community/blogs/81c130c7-4408-4e01-adf5-658ae0ef5f0c/entry/Are_hackers_targeting_your_industry_Find_out_in_the_2015_Cyber_Security_Intelligence_Index?lang=en

Web Accessibility Initiative. (2018). *Web Content Accessibility Guidelines (WCAG) Overview*. Retrieved from Web Accessibility Initiative: https://www.w3.org/WAI/standards-guidelines/wcag/

Section 4
Teaching Practices, Models, and Technologies

Chapter 22
Delivering Cybersecurity Education Effectively

Alastair Irons
University of Sunderland, UK

ABSTRACT

This chapter draws on current research and best practice into teaching in cybersecurity in higher education. The chapter provides a theoretical and pedagogical foundation for helping tutors make decisions about what topics to include and approaches to teaching and assessing the cybersecurity curriculum. There are of course a range of potential stakeholders in cybersecurity education ranging from government, policy, and law makers to all members of society. However, for the purposes of brevity, this chapter will focus on learners and those creating and delivering cybersecurity education in the higher education (HE) sector.

INTRODUCTION

The chapter discusses the opportunities for different and innovative ways of learning about cybersecurity – designed to provide deep learning and thus a greater understanding of principles, theories and applications of cybersecurity. The purpose of the chapter is to explore the differences between the delivery of cybersecurity education and the delivery of other computing-based subjects in Higher Education. Whilst the delivery of cybersecurity will utilize good practice from the delivery of computing, computer science and other subjects in HE the discussion in this chapter attempts to emphasize and examine the issues from a cybersecurity perspective.

In recent years, computing technology and computer systems have experienced dramatic growth. The growth in the number of systems (communications, information systems, Internet systems and e-commerce) and the advances in the scale, the functionality and the usability of systems have provided opportunities for malicious users to exploit insecure and non-robust systems. The pace at which companies and their customers have embraced technologies such as cloud computing, smart devices, mobile technologies, and the Internet of Things (IoT) has created an environment that is changing faster than organizations and legislators can keep abreast of. It's not only systems that are changing – the way people use the

DOI: 10.4018/978-1-6684-3554-0.ch022

systems and the expectations of speed and convenience means that cybersecurity can often be relegated in importance. Allied to the growth in systems technologies is the growth in the amount of data that is provided and the huge variety of ways in which data is collected, manipulated and stored.

The range of systems and technologies and the speed of implementation and adoption provide opportunities for cybercriminals to exploit. In addition to chance to take advantage of vulnerabilities in systems the advances in technology give computer criminals the opportunity to conceal their activities, to cover their tracks and attempt to destroy evidence of their actions. The ability to prevent cybercrime attacks and cybersecurity breaches that have taken place and the resultant requirement to examine the cybertrail have raised the need to develop specialists in cybersecurity – a set of practitioners who have the methods, skills and techniques to prevent, detect, recover and restore systems and data in the event of an attack.

The global news headlines frequently present cybersecurity attacks, vulnerabilities or failures, illustrating that there is an increasing loss of control over the cyber-threats to business. Recent years have seen high profile attacks to major corporations such as Tesco Bank, Talk Talk, Daimler Chrysler. In 2017 the NHS in the UK (along with 160 other organizations) were rocked by the "Wannacry" attack. Other headlines have reported belief and fear that the recent U.S. elections could be manipulated by a foreign power and speculation over whether development in artificial intelligence could lead to cyber attacks perpetrated by machines, without any human motivation.

The changing technology environment and the growth in threats and potential threats means that the role of cybersecurity is increasing in importance. As society and business becomes more reliant on cybersecurity the efficiency of cybersecurity education – what we teach and how we teach it – becomes an important objective. Similarly, there is a need to consider the learners, what they need and want to learn as well as how they learn as in integral part of cybersecurity education.

McGettrick (2013) argues for the need for cybersecurity education as opposed to cybersecurity training. In this chapter the focus is on cybersecurity education – but as tends to be the case with discussion on any aspect of cybersecurity there is overlap between the categories, so some aspects of training come in to the consideration of cybersecurity education. Part of the rationale for looking at this topic is because there are so many different providers offering a range of different cybersecurity learning products claiming to deliver education and training.

It is worth asking the question as to why there should be consideration given to examining the ways in which to deliver cybersecurity education. Cybersecurity is a complex and wide-ranging topic (or series of topics) to consider. The complexity associated with cybersecurity means that there is a need to consider different teaching approaches to enable cybersecurity learning. Rashid et al (2018) argue that "the foundational knowledge on which the field of cybersecurity is being developed is fragmented, and as a result, it can be difficult for both students and educators to map coherent paths of progression through the subject". There are many topic domains in which we potentially have interest in cybersecurity including (but not limited to) information security, systems security, network security and Internet security each with a set of fundamentals and principles and different theories and applications. In addition, there is an interesting mix of technical, policy, governance, ethical and human / society subjects which require different approaches to teaching and learning. As far back as 1997, Pfleeger et al (1997) suggested a broad range of sub topics making up the cybersecurity knowledge base, including "security policy, privileges, authentication, correctness and auditing", and how these relate "trusted systems, operating systems, database management systems, distributed systems, cryptography, protocols, system correctness, intrusion detection and mobile code". Hallet et al (2018) raise questions about the number of cybersecurity curriculum frameworks and indicate concerns about lack of equivalence across the different frameworks. The breadth of subjects to include makes the delivery of cybersecurity education even more complex.

Teaching cybersecurity as a subject in its own right is complicated enough. However, there is a further complicating factor because there is an additional expectation that cybersecurity is taught as part of the curriculum across the computing / computer science family of disciplines. Irons et al (2016) argue that embedding cybersecurity into computing science degrees presents a real opportunity to ensure that everyone involved in creating the digital economy – especially the technology underpinning it – understand the threats, vulnerabilities and mitigations that need to be managed. Embedding cybersecurity, and contextualizing cybersecurity, in other computing subjects such as programming, databases, and networks is important in the development of those subjects. The challenges in teaching cybersecurity in these disciplines runs in parallel with the effective teaching of cybersecurity as a specialist subject in its own right. Cybersecurity has recently (2017) been added to the components of the BCS accreditation criteria, reflecting the importance placed on cybersecurity and the expectation that all computing graduates should have knowledge and skills in cybersecurity as they move towards chartered status.

Cybersecurity is a rapidly changing and rapidly evolving discipline. This means that anyone involved in cybersecurity to a greater or lesser extent, from a technical to a managerial, from an organizational to an individual level needs to constantly review and update their knowledge on cybersecurity. This in itself presents a challenge for efficient cybersecurity education.

Anyone working or seeking to work in cybersecurity needs to develop a range of abilities and competencies in addition their technical knowledge of cybersecurity. For example, cybersecurity practitioners will come across situations where they are required as professionals to be able to make judgments when faced with uncertainty. Linked to this is the need to be able to have the confidence to react quickly to situations with robust and reliable solutions. Cybersecurity practitioners will need to be able to work both as part of a team and independently. Teaching these competences has an impact on the way that we seek to teach cybersecurity efficiently and effectively.

Invariably when we look how to teach cybersecurity education effectively there will be consideration given to the topics covered elsewhere in this book. Where appropriate there will be cross-reference to materials and topics covered other sections. In particular we will look at the links between the other chapters relating to cybersecurity curricula and the education program.

The remainder of this chapter covers the challenges in cybersecurity education; what to teach; how to teach effectively; approaches to learning and teaching cybersecurity; balance between theory and practice; use of technology in teaching; assessing cybersecurity knowledge, understanding and skills; and the need for continued professional development.

CHALLENGES IN CYBERSECURITY EDUCATION

There are many challenges in cybersecurity education, and these are discussed in this section. Understanding and overcoming the challenges in education will enable cybersecurity education to be delivered effectively. This section looks at the particular challenges in cybersecurity education and compare to the approaches used in other computing disciplines.

One of the key challenges in cybersecurity education is addressing the skills gap. (ISC)[2] report (2016) suggest that there are 350,000 open / unfilled cybersecurity positions unfilled worldwide and that this number is growing. Oltsik (2017) suggests that the skills gap in cybersecurity is getting worse. Oltsik identifies a growing problem with organizations indicating more than a doubling of "problematic shortage" of cybersecurity staff, increasing from 23% in 2014 to 51% in 2018. This provides a real challenge for cybersecurity educators.

The objectives of the cybersecurity education will depend on the level of learning to be achieved, the previous experience and knowledge of the participants, the subjects and topics of interest to the participants and the desired learning outcomes from the education. There are many challenges in cybersecurity education, as we shall see later in this chapter. However, the range of people potentially interested in cybersecurity and the variability in the depth and breadth of cybersecurity knowledge that they have, and that they need, mean the cybersecurity educators can collaborate with a wide range of colleagues to share their experiences and provide a wide variety of educational experiences.

The National Cyber Security Centre (NCSC) have produced a cyber attack categorization framework (2018) designed to indicate the priority that should be given to investigating different cyber attacks. The new framework increases the number of classifications from three to six (category 1 'national cyber emergency' to category 6 'localized incident'. Whilst the framework is designed to improve consistency around response and provide a better outcome for victims, the framework also illustrates the complexity of the cybercrime environment. The complexity can also be seen in the need for cybersecurity education – ranging from a general awareness that cybersecurity is a potential threat, through to what the threats are to what can be done about cybersecurity at a personal level to in depth technical expertise in creating and implementing cybersecurity infrastructure.

It is not the intention in this chapter to provide a framework on which topics to cover at which level – suggestions have been recommended in the previous chapters in this book. Harris and Patten (2015) provide a very good discussion relating cybersecurity skills and knowledge to levels of learning, linking cybersecurity to Bloom's and Webb's taxonomies. The ACM/IEEE (2017) report suggests a series of expectations for the cybersecurity curriculum and recommends which cybersecurity topics to consider. A common theme from all those who examine and evaluate the cybersecurity curriculum is the progression from remembering and understanding the cybersecurity fundamental principles and theories, to applying the principles and theories to cybersecurity problems, to making judgements based on those principles (and on standards and legislation) to creating solutions and providing strategic direction for cybersecurity. As indicated earlier the spectrum of subjects covered in the cybersecurity curriculum range from mathematically based, through technical cybersecurity and practical skills development to almost social science type subjects looking at the impact of cybersecurity on society.

This has a direct bearing on the way cybersecurity is taught. In particular there is a need to consider different ways of teaching for different aspects of the curriculum and using appropriate approaches to contextualize the expected learning for students and learners.

A further challenge in cybersecurity teaching is the interdisciplinary / multi-disciplinary nature of cybersecurity. Whilst there are a range of diverse discipline including criminology, psychology, sociology, law and mathematics which inform a range of cybersecurity topics including policy, human factors, ethics, and risk management, cybersecurity remains fundamentally a computing-based discipline. The challenge in teaching cybersecurity is that cybersecurity is both informed by the interdisciplinary content and driven by the needs and perspectives of the computing disciplines that provide the underpinning fundamentals of cybersecurity.

The multi-disciplinary aspect of cybersecurity is not necessarily a benefit – it could be argued that the multi-disciplinary aspects potentially dilute the core of the subject. However, it is suggested in this chapter that drawing from other disciplines strengthens cybersecurity in terms of rigor and robustness and also strengthens the suggestion that cybersecurity can stand as a separate and distinct discipline in its own right.

In order to allow students to apply theory and develop cybersecurity skills there is a need to analyze appropriately complex case studies and problems. The challenge for teachers is to develop materials that allow problem solving, analysis and application of theory and at the same time provide an environment to practice and make mistakes without falling foul of regulations (for example JANet regulations in universities in the UK) and to protect students and learners from exposure to inappropriate cases.

In any cybersecurity problems in the real world there are many complex and inter-related variables to consider, a number of legal considerations to contend with, many technical issues to be aware of and many cybersecurity principles, theories and guidelines to apply. There is a challenge for cybersecurity educators to put over this complex environment in teaching the subject without overwhelming students.

WHAT TO TEACH?

The curricula aspects are covered in later chapters of this book. In addition, the material covered in the UK's National Cyber Security Strategy (2017) and the Cyber Security Body of Knowledge (CyBOK) project has been established to codify the foundational and generally recognized knowledge on cybersecurity. At the time of writing the first two Knowledge Areas – Cryptography and Software Security – are open for public consultation. They can be viewed at www.cybok.org. The ACM have provided a comprehensive document outlining the curriculum Guidelines for Post-Secondary Degree Programs in Cybersecurity (2017). Hallet et al (2018) indicate that there are a number of different cybersecurity curricula. The different bodies promoting cybersecurity curricula include the Institute of Information Security Professionals (IISP), Joint Task Force (JTF), National Initiative for Cybersecurity Education (NICE), and the National Cyber Security Centre (NCSC). All of these bodies have indicated what they consider to be important components of the cybersecurity curricula. All of the frameworks in the examples above cover some overlapping but also some significantly different aspects of cybersecurity which makes it difficult for educators to decide what to include in cybersecurity teaching.

In this chapter consideration is given about what to teach about cybersecurity depending on the audience of learners and the relationship to how to deliver cybersecurity education effectively. What to teach and how to teach it effectively will vary depending on the audience and the experience of those in the audience. There is a large spectrum of potentially interested learners ranging from school pupils (all pupils), through school pupils studying computing and computer science at GCSE and A – level to students at college and university (again with a split between cybersecurity specialists, to computer science students to students in other disciplines such as business and engineering) and on to practitioners and professionals requiring continued professional development (CPD).

As indicated earlier in the chapter cybersecurity practitioners will come across situations where they are required as professionals deal confidently with uncertainty and make judgments about complex situations. One of the ways to address the potential issues of judgement and confidence is to consider computer ethics in the context of cybersecurity.

There is a significant challenge in teaching ethical awareness and embedding ethical principles into the cybersecurity teaching. There is a need to make students aware of the potential for misuse of cybersecurity tools and techniques as well as the need to instill ethical and professional behavior into cybersecurity practices. The teaching of computer ethics is normally embedded throughout computer science programs in order to meet professional body (for example BCS) expectations and requirements. Teaching cybersecurity requires emphasis on ethical issues early in the curriculum in order to instill the importance of appropriate ethical behavior right at the beginning of the students' cybersecurity program so that they have the ethical tools and mind set to allow them to deal with complex and challenging ethical dilemmas faced in cybersecurity education.

The coverage of computer ethics focuses on the professional responsibilities of a cybersecurity practitioner, namely using the skills and techniques of cybersecurity professional to the benefit of society and not to use cybersecurity knowledge for criminal activity or personal gain. A further thread of ethical consideration is to deal with cases sensitively and professionally maintaining the confidentiality and anonymity of participants in case or problem being studied.

There is also a "gamekeepers and poachers" dilemma in teaching cybersecurity. In order to develop the skills and techniques required to become a cybersecurity practitioner, students need to develop understanding and knowledge of the tools and techniques applied by cyber criminals. As students realize the security vulnerabilities and weaknesses in procedures and systems the temptation to utilize this awareness may arise. The concern in the "gamekeeper poacher dilemma" is that universities could become complicit in creating cyber criminals of the future rather than developing practitioners who are motivated to work against cybercrime.

There is potentially a different type of ethical dilemma associated with the teaching of cybersecurity, namely cybersecurity has the potential to put forward an unbalanced view and perspective in tackling computer crime, cyber attacks and misuse of data. One way to redress this potential concern is to include topics such as civil liberties and the Human Rights Act (1998) in the ethical consideration of cybersecurity.

DELIVERING EDUCATION EFFECTIVELY

In this section a brief discussion on what we mean by delivering education effectively will be presented – looking at engagement of learners, how learners learn, getting the learning materials and concepts to learners and metrics how to evaluate effectiveness of learning. These topics will be explored in the cybersecurity context.

In order to provide effective teaching in cybersecurity there is an expectation that the lecturer has a level of expertise and understanding of the subject, knows how the students learn and understands the range of pedagogic approaches that can be utilized. Subject knowledge is required to enable the lecturer to determine the most appropriate way to put across the subject and to organize and structure the teaching activities (and the series of learning activities if appropriate) in such a way that enables students to learn. In order for teaching to be effective it is important that the lecturer understands the level that students are at in their learning and us such appreciate what it is students know. Understanding the audience of learners will help the lecturer to identify the most appropriate approach to ensure clear communication and to determine the best ways to stimulate, inspire and excite the students.

As well will see with all the methods discuss in the next section, effective teaching is not only dependent on good lecturers and good lecturing. There is a responsibility on students to engage with the learning opportunities afforded them. One way to male teaching more effective is to work with students so that they understand their role in learning.

It is important for providers of cybersecurity education to consider the effectiveness of the learning opportunities to enable students develop the wide range of skills needed to be a cybersecurity professional. As well as the theoretical knowledge and technical skills involved in cybersecurity as a subject there is the need for cybersecurity professionals to have expertise in team working, the ability to make judgments (often under pressure) and the capability to become lifelong learners.

It is all well and good looking to have effective education, but what is meant by effective education and how will it be known when cybersecurity education is effective? Effective education can be viewed from a number of perspectives and different stakeholders will have different views on effectiveness. Suffice to say is that there is a need to measure something – but what?

The focus of this chapter is what makes effective cybersecurity education from a student perspective, but first consideration will be given as to what might be a suitable metric to use in determining whether the cybersecurity education is effective.

It has long been acknowledged (Lundstedt, 1966) that it is difficult to quantify what is meant by effective teaching. Quantifying effective teaching remains problematic today – there is an acceptance that effectiveness relates to the communication between teacher and learner, but that there is also an understanding of the learner needs in making teaching effective. Recently there has been a move towards considering "value" and "value added" in considering effective teaching. Barnett (1992) suggests that "value added" is one of the metrics in measuring the success of Higher Education. Although, Schleicher (2015) argues that although valued added has been on the HE agenda for a number of years it remains notoriously difficult to quantify as a measure. That said, the concepts of "value" and "value added" are particularly relevant in considering effective teaching in cybersecurity.

There are of course a range of perspectives on what constitutes effective teaching. From a government perspective there is a desire to drive down the cost of teaching in Higher Education and at the same time improve quality assurance, which gives an interesting dilemma for providers of Higher Education. Linked to cost, effectiveness might be measured in terms of class size, or the amount of contact time – it will depend what is important for the education provider.

Since the introduction of the National Student Survey (NSS) in the UK there has been an increasing emphasis on measuring student satisfaction and using student satisfaction as a proxy for effective teaching. There has been a significant amount of debate as the veracity of student satisfaction as a measure of effective teaching (for example Williams and Cappuccini-Ansfield, 2007), but whether it is correct or not, the NSS remains a metric which is utilized by Higher Education managers, government and creators of league tables!

Other drivers as far as measuring effectiveness of teaching in HE focus on research, research outputs and research income. Putting an emphasis on research in cybersecurity might conflict with providing effective teaching. However, if the principles of the teaching research nexus (Jenkins and Healy, 2005) are embraced then embedding current research, developing students' skills as researchers, and applying research informed teaching there can benefit to the students' overall learning experience. This begs a question as to whether there are unique research skills for those studying cybersecurity. There are a number of specific subject areas that are unique to cybersecurity including the impact of cybersecurity breaches; technical developments in cybersecurity; cybersecurity futures as well as a series of applications that are cybersecurity specific. The Engineering and Physical Sciences Research Council (EPSRC) has identified Academic Centres of Excellence (ACE) in Cybersecurity – based on the quality of academic research and publication in cybersecurity, critical mass of researchers, and investment in cybersecurity facilities – and these certainly illustrate that there is a range of cybersecurity topics worthy of research. The research skills cybersecurity students need to be on undergraduate and postgraduate degrees have much in common with the research skills required for other computing disciplines but should be contextualized to the cybersecurity environment. Of course, care needs to be taken in creating physical resources to enable cybersecurity research – this is particularly important when experiments are to be undertaken as part of research. For example, if students are building cybersecurity defenses against potential breaches and the defenses need to be tested it may be prudent to take the whole experiment to an autonomous network – certainly one which is removed from the standard university network.

Looking at efficiency in cybersecurity teaching from a pedagogic perspective the purpose is not have passive, compliant, surface learners in cybersecurity but to have participants who are independent, active learners who will be equipped with higher level skills in cybersecurity. In structuring learning and teaching activities (discussed in the next section) it is important that think about how to develop higher skills and encourage learners to be independent and active. This links in to key questions on learning and teaching in cybersecurity:

- What do should the students to learn (linked to curriculum and syllabus – see related chapters in this book)?
- What are the students actually learning (and how to measure a level of understanding)? The measurement of actual learning will be returned to in the ways in which student understanding is assessed in cybersecurity, later in this chapter).

The points above suggests a process of constructive alignment, whereas Biggs (1996) suggests the "aspects of teaching and assessment are tuned to support high level learning, so that all students are encouraged to use higher-order learning processes".

As well as technical skills there is the need to develop the softer skills in cybersecurity and include the development of these skills in cybersecurity teaching. There are the common soft skills such as problem solving, group work and communication that can be applied in a cybersecurity context. However, there are soft skills, which are potentially unique to the cybersecurity learner – for example

- How to raise awareness about the threats of cybersecurity;
- How to provide information to senior colleagues about the impact of cybersecurity breaches in language that will be understandable to non-cybersecurity people;
- How to do both of the above in a professional manner;
- How to give cybersecurity advice and feedback in non-technical language without being patronizing.

If effective teaching and learning is examined from a student perspective (it is suggested in this chapter that this is the most important perspective) then other variables come in to play. According to Cohen (1981) students want "systematic, stimulating and caring teaching that leads to success". In order to achieve this in cybersecurity is it suggested that learning providers try to ensure that:

- learning is transparent – i.e. it is clear to the learners what the learning objectives are and that the learners have the opportunity to put cybersecurity theory and principles into practice;
- teaching activities facilitate dialogue between teachers and learners and between learners; and

- there is the opportunity to develop communities of learners (based on Wegner (2000) and communities of practice.

The next section will examine tools and techniques for the delivery of cybersecurity teaching taking into account the aspiration and expectation that the teaching is effective.

APPROACHES TO LEARNING AND TEACHING CYBERSECURITY

In this section of the chapter a range of alternatives to enable learning in cybersecurity and encourage learner engagement, and effectiveness of the learning opportunity will be examined. Scheponik et al (2016) have argued that "despite the documented need to train and educate more cybersecurity professionals, we have little rigorous evidence to inform educators on effective ways to engage, educate, or retain cybersecurity students". Scheponik goes on to suggest that there is still a great deal of work to be undertaken in order to understand the most appropriate pedagogic approach in cybersecurity education. The different methods and approaches to teaching cybersecurity are not presented in any ranked order. The most appropriate method of delivery will depend on the subject matter and topic of cybersecurity, the level of cybersecurity experience of the learners and other variables such as group size and learning environment.

The benefits and issues associated with each approach will be presented. Each method will be discussed in the context of teaching cybersecurity and how they can enhance efficiency in the teaching of cybersecurity. Consideration will also be given as to where and how online learning and educational technology can be utilized to enhance the efficiency of the particular method.

Lectures

There is place for lecturing as a didactic learning method in cybersecurity, especially in situations where the audience is very new to cybersecurity or the speaker is particularly inspiring. Experienced cybersecurity practitioners are able to share real life examples or "war stories" which can be very beneficial in contextualizing cybersecurity theories, principles and issues for learners. Covill (2011) suggests that "students in a lecture-style class report learning a great deal, being involved in the learning process, and engaging in independent thinking and problem solving". Lectures continue to be a dominant form of teaching in Higher Education in the UK, despite the assertion lectures are not always the most effective way of engaging students. The learning that takes place as a result if a lecture depends on student engagement, the relevance of the subject matter and on the abilities and style of the lecturer.

Research carried out by Irons and Devlin (2012) on inspiring teaching identified (form a student perspective) what student considered to be important in lecture sessions and perhaps more importantly what they did not like in lecture sessions. The following list indicated what students didn't want from lectures or what they didn't like about lectures:

- Endless amounts of facts being dictated for long periods of time;
- Just reading from slides;
- Someone who is unprepared and uninspired by the subject they're teaching;

- Monotone, too many detailed slides, when the teacher is not interested in either the subject or the students' understanding;
- Boring;
- Teachers who talk down to you and treat you like you're back in secondary school;
- Too much information for 1 hour and we leave without complete understanding;
- When the teacher doesn't want to be there.

The detail provided by students on what the found to be uninspiring is a really useful list of things to avoid when lecturing on cybersecurity.

The following list suggests what make efficient lectures from a student perspective;

- Whenever someone gets up and is enthusiastic about what they're trying to teach you;
- When a teacher is comfortable enough about a subject to use examples of when they got it horribly wrong to help understanding;
- Yes – they're very knowledgeable and willing to help all of the time;
- They make jokes or use funny real-life situations;
- Use of stories or comparisons to help us learn;
- Their outlook and way of talking about things – friendly and approachable;
- Instead of just throwing information at you they got you involved in the subject;
- Passionate;
- They enjoy what they do;
- The way they delivered it – asked questions rather than giving answers;
- Their ability to make the subject relevant; and
- They broke down information into smaller more manageable sections.

The list of factors that appear to inspire students pertain to lecturing in cybersecurity. As well as the expectation of through subject knowledge it is important for those lecturing in cybersecurity to be enthusiastic, passionate and care about the subject matter. The subject matter and the relevance and currency of so many of the issues in cyber security and cybersecurity breaches can be drawn from current news stories. To this end, although it is a set of circumstances that should be avoided and prevented, the fact that there are so many news stories about cybersecurity, breaches of security, cyber attacks and cybercrime mean that it is possible to relate current affairs to the theories and principles that are conveyed in lectures.

Lectures can also be enhanced by use of technology – for example giving students access to lecture notes beforehand on virtual learning environments (VLEs) or by using lecture capture technology so that students can access materials outside the lecture session.

Flipped Classroom

The flipped classroom is an interesting way of changing the dynamic of lecture sessions. In a flipped learning session, the students have access to the planned material in advance, undertake learning before they come to the classroom and then use the class contact time to ask questions, discuss issues and explore the subject in more detail. Exponents of the flipped classroom (from example Alvarez, 2011, Johnston and Karafotias, 2016) suggest that this is an effective way to use student contact time for effective learning.

The author has used this approach in cybersecurity teaching and has had mixed results. When students engage in the process and come to the class prepared (having done the homework in advance of the class) then the teaching sessions can be very productive – in particular when students are willing to ask questions and to debate and discuss issues and principles the learning can be really exciting. From a teaching perspective it is important to a) be well prepared for a range of topics to be discussed (often not the ones that were expected) and b) to have a plan B when students haven't done the pre- work.

Webinars

Related to lectures in many ways, making use of technology, and much used in the cybersecurity subject area are webinars. Webinars enable those delivering sessions to deliver presentations to larger, geographically dispersed audiences. Webinars are live web-based video conference that use the internet to connect those hosting the webinar to the audience. The audience is not constrained by geography. Webinars are flexible in what is presented – audio, video, slideshows, demonstrations and can have multiple presenters from different locations. Some commentators, for example Joshi et al (2011) indicate that webinars are effective with "the most notable aspect of webinars was that it brought about the comparable gain in knowledge, skills and satisfaction".

Webinars and the technology supporting webinars enable a number of learning opportunities which contribute to their effectiveness. For example, webinars have the following features, including:

- **The Ability to Record the Webinar:** Which (like lecture capture) allows the material to be reviewed at a later date and re-used by the learner;
- **The Opportunity to Enable Chat Features:** Which allows students to type in questions and queries without disturbing the flow of the session. Chat questions can then be addressed later;
- **Application Sharing, Where Appropriate:** Allowing lecturers to share their desktops or applications, etc. to help the audience get a better understanding of the topic;
- **The Capacity to Conduct Opinion Polls:** By using this at strategic points in the webinar the lecturer can conduct polls and surveys for the audience, which helps in terms of getting a feel for audience understanding.

Practical Activities in Cybersecurity

In order to develop proficiency in cybersecurity there needs to be a balance between the theoretical and conceptual knowledge essential to understanding cybersecurity, and the practical skills that support the application of that knowledge. Weiss et al (2013) suggest that cybersecurity students learn best when they have hands-on experience. The challenge for lecturers and teachers is to ensure that the exercises enable student learning and push students to learn more about cybersecurity. As shall be illustrated later in this chapter when discussing case studies and problem-based learning it is difficult in cybersecurity to reflect the complexity of reality and at the same time design activities that can be successful at achieving in relatively short time periods. Practical activities can be standalone (not linked to other cybersecurity teaching) or more traditionally an opportunity to explore theoretical aspects of cybersecurity from lectures or research in a practical setting. The author has used practical activities in cybersecurity as short sharp learning opportunities, usually linked to a lecture session and as extended learning activities over a longer period of time. Longer activities start to move towards case studies and problem based / project-based learning approaches see below.

Case Studies and Scenarios

In order to address the challenge of realism a case study-based approach can be utilized. There are classic case studies already in cybersecurity such as the "Stuxnet", "Equifax" and "Wannacry" for example. Case studies and scenarios provide examples of people or organizations in real situations which allow learners the opportunity to examine and evaluate authentic problems, as well as apply potential solutions, that will provide clarity as opposed to trying to learn by the study of abstract theories or principles. Case studies attempt to mirror the type of situation that cybersecurity practitioners will encounter in the working environment by providing realistic learning opportunities. One of the interesting opportunities in teaching cybersecurity is the ever-growing number of instances that can be used to formulate case studies. It is almost the case that there is at least one significant breach every week that is worthy of study – ranging from attacks against individuals to attacks against organizations and even national states.

Use can be made of case studies in both teaching and practical sessions as well in the development of problem-solving approach and assessments. This approach provides the opportunity to illustrate the complexity of the cybersecurity environment and allows students to be guided through specific tasks in specific cases whilst at the same time developing their technical skill, their analytical skills and their problem-solving abilities. Scheponik et al (2016) have used scenarios in cybersecurity to develop students' skills in "adversarial thinking", a key skill in the analysis of cybersecurity situations and problems, helping students understand the issues from attack and defense positions but also from a legal perspective.

There is a difficulty in creating case studies from scratch both in terms of making them simple enough at one end of the scale to being complex enough at the other. At the same time the case studies need to be authentic and also motivate students. There are ethical considerations, which need to be taken into account when creating cases particularly around the use of live cases (albeit historical live cases) or simulations based on live cases. In order for case study creation to be efficient in the cybersecurity domain it would be very helpful for colleagues to work together to co-create and to share case studies. Recently (2016-17) there was an attempt by Higher Education Academy (now Advance HE) to establish collaborative projects leading to shared resources through a series of development grant funds.

The creation of case study material cases for analysis can potentially contravene the rights of those original involved in the cases (even when anonymity is used) issues. Case studies designed to provide students with appropriate experiences might actually infringe University regulations or even the law – for example when trying to simulate system breaches.

There is a further concern that using case studies based on reality might provide students with ideas for criminal activity that they didn't have prior to studying the case study. (see discussion on ethics in cybersecurity earlier in the chapter).

Problem-Based Learning

Problem-based learning (PBL) has been used to positive effect in a number of academic disciplines; Boud and Feletti (1997:1) advocate that PBL is the 'most significant innovation in education for the professions for many years. PBL has been used in many disciplines including computer science for a number of years to develop students' skills in solving authentic and realistic problems. Discussion of

PBL examples from the computing science literature include: Nuutila, Törmä, and Malmi (2005), Fee and Holland-Minkley (2010) and van Merriënboer (2013). Kessler (2007:264) discusses the use of PBL in problem solving:

Ill-defined problems or scenarios can be a fun and interesting way for students to synthesize and/or expand their knowledge, making abstract concepts more real. In PBL problems and scenarios tend to be real, relevant, and tangible, students usually are more motivated to work hard on these projects, often making many real-world assumptions that are applicable to them, further helping to improve their problem-solving skills.

The author was part of a team that developed PBL materials for cybersecurity and one of the objectives of the project was to "improve the efficiency of cybersecurity education and to help students develop the wide range of skills needed to be a cybersecurity professional". In particular the project attempted to give students the opportunity to develop their cybersecurity understanding by reducing 'information overload' and stopping students from learning huge amounts of unnecessary theoretical detail. As part of the application of PBL students had the chance to improve their control over their learning by designing the PBL activities to allow students to self-direct, to locate what they need to know and give them possession of their learning.

One of the key aspects identified in the project is that although problem-based learning may appear to be the application of common sense (student perception) it is actually a difficult learning skill (set of learning skills) to master. Therefore, it is important when using PBL in cybersecurity teaching to include learning guides for tutors and learning guides for learners.

An example of a PBL task in Cybersecurity is given in Box 1.

Box 1.

In this activity students are encouraged to reflect on the impact of Edward Snowden's disclosure of National Security Agency documentation. In particular consider the impact on the agencies in the UK, particularly GCHQ, MI5 and MI6.

Objectives
The objective of this activity is to analyze the impact of the actions of Edward Snowden in 2013 and the subsequent reaction of the public (impact on society), the security agencies in the UK, USA and around the globe, and an understanding of the legal issues that the scenario raises

Tasks
    1. Undertake research into the timeline of the main points of the Edward Snowden case
    2. Consider the legal, social and ethical issues that should be considered in light of the scenario
    3. Identify the implications for the cybersecurity community
    4. Relate to other similar scenarios – such as Bradley Manning

Outputs
At the end of this activity you should have developed
- Your own perspective on the correctness or otherwise of Snowden's actions and have created
- A report on the legal issues associated with gathering data on the public;
- A diagram to illustrate the relationship between cybersecurity and surveillance / dataveillance;
- A set of questions from your PBL work on the Snowden example to discuss with your tutor and class.

This type of PBL learning in the context of cybersecurity, as the example illustrates, encourages students to examine the complexities associated with cybersecurity and work as a group to further their understanding of cybersecurity topics.

MOOCs

MOOCs are another example of where technology can be utilized in the teaching of cybersecurity. A number of institutions, for example Harvard, provide Massive Open Online Courses (MOOCs) for the public. The Harvard program (gs.harvardx.harvard.edu/cyber-security/online-course) provides learners with the opportunity to obtain a Harvard certificate. Advocates argue that MOOCs are the future of on-line education. There has been an exponential growth in the use of MOOCs including in cybersecurity. Although MOOCs do not normally provide the full coverage of a degree, they are very useful in prepping students for study and providing introductions to the cybersecurity subject area. There are two distinct types of MOOC: cMOOC and xMOOC. cMOOCs are collaborative MOOCs that provide learning space for students to collaborate. On the other hand, xMOOCs put existing courses into an online format and as such tend to adopt a more traditional format to courses.

There are a number of UK examples of cybersecurity MOOCs – for instance Newcastle University have teamed up with FutureLearn to produce a 3 week introductory MOOC on cybersecurity, https://www.futurelearn.com/courses/cyber-security. The course covers topics such as privacy, payment safety and online safety at home. The Open University's Centre for Policing Research and Learning has also created a MOOC introducing cybersecurity.

Bootcamps

Bootcamps appear to be growing in popularity and these tend to be shorter, focused courses often running for a week or 10 days. Bootcamps offer a different approach to education often being run by industry experts. At the author's institution we have put in place a series of weeklong bootcamps for final year undergraduate and masters students run by visiting professors in cybersecurity. The feedback from students has been very positive about this approach, particularly when it is blended in with a more traditional structure of delivery. The cybersecurity Bootcamps that have been used at the author's institution have the added advantage of providing a test at the end of the bootcamp and a certificate for those succeeding the assessment. The author has then used the bootcamp and the test completion as material for an evaluative assessment exercise (see section on assessment later in this chapter).

Peer Learning

Students have the opportunity to learn from each other in Higher Education – working in groups, participating in discussion, reviewing demonstrations and undertaking problem-based learning are all examples where peer learning can take place in cybersecurity. Boud (1988) suggests that peer learning moves from independent learning to interdependent learning. The concept of interdependent learning would seem to be appropriate for cybersecurity learning.

There is the potential in peer learning for students to enhance their knowledge of cybersecurity concepts by explaining their understanding to their colleagues and to other students. Peer discussions allow for collaborative working, giving and receiving feedback and potentially evaluating their own learning.

Normally peer learning takes place between students in the same class / same level, but at the author's institution we have also introduced peer support between different levels through a peer mentoring project. The idea was to support learners at lower levels with peers who had been through those levels. Interestingly we found that it was peers at the higher level who benefited most and improved their understanding through the development of their skills in communication, organization and collaborative support.

Threat Sharing Platforms

Threat sharing platforms seek to protect against potential cyber attacks on organizations by providing the opportunity for sharing information on cyber threats via an online repository. The online repository provides a location to place intelligence on threats, attacks, vulnerabilities, and breaches in computer systems. A survey by Paloalto (2016) indicated that sharing increases resilience, "respondents believe that 39% of attacks can be prevented by shared intelligence". Whilst the majority of threat sharing platforms, such as the Cyber Security Information Sharing Partnership (CiSP) from the NCSC are closed member groups the concept of threat sharing platforms could be a useful educational tool in Higher Education, helping students understand the nature of cyber threats and appreciate the potential risk to business and industry.

ASSESSMENT AND LEARNING IN CYBERSECURITY

This part of the chapter examines the ways in which assessment can help learning in cybersecurity and what the assessment might indicate in terms of competence in cybersecurity. There are a variety of assessment instruments which can be used to help learning in cybersecurity including report writing, exams (written, multi-choice, oral), practical tests, portfolios, project work (including research projects, problem-based learning projects and work based learning projects) and reflective practice. The assessment strategy chosen will depend on the level and the amount of cybersecurity being taught (i.e. one module will be different to a whole specialist course).

Reviewing the literature suggests that assessment is one of the key motivators for students and is fundamental in determining what it is that students value in their education, and this can be applied to cybersecurity education. For example, Murphy (2006) suggests that it is assessment that indicates to students what really matters on a module or program of study and it is assessment that informs students about the goals of the module or program. As has been indicated earlier, the complexity of the cybersecurity environment can provide off-putting for students and assessment tasks may well help with their understanding. There is the potential for assessment to provide a mechanism for student learning and to act as a means of enabling student learning during assessment activities (Rowntree,1987). The concept of "assessment for learning" is proposed as a means to encourage student learning (Black et al, 2003; McDowell et al, 2005).

Brown et al (1997:7-8) put forward the argument that "assessment defines what students regard as important, how they spend their time and how they come to see themselves as individuals". Gibbs and Simpson (2004) support this perspective summarizing that assessment is seen to exert a profound influence on student learning; in areas such as: what students focus their attention on how much they study; the quality of engagement with learning tasks, and, through feedback, on their understanding and future learning. Hamdorf and Hall (2001) indicate that assessment is important because it has such a powerful influence on the learning behavior of students. Brown el al (1997:7) also identify one of the dilemmas in assessment in that "students take their cues from what is assessed rather than from what lecturers assert is important". So, in designing cybersecurity learning activities it is possible to consider utilizing assessment to help students focus on the important aspects.

The principles of assessment (Nicol and Macfarlane-Dick, 2004) require that assessment is reliable, valid, affordable and fit for purpose, i.e. usable. Reliability in assessment requires the assessment to be objective, accurate, repeatable and analytically sound, according to Knight (2001). In essence, reliability refers to the consistency of grades that are awarded and can be affected by marker consistency, inter-marker reliability and / or test / re-test reliability. Validity focuses on the extent to which an assessment measures what it intends to measure and as such contributes to assessing the things course specifications, course learning outcomes and module learning outcomes say are important and of value.

The author has employed a number of assessment instruments in cybersecurity to encourage students to use the assessment activities to enable student learning. The use of scenarios to encourage students to think both as attackers and defenders has been particularly helpful in enabling students to understand the cybersecurity environment. As an overall assessment strategy in cybersecurity attempts should be made to:

- get students to identify and critically evaluate threats – ranging from nuisance threats to "advanced persistent threats";
- design, develop and implement strategies to counter the threats;
- identify when breaches or attacks have taken place and critically evaluate the impact of those;
- design, develop and implement approaches to recover from attack;
- give students the opportunity to evaluate attacks and develop more robust cybersecurity defenses as a result.

The above can be done in the context of specific cybersecurity scenarios or case studies but can also be utilized to encourage students to think about and present policies and procedures for cybersecurity environments.

One particular assessment task that has been used by the author which helps pull together many of the cybersecurity threads and complexities is the use of "infographs". An extract from an assessment using infographs is given below.

The cybersecurity environment is a wide and complex one. For the first part of this assignment you are required to produce an infograph (1 page) outlining the typical threats that either a) individuals in society or b) organizations face from breaches of cybersecurity. The design of your infograph and the content of the infograph is left to you to decide but you should consider visual impact, key messages, data to support, examples and underpinning research. You will have the chance to present your infograph to your peers, academics and guests from industry. You should be able to discuss the points raised on your infograph, explaining the detail and answering any questions asked.

As well as allowing the student to analyze and evaluate a particular issue or concern the assessment enables the development and assessment of a series of professional competencies, including; communication, presentation skills, and the summarizing of complex cybersecurity issues.

One of the main functions of assessment is to provide a measurement of student understanding – and this can utilized in cybersecurity teaching to indicate to students where they are in the learning journey, but also to provide an indication to educators as to how well the students have grasped the cybersecurity concepts, [note – this can be an important aspect if assessment is to be used for certification, see discussion earlier in the chapter]. There is an argument put forward in Black (1999:118) who suggests summative assessment "serves to inform an overall judgement of achievement, which may be needed for reporting and review". Pelligrino et al (2001:42) support this position proposing that "assessment is a tool designed to observe students' behavior and produce data that can be used to draw reasonable inferences about what students know".

However, there has also been a level of concern regarding the appropriateness of this use of assessment for example, Biggs (1996) suggests that "testing has not always promoted good learning and indeed can have detrimental effects" and Black and Wiliam (1998), argue that summative assessment is not a particularly good means of finding out what it is that students know.

When students participate in assessment – both summative and formative – it provides an opportunity to give feedback to students. The provision of feedback is one of the primary functions of assessment and can enhance student learning. One of the key ways that assessment can be used to help with learning is through constructive feedback on assessment activities. When cybersecurity assessment activities are designed and when feedback is generated there is a need to make sure that students value the process and has time to engage in the process. Nicol and Macfarlane-Dick (2004:3) suggest that formative assessment and feedback should be "used to empower students as self-regulated learners and that more recognitions should be given to the role of feedback on learners' motivational beliefs and self-esteem". If the rationale of empowering and encouraging students in the direction of wanting to learn is used, then the value of assessment activities and the value of participating in those activities should become apparent.

Teachers in higher education put a great deal of time and effort into producing written, and indeed, oral feedback. It has already been shown that there is a huge amount of assessment and a growing number of students. Despite the changing environment of mass education students want the feedback process to be clear, explicit and fair (Holmes and Smith, 2003). If feedback is to contribute to student learning in cybersecurity and a great deal of effort is put into it by tutors – how can tutors be sure that it is having the desired effect on helping students?

Perhaps the simplest reason that students want feedback is that it will help them to learn. However, it is not quite as simple as that. The situation is also further complicated in that the types of feedback which are most effective will vary depending on the cybersecurity task being assessed. There is a need to make sure that the feedback that is provided will actually be useful and usable for students, and as such feedback should:

- **Be Understandable by Students:** There is the possibility that the feedback provided to students is often not understood by the students.
- **Be Valued by Students:** In order to be valued by students, feedback should be constructive and reflect the effort that they have put into any assessment activities but also be meaningful in the context of their future learning needs (feed-forward).
- **Allow Students to "Close the Gap" on Their Understanding:** If students know what to do to improve, they can "close the gap" between what they can do or know and what they need to do or know then there is the potential to make that learning opportunity effective.
- **Be of Appropriate Quality:** The quality of feedback given to learners has a significant impact on the quality of learning. The feedback should provide information that helps students trouble-shoot their own assessment performance and take action to close the gap between intent and effect.

- **Be Timely:** One of the key aspects in enhancing efficiency of learning is to ensure that feedback on assessment is timely. If students don't get the feedback soon enough then feedback is less likely to be perceived to be useful for their on-going studies.

Assessment tasks and the feedback associated with the assessment tasks provide an efficient and effective set of instruments to help students enhance their cybersecurity learning. It is important to think about the assessment design, the expectation of the assessment task and the resultant feedback (as well as the ways in which the student will be able to use the feedback).

Taking the above into account the author has used a phased approach in getting students to engage in assessment and to take into account the feedback provided on the assessment. Using this phased approach in cybersecurity enables the feedback on assessment to relate to the completeness of the assessment task but also to be specific to the cybersecurity environment. The following example illustrates the phased approach. This approach can be modified depending on whether the assessment is for one module or for a series of modules. The approach can also provide opportunities for the assessment(s) to be theoretical and / or practical in nature.

Phase 1: Identify and describe a series of cybersecurity threats (if practical is required, get students to design and potentially write a short program illustrating the algorithmic / logical nature of the threat).

Phase 2: Identify and describe defenses to the threats identified in phase 1 (again if practical get students to design and potentially write a short program illustrating the algorithmic / logical aspects of the defense – at this point only a very small portion of overall cybersecurity defense).

Phase 3: Discuss the implications and effect of cybersecurity threats as a series of attack vectors. At this point the concepts associated with impact can be introduced.

Phase 4: Get students to consider the risk (probability) and risk (business impact). Potentially also get students to think about continuity.

Phase 5: Depending on cybersecurity facilities available, simulate a real attack. This allows students to investigate the breach. The author has used this phase to develop digital forensics skills as well as introduce the consideration of how to improve cybersecurity as a result of what has happened in a breach.

Phase 6: Design and implement various levels of cybersecurity defense – depending on the students' level and the size of the assessment this can include programming the defenses.

Phase 7: Test and evaluate the defenses in phase 6.

Phase 8: If there is a need to take further then there is the opportunity to get students to think about policies and procedures required to improve cybersecurity.

There are various ways that the phases identified above can be utilized in assessment, either as a series of steps for an individual learner, or as a set of group activities. It is also possible to utilize the phases as an extended "capture the flag" type of activities.

Bootcamp assessment – as indicated earlier in this chapter Bootcamps can be a useful method for teaching cybersecurity. The author has used Bootcamp participation as an opportunity for students to undertake assessment. In this instance students are required to produce an evaluative and reflective report on what they have learned from the Bootcamp, how this can be applied to cybersecurity problems and how they have developed professionally as a result.

CONCLUSION

This chapter has drawn on current research and best practice on teaching and assessment in cybersecurity in higher education. Consideration has been given to the theoretical and pedagogical foundations for helping tutors make decisions about the methods and approaches to utilize in teaching and assessing the cybersecurity curriculum.

As has been discussed in this chapter there are many variables to take into account when considering effective teaching in cybersecurity. Irrespective of the variables or the objectives in the teaching it is important to focus on the learning needs of the participating student. The needs of the student will vary depending on the level of learning and the prior subject knowledge of the learner. The emphasis in this chapter has been to encourage providers to design cybersecurity teaching and learning opportunities that provide systematic and stimulating learning experiences that will give students the best chance to succeed in their learning. We have advocated that providers ensure that:

- learning is transparent;
- teaching activities facilitate dialogue between teachers and learners and between learners; and
- communities of learners are developed.

The principles and theories of cybersecurity and the associated application of those principles and theories exist in an ever-changing and rapidly developing environment. The environment is complex and complicated which provides further challenges for those seeking to teach cybersecurity effectively.

REFERENCES

ACM. (2017). *Cybersecurity Curricula 2017: Curriculum Guidelines for Post-Secondary Degree Programs in Cybersecurity. A Report in the Computing Curricula Series Joint Task Force on Cybersecurity Education*. Available at https://www.acm.org/binaries/content/assets/education/curricula-recommendations/csec2017.pdf

Alvarez, B. (2011). Flipping the classroom: Homework in class, lessons at home. Education Digest: Essential Readings Condensed For Quick Review, 77(8), 18 – 21.

Barnett, R. (1992). *Improving Higher Education: Total Quality Care*. Bristol, PA: OU Press.

Biggs, J. (1996). Assessment learning quality: Reconciling institutional, staff and educational demands. *Assessment & Evaluation in Higher Education, 12*(1), 5–15. doi:10.1080/0260293960210101

Biggs, J. (1996). Enhancing teaching through constructive alignment. *Higher Education, 33*(3), 347–364. doi:10.1007/BF00138871

Black, P. (1993). Formative and summative assessment by teachers. *Studies in Science Education, 21*(1), 49–97. doi:10.1080/03057269308560014

Black, P., & Wiliam, D. (1998). Assessment and classroom learning. *Assessment in Education: Principles, Policy & Practice, 5*(1), 7–74. doi:10.1080/0969595980050102

Black, P., & Wiliam, D. (1999). *Assessment for Learning: Beyond the Black Box. Cambridge.* Assessment Reform Group, University of Cambridge. Available at http://www.assessment-reform-group.org.uk/AssessInsides.pdf

Boud, D., Cohen, R., & Sampson, J. (1988). Peer Learning and Assessment. *Assessment & Evaluation in Higher Education, 24*(4), 413–426. doi:10.1080/0260293990240405

Boud, D., & Feletti, G. (1997). *The challenges of problem based learning.* London: Kogan Page.

Brown, G., Bull, J., & Pendelbury, M. (1997). *Assessing Student Learning in Higher Education.* London: Routledge.

Cohen, P. A. (1981). Student ratings of institution and student achievement: A meta-analysis of multisection validity studies. *Review of Educational Research, 51*(3), 281–309. doi:10.3102/00346543051003281

Covill, A. (2011). College students' perceptions of the traditional lecture method. *College Student Journal, 45*(1), 92–101.

Disability Discrimination Act (1995) with Amendments. (2000). Available at http://www.legislation.hmso.gov.uk/acts/acts1995/Ukpga_19950050_en_1.htm

Fee, S. B., & Holland-Minkley, A. M. (2010). Teaching computer science through problems, not solutions. *Computer Science Education, 20*(2), 129–144. doi:10.1080/08993408.2010.486271

Garet, M. S., Porter, A. C., Desimone, L., Birman, B. F., & Yoon, K. S. (2001). What Makes Professional Development Effective? Results from a National Sample of Teachers. *American Educational Research Journal, 38*(4), 915–945. doi:10.3102/00028312038004915

Gibbs, G., & Simpson, C. (2004). Conditions under which assessment supports students' learning. *Learning and Teaching in Higher Education, 1*(1), 3–31.

Hallet, J., Larson, J., & Rashid, A. (2018). Mirror Mirror on the Wall: What are we Teaching them at all? Characterising the Focus of Cybersecurity Curricular Frameworks. *ASE@USENIX Security Symposium 2018.* Available at https://www.usenix.org/sites/default/files/conference/protected-files/ase18_slides_hallett.pdf

Hamdorf, J., & Hall, J. C. (2001). The development of undergraduate curricula in surgery assessment. *The Australian and New Zealand Journal of Surgery, 71*(3), 178–183. doi:10.1046/j.1440-1622.2001.02031.x PMID:11277149

Harris, M. A., & Patten, K. (2015). Using Bloom's and Web's Taxonomies to Integrate Emerging Cybersecurity Topics into a Computing Curriculum. *Journal of Information Systems Education, 26*(3), 219–229.

HEFCE. (2002). *Successful Student Diversity.* Available at http://www.hefce.ac.uk/pubs/hefce/2002/02_48.htm

Higher Education Academy. (2006). *Embedding Success Enhancing the Learning Experience for Disabled Students.* York, UK: Higher Education Academy.

Holmes, L., & Smith, L. (2003, July). Student evaluation of faculty grading methods. *Journal of Education for Business*, 318 – 323.

Irons, A. D., & Devlin, S. (2012). *The Inspiring Teacher in Computing*. Paper presented at 1stAnnual Conference on Aiming for Excellence in STEM Learning and Teaching, London, UK.

Irons, A. D., Savage, N., Maple, C., & Davies, A. (2016, Summer). Embedding Cybersecurity in the Computer Science Curriculum. IT Now, 56 – 57.

Irons, A. D., & Thomas, P. (2016). Problem based learning in digital forensics. *Higher Education Pedagogies*, *1*(1), 95–105. doi:10.1080/23752696.2015.1134200

Jenkins, A., & Healy, M. (2005). *Institutional strategies to link teaching and research*. Higher Education Academy Publication.

Johnston, N., & Karafotias, T. (2016). Flipping the Classroom to Meet the Diverse Learning Needs of Library and Information Studies (LIS) Students. *Journal of Education for Library and Information Science*, *57*(3), 226–238. doi:10.3138/jelis.57.3.226

Joshi, P., Thukral, A., Joshi, M., Deorari, A. K., & Vatsa, M. (2011). Comparing the Effectiveness of Webinars and Participatory Learning on Essential Newborn Care (ENBC) in the Class Room in Terms of Acquisition of Knowledge and Skills of Student Nurses: A Randomized Controlled Trial. *In Indina J Pediatr*. Available at https://www.researchgate.net/profile/Anu_Thukral/publication/224914755

Kessler, G. C. (2007). Online education in computer and digital forensics: A case study. *IEEE Proceedings of the 40th Hawaii International Conference on System Sciences 2007*. 10.1109/HICSS.2007.407

Knight, P. (2001). *Formative and Summative, Criterion and Norm-Referenced Assessment*. LTSN Generic Centre, Assessment Series No. 7.

Lundstedt, S. (1966). Criteria for Effective Teaching. *Improving College and University Teaching*, *14*(1), 27–31. doi:10.1080/00193089.1966.10532492

McDowell, L., Sambell, K., Bazin, V., Penlington, R., Wakelin, D., Wickes, H., & Smailes, J. (2005). Assessment for Learning: Current Practice Exemplars from the Centre for Excellence. In Teaching and Learning. Northumbria University Red Guides, 11.

McGettreick, A. (2013). Toward effective cybersecurity education. *IEEE Security and Privacy*, *11*(6), 66–68. doi:10.1109/MSP.2013.155

Murphy, R. (2006). Evaluating new priorities for assessment in higher education. In Innovative Assessment in Higher Education. London: Routledge.

NCSC. (2018). *New Cyber Attack categorisation system to improve UK response to incidents*. Available at https://www.ncsc.gov.uk/news/new-cyber-attack-categorisation-system-improve-uk-response-incidents

Nicol, D., & Macfarlane-Dick, D. (2004). Rethinking formative assessment in HE. In C. Juwah, D. Mcfalane-Dick, B. Matthew, D. Nicol, D. Ross, & B. Smith (Eds.), *Enhancing Student Learning Through Effective Formative Feedback* (pp. 3–14). HE Academy.

Nuutila, E., Törmä, S., & Malmi, L. (2005). PBL and computer programming— The seven steps method with adaptations. *Computer Science Education, 15*(2), 123–142. doi:10.1080/08993400500150788

Oltsik, J. (2017). T*he Life and Times of Cybersecurity Professionals, ESG, ISSA Report.* Available at https://www.esg-global.com/hubfs/issa/ESG-ISSA-Research-Report-Life-of-Cybersecurity-Profession-als-Nov-2017.pdf

Paloalto. (2016). *2016 Prediction #10: Cyberthreat Intelligence Sharing Goes Mainstream.* Available at https://researchcenter.paloaltonetworks.com/2015/12/2016-prediction-10-cyberthreat-intelligence-sharing-goes-mainstream/

Pelligrino, J. W., Chudowsky, N., & Glaser, R. (Eds.). (2001). *Knowing what Students Know – The Science and Design of Educational Assessment.* Washington, DC: National Academic Press.

Pfleeger, C. P., & Cooper, D. M. (1997). Security and Privacy: Promising Advances. *IEEE Software, 14*(5), 27–32. doi:10.1109/52.605928

Rashid, A., Daneziz, G., Chivers, H., Lupu, E., Martin, A., Lewis, M., & Peersman, C. (2018). Scoping the Cyber Security Body of Knowledge. *IEEE Security and Privacy, 16*(3), 96–102. doi:10.1109/MSP.2018.2701150

Rowntree, D. (1987). *Assessing Students: How Shall we Know Them* (2nd ed.). London: Kogan Page.

Scheponik, T., Sherman, A. T., DeLatte, D., Phatak, D., Olivia, L., Thompson, J., & Herman, G. L. (2016). How students reason about cybersecurity concepts. *2016 IEEE Frontiers in Education Conference.* Available at http://doi.ieeecomputersociety.org/10.1109/FIE.2016.7757363

Schleicher, A. (2015). Valued-added: How do you measure whether universities are delivering for their students? *Higher Education Policy Institute (HEPI) Annual Lecture 2015.* Available at https://www.hepi.ac.uk/wp-content/uploads/2016/01/Andreas-Schleicher-lecture.pdf

Wegner, E. (2000). *Communities of Practice: Learning, Meaning, And Identity (Learning in Doing: Social, Cognitive and Computational Perspectives).* Cambridge, UK: Cambridge University Press.

Weiss, R., Mache, J., & Nilsen, E. (2013). Top 10 hands-on cybersecurity exercises. *Journal of Computing Sciences in Colleges, 29*(1), 140–147.

Williams, J., & Cappuccini-Ansfield, G. (2007). Fitness for Purpose? National and Institutional Approaches to Publicising the Student Voice. *Quality in Higher Education, 13*(2), 159–172. doi:10.1080/13538320701629186

This research was previously published in Cybersecurity Education for Awareness and Compliance; pages 135-157, copyright year 2019 by Information Science Reference (an imprint of IGI Global).

Chapter 23
A Practical Exploration of Cybersecurity Faculty Development With Microteaching

Darrell Norman Burrell
iD https://orcid.org/0000-0002-4675-9544
The Florida Institute of Technology, Melbourne, USA

Ashley Dattola
iD https://orcid.org/0000-0002-6480-3123
Capella University, Minneapolis, USA

Maurice E. Dawson
Illinois Institute of Technology, Chicago, USA

Calvin Nobles
iD https://orcid.org/0000-0003-4002-1108
Temple University, Philadelphia, USA

ABSTRACT

The growth and development of cybersecurity jobs and careers have created a need for new skilled faculty that can effectively teach the appropriate content to students at all levels. Often instructors are hired based on their academic credentials and professional experience without the use of assessment and faculty development methods to discover if these instructors can teach effectively or even improve the way they teach. Effective instructors have the ability constructively adjust teaching approaches when students are excelling or struggling based on skillful observation and constant assessment. If a student learns something with great ease, perhaps that approach would be of benefit to others. Part of what helps novices develop expertise here is their explicit attempt to understand how and why something works for students. The implementation and use of microteaching can provide a quality improvement approach to help cybersecurity instructors on all levels improve their ability to teach effectively.

DOI: 10.4018/978-1-6684-3554-0.ch023

BACKGROUND

Cybersecurity is a relatively new field of study when compared to other fields such as mathematics, biology, chemistry, and physics (Burrell & Nobles, 2018). As such, the field is collectively deficient and lags behind other areas in the quality of instruction and engagement of students in the classroom (Burrell & Nobles, 2018). The cybersecurity domain is growing increasingly complex requiring cybersecurity and information security professionals and associated specialists to evolve to keep pace with the technological revolutions continuously (Cabaj, Domingos, Kotulski, & Respício, 2018). Researchers postulate that 182 universities and colleges with Center of Academic Excellence in Information Assurance Certifications in the U.S. teach different undergraduate curricula (Cabaj, Domingos, Kotulski, & Respício, 2018). A 2013 report compared reputable universities in the U.S. and China and noticed a distinct difference between the curricula (Cabaj, Domingos, Kotulski, & Respício, 2018). The study revealed that China-based universities focused on telecommunication security while institutions in the U.S. concentrate on enterprise risk security (Cabaj, Domingos, Kotulski, & Respício, 2018). Over the past two decades, colleges and universities have struggled to adequately prepare cybersecurity professional due to rapid changes in the cybersecurity space, which includes recruiting enough students to sustain the ever-growing demand for computing professionals (Burrell et al., 2015).

By 2020, approximately half of Science, Technology, Engineering, and Mathematics (STEM) related jobs and more than 60% of all new STEM positions will be in computing fields (Burrell & Nobles, 2018). For those students pursuing computer science as a career path, there is a wide range of thoughts on how and what should be taught (Burrell et al., 2015). This is observable in the sub-field of cybersecurity, where the range of teaching methodologies and content varies dramatically between universities (Burrell at el, 2015). Recent growth and changes in cybersecurity continue to evolve so rapidly that educators struggle to update course material that will effectively prepare students to pursue advanced degrees and careers in cybersecurity (Burrell et al., 2015).

Unfortunately, many students lack exposure to cybersecurity concepts at the K-12 level (Burrell et al., 2015). Studies have shown this lack of exposure and a variety of misconceptions that students have about cybersecurity are factors in students not choosing to pursue degrees in the field (Burrell & Nobles, 2018). There are several reasons these issues exist. Computer science is currently not considered to be a core subject by many educational bodies and thus is not a high priority for school districts (Burrell at el, 2015). This leads to a lack of positions for teachers with cybersecurity skills, which in turn leads to a lack of training for teachers either during their college education or as part of their continuing education after they enter the workforce (Burrell at el, 2015).

Simply stated, there is a need to find ways to increase the number of students that choose to enter cybersecurity academic fields (Cheung at el, 2011). For those students who do choose cybersecurity as their career path, there is a wide range of opinions on how and what should be taught (Cheung at el, 2011; Burrell at el, 2015). This is observable in the sub-field of cybersecurity, where the range of approaches and content varies dramatically between universities (Burrell & Nobles, 2018).

Recent growth and changes in this field have occurred so rapidly that educators have not had the time to assess whether they are teaching this material in a manner that will promote student success in the classroom and encourage students to continue to pursue degrees and careers in the field (Burrell at el, 2015). Cybersecurity is currently not considered to be a core subject by many educational bodies and thus is not a high priority for school districts (Burrell et al., 2015). This leads to a lack of positions for teachers with skills, cybersecurity which in turn leads to a lack of training for teachers either during their college education or as part of their continuing education after they enter the workforce (Burrell et al., 2015).

Within cybersecurity, the sub-field of cybersecurity has seen tremendous growth over the past two decades (Burrell & Nobles, 2018). With the growth of the internet, the proliferation of network-capable computing devices, and the vast quantity of data being stored in digital formats, the need for professionals capable of securing communication channels and information storage has become a critical task for government entities, businesses, and individuals (Burrell & Nobles, 2018). This growth has occurred so rapidly that the academic pipeline has not been able to keep up (Burrell & Nobles, 2018).

Examining the status of cybersecurity education, it is evident that there are currently no definitive best practices (Burrell & Nobles, 2018). This problem is compounded by the variety of stakeholders attempting to address it (Burrell & Nobles, 2018). Government and industry are trying to keep up internally by developing their standards and training employees on systems that are continuing to change even as the training occurs (Burrell & Nobles, 2018).

In 2013, the Computer Science Teachers Association (CSTA) published a report that includes data from the Bureau of Labor Statistics predicting that by 2020 approximately 50% of all STEM-related jobs will be in computing fields (Burrell & Nobles, 2018). Their data shows that the growth rate of jobs in computing fields is expected to exceed 150,000 per year over that time span (Burrell & Nobles, 2018). While Cybersecurity graduates will fill not all these positions, the need for more students entering all fields of computing, including Cybersecurity, is undeniable (Burrell & Nobles, 2018). Meanwhile, the enrollment for undergraduate in computer science is still recovering from a rapid decline in enrollment occurring between 2001 and 2007 (Burrell & Nobles, 2018).

Given the difficulties in recruiting students into computer science departments discussed, departments should be doing everything within our power to provide high quality, engaging experience for those students who choose to enroll in our classes (Burrell & Noble, 2018). One area where this is especially needed is cybersecurity (Burrell at el, 2015). Meeting the need to develop the cyber workforce also requires new processes and approaches to develop more effective teachers, especially as new teachers enter the field (Fisher & Burrell, 2011).

DIVERSE CYBER CONTENT

Due to this rapid growth, and the breadth of cybersecurity content, a wide array of curriculum and pedagogical practices exist in today's cybersecurity curricula (Chisholm, 2015). While this diversity reflects the reality of cybersecurity education, it is a significant hindrance to the development of a comprehensive model for cybersecurity education which would allow for consistent and continuous improvement (Chisholm, 2015). For example, knowledge areas which could be incorporated into cybersecurity include computer architecture, criminology/law, cryptography, databases, human-computer interaction, information retrieval, information theory, management/business, mathematics, military science, mobile computing, networks, operating systems, digital forensics, philosophy, ethics, programming languages, software engineering, statistics (probability), and web programming (Burrell et al., 2015). Additionally, the expected outcomes from these courses may vary dramatically, with schools teaching cybersecurity as practical vocation skills, as good engineering practices, or as academic theories (Chisholm, 2015).

The pedagogical methods used to teach these courses are just as varied as the goals and content (Chisholm, 2015). Some courses focus on laboratory-based, experimental lessons. Others are lecture-based and involve the review and discussion of literature, and still, others are challenge-based courses where instructors and students work together to solve problems (Chisholm, 2015). This wide array of content and approaches shows how challenging it is to determine what might constitute the best practices in cybersecurity education (Chisholm, 2015). Adding to this problem is the fact that new technology and new vulnerabilities are thrown into the collective mix continuously, resulting in a constantly changing body of knowledge that must be incorporated into such courses (Chisholm, 2015).

NEW INSTRUCTORS

New instructors are being hired and face problems that they are not taught to handle in school (Sterrett & Imig, 2011; Melnick & Meister, 2008, & Le Maistre & Paré, 2010). Earning a degree, which includes practica, internships, and work-study programs, is not always adequate to prepare instructors for the classroom experience (Le Maistre & Paré, 2010). Newcomers to the teaching profession must be prepared for the experience through a transition process. In this fast-changing world, the roles of teachers and expectancies placed upon them are continuously evolving, as they face the challenges of new skills, requirements, technological developments, individualized teaching, special learning needs, and increasing social and cultural diversity (Wen, 2014).

Beginning teachers are those who have been teaching for three years (Melnick & Meister, 2008). The most serious problem areas for these teachers are motivating pupils, dealing with individual differences, assessing pupils' work, developing relations with parents, organizing class work, insufficient materials and supplies, and dealing with problems of individual pupils (Merc, 2015). Lesser problems are relations with colleagues; planning of lessons; effective use of different teaching methods; awareness of school policies and rules; determining learning level of students; knowledge of subject matter, the burden of clerical work, and relations with principals/administrators (Merc, 2015). Teachers must develop themselves in classroom management, in encountering students' varied needs, in distinguishing students' viewpoints (Merc, 2015).

New teachers need assistance with coping strategies due to a lack of classroom problem-solving strategies which is gained through experience (Merc, 2015). Academic administrators must recognize the gap between veteran and new teachers so that assistance can be given to help them gain the experience they need to be successful (Merc, 2015). Mentoring, technology, collaborative leadership, and working within professional organizations are four areas that were found to assist new teachers with gaining experience (Sterrett & Imig, 2011).

Sterrett and Imig (2011) strongly support the mentoring of new teachers by either an experienced teacher or colleague in the areas of classroom management, alignment of curriculum, and managerial minutia. New teachers need either a mentor or veteran colleague to assist with the completion of forms, meeting deadlines, and protocols which can be overwhelming (Fisher & Burrell, 2011). It is suggested that new teachers take on assignments by volunteering when given the opportunity with a veteran colleague review and validate what was done before final submission (Fisher & Burrell, 2011). Visiting colleagues will give a new teacher an opportunity to seek advice about pedagogy and working with students (Fisher & Burrell, 2011).

The changes in the cybersecurity domain are directly forcing modifications to faculty and teachers approach to providing instructions on cybersecurity (Topham, Kifayat, Younis, Shi, & Askwith, 2016). The high demand for cybersecurity professionals and continuous changes in the space coupled with the multidisciplinary aspects of cyber (Topham et al., 2016); consequently, requiring teachers to undertake new pedagogical methodologies to provide holistic curricula on an array of subjects related to cybersecurity. In some cases, experienced faculty members might lack the expertise on the emerging subjects and specialties areas in cybersecurity.

Researchers argue that contemporary real-world problems in cybersecurity require students to experiment with different technologies, tools, and techniques (Topham et al., 2016). Governments are taking an active role in collaborative efforts to shape cybersecurity practitioners training programs (Topham et al., 2016). Researchers and practitioners continue to advocate for experiential learning opportunities; therefore, requiring colleges and universities to leverage a myriad of laboratories environments (Topham et al., 2016). Teachers need to pursue different pedagogical methods to keep pace with the cybersecurity tools, technologies, and practices to adequately prepare future cybersecurity practitioners (Plachkinova & Maurer, 2018; Topham et al., 2016).

DEVELOPING TEACHERS

A 2010 study by the University of Saskatchewan in Canada discovered that beginning teachers found planning and collaboration with other teachers and professional development as the least need of support during their early years of study (Prytula, Hellsten, & McIntyre, 2010). The university's researchers examined two stages of teacher development: (a) pre-service, (b) and in-service that outline the need for modifying how teacher candidates receive training because universities and schools can teach using traditional methodologies and expect emerging techniques and practices from new teachers (Fisher & Burrell, 2011). A continuum of knowledge and learning must be entrenched with a generation of data that cascades over several generations of educators. The practice of collaboration and planning will enhance new teachers learning and student-centered practices (Fisher & Burrell, 2011).

At all academic levels, collaborative action research is important for providing diverse training materials, curricula, and theoretical discussions (Chisholm, 2015), which has had a positive effect on beginning teachers improving writing, mathematics, and problem-solving (Mitchell, Reilly, &Logue, 2008). The development of a community of practice that focuses on collaborative action research enables the beginning teacher to participate in learning relationships (Fisher & Burrell, 2011). New and creative methods of learning for beginning teachers are encouraged for learning must be continuous (Fisher & Burrell, 2011). Better teachers cannot be produced using the same old techniques so creativity is paramount (Fisher & Burrell, 2011).

In cybersecurity, the teaching subjects can range from digital forensics, ethical hacking, security and auditing, network security, cryptography, software development, malware analysis (Plachkinova & Maurer, 2018) threat and vulnerability management, risk management, and identity and access management. Researchers recommend for the teachers to use case studies to enhance students' knowledge and understanding of past data breaches given that case studies can enrich cybersecurity curricula (Plachkinova & Maurer, 2018) in which theoretical practices are executable in a laboratory environment. Given that teacher quality is not an observable metric, researchers use existential data such as student performance, and students' standardized testing scores and post-secondary is analogously as problematic (Carrell & West, 2010).

TEACHING METHODS

Another form of creative teaching is microteaching which is a proven and successful teaching technique (Fisher & Burrell, 2011). The importance of this technique is to prepare beginning teachers for actual classroom teaching by strengthening their approach to teaching, identifying their personal strengths, assisting with developing empathic understanding of students as learners, enhancing the student teacher's teaching style, and improve the student teacher's ability to receive feedback (Gavrilović et al., 2011; Satheesh, 2011). Microteaching can be used at undergraduate, masters or professorship levels of education as well as for other areas of learning (Fisher & Burrell, 2011). Student teachers are given 20 minutes to teach a lesson to their teacher and peers in a small group setting using flip charts, overheads, and handouts (Fisher & Burrell, 2011). Helpful tips for teaching are given as well as instruction on how to prepare their session (Fisher & Burrell, 2011). Effective feedback and questions for reflection are encouraged (Fisher & Burrell, 2011).

The purpose of microteaching is to strengthen instructors teaching skills by helping them understand both their strengths and their weaknesses through simulated teaching experiences (Fisher & Burrell, 2011). The teaching cycle includes planning, teaching, feedback, re-planning, re-teaching, and re-feedback (Fisher & Burrell, 2011). The rationale for the microteaching is based on behavior modification which involves the components of skill to be practiced during each step and receiving feedback on performance for improvement (Fisher & Burrell, 2011).

According to Fisher and Burrell (2011), core teaching skills include probing questions, explaining, illustrating with examples, stimulus variation, reinforcement, classroom management, and using Blackboard:

- Teaching is a complicated process, but it can be analyzed into simple teaching tasks called teaching skills;
- Teaching skill is the set of behaviors/acts of the teacher which facilitates pupils' learning;
- Teaching is observable, definable, measurable, demonstrable and can be developed through training;
- Micro-teaching is a teacher training technique which plays a significant role in developing teaching skills among the pupil teachers;
- The procedure of micro-teaching involves the following steps: Plan →Teach →Feed-back →Re-plan →Re-teach →Re-feedback. These steps are repeated until the pupil-teacher attains mastery in the use of the skill;
- The micro-teaching cycle consists of all the steps of micro-teaching;
- For practicing teaching skill, the setting of micro-teaching involves:
  - A single skill for practice;
  - One concept of content for teaching;
  - A class of 5 to 10 pupils;
  - Time of practice 5 to 10 minutes;
- Systematic use of feedback plays a significant role in the acquisition of the skill up to mastery level;
- After the acquisition of all the core skills, it is possible to integrate them for effective teaching in actual classroom-situations.

USING MICROTEACHING

Microteaching has been successfully used in the United States and in other countries to assist teacher students in improving their skills (Napoles, 2008; Butler, 2001; Popovich, & Katz, 2009; Mensa et al., 2008; Mastromarino, 2004; & Martin, & Campbell, 1999). In the field of music, microteaching has been very useful for teacher effectiveness and performance using the microteaching technique (Butler, 2001; & Napoles, 2008). Two studies are examined seven years apart in the field of music. The first study by Butler (2001) involved 15 undergraduate students and evaluated teacher effectiveness using microteaching during two sessions. It was found the microteaching helped shaped the students understanding of what it meant to teach. The second study by Napoles (2008) involved 36 students was conducted after each taught three microteaching segments. Later, the instructions, peers, and students evaluated the segments. The students evaluated themselves on areas they did well, suggestions for improvement, and effectiveness scores with ratings compared. A week later the students were asked to recall their evaluations an important aspect of the survey to see if students retained what they had learned from the sessions. This study developed by focusing on more than the teaching but the strengthening of students to assist them with self-development.

Teachers, educators, and all stakeholders in education must seek the best methods to help teachers understand and continuously work on, reform-oriented and technology-supported teaching and learning strategies (Fullan & Langworthy, 2014). Teaching is a demanding and on-going profession. There are constant fluctuation and evolution which requires improvement and enhancement. A portion of teaching is the ability to be able to adapt to various environments (Fisher & Burrell, 2011). Therefore, it is evident as a teacher a component would require the capability to adhere to existing practices (Fisher & Burrell, 2011). Teachers, like other professionals, should have a hungering need to update themselves, to engage in professional growth, and to expand and deepen their understanding (Seldin, 1993).

Microteaching can be thought of like one of those new practices; for teachers to collaborate. Arsal (2015) suggests through microteaching and group discussions, as well as the pre-service teachers sharing their experiences and collaborating with each other and the instructor, these strategies might play a role in the improvement of their critical thinking dispositions. The microteaching method offers different and new opportunities to pre-service teachers about planning and practicing a lot of theoretical knowledge which they have learned throughout their undergraduate studies (Gürbüz, 2015, p. 2). The concept of microteaching encompasses the teacher being videotaped while teaching a lesson (Fisher & Burrell, 2011). Once they have completed the lesson, the teacher is then evaluated and critiqued by other teachers as they watch the video (Fisher & Burrell, 2011). Micro-teaching is a cyclical process, comprised of the following phases: plan the activities, teach, criticize, re-plan, re-teach, and re-criticize (Fisher & Burrell, 2011).

The basic process of this cyclical process includes numerous steps (Gocer, 2016). Following their lessons, students are afforded the opportunity to think about their teaching episodes and analyze both the positives that occurred and the areas on which they can improve (Diana, 2013). The development of micro teaching is to present to the teacher ways to improve their teaching in a real-life environment (Fisher & Burrell, 2011). The goal is to give instructors confidence, support, and feedback by letting them practice a small part of what they plan to do with their students among friends and colleagues (Kusmawan, 2017). All educators know teaching in front of students is completely different from any form of a practice lesson (Fisher & Burrell, 2011).

Microteaching was incorporated in a professional development class (Popovich & Katz, 2009) and included communication skills, critical-thinking skills, and problem-solving abilities. The development of this class included a peer evaluation and a DVD of the student's presentation with a requirement to write a reflective essay of their performance. Microteaching is a valuable tool for assisting students with developing the skills of communication, critical thinking, and problem-solving so students can think on their feet (Fisher & Burrell, 2011). Their development is aided by classmates input for students' personal development.

Microteaching was used twice a month in a distance education program in Ghana, (Mensa et al., 2008) using a 78-item questionnaire collecting data from 895 female participants. Classes were established for female distance learners on weekends with face-to-face tutorials. Specific problems were found for the students based on their sex with advocacy for increasing integration of Information Communication Technology (ICT) systems such as e-portfolio, blackboard virtual learning environment for teaching and learning. Additionally, more use of audio and video conferencing, radio broadcast including the use of other electronic resources which are found in microteaching (Fisher & Burrell, 2011).

Microteaching is used in the field of therapy (Mastromarino, 2004) to help convert theoretical knowledge into practical applications during interaction with patients. Five techniques were used: (1) role-playing and video or audio recording, (2) self-observational and supervision (monitoring), (3) reinforcement (dissonance), (4) re-experimentation, and (5) practice of the acquired abilities. It shows people improve their performance using this method of teaching.

The United Kingdom used micro training for managing and participating in group discussion (Martin, & Campbell, 1999). Recommendations were made by the Dearing Committee (1977) to develop student skills in universities and colleges around communicative abilities. It was believed that the development of the participant's ability to communicate during their teaching is a critical aspect of being an effective instructor (Fisher & Burrell, 2011). The participants viewing themselves on video proved can be very helpful in developing their skills (Fisher & Burrell, 2011).

DEVELOPMENT OF NEW UNIVERSITY PROFESSORS

Microteaching is an excellent tool for preparing beginning teacher candidates for teaching at school to university professorship level (Fisher & Burrell, 2011). It was a technique first developed in the early and mid-1960s at Sanford University in the United States to improve verbal and nonverbal areas of teacher's speech and general performance (Gavrilović et al., 2011). Dr. Dwight Allen and a group of his colleague decided to improve student's teaching of science a model was developed that included teaching, with review and reflect, and re-teaching. (Gavrilović et al., 2011). Later it was used to teach language, and from there a similar model was developed named the Instructional Skills Workshop (ISW) for college and institute faculty (Gavrilović et al., 2011).

Since the 1960's microteaching has been used in many schools, universities, and other programs as it has a strong background of success and has been used for five decades (Gavrilović et al., 2011). Microteaching is an excellent tool for developing new university professors and can be conducted via the creation of a required course that includes collaboration and journaling as well as an assigned mentor (Fisher & Burrell, 2011). Videos should be made of the professor teaching and viewed with peers to focus on the elements of the lesson or teaching style (Fisher & Burrell, 2011). Observations may include clarity of lesson explanation, voice and body language, and level of group interaction (Fisher

& Burrell, 2011). It is suggested that new university professors also are included in collaboration with veteran professors as well as assigned a mentor (Fisher & Burrell, 2011). Even though microteaching can be given as a one-day event, it should be given as a longer course for new professors to assist with adjustment to academic activities (Fisher & Burrell, 2011).

Novice teachers learn through the mentor capabilities of experienced teachers while reviewing the tapes (Fisher & Burrell, 2011). The teachers can pause the video and provide feedback concerning a specific instruction of a lesson (Fisher & Burrell, 2011). Teachers can learn about different teaching strategies by observing the way their peers teaching and find the video recordings to be helpful for feedback and reflection (Bakir, 2014). The teacher can collect the knowledge and make a note to adjust their teaching in the future (Fisher & Burrell, 2011). It is a mirror for the teacher to view themselves to improve their skills (Fisher & Burrell, 2011). Teachers who have successfully incorporated professional development initiatives can see how these successful initiatives impact their teaching (Stair, Warner, Hock, & Conrad, 2016). Microteaching appears to have the potential to introduce best practices as well as instilling critical thinking which may emerge when contradictions are experiences (Davids, 2016).

Teaching consists of two components: the what and the how. The what can be determined by a syllabus, state standards, student interests, and testing capabilities (Fisher & Burrell, 2011). The how is the more difficult aspect of teaching. The how can be adjusted using numerous best practice techniques (Fisher & Burrell, 2011). The how is also noted as the authentic aspect of the teaching profession (Fisher & Burrell, 2011). Microteaching is a way to adjust the how (Fisher & Burrell, 2011). It is a tool for all teachers, novice ones, to be able to view themselves teaching and incorporate feedback from experienced teachers and mentors to fine-tune their abilities. Witterholt, Goedhart, and Suhre (2016) have emphasized that teachers learn through reflection on their teaching practices and microteaching allows teachers to experience teaching in a controlled environment.

The process of microteaching also provides the teachers the feedback from their peers, as a means of critiquing teaching behaviors and techniques (Fisher & Burrell, 2011). Teachers can tell one another techniques that have worked for them in the past, or others which have not worked out (Fisher & Burrell, 2011). It is a time for reflection and inquiry on the theory and practice of their teaching (Fisher & Burrell, 2011). Exchanging knowledge and experiences triggers reflection on each other's teaching practices and ideas, which may, in turn, result in an expansion of teacher knowledge and the refinement of one's teaching practices (Witterholt, Goedhart, & Suhre, 2016). During a microteaching exercise, the students can notice strong and weak points about their teaching skills (Bakir, 2014). Results confirm that this kind of training does make a significant and lasting impact on teaching (Gibbs & Coffey, 2004).

Although micro teaching can offer numerous benefits, it can also be utilized as a form of teacher collaboration (Fisher & Burrell, 2011). The significance of collaboration is emphasized in the field of teacher education over the past decades (Yuan & Zhang, 2016). Teacher collaboration can stimulate educational innovation and professional learning (Xu, 2015). Teachers working together can provide instances of best practices, classroom management, teaching styles, and curriculum assignments (Fisher & Burrell, 2011). Microteaching provides numerous opportunities for learning and reflective action as most respond positively regarding the guidance and advice that they receive (Davids, 2016).

Teacher collaboration can assist teachers with their teaching practices to improve their lessons and teaching materials (Kafyulilo, 2013). The use of collaboration provides learning and support for the teachers (Chiou-hui, 2011). Collaboration is vital to the progress of teachers within a functioning institution. While the teachers are reviewing their tapes, it is a time for them to converse with one another and discuss the concepts within the videos (Fisher & Burrell, 2011). Teachers working together can provide interaction focusing on the teaching within videos. Bowser, Davis, Singleton, and Small (2017) suggested that learning focusing on collaboration increases interactivity and provides an authentic environment for learning.

QUALITY MANAGEMENT AND PROCESS IMPROVEMENTS

Microteaching requires constant improvement to ensure teachers are using the most appropriate pedagogical methods and maximize practices to deliver high-quality instructions to students. Anttila and Jussila (2018) postulate that high-quality is a competitive advantage for organizations. In microteaching, a trait of high-quality is organizational learning as institutions seek to optimize knowledge base, practices, and integration to increase the quality of teaching output. Quality pertains to parameters and characteristics to achieve specific objectives (Anttila & Jussila, 2018); therefore, in microteaching quality pertains to teaching teachers how to optimize methodologies to ameliorate the quality of instruction. Quality management is the process by which organizations take to enhance integrated systems, processes, and procedures (Anttila & Jussila, 2018). Organizational leaders pursue quality assurance by ensuring all applicable stakeholders are confident with the existing quality management practices (Anttila & Jussila, 2018).

Tsarenko (2018) argues that quality management systems in higher education are in dire need of an overhaul to increase assurance standards to improve the level of quality of college education by focusing on process improvements. The quality of college academic programs face increased scrutiny as the quality of higher education undergoes monitoring and evaluation to compare different systems of higher education (Tsarenko, 2018). The quality management system and quality assurance efforts used to evaluate the quality of higher education programs are closely aligned to the International Standardization Organization (Tsarneko, 2018). The European Higher Education Area model consists of the following pillars: (a) the interests of students, employers, and society, (b) institutional individualism, and (c) leverage external quality assurance entities while not increasing the school's workload (Tsarenko, 2018). The abovementioned model is one of many models; however, most are comparable (Tsarenko, 2018) and lack details on assessing the teachers teaching methodologies and quality of teaching instructions.

Figure 1 illustrates a model for improving quality management systems which can be easily adaptable for microteaching. Constructive feedback to teacher candidates is an invaluable tool for continuous improvement (Bahçivan, 2017) given that quality of teaching ability aligns to product realization and can be assessed during the measure analysis and improvement phase of Figure 1 (ISO, n.d.). Improving the quality of teaching instruction by teacher candidates in an artificial environment can be effective (Bahçivan, 2017) using the above International Organization for Standardization (ISO) model (ISO, n.d.). Using traditional pedagogical methods to develop teacher candidates is a form of quality management and continuous improvement because experienced educators provide feedback to improve the teacher candidates' quality of instruction ((Bahçivan, 2017). The problem with quality management and process improvement for teacher candidates in cybersecurity is the frequent changes in technology, tools, techniques, the threat landscape, and regulatory requirements. The constant changes make it challenging to develop and standardized practices for cybersecurity educators and teaching candidates to enhance their quality of instruction.

There is a shortage of research addressing microteaching for cybersecurity educators. A significant challenge is duplicating a live network or environment in an academic setting to develop the theoretical and practical cybersecurity competencies (Topham et al., 2018). Topham et al. (2018) assert that cybersecurity practitioners are adversely impacted by the inability to establish real-world problems in an academic setting; thus, resulting in the under training of cybersecurity professionals and humans labeled as the weakest link in cybersecurity. This problem prevents cybersecurity teaching candidates from optimizing teaching methodologies due to the lack of research on microteaching in cybersecurity. A secondary level problem extending from this phenomenon is it limits research contribution to the quality management and process improvements regarding microteaching and cybersecurity.

Figure 1. The ISO 9001: 2008 Standard Model

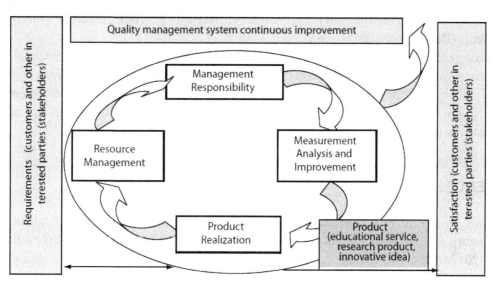

THE POSITIVE AND NEGATIVE CHARACTERISTICS OF MICROTEACHING

Some advantages of microteaching include a viable platform for teacher candidates to (a) hone teaching skills, (b) receive constructive feedback, (c) obtain mentorship from experienced teachers, (d) the ability to develop behaviors as a teacher, and (e) provide collective input to assess the overall quality of the education program (Elias, 2018). Pairing teacher candidates with experienced teachers allow the students to receive direct feedback, advice, and coaching from a veteran teacher (Elias, 2018). Another positive element of microteaching is teacher candidates can document their experiences and contribute to the body of knowledge to support theory development. Capturing microteaching data on cybersecurity educators would be helpful in shaping future iteration of developing teachers in the field of cybersecurity.

Regarding cybersecurity and microteaching, there are several negative attributes such as (a) dearth of microteaching and cybersecurity research, (b) unable to simulate an active or live cyber environment, (c) constant change in cybersecurity, (d) different collegiate curricula, (e) current cybersecurity educators lacking contemporary expertise, and (d) a shortage of empirical research on microteaching and cyber (Plachkinova & Maurer, 2018; Topham et al., 2018). Another negative attribute is that teaching candidates receive feedback from a limited population of experienced teachers. Institutions with poor teaching training programs lack the foundation and competency to develop future teachers resulting in a poor-quality course delivered to students (Husband, 2013). Constant change in the cybersecurity space makes it challenging for cybersecurity educators and those undergoing training to amass the teaching competencies accompanied by high demand for cybersecurity professionals.

CONCLUSION

With more schools offering specialized computer science degrees with an emphasis on security, finding qualified instructors is difficult (Burrell & Nobles, 2018). According to Stevenson (2017), an instructor's ability to create and deliver relevant course experiences is a critical job requirement in producing a well-versed security technologist. The goal is to produce cybersecurity program graduates with comparable industry skills (Burrell et al., 2015).

Translating tactical skills into practice for cybersecurity students is becoming an essential aspect of the computer security curriculum (Burrell et al., 2015). Having teachers that can effectively help students develop critical cybersecurity skills is a critical aspect of workforce training and development (Burrell et al., 2015). Microteaching provides a tool for developing cybersecurity professionals that are critical to the development of a skilled cybersecurity workforce.

REFERENCES

Anttila, J., & Jussila, K. (2017). Understanding quality – conceptualization of the fundamental concepts of quality. *International Journal of Quality and Service Sciences*, 9(3/4), 251–268. doi:10.1108/IJQSS-03-2017-0020

Anttila, J., & Jussila, K. (2018). Organizational learning in developing the integrated quality management. *Production Engineering Archives*, 18, 3–13. doi:10.30657/pea.2018.18.01

Aubry, L. (2011, March 17). Bad teachers are rarely fired. Why? *Los Angeles Sentinel*, A7.

Bahçivan, E. (2017). Implementing Microteaching Lesson Study with a Group of Preservice Science Teachers: An Encouraging Attempt of Action Research. *International Online Journal Of Educational Sciences*, 9(3), 591–602. doi:10.15345/iojes.2017.03.001

Blake, S. (2008). "A nation at risk" and the blind men. *Phi Delta Kappan*, 89(8), 601–602. doi:10.1177/003172170808900814

Burrell, D., Finch, A., Simmons, J., & Burton, S. (2015). The Innovation and Promise of STEM-Oriented Cybersecurity Charter Schools in Urban Minority Communities in the United States as a Tool to Create a Critical Business Workforce. In M. Dawson & M. Omar (Eds.), *New Threats and Countermeasures in Digital Crime and Cyber Terrorism*. doi:10.4018/978-1-4666-8345-7.ch015

Burrell, D., & Nobles, C. (2018). Recommendations to Develop and Hire More Highly Qualified Women and Minorities Cybersecurity Professionals. In *The Proceedings of the International Conference on Cyber Warfare and Security*. Academic Conferences International Limited.

Butler, A. (2001). Preservice music teachers' conceptions of teaching effectiveness microteaching experiences, and teaching performance. *Journal of Research in Music Education, 49*(3), 258–272. doi:10.2307/3345711

Cabaj, K., Domingos, D., Kotulski, Z., & Respício, A. (2018). Cybersecurity education: Evolution of the discipline and analysis of master programs. *Computers & Security, 75,* 24–35. doi:10.1016/j.cose.2018.01.015

Carrell, S., & West, J. (2010). Does professor quality matter? Evidence from random assignments of students to professors. *Journal of Political Economy, 3*(118), 409–432. doi:10.1086/653808

Carter, L. (2006). Why students with an apparent aptitude for computer science don't choose to major in computer science. *ACM SIGCSE Bulletin, 38*(1), 27–31. doi:10.1145/1124706.1121352

Cheung, R., Cohen, J., Lo, H., & Elia, F. (2011). Challenge based learning in cybersecurity education. In *Proceedings of the 2011 International Conference on Security & Management (Vol. 1).*

Chisholm, J. A. (2015). *Analysis on the perceived usefulness of hands-on virtual labs in cybersecurity classes.*

Clement, M. C. (2010). Preparing teachers for classroom management: The teacher educator's role. *The Delta Kappa Gamma Bulletin,* (Fall), 41-44.

Elias, S. K. (2018). Pre-Service Teachers' Approaches to the Effectiveness of Micro-Teaching in Teaching Practice Programs. *Open Journal of Social Sciences, 6,* 205–224. doi:10.4236/jss.2018.65016

Fisher, J., & Burrell, D. (2011). The value of using microteaching as a tool to develop instructors. Review of Higher Education & Self-Learning, 3(11), 86-94.

Gainsburg, J. (2009). Creating effective video to promote student-centered teaching. *Teacher Education Quarterly,* (Spring), 163-178.

Gavriliović, T. Ostojić, M., Sambunjak, D., Kirschfink, M., Steiner, T., & Strittmatter, V. (n.d.) *Chapter 5: Microteaching.* Retrieved from http://www.bhmed-emanual.org/book/export/html/36

Husband, T. (2013). Improving the Quality of Instruction through a Service Teaching Framework. *Journal of Effective Teaching, 13*(2), 73–82.

ISO 9000 standards (n.d.) From ISO 9001 checklist. Retrieved from www.iso-9001-checklist.co.uk/iso-9000-standards.html

Le Maistre, C., & Paré, A. (2010). Whatever it takes: How beginning teachers learn to survive. *Teaching and Teacher Education, 26*(3), 559–564. doi:10.1016/j.tate.2009.06.016

Martin, D., & Campbell, B. (1999). Managing and participating in group discussion: A micro-training approach to the communication skill development of students in higher education. *Teaching in Higher Education, 4*(3), 327–337. doi:10.1080/1356251990040302

Mastromarino, R. (2004). The use of microteaching in learning the redecision model: A proposal for an observation grid. *Transactional Analysis Journal, 34*(1), 37–47. doi:10.1177/036215370403400105

Melnick, S. A., & Meister, D. G. (2008). A comparison of beginning and experienced teachers' concerns. *Educational Research Quarterly*, *31*(3), 39–56.

Mensa, K. O., Ahiatrogah, P. D., & Deku, P. (2008). Challenges facing female distance learners of the University of Cape Coast, Ghana. *Gender & Behaviour*, *6*(2), 1751–1764. doi:10.4314/gab.v6i2.23418

Mitchell, S. N., Reilly, R. C., & Logue, M. E. (2009). Benefits of collaborative action research for the beginning teacher. *Teaching and Teacher Education*, *25*(2), 344–349. doi:10.1016/j.tate.2008.06.008

Napoles, J. (2008). Relationships among instructor, peer, and self-evaluations of undergraduate music education majors' micro-teaching experiences. *Journal of Research in Music Education*, *56*(1), 82–91. doi:10.1177/0022429408323071

Plachkinova, M., & Maurer, C. (2018). Teaching Case: Security Breach at Target. *Journal of Information Systems Education*, *29*(1), 11.

Popovich, N. G., & Katz, N. L. (2009). Instructional design and assessment. A microteaching exercise to develop performance-based abilities in pharmacy students. *American Journal of Pharmaceutical Education*, *73*(4), 1–8. doi:10.5688/aj730473 PMID:19657506

Prytula, M. P., Hellsten, L. M., & McIntyre, L. J. (2010). Perception of teacher planning time: And epistemological challenge. *Current Issues in Education*, *14*(1), 4-29. Retrieved from http://cie.asu.edu/ojs/index.php/cieatasu/article/view/437

Satheesh, K. (2008, November 15). Introduction to micro-teaching [Web log post]. *Sathitech*. Retrieved from http://sathitech.blogspot.com/2008/11/introction-to-micro-teaching.html

Sterrett, W. L., & Imig, S. (2011). Thriving as a new teacher in a bad economy. *Kappa Delta Pi Record*, *47*(2), 68–71. doi:10.1080/00228958.2011.10516564

Stevenson, G. V. (2017). *Cybersecurity implications for industry, academia, and parents: A qualitative case study in NSF STEM education*.

Topham, L., Kifayat, K., Younis, Y. A., Shi, Q., & Askwith, B. (2016). Cyber Security Teaching and Learning Laboratories: A Survey. *Information & Security*, *35*(1), 51.

Tsarenko, I. O. (2018). The quality management system in educational institutions of the Slovak Republic: Impact on the Ranking's position. *Bìznes Ìnform*, *3*(482), 71–80.

Wilson, M. (2010). There are a lot of really bad teachers out there. *Phi Delta Kappan*, *92*(2), 51–55. doi:10.1177/003172171009200213

This research was previously published in the International Journal of Applied Management Theory and Research (IJAMTR), 1(1); pages 32-44, copyright year 2019 by IGI Publishing (an imprint of IGI Global).

Chapter 24

Teaching Graduate Technology Management Students With Innovative Learning Approaches Around Cybersecurity

Darrell Norman Burrell
https://orcid.org/0000-0002-4675-9544
The Florida Institute of Technology, Melbourne, USA

ABSTRACT

Every year in the U.S., 40,000 jobs for information security analysts go unfilled, and employers are struggling to fill 200,000 other cybersecurity related roles. Colleges and universities have created certificates, undergraduate, and graduate programs to train professionals in these job roles. This issue becomes more complicated when you explore the that competent workers in this field need more than just book knowledge to be effective. Engaged and experiential learning approaches encourages experimentation and expanding teaching cybersecurity beyond the use of just classroom lectures, textbooks, and PowerPoint slides. The use of experiential and scenario-based learning approaches helps students to develop real-world problem solving and critical thinking skills that demonstrate expertise beyond course grades and degrees. Developing the ability to strategic and adaptive is vital to be effective. This case study research intends not to reconstitute theory but to influence the practice of cybersecurity education through the use of innovative applied and engaged learning approaches.

INTRODUCTION

Often university academic programs and faculty teach in the United States, Africa, and the Middle East with only textbook driven methods. Teaching only from the textbook is a problem when it comes to preparing employees to be cybersecurity managers around policy and operations. These antiqued pedagogy methods exclusively expose students to theory in ways only driven by book knowledge and PowerPoint presentations. This approach often leaves graduates with degrees but also limited practical

DOI: 10.4018/978-1-6684-3554-0.ch024

experience. Hofmann (2003) notably explains, "teaching management outside a business setting is just like teaching swimming without putting students in the water." He stated, "It's true, I've been teaching for almost a quarter of a century, but I've yet to meet another professor who took a course in how to be a professor. We learned by doing, not by watching from the sidelines. If business schools don't ensure that all students, management students, in particular, get this type of exposure through a required practicum of some form or fashion before they graduate, then we have failed them. Many educators entertain the assumption, a false one, that with enough knowledge about how to do something, one can do it. Well, folks, if you believe that works, read everything you can about flying and then go jump off a tall building." (p. 50). This applied research study functions with a goal to explore value and benefits of scenario-based learning could engage the academic development of graduate students.

Research by Meehan-Klus (2016) outlines the critical need for experience-based learning opportunities that mirror the workplace. Effective teaching requires new and innovative approaches that move beyond just lectures, formal exams, and academic papers (Meehan-Klaus, 2016). Good education involves using learning activities in which students can interactively develop the critical competencies, knowledge, and savvy that is expected to be highly effective in the real job (Meehan-Klaus, 2016). According to research by Tuberville (2014), academic programs can be grossly insufficient if they are missing elements for students to develop a core of marketable technical and soft skills to meet all aspects of the job role development needs of employers and job duty requirements.

ENGAGED AND ACTION LEARNING

David Moore (2013) outlined how teaching approaches and interventions should "induce the learner to look carefully at her experience, to question her own assumptions, to place the experience in relation to larger institutional and societal processes and discourses, to hear others' voices, to grapple with the question of why things happen the way they do, to imagine how things might be different, to read her experience in terms given by major social theories and to critique those theories from the perspective of her experience to engage, in other words, in serious critical thinking" (2013, pp. 201-202).

Engaged learning affords students with opportunities to engage deeply in their learning through high impact activities (Moore, 2013). These kinds of activities demand that students devote considerable time and effort to purposeful tasks to practice the transfer or application of knowledge across contexts (Moore, 2013). According to Moore (2013) in actual practice, actively engaged learning provides educational experiences that allow students to interact with other perspectives and voices, to receive frequent feedback about their performance, and to reflect on both that feedback and their learning.

According to Marquardt (2011), the crux of action learning, which is like engaged learning, comprises:

- Productive activities, actions, or interventions the foster and build individual and organization development through experiences;
- Problem-based learning that is driven and focused on real problems or areas of concerns that provide opportunities for reflection and education with and from their experience as participants attempt to improve things;
- An interactive process where participants have meaningful opportunities to make and comprehend meanings from direct experiences.

Marquardt (2011) outlined several interconnected reinforcing elements that make the use of action learning or engaged learning significant, including:

1. To actively participate in a variety of trial and error activities centered on making useful progress on solving problems or improving processes;
2. To help participants gain wisdom and knowledge through the problem solving or process improvement process that provides insights about how to deal, in the future, with other such similar problems or scenarios;
3. To allow participants to build confidence and self-efficacy through their successes or measurable progress in solving problems and improving processes;
4. To help participants create the conditions in which they can learn with and from each other in pursuit of a common task and the pooling of collective knowledge and intelligence.

Consider the vital idea that there are six elements is characteristic of high-impact educational practices (Kuh, 2008). High-impact instructional practices:

1. Require effort and participation;
2. Have constructive learning interactions that build bonds and familiarity that can lead to productive collaborative relationships;
3. Assist students in the engagement constructive, experiential, and perspective differences;
4. Allows varying opportunities for students to benefit from formative and constructive feedback;
5. Allows for students to benefit from trial and error through activities that help them apply and test what they are learning in new situations; and
6. Allows students to reflect on and observe their growth and knowledge development.

Juregens (2012) research outlined that actual work-based or on the job learning gives students to progressive responsibility This responsibility occurs through a series of structured, systematically linked real-world work experiences (Jurgens, 2012). These exercises allow the students the opportunity to gain progressive responsibility and growth opportunities to apply academic work while also learning specific competencies (Jurgens, 2012). According to Juergens (2012), experiential learning works because deeper learning occurs as the student increases his or her level of involvement in the activity.

Consider that many employers value actual work-oriented programs because they allow for the acquisition of more actionable knowledge about the real content of their degree programs (Meehan-Klaus, 2016). Experiential learning experiences that successfully connect students with the actual job functions of the workplace can better prepare students for realities and challenges of the actual job (Gault, Leach, & Duey, 2010).

Action and engaged learning experiences assist students in the crystallization of their vocational self-concept by facilitating the identification of relevant abilities, interests, and values and by performing job tasks pertinent to the chosen professional field (Tuberville, 2014; Meehan-Klaus, 2016).

Actual job role experiences can also create satisfying accomplishments that motivate students to continue along a career path, create realistic expectations about the world of work, and help clarify students' career intentions (Tuberville, 2014; Meehan-Klaus, 2016). Actual job role experiences also facilitate adaptability as they provide a unique form of a realistic job preview (Tuberville, 2014; Meehan-Klaus, 2016).

THE IMPORTANCE OF BUILDING SELF-EFFICACY IN CYBERSECURITY STUDENTS

The significance of using this innovative pilot approach to teach students about cybersecurity was to help them improve their professional ability and self-efficacy. Bandura's (1977) social learning theory explores self-efficacy as a product of diverse sources of knowledge acquired through mediated experiences. Bandura's research (2001) frames self-efficacy as a blueprint foundation of learning development. Bandura (2001) defines self-efficacy as having the "core belief that one has the power to produce effects by one's actions" (p. 10). According to Feltz (1982) Self-efficacy functions as progressive learning apparatus responsible for influencing cognitive behavioral reactions, thus, "perceived self-efficacy influences not only choice of activities but also the persistence of coping efforts in the face of anxiety-provoking situations" (p. 764).

Hughes, Galbraith, and White (2011) describe self-efficacy as dealing primarily with cognitive perceptions of individual competence, and as the combination of useful and competency attitudes. Thus, self-concept judgments are more general and are less context-dependent, relying on a comparison of social environments and the self (Hughes, Galbraith, & Whitem, 2011).

Bandura (1982) explains that efficacy is not a fixed act. Self-efficacy and confidence in one's ability are influenced by a variety of interconnected factors, including thoughts, feelings, emotions, previous experiences, social aspects, and behavioral components (Bandura, 1982). This factors significantly influence the ability to make decisions, understand things, and effectively solve problems (Bandura, 1982). Truthful assessments of efficacy are vital to dodge missteps and mistakes. Whether accurate or inaccurate, efficacy beliefs shape decision-making around the confidence to engage in action or fear and apprehension to engage in inaction (Bandura, 1982). Bandura (1982) describes how "people avoid activities that they believe will exceed their coping capabilities, but they undertake and perform assuredly those that they judge themselves capable of managing" (p. 123). Individuals who lack self-efficacy are more inclined to visualize instances of failure, which undermine performance capability and outcome (Bandura, 1977). This concept directly applies to students their comprehension and confidence in their ability to apply what they are learning in a course.

Bandura's (1977) research articulates that through valuable experiences, interactions, and observations, individuals learn and form conceptualizations of new actions, activities, behaviors and behavior patterns, which become a reservoir of knowledge that can be utilized in the future. Bandura (1977) states that those behaviors are then refined based on responses to performance outcomes that are either successful or unsuccessful.

Bandura's (1977) research describes the notable reciprocal relationship between efficacy expectations and performance. This interchange is indicative of individuals and how they view their levels of competency and ability in a given situation. Bandura's (1977) research describes the notable reciprocal relationship between efficacy expectations and performance. This reciprocal relationship ultimately leads to the idea that through experiential learning experiences, students can better develop their sense of self-efficacy they are more likely to function and perform better in the actual job (Tuberville, 2014).

When considering Bandura's social cognitive theory, Bandura (2001) explains that efficacy beliefs affect change through their impact on other determinants. Optimal performance is influenced by a combination of higher-order self-regulatory skills including assessment of task demands, evaluating potential routes of action, setting goals, managing attitudes, and navigating perceptions (Bandura, 2001; Bandura, 1982; Bandura, 1977).

However, Bandura (2001) also outlined that team accomplishments are "the product not only of the shared intentions, knowledge and skill of its members but also of the interactive, coordinated and synergistic dynamics of their transactions, thus perceived collective efficacy is an emergent group-level property, not simply the sum of the efficacy beliefs of individual members" (p. 14).

By focusing on experiences in which coping and competency efficacy increases, individuals will be able to see themselves overcoming previously feared/avoided situations that had yielded aversive outcomes (Bandura, 2001; Bandura, 1982; Bandura, 1977). Engaged and action learning experiences provide a platform for coping and competency efficacy to develop and increase. Using valuable lessons in ways that foster comprehension confidence and experiences can aid in the development of self-efficacy skills that are needed for future success in similar circumstances (Bandura, 1982).

Past performance plays an integral role in judging existing self-efficacy as well as setting future aspirations (Bandura 1990). Bandura (1977) defined "outcome expectancy" as a person's estimate that a selected level of knowledge can lead one to engage in effective behavior which will bear a likely specified outcome or performance result. He describes an efficacy expectation as the conviction that one can successfully make the decisions and engage in the actions and behaviors that results in a preferred product (Bandura, 1977).

THE PILOT PROGRAM

A pilot cybersecurity capstone course took place with a group of graduate students in a Master of Technology Management in Cyber Security. The subjects were chosen from students currently in a graduate program. The curriculum used an engaged learning approach (Moore, 2013) to apply the course content where students worked as project team consultants for actual small business owners of less than 100 employees but lacked an internal cybersecurity infrastructure. Before the capstone activity began, students spent class time engaged in case studies and cybersecurity lab sandbox. The students were given case studies on actual business and a series of virtual lab sandbox scenarios that allowed them to develop group strategies to advise these small business owners in areas that covered the following areas:

- Foundations of cybersecurity which includes exploring areas of Cryptography, Security Engineering, and the risks to the modern-day computing environment;
- Cybersecurity policy and governance which includes the creation of policies and processes that govern cyber operations;
- Emergency planning, business continuity, emergency response measures which are all about proactive measures around cybersecurity;
- Cyber defenses which are about creating strategies to defend an organization and network from attacks;
- Vulnerability assessments are about teaching students about vulnerability assessment and risk assessment.

New applied learning enlarges business program learning by serving students and the community with a win/win partnership between students and actual business owners. This approach is unique is because business owners with limited resources in the community to get free consulting assistance from graduate students and in return graduate students practical experience working with local businesses. Business owners were solicited through The Chamber of Commerce in state of Virginia USA.

Each small group of 4 graduate students was assigned a small business entrepreneur. Students spent two months meeting with small business owners working with them to assist them in aspects of their operations that required improvement. Students were also required to keep reflective journals that had weekly entries with prompts centered about the following areas:

1. What am I learning new?
2. How has this experienced challenged what I thought I already knew?
3. How has this experience confirmed what I already knew?
4. What have I identified as my personal and professional strengths that I would like to build on?
5. In what areas do I want to gain more knowledge-based off of my experiences?

At the end of the two months, there were a final presentation of each team's activities and results. Business owners even provided their evaluations and assessments of the impacts of the student interventions. Every business owner outlined the groups helped them improve processes and fix operational issues.

Ramsey and Fitzgibbons (2005) suggested that creative activities can provide plentiful learning opportunities if they are allowed to emerge. Every student brings personal experiences as workers or members of other organizations that can serve as incubators for growth and wisdom (Ramsey and Fitzgibbons, 2005). It is easier for them to take responsibility for their learning if they start from what they know and the journaling activity allowed the students to explore their knowledge and document their learning in real time, thus allowing every student, experience, reflection, and question become potential source of learning (Ramsey and Fitzgibbons, 2005).

Studies have shown that students engaging in reflective activities have reported increased self-awareness, self-confidence, and feeling of empowerment to recreate their self-concept (Morrison, 1996). Morrison (1996) stresses that contemplative leadership practices enhance professional skills such as decision-making, planning, listening, change management, critical thinking, and conflict management. Cunliffe's (2004) outlined an insightful approach to the reflection that includes:

1. Categorize an experience (What happened? What are my thoughts about my experiences? What impact has it made on me?)
2. Examine the significance of the course's subject area a level that allows for questioning one's assumptions (It what ways does the world of practice mimic the realm of theory? What theoretical aspects that I have learned have made me function better as a practitioner?)
3. Apply the learning to personal or professional lives (So what have I learned from my experiences? Now what will I do differently? What do I need to explore further? How will I think about this topic differently?)

The focus of this pilot was to help students move from learning that was only book driven and theoretical to engaged learning experiences that were practical through the use of problem-based learning approaches (Larmer, 2015). These approaches allowed business students with cybersecurity focuses and cybersecurity research interests to apply their textbook and theoretical knowledge to the real-life challenges of small business owners in areas of cyber and information security. Self-reflection is an essential skill in decision making (Marquardt, 2011). In application, this process included helping students comprehend entrepreneurial principles, business challenges, marketing strategies, financial constraints, profitability, and how several of them or all of them could be interconnected and dependent on each other. This approach comprehends the framework that abundant experiential learning opportunities are highly effective at helping students develop tacit knowledge and apply their skills to specific situations (Lee, McGuiggan, & Holland, 2010).

PROGRAM RESULTS

After the pilot was complete participants were engaged in a focus group interview that outlined listed the most significant things that were learned from the pilot engaged learning course experience. The collective group put together a list of 68 areas of new learning. Then the group was challenged to narrow the list to the most significant 15 areas of learning growth:

1. The experience built my confidence about my actionable knowledge about the subject;
2. The experience improved my business decision-making and problem-solving skills;
3. The experience improved my ability to be adaptable and resourceful;
4. The experience challenged my thinking in ways that improved my strategic thinking and planning skills;
5. The experience improved my ability to innovate because there were had limited resources;
6. The experience helped me improve my communication skills;
7. The experience helped me to improve my teamwork skills;
8. The experience helped me improve my conflict management skills;
9. The experience helped me improve my understanding of cybersecurity operations and processes;
10. The experience helped me before more proficient in business process improvement;
11. The experience improved my project management skills;
12. The experience improved my understanding of the importance of risk management and risk assessment skills.

Participant 1 said, "I feel more confident in making cyber operational decisions as a result of seeing the operations of a real business. I gained an increased readiness to take responsibility and initiative."

Participant 2 said, "This process required me to change the understanding of strategic planning and risk assessment. I realized that poor planning could lead to inferior outcomes that can destroy a brand, client trust, or a reputation with a cyber breach."

Participant 3 said, "I had no idea how difficult it was to function in a cyber role. Like many people that I know, picked this as a career change option because the pay is good and there is a shortage of jobs, but the job is pretty complex, and the approach requires committing to be an expert not just getting a job and getting a fat paycheck."

Participant 6 said, "Real business problems and their impacts can be very unpredictable. Working in this role for the first time was both a humbling and sobering experience. Before this experience, I thought this job only required textbook knowledge, grades, and a degree to be effective. I was so wrong. The work is not cookie cutter or like painting by numbers. I have spent a lot of my time memorizing processes from the textbook like I can follow them without failure almost like they are directions analogous to those in a cooking recipe. I was so wrong and surprised by how much I didn't understand and know."

CONCLUSION

This applied research study functions with a goal to explore value and benefits of scenario-based learning could engage the academic development of graduate students.

Consider the perspective that individuals who have self-doubts in their competencies and abilities prematurely settle for second-rate solutions (Bandura, 1990). In contrast, individuals with a strong sense of efficacy strive for results that are more comprehensive and effective (Bandura, 1990). Building competency and a stronger knowledge of efficiency is a critical aspect to building better performers, and practical learning experiences help in those areas of development (Larmer, 2015; Kuh, 2008).

Actual job role experiences provide a deeper understanding of subject matter, a higher capacity for critical thinking, the application of knowledge in complex or ambiguous situations, and expanded abilities for engaging in lifelong learning (Meehan-Klaus 2016). This idea fits well with Kolb's (1984) seminal learning cycle model. Kolb outlined the existence of our distinct stages of actionable learning: (a) an interactional experience, which leads to (b) a visible observation and (c) constructive reflection, which leads to the development of new approaches through trial, error, failure, and success, which leads to (d) progress driven experimentation, which leads to further experience. Learning can be more effective when it is coupled and anchored in experimentation and experience (Kolb, 1984).

Bandura (1990) outlined the importance of successful learning experiences and observing competency development as incubators that strengthens self-efficacy, cultivates critical thinking skills, enhances reflective thinking, and transforms self-confidence and self-perception from self-displeasure to self-satisfaction. Bandura (1990) states how successful results have been shown to fortify efficacy in ways that can lead to increased productively and improved abilities.

Creating approaches to teaching and learning that allow students to gain real-world experience is critical to the learning process, and it is relevant to employers that looking to hire graduates or lenders/investors that are looking to fund emerging entrepreneurs. Instructors and programs that teach cyber-security and cybersecurity policy should realize that new methods are needed to ensure that program graduates are more skilled and better prepared for the complex challenges that organizations face. The significant benefit of this research is to help curriculum managers and faculty in the United States, Africa, and the Middle East develop programs that are more effective in building actionable skills and competencies around cybersecurity.

REFERENCES

Academy of Management. (2018, March 21). Entrepreneurship. Retrieved from http://aom.org/Divisions-and-Interest-Groups/Entrepreneurtship/Entrepreneurship.aspx

Bandura, A. (1977). Self-efficacy: Toward a unifying theory of behavioral change. *Psychological Review*, *84*(2), 191–215. doi:10.1037/0033-295X.84.2.191 PMID:847061

Bandura, A. (1982). Self-efficacy mechanism in human agency. *The American Psychologist*, *37*(2), 122–147. doi:10.1037/0003-066X.37.2.122

Bandura, A. (1990). Perceived self-efficacy in the exercise of personal agency. *Applied Sport Psychology.*, *2*(2), 128–163. doi:10.1080/10413209008406426

Bandura, A. (2001). Social cognitive theory an agentic perspective. *Annual Review of Psychology, 52*(1), 1–26. doi:10.1146/annurev.psych.52.1.1 PMID:11148297

Bradley, S., & Price, N. (2016). *Critical Thinking: Proven Strategies To Improve Decision Making Skills, Increase Intuition And Think Smarter*. Seattle, WA: CreateSpace.

Cunliffe, A. (2004). On becoming a critically reflexive practitioner. *Journal of Management Education, 28*(4), 407–426. doi:10.1177/1052562904264440

Feltz, D. (1982). Path analysis of the causal elements in Bandura's theory of self-efficacy and an anxiety-based model of avoidance behavior. *Journal of Personality and Social Psychology, 42*(4), 764–781. doi:10.1037/0022-3514.42.4.764

Gault, J., Leach, E., & Duey, M. (2010). Effects of business internships on job marketability: The employers' perspective. *Education + Training, 52*(1), 76–88. doi:10.1108/00400911011017690

Hofman, L. (2003, September/October). Your turn. *AACSB International BizEd Magazine.*

Hughes, A., Galbraith, D., & White, D. (2011). Perceived competence: A common core for self-efficacy and self concept. *Journal of Personality Assessment, 93*(3), 278–289. doi:10.1080/00223891.2011.55 9390 PMID:21516587

Juergens, S. L. (2012). Experiential learning: How the utility of experiential learning within an MBA course enables the transfer of learning.

Kolb, D. (1984). *Experiential learning: experience as the source of learning and development*. Upper Saddle River, NJ: Prentice-Hall.

Kuh, G. D. (2008). High-impact educational practices. In G. D. Kuh (Ed.), *High-impact educational practices: What they are, who has them, and why they matter* (pp. 13–30). Washington, DC: Association of American Colleges and Universities.

Larmer, J. (2015). *Setting the Standard for Project Based Learning: A Proven Approach to Rigorous Classroom Instruction*. Alexandria, VA: Association for Supervision & Curriculum Development.

Lee, G., McGuiggan, R., & Holland, B. (2010). Balancing student learning and commercial outcomes in the workplace. *Higher Education Research & Development, 29*(5), 561–574. doi:10.1080/0729436 0.2010.502289

Marquardt, M. (2011). *Optimizing the Power of Action Learning: Real-Time Strategies for Developing Leaders, Building Teams, and Transforming Organizations*. Boston, MA: Nicholas Brealey.

Meehan-Klaus, J. (2016). Experiential learning and workforce preparedness of community college students.

Moore, D. (2013). *Engaged Learning in the Academy: Challenges and Possibilities*. New York: Palgrave Macmillan Publishing. doi:10.1057/9781137025197

Morrision, K. (1996). Developing reflective practice in higher degree students through a learning journal. *Studies in Higher Education, 21*(3), 317–16. doi:10.1080/03075079612331381241

Neck, H., Greene, P., & Brush, C. (2014). *Teaching Entrepreneurship: A Practice-Based Approach.* Northampton, MA: Edward Elgar Publishing.

Ramsey, V. J., & Fitzgibbons, D. (2005). Being in the classroom. *Journal of Management Education,* 29(2), 333–356. doi:10.1177/1052562904271144

Tuberville, K. A. (2014). A case study: Faculty perceptions of the challenges and successes in experiential learning at a public university.

This research was previously published in the International Journal of ICT Research in Africa and the Middle East (IJICTRAME), 9(1); pages 82-90, copyright year 2020 by IGI Publishing (an imprint of IGI Global).

Chapter 25
The Cybersecurity Awareness Training Model (CATRAM)

Regner Sabillon
Universitat Oberta de Catalunya, Spain

ABSTRACT

This chapter presents the outcome of one empirical research study that assess the implementation and validation of the cybersecurity awareness training model (CATRAM), designed as a multiple-case study in a Canadian higher education institution. Information security awareness programs have become unsuccessful to change people's attitudes in recognizing, stopping, or reporting cyberthreats within their corporate environment. Therefore, human errors and actions continue to demonstrate that we as humans are the weakest links in cybersecurity. The chapter studies the most recent cybersecurity awareness programs and its attributes. Furthermore, the author compiled recent awareness methodologies, frameworks, and approaches. The cybersecurity awareness training model (CATRAM) has been created to deliver training to different corporate audiences, each of these organizational units with peculiar content and detached objectives. They concluded their study by addressing the necessity of future research to target new approaches to keep cybersecurity awareness focused on the everchanging cyberthreat landscape.

INTRODUCTION

A satisfactory Cybersecurity Awareness Program must include adequate training that is aligned with the organization's objectives, the focus to raise cybersecurity awareness while performing employee's duties and an interactive communication between all stakeholders for any cybersecurity matter. Awareness programs may be unsuccessful if they are not designed to change people's attitude towards cyber incidents and likewise if a positive impact on any organization cannot be achieved. A cybersecurity awareness program is an organizational long-term investment that will help to create a cybersecurity culture if training is delivered on a continuous basis. A more energetic vision of the awareness aim is to go beyond the prevention of cybersecurity incidents.

DOI: 10.4018/978-1-6684-3554-0.ch025

We consider that the Cybersecurity Awareness TRAining Model (CATRAM) can represent a substantial foundation for the implementation of any organizational cybersecurity awareness program. CATRAM can also review any awareness training model that is steady and updated with the current cyberthreat landscape.

Cano (2016) points out that one of the consequences of current information security training methodologies is the "Bottom-up delegation"; this scenario does not allow end users to practice freedom and autonomy when it comes to data protection but instead follow and tolerate certain organizational information security policies.

BACKGROUND

This chapter look into an innovative model for creating, developing, planning, delivering and maintaining a Cybersecurity Awareness Training methodology or program that was validated in a Canadian Higher Education organization. The implementations in our target organization were part of a multi-case study research along with the CyberSecurity Audit Model (CSAM); another innovative model to conduct and deliver cybersecurity audits.

The Cybersecurity Awareness TRAining Model (CATRAM) was created distinctively to deliver cybersecurity awareness training to specific groups within any organization. CATRAM was designed to deliver the awareness training for the members of the Board od Directors, Top Executives, Managers, IT (Information Technology) staff and of course, end-users.

In this particular research scenario, CATRAM was implemented as the foundational model of our target organization. This organization did not have any Information Security policy in place for awareness training and CATRAM was validated to introduce cybersecurity awareness for their employees. These days, CATRAM is being used to develop the future cybersecurity awareness training program of this higher education organization.

LITERATURE REVIEW

As reported by the Gartner Magic Quadrant (2016) for Security Awareness Computer-Based Training (CBT) where leaders, visionaries, challengers and niche players are positioned. The Leaders are SANS Institute, Wombat Security Technologies, PhishMe, MediaPro, Security Innovation, Inspired eLearning, Terranova WW, PhishLine, Global Learning Systems, The Security Awareness Co.; Visionary vendors are Popcom Training and Security Mentor; Challenger vendors are BeOne Development, KnowBe4 and Optiv Security and last but not least are niche players like Junglemap, Digital Defense, Symantec (Blackfn Security) and Secure Mentem. Two years later (Gartner, 2018), we have seen relevant changes for the Security Awareness Computer-Based Training market where positions are different in all quadrants. The Leaders are Proofpoint (Wombat Security), MediaPro, Cofense, KnowBe and Terranova.; Visionary vendors are Inspired eLearning and Barracuda (PhishLine); Challenger vendors are SANS Institute, InfoSec Institute and Global Learning Systems and finally are the niche players like Junglemap, Security Innovation and Sophos. The new vendors placed as leaders, clearly identified market needs and incorporate new features on their CBT products, by including security topics aligned with the everchanging cyberthreat landscaping. Vendors continue to separate security awareness products and services by introducing a variety of formats, lengths and styles, by providing gamification, multilanguage support, supplemental internal marketing content like newsletters, intranet postings and security alerts, and integration with partnerships to offer endpoint detection and response, endpoint protection and data security. Another research study from Gartner (2018), indicates that by 2023 organizations that have implemented security awareness programs will go through 75% fewer account takeover attacks in comparison with other organizations, that is because effective security awareness programs must have a commitment from upper management and be in alignment with any organization's needs, practices and culture. Organizations face many challenges when deciding, delivering, implementing and maintaining a cybersecurity awareness training that is tailored to their specific business environment, strategy, needs and objectives. For example, choosing which topics to include when delivering the training, how to deliver training to personnel, how to verify the effectiveness of the training, updating the training program, implementing control measures to test cyber behaviors in the workplace and defining the frequency to re-train stakeholders.

A study from Ponemon Institute (2018) surveyed 1,021 IT and IT security practitioners in the USA and Europe, the Middle East and Africa (EMEA) to study Domain Name System (DNS) architecture, implementation and to identify responsibilities that manage cybersecurity activities in organizations. According to the results of the study, Ponemon Institute and Infoblox created the DNS Risk Index by categorizing five different areas: visibility, DNS attack protection, data protection and malware mitigation, threat intelligence and security operations. The most salient findings of this study show that most companies do not have dedicated staff to address DNS security, most companies are not tracking or identifying cyber assets, traffic analysis from firewalls is mostly used for malware mitigation and data assets protection, use of threat intelligence feeds is ineffective, measures to protect data assets include antivirus, endpoint security and data encryption and most cyberthreat investigations are conducted manually. The results show that the greatest concerns in terms of cyberattacks are advanced malware (63%), Advanced Persistent Threats (APTs – 59%), DNS-based data exfiltration (54%), unauthorized network access (51%), Ransomware (46%) and phishing/social engineering (45%).

The Global Security Awareness Report from SANS (2017), highlights that time and communication were identified as the critical takeaways to a thriving awareness program. The findings highlighted poor communication to engage people, the problem of time and lack of resources being assigned to a corporate awareness program. The participants revealed that they implemented awareness and behavior change (54.6%), had a compliance awareness program (27.1%), achieved long-term sustainment and culture change (9.8%), defined a program with robust metrics (0.9%) and did not have a cybersecurity awareness program at all (7.6%).

Symantec (2014) suggests that poorly trained personnel increases the risks of disclosure and loss of sensitive data like Personally Identifiable Information (PII) and Intellectual Property (IP). Its Security Awareness Program reduces vulnerabilities by creating a corporate culture and train employees to protect any organization critical assets from cyberattacks, exploitation, fraud and unauthorized access. The fundamental topics of Symantec's training program are information security, threats, vulnerabilities, countermeasures, securing the workplace, securing mobile users, protecting Internet information, social media mobile device security.

A study from Enterprise Management Associates (EMA, 2014) reported that 56% of personnel, not including IT and security staff, have not received any security awareness training in their organizations and 84% of participants recognized that the awareness training from their workplaces was also used to decrease cyber risks at home. In addition, the study findings confirmed that the existing security awareness programs lack the appropriate delivery periodicity, content and quality. Moreover, Company size, market and budgets have a significant impact on the existence and maturity of their corporate awareness training.

ESET (2017) provision free online cybersecurity awareness training to train employees and get a certification. The topics consist of an overview of threats like malware, phishing and social engineering; best practices for password management; best practices for email protection and preventive measures that cover best practices for cyber hygiene at the workplace and at home. PhishMe also provides access to a free of charge Computer Based Training (CBT) course called PhishMe CBFree which contains seventeen security awareness modules and four compliance training modules. The course is available in seven languages (English, Chinese, French, German, Portuguese, Spanish and Japanese). The Compliance modules are General Data Protection Regulation (GDPR), Payment Data, Personal Data and Health Care; The security awareness modules cover cybersecurity awareness, cloud computing, advanced spear phishing, business email compromise, ransomware, surfing the Web, data protection, insider threats, malicious links, malware, mobile devices, security outside of the office, passwords, physical security, social engineering, social networking and spear phishing (PhishMe, 2017). Table 1 introduces an overview of most models and frameworks linked to best practices for the definition and consolidation of cybersecurity awareness programs.

Industrial and critical infrastructure organizations can also be targets of any cyberattack, as these organizations rely their businesses on Industrial Control Systems (ICS). Global malware attacks such as NotPetya, WannaCry and Emotet as well more targeted ICS cyberattacks such as Industroyer and TRITON, are just a few examples that can impact production outages, clean-ups, catastrophic safety and environmental incidents. The Global ICS & Industrial Internet of Things (IIOT) risk report (Cyberx, 2019) analyzed data from 850 production ICS networks using Network Traffic Analysis (NTA) in conjunction with deep packet inspections. The major findings included that 40% of industrial sites have at least one direct connection to the Internet, 53% of sites have obsolete Windows systems, 69% of sites have plain-text passwords traversing their networks, 57% of sites are not running anti-virus solutions that include automatic signature updates, 16% of sites have at least a misconfigured Wireless Access Point (WAP) and 84% of industrial sites have at least one remotely accessible device without multifactor authentication controls.

Our literature review approach used mixed methods (Qualitative and Quantitative studies), to select the material as initial references in our multi-case study. The lead researcher used computerized databases and the Internet searching for keywords like "security training"; "information security training"; "SETA"; "cybersecurity awareness training"; "cybersecurity awareness training program"; "cybersecurity training framework" and "security awareness training program."

Axelos (2015) indicates that cyber-resilience specific training should be delivered on a regular basis, training should be designed and tailored to specific organizational roles and responsibilities of employees, awareness campaigns should be created to raise awareness and to address specific cyber risks. Nonetheless, we have to come up with finding innovative ways to deliver cybersecurity awareness training and most of all, keep people engaged with cybersecurity awareness activities.

Table 1. Cybersecurity Awareness frameworks and methodologies

Framework or Methodology that focuses on cybersecurity awareness	Phases
ISO/IEC 27001:2005 (2005)	There aren't any specific phases or recommendations for the security awareness delivery. Clause 5.2.2 highlights the importance of necessary personnel competencies to support the Information Security Management System (ISMS), providing training to satisfy needs, maintaining training records and that the organization is responsible for the awareness training of relevant personnel
ISO/IEC 27032 (2012)	Section 2.4 covers the training and awareness program. Defining training needs, designing and planning training, defining awareness program requirements and setting up training and awareness evaluation
Hewlett Packard Progressive Engagement Framework (Beyer et al., 2015)	1. Awareness Profiling · Company profiling · Awareness assessment · Gap analysis · Awareness maturity level report 2. Awareness Planning · Communication, education and training concept · Awareness improvement plan 3. Transformation · Creation, production and measures implementation · Support of internal core team 4. Optimization · Comparison between target and actual state · Adjust and optimize accordingly
SANS Security Awareness Maturity Model (2017)	This Awareness Maturity Model is organized in five sections: 1. Non-Existent: An awareness program does not exist 2. Compliance Focused: The awareness program is either aligned with a compliance or audit requirements 3. Promoting awareness and behavior change: This program is focused on training topics that have greatest impacts to support the mission of the organization 4. Long-Term Sustainment and Culture Change: This program is aligned with a corporate cybersecurity program. It has processes, resources and leadership support 5. Robust Metrics Framework: This is a mature awareness program with a robust metrics framework in place
MediaPro Adaptive Awareness Framework (2017)	1. Analyze: Use data to inform about the program 2. Plan: Draw a roadmap for planning the awareness program 3. Train: Build training to achieve real behavior changes 4. Reinforce: Battle the forgetting curve
Beyer-Brummel Comparative Cybersecurity Training Framework (2015)	Organized by levels: 1. Targeted: To produce non-IT cybersecurity skills to exact role specific performance 2. Education: To cultivate IT security insight and understanding 3. Advanced: To equip IT security professionals to address assurance, policy and training
NIST- Key steps leading to the implementation of the awareness and training program (2014)	1. Design Awareness and Training Program 2. Develop Awareness and Training material 3. Implement Program 4. Post-Implementation
PCI Data Security Standard (PCI DSS)- Best Practices for Implementing a Security Awareness Program (2014)	1. Assemble the Security Awareness Team 2. Determine Roles for Security Awareness 3. Target delivery of relevant material to the appropriate audience in an efficient and timely way 4. Define the Security Awareness training content 5. Define assessment metrics of the awareness training 6. Follow the Security Awareness Program checklist

continues on following page

Table 1. Continued

Framework or Methodology that focuses on cybersecurity awareness	Phases

Cano – Basic Model of the level of maturity of the Organizational Information Security Culture (2016)	To measure the maturity of several elements of the InfoSec culture
	Elements:
	  1. Culture foundations
	  2. Access foundations
	  3. Information understanding
	  4. Basic Instruments
	  5. Management compromise
	Maturity indicators:
	  1. Reactive
	  2. Unstable
	  3. Proactive
	  4. Sustainable

MITRE- Model to question the validity of any email (2010)	EARNEST utilizes a series of questions to challenge the validity of an electronic message: Expected: It the email expected? Ambiguous: Is it asking to open attachments? Relationship: Any prior relationship with sender? Normal: Are context, grammar, syntax and spelling consistent from your contact? Exposed: Any malicious links in your email? Sense: Does it make sense to receive a link or attachment? Time: Is there any time factor for responding?

Cyber Safe Workforce – Security Awareness and Training Program (2016)	The awareness lifecycle comprises the following phases:
	  1. Identify and Define: Define and create training plan
	  2. Baseline: Gather initial set of data for future trainining scope
	  3. Train: Deliver guidance and information training
	  4. Track & Measure: Audit participation and gather good metrics
	  5. Evaluate & Update: Keep updating your training program all the time

Whitman and Mattord - Framework of Security Education, Training, and Awareness (2019)	The Framework includes six components that are applicable to Awareness, Training and Education:
	  1. Attributes: It seeks teaching members the importance of security by focusing on what, how and why
	  2. Levels: Knowledge transfer from basic, detailed and in-depth levels
	  3. Objectives: Based on threat recognition, effective responses using learned skills and engagement of active defense
	  4. Teaching methods: Some examples include informal training, hands-on practice and seminars
	  5. Assessments: By using different evaluation techniques like problem solving and essays
	  6. Impact timeframe: Short-term, intermediate and long-term

Nguyen et al. – InCAT (Intelligence-based Cybersecurity Awareness Training). (2018)	A model for delivering cybersecurity training with a strong focus on drilling deep into the shared contexts among collected cyber awareness training results, cyberthreat intelligence reports, and other cybersecurity related data logs. InCAT feedback loop includes 8 steps:
	  1. Threat reports
	  2. Annotation model flow to knowledge discovery model
	  3. Derived knowledge from threat reports
	  4. Tests for users
	  5. Initial user reports
	  6. User report verification by the annotation model
	  7. User assessment reports
	  8. Final results in control dashboard system

THE CYBERSECURITY AWARENESS TRAINING MODEL (CATRAM)

The Cybersecurity Awareness TRAining Model (CATRAM), is an innovative model that can be implemented at any organization to consolidate the awareness foundations of a corporate Cybersecurity Awareness Program or to start the implementation of an organizational Cybersecurity Awareness Training Program (See Figure 1). The model design answers our main research question:

Figure 1. The Cybersecurity Awareness TRAining Model (CATRAM)

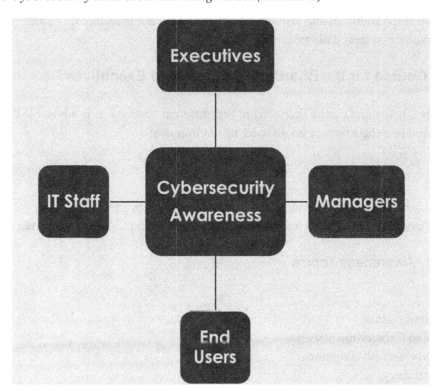

Why it is necessary to increase cyber awareness at the organizational and personal levels?

The aim of this research was to design a model for delivering cyber awareness training to support awareness education in any organizational environment. The Cybersecurity Awareness TRAining Model (CATRAM) has been created to deliver the initial cybersecurity awareness training at any organization or to re-introduce a better awareness training approach to an existing cybersecurity or information security awareness training program.

CATRAM has been designed to provide specific cybersecurity awareness training for personnel:

1. Board of Directors and Executives: Members of this group are trained based on the organizational cybersecurity strategy, governance and program.
2. Managers: Department managers are trained to support and lead cybersecurity initiatives in their corporate environment.

3. End Users: This group gets awareness training to improve cybersecurity practices in the workplace and their personal lives.
4. IT Staff: Information Technology specialists are trained in the use of advanced cybersecurity techniques, methods, procedures and best practices to support the corporate awareness program and the cybersecurity program.

Each awareness course has been developed with a specific outline, objectives, content and cybersecurity topics in alignment with the target audience, the organizational scope and aim, the cybersecurity awareness program and the corporate cybersecurity program. Cybersecurity topic choice are based on the group's main responsibilities and also on the cybersecurity domains that this group will be dealing with in the workplace on their daily tasks.

Awareness Course for the Board of Directors and Executives

The course lasts 2 hours and can be delivered in two different sessions. It is advisable that this course could be delivered in a classroom or board meeting environment.

Objectives

1. Provide a high-level overview of an effective cybersecurity awareness training for your organization
2. Create cybersecurity awareness for the Board of Directors and C-Suite Executives

Cybersecurity Awareness Topics

Initial Survey
Cybersecurity Introduction
Cybersecurity and Cybercrime Statistics
A Corporate Cybersecurity Program
Cybersecurity Strategy
Responsibilities of Stakeholders (Board of Directors and C-Suite Executives)
Cyberthreat Landscape
Cybersecurity Risk Management
Cybersecurity Frameworks
Cybersecurity Awareness and Training
Cybersecurity Business Continuity
Incident Response Management
Conclusions
Final Survey

Awareness Course for Managers

The course lasts 2 hours and can be structured in two different sessions. The course can be delivered in a classroom setting, online or a blended environment.

Objectives

1. Provide a high-level overview of an effective cybersecurity awareness training for your organization
2. Create cybersecurity awareness for Managers

Cybersecurity Awareness Topics

Initial Survey
Cybersecurity Introduction
Cybersecurity and Cybercrime Statistics
A Corporate Cybersecurity Program
Cybersecurity Strategy
Responsibilities of Stakeholders (Department Managers)
Cyberthreat Landscape
Cybersecurity Risk Management
Cybersecurity Frameworks
Cybersecurity Awareness and Training
Cybersecurity Business Continuity
Incident Response Management
Conclusions
Final Survey

Awareness Course for End Users

The course lasts 4 hours and can be established in two or four different sessions. The course can be delivered in a classroom setting, online or a blended environment. It is recommended to add a short video clip from YouTube as additional learning resource for your audiences.

Objectives

1. Educate end users to help protecting the confidentiality, availability and integrity of your organization's information and cyber assets
2. Create awareness of the importance of cybersecurity and cybersecurity controls

Cybersecurity Awareness Topics

Initial Survey
Cybersecurity Introduction
Cybersecurity and Cybercrime Statistics
You are a target for cybercriminals
Cybercrime
Hackers
Cyberthreats
Social Engineering

Phishing
Internet Browsing
Social Networks
Mobile device security
Passwords
Encryption
Data security
Identity Theft
Wi-Fi Security
Working remotely
Physical security
Protecting your online profile
Protecting your home network
Protecting our children online
Privacy
Avoiding Scams
Have you been hacked?
Conclusions
Final Survey

Awareness Course for IT Professionals

The course lasts 20 hours and can be structured in ten or twenty different sessions. The course can be delivered in a classroom setting, online, self-paced e-doing or a blended environment.

Objectives

1. Understand cybersecurity concepts
2. Recognize key cybersecurity objectives for the protection of cyber assets
3. Understand cybercrime operations
4. Recognize cybersecurity threat agents that could impact your organization
5. Understand any cyberattack architecture
6. Identify most common cyberattacks
7. Apply cybersecurity measures to defend against cyberattacks
8. Understand a cybersecurity program architecture and operation
9. Recognize the importance of developing, enforcing and maintaining cybersecurity policies
10. Understand the fundamentals of ethical hacking
11. Understand the architecture of penetration testing
12. Get familiar with most cybersecurity frameworks
13. Understand the basics of cyber threat intelligence
14. Understand the importance of proper cybersecurity training
15. Raise cybersecurity awareness in your organization
16. Apply cybersecurity architecture principles
17. Recognize the importance of hardening security in data, voice and video networks

18. Recognize the importance of security hardening for information, systems and applications
19. Identify cybersecurity vulnerabilities
20. Remediate existing cybersecurity vulnerabilities
21. Recognize the cybersecurity implications of new and evolving technologies
22. Understand the principles of Cybersecurity Incident Response and Management
23. Understand the fundamentals of Digital Forensics
24. Recognize the importance of the continual evaluation of a corporate cybersecurity program
25. Recognize the value of corporate cyber wargames to test cybersecurity
26. Identify the opportunities for cybersecurity education and professional development

Cybersecurity Awareness Topics

Initial Survey
Cybersecurity Fundamentals
Cybercrime
Cyberattacks
Corporate Cybersecurity Program
Cybersecurity Policies
Ethical Hacking
Penetration Testing
Cyber Operations
Cybersecurity Frameworks
Cyber Threat Intelligence
Cybersecurity Awareness and Training Program
Architecture and Networks
Information, Systems and Applications
Vulnerability Management
Evolving Technologies
Incident Response Management
Digital Forensics
Enterprise Cybersecurity Assessment
Cybersecurity Corporate Wargames
Cybersecurity Education
Final Survey

Alotaibi et al. (2016) point out that one of the best ways to deal with cybercrime is by creating awareness and by adopting effective cybersecurity practices for people.

MEASURING THE MODEL RESULTS

The results of CATRAM can be assessed once all training courses have been delivered. Most of the assessment could be measured at the end user level by evaluating changes in security behaviors and alignment with corporate cybersecurity compliance. If possible, end users must be advised that the effectiveness of the awareness training will be evaluated by performing announced assessments, and the delivery of non-announced assessment exercises as well.

Table 2 presents suggested awareness areas and participating groups to assess the compliance and the impact of the cybersecurity awareness model.

Table 2. CATRAM Metric Identifiers and Objectives

Metric Identifier	Group	Metric Objectives
Cybersecurity Awareness and Training Effectiveness	Executives	Identify training gap needs and approve training courses
Cyber policy-making assessment	Executives	Review, update and approve cybersecurity policies
Cyber monitoring, metric definition and reporting	Executives	Approve required cybersecurity metrics
Awareness training completion	Managers	Verify that all staff completes training for every department
Communication flow	Managers	Enforce the distribution of awareness communication and proper training documentation
Cybersecurity incidents volume	IT	Evaluate Help Desk monthly report
Cybersecurity skills	IT	Evaluate new cybersecurity skills of technical staff that is consistent with the organization growth and operations
Infected digital devices	IT	Identify percentage on a monthly basis
Phishing awareness and detection	End Users	Identify phishing victims and users that are able to avoid phishing attacks
Social Media risks	End Users	Evaluate percentage of user's time
Password management	End Users	Assess user's behavior for password management

Hayden (2016) presents a model to measure the levels of security culture strength. The strength of the security culture could be a function of the organizational awareness and training program or it could the result of a highly regulated industry: A weak security culture (80% occurrence of a bad decision); a moderate security culture (50% occurrence of a bad decision) and a strong security culture (20% occurrence of a bad decision).

We assess the cybersecurity awareness by measuring compliance by addressing the following criteria:

- Does your organization have a cybersecurity awareness program?
- Do you provide some kind of cybersecurity training to your staff?
- Is training delivered on a regular recurring basis?
- Do employees are following security policies of the organization?
- Are you delivering training to recognize and deal with social engineering?
- Do your staff know how to recognize and report a security incident?
- Is your staff able to detect and respond to any cybersecurity emergency?
- Do you enforce privacy and confidentiality requirements in your organization?
- Are your employees following security procedures for data and information protection?

- Is your awareness training focused and delivered to specific audiences like end users, managers, IT, C-Suite executives and Board of Directors?
- Is your awareness training covering multidimensional topics?
- Does your training outline cover technical, social and user behavior areas?

Evaluation Scorecard

We calculate the final cybersecurity maturity rating of the cybersecurity awareness training domain by using the criteria from Table 3. The score can be mapped to a specific maturity level.

Gartner (2018) suggests that security and risk management leaders must provision awareness training to employees in order to focus on protecting their online security and the personal aspects of cybersecurity, knowledge transfer of good practices to protect intellectual property and data in corporate environments. Gartner also suggests a series of best practices to develop and maintain a cybersecure worforce:

1. By nurturing a holistic cybersecure personal lifestyle that includes good hygiene for identity management and security awareness
2. By committing to training and awareness behavior that encircles corporate training, workshops and the use of the proper tools
3. By building trust that verifies employees' online behavior through timely tests of cybersecure hygiene

Table 3. Cybersecurity Awareness Training Maturity Rating

Rating	Description
Immature (I): 0-30	The organization does not have any plans to manage its cybersecurity. Controls for critical cybersecurity areas are inexistent or very weak. The organization has not implemented a comprehensive cybersecurity program nor an awareness training program.
Developing (D): 31-70	The organization is starting to focus on cybersecurity matters. If technologies are in place, the organization needs to focus on key areas to protect cyber assets. Attention must be focused towards staff, processes, controls and regulations. The Awareness Education domain is developing. The organization has a foundation model for cybersecurity awareness and additional efforts are required to develop a complete cybersecurity awareness program.
Mature (M): 71-90	While the organization has a mature cybersecurity awareness environment. Improvements are required to the key areas that have been identified with weaknesses.
Advanced (A): 91-100	The organization has excelled in implementing cybersecurity awareness training best practices. There is always room for improvement. Keep documentation up-to-date and continually review cybersecurity processes through audits.

METHODOLOGY

The Cybersecurity Awareness TRAining Model (CATRAM) has been tested, implemented and validated along with the CyberSecurity Audit Model (CSAM) in a Canadian higher education institution (Sabillon et al., 2019). The research project did audit the cybersecurity organizational strategy, implemented the CyberSecurity Audit Model (CSAM) and delivered cybersecurity awareness training to more than one hundred participants based on the Cybersecurity Awareness TRAining Model (CATRAM). The CyberSecurity Audit Model (CSAM) is an exhaustive model that encloses the optimal assurance assessment of cybersecurity in any organization and it can verify specific guidelines for Nation States that are planning to implement a National Cybersecurity Strategy (NCS) or want to evaluate the effectiveness of its National Cybersecurity Strategy or Policy already in place. The CSAM has 18 domains; domain 1 is specific for Nation States and domains 2-18 can be implemented at any organization. The CyberSecurity Audit Model (CSAM) contains overview, resources, 18 domains, 26 sub-domains, 87 checklists, 169 controls, 429 sub-controls, 80 guideline assessment and an evaluation scorecard.

The mutiple case study research included several phases like plan, design, preparation, collection, analysis, sharing and dissemination. We intended to perform qualitative research by utilizing interpretive material practices such as online and paper surveys, interviews, classroom and online training and analysis of documentation, processes and procedures of the target institution. We completed a multi-case study research following Yin's methodology (2018; 2014) to plan, design, prepare, collect, analyze and share phases by creating, implementing and validating two innovative cybersecurity models (CATRAM & CSAM). This initial validation of the CATRAM and CSAM took place in a Canadian Higher Education Institution. More recently, the CSAM has been validated for the second time in a larger Canadian Higher Education Institution.

The target organization provided their staff time to support the case study research, resources to conduct the cybersecurity audit, the provision of classroom space and time, computer use, Internet access for the delivery of the cybersecurity awareness training courses, the access to their computer systems to conduct the research and to design the online courses in their Learning Management System (Moodle).

RESULTS

Before initiating our case study research, our target organization did not own any cybersecurity awareness model nor any cybersecurity awareness education program whatsoever. The CATRAM delivery let the organization, to build a strong foundation for a future implementation of a comprehensive cybersecurity awareness training program. The cybersecurity audit of the awareness education domain was executed after the successful delivery and implementation of CATRAM. We conducted the audit of the awareness education based on the CSAM and the most relevant noncompliances are the lack of a corporate cybersecurity awareness training program and the confirmation that staff are aware that cyber training is not being delivered and it exists the necessity to eradicate this weakness (Table 4). The critical controls that need immediate attention are that the target organization does not have a valid cybersecurity awareness program, and employees were not aware how important is to keep training them in cyber topics to increase awareness and show a proactive participation in order for their potential awareness training program to be successful.

A series of tables are included to present the findings in this research scenario. Table 4 illustrates the assessment of the main cybersecurity awareness education controls. Table 5 contains the sub-controls findings based on the audit checklist. Major nonconformities need to addressed and corrected. Staff need to able to identify and report any cybersecurity incident, enforce privacy, confidentialy and protection for any Personally Identifiable Information (PII) for the internal and stakeholders of the institution.

Table 4. Control Evaluation of the Cybersecurity Awareness Education

Reference	Sub Area	Clause	Steps	Control Evaluation		Checklist
				Yes	No	CSAM-Awareness
13.1	Awareness	13.1.1	Organization deploys a cybersecurity awareness program	☐	☒	
		13.1.2	The awareness training program is delivered on an annual basis	☒	☐	
		13.1.3	Employees are aware of the need of this kind of training program	☐	☒	
		13.1.4	The training program is designed for different staffing levels	☒	☐	
		13.1.5	Training material is constantly updated as new cyber threats emerge	☒	☐	

Table 5. Control Evaluation of the Cybersecurity Awareness Education

Clause	No.	Checklist Questions	Findings		
			Compliant	Minor Nonconformity	Major Nonconformity
13.1.1	1	Does your organization have a cybersecurity awareness program?	☐	☐	☒
13.1.1	2	Do you provide some kind of cybersecurity training to your staff?	☒	☐	☐
13.1.2	3	Is training delivered on a regular recurring basis?	☒	☐	☐
13.1.1	4	Do employees are following security policies of the organization?	☒	☐	☐
13.1.1	5	Are you delivering training to recognize and deal with social engineering?	☒	☐	☐
13.1.1	6	Do your staff know how to recognize and report a security incident?	☐	☒	☐
13.1.1	7	Are your personnel able to detect and respond to any cybersecurity emergency?	☐	☐	☒
13.1.1	8	Do you enforce privacy and confidentiality requirements in your organization?	☐	☐	☒
13.1.1	9	Are your employees following security procedures for data and information protection?	☐	☐	☒
13.1.4	10	Is your awareness training focused and delivered to specific audiences like end users, managers, IT, C-Suite executives and Board of Directors?	☒	☐	☐
13.1.1	11	Is your awareness training covering multidimensional topics?	☒	☐	☐
13.1.1	12	Does your training outline cover technical, social and user behavior areas?	☒	☐	☐

Table 6 corroborates that the cybersecurity awareness training is at a *'developing stage'* and consequently needs improvement in our target organization. The higher education institution needs to implement a full cybersecurity awareness and training program for all stakeholders. Partial awareness training is ineffective. The validation of the CATRAM helped the target organization to implement a foundation for their future cybersecurity awareness training program. While the CATRAM implementation was delivered for the Board of Directors, C-Suite Executives, Managers, IT staff and end users thus a critical recommendation was to train their students and external stakeholders as well.

Table 6. Overall Cybersecurity Awareness Rating

Cybersecurity Awareness TRAining Model (CATRAM)			
Domain	**13-Awareness Education**		
Control Evaluation	**Ratings**		**Score**
	Immature	☐	
	Developing	☒	60%
	Mature	☐	
	Advanced	☐	
Developing (D): 31-70 The organization is starting to focus on cybersecurity matters. If technologies are in place, the organization needs to focus on key areas to protect cyber assets. Attention must be focused towards staff, processes, controls and regulations. The Awareness Education domain is developing. The organization has a foundation model for cybersecurity awareness and additional efforts are required to develop a complete cybersecurity awareness program.			

With regard to recommendations, we did suggest the creation and implementation of the corporate cybersecurity awareness training program, to define ownership to maintain the training program and the CATRAM update on an annual basis or as new cyberthreats emerge, to conduct "Train the Trainer" sessions for designated instructors or facilitators and, last but not least the constant evaluation of staff using scheduled and non-scheduled assessments to evaluate and understand cybersecurity awareness and behaviors.

CONCLUSION

The main objective of this multi-case study was to design and validate a cybersecurity awareness model; the Cybersecurity Awareness TRAining Model (CATRAM) to address the challenges to deliver cybersecurity awareness training based on staff roles. The cybersecurity model including all its components were successfully validated by a multi-case study performed in a Canadian higher education institution.

CATRAM could support the implementation of a foundation or for consolidating a cybersecurity awareness training program at any organization. The results of this research show that the delivery of cybersecurity training based on organizational roles and responsibilities tend to motivate personnel to create and maintain awareness in their workplaces as well in their personal lives.

The limitation of our case study is that CATRAM was validated in a single organization, time constraints, lack of interest for the topics and lack of engagement were some of the challenges that we have to overcome from some of the participants. Hence, future testing will enhance the model results by engaging more organizations. The case study results have implications for our target organization but at the same time, implications for future research to review and expand our proposed cybersecurity model. Future work would propose to transform CATRAM into a cybersecurity awareness training framework.

REFERENCES

Alotaibi, F., Furnell, S., Stengel, I., & Papadaki, M. (2016). A review of Using Gaming Technologies for Cyber-Security Awareness. *International Journal of Information Security Research*, 6(2), 660–666. doi:10.20533/ijisr.2042.4639.2016.0076

Axelos. (2015). *Cyber Resilience Best Practices.* Norwich: Resilia.

Beyer, M., Ahmed, S., Doerlemann, K., Arnell, S., Parkin, S., Sasse, A., & Passingham, N. (2015). *Awareness is only the first step: A framework for progressive engagement of staff in cyber security.* Hewlett Packard Enterprise.

Beyer, R., & Brummel, B. (2015). *Implementing Effective Cyber Security Training for End Users of Computer Networks.* Society for Human Resource Management and Society for Industrial and Organizational Psychology.

Cano, J. (2016). La educación en seguridad de la información. Reflexión pedagógicas desde el pensamiento de sistemas. *Memorias 3er Simposio Internacional en "Temas y problemas de Investigación en Educación: Complejidad y Escenarios para la Paz".*

Cano, J. (2016). Modelo de madurez de cultura organizacional de seguridad de la información. Una visión desde el pensamiento sistémico-cibernético. Actas de la XIV Reunión Española sobre Criptología y Seguridad de la Información, 24-29.

Cyber, X. (2019). 2019 Global ICS & IIoT Risk Report. A data-driven analysis of vulnerabilities in our industrial and critical infrastructure. *CyberX Labs.* Retrieved from https://cyberx-labs.com/resources/risk-report-2019/

ESET. (2017). *ESET Cybersecurity Awareness Training.* ESET Canada. Retrieved from https://www.eset.com/ca/cybertraining/

Fujitsu. (2017). *The Digital Transformation PACT.* Retrieved from https://www.fujitsu.com

Gartner. (2016). *2016 Gartner Magic Quadrant for Security Awareness Computer-Based Training Vendors.* Gartner, Inc.

Gartner. (2018). *How to Build an Enterprise Security Awareness Program.* Gartner, Inc.

Gartner. (2018). *How to Secure the Human Link.* Gartner, Inc.

Gartner. (2018). *Magic Quadrant for Security Awareness Computer-Based Training.* Gartner, Inc.

Hayden, L. (2016). *People-Centric Security: Transforming your Enterprise Security Culture.* Mc Graw Hill.

International Organization for Standardization - ISO. (2005). *ISO/IEC 27001:2005 – Information Technology – Security Techniques – Information Security Management Systems – Requirements.* ISO.

International Organization for Standardization -ISO. (2012). *ISO/IEC 27032:2012 – Information Technology – Security Techniques – Guidelines for Cybersecurity.* ISO.

LeClair, J., Abraham, S., & Shih, L. (2013). An Interdisciplinary Approach to Educating an Effective Cyber Security Worforce. *Proceedings of Information Security Curriculum Development Conference,* 71-78.

MediaPro. (2017). *A Best Practices Guide for Comprehensive Employee Awareness Programs.* MediaPro.

MITRE. (2010). *The Importance of Using EARNEST.* The MITRE Corporation. Retrieved from https://www.mitre.org/sites/default/files/pdf/mitre_earnest.pdf

MITRE. (2017). *Cybersecurity Awareness & Training.* The MITRE Corporation.

Monahan, D. (2014). *Security Awareness Training: It's not just for Compliance-Research Report Summary. Enterprise Management Associates.* EMA.

National Institute of Standards and Technology – NIST. (2003). *Building an Information Technology Security Awareness and Training Program.* NIST Special Publication 800-50.

National Institute of Standards and Technology – NIST. (2017). *An Introduction to Information Security.* NIST Special Publication 800-12 Revision 1.

Nguyen, T.N., Sbityakov, L., & Scoggins, S. (2018). *Intelligence-based Cybersecurity Awareness Training- an Exploratory Project.* CoRR, abs/1812.04234.

NTT Group. (2017). Embedding cybersecurity into digital transformation - a journey towards business resilience. *NTT Security.* Retrieved from https://www.nttsecurity.com

PCI Security Standards Council - PCI DSS. (2014). *Best Practices for Implementing a Security Awareness Program.* PCI DSS.

Penderdast, T. (2016). How to Audit the Human Element and Assess Your Organization's Security Risk. *ISACA Journal, 5,* 1–5.

PhishMe. (2017). PhishMe CBFree. *PhishMe Headquarters.* Retrieved from https://phishme.com/resources/cbfree-computer-based-training/

Ponemon Institute. (2018). Assessing the DNS Security Risk. Research report sponsored by Infoblox. Ponemon Institute LLC.

Sabillon, R. (2018). Scenario III: Data for a single cybersecurity domain audit (Awareness Education). *Mendeley Data, 2.* doi:10.17632/m4dk8n9sx7.2

Sabillon, R., Serra-Ruiz, J., Cavaller, V., & Cano, J. (2017). A Comprehensive Cybersecurity Audit Model to Improve Cybersecurity Assurance: The CyberSecurity Audit Model (CSAM). *Proceedings of Second International Conference on Information Systems and Computer Science (INCISCOS)*. 10.1109/INCISCOS.2017.20

Sabillon, R., Serra-Ruiz, J., Cavaller, V., Jeimy, J., & Cano, M. (2019). An Effective Cybersecurity Training Model to Support an Organizational Awareness Program: The Cybersecurity Awareness TRAining Model (CATRAM). A Case Study in Canada. *Journal of Cases on Information Technology, 21*(3), 26–39. doi:10.4018/JCIT.2019070102

SANS Institute. (2017). *2017 Security Awareness Report: It's time to communicate. SANS Security Awareness.* Retrieved from https://securingthehuman.sans.org/media/resources/STH-SecurityAwarenessReport-2017.pdf

SANS Security Awareness, . (2017). *2017 Security Awareness Report.* SANS Institute.

Symantec. (2014). *Symantec Security Awareness Program: Mitigate information risk by educating your employees.* Symantec Corporation.

Ward, M. (2016). *Security Awareness and Training: Solving the unintentional insider threat.* Cyber Safe Worforce LLC.

Whitman, M. E., & Mattord, H. J. (2019). *Management of Information Security* (6th ed.). Cengage Learning, Inc.

Yin, R. K. (2014). *Case Study Research: Design and Methods* (5th ed.). Sage Publications.

Yin, R. K. (2018). *Case Study Research and Applications* (6th ed.). Sage Publications.

ADDITIONAL READING

Choi, Y. (2018). *Selected Readings in Cybersecurity*. Cambridge Scholars Publishing.

KEY TERMS AND DEFINITIONS

Cybersecurity Awareness: Perception of cybersecurity matters to be incorporated at any job function.

Cybersecurity Awareness Education Maturity: Level of experience that an organization has implemented and acquired for cybersecurity training in accordance with the cyberthreat landscaping.

Cybersecurity Awareness Training: Cybersecurity areas that will be taught to any stakeholder in order to increase awareness and remediation.

APPENDIX

Template for Overall Cybersecurity Rating for Domain 13 (Awareness Education)

Table 7. Overall Cybersecurity Rating for Domain 13 (Awareness Education)

Cybersecurity Audit Model (CSAM)						
No.	Domain	Ratings				Score
		I	D	M	A	
13	Awareness Education	☐	☐	☐	☐	
Final Cybersecurity Maturity Rating of Awareness Education		☐	☐	☐	☐	
Immature (I): 0-30	The organization does not have any plans to manage its cybersecurity. Controls for critical cybersecurity areas are inexistent or very weak. The organization has not implemented a comprehensive cybersecurity program nor an awareness training program.					
Developing (D): 31-70	The organization is starting to focus on cybersecurity matters. If technologies are in place, the organization needs to focus on key areas to protect cyber assets. Attention must be focused towards staff, processes, controls and regulations. The Awareness Education domain is developing. The organization has a foundation model for cybersecurity awareness and additional efforts are required to develop a complete cybersecurity awareness program.					
Mature (M): 71-90	While the organization has a mature cybersecurity awareness environment. Improvements are required to the key areas that have been identified with weaknesses.					
Advanced (A): 91-100	The organization has excelled in implementing cybersecurity awareness training best practices. There is always room for improvement. Keep documentation up-to-date and continually review cybersecurity processes through audits.					

Chapter 26
The Three–Dimensional Model for a Community

Gregory B. White

CIAS, The University of Texas at San Antonio, USA

Natalie Sjelin

CIAS, The University of Texas at San Antonio, USA

ABSTRACT

The community cyber security maturity model (CCSMM) was designed and developed to provide communities with an action plan to build a viable and sustainable cybersecurity program focused on improving their overall cybersecurity capability. Not long after the initial development of the model, it was realized that there are intertwined relationships that needed to be addressed. This drove the creation of the three-dimensional model broadening the scope to include individuals, organizations, communities, states, and the nation. This chapter will provide an overview of the development and importance of the 3-D model and will describe the scope areas that were included.

INTRODUCTION

The 2-Dimensional model was the initial step to creating a roadmap for communities to follow when developing their cybersecurity program. The established characteristics help to define a community's cybersecurity posture at each level. As a reminder, the characteristics are organized by awareness, information sharing, policy, and planning dimensions. They also establish the three building blocks; a yardstick, a roadmap, and a common point of reference as previously discussed. It wasn't long after the characteristics were developed, that the CIAS researchers were discussing how cybersecurity guidelines affecting individuals in the community could be integrated into the CCSMM or how cybersecurity concepts for states should be integrated. This led to the realization that the model didn't have enough depth to address these other areas. After many discussions, it was determined that the model needed to

DOI: 10.4018/978-1-6684-3554-0.ch026

be 3-Dimensional (3-D). The model needed to be able to incorporate what individuals would need to do to improve their cybersecurity posture. It also needed to address organizations, states and ultimately the nation. There are two major considerations supporting this:

1) Everyone should have a role in cybersecurity
2) Effective cybersecurity is a collaborative effort

These concepts became the "The Whole Community Approach" theme for the Department of Homeland Security's cybersecurity initiatives many years later.

THE 3-DIMENSIONAL MODEL

The purpose of the 3-D Model is to broaden the capability of the framework allowing it to be flexible and scalable to address all aspects of a cybersecurity program. Consider the idea that individuals make up organizations; individuals and organizations make up communities; individuals, organizations and communities make up a state, tribe or territory; and the states, tribes and territories make up the nation. The change from a 2-D model to the 3-D model was a pivotal point in the creation of the Community Cyber Security Maturity Model. This shift created a model that can provide the improvement progression for everyone in the nation because the model can now support a roadmap for individuals, organizations, communities, states and the nation. In addition, it can integrate other frameworks such as the National Institute of Standards and Technology's (NIST) Cyber Security Framework (CSF) (NIST, 2018) outlining the security controls necessary for an organization. It can also support the National Initiative for Cybersecurity Education (NICE) Cybersecurity Workforce Framework (NICE Framework) (NIST, 2017) a resource that categorizes and describes cybersecurity work and the cybersecurity workforce. Communities should be able to advance their cybersecurity posture naturally, but a defined program that provides step by step guidance is the assistance that is realistically needed.

Once the 3-D Model was accepted, all the major concepts needed to be brought together. A visual was developed that could show the primary concepts in an easy and understandable fashion. The visual depiction of the 3-D Community Cyber Security Model is a cube as shown in Figure 1. The cube contains blocks representing the dimensions, the levels of improvement, and the scope areas. Across the top there are 5 blocks that identify the progression levels of cybersecurity maturity. The lowest level of maturity is Level 1 – Initial, and the most mature is Level 5 - Vanguard. Each level is a different color making the distinction of levels easier to see. The 4 vertical blocks represent the dimensions. The dimensions are the focus areas where cybersecurity is being improved. The blocks are 5 deep. Each of these blocks represents the scope areas. The scope areas are individual, organization, community, state and nation. These represent who is improving their cybersecurity posture.

The 3-D Model shown in Figure 1 shows the relationships of preparedness for the scope areas. As an example, the composition of a community includes individuals and organizations. The community's maturity level is influenced by the maturity of the individuals and organizations in that community. This dynamic shows how they are integrated together, and this directly affects the ability of the community's cybersecurity preparedness to address cyber threats. In fact, these relationships drive home the point that everyone has a role in cybersecurity.

Figure 1.

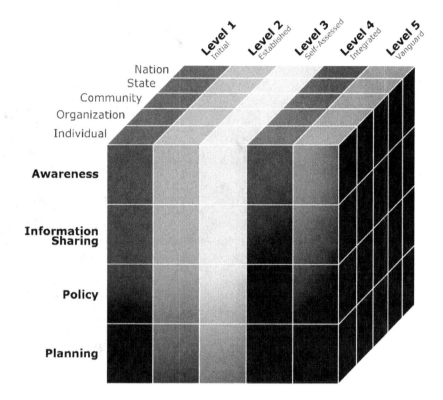

The last major concept that needed to be reflected in the 3-D Model is how the implementation mechanisms are used to transition from Level 1 to Level 2 and so on. This visual depiction is represented in Figure 2.

Each block in the cube individually represents the characteristics for the level and the **phase** activities to transition to the next level. Each phase is associated with a specific **scope area.** To transition from one **level** to the next, for a specific **dimension**, the **implementation mechanisms** listed in the block are utilized to provide the activities needed to transition.

To use Figure 2 as an example: the separated block represents an organization that is currently at Level 1 and working on improving their cybersecurity awareness. The activities they need to complete in order to improve their awareness are metrics, technology, training, processes and procedures and assessments.

THE SCOPE AREAS

The CCSMM identifies specific scope areas that have a role in cybersecurity preparedness. The scope is defined as the range or the extent of the area that is involved in maturing their cybersecurity posture. As mentioned previously, the scope areas are individuals, organizations, communities, states, and the nation. Each of these scope areas can determine their own maturity level which ultimately affects each of the other areas.

Figure 2.

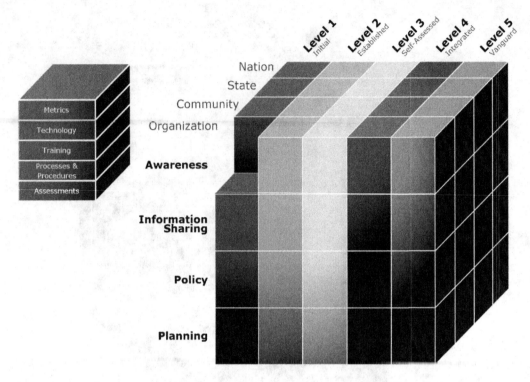

It is important to reinforce the idea that everyone needs to have some level of understanding of cyber-security. Technology touches every aspect of our modern lives. What once seemed to be science fiction, is reality today. Consider the technology and number of devices that connect to the internet found in homes, vehicles, and the extensive capabilities of smart phones. In addition, there aren't many jobs left that don't integrate technology to some degree. How secure individuals are at home can now impact the organization they work for. Working from home with a compromised computer and connecting to your organization's network; or moving information from home to work with a USB containing malware; or posting valuable business information on social media, are all significant risks to the business. This principle also exists between organizations in the community, the communities and the state and so on. This is the reason it is critical for the CCSMM to recognize each scope area.

Individual

The individual scope includes everyone who uses technology in some form. Improving an individual's cybersecurity preparedness, will start with the internet connected devices they use personally and are responsible for securing themselves, such as smartphones and their home wireless technologies. It should also include their computing habits while online.

Using the dimensions as a guide, individuals need to understand the following:

- **Awareness:** Individuals need to understand the threats they face using technologies, and if their device or online account is compromised, how this can impact them. They need to identify all the devices and data that is important to them and then learn how to protect them. They need to understand how to protect their privacy and why this is important. They also need to understand the importance of computer ethics especially as it pertains to downloading software, music or other licensed digital products.

- **Information Sharing:** What should be done when one sees malicious activity, experiences a cybercrime or incident? Individuals need to know who to report these activities to, when and how to report them.
- **Policy:** The individual needs to know what are good cybersecure practices they should be using while using their computers, laptops or other devices. They also need to understand good and bad practices while using email, social networking sites or purchasing online.
- **Plans:** What does the individual do if they are compromised? Here is where the individual should understand how to do backups, why they are important. They should also have some understanding of what to do if they have been compromised.

At each level of maturity, the activities of improvement will become more complex.

This scope area can support other frameworks and program initiatives that address cybersecurity at home, cybersecurity for the youth such as cyber bullying, cybersecurity gaming, cybersecurity competitions and cybersecurity educational activities. Cybersecurity initiatives such as the Culture of Cybersecurity shown in Figure 3. The Culture of Cybersecurity was created by the Center for Infrastructure Assurance and Security at the University of Texas at San Antonio. This and other programs should be considered to improve cybersecurity awareness for everyone. More information about programs such as this will be covered in more detail in the chapter for Awareness Programs.

Figure 3.

Organization

The areas covered by the organization scope includes small businesses, government agencies, non-profit organizations, mid-size companies and large corporations. Essentially, the organization is any business activity in a community. An organization's cybersecurity preparedness should include the individuals or employees, its customers, partners, and supply chain. Its preparedness capabilities should also include the organizations assets including information, computers, and networks.

Using the dimensions as a guide, organizations need to understand the following:

- **Awareness:** Organizations need to understand the threats they face. As an example, threats could be introduced to the organization through malicious or criminal attacks, system failures and glitches, human error, or exploited through social engineering tactics. Each threat should be identified.

Organizations need to know how the identified threats can impact the business. Attacks such as destructive malware, stolen credit card details, or mobile ransomware, to name a few, have shown attacks can impact not only the business operation, but can impact customers, employees, or supply chain partners by making information unavailable that is critically needed. Cyber incidents can also impact how secure the information is or modify the information making it untrustworthy. Organizations must safeguard all areas of the business including their reputation.

Organizations need to know how to detect malicious activities on their networks.

Organizations need to know how to protect their information and systems; understand how physical security plays a role in their cybersecurity program; and will need to address what level of cybersecurity awareness each employee, partner or supply chain associate needs to protect the organization.

- **Information Sharing:** Organizations should consider information sharing both inside their organization and outside. Employees should know who within the organization to report suspicious activity to. They should also address how to escalate cyber incident information to levels of management for their situational awareness and in more critical situations, to make decisions for the business. In addition, it should be determined what types of cyber incidents will be reported outside the organization, to whom and what threshold must be reached to trigger external reporting. It's a good practice to consult legal counsel to ensure compliance, privacy and other regulatory requirements have been considered. Establishing relationships and building trust with organizations and agencies before an incident will make the whole process easier because it is already known who to contact, what to expect and what to ask for. When the organization is in an emergency situation, not knowing what to do and who to contact will add stress to the situation and will add time to the response.
- **Policy:** Organizations need to document the cybersecure practices everyone associated with the organization should be using. Some examples are internet use, accessing social networking sites, connecting to the organization remotely, and technology disposal. How often policies should be reviewed and updated should also be implemented.
- **Plans:** Organizations should have at a minimum a plan to backup organizational information. Once established, organizations should implement plans for cybersecurity incident response, continuity, and disaster recovery plans.

At each level of maturity, the activities of improvement will become more complex.

Frameworks to improve organizational cybersecurity can be incorporated in this scope area for example, the National Institute of Standards and Technology's (NIST) Cyber Security Framework (CSF) (NIST, 2018) outlining the security controls necessary for an organization can be utilized in the policy dimension. The Department of Defense's new verification mechanism of cybersecurity controls called the Cybersecurity Maturity Model Certification (CMMC) can also be incorporated. To categorize and describe positions needed within the organization, the National Initiative for Cybersecurity Education (NICE) Cybersecurity Workforce Framework (NICE Framework) (NIST, 2017) can be used.

Communities

The area covered by the community scope is a defined geographical area. A community includes small, mid-size and large businesses, local government, emergency services, non-profit organizations, critical infrastructure, and the citizens living in that geographical area. The community will determine the area covered by the community scope that will be included in their cybersecurity preparedness; for example, a community may determine their cybersecurity program will include the surrounding cities and counties that are on the outskirts of the metropolitan area. Alternatively, the smaller cities or counties will have their own cybersecurity program but may look to the larger community as a mentor.

Using the dimensions as a guide, communities need to address the following:

- **Awareness:** Communities need to understand the threats they face and how these threats can impact the business operations, and critical services (essential functions) they provide. They will also need to determine what the potential cascading effects may be and how community services, organizations and citizens may be impacted. In the case of a cyber incident disrupting a critical service such as power, the community needs to recognize that additional communities, states or regions may be impacted. This could affect who the community could get assistance from.

Examples of ransomware attacks the past couple of years have shown how attacks such as this can disrupt local governments and public services with devastating financial impacts and potentially life-threatening consequences.

Communities need to identify what information and systems they will need to protect. They should also understand how physical security plays a role in their cybersecurity program; and will need to address who in the community needs what type of cybersecurity awareness.

- **Information Sharing:** Communities will need to consider information sharing both inside their community and outside; and will need to understand what cyber threat indicators are needed to recognize the community is under a cyber-attack.

Communities need to address how to escalate cyber incident information to state and national agencies. In addition, the types of cyber incidents that will be reported outside the community needs to be determined, who it should be reported to, and what threshold must be reached to trigger that reporting. Building relationships and establishing trust with these organizations and agencies before an incident will assist to ensure the information shared is timely, relevant and actionable.

- **Policy:** Communities will need to integrate cybersecurity concepts into established community policies. These policies will address at minimum, standard operating practices, communication methods, and establish the authorization hierarchy for the community. As an example, communities who augment their communications methods with the use of social media channels should ensure these policies include good cybersecurity behaviors with privacy and security considerations. Communities need to identify roles, and the authorization hierarchy to address cybersecurity practices for the community. As an example, who makes the final decision to take a server that supports a critical service "off-line".

- **Plans:** Communities should have at a minimum a continuity of operations plan (COOP) or an emergency management plan to address disasters that may impact the community. These plans should be reviewed to ensure cybersecurity elements have been incorporated. Additional plans that should be in place as the community matures, is a cybersecurity incident response plan such as a Cyber Incident Response Annex, and a disaster recovery plan, also called a disruption plan.

A very important consideration that must be addressed in the community plans is what will be done at the local level. All incidents occur at the local level and even if the incident must be escalated to the state or federal level for assistance, there could be a significant amount of time before assistance is on-site. The community should have a plan for what will be done, at a minimum, 72 hours after assistance has been requested. Recognize the time it takes to recover and get back to normal may be considerably longer. Communications with the media and citizens must be considered. Alternate operations methods for essential functions must be considered. There have been many examples of communities having to revert to paper and pencil for critical functions. How many people on staff will know what to do in this case? Does training exist to ensure this backup capability can be achieved?

The community scope area is where Fusion Centers, Security Operations Centers, and Community Information Sharing and Analysis Organizations (ISAOs) will be integrated into the community cybersecurity program. Professional organizations such as ISACA, ISSA, and InfraGard chapters should be established and integrated into the program to improve both cybersecurity and information sharing capabilities throughout the community. Initiatives such as cybersecurity workforce development may be established at local community colleges or universities.

States

The scope for a state includes its counties, cities, towns, critical infrastructures, state agencies, and citizens. While the scope area here only mentions the state, it is also intended to address tribes and territories. States, tribes, and territories are different in many ways, especially where planning for disasters is concerned; however, the cybersecurity practices that should be considered are very similar.

The cybersecurity preparedness of a state typically addresses the government agencies throughout the state and may include the critical infrastructures. Addressing the government agencies alone in a state is a tremendous task as there are likely hundreds of agencies in any given state. The issue, however, is all individuals, organizations and communities in the state can affect the states cybersecurity preparedness in both positive and negative ways. Simply put, if communities within the state are not prepared, they may need extensive incident response assistance and require significant resources. State cyber resources are most likely limited, which means a cyber-attack impacting multiple communities simultaneously may deplete all the resources available and in fact, there may not be enough resources to support multiple attacks. On the other hand, the private sector offers tremendous and valuable cybersecurity capabilities and skillsets. The state would benefit from public private partnerships such as this and may be able to supplement cybersecurity resources in the event a significant cyber incident occurs. This is also where the National Guard can be integrated to assist in responding to cyber-attacks and incidents.

Using the dimensions as a guide, states, tribes and territories need to understand the following:

- **Awareness:** States, tribes and territories need to understand the threats they face and how these threats can impact the business operations and critical services provided within the state. They will also need to determine what the potential cascading effects may be and how state and community services, organizations and citizens may be impacted.

States need to identify what critical services, information and systems will need to be protected. They should also understand how physical security plays a role in their cybersecurity program; and will need to address who in the state needs what type of cybersecurity awareness.

- **Information Sharing:** States will need to consider information sharing within the state and should also address how to escalate cyber incident information to national agencies. States need to understand what cyber threat indicators are needed to recognize the state is experiencing a cyber-attack.

In addition, it should be determined what types of cyber incidents will be reported, who it should be reported to, and what threshold must be reached to trigger that reporting. Building relationships and establishing trust with these agencies before an incident will assist to ensure the information shared is timely, relevant, and actionable.

- **Policy:** States will need to integrate cybersecurity concepts into established policies. These policies should address, at a minimum, the standard operating practices, communication methods, roles, and the authorization hierarchy to address cybersecurity practices for the state. This should include policies surrounding how communities in the state can request assistance regarding cyber preparedness and cyber incident response.
- **Plans:** States need to have, at a minimum, a continuity of operations plan (COOP) or an emergency operation plan to address "All Hazard" disasters that may impact the state. These plans should be reviewed to ensure cybersecurity elements have been incorporated. Additional plans that should be in place are a cybersecurity incident response plan such as a Cyber Incident Response Annex, and a disaster recovery plan, also called a disruption plan. This is where cyber incident response teams and the National Guard may play a role.

The state's plan should also address how, who, with what resources, and under what circumstances it will assist communities in the state to implement cybersecurity practices and respond to cyber-attacks or incidents.

The state scope area should also consider how the following organizations and agencies are integrated into the overall cybersecurity program for the state:

- Fusion Centers
- State Operations Centers

- Security Operations Centers
- Information Sharing and Analysis Organizations (ISAOs) to include community, regional, private sector
- Information Sharing and Analysis Centers (ISACs) associated with critical infrastructure

Nation

The scope for the nation includes states, tribes, territories, communities, critical infrastructures, federal agencies, and citizens. The role of the federal government is to ensure personal freedoms, economic vitality and to provide national security for the citizens of the United States. The federal government also has a role in cyber preparedness for the nation. "On November 2018, President Trump signed into law the Cybersecurity the Cybersecurity and Infrastructure Security Agency Act of 2018," which establishes the Cybersecurity and Infrastructure Security Agency (CISA), to "build the national capacity to defend against cyber-attacks and works with the federal government to provide cybersecurity tools, incident response services and assessment capabilities to safeguard the'.gov' networks that support the essential operations of partner departments and agencies.

For cybersecurity, CISA's main focus areas include:

- Combatting Cyber Crime and Cyber Incident Response
- Securing Federal Networks, Protecting Critical Infrastructure, and providing Cybersecurity Governance
- Promoting Information Sharing, Training and Exercises, and Cyber Safety information" (DHS, 2019).

Using the dimensions as a guide, the national scope area should address the following:

- **Awareness:** The federal government needs to understand the threats the nation faces and how these threats can impact critical services provided the federal government. They will also need to determine what the potential cascading effects may be and how services may be impacted.

The federal government needs to identify what critical services, information and systems will need to be protected. They should also understand how physical security plays a role in their cybersecurity strategy; and will need to address who in needs cybersecurity awareness and to what extent.

- **Information Sharing:** The federal government will need to consider information sharing within the nation. In addition, it should be determined what types of cyber incidents will be shared, who it should be shared with, and what constitutes a cyber incident that may impact the nation.
- **Policy:** The federal government will need to integrate cybersecurity concepts into established policies. These policies will address standard operating practices, communication strategies, and the protection of critical infrastructures.
- **Plans:** The federal government needs to have a continuity of operations strategy to address all hazard disasters, that includes cyber, that may impact the nation. They need to have a cybersecurity strategy that can be incorporated into all national policies. In addition, a national cyber incident

response strategy needs to be in place. This dimension is where cyber incident response teams and the Department of Defense plays a role.

The federal government has established a significant number of programs to increase public-private partnerships to improve situational awareness of cyber threats and improve cybersecurity capabilities; developed strategies that are cybersecurity focused or include cybersecurity; established information sharing initiatives to increase cybersecurity capabilities; and created plans that states and communities can use as templates to improve their cybersecurity capabilities.

Some examples of initiatives, programs and partnerships that have been established by the federal government to improve the nation's cybersecurity posture are:

- **Protected Critical Infrastructure Information Program:** Formed as a result of the passage of the Critical Infrastructure Act in 2002, the PCII Program affords protections to information provided by the private sector to the federal government. These protections include exemption from the federal FOIA, state and local disclosure laws, regulatory action, and civil litigation. Although DHS manages the PCII program at the federal level, states are encouraged to maintain their own programs in order to provide access to PCII protected information for state and local authorities with a need to know.
- **ISAO SO** - The ISAO Standards Organization is a non-governmental organization established through Executive Order 13691 on October 1, 2015. The ISAO Standards Organization's mission is to improve the Nation's cybersecurity posture by identifying standards and guidelines for robust and effective information sharing related to cybersecurity risks, incidents, and best practices.

As per the Executive Order, the ISAO Standards Organization, led by the University of Texas at San Antonio has been continuously working with, and will continue to work with, existing information sharing organizations, owners and operators of critical infrastructure, relevant agencies, and other public and private sector stakeholders to identify a common set of voluntary standards or guidelines for the creation and functioning of ISAOs.

- **National Training and Education Division**: The National Training and Education Division (NTED) provides tailored training to enhance the capacity of state and local jurisdictions to prepare for, prevent, deter, respond to, and recover safely and effectively from potential manmade and natural catastrophic events, including terrorism.
- **Cyber Security Advisors (CSAs):** are regionally located DHS personnel who direct coordination, outreach, and regional support to protect cyber components essential to the sustainability, preparedness, and protection of U.S. critical infrastructure and state, local, territorial, and tribal (SLTT) governments. CSAs offer immediate and sustained assistance to prepare and protect SLTT and private entities. They bolster the cybersecurity preparedness, risk mitigation, and incident response capabilities of these entities and bring them into closer coordination with the federal government. CSAs represent a front-line approach and promote resilience of key cyber infrastructures throughout the United States and its territories.
- **National Continuity Programs:** The Federal Emergency Management Agency's National Continuity Programs (NCP) serves the public by coordinating the federal programs and activities that preserve our nation's essential functions across a wide range of potential threats and

emergencies. On behalf of the White House, the Secretary of Homeland Security, and the FEMA Administrator, NCP guides and assists the planning and implementation of continuity programs that enable federal, state, tribal, territorial, and local governments to deliver critical services to survivors throughout all phases of a disaster. Continuity and sustainment of essential functions is a shared responsibility of the whole community. Development and maintenance of continuity capabilities helps build and sustain a more resilient nation equipped to sustain essential functions, deliver critical services, and supply core capabilities under all conditions.

- **The National Cybersecurity and Communications Integration Center's (NCCIC):** mission is to reduce the risk of systemic cybersecurity and communications challenges in our role as the Nation's flagship cyber defense, incident response, and operational integration center. Since 2009, the NCCIC has served as a national hub for cyber and communications information, technical expertise, and operational integration, and by operating our 24/7 situational awareness, analysis, and incident response center.

- **Critical Infrastructure Partnership Advisory Council (CIPAC):** Those who engage in these partnerships enhance their communication, planning, risk assessments, program implementation, incident response, recovery and operational activities.

- **The Regional Consortium Coordinating Council (RC3):** provides a framework that supports existing regional groups in their efforts to promote resilience activities in the public and private sectors. RC3 supports its member organizations with awareness, education, and mentorship on a wide variety of subjects, projects, and initiatives to advance critical infrastructure security and resilience, vulnerability reduction, and consequence mitigation.

- **National Risk Management Center:** is the Cybersecurity and Infrastructure Security Agency's (CISA) planning, analysis, and collaboration center working to identify and address the most significant risks to the Nation's critical infrastructure. Through the NRMC's collaborative efforts with the private sector, government agencies, and other key stakeholders, the CISA works to identify, analyze, prioritize, and manage high-consequence threats to critical infrastructure through a crosscutting risk management paradigm.

- **The National Cyber Incident Response Plan (NCIRP):** The NCIRP describes a national approach to dealing with cyber incidents; addresses the important role that the private sector, state and local governments, and multiple federal agencies play in responding to incidents and how the actions of all fit together for an integrated response. The NCIRP reflects and incorporates lessons learned from exercises, real world incidents and policy and statutory updates, such as the Presidential Policy Directive/PPD-41: *U.S. Cyber Incident Coordination*, and the National Cybersecurity Protection Act of 2014. The NCIRP also serves as the Cyber Annex to the Federal Interagency Operational Plan (FIOP) that built upon the National Planning Frameworks and the National Preparedness System.

CONCLUSION

The 3-Dimensional Model expanded the capability of the CCSMM framework allowing it to be flexible and scalable to address all aspects of a cybersecurity program. The 3-D Model provides the improvement progression for everyone in the nation. It is a roadmap to improve cybersecurity for individuals, organizations, communities, states and the nation, called scope areas. The scope areas can address cybersecurity by using the dimensions to improve their awareness of cyber threats and impacts, information sharing capabilities of cyber threat indicators, incorporate cyber into their policies and to understand what plans are needed for continuity, response and recovery.

The individual scope includes everyone who utilizes technology, no matter if it is a smart phone, smart television, laptop, tablet, iPad or some other device connected to the internet. This scope area will also include the youth of our country and should include safety topics such as cyber bullying. It should also include engaging initiatives such as cybersecurity gaming, cybersecurity competitions and other educational activities.

The scope for organizations includes small businesses, government agencies, non-profit organizations, mid-size companies and large corporations. An organization's cybersecurity preparedness will include all individuals associated with the organization. This could include individuals or employees, customers, partners, and those included in the supply chain. Organizational assets should be included in preparedness capabilities including information, computers, and networks.

The community scope is a defined geographical area, and includes small, mid-size and large businesses, local government, emergency services, non-profit organizations, critical infrastructure, and the citizens living in that geographical area. The community should define the area of scope included in its preparedness efforts. This could include smaller cities and counties surrounding the community. The larger community could, alternatively, become a mentor to adjoining smaller cities and counties.

The scope for a state, tribe or territory includes its counties, cities, towns, critical infrastructures, state agencies, and citizens. Cybersecurity preparedness for a state, tribe or territory most likely addresses government agencies and may also include critical infrastructures. In order to address other aspects that may impact the state, cybersecurity preparedness should also include individuals, organizations in the private-sector and communities in the state, tribe or territories. In addition, the role of Fusion Centers, State Operations Centers, ISAOs and ISACs should be considered in the overall cybersecurity program.

Finally, the scope for the nation includes states, tribes, territories, communities, critical infrastructures, federal agencies, and citizens. The federal government has a role in cyber preparedness for the nation and has established numerous initiatives, programs and partnerships to improve cybersecurity, information sharing and cybersecurity capabilities.

The next several chapters will expand the concepts of the dimensions and provide a mapping for the improving through the levels.

REFERENCES

About Us. (n.d.). Retrieved August 16, 2019, from ISAO Standards Organization website: https://www.isao.org/about/

CISA Cyber Infrastructure. (n.d.). *Protected critical infrastructure information (PCII) program.* Retrieved August 22, 2019, from U.S. Department of Homeland Security CISA Cyber Infrastructure website: https://www.cisa.gov/pcii-program

CMMC model v1.0. (n.d.). Retrieved February 25, 2020, from Office of the Under Secretary of Defense for Acquisition & Sustainment Cybersecurity Maturity Model Certification website: https://www.acq.osd.mil/cmmc/draft.html

County of Marin. (n.d.). www.marincounty.org/depts/ad/divisions/management-and-budget/ administrative-policies-and-procedures/administrative-regulation-no-1_25

Cyber Incident Annex. (n.d.). Retrieved August 13, 2019, from US Department of Homeland Security FEMA website: https://www.fema.gov/media-library/assets/documents/25556

Cybersecurity division mission and vision. (n.d.). Retrieved August 17, 2019, from US Department of Homeland Security CISA Cyber + Infrastructure website: https://www.dhs.gov/cisa/cybersecurity-division

DHS role in cyber incident response. (n.d.). Retrieved August 25, 2019, from US Department of Homeland Security CISA Cyber + Infrastructure website: https://www.cisa.gov/publication/dhs-role-cyber-incident-response

Information sharing and awareness. (n.d.). Retrieved August 22, 2019, from US Department of Homeland Security CISA Cyber + Infrastructure website: https://www.cisa.gov/information-sharing-and-awareness

National continuity programs. (n.d.). Retrieved August 2, 2019, from US Department of Homeland Security FEMA website: https://www.fema.gov/national-continuity-programs

National Institute of Standards and Technology. (2018, April). *Framework for improving critical infrastructure cybersecurity* (Publication No. Version 1.1). Retrieved from https://nvlpubs.nist.gov/nistpubs/CSWP/NIST.CSWP.04162018.pdf

NIST Special Publication 800-181. (2017). *National Initiative for Cybersecurity Education (NICE) Cybersecurity Workforce Framework (NICE Framework).* Retrieved from https://nvlpubs.nist.gov/nistpubs/SpecialPublications/NIST.SP.800-181.pdf?trackDocs=NIST.SP.800-181.pdf

The national cyber incident response plan (NCIRP). (n.d.). Retrieved August 19, 2019, from US Department of Homeland Security CISA Cyber + Infrastructure website: https://www.us-cert.gov/ncirp

U.S. Department of Homeland Security. (n.d.). *Cybersecurity strategy.* Retrieved October 27, 2019, from https://www.dhs.gov/sites/default/files/publications/DHS-Cybersecurity-Fact-Sheet.pdf

U.S. Department of Homeland Security. (n.d.). *Cybersecurity.* Retrieved August 24, 2019, from The Department of Homeland Security website: https://www.dhs.gov/topic/cybersecurity

Welcome to the national preparedness course catalog. (n.d.). Retrieved August 31, 2019, from National Training and Education Division | US Department of Homeland Security - FEMA website: https://www.firstrespondertraining.gov/frts/npcc

This research was previously published in Establishing Cyber Security Programs Through the Community Cyber Security Maturity Model (CCSMM); pages 55-74, copyright year 2021 by Information Science Reference (an imprint of IGI Global).

Chapter 27
Evolutionary and Ideation Concepts for Cybersecurity Education

David A Gould
City University of Seattle, Seattle, USA

Gregory Block
Syracuse University, Syracuse, USA

Simon Cleveland
ⓘ https://orcid.org/0000-0001-9293-3905
Georgetown University, Washington, D.C., USA

ABSTRACT

Evolution is a well-established biological theory, but some basic concepts can be abstracted and applied to non-biological domains such as the education domain for the purposes of knowledge sharing. There is a gap in the literature regarding how evolutionary processes can be applied to cyber security education. This article presents the general evolutionary algorithm and pairs it with an ideation technique (SCAMPER) to illustrate how certain evolutionary processes can be applied to cyber security education and learning. This paper does not attempt to close the gap, but rather offer a theoretical approach to address the gap.

INTRODUCTION

This research-in-process paper explores some evolutionary concepts and an innovative ideation technique or framework to find new approaches or applications to teaching cyber security. The paper extends a prior study on evolutionary systems and their application to cybersecurity learning (Gould, Block & Cleveland, 2018; Gould & Cleveland, 2018). Some definitions, examples, and frameworks are provided as a starting point, followed by some applications to cyber security. The paper concludes with a recommendation

DOI: 10.4018/978-1-6684-3554-0.ch027

for quantitative research measuring the effectiveness of evolutionary concepts in the preparation and execution of cyber defense educational curricula.

Evolutionary Concepts

Forrester (1971) argued that a system is a set of components that function together to achieve some purpose. A system can be viewed as a network with interactive nodes also known as agents, parts, components, elements, or objects. These agents may interact with each other as well as with their environment. Relationships between agents may be strong, weak, or null; with other descriptions possible as well. The type of network or networks illustrate systems structure as matter, information, or energy flow into, through, and out of the system; systems exhibit behavior, and some systems exhibit some form of change or dynamics over time such as transitional, transformational, adaptation or learning, or evolutionary.

Mobus and Kalton (2015) offered a more formal definition of a system as a 6-tuple, described by a set of subsystems, a network or networks, the set of nodes inside and outside the system, the boundary conditions, the interactions among the nodes, and the history of the system. While a variety of definitions of systems exist and there is no specific consensus on the definition of a system, an organization fits the Forester's (1971), Mobus and Kalton's (2015) definitions as a system.

Systems may evolve whether by biological or non-biological means. Solar systems, organizations, technology, culture, religion, and systems of knowledge are examples of non-biological evolutionary systems. Hull (1988) and Aldrich et al. (2008), argued for a concept called generalized Darwinism. That is, the general principles of Darwinism apply not only to biological evolution but also to evolution of societies and culture.

Fichter, Pyle, and Whitmeyer (2010) argued that if the definition of evolutionary change includes change in "complexity, diversity, order, and/or interconnectedness then there are at least three distinct mechanisms, or theories of evolution: elaboration, self-organization, and fractionation" (p. 59). The authors concisely identified the general evolutionary algorithm as the cycle of elaborate diversity, select from the diversity, amplify the selection, and repeat. Beinhocker (2010) further abstracted these key processes as variation, selection, amplification, and repeat.

Figure 1 illustrates a substrate-neutral model of evolution linking three principles: variation (differentiation), selection, and replication (amplification). These principles, abstracted from biological evolution, can be applied to other systems that evolve as well, although by other mechanisms than biology. While some minor differences in terminology exist regarding the abstract processes of evolution, they are useful in thinking about organizational change. Berlinski (2000) noted, "an algorithm is a finite procedure, written in a fixed symbolic vocabulary, governed by precise instructions, moving in discrete steps 1,2,3, …., whose execution requires no insight, cleverness, intuition, or perspicuity, and that sooner or later comes to an end" (p. xvii). Thus, the general evolutionary algorithm provides insight into systems change as all systems vary, they change due to endogenous and exogenous pressures, and not all changes are successful.

Evolutionary theory proposes that nature creates lots of experiments, yet few are successful (2010). This same principle can be applied to systems of knowledge. That is, multiple variations may be generated, with selection reducing the number that are successful.

Figure 1. A substrate-neutral model of evolution

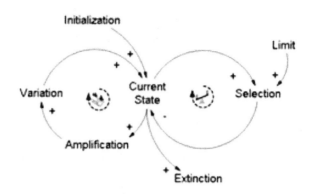

Arthur (2009) explored technology as an evolutionary system. For example, consider the ubiquitous technological product—the widget. Once a widget agent is developed and commercialized, it undergoes selection in the marketplace and if it survives, it will be replicated, and its numbers will increase and it may be considered successful. Widget derivatives, or variations, may be introduced to the marketplace to capitalize on its success. Innovation operates exogenously to create these derivatives or variations. Improving the capability to innovate increases diversity and reducing the time-to-market increases the velocity of the cycle. Arthur (2008) argued that technological evolution occurs exogenously as technologies combine or recombine to form new products or technologies. Mass production can create almost any number of identical copies given sufficient resources. Over time, one or more of these technologies can be combined with other technologies to create yet new technologies.

For example, both cybersecurity threats and defenses evolve as new techniques and technologies combine or recombine to form new techniques and technologies. This argument and example is consistent with Ziman (2000), who noted that theories, laws, and organizations evolve by processes of mutation and/or recombination.

Systems of knowledge follow similar patterns. For example, organizational learning is a critical factor for change and innovation in organizations and results from knowledge acquisition, information distribution, information interpretation, and organizational memory. Corporate performance is improved with the conversion of explicit to tacit knowledge (2000). The better a firm evolves the process of creating new knowledge and discarding obsolete knowledge, the more likely the firm will develop innovation behavior and gain a competitive advantage (Rebernik & Širec, 2007).

Aldrich and Ruef (2006) simplified or restated the general evolutionary algorithm as the processes of variation, selection, and retention and summarized a set of organizational perspectives (ecological, institutional, interpretive, organizational learning, resource dependence, and transactional cost economics) mapped to these evolutionary processes. Table 1, row 2 includes the ecological perspective. Extensions to the table include physical and cyber security perspectives.

Variation

Organizations introduce variation into cyber security via changes to cyber processes such as standards, guidelines, and practices; software products; hardware; networks; and algorithms. For example, the NIST (2018) Cyber Security Framework includes the five functions of Identify, Protect, Detect, Respond,

Table 1. Organizational perspectives mapped to evolutionary processes

Perspective	Variation	Selection	Retention
Ecological	Variation introduced via new organizations	Selection results from fit between organizations and environment	Retention through external pressures and internal inertia
Physical Security	Variation introduced via physical or structural requirements for organizational security	Selection results from the physical security fit	Successful changes are retained while unsuccessful changes are dropped.
Cyber Security	Variation introduced via organizational changes needed to defend against cyber threats	Selection results from the cyber security fit	Successful changes are retained while unsuccessful changes are dropped

and Recover. These specific functions of standards, guidelines, and practices are subject to variation or change as well. Some of these variations or changes may be successful and some may not. Success depends on the fitness to the resistance of cyber threats, which undergo variation or change as well. Cyber attackers are continuing to improve their approaches as seen from the trajectory of new cyber-attack software development. This pattern has been identified as the escalation archetype described by Senge (2006). As Senge (2006) noted, escalation occurs when two or more parties view success as depending on a relative advantage over the other. When one party gains an advantage, the other party feels threatened and redoubles its efforts to overcome the advantage to retake control. This pattern is observed in a wide variety of systems from children at play, to couples divorcing, to cyber security / cyber threats, to national and international disputes. This pattern may or may not stop peacefully or in a timely fashion.

Selection

Given a variety of agents, the process of selection, based on some fitness criteria, acts to reduce their numbers. Science and decision making are examples of a selection process in action as they both generate alternatives and select the fittest among them according to Hull (2001). For example, scientific experiments may generate several possibilities, from which testing and evaluations may select one or two of the best or fittest. Some, but not all cyber security variations in processes, products, or algorithms will be successful. Instead, they will fall on some continuum of failure to successful. Assessment is needed here to find those variations most successful. Selection in this sense is a filtering process, screening out the best from the not-so-best based on some fitness criteria.

Retention

Retention may be the easiest evolutionary process to conceptualize. Simply keep the most successful cyber security variations, drop the least successful cyber security variations, and deploy the best. Then repeat these evolutionary processes again, starting with variation of the best new processes, products, and algorithms.

There are several learning theories and the trial and error learning theory is used in this paper. As previously noted, nature experiments to drive variation and the more fit variations are selected to reproduce and the cycle repeats. Similarly, one approach to learning is trial and error. People experiment through trial and error to create or improve something; the more fit the creation or improvement is, the more likely it will be selected and retained for future use and/or improvement. This trial and error approach to learning is the evolutionary processes of variation, selection, and retention.

Extinction (Death)

As systems import and export material, information, and energy to survive, interruptions in the rate of input and/or output, the required amount systems require for survival, and/or the quality of these resources may cause a system to decline and at some point, become extinct. For example, a denial-of-service attack or distributed-denial-of-service attack disrupts normal Internet traffic and could crash one or more computers thus potentially leading to a temporary to permanent decline of an organization.

Another example is a cyber-attack leading to a disruption of a countries election process, which could result in up to a radical change in direction and/or political and social structure. Given the information content required for functioning supply chains, organizations, energy grids, and so on, information disruptions here could also cause declines up to and including the death of an organization or part of one. Additionally, as the number of information technology devices increases, such as laptops, servers, smart homes, smartphones, smart vehicles, wearables, and so on, these devices, as part of a system, are potential targets for cyber-attacks, with possible systematic decline.

Having examined evolutionary concepts and mapped organizational perspectives to evolutionary processes, a set of ideation techniques are assessed next for the purposes of facilitating knowledge creation and learning.

Ideation Techniques for Learning

In addressing a multifaceted challenge such as cybersecurity, professionals develop a causal mental model based on reflection, and improve the mental model through social interactions that may include argument, debate, and narrative construction (2013). The mental model is externalized through social exploration such that mental patterns emerge to leverage forward thinking to anticipate future patterns and events (2013). In the context of cybersecurity challenges, the ideation process must be goal-oriented, blending both creativity and innovation with utility and problem-solving (2003).

Ideation techniques can be categorized as intuitive, fostering innovative ideas to disrupt mental blocks, or logical, based on analysis and structural decomposition of the problem. Intuitive approaches to idea generation can be sub-categorized as follows:

- Germinal - fosters the creation of new ideas
- Transformational - modifies or augments existing ideas
- Progressive - uses iteration to improve ideas in discrete steps
- Organizational - focuses on group interactions to generate ideas
- Hybrid - combines one or more of the other approaches

Brainstorming is an example of a germinal technique. Brainstorming is a free-form, open-ended approach to eliciting idea formation in a solo environment or among group members (2006). While nominal groups perform better in the number of ideas generated than larger groups, the list of generated ideas must be pruned to select only the optimal ideas. Fishbone Diagrams are an example of an organizational technique, using a cause and effect diagram to illustrate the relationship between a problem and likely causes (1995). SCAMPER is a transformational, intuitive approach to idea generation (1996).

Logical techniques for idea generation can be categorized as history-based or analytical. Analytical methods decompose a problem to base principles and focus on relations and causal factors. TRIZ is an example of an analytical method. TRIZ (the theory of inventive problem solving) provides a set of tools that can be used to analyze a multitude of scenarios; specifically, forty rules are provided to describe how a system can be improved (1996).

In the realm of cyber security, many of these ideation techniques can be used to enhance cybersecurity learning. For example, extant studies of graduate students in a cybersecurity course showed that ideation techniques combined with the use of virtual environments lead to the development of higher level mastery of cybersecurity topics (2016). Moreover, this combination of technique and tools increased students' levels of enjoyment and trust in the courses. Similarly, Black, Chapman, and Clark (2018) demonstrated that the use of Enhanced Virtual Laboratory (EVL), a tool developed to enhance education for cyber security, helped students gain knowledge virtually, while giving instructors sufficient platform to share knowledge on the topics of cyber security in combination with ideation techniques. The authors argued that this approach was sufficient to deliver "a new and improved method of remotely delivering cyber security content to different users with variable depths of security knowledge" (p. 4).

Several studies have compared these ideation techniques for their effectiveness in generating ideas that have both novelty and utility. For example, Chulvi, Gonza´lez-Cruz, Mulet, and Aguilar-Zambrano (2013) compared a control group (using no specific technique) to groups using brainstorming, SCAMPER and TRIZ techniques and found that the SCAMPER technique achieved the most utility. SCAMPER stands for Substitute, Combine, Adapt, Modify, Put, Eliminate, and Reverse (1996) and was found to provide the most intuitive results in comparison with TRIZ and C-K theory, an analytical technique (2014); Moreno and Yang (2014) concluded that the cognitive load for participants using SCAMPER was low, enabling a higher degree of novelty, and that fixation supported idea refinement, while prompts enabled the participant to focus on a different design space.

Application of Scamper for Cybersecurity Learning

SCAMPER was proposed by Alex Faickney Osborn in 1953 and further developed by Robert (Bob) Eberle in 1971 in his book; SCAMPER: Games for Imagination Development. SCAMPER is a process or product improvement tool used to improve or create something. It is used as an ideation technique or idea generator and an easy-to-learn and easy-to-use creativity or improvement technique to change something into something else.

For example, Toraman and Altun (2013) found that in a seventh-grade course, using SCAMPER, students "were seen to have performed improvement in comparing ecosystems in terms of diversity of living creatures and climatic feature" (p. 181). Two implications here is that SCAMPER can be successfully applied in a variety of disciplines by people with a variety of educational levels.

The SCAMPER technique may be applied starting with anyone of its seven operators (S, C, A, M, P, E, or R). Consider some possible questions suggested by the operator to start searching the design space for ideas to consider (recall that SCAMPER is a brainstorming tool), then move on to another operator, and so on. Once a list of possibilities has been generated, begin a test and evaluation, and decision-making process to reduce the number to those that address the problem (fitness) to be solved. Sample questions that might come to mind from reviewing the SCAMPER operators include the following.

Many other questions could be asked depending on the objective.

- Could we replace all or some of the code with better algorithm? (R)
- Could this program be adapted to another cyber threat? (A)
- Could this program be streamlined by eliminating something? (E)
- Could this program be modified to better protect again current cyber threats? (M)
- What another agency could use this program? (P)
- Could two or more algorithms be combined? (C)
- Could we use a different algorithm in place of what exists? (S)

Moreno, Blessing, Yang, Hernandez, and Wood (2016) studied "two design by analogy (DbA) techniques WordTree and SCAMPER to overcome design fixation" (p. 185). They noted that "the creative design process may be inhibited by a focus on existing, standard solutions or variants of existing solutions, that is, by becoming fixated" (p. 185). Given rapidly evolving technologies such as information technology and potential threats related to cyber security, time as well as the quality may be critical in finding solutions.

Moreno et al. (2016) noted that compared with WordTree, SCAMPER generated more novel ideas. Clearly more research as Moreno et al. (2016) noted is essential as this is a relatively new field of study. Markman and Wood (2009) noted that ideation models come from serendipity, discovery, and analogy, thus continued research in DbA models such as SCAMPER and others is appropriate. Moreno et al. (2016) concluded analogy enables the identification of innovative or disruptive solutions based on the problem solver's experience.

This paper proposes that cyber security educators can leverage SCAMPER effectively to teach students how to prepare for cyber threats. Due to the tool's structured approach to arranging thinking processes, cyber educators can facilitate discussions with students that to generate rapid innovative solutions in critical scenarios.

Figure 2 identifies the SCAMPER stages as proposed by Daru et al. (2000). An illustration of a cybersecurity defense lesson using the tool is provided below.

Figure 2. SCAMPER stages

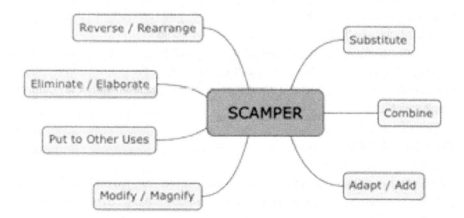

Substitute Stage

During the Substitute state, cyber security instructors can introduce students to the tool to prepare a cyber-threat assessment. For example, Gould and Cleveland (2018) argued that cyber security instructors can lead students in an informative questions and answers session at this stage. For contextual purposes, instructors can introduce an information system and ask students to assess its security level. During the discussion, instructors can probe students whether part of the system can be influenced by a threat without affecting the integrity of the entire system. Additionally, instructors can divide the students into teams and have each team work on brainstorming alternative scenarios to the proposed solutions of the other teams. The goal of learning in this stage is to train students to make a proper decision among alternatives solutions.

Combine Stage

During the Combine state, cybersecurity educators should instruct the teams to use various techniques and technologies to neutralize a possible cyber-attack. The goal is to teach students to seek the most effective and efficient ways to eliminate redundant steps, or ways to apply multiple security solutions simultaneously. The instructors should encourage and reward teams that find ways to combine resources with other teams to combat the attack, as well as use a variety of technologies to eliminate the threat.

Adapt/Add Stage

During the Adapt/Add stage, the cyber security instructors should continue to encourage students to work together and find ways to challenge their preliminary ideas and approaches. This can be done with the aim to obtain more favorable results through innovative hands-on lab tools and cyber games (e.g., cyber defense tower game as proposed by North (2016). Instructors should question and dare students to discover alternate ideas that are more flexible than previously thought.

Modify Stage

During the Modify stage, before a solution has been accepted, something may be modified for an improved solution; after a solution has been selected by the teams, instructors should lead the students in brainstorming session to examine the solution from a macro and then a micro point of view. The aim is to trigger new ideas about whether changing the process will lead to new results in the defense strategy. For example, a macro examination of the system defense mechanisms mean reveal that the proposed solution has exposed the system to additional vulnerabilities. Thus, the teams should continue to explore more efficient and innovative ways to secure the system as cyber attackers will likely continue to improve their cyber-attack capabilities.

Put to Other Uses Stage

During the Put to other use stage, the cyber security instructors can expand on the lessons by asking students to apply the solution to other areas of the enterprise or even related organizations. For example, if a solution could be generalized and put to other uses, it may be commercialized and sold to other organizations. Or, some solutions may become automated and be placed in a library for general use. This approach could open new organizational possibilities to protect against cyber-attacks. Specific topics for discussion can include enhancement of the security policies for other internal organizational systems.

Eliminate Stage

During the Eliminate stage, the cyber security instructors can encourage student teams to assess the outcomes associated with elimination of specific existing security measures and their role as potential cyber threats. Instructors can challenge the students with questions on whether the security protocols can be implemented with reduced resources. For example, are there aspects of cyber security that are no longer important or low priority that can be eliminated to free up time to focus on more important aspects of cyber security. In essence, this stage is about triage. The aim of this exercise is to build critical thinking skills associated with increased productivity and reduced amount of resources utilization.

Reverse/Rearrange Stage

Finally, during the Reverse/Rearrange stage, cybersecurity instructors should lead student teams to seek improved results by switching the order of solutions to foster creative brainstorming for improved results. This may include the reversal of selected security measures, the reversal of security roles, or other approaches to examine the overall defense mechanism. The key idea here is to find new or novel approaches for improvement.

Iterative SCAMPER

SCAMPER is not a one-time use function for innovation; rather it can be used iteratively as SCAMPER transforms something old into something new, which can then be used by SCAMPER to generate something new, over and over again. Thus, as cyber security instructors and students improve some aspect of cyber security V1 to cyber security V2, they can apply the SCAMPER function again transforming V2 to V3 and so on.

CONCLUSION

This paper proposed an innovative approach to leveraging concepts from the theory of evolution in the cyber security education domain. An examination of an evolutionary algorithm performed along with an innovative ideation technique to enhance the knowledge sharing process for cybersecurity education and learning. More specifically, variation is driven or increased via SCAMPER, selection occurs via testing and evaluation of options for fitness, and selection options survive to be implemented. This three-step process is iterated as necessary. Future studies should focus on quantitative research to measure the effectiveness of evolutionary concepts and SCAMPER in preparing and executing cybersecurity defense education programs.

REFERENCES

Aldrich, H. E., Hodgson, G. M., Hull, D. L., Knudsen, T., Mokyr, J., & Vanberg, V. J. (2008). In defence of generalized Darwinism. *Journal of Evolutionary Economics*, *18*(5), 577–596. doi:10.100700191-008-0110-z

Aldrich, H. E., & Ruef, M. (2006). *Organizations evolving* (2nd ed.). Thousand Oaks, CA: Sage.

Arthur, W. B. (2009). *The nature of technology: What it is and how it evolves*. New York: Free Press.

Barbara, M., & Stefano, F. (2014, June). Comparison of creativity enhancement and idea generation methods in engineering design training. In *Proceedings of the International Conference on Human-Computer Interaction* (pp. 242-250). Cham: Springer. 10.1007/978-3-319-07233-3_23

Beinhocker, E. D. (2010). Evolution as computation: Implications for economic theory and ontology. Retrieved from http://www.santafe.edu

Berlinski, D. (2000). *The advent of the algorithm*. New York: Harcourt.

Black, M., Chapman, D., & Clark, A. (2018). The enhanced virtual laboratory: Extending cyber security awareness through a web-based laboratory. *Information Systems Education Journal*, *16*(6), 4.

Chulvi, V., González-Cruz, M. C., Mulet, E., & Aguilar-Zambrano, J. (2013). Influence of the type of idea-generation method on the creativity of solutions. *Research In Engineering Design*, *24*(1), 33–41. doi:10.100700163-012-0134-0

Daru, R., Vreedenburgh, E., & Scha, R. (2000, December). Architectural innovation as an evolutionary process. In *Proceedings of the 3rd International Conference on Generative Art*. Academic Press.

Eberle, B. (1996). *Scamper on: Games for imagination development*. Prufrock Press Inc.

Fichter, L. S., Pyle, E. J., & Whitmeyer, S. J. (2010). Strategies and rubrics for teaching chaos and complex systems theories as elaborating, self-organizing, and fractionating evolutionary systems. *Journal of Geoscience Education*, *58*(2), 65–85. doi:10.5408/1.3534849

Forrester, J. W. (1971). *Principles of systems*. Portland, OR: Productivity Press.

Gould, D., Block, G., & Cleveland, S. (2018, September). Using Evolutionary Systems and Ideation Techniques to Enhance Student Cybersecurity Learning. In *Proceedings of the 19th Annual SIG Conference on Information Technology Education* (pp. 146-146). International World Wide Web Conferences Steering Committee. 10.1145/3241815.3241836

Gould, D., & Cleveland, S. (2018). Evolutionary systems: Applications to cybersecurity. *Proceedings of the Thirteenth Midwest Association for Information Systems Conference*, Saint Louis, MI. Academic Press.

Hackman, J. R., & Wageman, R. (1995). Total quality management: Empirical, conceptual, and practical issues. *Administrative Science Quarterly*, *40*(2), 309–342. doi:10.2307/2393640

Huber, G. P. (1991). Organizational learning: The contributing processes and the literatures. *Organization Science*, 2(1), 88–115. doi:10.1287/orsc.2.1.88

Hull, D. L. (1988). *Science as a process: An evolutionary account of the social and conceptual development of science*. Chicago, IL: University of Chicago. doi:10.7208/chicago/9780226360492.001.0001

Hull, D. L. (2001). The success of science and social norms. *History and Philosophy of the Life Sciences*, 23(3-4), 341–360. PMID:12472061

Markman, A., & Wood, K. (2009). *Tools for innovation, 5*. Oxford, NY: Oxford University Press. doi:10.1093/acprof:oso/9780195381634.001.0001

Mobus, G. E., & Kalton, M. C. (2015). *Principles of systems science*. New York: Springer. doi:10.1007/978-1-4939-1920-8

Moreno, D., & Yang, M. (2014). Creativity in transactional design problems: Non-Intuitive findings of an expert study using SCAMPER. *DS77: Proceedings of the DESIGN 2014 13th International Design Conference*. Academic Press.

Moreno, D. P., Blessing, L. T., Yang, M. C., Hernández, A. A., & Wood, K. L. (2016). Overcoming design fixation: Design by analogy studies and nonintuitive findings. *Artificial Intelligence for Engineering Design, Analysis and Manufacturing*, 30(2), 185–199. doi:10.1017/S0890060416000068

NIST. (2006). Cyberframework. Retrieved from https://www.nist.gov/cyberframework

Nixon, J., & McGuinness, B. (2013). Framing the Human Dimension in Cybersecurity. *ICST Trans. Security Safety*, 1(2), e2.

Nonaka, I., Toyama, R., & Nagata, A. (2000). A firm as a knowledge-creating entity: A new perspective on the theory of the firm. *Industrial and Corporate Change*, 9(1), 1–20. doi:10.1093/icc/9.1.1

North, M. (2016) War games: Simulation vs. virtual machines in cybersecurity education. *Issues In Information Systems*, 17(4).

Rebernik, M., & Širec, K. (2007). Fostering innovation by unlearning tacit knowledge. *Kybernetes*, 36(3/4), 406–419. doi:10.1108/03684920710747039

Rietzschel, E. F., Nijstad, B. A., & Stroebe, W. (2006). Productivity is not enough: A comparison of interactive and nominal brainstorming groups on idea generation and selection. *Journal of Experimental Social Psychology*, 42(2), 244–251. doi:10.1016/j.jesp.2005.04.005

Senge, P. (2006). *The fifth discipline*. New York, NY: Doubleday.

Shah, J. J., Smith, S. M., & Vargas-Hernandez, N. (2003). Metrics for measuring ideation effectiveness. *Design Studies*, 24(2), 111–134. doi:10.1016/S0142-694X(02)00034-0

Summers, T., & Lyytinen, K. (2013). How hackers think: A study of cybersecurity experts and their mental models. *Proceedings of the Third Annual International Conference on Engaged Management Scholarship*, Atlanta, GA. Academic Press. 10.2139srn.2326634

Toraman, S., & Altun, S. (2013). Application of the six thinking hats and scamper techniques on the 7th grade course unit "Human and environment": An exemplary case study. *Mevlana International Journal of Education*, 3(4), 166–185. doi:10.13054/mije.13.62.3.4

Ziman, J. (2000). *Technological innovation as an evolutionary process*. New York: Cambridge University Press.

This research was previously published in the International Journal of Smart Education and Urban Society (IJSEUS), 11(1); pages 13-22, copyright year 2020 by IGI Publishing (an imprint of IGI Global).

Chapter 28
Effectiveness of Increasing Realism Into Cybersecurity Training

Robert Beveridge
https://orcid.org/0000-0001-8884-4387
Robert Morris University, Moon, USA

ABSTRACT

This article describes how cybersecurity is a field that is growing at an exponential rate. In light of many highly publicized incidences of cyber-attacks against organizations, the need to hire experienced cybersecurity professionals is increasing. The lack of available workforce to fill open positions is alarming and organizations are finding that potential candidates with academic degrees and certifications alone are not as valuable as those with experience. Gaining rapid experience requires immersion into realistic virtual environments that mimic real-world environments. Currently, cybersecurity competitions leverage many technologies that immerse participants into virtual environments that mimic real-world systems to improve experiential learning. These systems are expensive to build and maintain, and to continuously improve realism is difficult. However, the training value of cyber competitions in which the participants cannot distinguish from real-world systems will ultimately develop highly experience cybersecurity professionals.

INTRODUCTION

Cybercrime is becoming more prevalent today than ever. Data breaches resulting in millions of records stolen are causing organizations to increase their cybersecurity posture and creating new organizational units and jobs for security professionals. Current statistics show a global workforce shortage of approximately 3 million information security professionals (ISC2, 2018). Private training companies have emerged offering cybersecurity certifications and universities are developing cybersecurity degree programs. However, employers have difficulty filling these positions due to the lack of qualified and

DOI: 10.4018/978-1-6684-3554-0.ch028

experienced cybersecurity professionals (Harris, Patten, & Patten, 2015). Part of the problem is that traditional academic settings and certification training often focus on teaching foundational skills through didactic classroom environments that lack the experience building opportunities for cybersecurity students (Anderson, 2017). The need to rapidly train cyber professionals as well as enable them to gain valuable experience will help meet the demand of the current workforce shortage across all industries (Manson & Pike, 2014). To build the experience that is needed in the workforce, experiential learning needs to be incorporated in the curriculum by building cybersecurity training ranges that allow immersion into mimicked real-world environments.

Cyber training ranges are being constructed and utilized to allow immersion into hands-on training environments that build valuable experience (Cankaya, 2015). These environments allow students into a virtual world that allows them to safely learn and experiment without the risk of damaging production systems. These active learning environments are created with varying degrees of realism to replicate real-world operational systems to increase learning. Military pilots train in simulators in order to gain valuable experience before allowing to fly aircraft where mistakes can be costly to equipment and lives. Training in simulated environments that bring as much realism as possible increases experiences needed for real-world employment. Without realism, training value and the ability to build valuable experiences decreases. According to Walcott (2017), training value decreases as realism decreases within these environments. However, increasing realism in cybersecurity training ranges also increases complexity and cost. Research into the effectiveness of injecting realism into cybersecurity training will be done. The purpose of this paper is to develop the understanding that increasing realism in these training environments also increases learning.

CYBERCRIME

Over the last decade, cybercrime has a detrimental impact on all facets of technology used in homes and businesses and continues to increase exponentially. The global economic impact of cybercrime in 2014 cost an estimated 345 million to 445 million dollars, or .62% of global Gross Domestic Product (GDP) (Lewis, 2018). As of 2017, the impact to global GDP increased to .87% or an estimated 608 billion dollars (Lewis, 2018). This cost, which includes loss of reputation, intellectual property, online fraud costs, and other financial impact, continues to grow. A successful cyberattack on an organization within the United States that results in a data breach is estimated to cost an average of 5.4 million dollars per incident (Reed, 2019).

Hidden within the Internet are illicit online marketplaces that specialize in buying and selling stolen information as well as other illegal products and services. These sites reside online in an area commonly referred to as the "Dark Web" and are only accessible by using specialized software that anonymizes the user and the owners of these sites to limit or negate attribution (Kim, Han, Ha, Kim, & Han, 2018). Novice users can pay anywhere between $1,000 - $5,000 to purchase custom malware from cybercriminals which gives them the ability to perform illegal actions such as disabling corporate websites and stealing personal information such as bank accounts and credit card numbers (Sharma, 2007). Due to the lack of attribution, cybercriminals are not the only ones using the dark web for nefarious purposes. According to Gabriel Weimann (2016), the Federal Bureau of Investigation (FBI) announced in 2015 that Islamic terrorists were using the dark web to recruit new members, publish book and guides on bomb-making and the effective use of them, and as a propaganda platform to encourage members to perform terrorist acts globally (Weimann, 2016). Using the Internet with no attribution allows anyone to promote their cause and rapidly disseminate information without accountability. Globally, security organizations have realized the importance of adequately funding and resourcing cyber professionals education and training to find and block these sites (VILIC, 2017).

INCIDENCES

Compromises to organizations are well-known and are often quickly publicized resulting in a negative impact to their reputations. Concern over the threat of personal identities being stolen is creating fear with consumers. Over 145.5 million personal credit records were stolen as the result of the Equifax breach in 2017 (Wolff, 2018). This breach resulted in an overall cost of $439 million and untold damages to the credit rating of consumers (Janofsky, 2017). In many instances, the cause of such incidences was due to a failure within the organization in having a lack of experienced staff. The Equifax investigation indicated that the breach was due to a failure of the Information Technology (IT) staff to install a software fix that would patch the vulnerability that allowed the breach to happen (Primoff & Kess, 2017). The well-known breach of having over 77 million records of sensitive user data stolen at Sony pictures in 2014 resulted in over $396,000 in fees, $30 million in recovery services to computer systems, millions in legal costs, and by giving away free games and services to users to rebuild their trust (Tuttle, 2011). A major contributing factor to Sony's failure is that out of a company of 7,000 employees, the information security team only comprised of eleven cybersecurity professionals (Tuttle, 2011).

NEW TECHNOLOGIES AT RISK

New technologies are being developed and used every day that attempt to make our lives more convenient, efficient, and tailored to our preferences. Within our homes, we have smart devices such as lightbulbs that change colors and dim on our command or smart thermostats that control air conditioning and heating systems by monitoring occupancy levels (Gartner, 2017). Using voice commands, we can shop online, turn the television channels, disable or enable security systems, and query the Internet for any information. Commercially, businesses are adopting similar smart devices to control manufacturing systems to use smart devices to mass produce anything from toys to commercial airplanes. These devices control cars that we drive, jet engines on airplanes, and even passenger and cargo rail systems, to name a few. Gartner (2017) reports that by the year 2020, it is estimated that there will be over 20 billion of these connected devices, commonly called the Internet of Things (IoT), that will be integrated into every facet of our lives (Seago, 2016). Shopping using IoT is a convenience; however, when IoT is used for keeping people alive and well, applying cybersecurity processes becomes critical. Current medical devices integrate IoT systems within it and can control artificial limbs, heart monitors, insulin pumps and other devices which are all referred to as "Internet of Medical Things" (Hudson, 2016). Access from the Internet to control these devices within home and businesses also opens these devices to cyber-attack from anywhere in the world. As integrated as these devices are in our environments today, and more so in the future, the need for qualified personnel to understand, engineer, and secure these devices are paramount (Gartner, 2017). According to Defranco, Kassab, and Voas (2018), it is estimated that a 30 percent increase in IoT job-related fields will occur by 2026.

THREATS TO THE UNITED STATES

Similar in technology as IoT, Supervisory Control and Data Acquisition (SCADA) systems monitor and control not just manufacturing systems and personal devices, but also our nation's infrastructure deemed critical. Devices that monitor and control critical systems, such as the electrical grid, nuclear power plants, communications systems, power generating dams were initially designed to control systems within the confines of the plant or within areas they were controlling and not exposed to externally accessible networks such as the Internet. Due to the isolated nature of these systems, they have very little, if any, security implemented in their design and focused on minimizing cost instead (Alexander, 2018). However, as SCADA systems were required to be integrated into business processes and connected into enterprise systems, exposure from external networks to these systems opened them up to attack (Alexander, 2018).

The threat of cyber-attacks against IoT or SCADA systems has different consequences depending on the function. An attack on infrastructure that control's the nations electrical grid would have disastrous consequences to the United States. Policy needed to be created that would identify critical systems and emphasizes the importance of implementing cybersecurity practices to ensure their health. An executive order was created to define and place the importance of cybersecurity on critical systems that would cause the most harm for the United States (The White House, 2013).

In the United States, there are over 2,800 power plants and 170,000 public water systems of which over 38,000 vulnerabilities in these critical systems were found by the Department of Homeland Security (DHS) during a site-assessment program (Koehler, 2019). Even minor incidents to any of these critical systems can have a significant impact on daily lives. In July of 2018, a water utility system operator accidentally activated a value that caused a loss of water pressure in parts of Washington D.C. which forced over 100,000 people under a boil order for two days (Koehler, 2019). Though this was a very minor incident, the impact would have been extremely detrimental if a cyber-attack caused a prolonged outage or permanent damage to the system.

As part of the deterrence and mitigation strategy to prevent attacks to our critical infrastructure, the National Cyber Strategy was developed in September of 2018 and signed by Present Trump (United States, 2018). This strategy outlines four important categories on how the United States will, "ensure the American people continue to reap the benefits of a secure cyberspace that reflects our principles, protects our security, and promotes our prosperity" (United States, 2018, p. 1). One main category focuses on the need to develop a highly skilled cybersecurity workforce, provide educational and training opportunities for those with diverse backgrounds, and develop a standardized framework that will identify workforce gaps (United States, 2018. p. 17).

WORKFORCE

With increasing cybercrime incidences, terrorism, threats to critical infrastructure, new technologies such as IoT being developed, the workforce shortage of cybersecurity professionals is alarming. As of 2018, the magnitude of the cybersecurity workforce shortage is almost 3 million unfilled security positions globally; the need to fill these gaps is urgent (ISC2, 2018). The top concern placing companies at risk is the inability to fill positions due to the lack of skilled and experienced cybersecurity professionals (ISC2, 2018). Employers have difficulty finding those with enough experience and skills to fill critical positions. This shortage is due to multiple factors contributing to the lack of skills and experience of applicants. One of the most significant factors is that real-world cyber threats rapidly evolve requiring knowledge and skills to be continuously updated, which is a challenge when trying to perform daily job tasks (Schaeffer, Olson, & Eck, 2017). Inadequate training to adapt to the rapidly changing threat landscape, coupled with a lack of human capital to educate, train, and employ, contributes to the ongoing workforce shortage gap.

INCREASING HUMAN CAPITAL

Several initiatives are currently undertaken to help reduce the workforce shortage gap by generating interest at a young age. Early training programs are being developed within middle and high schools to gain interest at an early age. Science, Engineering, Technology, and Mathematics (STEM) programs in elementary schools have integrated IOT concepts to generate interest in younger age-groups (Davis, 2017). To generate interest in cybersecurity in secondary education, students participate in cyber competitions throughout the country. High schools are partnering with government organizations such as the Civil Air Patrol, and the Reserve Officer Training Program (ROTC) to compete in cyber competitions created by the Air Force Association called Cyber Patriot (Manson, Curl, & Carlin, 2012). As interest in cybersecurity increases in primary and secondary education, many possible education and training avenues are available to continue developing cybersecurity professionals in postsecondary education.

CURRENT EDUCATION AND TRAINING

Learning cybersecurity effectively begins with learning foundational concepts. Academic degrees and certifications show knowledge competency in the field and, in many cases are required by employers. However, these do not necessarily build the critical thinking skills and experience needed to become highly proficient to levels that employers are wanting.

CERTIFICATIONS

Industry certifications not only serve as an avenue to learn cybersecurity, but to prove to prospective employers of being qualified with the required skills needed for employment. Obtaining certifications can be the determining factor when competing with others with similar skillsets for lucrative positions that also come with an increase in pay (Pierson, Frolick, & Chen, 2001). The Department of Defense, in accordance with DoD Directive 8570.1, requires its Information Technology (IT) workforce to have a certification such as the CompTIA Security+ certification without needing an academic degree (Walters, 2010).

There are several types of certifications, such as vendor certifications and industry certifications. Vendor certifications train on how to properly manage a specific device or technology developed and sold by the vendor, for example, Microsoft Windows (Pierson, L; Frolick, M; Chen, 2001). Industry certifications teach expert knowledge of a field or sub-field, such as ISC² Certified Information Systems Security Profession (CISSP) which focuses on leadership and operations within the cybersecurity domain (Hansche, Berti, & Hare, 2003).

Certifications typically discuss tools, techniques, and frameworks within the field of cybersecurity, but often lack the experiential, hands-on component in gaining valuable experience (Knapp, Maurer, & Plachkinova, 2017). Having the appropriate certifications may be adequate in many organizations to start working in entry-level cybersecurity positions. However, 50% of all companies require some academic degree in IT related field as part of their hiring practices, but only 15% required positions to have certifications (Wierschem & Francis, 2018). From a value perspective, employers valued work experience significantly higher than having an academic degree or certifications (Wierschem & Francis, 2018).

ACADEMIA

Colleges and Universities are slowly building cybersecurity curriculums for undergraduate and graduate programs. The need to understand what topics are relevant to build effective cybersecurity curriculums is challenging. Having to continuously update course content requires establishing partnerships and collaboration outside the academic circles. For newer technologies, such as IoT, fewer higher academic institutions are developing or even updating their curriculums. In many instances, IoT curriculums are just modified IT curriculums (Defranco et al., 2018). A survey of the top 50 colleges ranked shows that only 28 colleges had 49 IoT curriculums being taught, 39 of which were graduate-level courses (Defranco et al., 2018).

Partnerships between academia, industry, and governments have been formed to develop cybersecurity training (Vogel, 2015). As higher educational institutions rapidly build cybersecurity curriculums to meet the global demands for a trained workforce, building experience is challenging. The curriculums still focus on teaching theory and concepts rather than building experienced practitioners capable of critical thinking (Topham, Kifayat, Younis, Shi, & Askwith, 2016). According to Manson and Pike (2014), current cybersecurity education lacks the appropriate depth within its curriculum, and education starts too late to adequately develop cybersecurity professionals to meet demand. The importance of having hands-on experiential learning of at least one hour a day for cybersecurity practice will build experts with experience no differently than practicing on the field for sports, such as football, will build star athletes (Manson & Pike, 2014). Graduates are unprepared to enter the workforce because they may have the adequate technical knowledge but have not developed the critical thinking skills to solve problems adequately. According to Dark (2015), highly skilled cybersecurity professionals must possess critical thinking and problem-solving skills, comprehensive technical skills and abilities, understand and manage risk and uncertainty, and understand how adversaries think and operate.

EMPLOYER NEEDS

Academic education and certification training alignment with industry and government organizations to determine appropriate and effective cybersecurity curriculum is common in addressing workforce shortage issues. Focusing on what employers require and value to immediately fill employment gaps are critical to understand. As there are many avenues to acquire cybersecurity knowledge, focusing on the needs of employers is necessary for employment. Attaining advanced degrees and gaining certifications are valuable to employers; however, employers place more importance on hiring those with relevant work experience than having certifications and academic degrees. According to Wierschem and Francis,

(2018), employers indicated that work experience was valued at 50%, followed by 30% for academic degrees, and 20% for certifications for employee qualifications.

The Department of Defense (DoD) is one of the largest employers in the world training and equipping over 8,000 cyber mission force personnel responsible for defending and protecting critical infrastructure, DoD, and other federal agency systems (U.S. Government Accountability Office, 2019). The DoD refers to an adage, "Train like you fight and fight like you train" (Walcott, 2017, p. 7) when it comes to training and gaining valuable experience. This adage enforces the belief that without adequate realism in training, the value of that training decreases (Walcott, 2017). The realism is incorporated in varying degrees in cyber training ranges, which are being constructed and utilized to allow immersion into simulated real-world environments that build valuable experience (Cankaya, 2015). These active learning environments are created with varying degrees of realism to replicate real-world operational systems that rapidly increase learning and develop critical thinking and problem-solving skills.

PEDAGOGY IN TEACHING CYBERSECURITY

Didactic Learning

Illinois Institute of Technology developed a strategy for improvement by identifying learning outcomes for beginner, intermediate, and advanced topics within cybersecurity curriculums (Harris & Patten, 2015). By applying Blooms Taxonomy and Webb's depth of knowledge model, the faculty define concepts and skills that students need to learn and be able to demonstrate in each cybersecurity course (Harris & Patten, 2015). They applied these models to their cybersecurity curriculum and determined that different teaching methods would be appropriate depending on the level of knowledge: beginner, intermediate, or advanced. Depending on the level of instruction, the faculty would determine the type of learning that is most appropriate. For example, the beginner, or core courses, that required students to recall facts or explained ideas was determined that didactic methods or flipped methods would be sufficient (Harris & Patten, 2015). According to Harris and Patten (2015), "Within the "flipped" course model, rather than covering specific topics in class with lectures, faculty create videos and other learning material, which students study and review outside of the class time. This frees up class time for discussion on more in-depth newer, emerging topics" (p. 227).

Advanced cybersecurity topics that go beyond fundamental knowledge, hands-on learning approaches are necessary. The course that was developed at the Institute of Technology also used hands-on approach within the course, "The Security course goes further by utilizing hands-on projects to teach students concepts such as encrypting data on personal cloud storage, creating digital signatures, and using hashing function checksum software to verify file transfers" (Harris & Patten, 2015, p. 227).

Problem Based Learning

Problem-based learning (PBL) is learning through problem-solving. It requires the student to research, apply theory, and practice in order to solve problems and learn skills (Brilingaite, Bukauskas, & Juškeviciene, 2018). This type of learning requires self-motivation from the student and the teacher to act as a tutor. The teacher must be competent in the subject matter so that they can engage students with unfamiliar topics as well as answer questions that they, themselves may not have encountered (Ertmer, Schlosser, Clase, & Adedokun, 2014).

According to Mekovec, Aničić, and Arbanas (2018), PBL is effective for the development of critical thinking and solving complex problems that are often reflected in real-world issues, especially in a team environment. For PBL exercises to be effective, the problem should not be entirely clear, not all information should be available, and the problem should have multiple solutions (Mekovec, Aničić, & Arbanas, 2018). This requires the student or team of students to have to solve problems as if in the real world, requiring research and the application of theory, knowledge, and skills learned.

Active and Experiential Learning Methods

Active and experiential learning is often integrated into cybersecurity curriculum to increase learning and allow the student to gain experience. Traditional lecture within the classroom emphasis theoretical learning, but for practical application of skills, immersion into real-world replicated environments delivered through hands-on labs, or computer simulations, is preferred (Topham et al., 2016). If hands-on, skills-based labs are to be effective and improve learning, they need to provide rich and immersive learning environments that engage the student at the appropriate skill level. Simulations that are effective in producing rich and immersive learning environments allow for the student to actively learn by applying concepts into practice as well as increase interest in the subject (Arora, 2018).

Building labs can be challenging as many virtual simulators and LMS platforms are inadequate due to the lack of features needed to produce realistic and high-fidelity labs. Virtual labs are expensive to build and maintain, are often developed by technical experts not versed in educational frameworks, and do not provide current and engaging cyber simulation content that engages the student (Konak, Clark, & Nasereddin, 2014).

Understanding experiential learning frameworks and applying them to computer simulations can be very effective to maximize learning as it allows for the building of experience, instead of just learning concepts and theories (Botelho, Marietto, Ferreira, & Pimentel, 2016). This especially applies to any field in which it is important to develop hands-on abilities such as with many STEM-related fields such as engineering as Botelho et al., (2016) states, "In simulation labs, the students can be trained with practical experiences. It is an important skill to engineering students since Engineering is an applied science that requires hands-on abilities" (p. 81). Even in PBL development, success is dependent on the technology available to both students and teachers. Teachers use technology to plan and implement learning objectives, access problems to be solved, provide background information, and use capabilities to engage students to collaborate and address the challenges presented (Ertmer et al., 2014).

Kolbs-ELC Framework

Kolb's Experiential Learning (ELC) framework is one such framework that can be used to model cybersecurity simulations to maximize learning through hands-on activities that enable students to construct knowledge instead of just acquiring knowledge (Konak et al., 2014). Kolb's framework uses a four-stage learning cycle that begins with a hands-on experience building and learning process, called Concrete experience, then allowing the student to reflect on the experience, called Reflective Observation (Botelho et al., 2016). Abstract Conceptualization enables the student to understand the principles and build a theory behind the experience, and finally, the Active Experimentation stage allows the student to test the theory or model for the experience with different behaviors (Botelho et al., 2016).

According to Powner and Allendoerfer (2008), Kolb's ELC framework is an effective active learning methodology by stating, "Active learning techniques are uniquely capable of engaging all four stages of learning, and so they appeal to students with a variety of learning styles. Active learning techniques turn students into mentally engaged participants" (p. 77). Herz and Merz (1998) found that students participating in a simulation support the learning process as described by Kolb's learning cycle better than a traditional seminar. Konak et al., (2014) suggested that more complex student learning and higher levels of interest could be achieved with hands-on activities if designed with Kolb's ELC framework in mind within a virtual computer-based lab environment. A large part of students achieving competency in these virtual environments is to incorporate realism in the design, such as the ability to collaborate with other students. It was found that as students worked in groups, their interest increased as well as how competent they felt towards the subject they were learning (Konak et al., 2014).

Improving Experiential Learning in Training Platforms

The myriad of training and education opportunities are available to learn technical skills. Learning Management Systems (LMS) such as Blackboard, Moodle, and Canvas are fundamental tools that are often used in many curriculums and can provide foundational knowledge in cybersecurity (Kasim & Khalid, 2008). Massive Open Online Courses (MOOC) are designed to scale to teach many users at one time, but typically focus on a didactic approach that has prerecorded lessons, some type of formative assessment in the form of online quizzes and tests, and reading assignments (Smith, Caldwell, Richards, & Bandara, 2017). These solutions do not address critical thinking and problem-solving skills as well as incorporating realism that immerses the student in virtual training simulations that build experience.

Simulations

Computer-based simulations enable the replication of real-world environments, in this context, computer systems, and networks that reside in operational enterprises. According to Laurillard (2013), computer-based simulations are adaptive and provides the user with feedback on actions taken within the simulation. It is very useful for representing complex relationships and determining results of the relationships as variables within the simulations change (p. 128). Simulations provide the user with an immersive experience of the real-world instead of exposing the user to a descriptive experience that LMS and MOOC's provide.

Simulations that incorporate high levels of realism engage students in ways that are lacking in non-realistic training. It allows for a more in-depth learning experience for students to "master authentic tasks in personally relevant, realistic situations" (Dede, Grotzer, Kamarainen, & Metcalf, 2017, p. 167). Increasing realism in simulations supports the experience and knowledge that students already know and trust to be valid and allow them to build new skills and increase comprehension (Dede et al., 2017). This is especially important with realistic simulations that will enable the students to make decisions and take actions based on prior experience in the real world. Students found that simulations not only increase knowledge and critical thinking skills but also can have a side benefit of providing a fun learning experience (Shellman & Turan, 2006).

Cybersecurity Competitions

Computer-based simulations, in the form of competitions, are being used to not only develop an interest in cybersecurity at all ages, but it is used for training at all experience levels.

The popularity of cybersecurity competitions is due to allowing practitioners and students to operate in a simulated real-world environment and learn how to defend systems against adversaries, as well as learn how adversaries exploit systems. Competitions may only focus on teaching how to defend systems, teaching how to exploit systems, or can focus on both depending on the type of competition.

The Air Force Association developed a cyber competition, called Cyber Patriot, to generate interest at the middle and high school levels to bring students from all disciplines together in a collaborative, competitive environment (White, Williams, & Harrison, 2010). Cyber Patriot organizers leverage immersive training methodologies in virtual environments that are designed to generate interest by developing teams of students that work together to solve complex cybersecurity challenges (Manson & Carlin, 2011). It uses a gamified approach to training that contains simulations of real networks and systems, and are used by participants during competitions. Cyber Patriot uses immersive, hands-on, active learning methodologies, which, "involves students in doing things and thinking about the things they are doing" (Bonwell & Eison, 1991, p. 19). The program emphasizes on what is referred to as Cyber Citizenship, which teaches "Internet ethics and safety and defensive activity only" (Air Force Association, 2012, p. VI). This philosophy is to lay a positive foundation for young participants in order to generate interest in the field of cybersecurity.

Very popular and some of the best-known cyber competitions are known as Capture The Flag (CTF) events (Conti, Babbitt, & Nelson, 2011). These competitions, sometimes called Hacker competitions, require the participants to not only defend their environments but to attack other environments by exploiting vulnerabilities in opponent systems. These events are very useful for research purposes, innovation and industry collaboration, and may require advanced knowledge of exploitation techniques, engineering, and even knowledge of physical security subjects like lockpicking (Conti et al., 2011). According to Conti et al. (2011), "Hacker competitions touch on many aspects of computer science, information technology, electrical engineering, and information security education. They're powerful ways to teach, inspire, build teams, recruit students, and facilitate advanced skill building" (p. 56).

The Cyber Defense Exercise (CDX) is a four-day exercise for federal academy students and is sponsored by the National Security Agency (NSA). The objective is to train students in operating secure networks and to "foster education and awareness among future military leaders about the role of Information Assurance (IA) in protecting the nation's critical information systems" (Adams, Gavas, Lacey, & Leblanc, 2009, p. 1). The simulated computer environments that the participants work in are extremely realistic virtual topologies with intentional vulnerabilities that must be identified and mitigated. The participants, working in teams, must perform a survey of the systems and find vulnerabilities that can be used to exploit them by an adversary (Adams et al., 2009). The teams must not only mitigate these vulnerabilities and ensuring that the systems remain operational, but must do so taking into account the cost of hardware, labor, and licensing (Adams et al., 2009). Focusing on the business aspects within cyber competitions adds to the realism that is also required in operating real enterprise systems in many organizations today.

Considerations of Applying Realism

In any real-world organization, there can be thousands of users on computer systems to perform daily work tasks, such as e-mail or using the Internet for business purposes. Cybersecurity professionals protect the enterprise by monitoring and securing the IT systems within the boundaries of the organization. To provide an authentic learning environment, replicating these systems, including simulating thousands of users that can send e-mail and have the ability to connect to the Internet, should also be incorporated when designing and developing cyber exercise simulations (Braje, 2016). On the surface, simply allowing the exercise to be connected to the actual Internet and inviting real users to participate and act as organizational users that could send e-mail and conduct business over the actual Internet, would allow for increasing realism within the game space of competitions. Exercise developers could focus on simulating the organizational enterprise systems that participants would need to defend in the exercise environment.

Need for Isolation

In order to maintain a high level of realism within the exercise space, real-world malware is often used. Using active malware found on the Internet that are used against organizations to steal information allows for an authentic learning experience for students and practitioners trying to defend against them. Using live malware poses a risk of accidental leakage to the Internet. To prevent this, complete isolation of the game space is paramount, especially if the curriculum includes teaching topics like hacking techniques and hunting live malware (Topham et al., 2016). Building these isolated environments decreases realism and adds a level of complexity to the administration and design of the exercise environment (Mattson, 2007). If complete isolation is required, then connecting to the actual Internet cannot be done, and therefore inviting real users to act as fictional organizational users cannot be done. Additional effort and cost must be incurred to build systems that can simulate user activities and to simulate the Internet in an isolated environment. Researchers, programmers, and exercise developers must be hired to solve and develop solutions to these types of challenges.

Return on Investment of Increasing Realism

Cyber ranges that host these exercises are complex and expensive to build and maintain (Braje, 2016). To host, design and develop cyber exercises with high levels of realism and fidelity, including developing and integrating systems that mimic the Internet and simulate user traffic, is a complicated task requiring expertise and research of technologies (Braje, 2016). Keeping up with developing realistic exercises is challenging and to integrate the latest malware to maintain high levels of realism is extremely difficult if not impossible. According to Lewis (2018), there are about 300,000 new malwares released daily and 780,000 records stolen daily. The amount of effort, time, and cost to maintain high levels of realism will need to be reconciled with the training effectiveness and objectives required to be achieved.

Secondary Effects of Realistic Training

Ethics need to be considered if cyber competitions that teach hacking techniques, malware development, and understanding how cybercriminals operate, are used to teach complex cybersecurity concepts. Realistic cyber exercises teach tactics, techniques, and procedures used by cybercriminals to break into networks and computer systems to damage information systems in order to develop a defensive strategy (Hartley, 2015). However, educators and developers of cyber competitions need to understand the ramifications of teaching hacking techniques to students without also teaching them the consequences of performing illegal activities outside of the intended virtual computing platform.

The hesitation in teaching students hacking techniques is due to the concern from educators that it will encourage students to perform unethical activities, such as writing viruses or exploiting a system weakness to gain unauthorized access (Pashel, 2006). It also may be due to possible liability concerns that institutions are assuming by allowing hacking techniques to be taught.

According to Pike (2013):

Teaching ethical hacking is a serious responsibility given the destructive power of the skills being taught and the allure of negative influences on students. This is especially true when the cybersecurity challenges that the students face during and after their academic programs are complex, and it is often difficult to determine how to properly apply the ethics training received in courses. (p. 73)

Students who become cybersecurity professionals need to be able to make informed and ethical decisions when performing their duties. Often, students do not understand the ramifications of their hacking activities due to lack of ethics training. Building highly realistic training environments will allow students to practice illegal or unethical activities in an environment that replicates real-world environments so well, it may give less scrupulous students the confidence of trying it on real-world networks.

CONCLUSION

This paper serves to show that injecting realism into cybersecurity training and education is beneficial to rapidly training qualified, skilled, and experienced cybersecurity professionals. As cybercrime activity increases, employers are desperate to fill positions with employees that have adequate experience. Research shows that experiential learning is an effective way to gain experience that is needed. An extremely effective avenue for immersion into experiential learning is to participate in computer simulation exercises, also referred to as cyber competitions that replicate real-world environments. These exercises allow students to gain hands-on experiences while immersed in environments that mimic real-world operational systems. Highly realistic training allows students to gain valuable experiences employers are looking for. However, there are challenges and expense with maintaining realism due to the need for isolation, rapidly changing technology, and evolving real-world threats. Finally, there are ethical considerations when increasing realism within exercise environments. Making an exercise "too real" may persuade students to consider the possibility of undertaking unethical activities, because of the fear that they will not get caught after practicing on an environment that replicates real-world systems.

REFERENCES

Adams, W. J., Gavas, E., Lacey, T., & Leblanc, S. P. (2009). Collective views of the NSA/CSS cyber defense exercise on curricula and learning objectives. *Proceedings of the 2nd Conference on Cyber Security Experimentation and Test (CSET'09)*. Academic Press. Retrieved from http://dl.acm.org/citation.cfm?id=1855481.1855483

Air Force Association. (2012). CyberPatriot XI, *1198*(877).

Alexander, D. (2018). Fighting the Fight: Cyber attacks on industrial control systems are increasing. What can you do? *TCE: The Chemical Engineer, 923*, 45-48.

Anderson, D. L. (2017). Improving information technology curriculum learning outcomes. *Informing Science, 20*, 119–131. doi:10.28945/3746

Arora, B. (2018). Teaching cyber security to non-tech students. *Politics*. doi:10.1177/0263395718760960

Bonwell, C. C., & Eison, J. A. (1991). *Active Learning: Creating excitement in the classroom. ASHE-ERIC Higher Education Report*.

Botelho, W. T., Marietto, M. D. G. B., Ferreira, J. C. D. M., & Pimentel, E. P. (2016). Kolb's experiential learning theory and Belhot's learning cycle guiding the use of computer simulation in engineering education: A pedagogical proposal to shift toward an experiential pedagogy. *Computer Applications in Engineering Education, 24*(1), 79–88. doi:10.1002/cae.21674

Braje, T. M. (2016). Advanced tools for Cyber ranges. *The Lincoln Laboratory Journal, 22*(1), 24–32.

Brilingaite, A., Bukauskas, L., & Juškeviciene, A. (2018). Competency assessment in problem-based learning projects of information technologies students. *Informatics in Education, 17*(1), 21–44. doi:10.15388/infedu.2018.02

Cankaya, Y. (2015). Technical note: Exploiting problem definition study for cyber security simulations. *Journal of Defense Modeling and Simulation, 12*(4), 363–368. doi:10.1177/1548512915604585

Conti, G., Babbitt, T., & Nelson, J. (2011). Hacking competitions and their untapped potential for security education. *IEEE Security and Privacy, 9*(3), 56–59. doi:10.1109/MSP.2011.51

Dark, M. (2015). Thinking about Cybersecurity. *IEEE Security and Privacy, 13*(1), 61–65. doi:10.1109/MSP.2015.17

Davis, T. (2017). The Internet of Things for kids. *Science and Children, 54*(9), 84–91. doi:10.2505/4c17_054_09_84

Dede, C., Grotzer, T. A., Kamarainen, A., & Metcalf, S. (2017). EcoXPT: Designing for deeper learning through experimentation in an immersi...: EBSCOhost, *20*, 166–178. Retrieved from http://web.b.ebscohost.com/ehost/pdfviewer/pdfviewer?vid=11&sid=6c2f8843-b4b0-4318-b8eb-51e8600dfa1b%40sessionmgr102

Defranco, J., Kassab, M., & Voas, J. (2018). How do you create an Internet of Things Workforce? *IT Professional, 20*(4), 8–12. doi:10.1109/MITP.2018.043141662

Ertmer, P. A., Schlosser, S., Clase, K., & Adedokun, O. (2014). The Grand Challenge: Helping teachers learn/teach cutting-edge science via a PBL approach. *Interdisciplinary Journal of Problem-Based Learning*, *8*(1). doi:10.7771/1541-5015.1407

Gartner. (2017). Leading the IoT, 29. Retrieved from https://www.gartner.com/imagesrv/books/iot/iotEbook_digital.pdf

Hansche, S., Berti, J., & Hare, C. (2003). *Official (ISC)2 guide to the CISSP exam*. Taylor & Francis. doi:10.1201/9780203507872

Harris, M. A., & Patten, K. P. (2015). Using Bloom's and Webb's Taxonomies to integrate emerging cybersecurity topics into a computing curriculum. *Journal of Information Systems Education*, *26*(3), 219–234.

Harris, M. A., Patten, K. P., & Patten, K. P. (2015). Using Bloom's and Webb's Taxonomies to integrate emerging cybersecurity topics into a computing curriculum. *Journal of Information Systems Education*, *26*(3), 219–234.

Hartley, R. D. (2015). Ethical Hacking Pedagogy: An analysis and overview of teaching students to hack. *Journal of International Technology & Information Management*, *24*(4), 95–104. Retrieved from http://search.ebscohost.com/login.aspx?direct=true&db=bth&AN=122400154&lang=es&site=ehost-live

Herz, B., & Merz, W. (1998). Experiential Learning and the effectiveness of economic simulation games. *Simulation & Gaming*, *29*(2), 238–250. doi:10.1177/1046878198292007

Hudson, F. (2016). The Internet of Things is here. *EDUCAUSE Review*, *51*(4), 1. PMID:27441587

ISC2. (2018). Cybersecurity professionals focus on developing new skills as workforce gap widens table of contents. *Cybersecurity Workforce Study*.

Janofsky, A. (2017). Equifax Breach Could Cost Billions. *Wall Street Journal*.

Kasim, N. N. M., & Khalid, F. (2008). Choosing the right Learning Management System (LMS) for the Higher Education Institution Context: A systematic review. *International Journal of Emerging Technologies in Learning*, *11*(6), 55–62. doi:10.3991/ijet.v11i06.5644

Kim, S., Han, J., Ha, J., Kim, T., & Han, D. (2018). SGX-Tor: A secure and practical Tor anonymity network With SGX enclaves. *IEEE/ACM Transactions on Networking*, *26*(5), 2174–2187. doi:10.1109/TNET.2018.2868054

Knapp, K. J., Maurer, C., & Plachkinova, M. (2017). Maintaining a Cybersecurity Curriculum: Professional certifications as valuable guidance. *Journal of Information Systems Education*, *28*(2), 101–114. Retrieved from http://jise.org/Volume28/n2/JISEv28n2p101.html

Koehler, R. K. (2019). *When the Lights Go Out: Vulnerabilities to US Critical Infrastructure, the Russian cyber threat, and a new way forward* (Vol. 7). Georgetown Security Studies Review.

Konak, A., Clark, T. K., & Nasereddin, M. (2014). Using Kolb's Experiential Learning Cycle to improve student learning in virtual computer laboratories. *Computers & Education*, *72*, 11–22. doi:10.1016/j.compedu.2013.10.013

Laurillard, D. (2013). *Rethinking University Teaching : A conversational framework for the effective use of learning technologies* (2nd ed.). Hoboken: Routledge. Retrieved from https://reddog.rmu.edu/login?url=http://search.ebscohost.com/login.aspx?direct=true&db=nlebk&AN=606935&site=eds-live&scope=site

Lewis, J. (2018). Economic impact of Cybercrime—no slowing down report. Mcafee. Retrieved from https://www.mcafee.com/enterprise/en-us/assets/reports/restricted/economic-impact-cybercrime.pdf?utm_source=Press&utm_campaign=bb9303ae70-EMAIL_CAMPAIGN_2018_02_21&utm_medium=email

Manson, D., & Carlin, A. (2011). A League of Our Own: The future of cyber defense Competitions. *Communications of the IIMA, 11*(2), 1–11.

Manson, D., Curl, S., & Carlin, A. (2012). CyberPatriot : Exploring university-high school partnerships. *Communications of the IIMA, 12*(1), 65–78.

Manson, D., & Pike, R. (2014). The case for depth in cybersecurity education. *ACM Inroads, 5*(1), 47–52. doi:10.1145/2568195.2568212

Mattson, J. A. (2007). Cyber defense exercise: A service provider model. *IFIP International Federation for Information Processing, 237*, 81–86. doi:10.1007/978-0-387-73269-5_11

Mekovec, R., Aničić, K. P., & Arbanas, K. (2018). Developing undergraduate IT students' Generic Competencies Through Problem-...: GCU Library Resources - All Subjects. *TEM Journal, 7*(1), 193–200. doi:10.18421/TEM71-24

Nagamani, O., Sharma, M., & Pragati, G. (2011). Challenges and Countermeasures for Web Applications. *International Journal of Advanced Research in Computer Science, 2*(3), 381–385.

Pashel, B. (2006). Teaching students to hack: Ethical implications in teaching students to hack at the university level. *Proceedings of the 3rd Annual Conference on Information Security Curriculum Development, InfoSecCD 2006* (pp. 197–200). Academic Press. 10.1145/1231047.1231088

Pierson, L., Frolick, M., & Chen, L. (2001). Emerging issues in it certification. *Journal of Computer Information Systems, 42*(1), 17.

Pike, R. E. (2013). The "Ethics" of teaching ethical hacking. *Journal of International Technology and Information Management, 22*(4), 67–75. Retrieved from https://login.ezproxy.net.ucf.edu/login?url=http://search.proquest.com/docview/1518257238?accountid=10003%5Cnhttp://sfx.fcla.edu/ucf?url_ver=Z39.88-2004&rft_val_fmt=info:ofi/fmt:kev:mtx:journal&genre=unknown&sid=ProQ:ProQ:compscijour&atitle=The+&quotPowner, L. C., & Allendoerfer, M. G. (2008). Evaluating hypotheses about active learning. International Studies Perspectives. *International Studies Perspectives, 9*(1), 75–89. doi:10.1111/j.1528-3585.2007.00317.x

Primoff, W., & Kess, S. (2017). The Equifax data breach. *The CPA Journal*, (12), 14–17. doi:10.1099/00221287-144-10-2731

Reed, T. S. (2019). Cybercrime and technology losses: Claims and potential insurance coverage for modern cyber risks. *Tort Trial & Insurance Practice Law Journal*, *54*(1), 153–209. Retrieved from https://reddog.rmu.edu/login?url=http://reddog.rmu.edu:2060/login.aspx?direct=true&db=a9h&AN=13592 1582&site=eds-live&scope=site

Schaeffer, D. M., Olson, P. C., & Eck, C. K. (2017). An interdisciplinary approach to cybersecurity curriculum. *Journal of Higher Education Theory and Practice*, *17*(9), 36–40. Retrieved from https://reddog. rmu.edu/login?url=https://reddog.rmu.edu:3479/docview/2011213993?accountid=28365

Seago, J. (2016). A world of connections. *Internal Auditor*, *73*(4), 28–33. Retrieved from https://reddog. rmu.edu/login?url=http://search.ebscohost.com/login.aspx?direct=true&db=buh&AN=117767655&s ite=eds-live&scope=site

Shellman, S. M., & Turan, K. (2006). Do simulations enhance student learning? An empirical evaluation of an IR simulation. *Journal of Political Science Education*, *2*(1), 19–32. doi:10.1080/15512160500484168

Smith, N., Caldwell, H., Richards, M., & Bandara, A. (2017). A comparison of MOOC development and delivery approaches. *International Journal of Information and Learning Technology*, *34*(2), 152–164. doi:10.1108/IJILT-09-2016-0047

The White House. (2013). Executive Order 13636: Improving critical infrastructure cybersecurity. *Federal Register*, *78*(33), 1–8. Retrieved from https://www.gpo.gov/fdsys/pkg/FR-2013-02-19/pdf/2013-03915.pdf

Topham, L., Kifayat, K., Younis, Y., Shi, Q., & Askwith, B. (2016). Cyber Security Teaching and Learning Laboratories: A Survey. *Information & Security: An International Journal*, *35*, 51–80. doi:10.11610/ isij.3503

Tuttle, H. (2011). Sony faces lawsuits after data breach. *Fore Front*, *62*(2), 14. Retrieved from http:// go.galegroup.com.proxy.library.cmu.edu/ps/i.do?id=GALE%7CA405168899&v=2.1&u=cmu_ main&it=r&p=AONE&sw=w

United States. (2018). National Cyber Strategy.

U.S. Government Accountability Office. (2019). *DOD TRAINING U.S. Cyber Command and services should take actions to maintain a trained Cyber Mission Force*.

VILIC. V. M. (2017). Dark Web, Cyber Terrorism and Cyber Warfare: Dark side of the cyberspace. *Balkan Social Science Review*, *10*(10), 7–24. Retrieved from http://library.capella.edu/login?url=http:// search.ebscohost.com/login.aspx?direct=true&db=aph&AN=127927428&site=ehost-live&scope=site

Vogel, R. (2015). Closing the cybersecurity skills gap. *Salus Journal. Bathurst, New South Wales, Australia: Charles Sturt University.*, *4*(2), 32–46. Retrieved from http://hdl.handle.net/1959.14/1074749

Walcott, T. (2017). Training cyber forces without warfighting. *Journal of Information Warfare*, *14*(2), 1–11.

Walters, D. (2010). LandWarNet: Is your IT workforce ready? *Army Sustainment*, *42*(3), 26–28. Retrieved from https://reddog.rmu.edu/login?url=http://reddog.rmu.edu:2060/login.aspx?direct=true&db=a9h& AN=51974566&site=eds-live&scope=site

Weimann, G. (2016). Going dark: Terrorism on the dark web. *Studies in Conflict and Terrorism, 39*(3), 195–206. doi:10.1080/1057610X.2015.1119546

White, G. B., Williams, D., & Harrison, K. (2010). The CyberPatriot national high school cyber defense competition. *IEEE Security and Privacy, 8*(5), 59–61. doi:10.1109/MSP.2010.166

Wierschem, D., & Mediavilla, F. A. M. (2018). Entry Level Technology Positions: No Degree Required. *Journal of Information Systems Education, 29*(4).

Wolff, J. (2018). *You'll see this message when it is too late: The legal and economic aftermath of cybersecurity breaches.* MIT Press. doi:10.7551/mitpress/11336.001.0001

This research was previously published in the International Journal of Cyber Research and Education (IJCRE), 2(1); pages 40-54, copyright year 2020 by IGI Publishing (an imprint of IGI Global).

Chapter 29
Design of Cyberspace Security Talents Training System Based on Knowledge Graph

Xi Chen
Guizhou Normal University, China

Fangming Ruan
Guizhou Normal University, China

Lvyang Zhang
Yiwu Industrial and Commercial College, China

Yang Zhao
JiLin University, China

ABSTRACT

Internet, big data, global society, economy, life, politics, military, and culture are deeply integrated and have developed into an era of overlapping cyberspace and real society. Cyberspace security has become the most complex, comprehensive, and severe non-traditional security challenge facing all countries in the world. However, the talents in the field of cyberspace security cannot meet the practical needs of the development of cyberspace security. This paper puts forward the training scheme of network security talents, discusses the relationship between knowledge atlas and network space security, gives the construction and distribution of network space full knowledge atlas, and then constructs an education big data architecture for cyberspace security based on knowledge graph around the use of knowledge.

DOI: 10.4018/978-1-6684-3554-0.ch029

1. INTRODUCTION

Today, the emergence, development and popularization of the Internet are changing the whole world. While bringing convenience to people, they also bring many hidden dangers. In recent years, data information has leaked, malicious attacks by hackers, the emergence of blackmail viruses, various network destruction incidents have occurred, and the network is full of traps and dangers. Network security has threatened people's security, social security, economic security and even It is national security. As a brand-new technical specialty, cybersecurity involves the lifeblood of the country and is related to the security and sovereignty of the country. Without national security, there is no national security.

The competition in cyberspace is, in the final analysis, talent competition. Under the impetus of global network technology, the development of the whole society is inseparable from the network. The development of all walks of life depends more and more on the security of cyberspace security talents, and the demand for network security talents has reached an unprecedented height (Weng, Ma, & Gu, 2016). Network security involves various fields, network security threats are frequent, and network security connotation is expanded. However, there are problems such as large number of network security talents, low professional and technical capabilities, and unreasonable structure. In terms of subject education, the cybersecurity subject curriculum is unreasonable, and it is not integrated with the actual social needs, and there is no correct guidance for the development of learners. The traditional talent training model can no longer meet the development needs of cultivating cyber security talents. The cyberspace security discipline has its own characteristics. It can't just cultivate network security talents through the simple theoretical knowledge of cybersecurity and the transfer of technical knowledge. And practice is not to train high-end talents for network security. The emergence of educational big data has provided a new powerful weapon for solving this problem. It uses educational big data to analyze and mine valuable information for cultivating cyber security talents, change the traditional talent training model, and establish a sound cybersecurity domain specific. Talent development plan.

In view of the shortage of network security personnel and the unreasonable training mode of network security personnel cannot meet the demand, this paper analyses the current situation and problems of network security personnel training, and puts forward a gradient training standard model of network security personnel, and designs a large data body of network space education based on knowledge graph. Department structure, strengthen the construction of cyberspace security specialty and discipline system, so that a steady stream of cybersecurity personnel into the field of cybersecurity.

2. GOLDEN STONE CYBERSPACE SECURITY TALENTS TRAINING

2.1. Preliminary Exploration of Cyberspace Security Talents Training System Based on Education Big Data

On May 29, 2012, the United Nations Global Pulse released the white paper "Big Data for Development: Opportunities and Challenges (Pules, 2012)." The report points out that the world has entered the era of "Big Data", which brings both opportunities and challenges. On April 17, 2016, China's first report on the development of big data in the field of education, the Blue Book on the Development of Big Data in China's Basic Education, was officially released. The report combed the progress of policies related to the global big data in education, interpreted the connotation and uniqueness of the big data in education, and analyzed the source and structure of the big data in education. This paper introduces 13 kinds of educational data acquisition technologies, which are commonly used in four categories, and puts forward 7 typical educational data analysis models (Lu, 2016). Although there are a large number of universities, educational training institutions and educational products in China, they are very small compared with the huge potential market scale. For network security personnel training is still in its infancy. Education big data is not only reflected in the "quantity", but also in the "value". How to make full use of the "quantity" and "value" of big data in education to cultivate network security talents is a common problem faced by all countries in the world.

In the process of training network security talents, it is very important to fully understand the needs of the market and the field, and to understand the needs and abilities of learners. The "quantity" of big data in education helps educators grasp the development of network security through the analysis of big data, grasp the learners' own characteristics and learning cognitive ability, so that each learner can be taught in accordance with his aptitude. The "value" of big data in education helps educators fully dig out the valuable information behind these big data and use it to train network security talents.

2.2. Golden Stone Plan

Cyberspace security has received the attention of countries around the world. More than 50 countries including the United States, South Korea, Japan, and the European Union have successively issued national cybersecurity strategies. In terms of cyber security talent training, there are no exceptions. Many countries have plans to train cyberspace security talents. In the United States, there is a "National Cyberspace Security Education Program". It is expected that the general layout and actions of the country will be popularized in information security and regular academic qualifications. Education, professional training and certification have established a systematic and standardized talent training system to comprehensively improve the information security capabilities of the United States (Han, Wang, Huang, & Lu, 2012). There is a BOB program in Korea, which is a major program for cultivating cyber security talents in Korea. It trains 100 young hackers every year, and then selects the best among these young hackers to form a national hacker team.

On June 11, 2015, the Academic Degrees Committee of the State Council officially approved the addition of "cyberspace security" as a national first-level discipline (Zhang, Yu, & Zhai, 2016), which reflects the importance that the state attaches to the training of cyberspace security talents, and therefore designs a complete cyberspace security talent training. System and mode are particularly important (Yang, Zhou, & Liu, 2016). In this context, the author team has developed the Golden Stone Project, which provides a new engine for cultivating high-end network security talents in the future and leading the sustainable development of the network security industry. There are several main clues in thinking about the importance of cybersecurity and talent development in the new world order – big, understanding, knowledge, practice.

To say "big" first, if you want to be different, you must have a big perspective. The Confucius Institute promotes cultural concepts and philosophical systems throughout the world, which are worth learning from in terms of international cyber security talent development. Mr. Yang Yixian's "General Safety Theory" and "Safety History" have established a unified basic theoretical system of cyberspace security. Under the premise of almost no restrictions in science and engineering, it reveals some basics of hacker attack and defense and security evolution. law. These rules can be applied to all major branches of cyberspace security. Establishing an international network security talent training system requires a global perspective and a comprehensive understanding of the basic theoretical system of network security.

"Understanding", there are three important points in the process of cyber security talent training. The first one is "You want to understand him". The learner is our God. The needs and characteristics of learners are increasingly required to tailor them. The second one is "He wants to understand you". In the international network of talent training, effective communication is still the top priority. "You know him" and "He knows you too." After that, "you and he will understand it together." Security issues without borders have become a problem of pan-globalization, not only in the field of international cyber security talents, but also at the international level. The network security cooperation team will also be the future development trend, jointly promote the interconnection and sharing of network space, share the common governance, and jointly build a community of cyberspace destiny.

"Knowledge" is divided into four angles, strategy, tactics, battle, and war preparation. Strategically, to establish a sound international network security talent training system requires us to look at the world cybersecurity situation from top to bottom. In terms of tactics, we explore new ideas, new systems, and new mechanisms for talent training models from the shallower to the deeper. In the campaign, we will deploy talents from the outside to strengthen the joint training of universities and industries, and promote the in-depth cooperation and innovation in the talent training model among the various sectors of government, industry, and research. In combat readiness, there must be reserves for fighting, and high-end talents should be reserved from near to far.

Finally, it is "practice". In terms of the importance of practicing cybersecurity and talent cultivation in the new world order, there are two points. First, improve the top-level design of network security talent construction. Second, strengthen the construction of network security majors and discipline systems, accelerate the construction of network security talents and innovation bases, form a continuous training mechanism for school-enterprise cooperation as soon as possible, and promote the continuous development of high-level talents for network security.

Golden stone plans to set up three major positions according to the different needs of the current society for network security talents: strategic posts, research posts and technical posts. The strategic post requires network security personnel to conduct in-depth study of comprehensive knowledge in the field of network security, to grasp network security in general, to keep up-to-date information on network security, and to make corresponding strategic planning; The personnel conducted in-depth research on the events in the field of network security, analyzed the technical means and preventive measures contained therein, and issued research and analysis reports; the technical posts mainly required network security personnel to master the professional technical means in the field of network security. On the basis of these three major positions, each post was subdivided. In the strategic post, it is divided into data intelligence analysts and strategic planning analysts; in research posts, it is divided into application technology researchers and scientific and technical researchers; in engineering posts, it is divided into CTF competition engineers and network security system developers (Figure 1).

According to the requirements of social security talents and the characteristics of network security itself, the training process can be divided into three stages. The first stage is to learn the introduction of network security, the status quo, the main threats, etc., and lead learners to fully understand network security. To cultivate learners' interest in cybersecurity and to lead learners. In the second stage, we will increase the learning of technical courses that must be mastered by cyber security technology, deeply explore the characteristics and interests of learners, and conduct special task evaluation and selection. The tasks include technology, scientific research, and strategic perspective. Through the assessment to understand the learner's knowledge of the situation, and self-recommended courses, in order to achieve the purpose of personality training. In the third stage, we will focus on actual combat and conduct in-depth battles with cyber security companies. Through the training and assessment of the first two stages, learners will find a position of their own interest or show their strengths in this aspect, and can focus on this direction in the third stage.

Figure 1. Golden stone plan structure diagram

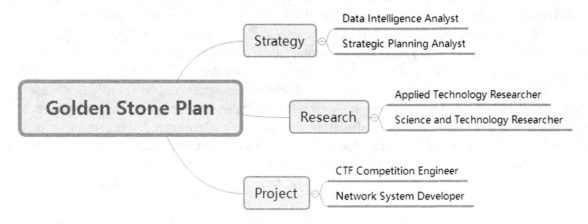

3. PRELIMINARY CONSTRUCTION OF KNOWLEDGE GRAPH OF CYBERSPACE SECURITY DISCIPLINE

According to the six positions set by the Golden Stone Project, the abilities required for each position are different. The courses and knowledge required to be learned in the process of training should also be different. However, from the current cyberspace security discipline system, the curriculum is too singular, targeted and practical, and the links between courses are often neglected. The knowledge learned by learners is fragmentation. Cannot be combined into a completed system. Although the discipline of cyberspace security has certain links with disciplines such as computer, mathematics, and communication, it also has its own characteristics that are different from other disciplines. However, the existing curriculum and training programs are mostly directly selected from these similar disciplines. They do not fully consider the differences in the discipline of cyberspace security, and specifically set up courses and develop training programs for this subject.

Constructing the subject knowledge graph can effectively solve the problem of unreasonable cyberspace security curriculum setting and help learners to fully understand the cyberspace security discipline. The knowledge graph is essentially a semantic network. It is a graph-based data structure composed of nodes and edges. That is, the knowledge graph is a structured semantic knowledge base that describes the concepts and their relationships in the physical world in symbolic form (Zhou & Ma, 2018). The points in the knowledge graph represent entities in the real world, and each edge represents the relationship between the entity and the entity. Each entity is represented by several attributes, and the entities are related by the attributes of the entities (Wu, Chen, & Zhao, 2017). The knowledge graph construction mainly includes three steps of knowledge extraction, knowledge representation and knowledge storage.

Knowledge extraction is the extraction of knowledge from data of different sources and different structures, and the formation of structured data is stored in the knowledge graph. The resources used for knowledge extraction are mainly divided into structured data, semi-structured data and unstructured data. The structured data includes the linked data and the relational database that have existed in the form of knowledge graph. For the linked data, the map mapping method can be used to extract the knowledge. For the relational database, the D2R conversion method is mainly used to extract the knowledge. Semi-structured data contains tables, lists, forms, and Infobox, which can be extracted using a wrapper. For unstructured data, this branch is extracted using information in natural language processing for knowledge extraction (Figure 2).

Figure 2. Knowledge extraction classification and inclusion of technical diagram

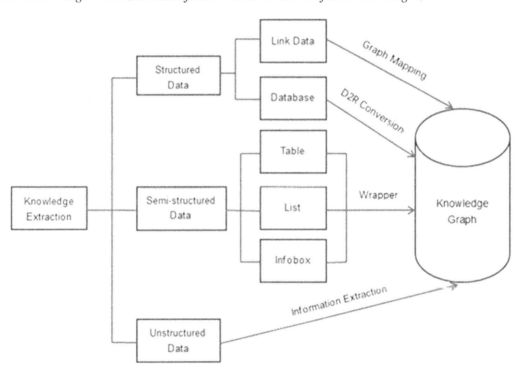

Knowledge representation is to realize the modeling of things in the real world and the relationship between things, to give data in line with the logical information expressed by human beings, and to enable barrier-free communication between people and computers (Ou, 2018). Early knowledge representation methods include first-order predicate logic, production systems, frameworks, semantic networks and so on (Li & Feng, 2017), but these methods all have various defects. At present, most of them use RDF, RDFS, OWL, XML and other representation methods to construct knowledge modeling and expression. Knowledge storage mainly stores knowledge graph in the form of graphs in the database. Typical databases include Google's Frecbase, Microsoft's Stori, OrientDB and PostgreSQL.

4. ARCHITECTURE DESIGN

The education big data architecture design of cyberspace security education based on knowledge graph includes three modules: learner module, domain module and visualization (Figure 3).

Figure 3. Cyberspace security education big data architecture design diagram

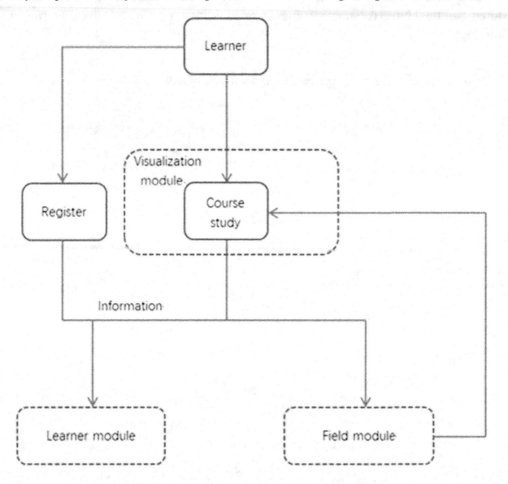

4.1. Learner Module

The learner model is a data structure used to represent the learner's current knowledge state (Polson & Richardson, 2013). It reflects the learner's personal characteristics, knowledge learning state, cognitive ability and so on. The learner model should include learner-related personal characteristics, interactive elements between learners and the system, learning situation of knowledge, and all behaviors related to teaching activities. The more information the learners have in the model, the better they can understand the positions, abilities and cognitive level of the learners who want to work in the field of network security and train the learners according to the current requirements of network security. Typical student models include lead plate model, cover model, cognitive model and so on. Different models have different emphasis. In order to reflect the learner's information comprehensively and update the student model dynamically, this paper synthesizes and simplifies the classical student model, and finally constructs a student model based on CELTS-11 specification. The model includes three parts: personal information, knowledge structure and learning behavior.

4.2. Domain Module

Domain module is used to describe the curriculum, knowledge points and their relationship by constructing knowledge map. The data resources of network security knowledge atlas mainly come from the training programs and courses established by different universities in the subject of network space security, and the professional training courses set up by network security enterprises. The original resource data are extracted by different technical means, and the pre-processed data are logically defined and described to build ontology database and form ontology model. The ontology model is mapped to the knowledge map, and the knowledge relationship of the subject is visualized to the learners in the form of knowledge map.

The specific construction process of this knowledge map is as follows:

1.   Identifying areas for knowledge mapping.

The knowledge domain of this system is network space security.

2.   Defining hierarchies.

This step is mainly used to determine the hierarchical structure of knowledge structure atlas, including the number of layers and the specific meaning of each layer.

3.   Extracting the main concepts in the knowledge domain according to the hierarchical structure.

According to the hierarchical structure defined in the second step, this step extracts knowledge concepts from the knowledge domain and determines the hierarchy of the concepts.

4.   Defining relational models.

This step determines the type of relationship between knowledge concepts and the level of nodes connected by each relationship.

5.   Designing knowledge structure atlas storage structure.

This step defines the storage structure for the designed knowledge structure atlas. The storage structure mainly includes node tables and relational tables.

6.   Constructing a Map of Knowledge Structure.

According to the defined hierarchical type and relational model, and the selected knowledge concepts, the knowledge structure atlas is constructed.

This paper divides the knowledge and skills system of Cyberspace Security talents into 14 subsystems, which are Web security, vulnerability mining and utilization, network penetration, malicious code, reverse analysis, traceability forensics, security operation and maintenance, cryptographic application, network key infrastructure security, endpoint and boundary protection, cloud security, Internet of Things security, mobile and wireless security. Secure block chain. Each first-level node is divided into several second-level nodes, and the second-level nodes are classified into several third-level nodes, not more than four-level nodes (Figure 4).

Figure 4. Knowledge graph of cyberspace security

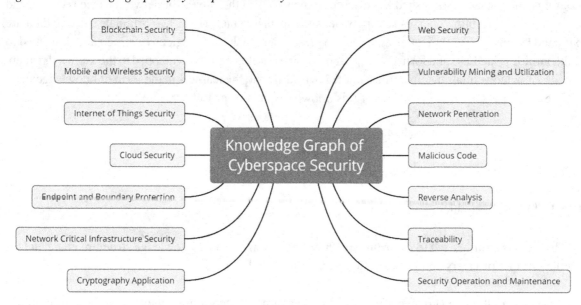

4.3. Visualization Module

Visualization module is the interface between learners and the system, and the display interface of the system. Based on the knowledge logic relationship of learners' cognitive level, post competence requirements and knowledge map, the corresponding courses are recommended and presented to learners through visual module.

5. CONCLUSION

Cyberspace has become the "second living space" of all countries in the world. The international competition and confrontation around cyberspace is increasingly fierce. The cyber warfare has obvious asymmetry. The network security prevention and control capability is weak, and it is difficult to effectively deal with organized organizations between countries. Cyber attacks, even a hacker can challenge a country and threaten the security of an entire country. Countries around the world have fully realized the importance of cultivating cyberspace security talents and have raised the cyberspace security talents to the strategic level of national security. There is a huge gap in cyberspace security talents, and the shortage of high-end talents is particularly serious. This has always been a shortcoming in the development of cyberspace security. Countries are improving the cyberspace security talent training mechanism, starting from the basic education of cyberspace talents, and accelerating the construction of a cyberspace discipline system. The rise of educational big data is changing the traditional talent training education model and accelerating the transformation and upgrading of the education model. Make full use of the two major advantages of the "quantity" of education big data and the "value", deepen the analysis and excavate the information that guides the training of cyberspace security talents, and help the establishment of cyberspace security personnel training programs. This paper proposes the network security talent training plan - the Golden Stone plan, and describes the relationship between cyberspace security and knowledge graph, and builds a cyberspace security education big data structure system based on knowledge graph. The training of cyberspace security talents has a long way to go. It needs to be oriented to the needs of the country and society, to the renewal and development of technology, to put capacity training at the core position, and to promote the continuous growth of network security talents.

REFERENCES

Jian, W., Ma, C., & Liang, G. (2016). Discussions on the talent cultivation of cyber security. *Chinese Journal of Network and Information Security*, *02*, 2–3.

Li, H. R., & Feng, H. P. (2017). *Review of Knowledge Graph Domain in Information Behavior*. Library Theory& Practice.

Lu, Q. (2016). Blue Book on China's Basic Education Big Data Development (2015). *Information Technology Education in Primary and Secondary Schools*, *5*, 4.

Ou, Y. (2018). A Survey of Knowledge Graph Technology Research. *Electronics World*, *13*, 55.

Polson, R. (2013). *Foundations of intelligent tutoring systems*. Psychology Press. doi:10.4324/9780203761557

Pulse UNG. (2012). *Big data for development: Challenges & opportunities*. Naciones Unidas.

Wei, H., Xing, W., Xue, H., & Lu, C. (2012). Analysis of the NICE Network Space Security Talent Team Framework in the United States. *Security Science and Technology*, *09*, 53.

Wu, Chen, & Zhao. (2017). Learning Path Recommendation Based on MOOC Platform Data and Knowledge Graph—Taking Software Engineering as an Example. *Industrial and Informatization Education*, (11), 33-38.

Yang, L., Zhou, X., & Liu, S. (2016). Research on the training mechanism and mode of cyberspace security talents under the background of big data. *Journal of Information*, *35*(12), 80–87.

Zhang, H., Yu, H., & Zhai, J. (2016). Planning suggestions for cyberspace security personnel training. *Journal of Network and Information Security*, *3*, 1–9.

Zhou, L., & Ma, Z. (2018). Intelligent Reference Architecture Design of Network Information System Based on Knowledge Graph. *Journal of Chinese Academy of Electronics*, *4*(13), 379.

This research was previously published in the International Journal of Digital Crime and Forensics (IJDCF), 12(4); pages 44-53, copyright year 2020 by IGI Publishing (an imprint of IGI Global).

Index

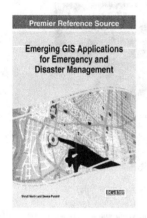
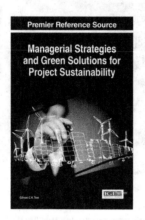

www.igi-global.com

Publisher of Peer-Reviewed, Timely, and
Innovative Academic Research Since 1988

IGI Global's Transformative Open Access (OA) Model:
How to Turn Your University Library's Database Acquisitions Into a Source of OA Funding

Well in advance of Plan S, IGI Global unveiled their OA Fee Waiver (Read & Publish) Initiative. Under this initiative, librarians who invest in IGI Global's InfoSci-Books and/or InfoSci-Journals databases will be able to subsidize their patrons' OA article processing charges (APCs) when their work is submitted and accepted (after the peer review process) into an IGI Global journal.

How Does it Work?

Step 1: **Library Invests in the InfoSci-Databases:** A library perpetually purchases or subscribes to the InfoSci-Books, InfoSci-Journals, or discipline/subject databases.

Step 2: **IGI Global Matches the Library Investment with OA Subsidies Fund:** IGI Global provides a fund to go towards subsidizing the OA APCs for the library's patrons.

Step 3: **Patron of the Library is Accepted into IGI Global Journal (After Peer Review):** When a patron's paper is accepted into an IGI Global journal, they option to have their paper published under a traditional publishing model or as OA.

Step 4: **IGI Global Will Deduct APC Cost from OA Subsidies Fund:** If the author decides to publish under OA, the OA APC fee will be deducted from the OA subsidies fund.

Step 5: **Author's Work Becomes Freely Available:** The patron's work will be freely available under CC BY copyright license, enabling them to share it freely with the academic community.

Note: This fund will be offered on an annual basis and will renew as the subscription is renewed for each year thereafter. IGI Global will manage the fund and award the APC waivers unless the librarian has a preference as to how the funds should be managed.

Hear From the Experts on This Initiative:

"I'm very happy to have been able to make one of my recent research contributions *freely available* along with having access to the *valuable resources* found within IGI Global's InfoSci-Journals database."

— **Prof. Stuart Palmer,**
Deakin University, Australia

"Receiving the support from IGI Global's OA Fee Waiver Initiative *encourages me to continue my research work without any hesitation."*

— **Prof. Wenlong Liu,** College of Economics and Management at Nanjing University of Aeronautics & Astronautics, China

For More Information, Scan the QR Code or Contact:
IGI Global's Digital Resources Team at eresources@igi-global.com.

Printed in the United States
by Baker & Taylor Publisher Services